Power, Wealth and Global Order

An International Relations Textbook for Africa

Edited by
Philip Nel & Patrick J. McGowan

Commissioned by
The Foundation for Global Dialogue

UNIVERSITY OF CAPE TOWN PRESS

1999

Power, Wealth and Global Order
An International Relations Textbook for Africa

University of Cape Town Press
Private Bag
Rondebosch
7701 South Africa

First published 1999

ISBN 1-919713-30-1

Set in 10 on 13 point Palatino; headings in ATRotis.

Cover design: Fritha Langerman
Maps: Susan Sayers
Typesetting: Red Setter, Cape Town, 8001, South Africa
Reproduction: Positive Image, Gardens, 8001, South Africa
Printing and binding: Creda Communications, Epping II, 7460, South Africa

Contents

Maps

How to use this book

This textbook was written with the interests of you, the student, at heart. To make life easier for you, we have included the following features:

There is an extensive Glossary on page 311. Whenever you come across a difficult word in the text (printed in bold), please look up its meaning in the Glossary. Bear in mind, however, that the meanings of many words used in the social sciences are contested, that is, various authors have different preferred meanings, and each feels strongly that his or her preference is correct. You should, therefore, not simply accept the meaning listed in this Glossary as being the only possible one. It is a good idea to refer to ordinary dictionaries, or dictionaries and encyclopaedias of the social sciences, to look up alternative meanings for words such as 'globalisation', 'interaction', and 'interdependence'.

To help you find your way around the book, we have included a detailed Index on page 333. While you will find the meaning of a word such as 'globalisation' in the Glossary, the Index will help you to find all the places in the book where this word is mentioned and discussed. The Index also contains concepts and names not included in the Glossary, and in each case lists the pages on which that particular concept or name is used or discussed.

We have also included two very useful Appendices from page 271. Appendix A deals with using the Internet – study this carefully in your own time. The Internet is fast becoming the main source of information for students of Political Science and International Relations, and if you are not yet familiar with it, you should aquaint yourself with it quickly. If you use a piece of information from the Internet in an essay, make sure you include enough information about the document (its name, the name of the author, and the date), as well as its location (URL), so that reader of your essay can look up that information.

Appendix B discusses the many job opportunities and career paths available to students who major in International Relations. Read this and discuss these career possibilities with your lecturer.

In the front of the book (from page x) you will find a number of useful maps of Africa, Southern Africa and the world. Geography is important and as a student of International Relations you should have a clear picture in your mind of the regions and states of the world, and how they differ in size and location. Please use the maps to orientate yourself, to locate states and regions mentioned in the chapters, and to check the correct spelling of the names of states.

At the beginning of each chapter is a brief overview of the contents of that chapter. Use this as a quick guide to the main sections of the chapter. If you have a clear idea of how a chapter is put together, you will find it easier to remember the finer details of the content.

Each chapter ends with a list of the key concepts discussed in that chapter, and a list of suggested readings covering the issues pertaining to the chapter. After you have studied the chapter, go through these key concepts and make sure you can remember their meanings, and that you are able to write them down from memory. If you cannot do this, go back to the section in which that concept is discussed, and study it again. Consult the list of suggested readings if you want to find out more about a topic. Remember, study at a university or technikon is primarily about finding out new things for and by yourself. Your library (and the Internet) are your best allies in this pursuit.

Finally, bear in mind that a textbook is not intended to provide you with a set of statements that you have to memorise as if it were the absolute truth. It is not meant to give you final, absolute answers to things, but rather to give you some insight into the type of questions asked by academics in a particular field, and how they try to find answers to these questions. The authors have written this textbook in this spirit, and we would like to extend an invitation to you, the reader, to join in the critical exploration of questions and puzzles. We would like to challenge you not to believe anything that is said in these pages before you have interrogated it. Generally, data and facts are almost always selected with a particular viewpoint in mind, and chapters inevitably reflect the opinions of the authors on their particular topics. Your safest bet, therefore, is not to accept anything at face value. Before you accept claims you should have been able to persuade yourself that you have understood why they were made, and that there are valid reasons to accept them as being true. Do not hesitate to ask critical questions of this book, and of the lecturer who is presenting it to you. It is only by asking critical questions that you will learn more about the exiting world of scientific research.

Acknowledgements

The editors wish to dedicate this book to the thousands of students in Africa who study the fascinating subject of International Relations, often under very difficult personal; and academic conditions. We hope that you get as much intellectual pleasure from studying this book as we gained from putting it together.

The idea of this textbook was born at The Foundation for Global Dialogue (FGD), an NGO based in Johannesburg that promotes international dialogue and understanding. The editors wish to thank the Executive Director of the FGD, Dr Garth le Pere, and his Board for their intellectual and financial commitment to this book. The views expressed in the book are those of the authors, however, and do not necessarily reflect the opinions of the FGD.

A special word of thanks goes to the Africa Institute in Pretoria for allowing the editors to use maps and charts from the institute's publication, *Africa at a Glance*. Thank you in particular to Mr Pieter Esterhuizen, the editor of *Africa at a Glance*.

Glenda Younge and her able staff at UCT Press also deserve our gratitude for putting up with late and messy manuscripts, and many last-minute changes. Somewhere there must be a special heaven for university publishers.

We would also like to thank Sandie Vahl for compiling the Index, and to Susan Sayers for drawing the maps. Maps 1 to 6 adapted from Allen, J.L. 1998. *Student Atlas of World Politics*, 3rd edn. Guilford, Con.: Dushkin/McGraw-Hill. Maps 7 to 10 from *Africa at a Glance*, 1997/8.

While every effort has been made to trace all copyright holders and obtain the necessary permission to reproduce material, this has not always been possible, and in a few instances we have not received replies to repeated permission requests. If there has been any oversight on our part, please accept our appologies and contact us with the relevant deatils.

The source for each Table, Box, or Figure is given on the page on which the item appears. We would like to take this opportunity to thank all those who have kindly granted us permission to reproduce material.

Contributors

Korwa G. Adar (Ph.D., South Carolina, USA) is a lecturer in the Department of Politics and the International Studies Unit, Rhodes University, Grahamstown, South Africa.

Chris Alden (Ph.D., Fletcher School, Tufts, USA) is Senior Lecturer and Director of the East Asia Project in the Department of International Relations, University of the Witwatersrand, Johannesburg, South Africa.

Kato Lambrechts (B.A. Hons, Witwatersrand, SA) is Senior Researcher at the Foundation for Global Dialogue, Johannesburg, South Africa.

Garth le Pere (Ph.D., Yale, USA) is Executive Director of the Foundation for Global Dialogue, Johannesburg, South Africa.

Anthony Leysens (M.A., Stellenbosch, SA) is a lecturer in the Department of Political Science at the University of Stellenbosch, South Africa.

Pat McGowan (Ph.D., Northwestern University, USA) is Professor of Political Science at Arizona State University, Tempe, AZ, USA. He is also the Visiting Professor of the Socio-political Environment of Business at the Graduate School of Business Administration, University of the Witwatersrand, Johannesburg, South Africa.

Chisepo J. J. Mphaisha (Ph.D., Graduate School of Public and International Affairs, Pittsburgh, USA) is Senior Lecturer and Head of Department of Public Administration at the University of the Western Cape, Bellville, South Africa.

Craig N. Murphy (Ph.D., North Carolina, USA) is the M. Margaret Ball Professor of International Relations at Wellesley College, USA, and Research Professor at the Thomas J. Watson, Jr. Institute for International Studies at Brown University, USA.

Philip Nel (D.Phil., Stellenbosch, SA) is Professor of Political Science at the University of Stellenbosch, South Africa.

Fred Ahwireng Obeng (Ph.D.) is Professor in the Graduate School of Business Administration, University of the Witwatersrand, Johannesburg, South Africa.

Eghosa E. Osaghae (Ph.D. Ibadan, Nigeria) is Professor and Head of Political Studies at the University of Transkei, Umtata, South Africa.

Maxi Schoeman (Ph.D., University of Wales, Aberystwyth, UK) is Senior Lecturer in the Department of Political Studies, Rand Afrikaans University, Johannesburg, South Africa.

Roger Southall (Ph.D., Birmingham, UK) is Professor and Head of the Department of Politics and the International Studies Unit, Rhodes University, Grahamstown, South Africa.

Lisa Thompson (Ph.D., Western Cape, SA) is Senior Lecturer and Director of Programmes, School of Government, University of the Western Cape, Bellville, South Africa.

Peter Vale (Ph.D., Leicester, UK) is Deputy Vice-Chancellor for Academic Affairs, and Professor of Southern African Studies at the University of the Western Cape, Bellville, South Africa.

Anthoni van Nieuwkerk (M.A., Rand Afrikaans University, SA) is Research Director of the Foundation for Global Dialogue, Johannesburg, South Africa.

Louise Vincent (Ph.D., Oxon, UK) is a lecturer in the Department of Politics and the International Studies Unit, Rhodes University, Grahamstown, South Africa.

Map 1: States of the world.

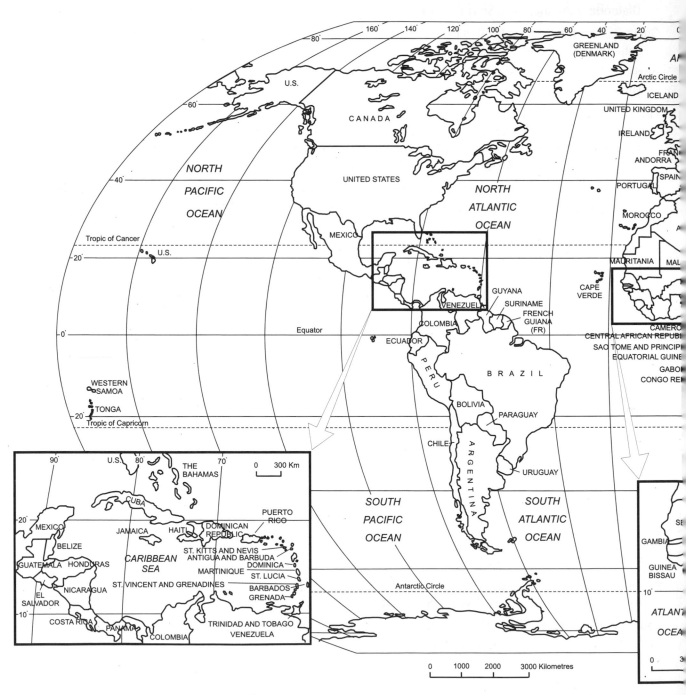

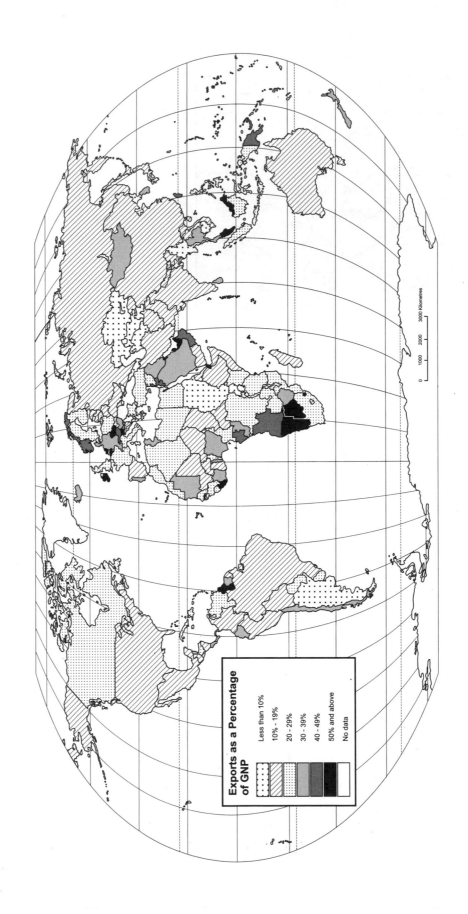

Map 2: World – exports as a percentage of Gross National Product (GNP)

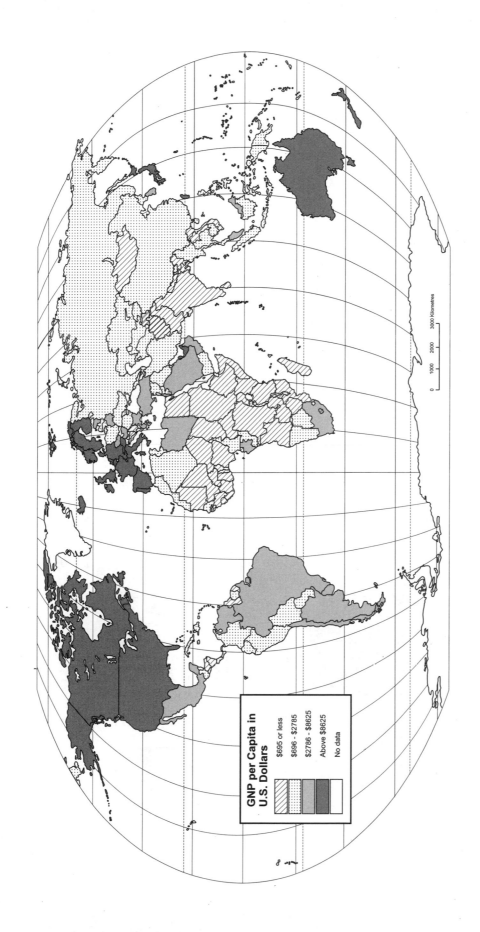

Map 3: Gross National Product (GNP) per capita of the world

GNP per Capita in
U.S. Dollars

$695 or less
$696 - $2785
$2786 - $8625
Above $8625
No data

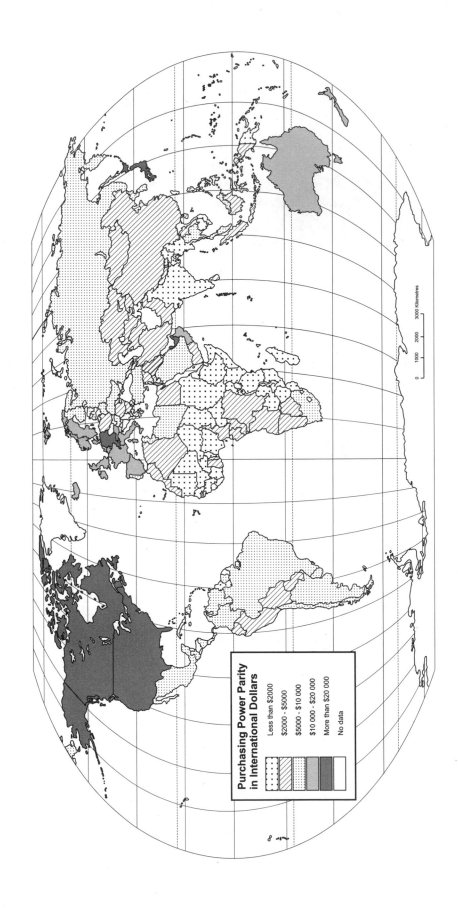

Map 4: Relative wealth of nations measured in Purchasing Power Parity (PPP)

Purchasing Power Parity in International Dollars

Less than $2000
$2000 - $5000
$5000 - $10 000
$10 000 - $20 000
More than $20 000
No data

0   1000   2000   3000 Kilometres

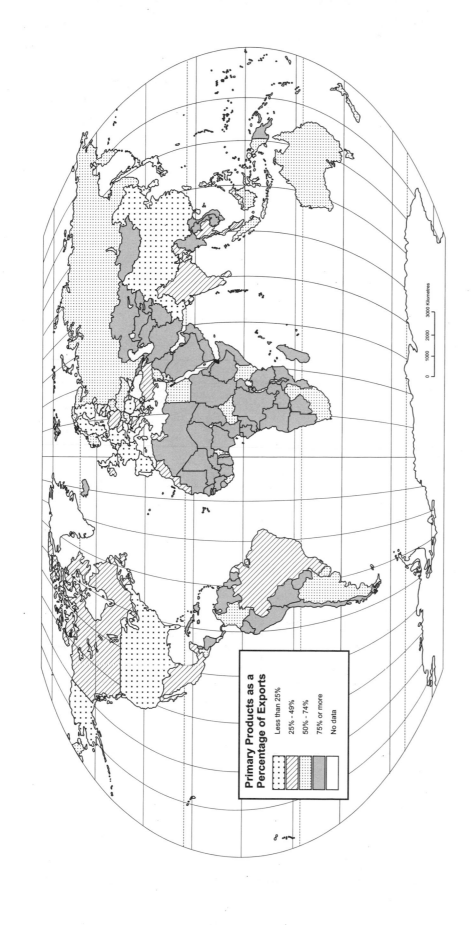

Map 5: World – dependence on exports of primary products

Primary Products as a Percentage of Exports

Less than 25%
25% – 49%
50% – 74%
75% or more
No data

0   1000   2000   3000 Kilometres

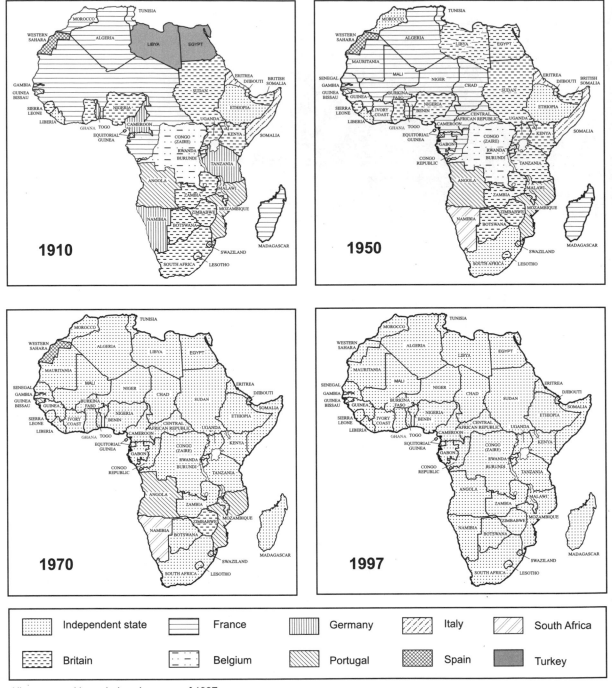

Map 6: The evolution of Africa, from colonialism to independence, 1910–1997

Legend:
- Independent state
- Britain
- France
- Belgium
- Germany
- Portugal
- Italy
- Spain
- South Africa
- Turkey

All names and boundaries shown as of 1997.

Map 7: Political map of Africa

SUB-SAHARA AFRICA (SSA)

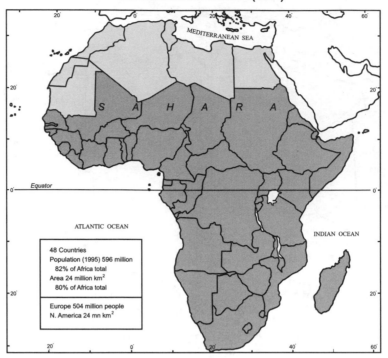

48 Countries
Population (1995) 596 million
82% of Africa total
Area 24 million km²
80% of Africa total

Europe 504 million people
N. America 24 mn km²

SUBEQUATORIAL AFRICA (SEA)

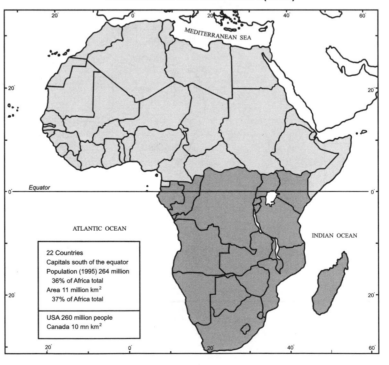

22 Countries
Capitals south of the equator
Population (1995) 264 million
36% of Africa total
Area 11 million km²
37% of Africa total

USA 260 million people
Canada 10 mn km²

Map 8: Sub-Saharan and sub-Equatorial Africa

ECOWAS AND UDEA/CEMAC

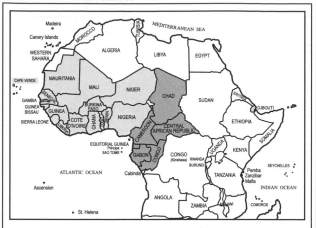

▨ Union douanière et économique de l'Afrique centrale (UDEAC)*

▢ Economic Community of West African States (ECOWAS)

	UDEAC*	ECOWAS**
Founding Date	1966	1975
Member states	6	16
Population (1995)	28 mn	209 mn
Area (km²)	3 mn	6.1 mn

* There is also the *Communauté économique et monétaire en Afrique Centrale (CEMAC)* with the same membership as UDEAC.
** Benin, Burkina, Côte d'Ivoire, Guinea-Bissau, Mali, Niger, Senega and Togo also belong to the *Union économique et monétaire ouest-africaine (UEMOA)*.

UAM AND COMESA

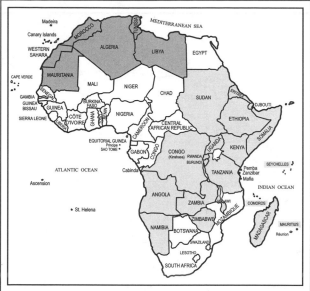

▨ Union of the Arab Maghreb (UAM)

▢ Common Market for Eastern and Southern Africa (COMESA) ratified in December 1994 (formerly Preferential Trade Area for Eastern and Southern Africa, founded in 1981)

	UAM	COMESA
Founding Date	1989	1981
Member states	5	21*
Population (1995)	74 mn	294 mn
Area (km²)	5.8 mn	12.5 mn

* In 1997 Lesotho and Mozambique withdrew from COMESA, retaining their membership of the SADC.

SADC

▢ Southern African Development Community (SADC), formerly the Southern African Development Coordinating Conference (SADCC)

	SADC
Founding Date	1980
Member states	14*
Population (1995)	176 mn
Area (km²)	9.3 mn

* Congo Kinshasa (formerly Zaire) and Seychelles joined the SADC in 1997.

SACU AND CMA

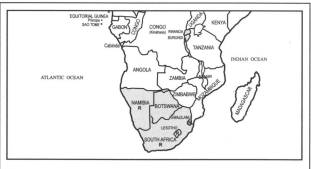

▢ Southern African Customs Union (SACU)

R Common Monetary Area (CMA). Currency linked to SA Rand

	SACU	CMA
Founding Date	1910/1969 1974	
Member states	5	4
Population (1995)	50 mn	48 mn
Area (km²)	2.7 mn	2.1 mn

Map 9: Regional economic groupings in Africa

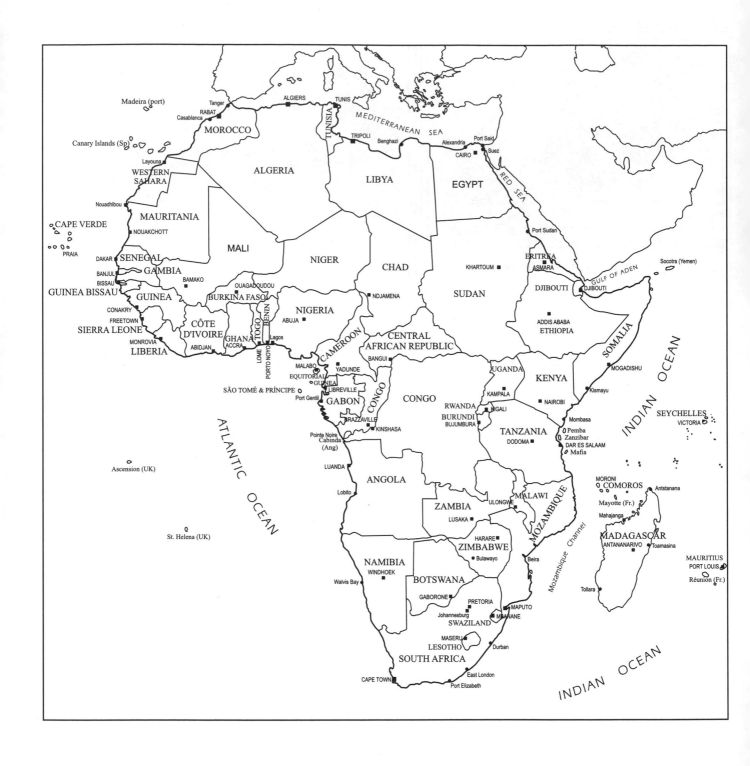

Map 10: Major railways, ports and dams in Africa

1 | The study of International Relations

Pat McGowan & Philip Nel

This chapter in outline
- What is International Relations all about?
    - The interdependent global system
    - The subject matter of International Relations
    - The concept of governance
    - A definition of International Relations
- Actors in International Relations
    - State actors
    - Non-state actors
- Science and the subject of International Relations
    - The importance of preciseness
    - The systematic nature of inquiry in International Relations

What is International Relations all about?

The interdependent global system

It has become commonplace to say that modern technology and the forces of **globalisation** are turning the world into one big 'global village'. This means that people from different countries and regions of the world have started to behave as if they all belong to one single village where everyone knows one another, and where each person's daily life is touched intimately by that of his or her 'neighbour', even if this neighbour is far removed in space and time. More and more, the world is becoming such a place. Today, people from all over the world intensively trade and have other commercial dealings with one another. Many people on a daily basis cross the borders of states in order to find work, visit relatives and friends, or just to see what other countries look like. We share lots of information with and about each other through modern means of communication such as the radio, television, the telephone and the **Internet**. Increasingly, people from all over the world are behaving in similar ways and are expressing similar value preferences: most youngsters, no matter where, want to wear Nike® shoes and Levi® jeans, and drink Coca Cola®; multiparty democracy has become the preferred form of government almost everywhere. Economically, the world is gradually being turned into a single market with countries following similar market-oriented roads to economic development.

Not all of these things are necessarily good, in the sense that they all enrich our lives and help us to develop our human potential, nor are they inevitable, in the sense that they are driven by an objective process over which we individually or collectively have no control. Nevertheless, they affect our lives in innumerable ways. One way of capturing the impact of the above is by saying that all of us, no matter where and how we live, are becoming part of an *interdependent global system*.

By that we mean that there is hardly any aspect of our lives that is not touched, in one way or another, by the decisions and preferences of people living outside our own national borders, and by the mechanisms humanity has developed to organise and manage interaction between people across natural and human-made borders. Similarly, many aspects of the lives of people in other countries, people whom most of the time we do not know and cannot see, are affected by what we prefer and how we act, and by the ways in which our interactions with them have been organised. Consider, for example, how your life as a student is affected by the decisions of 'foreigners' and by the operations of the global system.

First, the cost of your education is directly affected by the prices of the books and materials that you, and your university's library, must have. Many of these items have to be imported from outside our borders. We are not only exposed to ideas from people in other countries, but we are also exposed to the wishes of the book publishers and booksellers in other countries, not to mention the fluctuations in the **rate of exchange** between our own currency and that of the country from which we are importing the books. To determine how much in South African rands or Zimbabwean dollars we have to pay for a book produced in Britain and costing twenty pounds, a mechanism has to exist which can determine how many rands or Zimbabwean dollars can be exchanged for one British pound. Such an exchange-rate mechanism can either be provided by the South African or Zimbabwean central bank, or it can be left to the foreign-exchange market to decide how much buyers and sellers of currencies are prepared to pay for each currency. Whatever the case may be, the amount of money you as a student have to pay for your books and other materials is very often influenced by decisions made in other countries, and by a set of mechanisms that regulate or administer the interactions between the country in which you study and other countries.

Secondly, how much the state is prepared to contribute to your education is something that is affected not only by a decision taken by political or bureaucratic decision-makers in your government. When governments in Southern Africa today have to decide on such matters as support for education and student bursaries, their decisions are affected not only by the political will of their leaders and administrators, but also by a whole set of complex economic considerations that are influenced directly or indirectly by the wishes and behaviour of people and institutions outside of the particular country. Some Southern African states are heavily dependent on **foreign aid** or foreign loans to make up shortfalls in their budgets. This fact makes their decisions directly dependent on the wishes of people who are not citizens of the recipient country, but whose preferences affect local spending on education, health services, food subsidies and pensions directly.

All governments, even those in relatively better-off countries, find themselves constrained by the behaviour of investors on the international capital markets. Even if governments are prepared to overspend their budgets because they feel compelled to provide good education and other social services to their population, they try to keep these budget deficits to an absolute minimum. They fear that investors will lose confidence in their economy, and that money will start pouring out of the country, with all kinds of negative effects on the exchange rate of their currency and on **foreign direct investment**. Thus, the fact that many Southern African students on average pay more for their university education than do students in Denmark, for instance, has to do both with domestic and international reasons. Domestically, governments in Southern Africa raise less revenue than Denmark, because our economic base is much weaker. However, the differential in spending is also related to the fact that Southern Africa is much more constrained than Denmark in how big a budget deficit it can risk in view of the possible reaction by

international markets. We say that Southern Africa is *much more vulnerable to the vicissitudes of the international markets* than Denmark is. This means that you as a student and as a citizen are vulnerable to the decisions and wishes of overseas investors, and the quality of your life is closely affected by the mechanisms that organise the way in which people interact economically across borders.

Thirdly, the exposure of your life as a student to global interdependence does not mean that you are constrained only by trans-border forces and decisions taken in localities other than your own. The fact that we form part of a close-knit global network also provides us with many benefits. Universities are part of the network of knowledge that has allowed humans to transform their world into a habitable and cultured environment. Universities, by definition, are places of *world* learning and are therefore intellectually globalised. Although some aspects of what we are taught at university are not truly global, but rather ethnocentric and parochial, it is true that science and technology in general has a universal legitimacy that provides an intellectual bond and resource that is not restricted by borders. The fact that you are studying at a university makes you a citizen of the world of learning that, thanks to modern technology, is becoming increasingly intimate and cohesive. Just think about it: the very ideas that you are studying are very similar to the ideas that other students, thousands of kilometres away, are also grappling with, even though it may be in another language.

Decisions by people far away, and the mechanisms that we have devised to organise our interaction with one another across borders, affect our daily lives and that of our friends and family in innumerable other ways. All this means that the world is increasingly becoming an interdependent system in the true sense of the word, that is, *a tightly bound collection of units or actors whose behaviour affects one another directly or indirectly*. For a system to exist, it is not necessary that all the actors be equal in strength or size, nor is it necessary that the behaviour of each actor should affect every other actor equally. In the case of the global system, some actors are indeed richer and more powerful than others, and not all are equally affected by what happens in the system. **Interdependence** does not exclude asymmetrical relations of **dependence.** What it does mean is that there is **mutual dependence**, so the weak and poor have some power in an interdependent system. It is not only the weak that depend on the strong; the strong also depend on the weak, albeit in different degrees. Overall, the growth of an interdependent global system has become a crucial determinant of our daily existence. It has both negative and positive consequences for us individually, but also for the communities in which we live. The challenge we face is to develop the intellectual tools with which to identify the many ways in which the global system impacts on our existence, and to distinguish between those impacts that are negative – and which we have a right to resist – and those that are positive and which we might wish to encourage. Studying the subject of International Relations provides you with these intellectual tools. It also prepares you for one of the many job opportunities (*see* Appendix B) in which familiarity with and understanding of the global system is a prerequisite.

The subject matter of International Relations

The prominence of the global system in our lives has meant that quite a few academic fields of study have made it their business to study aspects of it. Thus, for example, International Economics studies the ways in which global resources and the decisions that underlie international financial and commercial interaction contribute to the creation and distribution of wealth in the world. International Law records, analyses and explains the emergence of a set of codified rules of behaviour to which international actors such as states and corporations adhere. Sociologists are interested in the emergence of

social and cultural patterns that include more than one society, while various environmental sciences are studying the global effects of the ways humans interact with the environment.

The field of International Relations also studies aspects of the global system. It is not always possible to decide clearly where the responsibility of the sociologist ends, and where that of the International Relations scholar begins. Neither is it easy to determine exactly what the ultimate difference between International Economics, International Law and International Relations is. Nevertheless, it is possible to identify a specific focus for International Relations that makes it possible to distinguish between its subject matter and that of other academic fields. This focus, as we will explain below, is the ways in which actors organise and manage their interactions in the global system, and how this leads to the establishment, maintenance and transformation of governance structures in the world.

To help us to understand what specifically it is that International Relations scholars are interested in, distinct from the foci of other scholars studying the global system, let us look at four news reports in Items 1.1 to 1.4. Although all four are taken from newspapers or news services, and they are therefore not scholarly pieces, they all report on matters that are of interest to a variety of subjects. However, it is possible in each case to identify a dimension of the news that is being reported that is of particular interest for us in the subject of International Relations.

At first glance, there seems to be a number of differences between these four news items. The first deals with the economic crisis which gripped parts of Asia in 1997 and 1998; the second with the number of people migrating from Nigeria to South Africa; the third deals with trade and aid relations between two countries; and the fourth item deals with a joint committee meeting held by a number of Southern African countries. Do these have anything in common?

By now, you will be able to see that they do have something in common. *All four news items*

Item 1.1: Crisis could hit South Asia

BANGKOK – A high-ranking United Nations official said yesterday that East Asia and Southeast Asia would not recover from economic crisis until at least 2000 and warned that trouble could spread to South Asia …

Adrianus Mooy, UN Under Secretary-General and Executive Secretary of the UN economic and Social Commission for Asia and the Pacific, called for more 'global governance' of capital flows and currency trading to try to avoid future economic shocks …

Mooy said the international community should consider setting up global organisations governing currency trading and capital flows. He suggested rules could be developed to encourage longer-term capital flows for investment by such measures as taxing short-term, speculative investment at higher rates.

Some of the blame for Asia's economic crisis belonged to lenders from developed countries who failed to heed clear warning signals that trouble was brewing, he said …

(*Business Day* – 98.04.09)

Item 1.2: Official SA figures hide Nigerian influx.

Nigerian emigrants are targeting SA which many perceive as a new El Dorado, writes Dulue Mbachu in Lagos

SLOW business in the past three years has forced Jude Orji, a 23-year-old vehicle spare parts trader in Lagos, Nigeria's commercial capital, to take what he considers the most important decision of his life: to sell up and move to SA …

Two broad categories of Nigerian emigrants to SA have become discernible. One group comprises largely unskilled youths seeking menial jobs and employment in street trading, such as Orji, while a second group comprises highly skilled professionals seeking better financial rewards for their skills …

Official SA figures do not correctly reflect the tide of Nigerians moving into the country. Out of 4 500 Nigerians applying for visitor's visas from January 1996 to October 1997, 3 478 were successful. Between January 1996 and July 1997, 100 applications for permanent residence were granted to Nigerians, while 12 were rejected.

Yet by some accounts every other family in Africa's most populous country of 104 million people has at least one SA-based relative. Those who entered SA legally are mainly qualified professionals, including medical professionals, engineers and academics, who, faced with poor pay at home, have taken up more rewarding job offers down south.

(*ANC News Briefing* – 98.01.19)

deal with decisions, events and/or statements that in some way or another have implications or effects in more than one country or that involve actors from different nations. As such, these news items all reflect what we said above about the interdependent global system. More specifically, we can say that they report on *international interactions*. What is the difference between 'international' and 'global'?

One way of answering this question would be to say that a global system would continue to exist, even if we removed the international order from it. The international order is a specific administrative and legal grid we have imposed on the global system over the past four centuries. The lines of this grid coincide with the boundaries of the independent, **sovereign states** we have today. Because the basic idea behind the existence of states is that they give a group of people, either a constitutionally or a culturally

defined **nation**, a territory over which they have exclusive say (sovereignty), we refer to these administrative and legal units as nation-states. The idea of an international order is thus derived from the recognition of the borders of **nation-states** as the determining lines between what is 'domestic' and what is 'foreign', what is 'national' and what is 'international'.

There is, of course, nothing eternal, nor sacred about the existence of the international order –

Item 1.3: Zimbabwe and France to sign three trade agreements

BULAWAYO – Zimbabwe and France will this year sign three bilateral agreements to improve trade and investment between them.

In an interview with Ziana news agency here on Saturday, French ambassador to Zimbabwe, Hadelin de la Tour-du-Pin, said the two countries would soon sign a financial protocol, where over 240 million Zim dollars would be made available to the Zimbabwe government to buy telecommunications and water supply equipment from France.

'The two countries have already agreed to the protocol and what is only left is the signing ceremony,' he said, adding the financial package would be part loan and part grant.

The second agreement, De la Tour-du-Pin said, would be an investment promotion and trade promotion agreement that seeks to give security to investors from both countries.

De la Tour-du-Pin said the third agreement would be for the establishment of a French development fund to finance rural projects in water, electricity and telecommunications.

Zimbabwe and France have already signed a double taxation treaty which protects investors from both countries from being taxed by both governments. The balance of trade is currently in France's favour with exports of mainly telecommunications and electronic equipment worth approximately Zd700 million while Zimbabwe in 1996 exported mainly horticultural and agricultural products worth Zd350 million.

(Sapa – 98.01.17)

Item 1.4: SADC defence body warns those supporting UNITA

LUSAKA – The 14-nation Southern African Development Community has warned that it will take drastic action against individuals and companies still providing war materials and logistics to the Angolan rebel movement, UNITA.

At a meeting on Thursday in Harare, the Zimbabwean capital, the community's ad hoc Committee of the Inter-State Defence and Security body noted that UNITA still received logistical supplies from individuals and companies violating the air spaces of certain Southern African states.

UNITA has been blamed for stalling full implementation of the November 1994 Lusaka Peace accord. Its inaction has effectively kept Angola in a situation of being neither at peace nor war. However, the United Nations has applied sanctions against UNITA and its officials in a bid to force its compliance with the accord.

The Harare meeting was attended by representatives from Angola, Malawi, Namibia, South Africa, Zambia and Zimbabwe. President Robert Mugabe of Zimbabwe is the head of this committee.

(PANA – 98.01.17)

the order formed by the recognition of nation-states as subjects of ultimate authority and objects of the highest loyalty. The international order is a recent invention in human history, and it surely will not last forever. It simply reflects the way humans have chosen to organise and govern the global system for the time being. It is important for you to remember that the words 'international' and 'global' are not synonyms, although people sometimes carelessly equate the one with the other. Similarly, the 'global order' and the 'international order' are not the same thing (Bull, 1977).

The fact that the international order is a recent invention does not mean that it is not important. Because nation-states are the bearers of ultimate authority in this order, and are the territorial and legal units to which people swear ultimate allegiance and loyalty, what happens in the international order is of major concern to us. When do we know that something or some event is part of the international order and when not? The simple answer is that whenever an event or an action crosses the borders of national states, or has implications that span such boundaries, we deem it to have an international dimension to it.

Returning now to our four news items, we can see that the fundamental thing that they have in common is that all report on events or actions with an *international* dimension. By that we mean that what they have in common is that the events or decisions that they report imply *the crossing of national borders* in one way or another. Thus, the first item deals with suggestions from a United Nations (UN) official about how the flow of investment capital from state to state can be better controlled in order to prevent crises caused by **capital flight**. Item two covers the movement of people from one country to another – migration; three deals with official agreements between two states; and number four deals with a policy statement by means of which a group of states would like to promote peace in another country – Angola. Although nation-states are not the main actors in each of these reports (*see* below), the existence and recognition of nation-states still form the implicit background or the grid within which these events and actions take place and receive importance as international events and actions. *Students of International Relations will be interested in the subject matter of these four reports, because they want to find out more about the characteristics of this international order that we have imposed on the global system, and how it functions.* This implies that these students are also keen to find out how and under which conditions the international order will survive, or will go under and be replaced with a new order.

There is a second fundamental feature in these four reports that will also tickle the fancy of the student of International Relations, one that is perhaps less obvious than the first. This is that all four items deal with issues that have some implication for the way or manner in which **actors** (*see* below for a discussion of the concept of 'actor') co-ordinate their behaviour and administer their relationships with other actors in the international order. Note that we speak about 'actors', a term that indicates a broader category than do the terms 'governments' or 'states'. As we have already noted, it is evident that it is not only

states that are involved as role-players in these four items. While states are the main actors in items three and four, individuals and their decisions to migrate feature in item two. In item one, investors of all sorts are implied, including private **portfolio** and private direct investors (*see* **foreign direct investment**).

The second feature that these four items have in common, then, is that they entail the co-ordination and administration of international activities. But is this true of all four items? Is it not only items three and four that can be said to involve the co-ordination and administering of relationships between two actors (item three), and between more than two actors (item four)?

At first glance, item two does not seem to fit into this pattern. This item reports on the decisions taken by private Nigerian citizens to migrate to South Africa to secure better living conditions for themselves and their families. This report seems to be a simple human-interest story.

Not so. The point of the whole report is to argue that the South African government is underestimating the numbers of Nigerians who illegally migrate to South Africa, and that its **public policy-making** in this regard may be inadequate. Furthermore, if this report is true, it may have implications for future South African policy towards migration from Nigeria, which in turn may have an impact on the relations between the two countries and their foreign policies towards each other. Thus, although the focus is initially on individual private behaviour, this behaviour clearly has ramifications for the way or manner in which these two countries are going to co-operate and administer their relations in future.

Item one also fits into the pattern. What is at stake is how international actors, not only states, but also private investors and international financial institutions, can better administer the flow of investment capital in the world, and so place the set of financial relations in the world on a surer, better co-ordinated level.

What specifically interests the student of

International Relations in these four items is exactly this last feature – a feature that we can best describe as the dimension of *governance*. By this, we mean the manner in which authoritative order is imposed on the numerous ways in which people interact in the global system. As we have seen, the current authoritative order in the global system is an *international* order, and it is therefore only natural that scholars in this subject focus heavily on the structures and sources of order and authority in the state system. However, many scholars are also interested in finding out more about alternative orders that existed before, and in the potential of alternative, non-state-based orders to replace the current state-based order.

The concept of governance

The concept of 'governance' should not be confused with 'government'. When we say that students of International Relations study forms of global governance, we are not saying that they are studying the possibility that a world government will come into existence. The word 'government' refers to either the form of political organisation of a political unit, usually a state ('South Africa has a government of national unity'), or a body or successive bodies of persons administering a state ('the Labour Party forms the current government of the UK'). 'Governance', in contrast, refers to the *manner* or *way* in which a specific domain of reality is administered or governed, that is, the way in which order is imposed in that domain. Governance in a system is possible, even if the system is not a political unit. The global system is not one political unit. In fact, it consists of a multitude of political units. Nevertheless, a specific order of governance can be said to exist in the global system at any one time.

Order, we can say, presupposes governance. Governance, in turn, presupposes authority, that is, the right to enforce obedience. Although we do not have a world government, the interesting thing about the current international order is that

people most of the time obey specific standards of behaviour or make use of established structures of interaction. The exchange of accredited diplomats is one example; another is the treatment of prisoners of war by belligerents in a war; a third is the respect people show for the principles of **international commercial law**. Whence this obedience? Put differently: what are the sources of authority in the current global system? Does it emerge from a communal sense of what is right and wrong that is shared by all in the world, or is it the function of the strong imposing their will on the weak? Remember, 'authority' implies power, that is, the ability to affect human behaviour, but it should not be equated with power (*see* Box 1.1). Authority is the right to use power, and this right can either be a legal right, or a right bestowed on someone or an institution because that person or institution may be highly valued by a community. In the absence of well-established norms and institutions of authority, governance is often a function of the use of power by the strongest members of a system.

It is this enquiry into the nature of global order, and the resulting questions about governance, authority, power, norms and institutions, that gives International Relations a unique focus on the global system in general, and on the international order in particular. From this focus flows the interest in international conflict and war that many scholars working in this field have. The extreme variety of actors and interest groups in the system makes conflict inevitable. The whole purpose of governance is to manage this conflict in order to maintain the equilibrium of the system. From this perspective, war is not a symptom of the breakdown of governance, but a manifestation of governance. Inter-state war in the international order is not unbridled violence; it is conducted according to some long-established and authoritative rules of behaviour.

But the academic subject called International Relations does not only study manifestations of military conflict. It also studies a wider domain of security issues, both human security and national security, in order to determine whom, and with what authority, is providing security for whom, and for what purpose. Similarly, International Relations scholars are keen to find out who is using what sources of power and authority to organise and steer international interactions in the spheres of trade, finance, production, transport, and science and technology. In all of this, the student of International Relations is also keen to find out who benefits from the way in which the international order in all its aspects is organised and administered. Governance is not an equitable activity in the sense that everyone who is involved in it benefits to the same degree. Although everyone will be worse off without governance, it always entails more benefits for some and less for others, and it imposes different costs on different actors. International Relations is one of the fields of study, therefore, that can help us to understand privilege and disadvantage in the global system.

Finally, the emphasis that the subject of International Relations places on the dimension of governance implies that it is also concerned about changes in the way the global system is managed. We have already noted that the international order, based on the co-existence and co-ordination between states, is the current governance order in the world (*see* Chapter 4). Governance orders in the global system (what some people call 'world orders') come and go, although some of them last for centuries. In this subject, you will also learn about the factors that maintain or transform governance orders.

A definition of International Relations

On the basis of what we have said so far, we can *define International Relations as the subject that studies global order:* how order emerges, is maintained and is transformed in the global system through the use of authority and/or power to structure and manage the relations among actors. These relations may involve states, in any combination of two or more, or it may exclude states, or it may involve states and actors that are not states. Thus,

the authority that is at stake is not that which only emanates from states. We are also interested in finding out how non-state-based authority – such as that which resides in, say, financial markets, or in the World Council of Churches, or in the moral stature of someone like Nelson Mandela – contributes towards the organising and managing of relations between international actors. Furthermore, when we study governance, we are looking not only at what is sometimes called 'global governance', which is the sum total of authoritative measures to structure and manage the system as a whole. Yes, some students of International Relations are interested in these broader patterns of global governance. Others, however, keep themselves busy with only one issue area, hoping to understand, for instance, how international interaction in the production of and trade in weapons is structured and what the sources of authority in that area are. Other scholars focus on a specific set of relations between two actors, France and Zimbabwe for instance (*see* Item 1.3), in order to understand how this relationship is structured and managed, and what influences it.

If you have not noticed, what we just did was to supply you with a definition of International Relations. In case you missed it, please consult Box 1.2.

In Box 1.3 there are some general comments about what a definition is and what makes a good definition. Please apply these comments to the definition of International Relations in Box 1.2 and make out for yourself whether this definition allows you to distinguish clearly between how the subject matter of International Relations can be distinguished from that of, say, a sociological look at the global system, or from the interests of an economist studying the dynamics of international trade.

It is important to distinguish our broader definition of the subject from narrower definitions that you may encounter in the literature. Sometimes, IR is equated with the study of 'interactions between state-based actors across state

Box 1.1: The variety of meanings of the word 'power'

'Multiple meanings of words may or may not produce confusion. It depends in considerable degree on the audience. Take the word *power*, for example. This is a technical term of political discourse. Yet the word carries several distinct meanings outside the boundaries of political discourse altogether. There is a mathematical concept of power: 'the product arising from the continued multiplication of a number into itself.' In the vocabularies of physics and engineering, power denotes 'the rate of transfer of energy, as in work done by an engine.' Then there is an optical concept of power: 'the degree to which an optical instrument magnifies.' Probably most of the readers of this book will suffer no confusion from these non-political meanings of the word *power*. But what of the two distinct meanings of power which one encounters *within* the frame of political discourse? One speaks of the power of Congress, and of the power of the United States. The first means *legal authority* to act; the second, *actual capacity* to affect human behaviour – two distinct and different referents.

To confuse matters still more, *power* in the political as distinct from the legal sense, carries various shades of meaning. To some readers of this book, we imagine, power will connote effective military force conceived in terms of prospective ability to win wars. To others, power may convey the idea of ability to override opposition by means of threats as well as actual warfare. In some contexts, power seems to connote only physical coercion, in others, non-coercive influence as well. Since power is a key term in the vocabulary of international politics, and since it carries different connotations or shades of meaning, its use presents constant risk of imperfect communication. It will be desirable, of course, to define such words very carefully. But so sloppy are prevailing linguistic habits in America, even among well-educated people, that there can be no assurance whatever that the most careful and precise definitions will be heeded when the term recurs in discourse.'
Sprout & Sprout, (1962:22–23)

boundaries' (Evans & Newnham, 1992:156). This clearly excludes a whole range of governance issues that are prevalent in the interactions by non-state actors (*see* below, and also Chapter 7) across national borders.

Some people still prefer to call our subject 'World Politics' or 'International Politics' (*see* Nossal, 1998), instead of 'International Relations'. These names are misleading, though, because they could create the impression that the subject is concerned only with *political issues*. In fact, today IR is increasingly concerned with *economic issues*, such as trade policy and the public policy implications of financial **liberalisation.** In addition, *communication, social, health* and *cultural issues* can all draw the attention of IR scholars, to the extent that they have trans-border and governance dimensions to them. There is, however, nothing wrong in calling 'International Politics' a sub-field of the broader subject of International Relations, just as we see 'International Political Economy' (*see* Chapter 2) as a sub-field of International Relations.

Now that we have given you at least some idea of what the subject of International Relations is all about, let us turn to some important concepts that we have used in developing our definition, but have left unexplained so far.

Actors in International Relations

We use the word *actors* when we speak about the individuals, groups of people, states and other institutions involved in the set of interactions and the dimension of governance on which the subject of International Relations focuses. The word 'actor' is useful because it is wider than 'state' (*see* above), and because it evokes the image of the world as a big stage on which individuals and groups can play a wide variety of roles. In broad terms, we distinguish between state actors, and non-state actors.

Box 1.2: Definition of International Relations

The subject International Relations (IR) is the study of how authority and/or power is used to organise and manage trans-border relations between actors, and how this contributes to the establishment, maintenance and transformation of order in the world system.

Note that when we speak about the academic subject 'International Relations' (IR), we use capital letters. When we refer to those events in the world that are studied by the subject, we use small letters and call them 'international relations' (the same principle applies in the subject Political Science, which is the study of politics).

State actors

It is common to distinguish between *state actors* and *non-state actors* in International Relations. State actors comprise the 194 states in the world and the **intergovernmental organisations** (such as the UN and SADC) that they form. Let us first look at states and the types of relations that they can have.

In Chapter 4, we deal with states, and the system that they form, in detail. Here we should merely note that we sometimes treat states as if each one represents one single actor. Thus, in news Item 1.3 we saw how the report spoke about *France* and *Zimbabwe* signing particular trade and aid agreements – each of the two in this case was treated as a single actor. It is of course problematic to speak about states as if they were single units. In real life, the state of France is made up of various individuals and groups, not all of whom always agree with one another. Although we often speak of 'the foreign policy of France' or 'the policy followed by Zimbabwe' (and there is nothing wrong with speaking like that for specific purposes), we have to be aware of the implications of our words, and what we leave out when we use such terminology. The point is, we have a choice of whether to speak

Box 1.3: Definition * Define

'• A precise description of something = **a definition**
• To give a precise description of something = **to define**

When defining something, you need to ensure that its meaning is made so clear that the definition can only refer to the thing that you are describing and nothing else. For example, the following *definition* is not a good definition of a caravan: "A caravan is something in which people live". This is not a very accurate or useful definition because it could refer to something other than a caravan, for example, a tent or a brick house.

A more accurate definition of a caravan would be: "A caravan is a house on wheels that can be towed by a vehicle". This definition refers only to a caravan; it excludes (cannot include) a tent or a brick house. When you define something, a good rule to follow is first to state the larger category in which the thing belongs (e.g. "A caravan **is a house** …") and then to state the characteristics that make the thing different from other members of the same category (e.g. "A caravan is a house *on wheels that can be towed by a vehicle*"). Further, only the most distinctive features must be included in the definition. For example, it would be unimportant to say that some caravans are silver and others green. These are not distinctive features.

In a university context, students are often required to define a phenomenon before proceeding to discuss or compare it with something else. For example, the nature of problem solving tasks in the humanities and social sciences is typically open-ended. If a student were asked to compare this open-ended nature with the puzzle-like nature of problems in the natural sciences, it is important first to define what is meant by 'open-ended'.

Note that a word's *denotation* (i.e. its usual or conventional definition, as found in a standard language dictionary), is different from the *connotations* or associations individuals may attach to such a word.'
Craig *et al.* (1994:62)

about the state as if it were a unitary actor, or highlight the different actors that together compose the state. Which of the two you choose depends on your intention and the theory that you are using (*see* Chapter 3).

If we treat states as if they were single, unitary actors, it becomes important to distinguish between two types of interactions that states can have with one another (naturally, states also have relations with non-state actors – see below). On the one hand, a state can have *bilateral* relations with another state. A good example of bilateral relations is provided by Item 1.3. This report covers an aspect of *the bilateral relations between France and Zimbabwe*. The prefix 'bi-' means 'two'. Bilateral relations are relations between two states.

States can also have *multilateral relations*. Multilateral relations involve three or more states that want to co-operate with one another in order to co-ordinate their policies concerning specific issues or sets of issues. Item 1.4 contains an example of multilateral relations. It reports on the multilateral efforts of a number of Southern African states who wanted to come up with a joint policy statement concerning the inappropriateness of further external help for UNITA (the National Union for the Total Independence of Angola).

The second group of state actors in which we are interested are *intergovernmental organisations* (IGOs), that is, international organisations that came into being through agreements among states. The United Nations Organisation (the UNO, more commonly known as the UN) is a prime example of an intergovernmental organisation, and other examples include the Southern African Development Community (SADC), the North Atlantic Treaty Organisation (NATO) and the Organisation of African Unity (OAU). These international organisations have to be treated as state actors, because they cannot act independently of the wishes of their members, which are states (*see* Chapter 6 for a discussion of international institutions, including IGOs).

Non-state actors

As the name implies, *non-state actors* include all international actors that are not composed of states. In this chapter, we have already mentioned different types of non-state actors who can have quite a significant global impact, for example individual political leaders, private investors and business concerns (such as banks and other private credit institutions). An important subgroup consists of business concerns that play an increasingly important role in international interaction and governance – **multinational** and **transnational corporations** (MNCs and TNCs).

To this list of potentially important non-state actors we should also add **international nongovernmental organisations** (INGOs), such as Greenpeace and the International Red Cross; **ethnonational** groups such as the Kurds and the Palestinians; **international religious movements** such as the Roman Catholic Church and Islam; and **transnational social movements,** such as the Anti-Slavery Movement in the nineteenth century, and the more recent world-wide Anti-Apartheid Movement. These non-state actors are discussed in more detail in Chapter 7.

Science and the subject of International Relations

International Relations is a subject, but it is not a discipline in the sense that Mathematics or Economics is a discipline (Berridge, 1997:1). It does have its own, distinct subject matter, but there is no single set of methods that scholars of International Relations all use in order to study this subject matter. As you will soon realise, scholars in this subject are very eclectic, and they use methods and conceptual tools from a whole range of disciplines to carry out their investigations. International Relations is a multidisciplinary subject, in which you will encounter methods and approaches loaned from Economics, History, Philosophy, Law, Statistics, Sociology, Anthropology and even Literary Criticism. This is one of the reasons why studying the subject is such a rich and rewarding experience!

Although students of the subject International Relations do not share one common set of methods or approaches, they do share a commitment to the *precise* and *systematic* study of their subject matter. It is this commitment that makes International Relations a scientific subject, worthy of being taught at tertiary level. What exactly does this commitment entail?

The importance of preciseness

The primary tool used by people studying International Relations is language, predominantly in its everyday variant ('literary language'), but also in its numerical variant (mathematics, the language of numbers). Because it is unlikely that you will encounter much mathematics in this introductory text, we focus here only on the standards which scholars expect from one another when they use literary language to discuss, analyse and explain international relations.

Above all else, the subject of International Relations demands that we be *precise* in how we use words. 'Being precise' can mean quite a few things, and below we shall mention two very important manifestations of it. In general, however, it means that we have to be aware of the way in which we use words. We should be aware of the various categories of words, the different operations that can be performed with them, and of the many connotations that concepts may have (*see* Box 1.3). Let us look specifically at two crucial manifestations of such self-awareness.

Different kinds of statements

Firstly, the linguistically self-aware scholar can distinguish between different kinds of 'intellectual operations' (Sprout & Sprout, 1962:25) that we can perform with words. In your study of International Relations (and other social sciences), you will frequently encounter the following five ways of using words:

- *Descriptive statements* are used to inform our readers or listeners about the features of objects, persons or states of affairs, such as an event. Description also implies spelling out, in as precise terms as possible, to which category of things an event or object belongs. (Very often, we use **typologies** or **taxonomies** to distinguish between a variety of similar objects and states of affairs. For instance, a taxonomy of the phenomenon of war will distinguish between civil [or intra-state] wars and inter-state wars.) Descriptive statements answer questions such as: *What is this object, person or event an instance of? What is it like? Where is it? What happened? When did it happen?*

- *Interpretative statements* are used to bring out the meaning we attach to something or some event, or how we evaluate it. Statements of this sort answer questions such as: *What is the relevance of this event or state of affairs? How important is it? What shall we do about it?*

- *Explanatory statements* are used to give an account of the reasons for or causes of something or why someone behaved the way she or he did. These statements are answers to *why* questions (*see* Chapter 3 for a further discussion of 'explanation'). They are usually oriented towards the past, asserting what the necessary and sufficient causes were for a state of affairs, such as World War I (1914–1918).

- *Predictive statements* are future oriented, and are used when we want to say what will happen in the future. In science, we do not rely on wild guesses to make predictive statements. Rather, we rely heavily on careful explanations and interpretations of past events to help us foresee what the future might be like.

- *Normative statements* are used to express our preferences in terms of what we believe is right or wrong, good or bad, desirable or undesirable, proper or improper. We use them to evaluate, often in moral terms, events, the behaviour of people or states of affairs. While there are scientists who believe that normative statements have no role in science, other scientists believe that they should play a central part in our scientific enterprise, if we want to contribute to making the world a better place (*see* Chapter 2 and 3).

Although it is not always possible or useful to distinguish too decisively between these categories of the intellectual operations we can perform with words, we should take care to know what type of operation is demanded of us in a particular context. If a lecturer asked you to explain the causes of poverty in the developing world, you would get very poor marks if you simply told him or her how bad poverty is, and how much it makes people suffer. What the lecturer wanted you to do was to engage in the language of explanation; instead, you used normative statements and described some of the effects of poverty. Similarly, if someone asked you whether a free-trade zone should be established in Southern Africa, you would be using an inappropriate type of statement if you explained how important and relevant a free-trade zone would be. In asking the question, s/he wanted you to engage in predictive statements; instead, you gave her interpretative statements. Communication often breaks down because we are not careful to ensure that we engage in the type of intellectual operation that is demanded by the specific context, or by our interlocutors.

Concepts

Of all the words that we use in the social sciences, none are more important than concepts. Concepts are more than mere words. A concept 'is the reflective thinking and rethinking or grasping together (holding) of an idea or a class of objects' (Craig *et al.*, 1994:38). As such, concepts form the basic tools with which we describe, interpret, explain, predict and make normative judgements. If we do not have a clear idea of the class of objects which we call 'wars' is, we will not be able to categorise an event as a war or not. Similarly, if we do not have a clear

understanding of what the concept 'important' means, we will not be able to interpret something as important or not. Also, if we do not have a clear idea of the concept of 'justice' (that is, what class of events or situations we can call just), we shall be unable to make a judgement about justice and injustice in international relations.

However, the problem with most interesting concepts in the social sciences is that they have different meanings (connotations) for different scholars. In fact, a lot of time and energy is used by scholars to convince one another of the correct or appropriate meanings that should be attached to specific concepts. Even concepts that may seem to be descriptive with straightforward meanings, such as 'state', 'authority', 'efficiency', 'peace', 'war', 'foreign policy' are, in fact, contested concepts. Different people attach different meanings to them, and we should, therefore, always specify what we mean whenever we use them. A concept such as 'International Relations' has different meanings for different people, and we should not simply assume that everyone has the same idea as we do when we use this term. The golden rule is: *always define the concepts that you use!*

The fact that core concepts are contested makes the social sciences somewhat different from the natural sciences, where important concepts such as 'gene', 'mass', 'velocity', 'gravitation', etc. have specified and universally accepted meanings. In the social sciences, we differ vehemently about the appropriate meanings that should be attributed to concepts such as 'democracy', 'power' (*see* Box 1.1), 'freedom' and 'justice'. In fact, we can view the evolution of the social sciences as the process whereby people discuss and refine the concepts that we use to make sense of our society. (*See* Box 1.4 for a further discussion of concepts.)

The systematic nature of inquiry in International Relations

Scientific discourse uses a different language to that used in everyday conversations; it is precise in its use of language, and attempts to be systematic in the way in which it investigates its subject matter. To be 'systematic' means that you are methodical (that you follow a specific method of investigation), that you work according to a plan, and that your investigation is not casual, sporadic or unintentional.

Like other social scientists, scholars of International Relations are able to choose from a series of standardised methods when investigating their subject matter. These methods range from the careful study of historical documents and artefacts, to the use of sophisticated statistical analysis to interpret large sets of data. While it is impossible to say which methods should or should not be used in the study of IR, the golden rule is that you should let your research questions determine your choice of methodology, not the other way round.

The breaking up of a larger issue into various dimensions that are then studied in a logical, sequential manner (called 'analysis') is also an important manifestation of a systematic approach. One of the techniques that scholars in the subject of International Relations have developed is what we call **levels of analysis**. When confronted with a large subject, say the causes of World War I (1914–1918), scholars will usually break this bigger issue down into smaller, more manageable portions. For instance, they might identify a number of levels on which specific factors contributed to the outbreak of the war, and distinguish between the individual, the state or national level and the systemic levels of analysis:

- On the *individual level of analysis*, we would inquire as to how the ambitions, desires and actions of specific individuals, usually leaders, contributed to the event that we are studying. In the case of World War I, we may focus on Kaiser Wilhelm II's great ambitions for Germany as being one of the important causes of the war.
- On the *state or national level of analysis*, scholars could use characteristics or attributes of the state as a whole, or of parts of the state, to

Box 1.4: Concept * Conceptualise * Conceptual

'• An idea or notion resting on a rich and often complex history of thought = **a concept**
- To engage in a process of working with ideas, of reflective thinking and rethinking = **to conceptualise**
- Describing that which is mental and involves the activity of conceptualising = **conceptual**

Examples of sentences using these three words are:

The concept of evolution concerns the development of a species over hundreds, thousands or even millions of years.'

'Students are often required to conceptualise the relationship between individuals and social structures.'

'The development of conceptual skills is very important for a university student.'

A concept expresses more than a word; it is the reflective thinking and rethinking or grasping together (holding) of an idea or a class of objects. For example, this is a **conceptual** dictionary rather than a standard English dictionary or a discipline specific dictionary (e.g. a dictionary of philosophy) because it aims to provide *a window into the further reaches of language*; that is, into the way in which a word, imbued with the history of thought, achieves a richness and complexity. (Think, for example, of how Marx's thoughts on the motor of history – class conflict – enriched the concept of 'class'.) This dictionary therefore aims to 'map' important concepts for students who are entering the study of the humanities and social sciences.

Concepts also vary in complexity. The meaning of certain concepts is easy to access while you can take years really to understand other, more difficult concepts. The way the concept of evolution is used in the example implies a general notion of (or an idea about) evolution; people share concepts in a general way and this enables them to communicate with one another. However, this concept is also complex and before you could claim that you have truly understood it, you would have to do a lot of hard work – reading, thinking and discussing – in order to develop a sound understanding.

Finally, when you describe something as being conceptual, you are referring to something that is mental, something that has to do with thinking – something involving the activity of **conceptualising**. Thus 'conceptual skills' are those abilities that enable you mentally to process or interpret information.'

Craig *et al.* (1994:38)

explain an event or a state of affairs. Thus, the internal weakness of the Austro-Hungarian Empire in the run-up to the war is sometimes cited as being an important cause of World War I. Others emphasise the so-called blank cheque that Germany gave to Austria-Hungary to deal with Serbia in any way they deemed necessary. A third group might focus on the rigidity of the military establishment in Germany as being a crucial factor that undermined the possibility of political compromise, and made the war inevitable.

- The causes of an event such as World War I can also be analysed on a *systemic level* (distinguish systemic word from 'system<u>a</u>tic'). Here, features or attributes of the larger system in which an event occurred are taken into consideration to account for that event. In the case of World War I, we could explain the outbreak of the war as being a consequence of the rigidity of the bipolar alliance system in Europe at the time. The members of the two alliances (Britain, France and Russia on one side; Germany and Austria-Hungary on the other) were so closely '**chain-ganged**' to other members of their alliance partners, that any confrontation involving one of the allies was bound to suck in the others. When one state from each camp became involved in a conflict (Austria-Hungary from the one pole, versus Russia from the other), it was only a question of time before all the allies of each side became involved. Other systemic factors include the prevalent normative or ideological mood in a system, the degree of trust in the system, and the level of militarisation. All of these systemic factors, in their own right, could have contributed to World War I.

We return to the issue of the level of analysis in Chapter 3. For the time being, it is important to remember that we can use these levels to develop different views of any event or state of affairs in international relations. A good scholar is someone who always attempts to interrogate his or her subject matter from different angles. Using different levels of analysis is one way of doing this systematically.

Later, in Chapter 3, we will see how we can also develop different theoretical perspectives on an issue, event or state of affairs. However, please do not confuse different 'levels of analysis' with different theoretical perspectives. A choice of a 'levels of analysis' determines on which unit (the individual, the state or the system as a whole) you are going to focus. A theoretical perspective suggests ways in which to account for the behaviour of your chosen unit of analysis.

When dealing with the causes of events or states of affairs, it is useful to distinguish systematically between different types of causes. One possible distinction is between:
- *'deep' causes*, which provide the broader background or fundamental circumstances without which the event would not have been possible;
- *indirect causes*, which contributed to the event, but which were neither necessary nor sufficient in themselves to cause the event; and
- *precipitating causes*, which are the causes that immediately preceded the event, and which directly triggered it, so to speak. (*See* Nye, 1993:65.)

When we combine this three-way distinction between types of causes with our earlier distinction between levels of analysis, we can come up with a two-dimensional systematic treatment of any event. Table 1.1 provides a systematic treatment of the causes of World War I.

As you delve deeper into the social sciences, you will become acquainted with the meaning of following a scientific approach, and with the wide variety of specific methods and research categories that scientists use to generate reliable knowledge about their fields of study. Behind it all, however, lies the desire to be precise and systematic.

Table 1.1: Causes of World War I (1914–1918)

	Precipitating causes	Indirect causes	'Deep' causes
Systemic level		Ideology of nationalism permeated the European system	Rigid bipolar system of alliance
National or state level	Germany's 'blank cheque' to Austria-Hungary		German élite tried to postpone internal reform by means of external adventures
Individual level	Assassination of Crown Prince Franz Ferdinand of Austria-Hungary by a Serbian nationalist in Sarajevo	Weak, tired leaders in Austria-Hungary and Russia	Ambitions of Kaiser Wilhelm II of Germany

The fact that International Relations is a scientific subject does not mean that it engages in matters that are abstract and which have no bearing on the real-life, practical concerns of our everyday existence. As you can see from the issues raised at the beginning of this chapter, the subject of International Relations is deeply involved with questions and problems that affect our daily lives. Because it looks for the origins and causes of these questions and problems on the broadest human dimension possible in the global system, International Relations can provide a breadth and depth of understanding that is a precondition for finding practical answers and solutions.

Key concepts in this chapter

Concept
Definition
Global
Governance
Interdependence
International

Levels of analysis
Non-state actors
Power
State actors
World system

Suggested readings

The following books have been cited in the text of this chapter. They can also be consulted in their own right as useful texts if you want to know more about the core concerns of International Relations. Please look at the *Conceptual Dictionary* by Craig and her colleagues for excellent discussions of some of the most important concepts you will encounter during your university education.

- Berridge, G. R. (1997) *International Politics: States, Power and Conflict since 1945*. New York: Harvester Wheatsheaf.
- Bull, H. (1977) *The Anarchical Society: A Study of Order in World Politics*. New York:

Columbia University Press.

- Craig, A., Griesel, H. & Witz, L. (1994) *Conceptual Dictionary*. Kenwyn: Juta.
- Evans, G. & Newnham, J. (1992) *The Dictionary of World Politics: Reference Guide to Concepts, Ideas and Institutions*. New York: Harvester Wheatsheaf.
- Kegley, C. & Wittkopf, E. (1997) *World Politics: Trend and Transformation* (6th edition). New York: St Martin's Press.
- Nossal, K. (1998) *The Patterns of World Politics*. Scarborough: Prentice Hall.
- Nye, J. (1993) *Understanding International Conflicts: An Introduction to Theory and History*. New York: Harper Collins.
- Sprout, H. & Sprout, M. (1962) *Foundations of International Politics*. Princeton: D, van Nostrand.

2 The evolution of the global political economy

Anthony Leysens & Lisa Thompson

This chapter in outline
- Introduction: combining politics and economics
- Understanding the global political economy
  - Five structures in the global political economy
- The origins of the modern global political economy
- The nineteenth century: from openness to closure
- World War I and the beginning of the end of European domination
- The inter-war years, or the twenty year 'armistice'
- The Bretton Woods era and beyond
  - The origins of the Bretton Woods system
  - The end of the fixed exchange rate system
  - Decolonisation and superpower rivalry
  - The oil crisis, the debt trap and the call for a new international economic order (NIEO)
  - The reconstruction of Western Europe and the rise of Japan
  - The rise of the newly industrialised countries (NICs)
  - The Cold War and its demise
- Globalisation
  - From GATT to WTO
- The global political economy and the developing states in the new millennium

Introduction: combining politics and economics

This chapter offers a concise overview and analysis of the events that have contributed to the formation and nature of the present global political economy. Before doing so, however, we need to point out that our discussion of this topic is informed by a specific theory. A distinguished international relations scholar and historian, E. H. Carr, reflecting on the selection and use of facts in history, remarked that, 'It was, I think, one of Pirandello's characters who said that a fact is like a sack – it won't stand up till you've put something in it' (1961:11). What does this mean?

What Carr meant when he was discussing the issue of the use of facts in historical accounts is that the mere collection and presentation of accurate facts (a basic skill of the historian) on its own is not good enough. What is missing? He points out that the scholar also needs to move through a process of thinking about why some facts are selected and some are left out. This we do by using theories (*see* Chapter 3).

The approach that underlies our analysis in this chapter is sensitive to the point made by Carr: facts do not speak for themselves. Facts are like the puppet of a ventriloquist: they have a voice only to the extent that a theory speaks through them.

According to certain theories, especially realism and liberalism, the 'facts' of politics can be divorced from economics. This we reject. That economic activities cannot be viewed in isolation from political events is illustrated in Box 2.1. Here, Irwin Stelzer, a respected economist, reflects on the recent financial crisis in Asia and the advent of a single currency (the euro) for some of the member states of the European Union on 1 January 1999.

It is therefore essential that we talk about the political economy of past (and present) events, instead of politics and economics separately. The discipline (within International Relations) that focuses on the political economy of the world is called International Political Economy (IPE) or Global Political Economy (GPE). Some prefer the term GPE because they want to focus on events and process that go beyond the inter-nation state system (*see* Chapters 1 and 4).

Box 2.1: Reflections on recent and future economic events and the importance of politics

'How long will the Asian crisis last? How deep will the recessions in that part of the world prove to be? Will there be an Asian contagion, or will the problems remain localised? Will the euro prove to be a viable currency? Economists cannot provide hard answers to these questions, because those answers would be as much a function of politics as of economics – more in fact. How deep and long the Asian crisis will be is going to be determined by politicians in Japan and China, not by market forces. To add to global uncertainty, we have the euro, about to become the standard of value and the means of exchange in place of the currencies of 11 of Europe's industrial economies. The debate over its long-run impact rages, with some reputable economists predicting a new era of inflation-free growth, and others a period of economic turmoil and the eventual collapse of the new currency. Which forecast will prove correct is more a question of politics than of economics … That will be determined by the politicians, who might decide, if the new monetary regime produces higher unemployment, that such joblessness is a price worth paying for what they see as an end to war on the continent.'

Irwin Stelzer, *The Sunday Independent (Independent Business)*, 98.06.28

Understanding the global political economy (GPE)

At its core, GPE looks at the mutual influences of the market and sources of authority, including the state. In this interaction between the market and authority, tates are actors that execute their authority over a particular geographical territory that is demarcated by 'national' boundaries (*see* Chapter 4). The market and its actors (particularly **multinational corporations** or MNCs and **transnational corporations** or TNCs, *see* below) are not easily restricted by the borders of states. One of the issues that students of IPE look at is how states try to control markets and market actors in order to achieve goals that they see as being in the national interest. The outcome is determined by whether the state or the market holds more power in any given situation.

The issue of power – who has it, how it is exercised, for what purposes and in whose interest – indicates the difference between GPE and the subject of International Economics. The latter tends to negate questions relating to power relations (politics). In our attempts to answer these questions we must, of course, also identify the important actors in the global political economy. As has been indicated above, states are not the only actors. Apart from MNCs we also find non-governmental organisations (NGOs), such as trade unions, and international non-governmental organisations (INGOs), such as Greenpeace, which concerns itself with the negative effects of uninhibited industrial growth and consumption on the global environment (*see* Chapter 7). States are also members of intergovernmental organisations (IGOs), such as the **World Trade Organisation** (WTO) (*see* Chapter 6 and below), which play an important role in the regulation and co-ordination of the activities of states in a specific area, in this case trade.

It is possible to simplify this complex global system of various actors and the power relations between them by viewing the global political economy in terms of a framework that emphasises different global *structures*. A global structure is a rule-governed pattern of repeated human actions and interactions in a particular sphere in the international arena (for instance, trade across borders) that, because of repetition, becomes predictable and relatively systematic. Structures

prescribe norms of acceptable behaviour and rules for the management of interactions, and can also contain specific institutions (such as the WTO, in the trade structure, for instance). In terms of the norms and rules that they contain, structures reduce uncertainty, but they also constrain the behaviour of those (human) actors who gave rise to them. To put it another way, structures are not impersonal: they are maintained by human interaction, but the rules and norms that develop can condition human behaviour in such a way that even while the names and faces involved in the interactions may change, the interactions themselves remain relatively constant. The framework that is offered below differentiates between the different structures of the global political economy and was developed and set out by Susan Strange (1988).

Strange explains the global political economy in terms of four primary structures – security, production, finance and knowledge. Although Strange views trade as a secondary structure (she argues that it is, in fact, shaped by the other four structures), we include trade here as a fifth (sub)structure. The reason for this is that trade was one of the most important motivators for the increase in international interaction between the various regions of the world, particularly from the eighteenth century onwards. In this respect, international trade contributed significantly to the formation and evolution of an integrated world political economic system (*see* Wallerstein, 1979).

Because we are students of political economy, it is important for us to understand how power arises and how it is used in international interactions. Again following Susan Strange, we can distinguish between *structural* and *relational* power. Relational power refers to the ability of actor A to coerce (force) or influence actor B to do something that B would otherwise not consider doing. Actor A manages to do this because, in relation to B, it possesses more power capabilities (military power or economic might, for instance) or because B thinks that A has greater capabilities. In 1991, for example, the United States was able to lead an international coalition against Iraq and force the latter out of Kuwait by utilising (among other power capabilities) its superior military technology.

In contrast, structural power is exercised within the five structures, not through coercion, but by the ability of an actor to determine the rules according to which other actors have to behave within that structure. For instance, the United States, because of the tremendous size of its economy, which makes it a lucrative market for the exports of other states, has been able to influence and shape the rules and norms that govern international trade within the WTO and to which other member states must abide (Strange, 1988:24–26).

Next, we look briefly at the five structures, bearing in mind that this division into five structures is to provide analytical clarity. In practice the patterns and norms governing the structures overlap and converge.

Five structures in the global political economy

Strange (1988:45–46) describes the *security structure* as follows: 'In the international political economy of modern times, the security structure is built around the institution of the state'. Strictly speaking, whenever a person or group provides security for another person or group of persons, a security structure is in place. This means that non-state actors can also provide security. However, Strange points out that states have come to dominate in the international security structure with profound effects on the global political economy. States are able to exercise coercive force legitimately. The international security structure is dominated by those states that have a monopoly on both forms of power, structural and relational. For example, during the Cold War (*see* below) the security structure was dominated by two superpowers, the United States (US) and the Union of Soviet Socialist Republics (USSR). International production, trade and finance interactions were affected by the relations that other states in the system had with the two dominant

powers and the rivalry between them.

Strange (1988:29) explains that the *production structure* refers to '(w)ho decides what shall be produced, by whom, by what means and with what combination of land, labour, capital and technology'. Who determines what is to be produced are those actors who, on a variety of levels, direct the course of 'free market' capitalism. Two powers have profoundly shaped the patterns of interaction taking place within the international production structure as we know it today – Britain, during the period of the Industrial Revolution in the 1800s up until World War I, and the US since then. Since the early 1960s this dominance has, to some extent, been whittled away by the economic recovery of Western Europe and Japan, but the US nevertheless has managed to maintain its position as a **hegemon**. The global production structure of the late twentieth century is characterised by the dominance of international production over national production. To this effect, the transnationalistion of production (through the activities of MNCs) has altered the shape of production during the post-World War II era.

The *trade (sub)structure* refers to the circulation of goods and services in the international economy. International trade drives production, although international trade does not always take place as a result of formal production in factories. For states and businesses, international trade plays an increasingly important role. The international marketplace is also very competitive in terms of goods and services entering the export market, thus states have to be sensitive to both international demand and supply. For example, one of the reasons why developing states struggle to be competitive in terms of international trade is that other more developed states can produce a greater range of goods (agricultural products, manufactured goods, industrial products) at relatively low cost, leaving little opportunity for developing states to enter and compete in the global market.

The *financial structure* is, according to Strange (1988:35–36), 'admittedly, rather more peculiar to

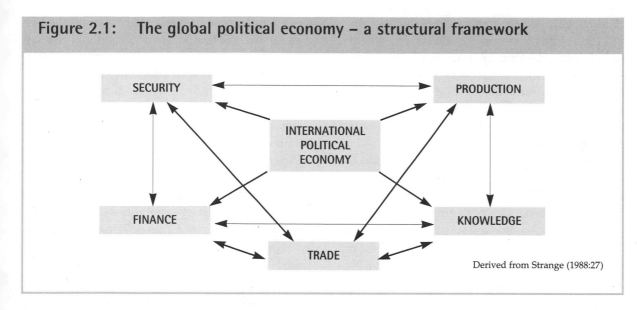

Figure 2.1: The global political economy – a structural framework

SECURITY

PRODUCTION

INTERNATIONAL POLITICAL ECONOMY

FINANCE

KNOWLEDGE

TRADE

Derived from Strange (1988:27)

advanced industrialised economies'. Understanding this structure is slightly more difficult because it includes not just the international flows of money in the forms of payment of imports, loans, foreign direct investment and aid, but also includes how, and on what terms, the value of currencies is determined by buyers and sellers in **financial markets**. This structure plays an extremely important role in the developing world, especially through powerful international lending institutions like the International Monetary Fund (IMF) and the World Bank. We will return to this point in the second half of the chapter.

The *knowledge structure* can be understood as accumulated information and patterns of belief that are regarded as legitimate in providing the most accurate understanding of the world around us. This structure is also of major importance to developing states. It is characterised by the generation of increasingly sophisticated technology, scientific discovery and the generation of new ideas, as well as the enforcement of dominant ideas, or what some analysts have called hegemonic knowledge. The *knowledge structure*, according to Strange (1991:37) is 'the … structure within which relational power is exercised, bargains are struck, and who gets what, is finally decided'. Strange is referring to the ways in

which dominant ideas come to shape our understanding of the world around us. These ideas are really values that are upheld by states that possess relational and structural power, mostly in the developed world. Western Europe and the US have, since the sixteenth century, dominated the knowledge structure, with profound effects on the developing world. Developing states have been characterised as backward by virtue of their lack of input into, and influence within, this structure.

Understanding the values that underpin these structures makes it necessary to briefly refer to the three main theoretical approaches to GPE. These approaches try to explain the development of the global political economy, but historically they have also played a very important role in determining the values as well as the actions of important actors within the global political and economic arenas.

The first approach, *mercantilism* or *economic nationalism*, emphasises the importance of the national interest when formulating economic policy. This approach shares much in common with realist theory (*see* Chapter 3). The national interest is seen to predominate as one of the main explanatory factors governing patterns of behaviour of states, and the approach underlines the need for state power to mediate between conflicting societal values in the global system.

The second approach, *liberalism*, explains the global political economy in terms of the primacy of individual interest. It is tied closely to neo-classical economics theory that emphasises the importance of free markets. The approach underpins the values of individual enterprise and equal opportunity.

The third approach, transformative *Marxism* (*see* Chapter 3) examines the global economy in terms of the dominance of classes or class interests. The defining aspect of this approach is its focus on the negative aspects of capitalist production, especially the way in which workers are exploited by those who own the means of production. It is a criticism of the way in which individual gain is prioritised over equity within and between societies. The value that this approach emphasises is equity (Balaam & Veseth, 1996:21–76).

In the next sections, we trace the evolution of the global political economy. Because the world has a market that is **capitalist** in nature, and because its major political units are states, we start our analysis with the origins of the modern state and the beginning of the development of the capitalist system as a means of production and trade.

At this stage you should take note that the expansion of the capitalist system from where it originated (Northwest Europe, specifically Britain, France and Germany – *see* Map 1) incorporated various parts of the world on an unequal basis. These inequalities are still features of the world today (for instance, the differences in wealth between the North and the South and between different states in the South, such as South Africa in comparison with other states in the Southern African region – *see* Chapters 13 and 14). The word 'evolution' in the title of this chapter therefore refers to how the global political economy changed with the passing of time. It does not refer to a process that has necessarily improved the lives of everyone on the planet.

Secondly, a historical overview that leads us to the global political economy of today will have to start in Europe, because that is where the origins of the contemporary international system are to be found. This does not mean that the characteristics of what we call the modern state can only be historically perceived in Northwest Europe. The Kingdoms of Ghana (fifth to eleventh centuries) and Mali (thirteenth to fourteenth centuries) in West Africa and the Central African Empire of Monomotapa (fifteenth century) were examples of highly organised societies that exhibited many of the administrative functions and military capabilities of the modern state (*see* Chapter 8). The development of the contemporary global economy can, however, be traced to Northwest Europe – and we need to trace its development in conjunction with the development of the modern state in the same region.

The origins of the modern global political economy

The beginning of the period in which the state is recognised as the primary unit of political organisation is usually dated to the **Peace of Westphalia** (1648). This event marked the end of a series of religious wars, as well as the demise of the political authority of the Pope and the Roman Catholic Church over **feudal** Europe. From 1648, the authority of the ruler (king) of a state was supreme and legitimate. States were regarded as sovereign, meaning that they were equal in their legal standing and that no higher authority could be exercised over them. Under the Westphalian system, states adhered to rights and obligations (rules) that they had to respect in their interactions with one another. These related, for example, to the right to form alliances, the treatment of envoys and diplomats, and the conduct of war (Papp, 1994:29–30).

When we want to determine a precise date or period for the origins of the capitalist economy as a mode of production we run into more difficulties. According to Cox (1987:51–52), it depends on whether we view capitalism as an economic system that increases the wealth (capital) of merchants by means of trade (exchange) or whether we regard it as a means of producing goods that enable the system itself to grow and spread. Cox (1987) uses the latter view, which leads him to focus on the nineteenth century as the century when capitalism became the *dominant* mode of production.

However, if we want to determine when capitalism first *emerged* (in embryonic form) as a way to trade and produce, we would agree with scholars such as Wallerstein (1974) who identifies the late fifteenth and early sixteenth centuries as the beginning of the development of modern capitalism, and Braudel (1982) who gives us a rich and detailed account of the historical development of capitalism from the fifteenth to the eighteenth centuries. Furthermore, Wallerstein (1979) rightly stresses that the development of the modern state and the development of the modern global (capitalist) economy cannot be understood in isolation from each other.

The early state system during the seventeenth and eighteenth centuries was characterised by the idea of 'state reason' ('*raison d' état*'). The idea or ideology of state reason demanded that the state should use every means and all the resources at its disposal to maintain and enhance its own continued existence among other states. The self-centred economic policy that went hand in hand with this principle is known as **mercantilism**.

Secondly, the early modern states were absolutist, in that the loyalty of those within the borders of the new states was directed at the monarch. This is illustrated in the often quoted words of Louis XIV, King of France, who stated: '*L'état, c'est moi*' ('I am the state').

Mercantilist policies (generally followed by European states during the seventeenth and eighteenth centuries) emphasised the continued existence and increase of state power through economic means. The acquisition of wealth (through trade, taxes and the hoarding of gold and silver bullion) was perceived as vital. This enabled monarchs to pay for mercenaries who fought their territorial wars for them, as well as the costs of state administration and the maintenance of law and order (Braudel, 1982:515).

At the time of the formation of the modern state system, European explorers (Portuguese, Spanish, French, English and Dutch) had already travelled to most parts of the world. These areas (incorporated during the first phase of colonisation) were the 'external and peripheral areas of the world-economy' (Wallerstein, 1979:302). They provided the mercantilist states of Northwestern and Southern Europe with silver and gold bullion (from North and South America, and West Africa), spices for the preservation of food (from Asia), which were paid for in gold and silver, sugar (from the West Indies and Central America), and wood and leather (from North and South America). By the second half of the seventeenth century, the Dutch had established a presence in the East Indies and the Cape of Good Hope. British expansion brought under its influence the colonies in North America, the Hudson Bay Territory (Canada), Gambia in West Africa and Calcutta in India. French colonisation extended from the Hudson Bay Territory to Louisiana in North America, South East Asia, and Senegal in West Africa. The Spanish Empire's borders in what is today known as Latin America ran from Mexico in the north, right down the continent to the river La Plata (the present-day border of Argentina). The Portuguese had colonised the area that roughly corresponds to present-day Brazil, and had also established themselves on the west coast (Angola) and east coast (Mozambique) of Africa. The French and Dutch also had a small presence in the north of South America (Guiana) (Kennedy, 1987:112).

The existence of a number of powerful sovereign states after Westphalia, and their policies of mercantilism and territorial expansion, led to the development of a system to ensure some form of stability and predictability in their interaction with one another. This system has been termed the '**balance of power**' system (*see* also Chapter 3)

Box 2.2: European wars during the late seventeenth and eighteenth centuries

1665	Second Anglo-Dutch War
1667–1668	France-Spain (Southern Netherlands)
1672–1674	Third Anglo-Dutch War
1672–1678	France-United Provinces (Netherlands)
1683	France-Spain
1689–1697	Nine Years War (France against Britain, Netherlands, Spain, Austria and the major German kingdoms)
1702–1713	War of the Spanish Succession (France and Spain against Britain, Austria and the Netherlands)
1699–1721	Sweden against Russia, Denmark and Poland
1735–1739	Austria and Russia against Turkey (the Ottoman Empire)
1740–1748	War of the Austrian Succession (Prussia, France and Spain against Austria and Britain)
1756–1763	Seven Years War (Prussia and Britain against France, Austria and Russia)
1776–1783	War of American Independence (Britain against American colonists, France and Spain; the latter two entered the war in 1778)
1793–1795	Prussia, Austria, England, Spain and Russia against revolutionary France
1798–1800	England, Russia, Austria, Turkey, Portugal and Naples against Napoleonic France

Derived from Kennedy (1987:100–139) and Bowle (1962:320–321)

and functions according to the principle that the weaker states will form alliances with stronger states (or one strong state) to protect themselves from the territorial ambitions of other stronger states. Strong states also form alliances with other strong states to counter the influence of a potential hegemonic power.

The eighteenth century balance-of-power system was not effective if we judge it in terms of the absence of war. War was generally accepted as a means to acquire wealth and territory and to maintain the balance of power. In fact, the latter half of the seventeenth century and virtually the whole of the eighteenth century were characterised by protracted wars between the major powers and the loss of sovereignty by a number of states (most notably Poland).

For example, the consolidated state inherited by Louis XIV (King of France) and his attempt to put his grandson on the throne of Spain posed an early threat to the commercial and colonial interests of the British and Dutch, who formed an alliance that defeated the French in the War of Spanish Succession (1702–1713). Before this, commercial rivalry between the Dutch and English had led to the outbreak of war between them (for instance, the Second Anglo-Dutch War of 1665). The British would later make peace with the Dutch to thwart French ambitions (1667) in the Southern Netherlands, which belonged to Spain. However, they were soon at war with the Dutch again (Third Anglo-Dutch War, 1672–1674). This time Britain was in alliance with France! French territorial expansion was later (1697) checked by a coalition consisting of the Netherlands, Britain, Austria, Spain and the larger German states (Kennedy, 1987:100–101, 104; Bowle, 1962:320–321).

In the east, the Turkish (Ottoman Empire) advance to Vienna was neutralised by an alliance between the Austrians, Germans and Poles. By the end of the seventeenth century the Ottoman Empire was no longer a threat to the survival of the Hapsburg Empire (Austria-Hungary). Russia's status (under Peter the Great) as a major power was confirmed by the defeat of the Swedes in 1721. The ancient medieval state of Poland, for all intents and purposes, ceased to exist in 1795 when it was divided between Prussia and Russia.

The wars fought during the eighteenth

the European balance of power (Kennedy, 1987:113). Box 2.2 summarises some of the major wars that took place during the second half of the seventeenth and eighteenth centuries.

In terms of the development of early capitalist production, an important difference between the feudal system and the emerging capitalist system was that, in the former, the extra agricultural produce of the peasant farmer was appropriated by the feudal lord who, in exchange, would allow the peasant to stay on the land. From the fifteenth century (and particularly after Westphalia), however, the tendency in some parts of Northwestern Europe was towards small-scale farming by independent peasants who sold some of their (surplus) produce in the town or village market. Overall, however, the political system was based on the power of the monarch and the land-owning (aristocratic) classes, who extracted rents from the farmers on their land. Employed labour, in the sense that we know it today, did not exist. Those peasants who could not remain on the land became 'wanderers', a vast, moving and unorganised class, who rarely found work and were paid little for it. Cox (1987:44) categorises them as 'primitive labour', while Braudel (1982:506) talks of paupers as 'a permanent mass of unfortunates unprovided for, with nothing left to do'.

Cox (1987:52–58) points out that the marketing of extra produce by independent farmers and the paying of wages by manufacturers (artisans) in the seventeenth and eighteenth centuries were necessary conditions for the development of the capitalist system, but not sufficient ones. It is to these other developments that we must now turn. But before we do so, we need to also highlight what was happening in other parts of the world during the period 1650–1800, and before (see Box 2.3; for a detailed account of the African experience during this time, see Chapter 8).

To summarise in terms of the five structures outlined in the first section, we can say that *security* during the period of the founding of the modern capitalist state system was centred on the state. Territorial expansion and the acquisition of

century centred mainly on French-English rivalry and the respective allies of the belligerents, as well as the maintenance and expansion of continental and colonial empires (the Ottomans in Turkey; the Hapsburgs in Austria and the Hohenzollerns in Brandenburg-Prussia). By the middle of the century, these wars had been extended to the colonies (for instance, French-English rivalry in North America). During the Seven Years War, both France and Britain admitted that trade and the colonies (which generated some of the wealth to finance these costly conflicts) made a vital difference to the outcome and wealth through *trade* and colonisation were undertaken in the name of 'state reason' and led directly to the wars of the period. In the realm of ideas (*knowledge*), the notion of the sovereignty of the individual state replaced the idea of a universalist European empire under the Holy Roman Church. This separation (between church and state) went hand in hand with a shifting of responsibility for education to the state, as those in power became aware of the importance of science and technology for the strengthening of capabilities. *Production* was still, to a large extent, based on agriculture, but a rapid shift towards manufacturing (particularly in England) was taking place during the second half of the eighteenth century. The importance of *finance* (and credit) is illustrated by Britain's ability to raise funds for its many wars with France through the Bank of England (established in 1694). Spain's inability to manage its finances (despite its gold income from the Americas) was one of the reasons for its gradual decline.

The nineteenth century: from openness to closure

The nineteenth century was, without a doubt, a crucial phase in the evolution of the contemporary global political economy. Paul Johnson (1991) argues that the origin of the modern system we know today can be traced to developments in 'world society' between the years 1815 to 1830. In many ways, the nineteenth century was Britain's century, just as the twentieth century would later be called the 'American century'. These events can only be understood by looking at how political and economic developments within Britain radiated outwards and dominated the world until the period just before the outbreak of World War I.

The seeds of the changes that took place were, of course, already sown during the last thirty years of the eighteenth century. The legitimacy of the absolute monarch was challenged by the American (1776) and French (1789) revolutions and had major repercussions for Europe and Britain in the years that followed. The example of the American revolution and the turbulence of the Napoleonic wars after the French Revolution (1789) led to the formation of independent states (and thus, the expansion of the European state system) in most of Latin America (Argentina, 1816; Brazil, 1822; Bolivia, 1825; Chile, 1818; Costa Rica, 1821; Ecuador, 1822; El Salvador, 1821; Nicaragua, 1838; Paraguay, 1811; Peru, 1824; Uruguay, 1828; and Venezuela, 1810).

The French Revolution, while rejecting the idea of the sovereign monarch and putting sovereignty in the hands of the people, also became a threat to the European state system itself. Napoleon Bonaparte, seizing the moment in the midst of the turmoil of revolutionary France, crowned himself emperor in 1804. Napoleon's idea of a united Europe with him as its ruler led to the conquest by the French Imperial Army of most of Europe. In 1812, he invaded Russia, but was defeated by the vastness of the country and the long Russian winter. In 1815, he was finally defeated at Waterloo by an alliance consisting of Britain, Prussia, Austria and Russia.

The defeat of Napoleon was followed by the Congress of Vienna in 1815, and the institutionalisation of a European balance-of-power system. This arrangement between the victorious powers (and defeated France) worked remarkably well and ensured peace and stability in Europe for the greatest part of the nineteenth century (the exceptions were the Crimean War from 1853 to 1856, in which France, Britain and Turkey were allied against Russia; and the Franco-Prussian War of 1870–1871). The unwritten rules of this balance-of-power system were: great power co-operation through diplomacy; territorial changes needed the approval of the major powers; the status of the major participants needed to be guaranteed; and the interests of the major powers could not be challenged, nor could their 'prestige and honour' be brought into dispute (Elrod, 1989:450–451).

The role of Britain in maintaining the

stability (acting as 'balancer') of the European system was extremely important as we shall see later, It managed to do this because it became the dominant power in Europe after 1815, and because the system was flexible (Papp, 1994:38). In the meantime, Adam Smith had published his *An Enquiry into the Nature and Causes of the Wealth of Nations* in 1776. His argument was a direct attack on the policy of mercantilism, and stated that free and open trade without government interference would increase productivity and would be of benefit to all states. This, in effect, meant that states would have to stop taxing the products of other states, and also abolish regulations that restricted the activities of their own merchants. The economic policy that followed the principles set out by Adam Smith is called free-market liberalism. The basic assumptions of this argument came into practice during the hegemonic leadership of Britain during the first half of the nineteenth century.

The liberal world system under the hegemonic leadership of Britain (the Pax Britannica) resulted from the consolidation of political stability in that country (this ensured hegemony 'at home' and avoided conflict between social forces); the role of Britain in maintaining the European balance of power; Britain's unrivalled naval power; and the technological advances in transportation and communications (the invention of the steam engine led to the development of Britain's railway system and its diffusion to the rest of the world; steam also speeded up sea travel, and led to the mechanisation of the manufacturing process), which greatly facilitated the expansion of trade and investment.

Box 2.4 presents a historical/explanatory summation of the process that led to Britain's gradual political economic transformation during the first half of the nineteenth century.

The result of the events referred to above was a type of state in Britain characterised by the hegemony of the middle classes (a reflection of the shifting of economic power to manufacturers and industrialists) in coalition with the old landowning class. The expansion of the doctrine of

Box 2.4: The consolidation of political–economic change in Britain (1815–1851)

1832 – First Reform Bill. Increases political participation by extending voting rights coupled to ownership of property. The effect is to incorporate the middle class (or manufacturers) into the state, and to exclude labour.

1834 – New Poor Law Act. Abolishes payment of a minimum amount, linked to the price of bread, to the poor (otherwise known as the 'Speenhamland' system). Effectively promotes labour mobility (to the cities) and wage labour.

1839 – Foundation of Anti-Corn-Law League by manufacturers and merchants to protest the protection of local corn farmers against cheaper imported corn. This protection, argues liberals such as Richard Cobden, increases food prices in the cities and necessitates the payment of higher wages.

1842 – Introduction of income tax. Provides the state with an alternative source of income and thus allows for the rapid abolishment and reduction of taxes on imported products.

1844 – Passing of the Bank Act. Currency issue by the Bank of Britain is coupled to gold. This introduces the 'gold standard'.

1846 – Repeal of the Corn Laws. Removes the reason for a budding coalition between manufacturers (the middle classes) and workers against the landowning aristocracy.

Derived from Cox (1987:123–147) and Thomson (1950:56–98)

free trade continued apace during the second half of the nineteenth century. Open trade between the major European states was promoted by agreements that reduced taxes on imported goods (the US was not included in these reciprocal arrangements).

Britain's final introduction of the gold standard in 1844 (the backing of the issuing of bank notes by gold) became generally accepted by other major trading states only after 1870.

Nevertheless, the example set by the Bank of England, as well as the example of Britain's policy of open trade, went a long way in stabilising international **monetary relations** and the promoting of the free exchange of goods (Walter, 1993:90–92).

The ideas that underpinned Britain's hegemony after 1815 and up to 1870 were derived from Adam Smith's doctrine of free trade and its own process of gradual political reform. In terms of the development of technology (*knowledge*), the period saw the development of efficient road and rail transportation networks, as well as the advent of steam power on land and sea. This facilitated more rapid transportation of people and goods and led to an increase in *trade*. *Security* was still the preserve of states, and stability was maintained through the balance-of-power system that had been negotiated in Vienna after the Napoleonic wars. The superiority of the British Navy facilitated trade, and the *production* capabilities that ensured Britain's predominance were rooted in its manufacturing and industrial base. Britain's introduction of the gold standard provided stability in international currency exchange, while credit (*finance*) was made available through British finance houses.

The transformation that took place under British tutelage in the second half of the nineteenth century amounted to the first phase of what we today call 'globalisation' (*see* below). The world economy moved from being restricted to a small amount of trade between mercantilist states to having 'an autonomy of its own' (Cox, 1987:107). The technological improvements that resulted in faster and safer transportation and better communication resulted in a type of expansion that rapidly saw the shrinking of time and space. During this time, important changes also took place in Africa's relations with the world, not the least of which was the abolishment of the slave trade, which was initiated by Britain and enforced by its navy (for a detailed account, *see* Chapter 8).

The decade that started in 1870 would see two major events that were destined to significantly affect the history of Europe and the rest of the world. In 1871, the twenty-five separate German states were unified under the leadership of Count Otto von Bismarck (Italy was unified in 1861). To accomplish this, Prussia had to fight three wars: against Denmark (1864), Austria-Hungary (1866) and France (1870). The second event was the downturn experienced by the global economy from 1873 to 1896. Both events can be connected to the last 'scramble' for colonies by the major European powers between 1875 and 1914, the outlines of which were drawn during the 1884–1885 Berlin Conference on West Africa (Carruthers, 1997:52; Hoogvelt, 1997:18).

German unification brought into being an enormous state whose population outnumbered those of the other major powers, except for the Russian Empire. The new state was determined to 'catch up' with the other European powers and embarked on a massive industrialisation programme. At the same time, to contribute to its great power status and to make inroads in an international market that was dominated by Britain, France, the United States and Japan, it began to compete with other colonial powers for overseas possessions. Japan, under the Emperor Meiji, had started its programme to 'catch up' with the European powers in 1868. By 1912, the country had reorganised itself into a significant military industrial power. This was illustrated in 1904–1905, when Japan defeated Russia in a war that was sparked by Japanese expansionist policies towards the Manchurian region of China.

Germany's expansionist potential was feared by other European powers and by the beginning of the twentieth century, Britain, Russia and France were bound by treaty in opposition to the Triple Alliance (1882), which consisted of Germany, Austria-Hungary and Italy. Furthermore, rapid competitive industrialisation (to enhance military capabilities) and the need to 'cement' capital and labour to the goals of the state (in Germany's case) led to a return to protectionist trade policies. Britain held out the longest, but by the beginning of World War I in 1914, the open trade system of the nineteenth century had all but disappeared.

Britain, in the meantime, was experiencing an important shift in the alignment of social groups (capital and labour) and in the way in which goods were being produced. In 1867, the vote was extended to the working class. This increased working class political participation and resulted in the demand for and the enactment of a number of social reforms that Cox (1987:158) sees as the beginning of the development of the **welfare state**. Secondly, the economic slump of 1873–1896 led to the downfall of many smaller companies and the subsequent concentration of capital in larger corporations. These larger companies were well placed to take advantage of a range of new technologies that were developed from 1896 onwards (for instance electricity, synthetics and the combustion engine), which were applied by manufacturers to develop a new form of production, called assembly line production. This reduced the cost of labour (less skills were needed) and removed labour even further from the control of production. Workers could, however, through collective organisation bring production to a halt. From 1900, the state would play a more active role in ensuring that the interests of capital and labour were harmonised in the national interest. This can be seen as the beginning of **tripartism** (Cox, 1987:159–162).

As noted above, colonisation became an important goal in the rivalry among the industrialising European powers. According to Hoogvelt (1997:18), whereas European rule encompassed 67% of the world's land area (acquired between 1800 and 1878), between 1878 and 1914 a further 18% of territory was added to the total. Some observers note that the European powers benefited more from trade with one another, and that the colonial territories provided small economic rewards in comparison. The main drive behind the final acquisition of colonies was political ambition and the perceived need to 'civilise' the world for commerce. We would agree with Hoogvelt (1997:21), however, that the changes in production relations referred to above, and the accompanying concentration of capital, played as important a role in the expansion of the European political economic system as political ambition/rivalry did.

World War I and the beginning of the end of European dominance

As we saw above, the challenge of a unified Germany gave a boost to imperialist rivalry (political and economic), and it changed the balance of power in Europe and led to the implementation of protectionist policies in international trade. Furthermore, the slow disintegration of the Ottoman Empire was causing instability in the Balkan region. Here, various disparate ethnic nationalities that were contained under Turkish hegemony were engaged in open warfare in an attempt to secure independence. One of the new states that emerged out of this was Serbia.

In June 1914, a Serbian nationalist assassinated the Archduke Franz Ferdinand (Crown Prince of the Austro-Hungarian Empire) in Sarajevo. The Austrians demanded that they be allowed to search for the assassin in Serbia. After the latter refused, Austria started making preparations to invade. Russia, however, was committed to the defence of Serbia in terms of a secret treaty between the two countries and the Czar ordered a general mobilisation. Germany, in terms of the Triple Alliance, started its own mobilisation. Austria-Hungary, relying on German support in case of a conflict with the Russians, ignored urgent communications from Berlin and invaded Serbia. In terms of a pre-prepared plan (the 'Schlieffen Plan'), designed to prevent a simultaneous engagement on two fronts (Russia and France), Germany launched a full-scale invasion of France. By August 1914, a world war had started that drew in most of the major powers and their dominions, and caused hitherto unseen devastation. It lasted for four years (until 1918).

By the end of the war, the economies of both the victorious and defeated states were in a state of decline. Britain and France owed large sums of money to the US, the Ottoman and Austro-Hungarian Empires were no more, and the US (who had entered the war only in 1917) played a major role in the shaping of the post-war order through its President, Woodrow Wilson. Wilson's influence on the Treaty of Versailles (1919) is encapsulated in his famous 'fourteen points' (*see* Chapter 3). The most important of these related to his proposed notion of **collective security**, out of which the League of Nations was born. This permanent international organisation of the world's states was to ensure that, through the application of international norms and mediation, aggression would be held in check. If required, all states would have to collectively act against an aggressor state.

Secondly, the principle of national self-determination would ensure that each nation had its own sovereign democratic state. This resulted in the creation of a number of new states (Hungary, Czechoslovakia, Austria, Hungary, Yugoslavia, Romania, Estonia, Latvia and Lithuania) and the restoration of Polish independence. Most of these states, however, did not reflect the principle of one nation one state (for instance, Yugoslavia and Czechoslovakia) and were regarded as weak states. Wilson also emphasised the importance of the removal of barriers to trade and the conducting of 'open' diplomacy (as opposed to the secret treaties that had contributed to the start of the war).

Another important change in the system had been brought about by the coming into being of a 'state of a different kind'. The Bolshevik Revolution had toppled the Russian Empire of the Czar in 1917 and, after the ensuing civil war (1918–1920) between the Czarist loyalists and the Bolsheviks had ended, the Union of Soviet Socialist Republics (USSR) came into being. The new state was perceived as a threat by the other major states because it was predicated on supporting (through the Communist International) and expecting working class (proletariat) revolutions in other parts of the industrialised world. This led to limited intervention by, among others, the United States, Britain, France and Japan in the war between the Bolsheviks and the Loyalists. However, after the consolidation of power by the Bolshevik Party (who renamed themselves the Communist Party of the Soviet Union – the CPSU) and the death of Lenin (the leader and driving force behind the revolution), the new leader of the CPSU, Joseph Stalin, declared that the USSR would first have to concentrate on 'building socialism within one country'. This reduced the immediate antagonism between the USSR, the US and Europe.

Lastly, Germany was severely dealt with after World War I. A 'war guilt' clause in the Treaty of Versailles blamed Germany for the war. Under this clause Germany had to pay reparations to the victors, restore lost land to France and Poland, and had to accept the French occupation of the Saarland (an industrial area) and the Rhineland (to ensure continued demilitarisation) (Carruthers, 1997:54–55).

The inter-war years, or the twenty year 'armistice'

Many observers criticised the Treaty of Versailles, after its conclusion. One of the French generals (Foch) stated that it would not bring lasting peace, but only a 'twenty year armistice' (Carruthers, 1997:57). The reasons given by the well-known British economist, John Maynard Keynes, were that the harsh war reparations that Germany had to pay would prevent the country from recovering economically. This would, in turn, negatively affect Europe's economic growth. Furthermore, and ironically, the US Congress refused to ratify the treaty and entered into a separate peace agreement with Germany (1921), which did not include the 'war guilt' clause. This signalled an unwillingness by the US to involve itself directly in European affairs and left the global political economy in a situation in which Britain was economically too weak to play a leadership role, and the US, because of its history of isolating itself from Europe, was not willing to fill the power vacuum that resulted.

During the years between World War I and World War II, the US economy outperformed its closest rivals by far. In 1929, it produced 42% of the world's industrial output compared to Britain, France and Germany, which together produced only 28% (Carruthers, 1997:57). Isaak (1995:121) states that 45% of the world's manufactured products came from the US in 1929. United States exports accounted for 20% of world exports, but made up only 6% of the US Gross National Product (GNP). During the same year (1929), the Wall Street Stock Market crashed and ushered in the Great Depression (1929–1933). The effects were felt world-wide (an indication of the growing interdependence of the world economy), but particularly in Germany. To protect itself from the impact of imports on its domestic producers, the US Congress passed the Smoot-Hawley Tariff Act (1930), which led to similar protectionist measures in the rest of the world. By 1933, world trade in manufactured goods had dropped by 40%, compared to 1930. Additionally, the US could not afford to continue to extend loans to an ailing Europe. The protectionist policies that followed, from the example set by the US, led to a serious decline in trade and contributed directly to a world-wide recession. The Trade Act that was passed by the US Congress in 1934 delegated the authority over tariffs to the executive and was the first indication that the US would henceforth use its power to manage trade to its own benefit (*see* below).

The hyperinflation, unemployment and increasing poverty of the early 1930s in Germany, together with continuing resentment of the terms imposed by the Treaty of Versailles, were fertile ground for the emergence of extreme right-wing movements, such as Adolf Hitler's National Socialist (Nazi) Party. Japan, too, was hard hit by the world economic depression and (even though it was against Germany during World War I) was unhappy with the terms of the Treaty of Versailles. The Japanese had expected more territory in return for their role in the war. Moreover, the Japanese did not manage to have a clause on racial equality included in the Treaty. Furthermore, the Washington Treaty (1921–1922) was resented for its attempt to limit the growth of the Japanese Navy. In 1930, the Japanese, on the pretext of a border skirmish, invaded and occupied the Chinese region of Manchuria. Mediation by the League of Nations in 1933 resulted in a Japanese walkout. In the same year, Adolf Hitler was elected as chancellor and took Germany out of the League of Nations. By 1937, Germany, Italy and Japan had joined in the Anti-**Comintern** Pact. Britain and France entered into treaties with the new states of Central Europe to guarantee their independence.

The road to war in Europe was characterised by a series of expansionist movements: 1936 – the German occupation of the Rhineland demilitarised zone; 1938 – Germany annexes Austria; 1938

– Germany 'enters' Czechoslovakia; 1939 – Germany occupies remainder of Czechoslovakia; 1939 – Germany invades Poland. The invasion of Poland by Germany resulted in a declaration of war by Britain and France on 3 September 1939. Japan had declared war against China in 1937, and attacked the US Navy in Pearl Harbour in 1941. Italy entered the war in 1940.

The end of the war in 1945 saw the first (and to date only) use of nuclear bombs when the US attempted to force Japan into submission. The end of the war was also the end of a long period during which European states had managed to dominate the world political economy. The United States emerged from the war as the strongest political economic power and was determined to prevent a repeat of the economic instability that had created the ideal circumstances for the rise of Fascism and Nazism. Consequently, it convened a conference with its major allies in Bretton Woods (New Hampshire) in 1944. Here the rules that were to underpin the post-war economic system were set out. When the US accepted and carried out the role of global hegemon, a position that had been vacated by Britain towards the end of the previous century, a new period was ushered in.

The inter-war period was, in sum, supposed to be based on the ideas of collective security, open diplomacy, national self-determination and open trade. The institution that was to be the instrument of ensuring stability was the League of Nations, while the Washington Treaty was an attempt to prevent the extensive arms build-up that had occurred before World War I. However, in the absence of a hegemon with the will (and the capacity) to ensure that the proposed 'rules' were adhered to, the inter-war order was one which was characterised by global political economic instability. Credit was in short supply, because war-ravaged Europe could not provide it and the US was unwilling to do so. In fact, money flowed from Germany to France and England, both of whom had to repay war debts to the US. In terms of production, US manufacturers were making impressive advances. World trade was greatly reduced by the protectionist policies that were followed during the 1929–1933 recession.

The Bretton Woods era and beyond

The origins of the Bretton Woods system

We have discussed how crises occurring at the level of global production and finance during the late 1920s and early 1930s helped considerably to make the rise of Hitler possible. The international community, and particularly the US, was determined that this should not occur again. High on the list of priorities for the US, emerging as the dominant state leader, or superpower, of the West, was the stability of the international financial order, particularly currency stability. The US and its Western European allies wanted to ensure that the value of domestic currencies would never again be subject to wild fluctuations and devastating devaluations of the nature experienced by Germany in the 1930s. This led to the establishment of the Bretton Woods institutions in 1944. These institutions, the International Monetary Fund (IMF) and the International Bank for Reconstruction and Development (IBRD) (colloquially known as The World Bank), together with the General Agreement on Tariffs and Trade (GATT), which became the World Trade Organisation (WTO) in 1995, have had a profound effect on the nature and shape of the global political economy (Williams, 1994: 1–24). The reasons for their establishment went hand in hand with the commitment of the US to uphold the stability and coherency of the world capitalist system and to ensure the reconstruction of the devastated Western European states. It was through the establishment of these institutions, and particularly the dominant role of the US within them, that the US extended its sphere of influence in the West. The Soviet Union also established its hegemony in Eastern Europe through the establishment of the Council for Mutual Economic Assistance (CMEA, also known as COMECON) in 1949. However, the CMEA did not have the financial resources of the IMF and World Bank and functioned more as a Soviet-dominated forum for co-ordinating the centrally planned economies of communist states in Eastern Europe. Nonetheless, in spite of the ideological battlelines, the East and West were never totally separate in terms of trade and finance (Gill & Law, 1988, 310–312).

It is through dominating the finance and production structures that the US and the USSR directly affected the economics of the global system: the United States, through upholding the values, ideology and institutions underpinning free-market capitalism; the Soviet Union through its role as the most powerful communist state in the world. This state of affairs came to be known as the bipolar state system.

The establishment of the Bretton Woods institutions also effectively split the world economy into two: the Eastern bloc and the Western bloc, with the US and the USSR as respective superpower leaders of each. This did not mean that production, trade and finance were totally divided, but there were significant differences between the ways in which the US and USSR maintained their ideological spheres of influence, specifically on the question of private property ownership. The US remained a defender of the rights of individuals to own private property in the production process. The USSR, on the other hand, promoted public ownership of the means of production and over private property.

The role of the Bretton Woods institutions are set out in some detail in Tables 2.1 and 2.2.

The core component of Bretton Woods was the **gold exchange standard** whereby the US, as the strongest capitalist state in the post-war system, undertook to peg the value of the dollar to gold at a rate of $35 to an ounce. This meant that the US assumed responsibility for ensuring the currency stability of the capitalist world economy. The IMF and the World Bank were also to play crucial roles in ensuring the stability and coherence of the Western financial structure. The role of the IMF would be to ensure that if a state, for instance, Belgium, experienced difficulties with its currency value, the IMF would step in to help with short-term **balance of payments** (BOP) problems and other possible currency-related problems. If Belgium imported extensively in any given year, that is, bought many goods from other states, and did not manage to export much or somehow attract an inflow of foreign funds, it might experience a shortfall or a balance-of-payments deficit. If requested to do so, the IMF would then step in to negotiate financial assistance for Belgium to overcome its difficulties, and to protect the value of the Belgian currency.

The IBRD or World Bank, on the other hand, was established to help ensure that the economies of war-torn Europe were rebuilt, with a secondary role of helping former colonies to build similar economies to those of Western states. This secondary role was called its developmental role; the other, more important role was its reconstructive role. But the IBRD soon shifted its focus onto the developing world, since it became clear as early as 1947, that it did not have the financial capacity to effect the rebuilding of Europe. The **Marshall Plan** was introduced, spearheaded by the US, and channelled largely through the **Organisation for Economic Co-operation and Development (OECD)**. This effectively replaced the World Bank's reconstruction role, which left the Bank in the position of having to readjust its institutional focus or become largely defunct.

The IMF and World Bank group have, over the years, gradually played an increasingly influential role in the economic development of the developing states. However, although some analysts, notably more critical theorists, would say that both institutions have contributed to the lack of development in these states (Walters & Blake, 1992:57). Whatever one's theoretical or ideological perspective, it is clear that these two institutions together with the GATT/WTO have helped to shape the world economy of today,

Table 2.1: The World Bank group

World Bank group	Principle functions
IBRD (International Bank for Reconstruction and Development)	International bank; leader of last resort
IDA (International Development Association)	Soft loans to poorest developing states
IFC (International Finance Corporation)	Provides funds to private companies in the developing world
MIGA (Multilateral Investment Guarantee Agency)	Provides investment insurance

Derived from Williams (1994:51–93)

Table 2.2: The International Monetary Fund

Services	Principle functions
Buffer Stock Finance Facility	Contributions to buffer stock agreement
Compensatory and Contingency Financing Facility (CCFF)	Bridging finance to primary producers experiencing shortfalls in export earnings
Structural Adjustment Facility (SAF)	Medium-size loans for developing states
Enhanced Structural Adjustment Facility (ESAF)	Large loans for developing states

Derived from Williams (1994:101–136)

particularly concerning what is understood as acceptable economic policies in the developing world.

The GATT/WTO, as the third 'leg' in the Bretton Woods system, was established in 1947 to free global trade. Initially it was seen as an interim agreement which would lead to the establishment of the International Trade Organisation (ITO). The withdrawal of the ITO proposal in 1950 by President Truman of the US (because of lack of support in the US Congress) saw GATT remaining the semi-institutional vehicle for maintaining consensus on free trade, the most important of which was the Most Favoured Nation principle (MFN). This principle can be described as that of 'every child is my favourite'. Just as parents are told not to favour one child over another, and to extend privileges equally because otherwise hostility, rivalry and other problems may arise, so the MFN principle enshrines the norm that a favour or concession to one state must be extended to all other states. The WTO, established in 1995, continues the central goals of GATT, that is to promote free trade in the international system. How fair the free trade principle is remains an area of dispute, specifically with regard to the position of the developing world in the global economy (*see* the discussion on the NIEO, and Chapter 3).

The emergence of the US as the dominant power in the West after 1945 allowed for the creation of an international, rule-governed economic order. The US, through its dominance over the finance, production and trade structures managed to entrench rules, regulations and norms governing the IPE through the Bretton Woods institutions, the Marshall Plan and GATT.

In the case of international finance institutions (IFIs), the 'surveillance organisations', the IMF and the World Bank grouping allowed the US to exercise structural and relational power within the Western economic order (Cox, 1987). While the USSR acted in a similar hegemonic fashion in Eastern Europe, because of the nature of centrally planned economies, it had a more coercive (relational) form of power over the Eastern economic order (Gill & Law, 1988: 302–312).

Of the major events that have occurred within the global political economy since 1945, the following are central: the end of the gold exchange standard from 1971 onwards; the economic recovery of Western Europe and Japan; decolonisation; transnationalisation; and the end of the Cold War.

The end of the fixed exchange rate system

From the creation of the Bretton Woods institutions just prior to the end of World War II, until the 1960s, the US allowed a vast amount of dollars to flow out into the international system. This was to help Western Europe and Japan to recover economically, but was also good for the US. It enabled the US to extend its sphere of political influence as part of its **containment** of communism policy and it also strengthening its trade partners. Unfortunately, the US failed to closely monitor the balance between the amount of dollars it was sending into circulation internationally, and its gold reserves.

Between 1944 and the late 1960s, the US slowly developed both balance of payments and a balance of trade shortfall as it imported more from the recovering economies of Western Europe and Japan. This situation was made worse by the large amounts of money that the US was spending on wars against communism in Vietnam and Korea. In 1971, US President Richard Nixon announced that the US would no longer be able to maintain the fixed exchange rate of the dollar. The US's gold reserves were too small to back up the amount of dollars it had released internationally. In other words, if all the states in the system had asked for gold in exchange for their dollars, the US would not have had nearly enough to meet its financial obligations. In 1952, the US held 68% of the world's monetary reserves. By 1977, the US held only 6% (Ray, 1992: 253). The implications of this were severe. Although the US had instigated the fixed exchange rate system to stabilise the global economy, it had, in effect, landed up causing great financial instability in world finance and production structures. The fixed exchange rate system was replaced by a **floating exchange rate system** that is currently still in place.

The floating exchange rate system means that currency values are largely linked to, and determined by market forces, but also increasingly by financial market speculation. This means that the value of a currency, the rand for example, will move up and down according to what banks and other private buyers are prepared to pay for it. Fluctuations occur daily, and usually more than once on any given day. Such fluctuations can be in response to good or bad media reports of political or economic indicators or events, or combinations of these. For example, since 1994, bad news about President Nelson Mandela's health has affected the value of the rand, even when such 'news' is based on rumours and hearsay.

The floating exchange rate has brought back financial uncertainty of the kind that the Bretton Woods institutions were set up to avoid, but it does serve as a mechanism to weed out economic inefficiency and the lack of transparency. While the fixed exchange rate system did provide the financial stability needed to rebuild Western Europe and Japan, its collapse had a very negative effect on the international economic system, especially on the newly independent states of the world. This was made far worse by the ensuing OPEC oil price hikes during the 1970s.

Decolonisation and superpower rivalry

The establishment of the United Nations (UN) in 1945, to replace the defunct League of Nations, also brought about an increased international awareness of the importance of the principles of national self-determination, human rights, non-racism and, consequently, the lack of such rights in colonial territories. The UN Charter set the framework of international norms and values that helped to bring about the end of official colonialism, although this process was slow and not uniform. Many developing states today still experience the effects of colonialism, if not politically then certainly economically. Nonetheless, since 1945, every colony in the world has finally become independent, either by force (through revolutions or armed struggles) or peacefully, by means of the right to independence being granted by the colonising state. However, it should also be remembered that since 1945 other states have been occupied, notably Tibet (by China in 1950) and East Timor (by Indonesia in 1975).

The decolonisation process was also affected by superpower rivalry for spheres of influence in Asia and Africa. A classic example is the involvement of United States in the war between North and South Vietnam. Some of the most important proxy wars between the two superpowers occurred in decolonised states in Southern Africa. In the 1970s and 1980s Mozambique and Angola were two states in which the USSR and US tried to exert influence over rival guerrilla movements and political forces (Barber & Barratt, 1990). Colonisation and decolonisation are vital to the understanding of the situation of the developing world in the global political economy (*see* also Chapters 8 and 11).

The oil crises, the debt trap and the call for an NIEO

Many former colonies entered the global political economy as sovereign and politically independent states between 1960 and 1980. Unfortunately, those states that began to try to develop and restructure their economies along the lines of Western Europe, the US and Japan soon ran into difficulties. The collapse of the fixed exchange rate system created great economic uncertainty in the early 1970s, and this was aggravated by the decision of the Organisation of Petroleum Exporting Countries (OPEC) to raise the price of oil 400% in 1973. OPEC, one of the first primary export commodity cartels to be established in the developing world, was celebrated by other developing states for an economic show of muscle in a global economic situation, which most developing states had come to understand as unequal and unfair. The consequences of the oil price hikes were, sadly, felt more by the developing states in the long run than by the developed world.

Oil-producing states deposited their newly acquired riches in banks in the West, who then lent large sums of money to developing states so that they could meet their import needs (particularly oil). In this way, 'petrodollars' were recycled. Initially this led to moderate growth rates in the developing world. The cash honeymoon ended in 1979 with the second OPEC price hike. The US and Western Europe responded by trying to counter **inflation**, that is, the steady rise in the price of goods due to rising production costs. One step was to raise interest rates, since this stops producers from borrowing money (and usually slows production). The effect on the domestic economies of the West was a recession (negative or no economic growth). The effect on the developing states was even more devastating. Suddenly, loans to developing states that had been lent at low rates of interest were raised. This was the start of the debt trap cycle into which many developing states have fallen. Many states in the developing world, including a large number of African states, Mozambique, Zambia and Nigeria, to mention but three, are so heavily in debt that paying the interest on their loans sucks up more than the total value of their exports in a year.

Another consequence of OPEC flexing its muscles was a wave of confidence on the part of the developing states. The Group of 77 (also known as the G-77), a coalition of developing states, consolidated their call for a **new international economic order (NIEO)** in the 1970s. This goal had been inspired and informed by **dependency theorists** and had taken shape through the UN Conference on Trade and Development (UNCTAD) in the 1960s. UNCTAD was established to help foster the interests of developing states in a global economic situation, which they saw as representing the interests of the developed countries. These countries promoted the principle of free trade to serve their own interests, but engaged in protectionist economic policies when it suited them. Indeed, at UNCTAD I the G-77 proposed that UNCTAD should become the forum for discussing and negotiating trade, production and financial issues with the developed world in place of GATT. The proposed NIEO suggested:

- an integrated programme for commodities (IPC) to control and stabilise commodity prices;
- the extension of the **Generalised System of Preferences** (GSPs) on tariffs for developing country exports;
- the development of a debt relief programme;
- increasing official development assistance (ODA) flows from North to South;
- changing the decision-making process in international financial forums such as the UN, the IMF and the World Bank so that the developing world had more decision-making power; and
- promoting the economic sovereignty of developing states through, for example, ensuring greater control over their own

natural resources; gaining increased access to technology; regulating MNCs and TNCs, and gaining greater access to the markets of the developed states (Kukreja, 1996:317).

It is fairly evident then, that in terms of the above demands developing states were buoyed by the activities of OPEC, at least initially. However, as the economic power of OPEC waned, and the debt problem raised its ugly head, so too did the calls for the NIEO become fainter. The demands for a NIEO and the solidarity that UNCTAD was supposed to give rise to were also undermined by the failure to forge an effective alliance on the part of developing states. This was a result of ideological differences as well as differing economic situations and priorities. Regional and cross-border rivalries have also played their part. However, since the end of the Cold War the ability to develop common values to strengthen the position of developing states has again been enhanced. The successful UNCTAD IX held in South Africa in 1996 indicates that the developing states continue to work towards building a closer alliance so as to represent their interests in global economic forums.

It is in the context of the economic developments sketched above that the IMF and World Bank have come to play an increasingly important role in the developing world. Since the end of the fixed exchange rate system, the IMF, like the World Bank, had to redefine its role in the international economic system. Both IFIs have functioned to help developing states with development through a variety of different types of concessional loans (*see* Tables 2.1 and 2.2) and what are called structural adjustment programmes (SAPs). The changing role of these two institutions has been criticised by a number of sources. The main criticism from the developing states is that both institutions uphold a very fixed view of how economic development should be pursued. Since both institutions, as sources of finance, are in a position to impose conditionalities on their loans, both academics and practitioners in developing states have concluded that the IMF and World Bank enforce orthodox neo-liberal economic policies, the cornerstones of which are open markets, minimum protectionism, minimal state intervention and the inviolability of private property ownership (*see* Chapter 11).

The reconstruction of Western Europe and the rise of Japan

At the end of World War II, large parts of Western Europe and Japan were destroyed, so the US poured vast sums of money into their reconstruction. The Marshall Plan for Western Europe channelled US$ 12 billion into Europe through the OECD. The US also accepted protectionist measures introduced in Western Europe, such as the Schuman Plan of 1950, which led to the establishment of the European Coal and Steel Community (ECSC), a historic act of economic co-operation between two arch enemies, France and Germany. The ECSC laid the basis for what we now know as the European Union (EU), a form of economic integration in Western Europe that was founded on the principle of certain forms of regional protectionism. The US supported the rise of the European Economic Community (or EEC, as the EU was first called) in 1957 as part of its commitment to the revival of an international economy based on capitalist principles.

The recovery of Japan, especially after the devastation caused by the two nuclear bombs dropped on Hiroshima and Nagasaki, was also an economic priority for the US. Financial aid and concessions on protectionist policies utilised by Japan to reconstruct its economy allowed for Japan's rapid recovery. In the 1980s, however, Japan's continued use of protectionist policies led to political tensions with the US, especially because Japan continued to maintain a very high trade surplus with the US; that is, Japan exported far more to the US than it imported. By the 1990s, this trade surplus had reached $50 billion. Thus, since 1945 Japan's economy has come to play an extremely important role in the world economy,

and in the economy of the US.

Tensions also began to emerge between the US and the EEC in the 1980s, which related to the EEC's agricultural protectionism in the form of its Common Agricultural Policy (CAP). This has been the subject of extended negotiations in GATT/WTO trade negotiations, especially the Uruguay Round.

The rise of the newly industrialised countries (NICs)

At the same time as states in Africa were gaining their independence, so too were four newly independent Asian states (Hong Kong, Singapore, Taiwan and South Korea) rapidly expanding their economies to the extent that, by the early 1980s, these states were being respectfully called the 'East Asian Tigers'. Each of these states has been relatively successful in achieving the kind of industrialisation and economic growth that Western states have taken to be the measure of economic development. Between the early 1950s and the 1980s, they consistently reached growth rates of between 5% and 8%, and sometimes higher. Two of these states, Taiwan and South Korea, are often cited by neo-liberal economists as proof that critical, transformative theorists are wrong, and that if free market policies are applied, economic growth will follow.

The four 'tigers' were joined in the 1990s by Malaysia, Thailand and Indonesia. However, it is important to note that none of these states have very good records on political freedom and democratic rights, and the environmental damage caused by rapid industrialisation has been severe (Bello & Rosenfeld, 1990). Even more troubling are the recent signs of financial instability, especially in South Korea, Malaysia and Indonesia, caused by a loss of confidence by speculative investors in these so-called **emerging markets**.

The Cold War and its demise

The post-war rivalry between the Soviet Union and the United States, to which we referred earlier, had a major effect on the nature and shape of the global political economy between 1945 and 1990, primarily because of the competing ideologies of communism and capitalism, and the ensuing strategic rivalry in Europe, Asia, Latin America, the Middle East and Africa.

How did the Cold War start? It is generally agreed that one of the most important events early in the Cold War, and the ensuing arms race between the superpowers, was the Berlin blockade of 1948, whereby Stalin, who was leader of the USSR at the time, cut off all transport and communications links to the city. This led to a US deployment of nuclear weapons to Britain and the signing of the North Atlantic Treaty Organisation (NATO) in April 1949. The blockade ended shortly thereafter, but Berlin remained a symbol of East-West rivalry, characterised by the Berlin Wall which was erected in the early 1960s by the East German government to separate East Berlin from West Berlin. It is equally symbolic that the fall of the Berlin Wall in 1989 is said by many analysts to have heralded the end of the Cold War.

There were other 'trigger events' that led to the escalation of hostilities and the speeding up of the arms race. Conflict in Asia proved to be one of the key areas of superpower rivalry. The end of the Chinese civil war in 1949 led to US fears of an alliance between the Chinese and the Soviets. For this reason, the US was particularly interested in building up Taiwan.

Similarly, when the forces of the Democratic People's Republic of Korea (North Korea) attacked the Republic of Korea (South Korea) in 1950, the US saw this as the beginning of a 'communist' offensive. The resulting war caused the death of several million people, and a lingering antagonism between the two Koreas that has outlasted the collapse of the USSR.

Perhaps the best example of the extent of the ideological rivalry that characterised the Cold War was the war in Vietnam. The war started as a war against the coloniser, France, and ended as a war between the communist government in North Vietnam and successive capitalist-friendly regimes in South Vietnam, upheld initially by the French and later by the US. American involvement in Vietnam began in earnest in 1965 and ended in 1973, during which time the superpower was militarily humiliated by the guerrilla warfare of the Vietcong, who were supported by the North Vietnamese.

For Southern Africans, there are many examples of Cold War rivalry in the region. Some of you may even live in a state where Cold War rivalry played an important part in shaping historical events in the 1970s and 1980s. The war between RENAMO and FRELIMO in Mozambique, for instance, was maintained by superpower rivalry. It is now known that the US Central Intelligence Agency (the CIA) was involved in giving assistance to RENAMO; the USSR was always open about its support for FRELIMO. Unfortunately for Mozambique today, this war, made worse by South African **destabilisation**, devastated the economy and lives of a great many Mozambicans. As a result of the war, Mozambique is one of the poorest states in the world.

The Cold War has been characterised as having gone through stages of being hot, that is where the danger of nuclear warfare between the two superpowers and their allies was great, and times of *détente* (between the US and USSR) and *rapprochement* (between the US and the Chinese) when relations calmed down. In terms of the global political economy the most important events of the Cold War were, firstly, the *rapprochement* that began to occur between mainland China and the US in the late 1960s, culminating in the granting of the China seat in the UN to the People's Republic of China (mainland China) in 1971. Second was the final *détente* phase between the USSR and the US, signalled by the coming to power of Gorbachev and the introduction of his two policies of *glasnost* (openness) and *perestroika* (restructuring), which led the way to the disintegration of the USSR and the end of Soviet-style communism. Ironically, it was the opening up and deregulation of the USSR's economy that led to the disintegration of the monolithic state into the Commonwealth of Independent States (CIS), not a wholesale revolt against the authoritarian-style politics that characterised Soviet and Chinese communism.

The end of the Cold War has, unfortunately, not meant the end of the threat of nuclear war, even though negotiations between the United States and the Soviet Union (now the CIS) have moved from agreements on Strategic Arms Limitations (SALT I and II in 1972 and 1979 respectively) to Strategic Arms Reductions Treaties in the 1990s (START I and II in 1991 and 1993). However, the break-up of the USSR has meant that four of the newly formed states in the CIS has nuclear capacity, namely Belarus, Kazakhstan, Russia and the Ukraine. Negotiations between these states and the US have brought agreement that nuclear weapons will be returned to Russia or destroyed, but the danger of nuclear capacity in states other than Russia remains. Both the US and Russia have also agreed to cut their nuclear capacity in half by the year 2003 (according to START II) but this still means that both have sufficient nuclear capacity to launch a nuclear war, as each will retain 3500 nuclear warheads. It is also important to note that other states, for example France, Iraq and India, have continued to build their nuclear capacity beyond the levels set by START II. Although it is unlikely, in the current wave of economic globalisation, that another militant state such as Hitler's Germany of the 1930s will emerge, the danger of a nuclear-based international war remains as long as there are nuclear weapons, and given that the common 'wisdom' of international history holds that preparing for war is good for a state's economy.

However, the end of the Cold War has brought about the end of a bipolar security structure. This has also meant that the values underpinning interactions in the trade, finance, production and knowledge structures are now unchallenged by any state or group of states exercising significant structural or relational power. Consequently, the globalisation of the

Figure 2.2   World trade – growth and main actors

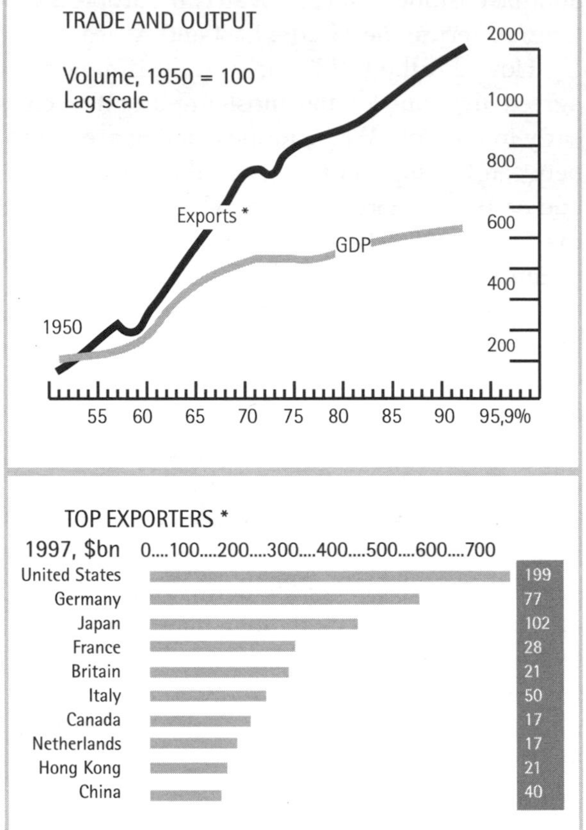

TRADE AND OUTPUT

Volume, 1950 = 100
Lag scale

The Economist 98.05.16   Trade balance $bn

global political economy is now a key area of discussion and analysis.

Globalisation

As we said earlier, the globalisation of the world economy started in the previous century. Globalisation, understood as increased trade, is therefore not a new phenomenon, nor are the current high levels of trade compared to world production unique (Hoogvelt, 1997:115). If we look at the ratio between world production and world trade in goods and services, the extent of

Table 2.3: World trade in services, 1980–1993

	1980	1990	1993
Trade in commercial services ($billions)	358	791	934
North	283	648	752
South	75	143	182

Adapted from Kegley & Wittkopf (1997:264)

trade occurring in 1913 in comparison to 1997 is not that different. Nevertheless, the growth rate of world trade has consistently outstripped the rate of growth of world output (production), meaning that trade of goods and services in the global political economy has become increasingly important for national economies as they rely more and more on exporting certain commodities and importing others (*see* Figure 2.2 and Table 2.3).

But globalisation means more than simply the growing importance of trade. Some analysts use it as a short-hand way of referring to the overall trend that began in the early to mid-1980s and which is characterised by the declining importance of national boundaries to production, finance and trade. For example, today a company like Mercedes Benz, initially known as a 'German' company, will locate the manufacturing plants of Mercedes components in several different states to ensure the best balance of labour costs to production costs. Car parts may be made in several different states and put together in yet another state. In the light of this trend, it is difficult to call the finally completed car a 'German product' because it has been produced in a number of states and as a result of trade between firms.

From a transformative perspective, it is possible to depict this process as a form of neo-colonialism, because technological innovations and production flows are controlled by MNCs,

located in the developed states. This control leads to what Strange identifies as the structural power of the major actors in the highly industrialised part of the world over production structures. In addition to this, certain actors have more structural power than do others in the global production structure. Indeed, it is not just the developing world who complains about the neo-colonialism of production, the governments of France and Britain have also voiced their objection to the globalisation of the 'shopping mall culture', which is linked to US-style consumerism. This consumerism is fed not only through the goods that the US exports, but also through telecommunications, a sphere in which the US clearly dominates. Even in a state like France or Belgium, many of the television programmes people watch and much of the lifestyle they lead is based on US production and consumer goods and values. In a sense, the most striking thing about globalisation is the way it has changed social relations globally. More and more, we watch the same television and films, listen to the same music and dress in similar clothes. I can contact my friend in France or the US in the same amount of time that it would take me to walk next door to talk to my neighbour. Via e-mail or the Internet, I can even have lengthy debates or discussions with colleagues and far-away friends. The idea of 'the global office', 'the global market' and 'global business' refers to this intermeshing of relations that cancel out space and time distances between people across the globe.

Globalisation has also meant a change in world production and financial trends, especially in terms of the functions of transnational or multinational companies. These companies now tend to produce less, but work faster, relying on constant innovations to sell products. The importance of technological innovation has become the key to global production and marketing success. Transnational production has moved from a Fordist 'just in case' production structure, where many goods of the same type were produced 'just in case' there was heightened demand, to a post-Fordian 'just in time' production structure where limited amounts of technologically sophisticated goods are released onto the market to maintain consumer demand. This change in production structure is very important because it also characterises a movement away from the principle of national economies of scale that basically works on the principle that more production makes the cost of goods cheaper. 'Just in time' (JIT) production, on the other hand, works on the principle of keeping the cost of production low by going for zero-defect, high-quality products balanced against skilled labour costs and the costs of limited quantities of constantly updated production materials. Also, in terms of labour, there is an increasing trend for companies to relocate wherever labour is cheapest. It is accepted by employees that if a company relocates they will be dismissed with very little compensation. Workers rights are thus now becoming a more global than national issue (Hoogvelt, 1997).

Globalisation has contradictory effects and possible prospects for developing states, since they now have to try to become economically competitive in a global economy that values high technology goods, but at the same time, states with export capacity can benefit from freer markets. The positive outcomes of globalisation will thus differ from region to region and state to state in the developing world. Developing new technology or maintaining technological innovation is expensive and this makes it difficult for

Box 2.6:   A GATT/WTO chronology

1947	Birth of GATT, signed by 23 countries on 30 October at the Palais des Nations in Geneva.
1948	GATT comes into force. First meeting of its members in Havana, Cuba.
1949	Second round of talks at Annecy, France. Some 5000 tariff cuts agreed to; ten new countries admitted.
1950–51	Third round at Torquay, England. Members exchange 8700 trade concessions and welcome four new countries.
1956	Fourth round at Geneva. Tariff cuts worth $1,3 trillion at today's prices.
1960–62	The Dillon Round, named after US Under-Secretary of State, Douglas Dillon, who proposed the talks. A further 4400 tariff cuts.
1964–67	The Kennedy Round. Many industrial tariffs halved. Signed by 50 countries. Code on dumping agreed to separately.
1973–79	The Tokyo Round, involving 99 countries. First serious discussion of non-tariff trade barriers, such as subsidies and licensing requirements. Average tariff on manufactured goods in the nine biggest markets cut from 7% to 4,7%.
1986–93	The Uruguay Round. Further cuts in industrial tariffs, export subsidies, licensing and customs valuation. First agreements on trade in services and intellectual property.
1995	Formation of WTO with power to settle disputes between members.
1997	Agreements concluded on telecommunications services, information technology and financial services.
1998	Today the WTO has 132 members. More than 30 others are waiting to join.

The Economist 98.05.16

debt-ridden states to compete, especially where their export capacity is minimal. These obstacles have become even more pronounced by some of the new regulations in GATT/WTO.

From GATT to WTO

The evolution from the General Agreement on Tariffs and Trade (GATT) to the World Trade Organisation (WTO) has occurred via a succession of negotiations, called Rounds, which have marked the major decision-making events of the original agreement. The final round of GATT, known as the Uruguay Round, began in 1986 and was concluded in 1994. The WTO replaced GATT the following year (*see* Box 2.6).

The conclusion of the Uruguay Round has led to some significant changes to trade regulations in the world economy, particularly with regard to agricultural protectionism, as well as **Trade Related Intellectual Property Rights** (TRIPs) and **Trade Related Investment Measures** (TRIMs). Tariff and non-tariff barriers are, in terms of the Uruguay Round agreement, set to drop even further, and protectionist measures adopted by regional groupings such as the EU have been restricted.

What does this hold in store for developing states such as those in the Southern African Development Community (SADC)? The impact of restricting protectionist measures is twofold: on the one hand it makes it more difficult for developing states to protect young industries or to regulate the price of agricultural products; on the other hand, the multilaterally-agreed anti-protectionist rules of the WTO also place pressure on richer states to open their markets more for developing country exports. An example of the latter is that the EU has for many years relied on its protectionist Common Agricultural Policy (CAP), which was the subject of heated argument between the US and EU members during the Uruguay Round. The EU has agreed to lift the many of the protectionist measures contained in CAP, for example the subsidisation of beef exports. However, rules against agricultural subsidies that are being built into the framework that the WTO regulates make it also harder for a state, or grouping of states, say Zimbabwe or SADC, to enforce protectionist measures if they become members of the WTO. Developing states do get concessions in terms of WTO but are expected to move into line with WTO rules and regulations as soon as they can.

In terms of TRIMs developing states are limited in their capacity to regulate investment flows, and in terms of TRIPs restrictions are placed on the imitation of new technologies or ideas originating elsewhere. All of this makes it difficult for them to catch up with the highly industrialised countries of the world, and to find a competitive edge in the world economy.

The global political economy and the developing states in the new millennium

The world is perceived to be moving towards what has been called the 'global village'. This implies that widespread communications, rapid transport, and shared community norms and values tie us together globally in the same way that a village is understood to function (*see* Chapter 1). Developing states, however, run the increasing risk of remaining the village outcasts.

The effect of the emergence of strong regional economic groupings in the West, and the emergence of lucrative East European markets after years of economic stagnation under communist command economics, has led to a growing lack of interest in states who have little consumer demand for goods and services, bad transport and communications networks, shaky political structures and huge amounts of external debt. This is the profile of many African and Latin American states. One can conclude that the world may be becoming a global village, but patterns of economic inequality are not necessarily disappearing as a result of this. In many instances, these are set to deepen over the next decade unless a major economic intervention is made on the part of the developed world towards the developing world. One suggestion is that the IMF and World Bank write off the multilateral debt of heavily indebted developing states so that they can start with a clean slate. Another suggestion is that developing states develop stronger regional groupings themselves to ensure that they develop together. At this point, the latter option appears the most realistic. Nonetheless, given the current distribution of structural and relational power in the global political economy it is unlikely that the developing world's influence over the production, finance, security or knowledge structures will increase significantly in the short to medium term.

However, states in the developing world do have the option of trying to enhance the level of human development in their societies. Human development is distinguishable from economic growth (reflected in indicators such as GNP) because it emphasises societal development in a more holistic way, not just in terms of the amount of income per capita. Human development is measured by quality of life indicators such as life expectancy at birth, ratios of levels of education and income. Developing countries can improve the quality of life of their people through **sustainable development**, which prioritises health, environmental and welfare aspects of state-societal relations and the evolution of economies (*see* Chapters 8, 11, 14 and 15). In terms of the evolving nature of the global political economy, notions of sustainable development reflect a shift towards trying to combine further integration into the world economy with community values rather than purely liberal individualistic values. The ability of developing states to do so will depend on their ability to jointly secure a fairer deal for themselves in the security, financial, trade, production and knowledge structures of the global political economy. It also depends, however, on the degree to which developing states can build regional economic partnerships and institutionalise responsible and accountable governance in their countries.

Key concepts in this chapter

Balance of power
Collective security
Economic integration
Globalisation
Hegemony
Mercantilism
New international economic order
Political economy
Protectionism
Structural adjustment programmes
Structural and relational power

Suggested readings

- Chase-Dunn, C. (1989) *Global Formation: Structures of the World-Economy*. Oxford: Blackwell.
- Hirst, P. & Thompson, G. (1996) *Globalization in Question: The International Economy and the Possibilities of Global Governance*. Cambridge: Polity Press.
- Hobsbawm, E. (1994) *Age of Extremes: The Short Twentieth Century 1914–91*. London: Michael Joseph.
- Hogan, M. (ed.) (1992) *The End of the Cold War: Its Meaning and Implications*. Cambridge: Cambridge University Press.
- Pettman, R. (1996) *Understanding International Political Economy – with Readings for the Fatigued*. St Leonards: Allen and Unwin.
- Said, E. S. (1994) *Culture and Imperialism*. London: Vintage.
- Stubbs, R. and Underhill, G. (eds) (1994) *Political Economy and the Changing Global Order*. Basingstoke: Macmillan.

3 Theories of International Relations

Philip Nel

This chapter in outline
- What is a theory?
- Realism as a political attitude and as theory
  - The political attitude of realism
  - The assumptions of realist theory
- The political attitude and theory of liberalism
  - Liberalism and idealism
  - The main assumptions of liberalism
- A transformative theory of International Relations
  - Transformative versus conservative theories
  - A transformative view of privilege and marginalisation in the global economy
  - The main assumptions of a Marxist transformative theory of International Relations

What is a theory?

The amount of official development-oriented **foreign aid** provided by the rich countries of the world to poorer nations is not very large. The maximum yearly figure during the 1990s was only US$53 billion (1993). This is less than what the United States (US) and its allies spent on the Gulf War in 1992 (roughly US$61 billion), and about equal to what the world spends in a year on keeping infant buttocks dry, that is, the amount of money spent on nappies, baby powder, etc. (Raffer & Singer, 1996:39).

Nevertheless, foreign aid of this type is an important source of additional finance for poorer countries. In 1996, foreign aid amounted to 13% of the **gross national product** (GNP) of the least developed states of the world, and some states in sub-Saharan Africa are crucially dependent on it to relieve the shortfalls on their **balance of payments**.

Because of its importance, people interested in international relations pay considerable attention to foreign aid. They do so, however, with wide-ranging purposes in mind. Some scholars are interested in finding out exactly how much aid is provided by the richer states, in particular the twenty-nine members of the **Organisation for Economic Co-operation and Development** (OECD), and who the main recipients of this aid are. To do this, they engage in what we call description and analysis. This means that these scholars collect and investigate the available information about the flow of foreign aid in the world, try to break this information up into its various elements and present it in such a way that we can detect clear patterns.

Figure 3.1 contains the results of a simple application of description and analysis. It reports by year the foreign aid contribution of Japan to sub-Saharan Africa during the period 1985–1995.

A lot of academic work in International Relations is devoted to collecting information of the type reflected in Figure 3.1, and to its description and analysis. Without these activities, we would not have reliable **data** about such things

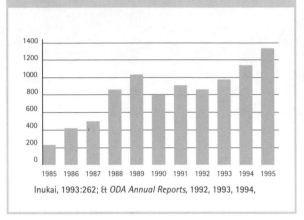

Figure 3.1: Japan's total bilateral overseas development assistance to sub-Saharan Africa, 1985–1995 (net disbursement, US$ million)

Inukai, 1993:262; & *ODA Annual Reports*, 1992, 1993, 1994,

as foreign aid, the flow of tourism in the world and the military spending patterns of states, to name but a few. Obviously, description and analysis can entail much more complicated operations than those presented in the figure.

However, some scholars are not interested only in describing and analysing data about foreign aid flows, important though these data may be. Some of them would also like to explain *why states engage in aid activities at all*. The answer to this question is not so obvious, especially if we take into consideration that large-scale and sustained aid from one group of states to other states is something that has taken place only since the end of World War II in 1945. *Whenever we encounter a surprising fact or something that is not obvious, scientists look for explanations.* Explanations, we can say, are answers to *why* questions (Nagel, 1971:15).

Why do states provide aid? Do wealthy states provide aid because they perceive it to be in their own interests (as a means of securing political support, or of encouraging recipient countries to buy their exports, for example), or do donors give aid because of humanitarian concerns about poverty and destitution?

To answer *why* questions of this nature,

scholars have to engage in somewhat different activities than do those who are only interested in finding out who gives what type of aid to whom, and how much of it. In trying to find explanations it is not enough to only collect, describe and analyse information. Yes, we must find out exactly how much aid is given, by whom, to whom, and for what this aid is used, but this does not answer the question of *why* states engage in giving aid at all.

We are confronted with many why questions every day. *Why did my car not start this morning? Why can't the government give larger bursaries to all students?* Finding answers to these questions often involves looking for some factor or occurrence or reason that lies behind the events we want to explain. Hence, a sufficient explanation for the puzzling fact that my car would not start could be that the petrol tank was empty, or that the spark plugs were so dirty that they could not fire, or that the battery was flat. We say that *we explain the fact of the car not starting by identifying a factor or occurrence that caused the breakdown*. This we call a causal explanation. Similarly, a causal explanation for the fact that the government gives students such small bursaries could be that the government has a limited budget, and that it has to spend that limited amount on many services and projects, such as housing, hospitals, schools and the police service. Here, the absence of surplus funds is taken to be the cause of the limited spending on bursaries.

Most of the time we are quite satisfied with an answer that tells us what caused something. But sometimes we want to know more. For instance, we may be curious to find out why it is that dirty spark plugs cause cars not to start. To answer this further why question, we now have to start developing an understanding of how the internal combustion petrol engine works; that is, we have to learn about all the parts in the engine, their relations with one another, and how they work together as a **system** to produce a specific result. Similarly, we may not be satisfied with the causal answer given to our question about the government's small bursary scheme. Maybe

some of us would like to know why the government does not cut some of its spending on defence, for instance, to free more money for bursaries for university students. In attempting to answer this further question we now have *to start exploring how governments work, and how they make decisions*. Perhaps we could argue that government expenditure is eventually influenced by the political bargaining that takes place in the Cabinet between representatives of the various interest groups in the civil service. Departments of defence are normally represented by a Minister of Defence who bargains very hard for money to modernise and expand the defence forces. Students, however, are normally not represented directly in Cabinet and so they have less influence on budgetary decision-making than do defence forces.

So, to explain why the government spends so little on bursaries, we were called upon to present a general 'picture' of how governments make decisions; similarly, we had to present a general picture of the internal combustion engine so as to explain the function of spark plugs. These 'general pictures' are what we call *theories*.

Thus, if we now return to our example of foreign aid, it should be clear that we could try to answer the question *Why do states give foreign aid?* by means of providing a *reason* for the behaviour of states. We could say that states give aid *because* they want to promote their own interests in the recipient state, for instance in getting that state to buy more products from the donor state. Or we could argue that donor states are motivated by a desire to eliminate poverty and suffering in recipient states, therefore, they provide aid. In doing this, we have provided two possible motivations (or 'causes') for donor state behaviour. Say, further, that through investigation of the behaviour and statements of donors, we find that most donor states provide aid for what can be termed 'selfish reasons'. Have we now completed our explanation?

As our examples of the internal combustion engine and student bursaries have shown, it is always possible to go one step further and to ask, *why is it that states act selfishly?* To answer this question, we will have to produce a theory of the behaviour of states in the international system. Put differently, we will have to paint a picture of how states relate to one another to form the bigger whole that we call the international system. Below we will review three different pictures of how states (and other actors – *see* Chapter 1) relate to one another, and how the international system is constituted. Before we get to that, let us summarise this discussion about what theories are, and let us look at some important things that you have to remember about theories.

The simplest definition of a theory is that it is a *mental picture of how things in a specific segment of reality hang together or are connected (see* Box 3.1 for other definitions). Theories are very important, because they allow us to detect links between factors and events that we may have regarded as independent of one another. We say that theories help us to *understand* our world, that is, to appreciate things in their context and to see how they work together to produce a specific result.

Thus, the first thing to remember about a theory is that it is a set of ideas that we develop in order to make it clear to ourselves how certain aspects of reality stand in relation to other aspects. Because these relations are often hidden, we have to think them out, so to speak. *Theories help us to understand and explain aspects of reality that are not obvious or immediately visible.*

A second important point about theories is that they are built upon **assumptions**. Assumptions are ideas that we take to be true, even if we have no proof for them. For instance, when I go to bed at night, I *assume* that the sun will rise the following morning, but I have no proof that it will. Yet, I take it for granted, and I plan tomorrow on that assumption. Similarly, theories are built on certain basic assumptions that are necessary for the development of the theory's argument or explanation, but about which there cannot be absolute certainty. We simply take assumptions for granted.

We shall now see how people make different assumptions about:

- the most important actors in international relations (some theories emphasise states; others argue that non-state actors are becoming increasingly important – *see* also Chapter 1);
- the fundamental characteristics of the international system;
- the degree and direction of change in international relations;
- the basic features of human nature (some theories assume that humans are by nature selfish brutes, while other theories assume that humans are capable of learning and improvement); and
- the role of moral beliefs in international relations.

In order to understand a theory, we have to understand the basic assumptions underlying the theory. Similarly, in order to understand a particular piece of writing on international relations, the reader first has to try to find out what the main assumptions of the author are. This is often difficult to do, because not all authors tell us explicitly what their assumptions are.

A third important point to remember about theories is that in International Relations *there is always more than one possible theory to explain a particular set of facts*. This is because theories are inventions, not discoveries. When we say that 'a botanist has discovered a new species of plants', we mean that the botanist has found something that was already there in reality, but of whose existence we were not aware up to the point of discovery. Theories cannot be discovered. Theories are creations of the mind: they have to be thought up, dreamed up or sucked out of your thumb.

Different people will, therefore, usually come up with different theoretical attempts to understand the same set of facts, and most of the activities of scientists go into long debates about the merits of one theory over its rivals. The point of these debates is not simply argument for argument's sake. No, scholars have these debates because they believe that rational debate is the

Box 3.1: Definitions and descriptions of 'theory'

There are many definitions and descriptions of theories. Look at some of these and decide which one helps you to understand best what a theory is.

- A theory is 'an ordered set of ideas, assumptions and concepts which tells us something about the world, ourselves, or an aspect of reality' (Craig, A. P. *et al.*, 1994:193).
- 'A theory is a set of logically interrelated propositions and the implications that follow from them, which is used to explain some phenomenon. Implicit in any theory is a set of underlying assumptions and methods that are rarely questioned' (Johnson, 1995:297).
- 'Laws are "facts of observation"; theories are "speculative processes introduced to explain them". Experimental results are permanent; theories, however well supported, may not last. Laws remain, theories come and go' (Waltz, 1979:6).
- *A humorous definition*: 'A theory is a hunch with a college education' (Levinson, 1963:227).

Theories are abstract, in the sense that they help us to understand a whole set of facts or events, not any specific event or fact. To grasp this point, think about the following two citations:

- 'An important point to keep in mind, however, is that attempts at theory building are focused on explaining and predicting general trends or phenomena, such as the conditions under which war is most likely to occur. The theoretical enterprise is not devoted to attempting to predict on what day Country X will attack Country Y. To state it in simple language, theorists are interested in the forest, not in particular trees.' (Viotti, & Kauppi, 1993:4)
- 'A theory should be likened to a map. Like a theory, a map provides an unrealistic account of the world, if by unrealistic we mean that there is not a one-to-one correspondence between what appears on the map and what appears in that part of the world under consideration. The more realistic a map is, the less likely it will be of assistance. Imagine trying to find one's way around Pretoria with the aid of a map the size of several rugby fields. In the first place, the map will not fit into your car. In the second place, the profusion of detail would confuse you. A map the size of Pretoria would be of no assistance at all. Since theory is by definition unrealistic, a good theorist must know what to leave out of his analysis. Such a decision is at least as important as knowing what to leave in.' (Christopher Torr, during his inaugural lecture as Professor of Economics at the University of South Africa, cited in Mohr, P. *et al.*, 1995:149)

---

only way in which they can weed out the poor theories, and identify the better ones. The fact that theories are invented means that there will always be competitive theories. Although no single theory can ever claim to represent the truth all on its own, it is possible to distinguish between better and worse theories. Being a scientist (as distinct from being a religious believer) means that you are critical about people's claims, and that you accept a statement or theory only if you have good, rational reasons to do so. Scientists use the following criteria or questions to distinguish between a bad and a good theory:

- Are the concepts used in the theory well defined or not?
- Is the theory based on ideas and/or facts that are widely accepted as the truth?
- Does the theory contain a logically consistent line of argument?
- Can the theory be put to the test (a theory that cannot be tested is usually regarded as a waste of time)? A theory that has survived empirical tests is not necessarily regarded as the final truth, but only as 'robust' and 'corroborated', which means that it is accepted until such time as a better theory emerges.
- Does the theory explain more than its rivals do (scientists prefer more inclusive theories to narrower ones)?

- How complicated is the theory? All else being equal, scientists prefer a simple (parsimonious) theory to a complex one.

There is one final point about theories that we need to understand before we discuss different types of theories in the field of International Relations. This is that there are some scholars who wish to make a distinction between *empirical theories* and *normative theories*. By this they mean that there are theories that exist only to explain empirical reality so that we may better understand it (empirical theories). Then there are theories that explain reality in order that we might evaluate and perhaps even change it. These are called normative theories because they work with a norm or a set of norms (standards of good and bad) in terms of which existing reality is evaluated.

Scholars who want to distinguish between empirical and normative theories argue that it is possible and desirable to do so. It is possible, they say, because theories in the natural sciences hardly ever have normative goals. Sir Isaac Newton's theory of gravity (through which he tried to explain the motions of heavenly bodies and the fact that we as people do not fly off the face of the Earth) describes what reality is like, not what it *should* be like. Similarly, as social scientist we have to try to understand reality in order to enlarge our knowledge of ourselves and our world, and should not get involved in attempts to change it.

In any case, scholars argue, it is dangerous for scientists to introduce norms and values into their scholarly work, because they could start to 'bend' reality to fit their normative schemes. Scientists 'bend' reality when they start to select only those facts that fit their normative views, and ignore other 'uncomfortable' facts. If we, as scientists, do this, we will never produce reliable knowledge, only opinions. Yes, we can study norms and how people behave in terms of them, but the scientist cannot choose one set of norms beforehand as the 'right' one.

There are other scholars, however, who

Box 3.2: Theories are not the same as 'generalisations' or laws

It is important to distinguish clearly between a generalisation and a theory (see Waltz, 1979:1–7). A generalisation (sometimes called 'laws') can be based on repeated observation of the simultaneous occurrence of two or more factors. The British scientist, Sir Isaac Newton, formulated such generalisations for the behaviour of physical forces. For example, every application of force encounters a counter-force (that is why your toe hurts when you kick a stone).

We have one famous generalisation in International Relations, namely that 'democracies do not make war against other democracies'. Although generalisations in the social sciences seldom hold for all possible cases, research has shown that an overwhelming majority of democratic states behave peacefully toward other democracies.

Thus, a generalisation states what is the case most of the time (or always). A theory, on the other hand, attempts to explain why a specific generalisation holds. As soon as you ask, 'Why is it that democracies do not fight each other?' you have taken the first step towards developing a theory. Similarly, as soon as physicists start to ask for the reasons why Newton's generalisations hold, they engage in theoretical discussions.

---

believe that it is impossible not to choose in favour of a set of norms, and who thus say that scientists should do so openly and explicitly. The point is, they say, that even if you only want to focus on understanding the world, you are already taking a normative position: *you are leaving the world as it is, and you are therefore implicitly expressing support for the political, economic and social status quo.* Empirical theory is already *normative* theory; it is simply not aware of its conservative bias. Instead of fooling yourself that it is possible to be a detached scientist without normative preconceptions, rather be open about your unavoidable normative preferences. All theory in the social sciences is, and should be, normative, they claim.

Most of the authors in this book would tend to agree with those who say that theory is always already normative theory, and that we should openly say what we stand for and not hide behind the smokescreen of 'objectivity'. To the extent that the current set-up of the world stabilises or enforces patterns of inequity and marginalisation, we would like not only to understand it, but also to contribute towards changing it for the better.

However, as *scientists* we believe that it is wrong to select only facts (and theories) that support our own normative conceptions, and to ignore evidence, and other points of view, that may contradict or challenge our norms. Being a scientist means that you must be willing to let yourself be convinced by the better argument, even if this argument refutes your deepest-held beliefs. Scientists are not members of a religious sect that have to believe against all the odds and evidence. Scientists believe in pursuing the truth, whatever that may be.

We can summarise what we have said about theories thus:

- Scholars are not only interested in gathering, describing and analysing facts. The interesting part of science is the attempt to understand 'how things hang together', and to search for explanations of puzzling occurrences. To do these things, we need imaginative constructs that we call theories.
- Although no single theory can claim to represent reality fully and accurately, scientists do have ways in which to compare theories with one another in order to distinguish between better and worse theories.
- All theories have normative implications, and a 'neutral' or 'objective' theory is an illusion. Nevertheless, it should be rational argument, with a healthy respect for evidence, which determines theory choice in science, and not simply normative preferences.

Realism as political attitude and as theory

Now that we have a better idea of what a theory is, let us look at some examples of theories that you will come across in your study of international relations. We start with *realism,*, not because it is necessarily the 'best' theory, but because it is by far the oldest, and arguably the most influential, theory in the discipline of International Relations. Let us begin by looking at one of the earliest recorded manifestations of realist thinking.

The political attitude of realism

In the year 416 BC, during what has become known as the **Peloponnesian War**, the powerful Greek city-state of Athens laid siege to the island of Melos, a colony of Athens' bitterest enemy, Sparta. Because of its overwhelming military might, Athens could easily have overrun Melos. But before doing so, the Athenian generals sent representatives to Melos to negotiate the conditions of Melos' surrender. The Melians refused to consider surrender, however, putting forward the argument that justice and fairness demanded that the Athenians respect Melian neutrality. This is how the great Greek historian, Thucydides, reports on the reply of the Athenian representatives and the ensuing dialogue with the Melians:

Athenians: What we shall do now is to show you that it is for the good of our own empire that we are here and that it is for the preservation of your city that we shall say what we are going to say. We do not want any trouble in bringing you into our empire, and we want you to be spared for the good both of yourselves and of ourselves.

Melians: And how could it be just as good for us to be the slaves as for you to be the masters?

Athenians: You, by giving in, would save yourself from disaster; we, by not destroying you, would be able to profit from you.

Melians: So you would not agree to our being neutral, friends instead of enemies, but allies of neither side?

Athenians: No, because it is not so much your hostility that injures us; it is rather the case that, if we were on friendly terms with you, our subjects would regard that as a sign of weakness in us, whereas your hatred is evidence of our power.

Melians: Is that your subjects' idea of fair play – that no distinction should be made between people who are quite unconnected with you and people who are mostly your own colonists or else rebels whom you have conquered?

Athenians: So far as right and wrong are concerned they think that there is no difference between the two, that those who still preserve their independence do so because they are strong, and that if we fail to attack them it is because we are afraid …

(Thucydides, 1985:400–409).

The words of the Athenian representatives are one of the classic statements of the principles of *political realism* (called '*realpolitik*' in German). Because the academic theory of *realism* is based on *political realism*, it is important to first try to understand the latter.

What the Athenians were saying was that *the very survival of one's state is a value that overrides all other values in international affairs.* The reason they refused to grant the Melians their wish to remain neutral, and why the Athenians had to subjugate the Melians, was not because they did not like the Melians. It was simply that if the Athenians did not establish their rule over Melos, other Athenian subjects might have started to suspect that Athens was weak. This would have given these subjects the self-confidence to perhaps stage a revolt against Athens, and before they knew it, the whole Athenian Empire would have been in ruins. To survive, the Athenians had to

show that they had power, even if this meant that they had to trample on the interests of the weak. Elsewhere in their debate with the Melians, the Athenian representatives gave the following summary of the basic principle of political realism:

'[W]hen these matters are discussed by practical people the standard of justice depends on the equality of power to compel and that in fact the strong do what they have the power to do and the weak accept what they have to accept' (Thucydides, 1985:402).

It is important to note that political realists are not cynics, that is, people who argue that values are a waste of time. Rather, political realists have a clear hierarchy of values, and the highest value for them is the survival of the political unit (state) of which they are citizens. Everything else, including virtues such as friendship, mercy and seeking peace, can be considered only when they contribute to the survival of the state. Political realists would agree with the advice penned down by the great Indian strategist, Kautilya (360–280 BC), when he wrote:

'Agreements of peace shall be made with equal and superior kings; and an inferior king shall be attacked. Whoever goes to wage war with a superior king will be reduced to the same condition as that of a foot-soldier opposing an elephant' (1992:127).

What is important for a political realist in securing the survival of the state are not lofty ideals such as justice, freedom and equity, but the simple hard realities of which state has the power, and how much of this power does it have. If the balance of power is in your state's favour, then you will survive. If not, you had better start doing things to make it so.

Although this type of advice sounds cruel, political realists point out that being hard-nosed about power is actually the only way to secure peace and save the world from the endless wars in which humanity is prone to get involved. It is the prudent use of power, they argue, that will secure peace, not an appeal to people to be nice to one another.

The assumptions of realist theory

The contemporary *theory* of realism is based on the political outlook or world-view of political realism, but it is less concerned with prescribing what the correct (wisest, most prudent) political practice is than it is with developing an understanding of the basic patterns of international relations. The theory of realism is based on five fundamental assumptions, which will be discussed below.

The first main realist assumption is that *states are selfish actors who always seek to maximise their own interests, even at the cost of risking benefits that more than one state can share*. How else, will a realist ask, can we explain the seeming madness of arms races? During the **Cold War**, for instance, the United States (US) and the Union of Soviet Socialist Republics (**USSR**) spent huge amounts of money on building up gigantic arsenals of nuclear weapons – money that could have been used for social development in the two countries. Why did they not come together at an earlier stage to sign agreements to limit the nuclear arms race, so that they could save money for their mutual benefit? The same question applies in the Middle East, for instance, where today Israel and some of its neighbours are spending large amounts on building up their military might against one another, instead of using the money for social and economic development in the region, which will be to the benefit of everyone. This looks completely irrational, does it not?

Realists, however, argue that it is not so irrational for states to behave in such a seemingly irrational and selfish way. Instead, they argue, it is safe to assume that states most of the time act very rationally, that is, they are sensible and calculative. To understand this, realists say, we need to appreciate the fact that states act selfishly not because of some inherent evil in them, but because the international system leaves them with no other choice: *the structure of the international system condemns states to selfishness and self-reliance.*

The big difference between the international system and the local political set-up in any country is that in the case of the latter, there is a central authority that enforces rules of co-operation on everyone within the boundaries of that country. Thus, in most countries people gradually learn to live in relative peace with one another, to respect one another's property, and to resolve their differences by means of institutionalised political processes and courts of law. These things become possible because countries have legitimate governments that have the right to use the power of the courts, the police, etc. to enforce political and civil rules on the population. Co-operation and peaceful co-existence prevail inside countries because of the existence of an institution that has the monopoly on legitimate violence to coerce subjects, and to protect established rules of co-existence. This institution we call *the state*.

There is nothing similar in the international system, however. While there is an authority that can enforce rules of co-operation *inside* states, there is no central authority in the world that can enforce co-operation *between* states. Our state system consists of 194 **sovereign** states that are all legally equal, with no authority that can rule over them. To express this fact, realists describe the international state system as **anarchical** (*see* Box 3.3). Anarchy does not mean that there is no order, or that the state system is chaotic. It simply means there is no central authority that can make states obey rules that they do not want to obey. The United Nations, or UN, has no authority independent of what it gets from its member states, and therefore cannot be seen as a 'world government'. Although we have a world court – the International Court of Justice located in The Hague, Netherlands – this court has no compulsory jurisdiction, and cannot enforce its decisions on states.

In these circumstances, realists say, it is perfectly rational for states to look out for their own interests exclusively. If someone steals your car, you can run to the police for help. States have no body to run to. So to be safe, every state has to look after itself, arm itself to the teeth, and also make sure in other ways that it is powerful enough to dispel any possible attack. In such circumstances, the normal, rational thing to do is to protect yourself at all costs, even if it means that you have to forego the opportunity to pursue mutual benefits with other states. *The pursuit of **power** is intended to guarantee national security, the main national interest of all states, a realist would say.*

This self-help pursuit of power in order to establish security leads to a *security dilemma*, however. The more a particular state builds up its power – traditionally through establishing a strong military force – in order to improve its security, the less secure and more threatened its neighbours feel. They, in turn, then start to build up their own power resources, for instance by enlarging their military forces, or by forming **alliances**. The outcome is that the state that originally tried to improve its security ends up with a *worse* security situation than before. This dilemma is faced by every state. The tragedy of the anarchic nature of the international system is that states are condemned to this never-ending cycle of the security dilemma.

The second main assumption of realism is that *the distribution of power between the actors in the international system is the one factor that has the biggest effect on what happens in international relations.* Realists argue that states – the most important political actors in international relations – are formally equal, that is, they can all claim **sovereignty**. States are not equal, however, in terms of their *power capabilities*: some are strong, that is, they control effective power resources such as a big military force or a strong economy, while other states are weak. The history of international relations is the story of how the strong try to maintain their power and how the weak try to become stronger. Realists believe that the one factor that best explains the dynamics of

international relations, be it characterised by change or stability, is power.

Based on such arguments, realists conclude that conflict and strife are not the exception, but the rule in international affairs. This does not mean that there is no order in international politics, however. Order emerges in international affairs not because there is a set of rules that everyone obeys in fear of being punished by a central authority. Order emerges in the inter-state system primarily because of particular sets of power configurations, or **balances of power**. Sometimes there is one state that is powerful enough to force everyone else to behave as the strong state would like them to behave; sometimes the power of strong states are roughly equal and no one state can dominate the others and there is an **equilibrium** in the system (other configurations of power, with more or less stabilising effects than those mentioned, are also possible).

Thirdly, realists tend to be very *sceptical about explanations that place emphasis on the role of morality in international affairs.* Again, they are sceptical not because they do not believe in moral principles themselves, but simply because they believe that the nature of the international system is such that it does not encourage states to behave in terms of moral principles such as altruism, justice, etc. While this holds true for all times, it has become especially relevant in the nineteenth and twentieth centuries. Because of the rise of the **ideology** of nationalism, today states are even more conditioned to think in terms of their narrow self-interests, than about the welfare of the world, or about the common good (Morgenthau, 1973:250–256). This state of affairs is not necessarily welcomed by realists. They claim that it is a reality, however, and that we cannot simply wish it away.

Fourthly, it should be clear from the three main assumptions already mentioned that *realists regard the state as the major actor in international relations.* That does not mean they ignore the importance of other actors, such as **transnational companies**, international crime syndicates or

The word anarchy comes from the Greek words 'an' and 'arche', which literally mean no authority. Following this original meaning of the word, IR scholars usually mean the following when they refer to the international system as anarchical: there is no central authority that can make and enforce rules for all the participants. This point is sometimes translated as follows: there is a decentralisation of power in the international system.

It is important to keep this original meaning in mind, because students sometimes confuse this original meaning of the word with another meaning that the word gradually acquired. In our everyday speech, we also associate the word 'anarchy' with meanings such as 'chaos' or 'lack of order', but it is important to realise that this is not the only meaning that the word has. This point becomes very important for realists when they argue that the fact that there is no central authority in the international system (and every state is its own lawmaker, so to speak) does not mean that there is no order in the system, or that chaos reigns. There can be order, a realist will say, even if there is no central authority. A strict **bipolar** balance of power, for instance, establishes stability in a system, although there is no central and overarching source of authority in the system (*see* Waltz, 1979; Miller, 1996.

international organisations, to name but three (*see* Chapters 1, 6 and 7 for discussions on the various actors in international relations). Realists would argue that analytical concepts, such as power, can also be applied to these actors, and that a realist analysis can be applied to these other actors as well. At the same time, though, realists would say that states are crucially important actors in international politics because:

- they control the means of legitimate violence (via their control over the police force and the military);
- the state is the only institution that can wage war legally and legitimately;
- states determine the movement and employment of people (it is only the state that can issue a visa, a passport and a work permit);
- in many countries the state continues to be the only institution with the resources and the capacity to facilitate and co-ordinate national development; and
- the state has a large role in managing the economy, through mechanisms such as monetary and tax policies, for instance.

Some of these traditional roles of states are being eroded by current global developments such as the rise of global crime syndicates, and the **globalisation** of economic affairs. Nevertheless, on balance, states remain the major coercive and regulatory institutions in the world, a realist would argue.

Finally, realists assume that *there is a basic continuity in international relations*. Wars, for instance, start today for very much the same reasons as they did during the time of the Peloponnesian War, or during the era of Shaka's great conquests: one side has too much power and this leads to a situation in which the stronger tries to impose its will on the weaker, or where the weaker side collects allies in order to attack the stronger. Because of this continuity, it is possible to formulate scientific generalisations about the inter-state system; for instance, a tight **bipolar** system, where two major poles (states or empires) keep each other in a balance of power, has fewer wars than a system where there is an unequal distribution of power among many big states or empires. This explains, realists would claim, why Europe experienced an absence of war from 1945 to 1990. During this era, two major groupings of states, the allies of the capitalist US on the one hand, and the allies of the communist USSR on the other hand, kept each other in a near perfect balance of power, and no one dared to attack the other for fear of massice retaliation. What holds true for Europe is also true for any other part of the world: as long as there is a balance of power, peace will be secured.

The political attitude and theory of liberalism

Liberalism and idealism

Realism's main contender in contemporary debates about international relations is called *liberalism* (sometimes *pluralism*). This is a very confusing label, because the word liberalism means different things to different people. The word comes from the Latin word which means 'a free man', and originally liberalism was associated with philosophies and political programmes that tried to establish the freedom of the individual and of civil society over and against the power of the monarch or of the state. Political liberals believe that people are born with many talents to achieve the best and a capacity to be good. Politics should be about creating the right circumstances and institutions in which these talents and propensity for the good can blossom. These circumstances, they believe, exist where individuals are given maximum freedom of choice and opinion, as long as they do not interfere with the freedoms of others.

In certain circles the political philosophy of liberalism is also translated into an economic policy that promotes maximum freedom of choice for the producer and consumer, and minimum interference from the state or other authorities in the running of the economy. In this respect, economic liberalism is very often equated with an absolute belief in the merits of the 'free market'. In this sense, liberalism stands over and against socialism or social democracy, both of which emphasise state involvement to rectify the shortcomings / failures of the market. Today we find these oppositions in debates about the market-driven policies suggested by the **International Monetary Fund** (IMF) and the **World Bank** for countries in Africa. Opponents of these policies often refer to the IMF-World Bank policy recommendations as the 'neo-liberal Washington consensus'.

When it comes to the various economic policies that are all called 'liberal', there is one aspect of the political belief of liberalism that is shared by all people who call themselves liberals. When an English liberal such as John Stuart Mill writes that 'all silencing of discussion is an assumption of infallibility' (1983:77), or a European liberal such as the Austrian economist Frederick von Hayek (1960) writes about 'the creative powers of a free civilisation', or when President Franklin D. Roosevelt in 1944 called for a 'New Bill of Rights' to establish the welfare state (Roosevelt, 1958:396), they all have in mind the *creation of circumstances in which individuals can flourish, and the cause of humankind can be advanced*.

Liberals, we can therefore say, are *idealists* when it comes to politics. Political realists, you will recall, are fairly sceptical about human nature, and they emphasise that humans are selfish and, as a result, conflict will be with us always. Idealists, in contrast, believe that people are by nature given to learning and improvement, but circumstances often prohibit them from putting those inclinations into practice. Idealists believe in the *progressive perfectability* of humankind: that over time humans can become more perfect, that is, can be brought to live according to moral precepts and in harmony with one another.

One of the best examples of liberalism applied to international relations is President Woodrow Wilson's 'Fourteen Point' speech to the US Senate on 22 January 1917. Deeply impressed by the destructive character of modern warfare shown in World War I, Wilson came up with an idealistic vision of how the world could be reformed in order to encourage people to live in harmony and peace. Here are some of the things that he proposed (these items still form part of the beliefs of liberals):

- Democracy should be promoted in all countries, because (as we have seen) it is one of the well-established generalisations of international relations that democracies do not fight one another. Throughout history, democracies and non-democracies have regularly engaged in warfare against one another, but the record shows that democracies rarely, if ever, fight one another. The institutions of democracy, namely free public opinion and parliamentary accountability, are important controls over the dangerous ambitions of national leaders. In addition, democracies share the same values, and they seldom have reason to engage in ideological competition.

- 'Self-determination' of subjected peoples and nations should be encouraged. When colonial peoples or minority national groups are able to rule over themselves, the destructive forces of nationalism are constrained (note, it was an act of revenge by a Serbian nationalist that triggered World War I).
- Lowering barriers between countries encourages **interdependence** and raises the costs of conflict, Wilson argued. In line with this, liberals tend to favour unhindered cross-border flows of information, individuals, capital and goods, and the removal of obstacles to trade such as **tariffs** and **non-tariff barriers**.
- Strengthening **international law** and creating international organisations such as the **League of Nations** (later, the United Nations Organisation or UN) will also promote peace and co-operation. Respect for international law makes the behaviour of actors predictable and reliable. International organisations, in turn, create opportunities in which the states of the world can co-operate on functional issues such as health, security, economic development and labour issues. The more areas in which states co-operate, the better they share information about each others' interests and concerns, and the more opportunities there are for them to sort out their differences peacefully (*see* Kegley , 1995:10–14).

The main assumptions of liberalism

These idealistic political attitudes have given birth to a distinctive *liberal* theory of international

Box 3.4: A realist looks at foreign aid

'Bribes proffered by one government to another for political advantage were until the beginning of the nineteenth century an integral part of the armoury of diplomacy. No statesman hesitated to acknowledge the general practice of giving and accepting bribes, however anxious he might be to hide a particular transaction. Thus it was proper and common for a government to pay the foreign minister or ambassador of another country a pension, that is, a bribe …

Much of what goes by the name of foreign aid today is in the nature of bribes. The transfer of money and services from one government to another performs here the function of a price paid for political services rendered or to be rendered. These bribes differ from the traditional ones exemplified above in two respects: they are justified primarily in terms of foreign aid for economic development, and money and services are transferred through elaborate machinery fashioned for genuine economic aid. In consequence, these bribes are a less effective means for the purpose of purchasing political favours than were the traditional ones …

It is in fact pointless even to raise the question of whether the United States ought to have a policy of foreign aid – as much so as to ask whether the United States ought to have a foreign political or military policy. For the United States has interests abroad which cannot be secured by military means and for the support of which the traditional methods of diplomacy are only in part appropriate. If foreign aid is not available these US interests will not be supported at all.'

Morgenthau (1962:301, 302)

relations, which differs markedly from realism in the explanations that it offers for events and tendencies. This can be illustrated very clearly if we contrast a typical liberal discussion of foreign aid (*see* Box 3.5) with Hans Morgenthau's realist views, which we encountered in Box 3.4.

The following are the five main assumptions on which a liberal understanding of international relations is based:

1. Liberals agree with realists about the basic anarchic nature of the international system, but they do not agree that the absence of a central authority condemns actors to a perpetual competition where everyone only looks after himself. The reality of international relations belies the pessimistic conclusion reached by realists: despite the fact that there is no effective central rule-enforcer in the world, we nevertheless find that states co-operate on many more issues than they fight about. Yes, there is competition in the international system, but humans, fortunately, can learn from experience. Once they realise that all-out confrontation on a specific issue, say trade, only leads to mutual disappointment and losses, they become more willing to consider options that provide some chances for mutual gains, even if these gains are not the maximum the states aimed for at the beginning. Through interaction with one another, states learn to modify their behaviour.

Thus, the big mistake made by realists is to assume that the international system can be reduced to its anarchic structure. Overlaying this structure and softening its effects, liberals argue, is a rich network of transnational interactions between the actors in the global system which provides them with opportunities to share information, to understand their own interests (and those of others) better, and to learn to appreciate that mutual benefits are possible (and that international relations is not necessarily a **zero-sum game**).

States co-operate to their mutual benefit on an increasing range of issues, such as human health, the environment, securing a global postal service, managing sea and air transport, the control of radio frequencies, the launching and orbiting of satellites, making and keeping peace in conflict situations between and inside countries, promoting economic development, controlling the world banking system and freeing international trade, to name only a few. Co-operation on some of these issues is sometimes structured via international organisations (such as the World Health Organisation, WHO, in the field of health). Often, though, co-operation takes place based on shared understandings about the correct way to deal with a specific issue. These understandings, and the rules and principles to which they give birth, are called **regimes**.

2. Liberals also challenge the assumption by realists that the distribution of power is the main factor that determines outcomes in international affairs. In turn, liberals assume that power is only one factor amongst many others that have an effect. Thus, liberals will not always look for a breakdown in the balance of power when they try to explain the outbreak of a specific war. Often, they will also look for explanations in factors such as **misperceptions** that the opposing sides may have had of each other's intentions and capabilities.

Despite modern communications, states still keep many secrets from one another, and this sometimes leads to misunderstandings and wrong calculations. Conversely, the absence of war cannot always be explained in terms of an existing balance of power. Liberals will try to explain peaceful relations between countries by also looking at, amongst others, which values they share, and at the level of their economic and/or environmental interdependence.

3. As we can see from the citation from Lumsdaine's book in Box 3.5, liberals assume that morality plays a bigger role in international affairs than realists are willing to concede. The ability to make conscious moral decisions is what distinguishes humans from other animals, liberals say, and it is unthinkable that such a distinguishing feature would play no role in international human

interaction. Again, liberals point to the historical record to prove their point. Throughout the past 350 years (that is, since the establishment of the modern state system), states have established many international moral principles and regimes through co-operation with one another. Religious freedom was established, slavery was outlawed and abolished, humane rules of warfare have been accepted, a Universal Declaration of Human Rights has been accepted by most states in the world, torture has been outlawed and the world community has taken steps to punish perpetrators of **genocide**, to name but a few examples.

4. Liberals also regard the state as a very important actor in international affairs, but they refuse to regard it as necessarily the most important actor. There are many actors in international affairs, who all contribute to the rich texture of interactions that overlie the basic anarchic structure of the world (*see* Chapter 1). We cannot say in advance which type of actor is the most important; it all depends on the issue at stake. In international economics, for instance, states are no longer the only or necessarily the most important actors: **transnational** and **multinational corporations** (TNCs) and individuals today are as important, if not more important, than states (*see* Chapter 7).

Because they emphasise a plurality of international actors, liberals are often also called *pluralists* (*see* Viotti & Kauppi, 1993). But their pluralism also extends to the state itself, where liberals argue that realists are often too much inclined to see the state as a single, monolithic actor, or as a single 'billiard ball'. Thus, realists will say that 'Iraq thought that it was in its national interests to invade Kuwait in 1990', while it is probably more correct to say that 'Sadam Hussein, the leader of Iraq, thought that it was in Iraq's interest to grab the oil fields of Kuwait'. 'Pluralists' point out that states are composed

of layers of people in authority who are often divided in terms of their understanding of what the interests of the state/nation are. In the case of Iraq, Sadam Hussein probably does not allow any other person in a leadership position to differ from him, but in many other countries, policies are often the result of political bargaining and struggle between various interest groups, and leaders. Thus, it

Box 3.5 A liberal looks at foreign aid

'How can the international system be changed to make the world a better place? Can it be changed at all? Certainly, changes occur; but if human efforts cannot affect how things change, there is little hope of building a better world. Some assume that everything in politics is a matter of calculated self-interest. Others hold that international anarchy and the distribution of power alone determine the basic character of international politics. I, in contrast, argue that efforts to build a better world can effect significant change in international politics: vision, hope, commitment, conviction sometimes make a big difference.

Many converging lines of evidence show that economic foreign aid cannot be explained on the basis of donor states' political and economic interests, and that humanitarian concern in the donor countries formed the main basis of support for aid. The same conclusion emerges whether one examines where donor countries spent their money, what countries contributed a lot of aid, which groups and politicians supported aid, what the public thought, how aid started, or how it changed over time. Support for aid was a response to world poverty which arose mainly from ethical and humane concern and, secondarily, from the belief that long-term peace and prosperity was possible only in a generous and just international order where all could prosper.'

Lumsdaine (1993:3)

is a gross oversimplification to speak about, for instance, 'US policy towards Angola'. A liberal will say that it is more correct to speak of 'the Clinton administration's policy', which may or may not differ from the policy advanced by the legislative authority in the US Congress.

5. Finally, liberals assume that change for the better, progress, is possible in international affairs, as is well illustrated by the citation in Box 3.5. While realists assume that there is a basic continuity in world affairs, and that states today are subjected to very much the same pressures and demands as they were centuries ago, liberals emphasise adaptation of actor behaviour on account of a learning process. Because there are such high levels of interdependence in the world today, and an increasing degree of moral consensus, and because actors interact so often, and in so many ways, we can begin to speak of the emergence of a world community. This means that the world is qualitatively a different and better place today than it was when Athens fought Sparta during the fifth century BC, or when the Roman Catholic royals of Europe made war on the Protestants and their dukes, princes and kings during the seventeenth century, or when colonial powers seized territories in Africa, South America and Asia during the eighteenth and nineteenth centuries.

A transformative theory of international relations

Transformative versus conservative theories

Although *realism* and *liberalism* are the two theories that dominate academic writing on international relations, and are also the two theories most often subscribed to by diplomats and policy-makers, there are many other contending theories in the field (*see* Groom & Light, 1994; Dougherty & Pfaltzgraff, 1981; Viotti & Kauppi, 1993 for useful overviews). One way of getting an initial grasp on this variety is to divide it into groups of theories. For our purposes, we may identify two main groups of theories, namely *conservative* theories on the one hand, and *transformative* theories on the other.

Despite the many differences between realism and idealism, they share one feature, namely that both of them take the explanation of international reality as the most important function of theory. Theory, realists and idealists would say, is there to help us understand the world, and nothing more. Understanding enlightens us, and frees us from false ideas and superstitions, and this is a value worth pursuing in its own right.

There is, however, a second attitude that we can take towards theory. This attitude would agree that understanding the world is an important enterprise, but would add that understanding for its own sake cannot be the highest value. Instead, understanding should be in the service of transforming the world in order to make it a better place. This attitude is well reflected in the well-known aphorism formulated by the father of Marxism, Karl Marx (1818–1883), when he wrote that up until now, 'the philosophers have only *interpreted* the world in various ways; the point however is to *change* it' (Marx, 1935:231).

Generally speaking, realism and liberalism are not theories that set out to *transform* the world, if what we mean by 'transform' is what Marx had in mind when he used the word, namely 'radical change' (literally, 'change that goes to the root of things').

Realism and idealism can give birth to attempts to change circumstances and / or aspects of the behaviour of people. Thus, a realist such as Hans Morgenthau fought long and hard to try to change the way in which the US formulated its foreign policy during the 1950s and 1960s. He warned, for instance, against taking up ideological crusades (anti-communism, for example) in foreign policy, because such crusades often prevent decision-makers from seeing where their country's real national interests lie (*see* his masterful 'The promise of diplomacy: its nine rules', in Morgenthau, 1973:538–546).

As we have seen, liberals also believe in change and actively promoting the changing of circumstances and institutions in order to bring out the best in people. Woodrow Wilson's 'Fourteen Points' was a plea for widespread reform in international affairs.

The point is, however, that the type of change that realism and idealism can lead to is only *piecemeal change*, or *reform*. It is not *radical* change, because it leaves the roots of the world situation unaffected. In this sense of the word, realism and liberalism are not *transformative* theories, and because they leave the basic constituents of the world situation intact, one is justified in calling them politically *conservative* theories.

Transformative theories are theories that propose radical change, we said (the English word 'radical' comes from the Latin word *radix*, which means 'root'). This implies, however, that we have to first get clarity about what the roots of international relations are before we can uproot the present system and replace it with something that is presumably better.

A transformative view of privilege and marginalisation in the global economy

The dominant transformative theory of our time takes its cue from Marxism in that it identifies the *relations of production* as the fundamental roots of the world system. It argues that *the manner in which humans have organised the way in which they use capital, technology, raw materials and labour power to produce economic value forms the foundation of society and of international relations*. In the modern world, the dominant manner of creating economic value is the *capitalist mode of production*, that is, a manner of production in which:
a) the means of production are privately owned;
b) labour power is hired as a commodity; and
c) goods and services are produced for sale in a market in which the objective is to realise maximum profit (*see* Chapter 2).

This mode of production is fundamentally unjust, Marxists have argued, because it concentrates wealth in the hands of the owners of the means of production (called 'capitalists'), while the rest of the economically active population ('the workers' or 'proletariat') have no other means to stay alive than to sell their labour power to these owners.

Over the past five centuries, the capitalist mode of production has gradually spread to all corners of the world, often by means of violent conquest and displacement of non-capitalist modes of production (Wallerstein, 1996:87–107). Today, the world economy is organised as one huge capitalist economy, with an unequal pattern of ownership, and an unequal division of labour. These unequal relations of production tend to reproduce themselves in the dynamics of international economic exchange. Trade, for example, is supposed to be the one form of international economic exchange in which all participants gain. According to the well-known theory of comparative advantage first proposed by David Ricardo, trade allows the participants in a trading system to specialise in what they can produce best, which leads to higher productivity. Trade thus spreads the benefits of higher productivity throughout the system.

The reality is, however, that many of the poorer countries of the world, for historical reasons, rely very heavily on the export of a single raw material or agricultural product, while they have to import a whole range of consumer and luxury goods. Because the price of raw materials and some agricultural goods tend to decline over time, while the price of manufactured consumer goods rises, the **terms of trade** of the poorer, single-commodity exporters gets worse, and they have to borrow more and more to stay afloat. In this way inequality in the world economy is reproduced and perpetuated.

The international flows of investment capital also reproduce inequality, it is argued. According to economic theory, the poorer countries should benefit from the relatively free flow of investment capital, which searches for the best returns on investment. Because labour and infrastructural costs on average are lower in developing countries than in developed countries, opportunities for higher returns exist in the so-called emerging markets of the world economy. The problem is, however, that most of the capital that comes into these emerging markets is short-term capital (which is invested in stocks and bonds). Being short term, it can leave as easily as it enters, which often leads to high levels of volatility on the stock and capital markets of these countries, as Mexico (1994), South Africa (1996), Thailand, Malaysia, South Korea and Indonesia (1997–1998) have experienced. Again, fundamental inequalities in the world economy are exacerbated by the 'free market', not relieved by it, Marxists would say.

The problem with realism and liberalism, therefore, is that neither offers an adequate understanding of the unequal economic roots of the international system. Both these theories largely stay on the level of politics, and therefore cannot expose the ultimate sources of privilege and marginalisation, and of conflict and strife in the world.

The Marxist transformative theory emphasises that politics flows from economics, not the other way round. Even the state as the dominant political unit in the world, which realists and liberals take for granted, is related to and determined by fundamental economic forces. It is no coincidence that the system of nation-states with exclusive sovereignty over nationally defined territories arose at the same time in world history as did the world capitalist system. We can argue that a system of sovereign nation-states fitted in well with the demands of expanding world capitalism. Capitalism on a world scale required political units in which strong central control over labour could be enacted, and in which the laws of property ownership and transfer were codified in a much clearer and rational manner than had been the case during the age of princely and monarchic control over the division of land in pre-capitalist modes of production (such as feudalism). In this sense, colonialism was also a matter of grabbing territory not only for for its wealth-creation sake. The expansion of the world capitalist system depended on the application and enforcement of the rules of private property, not only in the so-called 'civilised' countries of the world, but also in the 'backward' territories where pre-capitalist modes of production, and concomitant modes of property ownership, resisted the forces of 'modernisation'.

Thus, the international system of states as we know it today is a creation of world capitalism. It is not states that have created the international system, but rather the international (capitalist) system that has created states. This same logic applies today. The state is not so much the conveyor of the interests of its population to the international system. It is rather the other way round: the contemporary state is a vehicle for translating the demands of an international capitalist system to its population, and for enforcing the rules and ideology demanded by that system. This 'internationalising' of the state (*see* Box 3.6) does, of course, not affect every country in the same way. Rather, it is clearly hierarchically ordered, so that we can speak in general about *core states* (roughly the twenty-nine members of the OECD), and a large group of *peripheral* or *semi-peripheral states* (the developing countries of the world). This division, and the patterns of privilege and marginalisation that go with it, are justified by the ideology of the 'free market' or 'the open world economy', an ideology that at the end of the twentieth century is shared by a large economic élite all over the world. It is also actively promoted by institutions such as the World Bank and the IMF.

However, we should not see these processes, and the ideological **hegemony** that goes with them, as inevitable. Marxist theoreticians emphasise that world history fundamentally is a **dialectical** process. This means that every development and every tendency, no matter how strong it appears to be, always evokes resistance or, what Cox (in Box 3.6) calls, 'countertendencies'. Thus, the growth of capitalism in Europe in the nineteenth century led to the growth of the labour movement that actively resisted many of the harsher forms of capitalist exploitation. Similarly, colonialism evoked the countertendency of national liberation struggles, and today direct colonialism is something of the past. Extending this logic, we can argue that the current tendency of the internationalisation of the market economy is giving birth to all forms of localised and international resistance, led by those groups and countries who are disadvantaged by these

Box 3.6: The internationalising of the state

'The internationalising of the state is the global process whereby national policies and practices have been adjusted to the exigencies of the world economy of international production. Through this process, the nation state becomes part of a larger and more complex political structure that is the counterpart of international production. The process results in different forms of state corresponding to the different positions of countries in the world economy. The reshaping of specific state structures in accordance with the overall international political structure is brought about by a combination of external pressures (external, that is, to particular countries though arising within the overall international political structure) and realignments of internal power relations among domestic social groups. Like the internationalising of production, the tendency toward the internationalising of the state is never complete, and the further it advances, the more it provokes countertendencies sustained by domestic social groups that have been disadvantaged or excluded in the new domestic realignments. These countertendencies could prove capable of reversing the internationalising tendency, especially if the balance tips simultaneously in a number of key countries. There is nothing inevitable about the continuation of either the internationalising of the state or the internationalising of production.'

Cox (1987:253–254)

processes (*see* Box 3.6). Herein lies the hope for transformation: once these disadvantaged groups and countries get together and launch a counter-hegemonic assault on the forces of world capitalism, things can start to change fundamentally, from their roots upward, so to speak.

Whether we think that these expectations of fundamental change are realisable or not, there is no doubt that we have here a very distinct way of understanding the world of international relations. Proponents of this transformative, Marxist theory explain events and tendencies in ways considerably different from those of realists or liberals. For instance, while a realist would look for the explanation of the outbreak of war between two sides in the breakdown of the balance of power, the liberal would look for value differences and possible misunderstandings between the two which led to the conflict. Transformative Marxists, on the other hand, would investigate the position of the two warring sides in the world economy, and the dominant economic interests of the decision-makers in both as clues for the explanation of the war.

Transformatists in general also focus on different sets of problems than do realists and liberals. While realists are very concerned about the (military) security of states, and liberals about patterns of integration in international society, transformatists focus on the global political economy of development, and the problems associated with the plight of the poorer, marginalised states in the global economy. Problems such as the heavy indebtedness of some developing countries, and the impact of structural adjustment policies imposed by creditors on the developmental function of the state in these countries, receive considerable attention, as do the challenges posed by the international **liberalisation** of trade and financial transactions. As we can see from the example in Box 3.7, transformatists view the world from the vantage point of the developing countries, from where an issue such as foreign aid and the financial flows between the *peripheral* states and the *core* looks very different than if viewed from a traditional realist or a liberal point of view.

The main assumptions of a Marxist transformative theory of international relations

By focusing on the following five main assumptions of the theory we have discussed in this section, it is possible to draw the following contrast between a Marxist transformative theory and the theories of realism and liberalism:

1. Like realism, Marxist transformative theory also assumes that the **structure** of the international system is an important factor to consider when we want to understand international relations. Whereas realism places emphasis on the *anarchic* political structure of the world, Marxist transformative theory emphasises the fundamental *production* (economic) structure, and the different places taken up by states, societies and classes in that structure.

   The reader will recall that realists argue that the structure of the international system condemns state actors to be selfish and to compete constantly with one another. Realists assume that conflict is the rule, rather than the exception, in the international system. Marxist transformatists tend to agree that the world is basically a place where conflict is the rule, but they do not see this conflict as arising so much between individual states, but rather as involving groups of states which compete against one another for control over the means of production. In the capitalist world system, the core states, organised in the OECD, have established firm control, but the peripheral states, organised as the **G-77** (Group of 77) in the United Nations Conference on Trade and development (UNCTAD), or as the **Non-Aligned Movement**, are trying to wrest control away from them, or at least are trying to offset some of the harsher forms of the core's control. Conflict, therefore, is the name of the

Box 3.7: A transformatist looks at financial flows between the core and the periphery during the 1980s

'If the 1970s marked the massive expansion of Third World debt, the 1980s became the decade when the chickens came home to roost …

The core creditor countries, amongst which the USA is still dominant, issue and control the value of the currencies in which most debts are denominated. In a world economy dominated by global financial markets, by money careening around the globe at a frenetic pace, the principal national economic objective of the core countries has to be … one of maintaining the comparative strength of their currency *vis-à-vis* each other … and trying to catch as much as possible of the careening capital flows into the net of their domestic currency areas …

It is therefore no coincidence that the 1980s, at least until the Louvre Accord in 1986, stands out as a period of … high and rising interest rates of the core currencies. Most of the outstanding stock of Third World debt was originally contracted at low and fixed interest rates in the mid-1970s. They were, however, rescheduled in the early-1980s when floating (and rising) interest rates prevailed …

The upshot was that since 1983, and for the first time in the postwar period, officially recorded capital outflows from the Third World to the core countries have annually exceeded the monies flowing to it.'

Hoogvelt (1997:165–166)

game in international relations in that class struggle between capitalists and workers within particular countries is manifested at the global level as struggle between the rich and the poor nations.

The conflictual views of realists and Marxist transformatists contrast starkly with the more co-operative assumption made by liberals. Liberals argue that dense patterns of transnational interactions between a whole range of actors soften the conflict-generating effects of structure (*process mitigates structure*, one could say).

2. We saw how realists view the distribution of power as the most important explanatory variable in international relations, while liberals introduce a whole range of other factors which, depending on the context and issue, can be used to explain events and tendencies. Here, again, Marxist transformatists are closer to realists than they are to liberals, insofar as they also privilege power differentials as an important factor. The big difference, of course, is that realists focus on state power in general, and specifically on military power, while Marxists tend to emphasise *structural economic power*, that is, the relative position that groups of states and classes have in the structure that determines who has control over the means of production in the world economy.

3. Marxist transformatists also share realism's sceptical attitude towards the role of morality in international relations. Marxists assume that morals are often just an ideological smokescreen that is used to hide the real, and determining, economic interests which motivate the behaviour of actors. Liberals, in turn, assume that moral considerations do sometimes motivate people, and should be treated as a credible explanatory factor in certain circumstances and concerning certain issues (foreign aid, for instance).

   The fact that Marxist transformatists are sceptical about the role of morality in international affairs does not mean that they discount morality altogether, though. In fact, their whole view of the world is infused with a strong moral commitment to the plight of the oppressed, the downtrodden and the marginalised in the world. Marxists entertain a moral assumption, namely that the capitalist world is a fundamentally unjust place, and that it therefore must be transformed.

4. Liberals and Marxists reject realism's almost obsessive pre-occupation with the state. Liberals argue in favour of a pluralist point of view, namely that there are many and varied types of actors in international relations, and that it is the context and issue which determine which type of actor plays the dominant role. While agreeing that realism overemphasise the state, Marxists are not pluralists. They regard only a few types of actors as crucial economic players. Firstly, there are *classes* which are distinguished according to their relative control over the means of production. These classes are organised not only within the confines of nation-states, but also transnationally. Secondly, there are groups of states that internationally compete with one another for economic dominance (core versus periphery; the third world versus the first world; South versus North). Thirdly, big economic conglomerates which are organised transnationally – the so-called transnational corporations – are also regarded as increasingly important players in the world economy which establish new patterns of privilege and exploitation. Marxists do not ignore the role of the state; they only argue that the state is not an independent player, but very much the captive of economic interests and forces.

5. On the question of whether international relations display a basic continuity or not, Marxist transformatists find themselves somewhere between realists and liberals. With realists, they believe that there is continuity. For Marxists, this continuity exists in the fact that throughout history there have been groups that controlled the means of production – and were privileged because of that – while there were simultaneously groups who had little or no control, and therefore bore the brunt of this privilege. World history is the story of privilege and exploitation, they would say.

   On the other hand, Marxists also believe that this basic continuity does not rule out the possibility of fundamental transformation. Like liberals, Marxist believe that the

Table 3.1: A comparison of realist, liberal and Marxist transformative thinking on international relations

	Realism	Liberalism	Marxist transformative
Basic feature of the structure of international relations	Anarchic state system	Anarchy, softened by rise of international community	Division on the basis of differential positions in capitalist production structure
Process of international relations	Struggle for power	Multiple interaction and interdependence	Class struggle on a global scale
Main explanatory factor	Distribution of state power	Variety, including power, ideas, moral beliefs	Economic interest in terms of degree of control over the means of production
Causes of war	Disturbance in balance of power	Misperception, lack of ideological consensus	Conflicting economic interests
Role of morality in international affairs	Diminishing role	Growing role	Secondary role, subordinated to economic interests
Types of actors	States, predominantly	Plurality of actors	Classes, groups of states, TNCs
Continuity or change?	Basic continuity	Progress towards an international society	Basic pattern of exploitation; can change, however
Leading norms	Autonomy, security, balance of power, national interest	Co-operation, prosperity, freedom, human rights	Justice, equality
Status of theory	Conservative	Conservative, with a touch of reformism	Transformative

world can be made a better place. Where they differ from liberals, however, is that Marxists do not see this improvement as a 'natural' process of progress, but as something that has to be deliberately fought for. Transformation does not come to those who sit and wait; only to those who go out and wrest economic and control from the hands of their exploiters.

In conclusion

Although the concepts discussed in this chapter are reviewed as important academic concepts, it does not mean that they have no impact on the practical world. Despite the incorrect belief that theories have only academic interest, we can say that all practical matters and real-life decision-making are based on one or other kind of theory, often without the people involved being aware of it. Thus, training yourself to think in terms of theory will help you to identify the implicit, unexpressed theoretical assumptions of others, and will empower you to state and defend your own theoretical assumptions explicitly and clearly. Since we can never escape thinking and acting in terms of assumptions, is it not better to bring them into the open and to expose them to scrutiny?

Key concepts in this chapter

Anarchy
Explanation
Idealism
Liberalism
Marxism
Political realism
Realism
Theory
Transformative theories

Suggested readings

- One of the most accessible brief introductions to realism and liberalism, and how they would differ in their explanations of modern conflicts, is Nye, J. S. (1993) *Understanding International Conflicts: An Introduction to Theory and History*. New York: HarperCollins. This book is based on the course on international conflicts that the author has taught for more than a decade as part of Harvard University's core curriculum.
- Morgenthau, H. (1973) *Politics Among Nations: The Struggle for Power and Peace*. New York: Alfred A. Knopf. To this day this remains the classic statement of realism in international relations. Carr, E. E. (1966) *The Twenty Years' Crisis, 1919–1939*. London: Macmillan, probably contains the most forceful statement of the political attitude of realism (*realpolitik*) and a defence of it against moral idealism (liberalism).
- The very best contemporary re-statement of realism's contribution to international relations theory is Buzan, B., Jones, C. & Little, R. (1993) *The Logic of Anarchy: Neorealism to Structural Realism*. New York: Columbia University Press.
- Hoffman, S. (1981) *Duties Beyond Borders: On the Limits and Possibilities of Ethical International Politics*. Syracuse: Syracuse University Press, contains an excellent statement of the theoretical issues involved in considering the role of moral beliefs in international relations.
- Baldwin, D. A. (ed.) (1993) *Neorealism and Neoliberalism: The Contemporary Debate*. New York; Columbia University Press, and Kegley, C. W. (1995) *Controversies in International Relations Theory: Realism and the Neoliberal Challenge*. New York: St. Martin's Press, are the two best contemporary collections of discussions of the relative merits of realism and liberalism. Both are aimed at the more advanced student, rather than the beginner.

- One particular brand of transformative Marxist thinking on international relations is based on the world-system approach defined by Immanuel Wallerstein. See Wallerstein, I. (1979) *The Capitalist World-Economy*. Cambridge: Cambridge University Press. Another important contemporary influence has been the approach taken by Robert Cox. See Cox, R. W. (1987) *Production, Power, and World Order: Social Forces in the Making of History*. New York: Columbia University Press.
- There are many collections of 'readings' taken from classic writings on international relations. Two of the more useful are Luard, E. (ed.) (1992) *Basic Texts in International Relations*. London: Macmillan, and Vaquez, J. (ed.) (1990) *Classics of International Relations*. Englewood Cliffs: Prentice Hall.

4 States and the inter-state system

Korwa G. Adar

This chapter in outline
- The modern inter-state system
  - What is a system?
  - The origins and principles of the modern inter-state system
  - Configurations of the modern inter-state system
- The units of the modern inter-state system: states and their attributes
  - Nations and states
  - Sovereignty
  - National power
  - National interest
- Forms of interaction among states
- The end of the inter-state system?

The modern inter-state system

What is a system?

System remains one of the most commonly used concepts in Internationals Relations and Political Science in general, as well as in other disciplines. In this chapter, the focus will be on the inter-state system. However, before examining the inter-state system, it is necessary to explain the meaning of the concept 'system'.

Think of a classroom scenario in which a lecturer and students interact. The classroom constitutes the 'whole' and the lecturer and the students are its 'units or parts'. Each of these, the whole and its units or entities, has influence over the other. A lecturer may not necessarily determine what is going on in the classroom all the time. He or she may also be influenced by the whole and its units. The concept 'system' can therefore be defined to mean a set of interrelated or interacting units. It is a 'whole which functions as a whole by virtue of the relationships between its units or entities' (Rapport in Buckley 1968:xvii). Further definitions of the concept 'system' are provided in Box 4.1.

What I have explained can also be conceptualised within the context of the international system. The concept international system can be defined as the whole formed by all the units (actors) in the world plus the sum of all interactions among these component units or actors. As we saw in Chapter 1, these units or actors can be nation-states (South Africa, Kenya and Malawi), inter-governmental organisations, or IGOs (the United Nations, Organisation of African Unity, and Southern African Development Community) or international non-governmental organisations, or INGOs (the International Red Cross, Total Oil and the World Council of Churches).

Apart from the modern international system, there are other inter-state systems that have existed in history. They include, for example, more localised (regional) systems such as the Songhai Dynasty (*c.*1335–1600) and the Ashanti Empire (*c.*1680–1900) among others in Africa

Box 4.1: Aspects of a definition of 'a system'

1. A system is 'a set of component parts which together can perform some purposeful activity'.
2. But a system is also a 'functional interrelationship of the parts. The various components are necessary if the system is to work properly. The absence of one or more doesn't necessarily mean the system will collapse, just that it won't work to capacity.'
3. Finally, there exists 'an ongoing interrelationship between this set of component parts and the environment' (that which falls outside the system). 'This means that these parts monitor the environment, respond to it, may even be able to influence it.'

(Lovell, 1970:211–216).

(Davidson, 1974). Both of these systems established influential administrative authorities and strong armies centralised within the ambit of kings. Under the leaderships of Opoko Ware (1720–1750) and Osei Tutu Kwame (1801–1824), the Ashanti established one of the strongest empires in Africa, which occupied an area larger than that of modern Ghana. The Ashanti traded extensively with other empires and states, as well as with the Dutch and the British (Davidson, 1974:207).

In Asia and Europe the Chou Dynasty (1122–221 BC), the Greek city states (800–322 BC), the fifteenth-century city states of Renaissance Italy, the Ottoman Empire (1300–1922), and the eighteenth- and nineteenth-century European colonial empires, all formed localised systems that thrived for a number of centuries.

What makes the modern state system unique is the fact that it is not localised in only one region of the world, as are all the examples of systems mentioned above. The modern state system is a truly universal system. By that, we mean that this system incorporates the whole world, and that the organising principles of this system apply to all the units of the system.

The origins and principles of the modern inter-state system

The origins of the modern state system go back some 700–800 years to the end of the **feudal era** in Europe, and started with the consolidation of the Capetian dynasty between the tenth and thirteenth centuries (Spruyt, 1994:77–108). These origins were tied up closely with:

- expanded trade in Europe during that period and the consequent growth of towns and cities as centres of exchange;
- the resultant need for standardised measures for weight, volume and value on the one hand, and on the other, the need for a secure legal order to reduce transaction and information costs;
- the growing demand for effective security that could only be provided by larger, more centralised military powers. With the ability to provide effective security also came the ability to penetrate society more effectively in order to extract resources, and to forcefully subdue resistance and incorporate peripheral regions.

There was no historical inevitability in the fact that the idea and practice of consolidated, centralised territorial rule by a sovereign since the fourteenth century – the modern state in other words – gradually overcame all other political contenders in Europe. As the personalised and localised form of rule in feudal Europe began to disintegrate, three different contenders emerged as possible political successors. The first was the loose confederation of Hanseatic trading states (the Hansa League) in Northern Europe. The second was the Italian city-states, such as Venice, Genoa, Pisa and Florence, which successfully resisted monarchic inclusion and maintained a large degree of local sovereignty until about 1450.

The reasons why it was the third contender, the territorial, sovereign state that eventually emerged as the sole successor of feudalism, and not leagues such as Hansa, or autonomous city-states, are many. Important for our purposes, however, is to note that the absence of an exclusive territorially defined jurisdiction in the case of Hansa, and the divided sovereignty within many of the city-states, meant that they could not solve the **public goods** problems brought about by expanded interaction and commerce. These public goods, namely legal certainty, effective security and standardisation, could be supplied, however, by the territorially inclusive state with one single centre of sovereignty (*see* Nel, 1998).

When the globalisation of capitalism started in the sixteenth century (Wallerstein, 1974) the logic that selected the territorial state as the desired, most effective form of political organisation from the viewpoint of providing public goods also played itself out in other parts of the world. As more and more regions of the world became incorporated into trade and commerce for the sake of privately appropriating surplus value (capitalism), the demand grew to limit transaction and information costs through standardisation and legal customisation.

The Peace of Westphalia, that is, the signing of the Treaties of Münster and Osnabrück in 1648, is often referred to as the founding date of the modern state system. As we saw above, states in the modern sense of the word had already existed in Europe since at least the rise of the Capetian state in France, so the Peace of Westphalia can therefore not be seen as the starting date for the state system. However, the two treaties that constituted the peace agreement did legitimise the idea of a state system by 'solving' two fundamental issues of the Thirty Years' War. The first was the problem of religious intolerance (the main cause of the war was the contest between the Roman Catholic and Protestant strands of Christianity), and the second was concern over the hegemonic ambitions of 'the Ha[b]sburg family complex' (Holsti, 1991:34). The problem of freedom of conscience was addressed via the invocation of one of the principles of the 1555 Peace of Augsburg, *cuius regio, eius religio,* and the safeguarding of private worship, private religious education, the establishment of the Lutheran church, and the recognition of Calvinism as a legitimate branch of Christianity. Hapsburg hegemony was broken by safeguarding the rights of individual units of the empire, and giving them control over foreign policy matters. As Holsti notes, the Treaty of Osnabrück in effect rewrote the constitution of the Empire: 'over three hundred political entities were now entitled to conduct foreign relations (make alliances), and the Holy Roman Emperor could not employ force in the conduct of foreign policy, or even make alliances, without the consent of the individual members of the Empire' (Holsti, 1991:35). Religious diversity was ensured, and religion never again became an issue of confrontation in Europe. At the same time, the right of political self-determination became the central rule or norm of the state system (Nel, 1998).

Some of the cardinal principles of inter-state relations provided for in the Treaty of Westphalia are mutual respect between states for each other's sovereignty, and the principle that states should not interfere in the affairs of another state (Brown, 1922:74). Mutual respect for sovereignty and territorial integrity has since become accepted norms of inter-state behaviour in the international system. This practice did not, however, preclude the right to violate the sovereignty of another state in defence against an aggressor. Remember the 1990 Iraqi invasion of Kuwait and the subsequent reaction of members of the United Nations (UN).

Configurations of the modern inter-state system

Having examined the concept system, and having looked at the origins and fundamental principles of the modern inter-state system, it is now necessary for us to discuss the specific configurations of the modern inter-state systems to illustrate further what underpins the international system. These configurations (or organising patterns) are bipolar, unipolar and multipolar systems (Rosecrance, 1966: 314–327; Holsti, 1995).

A *bipolar system* is a system in which two states or two groups (blocs) of states have a preponderance of power over the other actors. It is characterised by a leading actor within each of the two. The end of World War II culminated in a bipolar system dominated by the United States (US) and the Union of Soviet Socialist Republics (USSR). The formation of the Warsaw Pact (1955) and the North Atlantic Treaty Organisation (NATO) in 1949 only solidified the dominance of the USSR and the US respectively. NATO and the Warsaw Pact operated as block actors (regional actors) as well as participants in the international system.

The bipolar system was characterised by the pursuit of opposing ideologies by the **hegemons**, resulting in what became known as the 'deep' Cold War (1946–1962). Nuclear weapons played an important role in the power equation in the bipolar system. The objectives of universal actors such as the UN, as well as the regional blocs (NATO and the Warsaw Pact) were constrained by the members, particularly if the interests of the two opposing hegemons were in conflict.

Kaplan (1970:11) has suggested a number of rules that are necessary for the maintenance and stable existence of small and great powers in a bipolar system. These rules presuppose that:

- the two blocs increase their capabilities as a necessary mechanism for the maintenance of the system;
- the blocs should be ready to risk eliminating the rival bloc, a suggestion that would be devastating in the nuclear age;
- the question of dominance by any bloc is ruled out and in such a situation war would be likely to occur;
- each of the blocs accepts non-alignment and permits new members to join their ranks in the group;
- non-aligned states should engage in diplomacy that reduces the risk of war among the blocs;

- the UN is used by the non-aligned states as a means for the neutralisation of the power of the two blocs;
- the issue of neutrality by the non-aligned states *vis-à-vis* the blocs is important, but, the non-aligned states can take sides with any of the power blocs in the UN on fundamental issues affecting them; and
- the rival blocs should subordinate the objectives of the UN if the objectives are in conflict with their own interests, but any of the blocs should subordinate the objectives of the adversary to those of the UN.

The dominance of the two superpowers during the Cold War bred insecurity with competition taking the form of a **zero-sum game** (Spanier, 1975). This meant that both sides viewed any military, diplomatic or economic gain as an equal loss for the other.

A *multipolar system* is one in which there are at least three 'poles' or actors that can be identified as predominant. Because there are more than two centres of power, this configuration makes it possible for two of the poles to join forces against the third. Historically, this was done in order to balance the power of the third, and to prevent it from becoming the single predominant power. The balance of power system that characterised Europe from 1815 to 1914 is thus a classic example of a multipolar system (*see* Chapter 2).

Scholars such as Crabb (1968) argue that by the late 1960s, particularly after the establishment of *détente* between the US and the USSR during the Nixon-Kissinger administration, the world moved into the era of a multipolar system. *Détente* established by President Nixon and Secretary of State Kissinger was based on a policy of co-operation and restraint between the US and the USSR. The policy reduced tensions between the superpowers. Apart from the US and USSR, Japan, China and Western Europe played increasingly dominant roles in the distribution of power. Economic power (Japan, Germany) became an increasingly important factor.

Some scholars (for instance Eagleburger in Hamilton, 1989:242–260) suggest that today, after the collapse of the USSR, we again have an example of a multipolar system in the world. Russia, Germany, Japan and China are rival powers to the US, with Germany and Japan taking leading roles in the economic field. The role played by the European Union as an actor can be added to the multipolar equation. What needs to be stressed here is that power (a concept to be discussed later) is not conceptualised only in military terms. Economic resources also play important roles in power distribution (Thurow, 1992).

The *unipolar system* is rare in history, although the Roman Empire at the start of the Christian era was a clear case of a system with one pole being the clear predominant actor. It has been suggested that immediately after World War II (1945–1949), the US was such a single predominant pole in the world, and that perhaps today it is again in such a position of dominance.

One of the questions that arises from a discussion on types of inter-state systems is, how does each type impact upon stability or instability in the system as a whole? Is a unipolar system more or less stable than a multipolar system, for instance? The word 'stability' refers to the relative absence of significant changes and/or conflict in the system.

Questions such as these are hotly debated in the International Relations literature. A number of viewpoints have been advanced. One perspective posits that 'as the system moves away from bipolarity toward multipolarity, the frequency of war should be expected to diminish' (Deutsch & Singer, 1964:390). This viewpoint emphasises that alliances reduce the possibility of system-wide interactions, which in turn increases the chances of conflict. Alliances tend to control their members, thus limiting interactions with members of other alliances. For example, both NATO and the Warsaw Pact members had limited interactions across the bloc lines compared to within the blocs. This perspective would advance the argument that with the end of the Cold War and the emergence of other power centres – the European Union (EU), Germany, Japan and possibly China – stability is going to prevail. An arms race reminiscent of the bipolar deep Cold War era is unlikely in such a multipolar system.

Another school of thought posits that a multipolar system is prone to conflict because of the existence of the **balance of uncertainty** (Hoffmann, 1972:618–643, Waltz, 1967:215–231). The Cold War bipolar system, according to this perspective, minimised international conflict because of the ever-present threat of a full-blown nuclear confrontation. Large-scale wars were therefore deliberately avoided by the US and the USSR, and they chose to confront one another more in localised regional wars in the periphery, such as the war in Angola (1974–1990) or in Afghanistan (1980–1990). This school would blame the proliferation of conflict in the 1990s in certain regional areas on the collapse of both the Cold War and the superpower rivalry.

Distinguishing between different types of systems is important in understanding inter-state relations. Whereas NATO and the Warsaw Pact, and for that matter the US and USSR, played important global balancing roles, it is also important to explain the roles of regional actors, that is, actors that are not part of the direct power play between the major powers, but who can still affect the power balance in parts of the world.

In different regions, certain powers stand out as dominant actors with respect to conflict management and stability. Stability largely depends on such regional balances (or subsystems) and in some cases, the global powers have used the regional powers to further their own interests. Apart from their global security responsibilities, the US and the USSR used the European theatre as their military balancing front, with each side deploying sophisticated weapons in the name of maintaining stability.

Ethiopia and Kenya entered into a balance-of-power military alliance in 1964 to balance the immense military expenditure by Somalia, a country known for its Greater Somalia (Pan-Somalism) policy objectives, at least before its collapse in 1991 (Adar, 1994). In Southern Africa and West Africa, South Africa and Nigeria remain central regional hegemons respectively (the role South Africa plays in the Southern Africa region is clearly articulated in Chapter 14). Nigeria, as a dominant regional hegemon in West Africa, played an important role within the framework of the Economic Community of West African States (ECOWAS) in bringing peaceful resolution to the civil wars in Liberia and Sierra Leone in the 1990s. It is an interesting question as to whether this means that we have a unipolar system in West Africa or in Southern Africa. Is the nuclear arms race between India and Pakistan perhaps a sign of the beginning of a bipolar system in South Asia?

The units of the modern inter-state system: states and their attributes

The preceding section focused on the concept system, its characteristics and configurations. In this section, the emphasis is on the concept **nation-state**, its component parts, its elements and how it exerts power and influence over other units or actors in the international system.

Nations and states

For a clear understanding of the concept state, it is necessary first of all to distinguish between concepts **nation** and **state**. Nation refers to people who regard themselves as comprising a distinct cultural, geographical or political unity and identity. It has a psychological and emotional basis to it, encompassing shared descent, geographical area, language, religion and economic order (Connor 1987, Danziger 1991). For example, Canadians, Americans, Jews, South Africans, Xhosas, Zulus, Luos, Ibos and Somalis are all 'nations'. Some of them (Americans and Canadians, for instance) share a common political and geographical identity, but not necessarily one language or culture. Other nations, such as Jews, share a common culture but not necessarily the same geographical or political identity.

One of the important forces in the formation of the modern state system has been the rise of nationalism, that is, the belief or ideology that every distinct nation should have its own nation state. Many states, especially in Europe, were formed in this way, and we therefore still find textbooks that refer to states as nation-states. Elsewhere, however, states were often formed on the basis of political and geographical identity, and not on the basis of all citizens sharing the same culture or language. The result is that in many parts of the world states cut across nations.

As our discussion suggested, a state is a legal-political entity which has ultimate power over its own affairs (sovereignty). States have the authority, therefore, to make legally binding decisions over a specific territory and over the population living in that territory. One of the rules of the inter-state system is that if an entity cannot claim authority and control over a permanent population and over a clearly specified territory that is not claimed by another state, that entity will not be recognised as a state.

The processes that have led to the formation of states in history have taken two paths. First, groups that identify themselves as a 'people' (nation) have governed themselves through a legal and sovereign entity, the state. There are still examples today of this process of nation-state formation (Bulmer & Scott, 1994; Sakamoto, 1994). Take the case of the former Yugoslavia, where Serbs and Croats have established Serbia and Croatia as nation-states respectively. In Africa, the Eritreans fought a war against Ethiopia for thirty years and succeeded in the formation of the Eritrean nation-state in 1993.

Second, there are states whose citizens comprise different historical nations and cultures. Here, unity among the citizens is political and not cultural – often in terms of shared loyalty to a constitution. In Africa, the colonialists created states with less regard to the African peoples

(nations) than to creating manageable political units. State boundaries cut across cultural and national lines (*see* Figure 4.1).

The problem with the concepts 'nation' and 'state' is that they are often confused with one another. The prime example is the idea of 'nation-building'. African governments have since independence embarked on policies of **nation-building** to augment and solidify the 'we-feeling' among the different 'nations' embraced by the newly created state (Russett & Starr, 1981:46; Connor in Weiner & Huntington, 1987). The concept 'nation-building' thus actually means transferring a sense of belonging from a people (nation) to the state (Zartman, 1997:10), and it is thus clear that we should actually use the term 'state-building' for this process. Nevertheless, the confusion is cleared up when we remember that the word 'nation' can have two meanings: one, referring to a cultural entity ('volk' or 'people'); the other referring to the nation as a political identity of all the people living under one political authority.

Sovereignty

The term **sovereignty** is centred on the premiss that every state has complete or supreme authority over the territory without limitations, at least in the traditional sense. Sovereignty is, therefore, the main characteristic that confers on the state 'supreme powers over citizens and subjects unrestrained by law' (Sabine, 1961: 405). It means that the state has internal and external autonomy. It also implies in principle that states are legally 'equal' (sovereign equality) and that no state has more rights than any other in international relations.

The concept 'sovereignty' has three historical conceptual roots. The first person to abstract and clearly define the concept 'sovereignty' was the French philosopher Jean Bodin (1530–1596). He was concerned with the issues of fragmentation, sectionalism and wars that plagued France at the time. He was therefore interested in strengthening the authority of the king. Bodin

Figure 4.1: Ethnic Africa

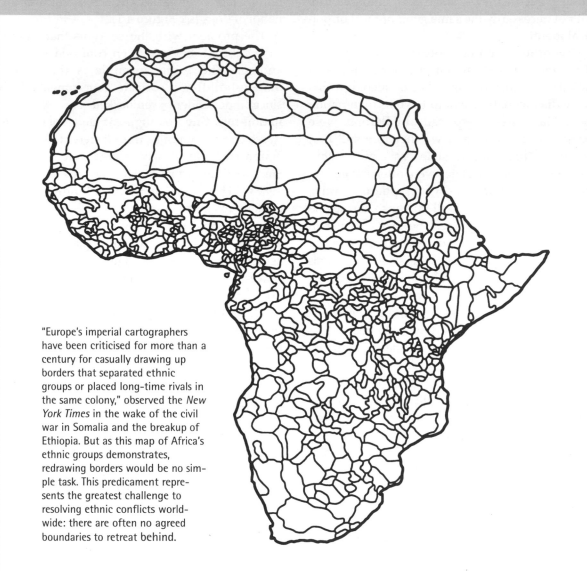

"Europe's imperial cartographers have been criticised for more than a century for casually drawing up borders that separated ethnic groups or placed long-time rivals in the same colony," observed the *New York Times* in the wake of the civil war in Somalia and the breakup of Ethiopia. But as this map of Africa's ethnic groups demonstrates, redrawing borders would be no simple task. This predicament represents the greatest challenge to resolving ethnic conflicts worldwide: there are often no agreed boundaries to retreat behind.

Source: George J. Demko *et al.* (1992) *Why in the World? Adventures in Geography*. Anchor Books/Doubleday. Reprinted with permission of Jerome B. Agel Publishing Co., New York.

defined the state as 'a lawful government of several households and their common possessions, with sovereign power' (Sabine, 1961:402). He emphasised that the king had the sole right and authority to make, interpret and execute the law without restrictions. The king was subject only to God and was to adhere to natural laws.

The second version of sovereignty was introduced by the British philosopher, Thomas Hobbes (1568–1679). Hobbes was also concerned with the factionalism and wars that were common in England and in Europe at the time (among them, the Thirty Years' War of 1618–1648). As was the case with Bodin, Hobbes' main objective was to strengthen the authority of the king and his government. For him the solution to conflict among people in the same territory was to centralise more power and authority on the sovereign. What was the sovereign? The sovereign was the state 'equated with the government' (Couloumbis & Wolfe, 1978:47). He thus depersonalised the sovereign. The sovereign was not a person, the monarch, as with Bodin, but an institution (government).

The third conception of sovereignty has its roots in the American (1776) and French (1789) revolutions. In this case, sovereignty is shifted away from the king and the institutions of government to 'the people'. The people are the ones who govern or rule ultimately (democracy). To put it differently, governments rule in the name of the people who put them into power. This means that governments come and go. The people and, by extension, their state remain.

In the contemporary international system, the three versions are incorporated at different levels. For example, which version of sovereignty do most African leaders apply when carrying out oppressive and discriminatory policies internally? Think of the detentions, banning of print and other media, assassinations, disappearance, murder and hanging of the critics of African governments. This leads us to another meaning of sovereignty, which links the state with the international system.

What we have dealt with thus far are concepts of **internal sovereignty**. However, as an actor in international relations a state also exercises what is called **external sovereignty**. The Dutch jurist Hugo Grotius (1583–1645) defined sovereignty as 'that power whose acts are not subject to the control of another' state (Couloumbis & Wolfe, 1978:48). In other words, nation-states recognise the independence and territorial integrity of others and, in theory at least, refrain from interfering in the internal affairs of other states.

External sovereignty is an important principle that protects us from the aggression of and intervention by other, more powerful states. African states in particular have tried to protect their sovereignty against the intrusive economic and political interference of major powers (neo-colonialism). However, sovereignty also provides a wall behind which dictatorial leaders can hide, and continue to oppress and exploit their people while claiming that no one has the right to interfere in their domestic affairs.

Because of the weakness of many African states today, some scholars have put the sovereignty of African nation-states into question, arguing that a number of them have or are about to collapse (Zartman, 1995; Callaghy, 1984). The concept *state collapse* refers to a situation in which the legitimate power of the state, such as administrative structure, law and order, have disintegrated, and where the institutions of the state can no longer exercise authority over a territory and a people (*see* Chapters 10 and 11).

National power

It would be simplistic to assume that nation-states (or sovereign nation-states as they are also called) are equal in their power relations. Certain states enjoy more power and exert more influence than do others. In order to get a clear picture and understanding of the prevailing inequality of states it is necessary to look briefly at the concept of power (*see* also Chapters 1 and 2).

Power, as it relates to actors in international relations, is the ability to control or to influence others. In Chapter 2, we made a distinction between relational and structural power. In the case of the inter-state system, relational power refers to those tangible resources that state A can use to get state B to do what B would otherwise have not done.

Power can be used to change the actions or control the behaviour of another state. Take for example the 1997–1998 US–Iraq confrontation over the question of the United Nations weapons inspector team. Iraq insisted that the UN team could not visit presidential buildings within its territory. According to Iraqi officials, inspection of the buildings would violate Iraqi sovereignty, a principle that is accepted internationally. The US, on the other hand, insisted that Iraq must comply with the UN resolutions and allow the weapons inspectors to visit any area within Iraq. To achieve this objective the US deployed its sophisticated warships and submarines around the Gulf, ready to force Iraq to comply. Iraq eventually allowed the inspection of the presidential buildings by the UN team. In this example, it is the US military power, let alone the pressure by the international community, which was used as a means to control the behaviour of Iraq. In one of his major treatises, Machiavelli advised the prince to think and act in terms of power if he did not want to lose his authority. Machiavelli saw power as an important means and an end to achieving one's objectives. For him there was no neutrality in war. A prudent prince had to: increase his prestige and diminish that of his opponents; keep the masses passive and loyal; use force to rule to instil fear and obedience in the people; and increase his power capabilities. His idea of power was based on the conception that power is a means to an end.

However, power can also be used as an end in itself. According to realist theory (*see* Chapter 3), the survival of a state in the anarchic international system is central. Anarchy does not necessarily mean war. It simply means that there is no world authority or government that can authoritatively control its parts as nation-states do internally. In this case, it is the state power that translates into its ability to maintain secure borders. For example, it is unlikely that Lesotho would, at any time, attack South Africa militarily even if strong differences existed over an issue that would otherwise necessitate such an action. In this case, the South African retaliatory capacity or, simply, military power, prohibits Lesotho from taking such unwarranted suicidal action. In this case, power is conceptualised as an end.

We cannot always assume that if state A is militarily stronger than state B, A will always be able to change the behaviour of B. Sometimes military dominance on paper cannot be translated into usable power, because military power may not be relevant to the relationship or to the issue over which two states interact. In such circumstances, we speak of the low **fungibility** of military power. The effectiveness of power is context dependent, we can say.

There are certain elements or attributes of power that give a state its capacity or potential to act and to exert influence on other states. These attributes are either tangible or intangible. In some cases, a tangible element of power may also be determined by qualitative and not only quantitative features. Population, territory, natural resources, agricultural capacity and military strength are some of the tangible attributes.

- Population is a tangible power asset. It is unlikely, for example, that a country with a small population like that of Swaziland would be able to sustain an invasion of South Africa irrespective of the differences that might arise. However, population also has qualitative elements to it. A malnourished, diseased, illiterate, disloyal and disunited population is not much of an asset.
- Territory or size of a country is an important power asset a state can have in relation to others. Some of the intangible attributes of territory relate to climate, geographic location and natural boundaries. A mountainous state is more difficult to overrun in war than a flat state.
- Military might is a third important element of power. The ability of a state to deploy its armed forces outside its own territorial boundaries is an important factor in its relations with others in the international system. The number of armed forces, ammunition and military expenditure is an important measure of a state's power. The intangibility of a state's military strength relates to the readiness, training, morale, leadership and quality of the armed forces.
- Economic power, the fourth attribute, is measured in terms of a state's natural resources, the quality of its human power, its

technological sophistication, the size of its domestic market, its level of industrial development and its agricultural capacity (or the ability to feed its population).

A state's intangible power resources include things such as the leadership style or personal standing of its leaders. Another such intangible asset is provided by the effectiveness of the state administration or bureaucracy. A powerful state has an administrative bureaucracy that can effectively penetrate society, but is also free of untoward societal dependence (such as corruption). Societal cohesiveness is another important intangible ingredient of a state's power. A divided state is a weak state internally, but also in terms of its external relations.

As we noted in Chapter 1, power is an illusive concept. It has many meanings and elements, some of which cannot be measured accurately. Even if some of the elements can be measured, they do not always correlate with the desired outcome. For example, the US has tried for many years to change the system and leadership in Cuba without any success. The power of Cuba is not comparable with that of its giant neighbour, the US. The other problem is with the issue of ranking attributes. It is not easy to clarify which attribute may have the dominant influence vis-à-vis other attributes as they relate to policy outcome. For example, which attribute can we say better explains the Tanzanian defeat of Uganda in 1978? Was it Tanzania's military capability that played a role or was the morale of the Tanzanian soldiers better than those of the Ugandans? Would the outcome of the Tanzania-Uganda conflict have been different if it occured today under the leaderships of Museveni (Uganda) and Mkapa (Tanzania)?

National interest

The concept 'national interest' is used in at least two different senses in International Relations. In the first usage, it refers to the goals or objectives of a state's foreign policy (*see* Chapter 5). Thus,

we can speak about how Zimbabwe pursues its national interests by means of playing a leading role in the Southern African Development Community (SADC). According to the second usage, the national interest can be used as justification for any state policy. Very often state leaders justify an unpopular action by telling us that it was done 'in the national interest', and they then expect us to accept the decision.

Here, we are of course interested in the first usage of the term. As we noted in Chapter 2, the notion of 'state reason' or *raison d'état* was devised in the sixteenth and seventeenth centuries to indicate that states may have interests to protect in competition with other states. The word national interest today has replaced the notion of '*raison d'état*. It is used mainly by realist scholars (*see* Chapter 3) who claim that it provides a better explanation of state behaviour than explanations that relate everything a state does to its official ideology. For realists, the motives for Sadam Hussein's invasion of Kuwait in 1990 lie in the power interests of Iraq, not in the specific strand of Islam that Sadam professes. Similarly, realists would say that the USSR acted like it did not because of its communist ideology, but because its national interests pushed it into confrontation with the other contender for superpower status, the USA. Thus, the Cold War erupted not because of capitalism or of communism, but because the national interests of the two states collided head-on.

Hans Morgenthau, one of the leading advocates of realism, defines national interest in terms of power. According to Morgenthau, statesmen who act on behalf of the nation-state 'think and act in terms of interest defined as power' (Morgenthau, 1978:5). In this respect, power is crucial for survival in the anarchic international system. What this means is that there is no clear distinction between national interest and national survival, with statesmen as the main custodian (Dougherty & Pfaltzgraff, 1981: 84–127). The central point to reiterate is that in relation to other states in the international system a state's own interest is supreme. A state's national interest must, therefore, be proportionate to its capabilities, a realist ould say.

However, some scholars claim that the concept of national interest is not much use because different analysts would identify the basic national interests of a state in different ways. There is no reliable objective measure to use in determining whose list is the correct one. These scholars therefore suggest that we should drop this word altogether and rather use the word 'goals of the government of the day'. By doing this, we make it clear that it is a government that formulates foreign policy goals, and that national interests are not metaphysical qualities that belong to a state, independent of whom the government is and how it governs. National goals can be influenced by the voice of the people; 'national interests' cannot.

Forms of interaction among states

Strictly speaking, states engage in only two forms of interaction with one another: they can make war with each other, and they can conduct diplomacy with one another. For some analysts war would be only another form of diplomacy, so maybe there is only one form of interaction: diplomacy. Naturally, there are many types of interactions between the citizens of one state and the citizens of another. It is not one state that trades with another state, but a corporation in one state that trades with a corporation in another.

For centuries, governments, irrespective of their form or character, have engaged in some degree of reciprocal dealings. This form of mutual exchange, or simply the way two or more governments engage in business with each other, is called **diplomacy**. It involves government-to-government on a one-to-one basis, performing certain substantive functions. These may include conflict management (including war), problem-solving, country-to-country communication, negotiation and programme management (Russett & Starr 1981:161).

Negotiation is one of the main diplomatic instruments for reaching an agreement over an issue. For purposes of arriving at an amicable solution, representatives of two or more states will discuss aspects of the issues in question with the assumption that the participants have an interest in solving the issue at hand. This is what is often referred to as 'negotiation in good faith'. This is an important aspect of diplomacy. The consent of the parties is fundamental before the process begins. Once an agreement is reached, the details are arrived at by the parties concerned through bargaining. Bargaining involves influencing the other side to agree to your proposals, that is, making your opponent see it 'your way'.

Diplomatic practice is traditionally the province of nation-states and may be in the form of bilateral or multilateral interaction (*see* Chapter 1). State practices concerning their diplomatic relations were codified into the 1961 Vienna Convention on Diplomatic Relations, which also specified the categories of diplomats, ambassadors, nuncios (Papal representatives), envoys extraordinary, ministers plenipotentiary, ministers resident and chargés d'affaires that one state can send to others. Ambassadors and nuncios are the highest-ranking diplomats, with 'embassy ministers' just below them. The head of state of the host country normally directly receives the ambassadors and ministers at the time they present what is called 'letters of credence' in a brief ceremony known as 'presentation of credentials'. Symbolic as it may be, it shows that the host state accepts the ambassador as the full representative of the other state.

The ambassador and other high-ranking diplomats must be acceptable to the host state. Usually the host state issues what is called **agreement** (consent). Agreement indicates that the mission in question is acceptable to the host state. The host state has the right, however, to withhold the agreement without an express explanation. In most cases, this happens in situations where the host state is still investigating the background of the envoy in question. Once the process is over and the ambassador becomes fully accredited, certain international implications are conferred on the ambassador and the mission. Only a few examples will be given here. Firstly, the diplomats accredited to the mission become immune from criminal and civil jurisdiction. He or she cannot appear in court as a witness. They do not pay taxes. They obey the laws of the host state on a 'voluntary' basis. This is not to say that they are free to commit crimes. What is important to note here is that in situations where they may have committed a crime they may be deported (declared *persona non grata*) to the sending state for trial.

Second, the premises and the surrounding properties of the mission constitute 'islands of sovereignty'. In other words, the premises and properties are considered part of the sending state. To put it differently, it simply means that the premises are considered not to be part of the host state. The practice is based on the principle of **extraterritoriality**. The premises are inviolable. The 1978–1979 taking of US hostages within the American Embassy in Tehran by Iranian terrorists was in direct contravention of the principle of extraterritoriality and international law in general.

What needs to be emphasised here is that diplomatic relations are based on mutual consent of the parties concerned. It is not automatic. However, it has to be noted that diplomats are subject to civil and administrative jurisdiction if the diplomat is involved in private commercial activities and any other matter relating to the diplomat as a private person. Such situations are, however, rare.

Diplomats perform many functions, some of which include representation of the sending state, protection of nationals of the sending state and gathering information. Ambassadors attend official, ceremonial and social functions, a demonstration of political, economic, cultural and social interests of his or her country. Representation of the nationals of the sending state in crisis situations, when jailed or when their properties are being violated, is an important responsibility of ambassadors. These services are available to the nationals of the sending state if the host state is unable to provide such services or if the available services are unsatisfactory. On a number of occasions, foreign nationals have been evacuated in crisis situations. Information gathering is an important aspect of the duties of ambassadors. It may range from gathering information at cocktail parties, by reading papers and reports, and through debates and courtesy calls. Ambassador's reports concerning the economic, political, military and social situations of the host state – generally called **intelligence** gathering – are important duties he or she has to perform. These intelligence gatherings may take different forms depending on the interests of the sending state. Indeed, ambassadors are not the only officials who rely on information gathered from the host state to perform their duties. There are other government departments in all countries in the world whose duties are mainly intelligence gathering. We are not concerned with these in this study.

Another technique employed by ambassadors on a number of occasions is **propaganda**. Propaganda is a technique that ambassadors and diplomats in general use to influence the behaviour of a population or a section of that population. A diplomat could, for instance, issue statements concerning a particular issue with the view to influencing both the host government and the population. In most cases, such a statement is usually directed towards a target group who, in turn, would influence the government. However, the customary practice of diplomats is not to interfere in the internal affairs of the host state. Instead, they conduct their business through contact with officials of the host government. This trend is changing, however, with diplomats getting more and more directly involved in the affairs of host states. This practice is becoming common in Africa in the post-Cold War era where diplomats openly support the pro-democracy and human rights advocates. Propaganda is, therefore, normally employed to change the cognitive and emotional perspectives of a target group, particularly to make the group act in conformity with the demands of the sending state. In some cases, a diplomat may make a statement targeting a group or he or she may join certain mass actions as we witnessed in Africa and Eastern Europe in the 1980s and the 1990s.

We cannot deal with diplomacy in the inter-state system and ignore war. **War**, according to a Prussian strategist, Karl von Clausewitz, is an extension of diplomacy or politics by other means. War is one of the ways in which humans engage in armed conflict across national borders (another is **terrorism**), but it is the only one which is acceptable, under certain strict conditions, in terms of **international public law**.

However, it is not only states that can resort to war. Different groups inside a state can also engage in large-scale and organised violence against each other. This we call civil war. Thus, war can be defined as organised physical armed conflict between states or social groups within a state to resolve a dispute. Fortunately, not all disputes lead to war. A dispute becomes a war when states find that the pursuit of incompatible goals cannot be confined to non-violent modes of diplomatic interaction.

In this study, we are not concerned with the causes of war as such. The central concern is how it is used as a form of diplomacy. Take the case of the 1977–1978 Ethio-Somali War. Somalia went to war with Ethiopia with the aim of incorporating the Ogaden (or Western Somalia, as Somalis call it) within its territory. The Ogaden is inhabited mainly by Somali-speaking peoples. Somalia resorted to war to achieve its objective. Many other examples can be included here.

According to the so-called 'just war' tradition in international public law, an inter-state war may legitimately be started by state A against state B if B threatens the survival of A, if A has a legitimate government, if all other forms of conflict resolution have been exploited, and if there is a reasonable chance that the war will succeed without extensive loss of life. However, if A wants to act 'justly', it must also stick to acceptable standards of warfare and the treatment of

prisoners of war. What makes a war just is thus not only its purpose (*jus ad bellum*), but also the way in which it is conducted (*jus in bello*).

Attempts have been made in the twentieth century to outlaw inter-state war altogether. One such (unsuccessful) attempt was the Kellog-Briand Pact (or Pact of Paris) of 1928. Within the UN system a number of norms have also evolved which indicate that war is regarded as undesirable by the world community. The United Nations Charter, Article 2 provides, *inter alia*, that members are 'to settle their international disputes by peaceful means ... in such a manner that international peace ... and security, and justice are not endangered'. Similarly, members are to refrain 'from the threat or use of force'. However, under Chapter VII, the Charter authorises the UN to use 'all necessary means' as well as the use of force when international peace and security are threatened. On a number of occasions – the 1990–1991 Gulf War, the 1950 Korean war, the 1992–1993 involvement in the Somali Civil War – the UN has invoked its Charter to use military means to brings about international peace and security. Fortunately, today inter-state war is something that is occurring less and less frequently, as Table 4.1 indicates. On the other hand, intra-state wars, or civil wars between groups within a state, are still a far too regular phenomenon (*see* Table 4.2).

The end of the inter-state system?

Despite the global human catastrophes witnessed at the end of World Wars I and II, regional fissions culminating in the division and the unification of states (Korea, Vietnam, Germany, Yugoslavia, the USSR, Ethiopia), and internal centrifugal and centripetal forces leading to the untold human suffering (Rwanda, Liberia, Nigeria, Somalia, Sudan, Yugoslavia) states remain the dominant actors in international relations. The number of states have steadily continued to multiply in the twentieth century, with

Table 4.1: Frequency with which 185 wars between states have begun over six historical periods, 1816–1994

Period	Key system characteristics	Number of wars initiated	System size (average number of states)
1816–1848	Concert of Europe	33	28
1849–1881	Wars of European unification	43	39
1882–1914	Resurgent imperialism	38	40
1915–1944	The Great Depression	24	59
1945–1988	The Cold War	43	117
1989–1994	Post-Cold War multipolarity	4	174

Derived from Kegley & Wittkopf (1997:365)

Table 4.2: The frequency and severity of 162 civil wars, 1816–1992

Period	Number of civil wars started	System size (average number of states)	Battle deaths
1816–1848	12	28	93 200
1849–1881	20	39	2 891 600
1882–1914	18	40	388 000
1915–1945	14	59	1 631 460
1946–1988	60	117	6 222 020
1989–1992	38	172	Not available
Totals	162	Not applicable	11 226 280+

Derived from Kegley & Wittkopf (1997:367)

some of them disintegrating and re-grouping into new states (USSR, Yugoslavia, Ethiopia) even in the late twentieth century.

The state as a legal entity is endowed with certain international rights, duties and obligations that the other actors do not possess. For example, even with the rapid growth of other actors in international relations, nation-states still have more legal say on the question of the use of force as an instrument of policy. In other words, there is no global legal authority or entity that has the capacity over states comparable to, for example, Canada over its provinces, Nigeria over its federal regions or the US over its states.

However, states are increasingly being challenged by rapid globalisation of economically relevant activities (*see* Chapter 2) and the prevailing complexity of the international system. States are increasingly unable individually to manage such crucial economic factors as the exchange rate of their currencies, or to manage the environment. Environmental problems do not respect state boundaries, and nature has a sovereignty of its own which does not coincide with the sovereignty of states. Some states are also faced with serious internal problems, so much so that some of them are becoming increasingly unable to provide internal order and security within their boundaries (Somalia, Rwanda, Yugoslavia, Sri Lanka, Sudan). In many areas, non-state actors are increasingly taking over the role of nation-states (Caldwell, 1992; Camillieri & Falk, 1992; Hurrell, in Dunn, 1995:146–165; *see* also Chapter 7).

However, states and the inter-state system still control much of our lives. It determines where one may live and work, where one may travel, and what one can or cannot do, legally speaking. In this sense of the word the state and the state system is still very much alive and kicking, and reports of its imminent death are grossly exaggerated. This is a good thing because for many of the poor people of the world, the state and its resources are the only chance they have to develop (*see* Chapters 11 and 15). Furthermore, the state system up to now has provided the only workable framework within which democracy is possible. To give power to the people you first have to decide who the people are. By establishing sovereign states the world has come up with a mechanism to do just that, and in principle at least has ensured that no one can prescribe from the outside how the people should govern themselves. State sovereignty is, therefore, not something to be given up lightly.

Key concepts in this chapter

Armed conflict
Bipolarity
Diplomacy
Globalisation
Multipolarity
Nation
National interests and national goals
Power
Sovereignty
State
System
Unipolarity
War

Suggested readings

- The issues of the formation of nations and their ethno-centric linkages are well discussed and documented in Connor, W. (1994) *Ethno-Nationalism: The Quest for Understanding*. Princeton: Princeton University Press, and Eriksen, T. (1993) *Ethnicity and Nationalism: Anthropological Perspectives*. London: Pluto Press.
- Vasquez, J. (1983) *The Power of Power Politics: A Critique*. New Brunswick, NJ.: Rutgers University Press, offers a detailed critique of power as a useful concept, dwelling on its limitations and use by its advocates. He examines the theoretical underpinnings of realism. One of the most detailed treatments of the balance of power system and its limitations is covered in Wright, M. (1975) *The Theory and Practice of*

the Balance of Power. London: Dent. For a discussion of forms of power, see Nye, J. S. (1990) *Bound to Lead: The Changing Nature of American Power*. New York: Basic Books;

- Diplomacy is increasingly occupying an important role in the inter-state system, particularly at the end of the Cold War bipolar system. Some of the works contributing to the theory and practice of diplomacy include, for example, Fisher, G. H. (1972) *Public Diplomacy and the Behavioral Sciences.* Bloomington: Indiana University Press; Schmidt, H. (1990) *Men and Power*. New York: Random House; McDonald, J. W. (ed.) (1990) *Conflict: Readings in Management and Resolution*. New York: St Martins Press.

- Many studies have been undertaken on the issue of globalisation, some of which view it as a real threat to the existence of the inter-state system, while others view it as a means to increase the role of the state. On the rise of the power of the state, irrespective of globalisation, see Robinson, W. I. (1996) *Promoting Polyarchy: Globalization, US Intervention, and Hegemony*. Cambridge: Cambridge University Press; Robertson, R. (1992) *Globalization: Social Theory and Global Culture*. Newbury Park: Sage; and Dunn, J. (1990) *Interpreting Political Responsibility*. Cambridge: Polity Press.

5 Analysing and evaluating foreign policy

Peter Vale & Chisepo J. J. Mphaisha

This chapter in outline
- Defining foreign policy
- Understanding foreign policy: the toolbox
  - Foreign policy-making: four environments
  - The goals of foreign policy
- Foreign policy-making: an evaluation
  - Some characteristics of foreign policy-making
  - Ethical questions about foreign policy-making

Defining foreign policy

Early in 1995, the South African government decided not to grant permission to South African producers of heavy artillery to sell such weapons to the Turkish government. The official reason given was that the Turkish government was conducting a civil war against some of its own citizens, the Kurdish guerrilla movement, which agitates for Kurdish autonomy. South Africa, so the explanation continued, preferred not to add to the misery that such a virtual civil war was producing, by providing one side in the conflict with sophisticated, long-range guns.

A decision such as this belongs to what we call the **foreign policy** of a country. In the example, South African decision-makers had to make a choice that would have had, and still has, an impact on an environment beyond the sovereignty of the South African state, or, to put it differently, *an impact on South Africa's external environment*. In this sense, the decision is part of South Africa's *foreign* policy.

At the same time, though, it is clear that this decision forms part of an official and general plan in terms of which the decision-makers wish to conduct South Africa's relations with its external environment. This official and general plan or approach is what we call a *policy*.

A decision concerning the sale of weaponry further belongs to what can be called the *high politics of foreign policy*, where it shares space with issues such as establishing trade relations with another country, establishing diplomatic relations, providing development assistance to a poor country, joining international organisations, and declaring war or making peace. These issues usually draw the attention of the media, and we are easily seduced into thinking that these high politics issues alone constitute foreign policy. However, much of a country's foreign policy is taken up by *low politics*, that is, those mundane day-to-day affairs that take up most of the time of the diplomatic and consular services of the Department of Foreign Affairs. These include events such as state A sending a diplomatic note to state B in order to secure the release of a citizen of state A who is being held in B's prison; the establishment of a telephone link between two states; and/or attending the endless stream of formal diplomatic receptions and cocktail parties that ambassadors and other senior diplomats regularly host. These relatively insignificant events are, however, the stuff from which most of the exchanges between states are made.

The word **diplomacy** comes from a Greek word that means 'a folded piece of paper'. Diplomats are people whose official tasks are largely taken up by the practice of exchanging pieces of folded paper with the governments or citizens of other countries, and with international organisations.

However, both the high and the low politics of foreign policy are concerned with those things that governments do to achieve certain results in the external environment in which the state must operate. These results can include getting another government/state to do things that it otherwise would not have done (exerting influence), or simply maintaining cordial relations with institutions and individuals in the external environment. In all cases, though, the point is that foreign policy decision-makers, through their decisions and actions, try to have an impact on their state's external environment.

Foreign policy is the result of a process that has normally been related to the way in which states react to their external environment. Scholars who study the foreign policy process do so in terms of various analytical frameworks, but essentially, they look at how a particular international actor arrives at specific policy decisions. This is done by taking into account the different factors and actors that influence the process.

We can define foreign policy as *the sum total of all activities by which international actors act, react and interact with the environment beyond their national borders*. Although we mostly speak of the foreign policy of states, states are definitely not the only significant actors in international relations (*see* Chapter 7), and there are no good reasons why we should not also study how big companies, such as Anglo American, respond to their external environment and how they try to have an impact on that environment. The same applies, *mutatis mutandis*, in the case of an organisation such as the South African Cricket Board. It may be true that it is more difficult in the case of an organisation or a company to define the external environment, but that is not an insurmountable problem and should not prevent us from taking up the challenge to try to understand the foreign policies of these actors as well.

At the same time, though, the state needs special attention because of the tremendous implications that the foreign policy decisions of states have on our lives. It is still only the state that can legitimately declare war, issue passports to its citizens to travel outside its borders or guarantee the currency in which citizens do their international business. Because of these (and other) considerations, the literature has tended to focus predominantly on the foreign policy decisions of states.

However, we do have to realise that it is wrong to suggest that the foreign policy of a country is something that is made only by the central administrative institution that we call 'the state'. Although this institution has to articulate and represent the international interests of the country as a whole, the making of foreign policy is something in which all layers of society can and should be involved as part of the process of democratic decision-making. Analytically, this implies that that we should be aware of the many actors inside and outside a country that can contribute to the making of the foreign policy of that particular country. A useful starting point in this regard is to remind ourselves of the various levels of analysis that were mentioned in Chapter 1. Whether we choose to approach foreign policy as something that should be explained on the level of the international system, or on the level of the state, or on the level of the society within which that state operates, or on the level of the individuals in that society, has fundamental implications

for how foreign policy is analysed and what conclusions are reached.

Understanding foreign policy: the toolbox

Foreign policy–making: four environments

The making of foreign policy is set within reciprocal sets of relationships with four distinct environments that are constantly changing. These environments are the domestic environment, the international environment, the psychological environment, and the bureaucratic or organisational environment. Let us look at these three environments in turn.

The domestic environment

Invariably, foreign policy decisions emanate from within the state itself and, therefore, it is important to understand some of the internal factors that influence foreign policy-making. These include the economic and political situation; natural resource endowments; certain national attributes; government structures and philosophy; and public opinion, interest groups and political parties.

To consider each in turn is to appreciate that individual facets of the policy process enjoy the support of different domestic constituencies. An understanding of this offers us a finer appreciation of the boundary-line positioning of foreign policy, and its making. All government decisions begin with the socio-economic and political situation. The idea (certainly in theory) that the duty of government is to help reallocate public goods suggests, for instance, that foreign policy must be adopted to sustain and foster the national economy.

This goal is intimately linked to geography and its twin, the endowment of natural resources; that is, some states are richly endowed while others are resource poor. Not surprisingly, geographical and topographic characteristics result in various opportunities, vulnerabilities and constraints for and on a state's foreign policy-making, but it is true that technology can (and does) play a role in changing the significance of natural resource endowments (Holsti, 1995). Traditionally it has been argued that states that are able to bring natural wealth and technology together can use foreign policy to enhance the range of domestic options available to a government (Singer, 1972). However, things are changing: in the globalising world – financial flow now seem able to effect political changes faster than governments and technology, or both, can.

The idea of national attributes – territorial size, military forces, population and the level of economic development (*see* Chapter 4) – is freely associated with the capacity of individual states to exercise power and influence across a range of foreign policy issues. Because it seems less concrete, the environment provided by government structures and political beliefs appears able to explain very little about the substance of foreign policy-making. However, it is useful as an analytical category – it suggests some constraints on state behaviour and, simultaneously, indicates the need for domestic consultation and co-ordination. Quite obviously, the freedom to exercise foreign policy choice is more limited in a parliamentary democracy than it might be in a personalised authoritarian state where foreign policy-making is not subjected to pressure from opposition parties or domestic lobbying. Governing parties in democracies can, however, experience constraints even closer to home: making foreign policy in a coalition government may be a painful process. Major foreign policy initiatives can often become the subject of tough bargaining between political parties in government, and in some cases may lead to the collapse of the coalition, particularly if foreign policy is the persistent source of irritation.

There are also other forms of domestic pressure on foreign policy. In developed democracies, parliamentary committees on foreign policy can sometimes play a decisive role in the making of policy. For example, in some countries (Norway is a good example), the parliamentary committee on foreign policy is a formal player in the decision-making process. In addition, multiple and sometimes quite autonomous groupings within government can also fight each other for influence over the foreign policy agenda. As the debate over sanctions against apartheid South Africa in the United States (US) has taught us, powerful groupings can position themselves so as to veto foreign policy decisions of the executive authority. In this case, public opinion mobilised by interest groups affected the positions that were formally held by the two political parties in the US. As the debate over apartheid deepened, cities, and even universities – by divesting themselves of stocks in companies doing business with the minority-ruled state – eventually put further pressure on foreign policy-makers. This example suggests why in most liberal democracies, governments cannot ignore public attitudes in the making of foreign policy. This interpretation tends to support the claim made in 1936 by US Secretary of State, Cordell Hull, that 'public opinion has controlled foreign policy in all democracies' (as quoted in Eigen & Siegel, 1993:226).

The effects of these constraints are, of course, not universal; they differ from country to country and from issue to issue. In general, we might suggest that pressure on foreign policy-makers is effective in countries where the public is literate and where there is an awareness of the international environment.

Here, the role of dedicated foreign policy expertise has become a decisive one. A relatively new constituency in foreign policy-making, think-tanks or (as can happen) universities, appear to have made access to foreign policy easier to the general public. Their intervention in the media, thus highlighting the issues of foreign policy in clear and succinct ways, seems to have brought the making of foreign policy within the grasp of the ordinary citizen. But the role of these knowledge workers, as some have called them, is not without question. Recent research suggests that, rather than opening up the process to wider participation, these communities close it down by wrapping issues in jargon and sealing off the decision-making process from public participation. Issues that might possibly have been debated in the public domain are therefore contained within closed communities that share a desire to control the public agenda around a foreign policy and its making.

The participation of the public in foreign policy-making depends, of course, on who is expressing opinions concerning what foreign policy issues and in which situations. Often small, well-organised and articulate groups can play an enormously influential role in foreign policy-making. So, significant immigrant communities within a particular nation-state, especially when they are not fully assimilated, can seek (and play) out roles in defining the foreign policies of their host country towards their home country.

It needs, however, to be appreciated that what people know, or come to know, about situations abroad may be initiated by their own government. Foreign policy-makers can use a range of democratic instruments – press conferences and releases, political speeches or parliamentary debates – to develop a favourable political environment within which to develop foreign policy. This is obviously easy in political systems where the government controls most of the sources of information, but often these are the very cases where public opinion is not all that important in the making of foreign policy. In democracies, this process is very uneven, however. Rosenau (1961) and Abravanel & Hughes (1973) demonstrated that governments can also be instrumental in the creation of public opinion that may well come to constrain their freedom of action. On the other hand, opponents of a government's foreign policy invariably experience great difficulty in establishing sources of information independent from the official one.

It is also possible to suggest that the public

and elected politicians are lesser players in the making of foreign policy: their ultimate role, despite their prominent formal positioning in the political system, is subservient to bureaucrats, who are considered by some as the most powerful participants in any policy process. Policymakers, bureaucrats (and here we include diplomats) define situations in terms of what is (and is not) possible from a bureaucratic point of view. Moreover, most non-critical links between governments are carried out by the lower echelons of policy-making organisations without the direction of the political leadership. Being positioned at the transaction moment of foreign policy, even the lowest bureaucrat can exert power on the direction and goals of the policy process.

The international environment

The international environment comprises a range of actors – nation-states, international organisations, multinational and transnational corporations and transnational social movements. Each is capable of independent decisions and behaviour that can affect foreign policymaking. In its primary setting – an association of nation-states – the international system is asymmetrical in that it consists of powerful states and weak ones. But the international environment operates in other settings, too; for instance, it gives licences to international companies, many of which are very often richer (and potentially more powerful) than states (see Chapter 7). And, although policy-makers are encouraged to view the international environment as rational, it is often highly unpredictable – it sanctions permissive behaviour in some cases, and in others not.

The hierarchical structure of the international environment, perhaps more than anything else, helps to set the agendas and determine outcomes. This is why, as we have noted, weak governments are often compelled to trade off certain amounts of political autonomy for the sake of their national security or their economic survival. An understanding of this enables us to reinforce a central theme of this chapter. While the notion of national security remains important, no issue in the late twentieth century is emphasised more in the international environment than the global economy. Trends and developments in the world economy can, and do, have both structural and immediate impacts on the foreign policy goals of individual governments (Blake & Walters, 1992; Isaak, 1995). The rise of the primacy of the market has also deepened the power of those arguments that suggests that foreign policy should be based purely on the principle of trade, trade, trade. As a result, states are being encouraged to believe that they endanger their best interests if they choose to disregard what many suggest are the iron laws of the international economic system. These 'iron laws' discriminate against weak and poor states, however, and strongly favour the rich and powerful (*see* Chapter 2).

This reading of contemporary international relations suggests that the economic structure of the international system offers more constraints than opportunities to weak states, thus narrowing their foreign policy options. In the 1960s and 1970s, however, weak states were not without power. Sometimes they bonded together to press home to the wider international community their common concerns (Mphaisha, 1997). A good example of this is the rise of the Non-Aligned Movement, which sought to offset the hostile and security-driven international environment that marked the Cold War. But the economic debate that has come to set the international environment in the final years of the twentieth century has exerted immense power on foreign policy-makers. This is why many suggest that international relations at the end of the twentieth century is no different to the security debate that set the tone in the middle of the century. As a result, we inevitably conclude that despite a change in emphasis, power relations in international relations remain 'largely the game of the powerful ... [they] ... extract what they will, the weak must surrender what they cannot protect' (Tandon, 1995: 390–391).

If, at the macro level, security and economics set the stage for the international environment

within which foreign policy is made, a significant number of constraints are obviously found at the micro level. The most obvious are the policies and actions of other governments, which determine a response in the form of foreign policy-making. Recognising this reinforces the earlier point about the power of bureaucracy – the first line of interaction with these (and other) issues are the foreign service personnel, embassies, legations and other forms of diplomatic representation, which are the primary sources of information on the policies and actions of other governments.

This opens a small window for us to consider the role of the diplomatic profession in the making of foreign policy. A skilled diplomatic corps is a prized asset for any country, and it is easy to see why this is so. A well-trained and effective service invariably includes individuals skilled in a range of fields relevant to the interests of a state in the globalising world. These might include expertise in labour, science and technology, commerce and industry, and military affairs. But diplomats are also expected (as the Florentine historian and statesman Francesco Guicciardini observed in the sixteenth century) to be the eyes and ears of states. As a result, they must be dedicated to gathering as much information as possible for their own foreign policy-making purposes. Access to information is readily available through public debate – in the electronic and printed media, for instance – in host countries. Despite the power of the information revolution, the diplomats' reporting and interpreting of first-hand impressions, experiences and incidents for their home government remains important for the understanding and appreciation of the policies and actions of other governments. In short, it is essential in the making of foreign policy. This can lead to tension, as indicated in the following open question: to what extent are foreign diplomats free (through the routine procedures of both protocol and their diplomatic immunity) to pry for state secrets without transgressing the bounds of immunity?

Inter-state diplomacy, however, is not the

only force in the making of foreign policy. The activities of extra-state players and private individuals – non-governmental organisations (NGOs), corporations, ethnic and special interest groups, the media and private individuals – can also play a significant role in setting the agenda. Although varied, their influence on foreign policy-making is central (Neack *et al.*, 1995; Holsti, 1995). Because they are not bound by the considerations of sovereignty, and the resulting prioritisation of policy within the confines of national interest, the activities of non-state actors and private individuals can often become a foreign policy headache for governments. The influence of the international Anti-Apartheid Movement offers a powerful illustration of the cumulative impact of an international NGO, and suggests how, with sustained effort, a non-government movement can shift the foreign policy agenda of even the most powerful internal coalition.

The psychological environment

A consideration of the psychological environment draws us away from strictly 'foreign' issues to the broader questions of policy-making and towards the idea of constructionism – an approach to understanding the social world, which believes that ideas, not organisational structures, create reality.

To make policy, in this view, is to make decisions based on interpretations about the nature of the domestic and international environments. Thus, making policy is fundamentally about perceptions of reality. In this view, all humans behave as they do because of the ways in which they perceive their own external world. It follows from this that the same stimuli are perceived differently by different individuals and groups because for them only subjective constructions of reality seem to exist. As a result, the understandings of 'reality' that foreign policy-makers hold explains their objectives, and determines their choices from a range of possible actions. In the making of foreign policy, therefore, 'objective

conditions' do not matter as much as what government leaders (and, more importantly, the officials who serve them) believe 'reality' to be. Each actor reads different sets of meanings into a foreign policy situation, and, because actors characterise a situation they see, different responses to the same problem are the only logical result. Individuals only 'see' information that conforms to their values, beliefs or expectations because only a fraction of what they 'see' may be relevant to the particular situation.

What seems to be subjected to interpretation too seldom when it comes to the daily making of foreign policy is the question of attitude. Policy-makers operate within a certain framework of evaluative assumptions about the following opposites with regard to the nature of their craft: friendship/hostility, good/bad, trust/distrust or fear/confidence towards other governments. These attitudes tend to have important effects on how policy-makers react to the actions, signals or demands of others; on how they perceive their respective policy intentions; and on how they define their own goals/objectives towards them. Quite clearly, these are linked to the question of values that serve to frame standards against which policy-makers can judge their own actions and those of their counterparts, but adherence to values can also be cited as the reasons and/or justifications for policy goals, decisions and actions. The rhetoric of the Cold War provides an outstanding example of this: the US continuously sought to intervene to defend 'Western values', but often this was a cover to advance its own interests.

A central problem is that policy-makers, like everyone else, often hold certain propositions to be true even if they cannot be verified (that is, beliefs). Beliefs are a foundation of national 'myths' and ideologies, which is why efforts to question them systematically are usually met with hostility or even persecution. Policy-makers dislike being told that their beliefs are wrong, or that the bases upon which they made decisions were in conflict with reality. This is intimately tied to the conditioning factor provided by ideology and doctrine, which, all too often, seems to provide the only available means for framing foreign policy, both at the abstract and practical level. The powerful role of former Zambian President Kenneth Kaunda's philosophy of 'humanism' was the major influence in the approach of that country to major foreign policy issues – including the liberation of Southern Africa and the issue of Pan Africanism (Anglin & Shaw, 1979:39–71). The Zambian example demonstrates how ideology prescribes both the national role and self-image of the state within the international system, and establishes the framework through which foreign policy-makers observe reality and make choices.

Ideology becomes 'a kind of lens' through moral and ethical framings as well as long-term goals (Evans & Newnham, 1992:135). As such, they help to prescribe the 'correct' attitudes and evaluative criteria for assessing the response of policy-makers. In every way, ideology provides profound limitations for the process of making foreign policy, limiting the scope for the exploration of innovative policy options, but it often offers some order to the perceived randomness of the environment that a policy-maker encounters.

Finally, because of the high public profile nature of foreign policy, the role of personality has been much explored in the literature on decision-making. The powerful media appeal of the American diplomat and historian Henry Kissinger (which he undoubtedly encouraged) considerably reinforced popular appeal of this topic. Quite clearly, the psychological environment of foreign policy-makers helps in the identification of their attitudes, values, beliefs and personality. Each quality is (or could become) relevant in the making of foreign policy. Even in democracies, it seems important to think about the role of personality in foreign policy-making. Key decisions are often made to create maximum domestic impact in order to offset an individual leader's sagging political fortunes (Cottam, 1977).

The bureaucratic or organisational environment

The fourth environment is the bureaucratic or organisational environment. This is perhaps best understood in the light of an analysis Graham Allison did of the Cuban missile crisis.

In October 1962, the United States (US) and the Soviet Union (USSR) were involved in a major confrontation over Cuba. This became known as the Cuban missile crisis. Following an abortive CIA-sponsored invasion of the island at the Bay of Pigs, the USSR secretly began building missile launching sites in Cuba. After the construction was detected by US reconnaissance flights, US President John F. Kennedy demanded the demolishing of the missile sites, and imposed a naval blockade on Cuba. For six days, the world appeared to be on the brink of a nuclear war; then, the Soviets agreed to dismantle the missile sites, and the crisis ended as suddenly as it had begun. Nineteen years after these events, the Harvard political scientist Graham Allison (1971) assessed the decision-making processes that were taking place around President Kennedy.

Extrapolating from his findings, Allison established three conceptual models for explaining what happens (or could happen) when groups in a government charged with making policy meet, deliberate and recommend options. While recognising the controlled nature of the exercise, Allison suggested that both professionals and informed citizens come to think about problems of foreign and military policy largely in terms of three implicit conceptual models.

Graham Allison called these conceptual models of the policy-making process, the rational actor model, the organisational process model and the bureaucratic politics model. Let us look at each in turn.

The **rational actor model** is drawn directly from the work of Max Weber. The activity of foreign policy-making in this model is between identified players (Allison called them actors) – these have very set goals and each makes clearly defined and informed choices about how to achieve them. In Allison's model, the challenge for a decision-maker – the essence of decision as he put it in the title of the book – is to choose between competing alternative options. The making of policy, in this case, means rationally evaluating each set of consequences that would result in foreign policy actions.

In foreign policy-making, a range of assumptions underpin this approach: the existence of a centrally controlled, informed and value-maximising government; that behaviour follows calculated choices from informed and rational leaders; and that the government will act on the basis of either opportunities or threats originating from the international environment. Put differently, foreign policy actions are formed in response to a series of strategic problems that confront decision-makers at any given moment. As government decides, it rationally weighs the consequences of each separate policy option in terms of advantages and disadvantages of defined foreign policy goals and objectives. So, those who make foreign policy select the course of action whose anticipated consequences rank highest in terms of the national goals that are pursued by their government.

The rational actor model has been criticised for simplifying the decision-making world, and for the unreliability of the assumptions which underpin it. In the latter vein, Lindblom (1968) believes that for policy choices to turn on rational assumptions, they would have to meet a series of six conditions.

Let us examine each in turn. Government must, first, identify a foreign policy problem on which there is consensus among all relevant stakeholders. In a quickly changing and complex world, this is highly unlikely, however. Secondly, decision-makers define, and place in order of ranking, all their goals and objectives regarding the specific foreign policy problem that requires resolution. This is also unlikely because decision-makers often differ on objectives and goals. Thirdly, governments identify all policy alternatives that would lead to the achievement of each

separate goal and objective. Again, this is unlikely since new options often unfold within the dynamic of a situation. Fourthly, the government must be positioned to predict all the consequences that would emerge from the selection of each alternative. Fifth and following from four, each alternative must be weighed, in cost and benefit terms, against each goal and objective. Finally, the government must choose the policy alternative that maximises the achievement of foreign policy objectives (Dunn, 1994; Lindblom, 1968). In practice, however, all these are unlikely. Because policy choices are invariably constrained by the practical circumstances under which they occur, and by the lack of information, in practice no government can possibly make foreign policy decisions in the manner depicted by the rational actor model (Lindblom & Braybrooke, 1963).

Allison's second model, **organisational process**, is grounded in empirical observation and rests on the understanding that the pursuit of policy (any policy; however, in this case, foreign policy) is determined not by the activities of rational calculations or the inputs of particular individuals, but by the routine behavioural habits of the organisation (or organisations) involved in the decision. Each member in an organisation operates within the standard operating procedures, or the culture of the organisation. As a result, when faced with the need to make a decision, an organisation often draws on its past experiences to make the appropriate response. In this way 'organisational activity seems to have more to do with process than with the pursuit and achievement of goals ... and organisations operate through routines: new situations are analysed in terms of past practices' (Colebatch, 1998:80).

In his study, Allison suggests that three important agencies (the State Department, the Central Intelligence Agency, or CIA, and the Department of Defence) each approached the problem of the Soviet missiles in Cuba from the institutional perspective that was offered by their organisation – its history and culture. Each therefore addressed the problem in a different way.

This contrasts with the rational perspective. Governments are not the proverbial 'black boxes' – unitary actors in the making of policy. Instead, governments consist of a number of loosely allied organisations, each with a life and experience of its own. As a result, when it comes to making a decision, government perceives policy problems through a series of historical filters determined by the experience of particular semi-autonomous organisations, which at times co-operate with each other, and other times clash.

How are we to assess this approach? Again, let a chain of commentary put the model in some perspective. Because organisational output is the unit of analysis, the use of policy resources, rather than policy itself, determines the scope of effective alternatives. More than anything else, these outputs structure the decisions within which leaders must make policy. To view policy-making in this way encourages parochialism because the goals and objectives of each organisational unit emerge as a set of constraints that define acceptable performance. Experience suggests that standard operating procedures are slow to change, with the net result that organisational behaviour within government is formalised, sluggish or inappropriate in crisis situations. Because organisations are geared to protect narrow interests, each organisation will approach an issue from a different perspective. Each reads into a situation different information and each sees different policy alternatives, but organisational interests, rather than the issue at hand or its interpretation, determine the final decision.

Like its predecessor, Allison's third model, the **bureaucratic politics model**, begins by assuming that government is not a unitary actor in the making of foreign policy. The central focus is on conflict and co-operation between the departments charged with the decision-making and administration of foreign policy, and suggests that the outcome of this is infinitely more important than the issue at hand.

As Colebatch puts it 'specialised bodies (in government) have different interests and powers, and the policy process is about power relationships and bargaining between them' (1998:79). Government and its processes are the sum of many competing organisations, and, if this is taken to its logical conclusion, the individuals within these organisations are not a monolithic group either. In their own individual right and their organisational embodiment, they are 'players' in a competitive game of politics – bureaucratic politics, to be sure. As such, the players compete 'for resources, for attention and for the right to frame the policy question' (Colebatch, 1998:80). The result is conflict, although it can (and frequently is) about the building of coalitions between the competitors. However, the outcome of this politics affects policy. So it is that the 'players' bargain (or negotiate) among themselves – sometimes along regular channels, sometimes not – within the structures of government. The bureaucratic politics model, therefore, sees many actors focusing on many diverse intra-national foreign policy problems, with each player holding different conceptions of national, organisational and personal goals. The actual process of making foreign policy takes place through a 'pulling' and 'pushing' of interests – policy-making is itself the subject of intense politics. It may not necessarily be crude politics, of course. Conceivably, actors might think strategically – doing 'deals' with their bureaucratic opponents or opting out of some decision-making processes in order to concentrate on others.

The central 'players' in this process are political leaders and senior public servants. Each enjoys considerable organisational discretion in foreign policy-making and their respective and often very distinct roles are guaranteed by the principle of bureaucratic decentralisation. The nature of foreign policy-making, in this framing, permits basic disagreements among the 'players' regarding what must be done to solve a given foreign policy problem. In addition, differences in perceptions and priorities are encouraged by the separate responsibilities individuals and the interests they represent shoulder within the entire mosaic of government. Thus, the fundamental idea in the bureaucratic politics model is the idea of policy as political outcome, and the central problem is how the decision was made.

These three conceptual models of policy-making are not mutually exclusive. As Colebatch (1998:81) aptly concludes: 'In any policy situation there will be elements of choice (rational actor) and routine (governmental process) and contests (bureaucratic politics), but they will not be the same for all the participants, or at all times, or in all policy fields'. Now, what difference does it make to us in Southern Africa as regards which of the views of Allison we take seriously?

The goals of foreign policy

Foreign policy, we said, is the sum total of all activities by which states act, react and interact with the external environment. Those who make foreign policy straddle two environments – one is domestic and the other is international. Foreign policy-makers and the craft they represent both stand at the point where two worlds meet; often they mediate between the two (Evans & Newnham, 1992:100). So where does their loyalty lie? Primarily because they are appointed by their governments, foreign policy-makers appear to owe loyalty to the domestic environment, although professional diplomacy attaches more weight to the idea that it is not bound by the constraints of domestic loyalty.

For this immediate argument, we can identify four clusters of goals a government might seek to achieve in its foreign policy. They are:

1. national security,
2. the promotion of political and economic autonomy,
3. the enhancement of public welfare, and
4. the enhancement of status or prestige.

Although these goals are constructed entirely to give the appearance of fixity, they seldom are – citizens can be mobilised to support those goals, or a government can stress one of these in order to maximise its influence in one area of policy. Before opening these up for further discussion, we need to make a few quick comparative points. The search for these goals may be clear and explicit in the case of a state like the US, or they may be poorly defined in the case of a state like Haiti, or they may be implicit, as in the case of a country such as Britain. They may also be understood differently by different groups within or opposing a government or nation-state. Here, apartheid South Africa offers a compelling example: the African National Congress (ANC) in exile held far more sharply differing views on South Africa's international position and its role in the world than did the incumbent minority-ruled government (Vale, 1997).

Realist theorists (*see* Chapter 3) argue that the oldest, most powerful impulse of a state is self-preservation. For states, self-preservation begins with efforts to reduce threats from other states, especially states that are hostile. As a result, states are invariably preoccupied with enhancing their national security and with defending their interests. The first of these, national security, was emphasised during the Cold War; in recent times, however, this has been superseded by economic concerns.

Threats to national security are held to take the form of demands or claims on territory, armed invasions or control over strategic territorial assets. They may be in total or partial violation of national sovereignty – sovereignty is the enabling concept in international relations that allows a state to assert its authority within a distinct geographic territory. Threats may also be conceived in terms of deprivation of national economic assets or resources. So, for instance, a state may be vulnerable to economic blockade, or sanctions, or the cutting off of energy supply sources or drastic declines in the world price of its major export commodities. Articulated as threats to 'national interest', these may persuade a government to pursue foreign policy options that would protect its national security above all else. (*See* Chapter 4 for a critique of the concept of 'national interest'.)

The governments of most states aim to make foreign policy in terms of their own political priorities; in other words, a government seeks to withstand influence of or coercion from others. But let us stop to consider this more carefully. In important ways, the goal of political and economic autonomy is pursued only in principle by many governments across the world. Economic coercion, and the practice of globalisation, means that states are increasingly under voluntary restraint to comply with a range of external obligations. In some cases, weak, poor states are subject to the direct political and economic influence of international financial institutions such as the International Monetary Fund (IMF). In Southern Africa, this has been the case since the early 1980s, the date when structural adjustment programmes (SAPs) were first implemented. The conditions attached to these international engagements substantially reduced the capacity of recipient governments to set their own agendas – either foreign or domestic.

This experience suggests how foreign entanglement can limit, rather than increase, government efforts to satisfy the economic and public welfare requirements of citizens. This was not always the case, for example, the Canadian theorist Robert Cox noted that 'neo-liberal ... [economics] ... is transforming states from being buffers between external economic forces and the domestic economy into agencies for adapting domestic economies to the exigencies of the global economy' (1995:39).

While the power of the discourse of trade and finance seems uncontrollable, the counter-pressure to the dominating view that foreign policy can only be economic policy is increasingly to be found in the NGO community, which is exploring ways to resist the ideology of globalisation. In a parallel vein, the latent clash between economic growth and concern for the planet's carrying capacity has also been taken up by NGOs. Both these developments represent important challenges to international society, let alone foreign policy-making, in the twentieth century. As a result, the looming struggle between foreign

policy-makers and global NGOs will be important to the way the world will look in the new millennium. Foreign policy-makers may well have to negotiate a path between the power of economic forces and the capacity of non-government players, world-wide, to launch and sustain forms of resistance to state power.

Does this engagement of foreign policy-makers with NGOs and the like represent a shift in the nature of states? Are states becoming lesser players in the international community? The answer to both is yes, partially. We can, however, only provide an incomplete answer to these questions in this chapter (*see* Chapters 1 and 7).

Contemporary social theory suggests that states are the product of the way we talk about them, especially concerning the idea of nationalism, which feeds a series of unfolding myths. To ensure their own survival, and that of the state, governments become involved in the promotion and enhancement of national status or prestige. This has become a major item in the foreign policy-making process of states, rich and poor. Domestic discussion of this issue invariably turns on protection of the 'values' and 'ideals' which brought about the nation, but scholars (*see*, for instance, Cottam, 1977) suggest that preoccupations with prestige, dignity and international positioning can also be the primary motivating force behind the foreign policy of a country.

Accordingly, any loss or gain in influence tends to affect the understandings of the status or prestige of the state. There are many indicators of national status or prestige, and governments can certainly manipulate these to pursue narrow domestic or foreign objectives. Blatant ways are by staging military displays and demonstrations of the use of force, but more benign means can also play a role. The latter can include the sponsorships of events such as the Olympic Games, the Africa Cup of Nations and the World Soccer Cup, which have become very powerful indicators of national status or prestige.

Foreign policy-making: an evaluation

If we accept that most people when viewing a problem do not share the same opinion about what 'reality' is, how are we to evaluate decision-making in the field of foreign policy? Three further questions almost naturally follow: Are we interested in the formal outcome of a decision as this affects the power and influence of a state? Or, at the other side of the spectrum, are we interested in the way in which a foreign policy decision will touch the lives of individuals? What is the role of evaluation in foreign policy-making?

Evaluation of foreign policy-making is as complex a process as the policy process itself. At a primary level, it asks two interlinked questions of the experience: whether the goals were desirable and if they were achieved. But rational evaluation also asks questions for the future: what difference would another course of action make to the resolution/alleviation of a similar problem? All these questions focus on the desirability of certain foreign policies and programmes.

Evaluation is also used to provide information about policy performance. This includes an examination of the policy strategies designed to change the situation to the benefit of the government; the careful reassessment of the manner in which the chosen course of action was formulated and the manner in which it was implemented; the account of the main governmental units responsible for policy implementation; the consideration of the available option; and the presentation of the overall assessment of the course of action. A different set of managerial issues is addressed by raising counter-factual questions. These might begin with these questions: What were the alternatives to policy? Was this a domestic rather than a foreign policy issue?

Some characteristics of foreign policy-making

Given the profound limitations in the policy process, it seems a miracle that foreign policy decisions happen at all, but they do. It is also a miracle that efforts to understand and explain these decisions have been undertaken, but as we have sought to illustrate, they certainly have.

And as the chapter ends, we need, perhaps, to give some generalised characteristics of foreign policy-making. These four seem to follow upon the points we have raised:

- Foreign policy-makers often avoid thinking through or at least spelling out their objectives. They proceed cautiously by making incremental changes to existing policies from a baseline of what is known, rather than take risks on uncertainties.
- Foreign policy-makers seem to accept that problems are rarely completely solved and, therefore, all steps in the policy-making process will be repeated as (and when) the need arises.
- Foreign policy is invariably made by the interaction of many individuals operating in various organisational settings who bargain, negotiate and compromise with each other, often many times over.
- As diplomats, foreign policy-makers invariably seek consensus – the policy option that finally emerges is the one on which most groups agree rather than what might be thought of as the 'best' policy option (Lindblom, 1968; Hogwood & Gunn, 1984; Bloomfield, 1974).

Foreign policy-makers, therefore, have an interest in both outcome and process; put colloquially, the proverbial chase seems as important as the victory. There is one final topic that must engage us. Indeed, we still have an unanswered question. What is the role of ethics and morality in the making of foreign policy? In seeking an answer, we must recognise that we have left the deepest question for last.

Ethical questions about foreign policy-making

Because decision-making in foreign policy is literally about life and death, the central issue in the making of foreign policy is ethical. To explain this, however, raises a complex set of questions (with few answers) about the nature of international relations, foreign policy and, indeed, life itself.

Let us consider the view that both ethics and morality are central to foreign policy-making because the legitimacy and authority of the government (and therefore the decisions it makes) are enhanced when its own citizens and other governments believe that its actions are informed by ethical considerations. It is easy to see why claiming the moral high ground makes it easy for policy-makers to believe in the correctness of their position. The problem is that, invariably, foreign policy decisions are taken around the idea of **self interest**. The result is invariably violence, of which war is the most obvious example.

But there are areas of co-operation in international relations, and many of these are ethical (*see* Chapter 3). A good example of this is the preoccupation with human rights that has flourished since the end of World War II. But because concerns for these and other issues (such as nuclear weapons) are framed within states, they remain located within foreign policy-making that considers national self-interest as central. Is there a way to break the claim that states will always be ethical in their approach to foreign policy-making?

As we have learnt in Chapter 3, normative theory suggests we should concern ourselves with the way international relations ought to look – with a concern for the future of the planet. If states are truly concerned with ethics, many believe they should place less emphasis on protecting their respective national interests (or national goals), and concern themselves more with their obligations to the entire community of states. For some thinkers however, states – even within a selfless community of them – are themselves violators of ethics. For these **critical thinkers**, the focus of international relations and foreign policy-making should not be with sustaining power, maintaining boundaries and

preserving national interest, but the suffering of humanity as a whole (Booth & Smith, 1995:8).

This chapter has opened up a series of debates around life on the boundary-line represented by foreign policy and its making. Because of the need to understand deep changes in the world, in the aftermath of the ending of the Cold War, the operational context of foreign policy-making – the questions of how decisions are made – remains of interest to policy, but, as our conclusion suggests, the concern of scholars appears to be moving towards the ethical issues involved in the making of foreign policy.

Key concepts in this chapter

Bureaucratic or organisational environment
Bureaucratic politics
Diplomacy
Domestic environment
Ethics
Foreign policy goals
International environment
Organisational process
Policy
Psychological environment
Rational actor

Suggested readings

- For general introductions to the study of foreign policy, see Clarke, M. and White, B. (eds) (1989) *Understanding Foreign Policy: The Foreign Policy Systems Approach*. Aldershott: Edward Elgar; Neack, L. *et al.* (eds) (1995) *Foreign Policy Analysis: Continuity and Change in its Second Generation*. Englewood Cliffs: Prentice-Hall; and Holsti, K. (1995) *International Politics: A Framework for Analysis* (seventh edition). Englewood Cliffs: Prentice-Hall.

- For a discussion on how foreign policy is made in developing states, *see* Korany, B. *et al.* (1986) *How Foreign Policy Decisions are Made in the Third World.* Boulder: Westview.

- For more advanced treatments of foreign policy, see Hermann, C. *et al.* (eds) (1987) *New Directions in the Study of Foreign Policy.* Boston: Allen and Unwin; and Rosenau, J. (1971) *The Study of Foreign Policy.* New York: Free Press.

6 | International institutions

Craig N. Murphy

This chapter in outline
- The problem of co-operation among sovereigns
- International law
- Regimes and multilateral conferences
- 'Global' international organisations
- Regional organisations
- Explaining international institutions

The problem of co-operation among sovereigns

When I was a boy, some of my favourite stories were the Viking sagas – tales of those blood-thirsty and brave ocean-going pagans who ter-rorised northern Europe a thousand years ago. The Vikings lived in a world that was violently anarchic, full of pitched battles, drunken skull splitting and villages set aflame.

Here is a typical story. After years of war two Viking kings both claimed victory because each had become the undisputed sovereign over what each thought was the only valuable part of the world. Nor (the legendary first king of Norway) controlled the land, while his brother Or (the leg-endary first earl of Orkney, an island province of north Scotland) controlled the sea. The only problem was that Nor's people no longer had access to the ocean, to the fish and animals there, and to the sea passages through Orkney south to the rich European cities that the Norwegians loved to raid. Or's people, on the other hand, had lost access to the land, to the fruit trees and corn fields that sustained them, and to the paths that led east to lands where precious amber, bears and gold could be found. Thus, self-interest forced the old enemies to make peace. They established rules under which their people could trade and travel through each other's countries without harm. In modern terms, we would say that Nor and Or created **international institu-tions** – regular, mutually accepted and mutually created patterns of relations between sovereign states.

International institutions are just as much a part of international relations as sovereign states themselves. In fact, many scholars and policy-makers would argue that today's system of inter-national institutions should be thought of as the logical predecessor of the sovereign state, that international institutions create and constantly recreate sovereignty. Daniel Patrick Moynihan, a United States (US) Senator who once served as Ambassador to the United Nations (UN), notes that of the 194 sovereign states that now exist, all but a handful were granted their sovereignty, at least in part, *by* international institutions (Moynihan, 1993). This group of nations not only includes those that were colonies in this century, but also former sovereign states that were defeated in war, occupied and then returned to sovereignty by the victors' actions – nations such as France, Norway, Germany and Japan.

Moynihan says that as a practical consequence of this, politicians in most countries are quite familiar with international institutions. Consider legislators in Zimbabwe or South Africa, many of whom gained experience working with and within the UN during the anti-colonial and anti-Apartheid struggles. Ironically, it is only in two or three unusually powerful countries, including Moynihan's US, that policy-makers are likely to be relatively ignorant of international institutions.

So, after you have finished reading this chap-ter you may know more about institutionalised international co-operation than most US sena-tors, British members of parliament or perhaps even representatives in the Russian Duma. You will know a bit about **international law**, **multi-lateral conferences**, **regimes** and **international organisations** at the global level (such as the UN), and regional organisations (both in the industrialised North and in the South). You will know something about the different theories that have been advanced to explain the rise, impact and fall of different international institutions, and you should be left with some questions about their future, and about the ethical dilem-mas associated with institutionalised interna-tional co-operation as it is done today.

International law

As the story of the mythical Nor and Or is meant to suggest, institutionalised, regularised co-oper-ation between sovereigns almost always has two sides. On the one hand, there are rules, proce-dures and patterns of expected behaviour that apply to the transnational interactions between citizens and non-state actors such as private corporations – rules that apply to things like travel and trade. On the other hand, there are rules that apply to the relations among governments themselves. When those rules are considered to be authoritative or binding, we refer to them as constituting part of international law. The law that applies directly to the transnational interactions of citizens and their private associations is *private* international law. The law that applies to states in relation with each other is *public* international law.

Scholars of International Relations and most foreign policy-makers in most governments understand the current *global* system of international law as having its origins in the *regional* system of European states in the seventeenth century. As part of the effort to resolve the religious wars that had plagued Europe for more than a century, monarchs began to recognise each other's absolute authority within domestic affairs. In doing so, the argument goes, European monarchs created an **international society** based upon mutual recognition of sovereignty. As time went by, non-European countries became part of this particular 'society of states,' mostly as a consequence of European imperialism and then decolonisation.

Contemporary international law grew out of the rules that bound this European international society. International lawyers write that such law had three sources: *custom, treaty* and legal *scholarship.*

Customary international law stems from the common practices of states in their dealings with each other. For example, it is a principle of international law that governments are not supposed to kill or imprison the ambassadors of other countries. Even if they happen to end up at war with a neighbour, a government is expected at most to expel the ambassador of its new enemy. The root of this law is simply the self-interested practice that had become the custom of Europe's warring monarchs, even in the seventeenth century.

Treaty law comes from agreed-upon written contracts between states. For example, most governments negotiate explicit agreements about the treatment of foreign workers with all the countries in which significant numbers of their citizens are employed. Because treaties are carefully negotiated and written down, they can provide greater certainty than appeals to custom. In addition, treaty law is often made more widely legitimate within society through ratification – the submission of a treaty to a country's legislative body for its approval.

In most societies international law is, today, the only law that has a source other than custom or the acts of legislatures. Texts of international law written by scholars are also treated as sources of law by the courts that act as part of the international legal system. Through the contribution of non-European scholars to such **legal doctrine**, as well as through the customary practices of non-European states, and the treaties that they have initiated, the originally narrowly European system of international law has become truly global. Since the period of rapid decolonisation in the 1950s and 1960s, the third world majority within the UN has also used the process of passing non-binding resolutions of their diplomatic representatives as a way of further reinforcing various legal doctrines and as preparation for exercises in multilateral treaty-making.

Many people find it strange that the customary practices of sovereign states, the treaties they ratify and certain legal doctrines identified by scholars are called *law*. After all, they argue, is not the whole point of *sovereignty* that sovereigns recognise no higher authority? Can sovereign governments not always just say that they have the *right* to ignore international law, whatever its source? This is an interesting point, and one that is the subject of a long and fairly complicated debate. The most important argument in that debate is that if sovereigns exist only as part of an *international society* that recognises their sovereignty, then, in order to maintain their sovereignty, they are *obligated* to abide by the laws that make their international society possible.

Moreover, one of the (quite minimal) rules that makes an international society possible is the principle that states will live up to the obligations they undertake with each other. Thus, the obligation to abide by the treaties you have made can be thought of as one of the constitutional principles of international society.

The question of whether or not international law is truly law – whether it is truly obligatory and binding – is actually less troublesome than the related question of what can be done when states violate international law. Sometimes some journalists or politicians will say that international law is unimportant because it is 'unenforceable'. This is only a very partial truth.

A great deal of international law, especially international private law based on treaty, is enforced domestically by the courts and police of each of the countries that are party to a treaty. If, for example, Zimbabwe and South Africa have a copyright treaty designed to protect the interests of recording companies, performers and songwriters in both countries, and if a South African band visiting Harare finds street vendors selling illegal recordings of its performances, the band simply sues for its rights in the Zimbabwean court.

In some parts of the world, and for some purposes, international courts exist, although primarily to deal with issues of international public law. The courts grew out of international treaties of 1899 and 1907 that set up a system of international courts of **arbitration**, where states with particular disputes would give them to international panels of jurists to resolve. In 1919, the victors in World War I established the International Court of Justice on the foundation of the older system of arbitration. In 1945, the Court was reconstituted as the judicial arm of the UN. It is located in The Hague, the Netherlands, and has fifteen judges who serve nine-year terms.

Throughout the first two-thirds of this century the international courts were Western-dominated institutions that significantly helped some Western European states resolve a few major disputes, but that did little to enforce international

law on a truly global basis. For example, in 1966 in what is perhaps the Court's most notorious decision, South West Africa, Second Phase, the Court found unusually narrow and abstract procedural grounds on which to refuse to intervene to prevent the extension of the policy of Apartheid to Namibia (then, South West Africa), which South Africa had controlled first as Mandate of the League of Nations and then as a Trusteeship of the UN.

Since the mid-1980s the International Court has gained a much wider legitimacy, especially as it works with and alongside new international tribunals designed to cope with the consequences of many of the protracted conflicts that intensified at the end of the Cold War, such as the international tribunals concerned with war crimes in Bosnia and with genocide in Rwanda. Perhaps even more significant has been the development and expansion of international courts at a regional level, especially in Europe, but also, in the field of human rights, in the Americas.

Of course, international courts are only one part of a solution to the problem of enforcing international law. Within countries, the courts always work hand-in-hand with the police and the prisons. When a state violates international law it is only other states that can act as the police – by using their military forces to force the violation to end – and as prisons – by using diplomatic and economic sanctions to punish violations or to make the rogue state incapable of repeating its actions. It is, therefore, impossible to enforce international law against powerful states or powerful coalitions of states. That is what makes international law look so ineffective.

Consider what happened in 1935 when Fascist Italy invaded and eventually annexed Ethiopia, which, along with Liberia and white-ruled South Africa, made up the African members of 'international society'. International law demanded that Italy be punished and its action reversed, but the realist principle of forming alliances against a powerful state that might be capable of threatening one's own vital interests convinced

French and British policy-makers to impose only weak sanctions on Italy in the hope that Italy might eventually join them in an alliance against the larger threat from Hitler's Germany. A half a century later, at the beginning of the UN debate on using force to reverse the Iraqi take-over of Kuwait, the US Secretary of State invoked the precedent of French and British policy in the 1930s. He said that it was a mistake to let Italy violate international law then, and it would be an equal mistake to allow Iraq to get away with a similar violation of international law today. Many historians of international relations agreed, but they also recognised that international law was enforced against Iraq only because its invasion harmed vital US interests in Persian Gulf oil.

Questions about the enforcement of international law can become even more troubling, both in practical and ethical terms, as is suggested in Box 6.1. As a consequence, many scholars and diplomats, even those outside the 'realist' camp, urge governments to limit their treaty-making to agreements that can become somewhat 'self-enforcing' by reinforcing the long-term mutual interests of all parties in the outcomes achieved by the treaty.

Political scientist Robert O. Keohane argues that international co-operation is best thought of as an active process of discovering and reinforcing previously unrecognised mutual interests of sovereign states (Keohane, 1984). The institutions created as a part of this kind of active co-operation – including the customary practices of states and the treaties they make – have the long-term self-interest of the states involved to strengthen their enforcement at any time that irrational policy-makers or the short-term interests of one or another state might lead them to violate that part of international law.

Regimes and multilateral conferences

Scholars and policy-makers are apt to call the combination of customary practices, treaties and enforcing institutions that apply to a specific area of common international interest the '**regime**' for that particular aspect of international social life. Thus, for example, the treaties under which some states pledge not to build nuclear weapons, the incentives to make those pledges – especially the promise of shared technology – given by states with advanced nuclear industries and the monitoring by various international organisations of sites where radioactive materials are used can be said to constitute the *'nuclear non-proliferation regime'*. Similarly, the global treaty banning international trade in endangered animals and plants, the regularly renewed pledges of many countries to ban the domestic sale of the bones of tigers, and the monitoring of these agreements, which is done by the various private environmental groups around the worl, as well as the transnational, often government-funded, co-operative research on preserving tiger habitats, can be thought of as the *'international tiger regime'*.

Hundreds or perhaps thousands of international regimes exist. In fact, because the idea of an 'international regime' is an intellectual concept, people can disagree about whether a particular pattern of international behaviour constitutes a 'regime' or not. Nonetheless, the wide range of scholars and policy-makers who agree that the concept of 'regime' is useful would also agree that there are regimes that cover an astonishingly wide range of human activities. Some international regimes involve only two states, for example, regimes that regulate activities on lakes that lie between two nations. Other regimes include virtually all nations.

Despite the wide diversity of contemporary international regimes, almost all of them grew out of the same standard form of international, co-operative practice, the same 'meta-regime' or 'regime for creating international regimes' – the **multilateral conference**. Beginning in the early 1800s, when what was to become today's 'international society' was still just a club of European governments under emperors and kings, the representatives of different states began the practice of holding *ad hoc* multilateral meetings to discuss

Box 6.1: Who is to blame when international law is not enforced? Questions for research and debate from the case of the Rwandan genocide

In April of 1998, the Rwandan government began executing people who had been tried in Rwandan courts and convicted of responsibility for the genocide of a stigmatised group of Rwandan citizens (Tutsis and their non-Tutsi supporters) four years earlier. Officials of many governments asked the Rwandans to suspend further executions and trials. They argued that genocide was a crime under international treaty law, that an international tribunal had been established to try those responsible and that the tribunal had already convicted one man. The Rwandan government refused, arguing that international courts were notoriously ineffective. They lack police power and can only bring to justice those people that powerful states wanted to bring to justice. Was the Rwandan government right to take matters into its own hands even if that could be interpreted as violating its own treaty obligations and as further undermining international law?

In the same month, a number of newspapers and magazines published a UN memo written in January of 1994 from the Peacekeeping Office, which was then headed by Kofi Annan, who later became UN Secretary General. The memo indicated that the UN general who was then in the field had reported excellent intelligence that the genocide was about to take place. He had asked for the authority to try to use his forces to stop it. Annan's office refused, citing (spokespeople now say) the lack of interest of many Security Council members in beginning any new military action in which there was any possibility that Western soldiers would be killed. But the reporters accused Annan of not giving Security Council members all the information that the UN had about the high probability that genocide was to take place. If that were true, should Annan have been held responsible for the genocide? Should he be brought before an international tribunal?

In response to the criticism in the press, Annan pointed out that at least a division of rapidly deployed troops would have been needed to prevent the genocide and that only Belgium, France and the US had the combination of trained troops and the ability to deploy them rapidly in Central Africa. Annan says that those governments refused, something confirmed by US President Clinton, who later apologised to the people of Rwanda for his country's inaction. Is an apology enough? Would international law demand that countries with the ability to intervene should be held accountable? Should the US President be brought in front of the international tribunal?

Shortly after the overthrow of the government that had sanctioned the Rwandan genocide, Archbishop Desmond Tutu and a number of other recognised moral leaders of the continent visited the devastated country. Many came away from the horror with sharp words for other African governments who had not intervened to stop the genocide and who had not developed the military capacity to launch co-ordinated efforts to stop such outrages, even though the earlier tragedy in Somalia made it clear how great the need might be, and how futile it was for Africans to expect that well-armed Northern states would act morally and consistently. How responsible were other African governments for allowing the genocide to take place? Should African leaders be asked to appear before an international tribunal to justify their 'sins of omission'?

particular topics of potential mutual interest such as piracy on the open seas, the international transmission of diseases or the loaning of works of art among national museums.

Typically, the idea for a particular multilateral conference would arise from an international non-governmental organisation (an **NGO**) – often a professional group or a social movement concerned with the issue. The groups were invariably motivated by the belief that there was a mutual, but perhaps as-yet-unrecognised, interest of states in establishing a regime to regulate some aspect of international society. For example, in the 1850s museum directors and art educators throughout Europe convinced their governments to meet and agree upon a regime to promote the exchange of copies of great works of art using what were, in those days, new technologies such as photography.

In the 1800s, NGOs frequently convinced governments to attend such conferences by convincing Europe's monarchs to sponsor them. In the last third of the century there was even a peculiar sort of division of labour that had been worked out among Europe's princes to cover all the areas of human life in which new conferences might be called, with the Italian King responsible for questions of agriculture, the German Kaiser for issues involving industrial labour, the Danish King concerned with questions about the oceans, the French Emperor (and, later, the French presidents) with questions of communication, the Belgian King with issues of trade, the Dutch with questions to do with money and, perhaps somewhat ironically, the Russian Czar with general questions about war and peace.

This system for sponsoring international conferences was bound to change as monarchs either disappeared or became constitutional figureheads. In this century, it is either governments themselves, or existing international organisations, that end up sponsoring the large multilateral conferences that do much of the business of creating international regimes. Beginning in 1972, with a Swedish-sponsored global conference on international environmental matters, a regularised but informal **global conference system** has developed (*see* Box 6.2). Governments return to the same topics over and over again, often in a ten-year rotation. Thus, there were global conferences on women in 1975, 1985 and 1995, conferences on population in 1974, 1984 and 1994, and governments most recently returned to the environmental questions in a 1992 meeting in Rio de Janeiro, Brazil.

Critics of the global conference system say that the conferences have become costly media events that just give NGOs (who always meet nearby at the same time) an opportunity to meet, share strategies and pressure governments to agree to things that they might not agree to if it were not for the presence of newspaper reporters and television cameras. Advocates argue that this is actually one of the strengths of the conferences: they strengthen international grass-roots politics and help to force governments to live up to their rhetoric about international co-operation. Advocates argue that it is in the global interest that the conference system has started to take on a kind of 'legislative function' in the emergent, but still incoherent, system of **global governance** that they believe is essential in a world in which there is a single, global economy.

UN Secretary General Kofi Annan has responded to critics' concerns about the high costs of the global conferences by advocating that they should be superseded by a system of special sessions of the General Assembly (the one part of the UN in which every state is involved) that would replace much of what is currently a rather stale annual debating exercise in New York (Annan, 1998). In fact, the impact of Annan's proposals could be to further institutionalise this 'legislative' aspect of global governance, including the direct involvement of NGOs. Annan has proposed that the physical and institutional structures of the UN's Trusteeship Council be turned into a permanent base for NGO forums that would take place each year alongside the special UN sessions.

'Global' international organisations

Many people would argue that eventually something like Annan's proposal will have to be put in place. They point to the post-**Industrial Revolution** tendency for industrial economies to 'outgrow' existing states. Many observers call the current manifestation of this tendency economic **globalisation**, in part because it looks to some as

Box 6.2: Major global conferences, 1972–1996

Human Environment	June 1972	Stockholm
Law of the Sea	1973–1982	New York, Caracas, Geneva
Population	August 1974	Bucharest
Food	November 1974	Rome
Human Settlements	May–June 1976	Vancouver
Employment	June 1976	Geneva
Water	March 1977	Mar del Plata
Technical Co-operation for Development	September 1978	Buenos Aires
Primary Health Care	September 1978	Alma Ata
Agrarian Reform	July 1979	Rome
Science and Technology for Development	August 1979	Vienna
Desertification	September 1979	Nairobi
Women	July 1980	Copenhagen
New and Renewable Sources of Energy	August 1981	Nairobi
Least Developed Countries	September 1981	Paris
Ageing	August 1982	Vienna
Population	August 1984	Mexico City
Women	July 1985	Nairobi
Drug Abuse	July 1987	Vienna
Social Welfare for Development	September 1987	Vienna
Disarmament and Development	August–September 1987	New York
Education for All	March 1990	Jomtien (Thailand)
Least Developed Countries	September 1990	Paris
Water and Development	January 1992	Dublin
Environment and Development	June 1992	Rio de Janeiro
Human Rights	June 1993	Vienna
Natural Disaster Prevention	May 1994	Yokohama
Population and Development	September 1994	Cairo
Social Development	March 1995	Copenhagen
Small Island Countries	April–May 1995	Barbados
Women and Development	September 1995	Beijing
Habitat II	June 1996	Istanbul
Food	September 1996	Rome

Fomerand (1996:374–75)

if a single, world-wide industrial economy has either already developed or is now inevitable. In either case, the need for a system of **global governance** – a system of institutions to regulate and/or to promote a truly global economy – would seem to be on the horizon.

Whether or not we have reached this stage (and I, for one, doubt that we have) the same process that many people now call 'globalisation' has been a feature of world society for at least two centuries. Industrialists are compelled by the economic logic of capitalism to look constantly for ways to produce more goods that can be sold at a profit. This eventually forces all of them to look beyond their country's borders for cheaper labour, cheaper raw materials and the wider markets in which they can sell the goods that they produce. To the extent to which states support or respect capitalist interests, they, too, become motivated to extend market areas beyond the confines of the individual nation. While it may be true that, at certain times, a policy of **imperialism** has been sufficient to open new markets for labour and raw materials, it usually takes international co-operation among industrialised states to extend the market for industrial goods. For over a century that co-operation has included the establishment of formal international organisations that are open to membership for almost all the states within international society.

Part of creating a larger market area for industrial goods involves removing any tariff or non-tariff barriers to the purchase or sale of those goods from companies in other countries. This is the sort of work done by the World Trade Organisation (WTO) in Geneva, a bureau that supports and monitors periodic reductions in international barriers to trade. But trade rules are actually only a very small part of market creation. International organisations exist to promote the physical infrastructure of international markets – the transport and communications systems that make it possible to buy and sell goods and move them from place to place. International organisations also help to create and govern the monetary and financial systems that support trade. They also set industrial standards – for example, standards for the shape of electrical plugs and computer software – and they protect intellectual property, such as patents, trademarks and copyright.

International organisations not only create wider international markets, they also 'secure' them by making it easier for states to co-operate to overcome the resistance to 'globalisation' that emerges at every stage. Industrial workers oppose the lack of democratic control over pro-duction – including the introduction of new technologies and the shifting of work to other places – and international organisations, such as the current International Labour Organisation (ILO), have been created to help manage this dissent. In every era of industrialism some farmers and those connected with older industries have opposed the market-expanding activities that led to the introduction of whole new major industries, and international organisations, such as, in its early days, the UN's Food and Agriculture Organisation, have worked to placate those interests. Equally, in every era there have been large regions of the world that have provided raw materials and labour for the centres of advanced industry, but they have not received corresponding degrees of new technologies and high levels of investment in industry. International organisations have been created to reduce the resulting potential for international conflict. This is part of what was achieved by the UN's support of decolonisation and development assistance (foreign aid) throughout the Cold War. Some observers, such as Canadian political scientist Robert W. Cox, argue that in the 1990s the role has shifted to one of 'famine relief and riot control' through the new forms of UN military intervention and refugee services in many parts of the increasingly marginalised and politically weakened South (Cox, 1992).

Nonetheless, despite that bleak assessment, even those who agree with Cox would readily admit that today, as in the past, 'global level' international organisations have helped to reduce violent conflict and have created other opportunities for those who promote social transformation. In part the opportunities have been created by the existence of cycles in the system of 'global level' international organisations. Sets of organisations seem to have a regular lifespan: they are created, they thrive for a while and then they wither and have to be reformed or else replaced by entirely new organisations. Almost invariably, when organisations are reformed and new organisations are created, 'progressive' NGOs play a significant role, and, in doing so, they have had the opportunity to add their own agenda items to each successive system of global intergovernmental organisations.

The first set of 'global' international organisations were established by European states in the second half of the nineteenth century, the so-called 'Public International Unions' for the telegraph, railroads, trade, intellectual property, labour, agriculture and other fields. After World War I, most of the same organisations were reconstituted as part of the League of Nations system. After the failure of the League, the victors in World War II – an alliance that was officially called 'the United Nations' – established the UN system, reconstituting most of the League organisations. Arguably, an analogous process is going on in the 'reform' of the UN system after the Cold War.

At each stage the design of the new set of organisations was influenced by NGOs that were part of transnational social movements promoting what were relatively progressive, egalitarian positions (at least for their time): the abolition of slavery and the right of workers to organise in the nineteenth century, the enfranchisement of women and decolonisation in the first half of this century, and environmental justice and some degree of democratisation of the global economy today.

These social movements have not succeeded in making their utopian visions a reality, but the NGOs' significant role as innovators and promoters of new international organisations – especially those institutions that help to resolve conflicts that might otherwise impede the next stage of economic globalisation – have assured that some of the progressive doctrines of an earlier age have been incorporated into each of the successive systems of global organisations. In practical terms, this has meant that the organisations have at least served as forums in which stronger national and regional political forces advancing similar goals can have their positions aired and amplified to a larger world. Thus, for example, the UN was able to play a substantive role in the struggle against colonialism and

minority rule in Southern Africa, despite the fact that some of the UN's most powerful members (for example, the US and Great Britain) supported the Apartheid regime.

Critics of the UN and other global institutions often complain that they do not do enough to support human rights, meet human needs or advance other progressive causes. This kind of criticism is usually based on a misunderstanding of how few people and resources these institutions have. Formal international organisations are usually relatively small bureaucracies, rarely with more than a few thousand employees and usually with only a few hundred. The people who work for international organisations typically arrange multilateral conferences, do research relevant to uncovering common interests or monitor prior international agreements. Traditional peacekeeping falls under the last category; soldiers loaned by governments to the UN keep watch to make sure that governments in conflict do not violate cease-fire pledges. In a few cases the employees of international agencies actually provide resources or services directly to their nation-state members or to their citizens, for example, when the World Bank loans money to governmental development projects or insures private companies that have invested in the third world. But in most cases in which international organisations have some responsibility for providing a service – for example, in caring for refugees – the international agencies only serve as a co-ordinator of efforts performed by private voluntary agencies, which are NGOs such as Oxfam, Catholic Relief, or the Red Cross and Red Crescent societies.

In the last ten years, the UN's role in providing or co-ordinating services to people involved in conflicts has greatly increased. However, one of the major characteristics of almost all the UN's new peacemaking and peace-maintenance operations – whether in Bosnia, Somalia, Cambodia or elsewhere – is that most of the operational staff and resources used by the combined operation are seconded by UN members or else provided by private NGOs (*see* Chopra, 1998; Weiss, 1998).

Box 6.3: Some major global international organisations, by function

Creating markets

Trade	World Trade Organisation (Geneva)
Infrastructure of transport and communication	International Telecommunications Union (Geneva)
	INTELSAT (Washington)
	International Maritime Organisation (London)
	International Civil Aviation Organisation (Montreal)
Intellectual property	World Intellectual Property Organisation (Geneva)
Industrial standards	International Organisation for Standards, ISO (Geneva)
Money and finance	International Monetary Fund (Washington)
	Bank for International Settlements (Basle)

Securing markets

Labour	International Labour Organisation (Geneva)
The third world and	World Bank (Washington)
alternative social systems	UN Development Programme (New York)
	UN Security Council (New York)

Securing human rights, meeting basic needs, protecting the environment

UN Human Rights Commission (Geneva)
UN High Commissioner for Refugees (Geneva)
UNICEF (New York)
UN Environmental Programme (Nairobi)

Murphy (1994:3)

Another source of organisational weakness for the UN system is the relative autonomy of its many parts. Most of the work of the UN is done by so-called **specialised agencies** such as the ILO, the World Bank and the WTO. Someone who looks at the organisation chart of the UN (*see* Figure 6.1) and reads the UN Charter might conclude that all of these specialised agencies work together just like the many bureaux of a national government. After all, the organisation chart shows all of them as 'under' the Economic and Social Council (ECOSOC) of the UN and the Charter makes it clear that ECOSOC, in turn, is a

sort of executive committee of the General Assembly. But, in fact, the specialised agencies are only required to *report* on their activities to ECOSOC, something that is a historical consequence of the fact that almost all the specialised agencies have either existed for longer than the UN itself, or else they were designed from the beginning to be free from the one-nation/one-vote system of governance that is used in the UN General Assembly.

Each specialised agency is actually *governed* by its own board and many of those boards employ voting procedures that give the major economic powers a much greater say than other nations. For example, in both the International Monetary Fund (IMF) and the World Bank, the US has, from their beginning, held an effective veto over any action. That does not mean that these organisations are completely controlled by the US and are, thus, simply instruments of US foreign policy. Americans cannot *make* the organisations do things that a majority of other economic powers do not want; the Americans can only *prevent* the organisations from doing things that damage US interests.

Significantly, there is one type of UN work that is not done by the specialised agencies and that remains the responsibility of the central organs of the UN, that is work concerned with peacekeeping, peace enforcement and conflict resolution. Again, though, this work is effectively governed by the great powers. It is under the authority of the Security Council, a fifteen-member body that at present includes five 'permanent' members – the US, the United Kingdom, France, Russia and China – each of which is given the power to veto any proposed action. Throughout the Cold War, the existence of the veto assured that the UN engaged in few peace-related military actions because most world conflicts divided allies of the Soviet Union from allies of the US, each of which could prevent Security Council actions. In the first half of the 1990s the great powers were willing to allow many more Security Council actions, but in recent years the number has again declined, now because the great powers are relatively uninterested in devoting funds and forces to many of the regions of world in which conflicts are the most prevalent, especially Africa.

Regional organisations

There are more powerful international organisations at a regional level in some parts of the world. Of course, there are regional organisations in every continent, for example, the Organisation of African Unity (OAU), the Association of Southeast Asian Nations (ASEAN), the North American Free Trade Area (NAFTA) and the Islamic Conference, but only in a very few places are there international organisations that have become quite a bit more than the sum of their parts, that is to say, more than the sum of the sovereign states that make up their membership.

At present, the European Union (EU) is probably the international organisation with the widest range of powers, resources and responsibilities. The EU has emerged relatively slowly over the last fifty years. At the end of World War II, the US encouraged the Western European, non-communist nations to co-operatively rebuild their industrial economies. Initially that co-operation was restricted to unifying the coal and steel industries along the German-French border because this region, and the important industries located there, had been a central issue not only in World War II (1939–1945), but also twenty years earlier in World War I (1914–1918), and even in the Franco-Prussian War (1870–1871). In the 1950s, Western European states also united, under the urging of the US, to form a union to develop peaceful uses of atomic energy, and many Western European states joined the US, Canada, Iceland and Turkey to form the anti-Soviet North Atlantic Treaty Organisation (NATO) of the Cold War era.

In 1960, six of the countries that had been part of all of these co-operative endeavours (Belgium, the Federal Republic of Germany, France, Italy, Luxembourg and the Netherlands) formed a customs union, the European Economic Community (EEC), which eventually evolved into today's EU, covering almost all of Western Europe. As a customs union, the EEC's purpose was to abolish barriers to trade among its members and to set up a common external tariff. This was meant to encourage economic efficiency, in particular through the establishment or reform of industries that invested in large, modern factories to sell goods to the entire industrial market area united by the Community.

In the nearly forty years of the EEC/EU's

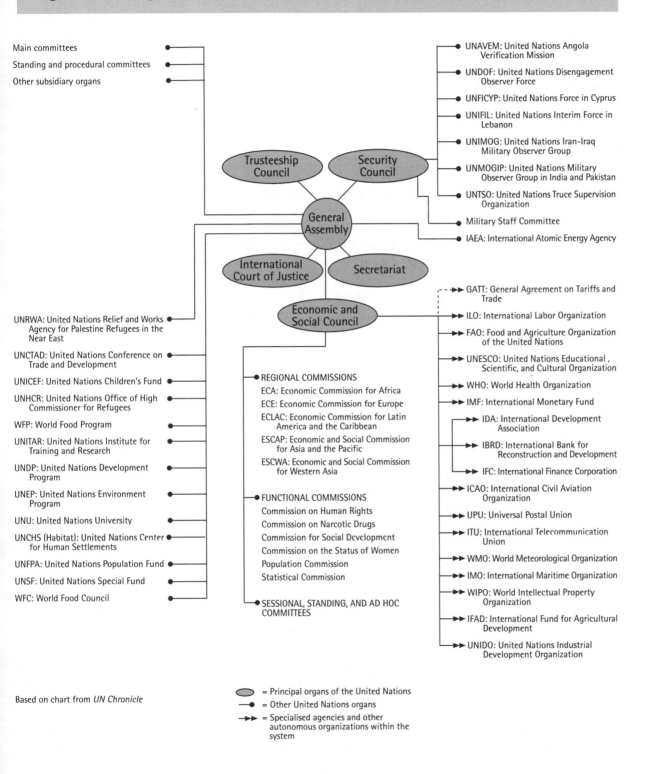

Main committees

Standing and procedural committees

Other subsidiary organs

Trusteeship Council

Security Council

General Assembly

International Court of Justice

Secretariat

Economic and Social Council

UNAVEM: United Nations Angola Verification Mission

UNDOF: United Nations Disengagement Observer Force

UNFICYP: United Nations Force in Cyprus

UNIFIL: United Nations Interim Force in Lebanon

UNIMOG: United Nations Iran-Iraq Military Observer Group

UNMOGIP: United Nations Military Observer Group in India and Pakistan

UNTSO: United Nations Truce Supervision Organization

Military Staff Committee

IAEA: International Atomic Energy Agency

GATT: General Agreement on Tariffs and Trade

ILO: International Labor Organization

FAO: Food and Agriculture Organization of the United Nations

UNESCO: United Nations Educational, Scientific, and Cultural Organization

WHO: World Health Organization

IMF: International Monetary Fund

IDA: International Development Association

IBRD: International Bank for Reconstruction and Development

IFC: International Finance Corporation

ICAO: International Civil Aviation Organization

UPU: Universal Postal Union

ITU: International Telecommunication Union

WMO: World Meteorological Organization

IMO: International Maritime Organization

WIPO: World Intellectual Property Organization

IFAD: International Fund for Agricultural Development

UNIDO: United Nations Industrial Development Organization

UNRWA: United Nations Relief and Works Agency for Palestine Refugees in the Near East

UNCTAD: United Nations Conference on Trade and Development

UNICEF: United Nations Children's Fund

UNHCR: United Nations Office of High Commissioner for Refugees

WFP: World Food Program

UNITAR: United Nations Institute for Training and Research

UNDP: United Nations Development Program

UNEP: United Nations Environment Program

UNU: United Nations University

UNCHS (Habitat): United Nations Center for Human Settlements

UNFPA: United Nations Population Fund

UNSF: United Nations Special Fund

WFC: World Food Council

REGIONAL COMMISSIONS

ECA: Economic Commission for Africa

ECE: Economic Commission for Europe

ECLAC: Economic Commission for Latin America and the Caribbean

ESCAP: Economic and Social Commission for Asia and the Pacific

ESCWA: Economic and Social Commission for Western Asia

FUNCTIONAL COMMISSIONS

Commission on Human Rights

Commission on Narcotic Drugs

Commission for Social Development

Commission on the Status of Women

Population Commission

Statistical Commission

SESSIONAL, STANDING, AND AD HOC COMMITTEES

Based on chart from *UN Chronicle*

= Principal organs of the United Nations

= Other United Nations organs

= Specialised agencies and other autonomous organizations within the system existence the co-operation among members has constantly deepened. EU citizens can now work in any country of the Union. Their passports identify them first as EU citizens and then as nationals of their own countries. Many EU countries no longer have border controls. In 1999, eleven EU members began to share a single currency (the euro), and more are expected to join the currency system in the near future. EU members also co-ordinate much of their foreign policy toward non-EU regions of the world and a European parliament with limited but growing powers exists to bring some degree of democratic representation to the process of on-going co-operation.

At the same time that European co-operation has deepened, the Union itself has expanded. Today, the population of the original six members of the Union would be about 200 million, which is about 60 million fewer than that of the US. The population of the current fifteen members of the union is more than 360 million, 100 million greater than that of the US, and almost double the size of the original EEC.

The deepening and the widening of the EU has had complementary results: Western Europe has become the largest unified industrial market area in the world. These economic consequences were, of course, one of the reasons for the formation of the Union in the first place, and they link the history of the Union back to earlier, similar experiments. In the 1800s the United States of America (after its Civil War of 1861–1864), Germany and Italy all went through processes of integration that bound previously separate and relatively sovereign states into larger entities of shared sovereignty. These larger entities were able to become increasing powerful industrial states due to the industries that grew within their expanded market areas.

In addition, Germany, Italy and even the US unified, in part, due to military competition with other powers. Nineteenth-century Italians worried about the Austrians and the French; Germans competed with the French and Austrians. Similarly, the strategic competition

with the Soviet Union provided much of the original motivation for the EU, while more recently, Europe's economic competition with the US and Japan has encouraged the development of the euro and the further integration of the continent.

Outside the industrialised world, the same types of strategic and economic motivations also account for much of today's regional co-operation. For example, in 1980 Angola, Botswana, Lesotho, Malawi, Mozambique, Namibia, Swaziland, Tanzania, Zambia and Zimbabwe formed the Southern African Development Co-ordination Conference (SADCC) to promote regional economic development and reduce dependence on Apartheid South Africa. The organisation continues after Apartheid as the Southern African Development Community (SADC), and, like many regional groupings in the developing world, it serves as a forum and information-gathering agency that encourages deeper levels of economic co-operation.

Ironically, perhaps, even though economic integration may have greater economic payback for nations that are the least industrialised, the historical record suggests that it is much harder to establish economic co-operation among least developed countries. In part this may be because in the early stages of economic co-operation some state or states need to be willing to sponsor the co-operation, that is, to absorb some additional costs in order to demonstrate the importance of that co-operation to other countries. This is a role that has traditionally been taken by relatively benign **hegemonic powers**, such as the US in its relation to Western Europe immediately after World War II (Keohane, 1984). A successful hegemonic power may appear unusually generous, but is not really altruistic. It is not acting against its interests; it is acting in its own long-term interests by bearing some high costs in the short-term, such as the cost of European reconstruction that were partly borne by the US in the 1950s in order to ensure that Europe became associated with the Western world order rather than with the system the Soviets were

Box 6.4: Unexpected benefits from a politically questionable customs union

'Since 1910 the colony and then the nation-state of Botswana has been a member of a customs union with South Africa, Lesotho, Swaziland and Namibia. The practical experience with that union is often cited as a reason that Botswana was able to contribute to a relatively realistic, long-lasting economic institution when SADCC was formed in 1980, even though there is no question that the earlier Southern African Customs Union (SACU) was primarily designed to serve Southern African interests.

Nonetheless, some economists credit the older SACU with helping institutionalise some aspects of the quite successful economic and political order that Botswana developed after independence. Botswana, with its consistent and high rates of growth, is, in economic terms, one of the success stories of sub-Saharan Africa. It is also one of the few countries on the continent to maintain a system of liberal democracy since independence. Some economists argue that part of the reason for Botswana's economic success is that the long experience with the customs union had created domestic economic interests that were relatively committed to free trade. Moreover, the customs union actually prevented Botswana's government from instituting trade and currency restrictions that many other African states established or strengthened immediately after independence. Since these economists believe that these trade and currency restrictions ultimately proved detrimental to other African states, they argue that Botswana actually gained one small benefit from its dependency. In addition, Botswana's 'demonstrated' commitment to 'sound' economic policy, which helped attract foreign investment, including the Hyundai auto assembly plant in Gabarone, whose primary market is in South Africa. Finally, about 15% of Botswana's government revenue comes from its share of the SACU Common Revenue Pool (*see* chapter 15; Harvey & Lewis, 1990).'

Courtesy of David Lindauer

creating. In many cases in the less industrialised world the countries that have attempted to act as hegemonic leaders of regional co-operation have faced political opposition at home simply because the costs of sponsoring co-operation were too high relative to the country's limited resources. This is what some scholars believe happened with Ghana under Kwame Nkrumah relative to Pan-Africanism and to Tanzania under Nyerere relative to East African integration (Murphy, 1987).

Explaining international institutions

Until World War I the dominant way of thinking about international institutions was a liberal idealist view that was shared by many of the NGOs that played an important role in designing the League of Nations as well as the earlier Public International Unions. This view assumes that such institutions were established to achieve the public good and imagines that they will be successful. From this point of view, the mere growth of international institutions may be assumed to be a positive phenomenon. But a quick glance at the data on the growth of international organisations of different types reveals some problems with this assumption (*see* Table 6.1).

The number of international organisations has grown dramatically throughout this century, but neither world peace nor prosperity for all has followed. Unfortunately, the history of the League of Nations has been typical, and that history led many scholars to explain international institutions in a very different way: After the League's failure to stop the Italian occupation of Ethiopia and the other conflicts that led to World War II, some scholars and policy-makers adopted a realist view of international institutions, arguing that they merely reflected the power of their dominant members.

A contemporary, somewhat eclectic, understanding of international institutions that shares

Table 6.1: The growth of international organisations

Type of organisation	Before World War I (1909)	Beginning of Cold War (1956)	After Cold War (1996)
Regular intergovernmental organisations (IGOs)	37	132	260
Regular non-governmental organisations (NGOs)	176	4 265	5 472
All international organisations (IOs)*	213	14 273	44 128

* including relatively autonomous programmes of regular IGOs and international scientific associations that may reflect the existence of different epistemic communities

Union of International Associations, http://www.uia.org/uiastats/stybv296.htm

some of this realist insight is that of Susan Strange (1996). She holds that, for the most part, international institutions are established to serve the interests of their most powerful members, and that, as a result, much of the UN system, and certainly the IMF, the World Bank and the WTO, is best thought of as part of the 'informal empire' that the US has established throughout the Americas, Western Europe, much of the Middle East, Africa and parts of East Asia. But, Strange argues, the institutions, once established, do have consequences. In particular, she argues that the trade and monetary institutions established by the US and its dependent partners have had the consequence of weakening *all* states, including the US, making all of them susceptible to the increasing power of the very global markets that those institutions were designed to establish.

From Strange's point of view the growth in the number of international organisations is explicable simply because international organisations represent an institutional form that the US has found useful in establishing and maintaining its 'empire'. The argument would be similar to that used by historians to explain the proliferation of 'durbars' during the period of the British Empire. Durbars were ritualised gatherings of local Indian princelings that the British first used as opportunities to cement Indian fealty to British governors. They later exported the custom throughout the world as a way of symbolising British 'indirect rule' and giving collaborationist 'traditional chiefs' opportunities to manifest their power. Eventually the custom was copied by African traditional leaders, even in territories that were not governed by the British, and now in many parts of the continent, people are convinced that the durbar is a long-standing 'African' tradition with deep local roots. Similarly, a follower of Strange might argue that the US has promoted international organisations to cement its own 'indirect rule,' sometimes, as in the case of the EU, demanding that it allies create organisations that eventually served other purposes. Similarly, leading states in other regions have copied this American custom in order to cement their more local 'empires'; that would be one way to explain the Soviet Union's construction of an international organisation system in Eastern Europe (the Warsaw Pact and the Council for Mutual Economic Assistance). It would also explain Apartheid South Africa's construction of the SACU.

A number of transformationist theorists, including Robert W. Cox (mentioned earlier) and myself, agree with part of Strange's realist characterisation of the original purposes served by many international institutions, but we urge observers to look at the longer history of capitalist globalisation in order to understand why many states, and not just regional powers or the major capitalist powers, might have an interest in creating a more and more global economy. We are also more apt to discuss the role that social struggle – domestically and internationally – has played in the emergence of particular configurations of international institutions and their related eras of the world economy.

On some subjects, these contemporary 'neo-Marxist institutionalist' theories of international organisation are often quite compatible with contemporary 'neo-liberal institutionalist' theories that de-emphasise the utopian side of the liberal tradition. The neo-liberals see themselves as having a realistic appreciation of state power, but, like Strange, they recognise that institutions themselves have consequences, especially, according to the neo-liberals, in the ways in which institutions can shape states' perceptions of their self-interests by changing the costs and benefits of alternative courses of action (Keohane & Murphy, 1992:882).

Both liberal and transformative accounts of international institutions have been deeply affected by studies of the impact of **epistemic communities** on agenda setting for international co-operation. Epistemic communities are communities of knowledge, such as the scientific and

policy-making groups that deal with a particular topic area. You will recall that earlier I mentioned the idea of an 'international tiger regime'. There really is such a regime. It is based upon the ideas that animal conservationists have about the best way to preserve a species without creating excessive economic hardship for people living near the species (Meacham, 1997). For better or for worse, in the case of this and many other regimes, states base their agreements almost solely on the current expertise of a scholarly community. Usually that works out well, and it certainly makes agreements easier to reach, but it is not necessarily a perfect policy. Some conservationist point out, for example, that in the case of attempts to preserve elephants, countries that followed the policies most recommended by the relevant scientific community, such as Kenya, turned out to be less successful than countries that were not able to, such as Zimbabwe due to its long civil war. The well-managed population of Kenyan elephants declined while the unmanaged elephants of Zimbabwe thrived. The author of the tiger book mentioned above is cynical enough to suggest that the non-human world might best be served by that most typical of international institutions – war.

This view may be too radical, but it does, at least, help us to bear in mind that international institutions, and the international co-operation that these foster and require, are not necessarily good things for every member of the international society, even though they are relatively common. If international institutions are created by bloodthirsty states, that is the interest that they will serve, at least initially. In the medium term, of course, if international institutions are created to serve interests of trade and commerce – as they often are – they may contribute to a more peaceful world. The Viking sagas mentioned at the beginning of this chapter almost always end with trade leading to a settled life and to relative peace. But the history of Northern Europe in the thousand years since the Vikings should remind us that trade and international institutions do not guarantee either prosperity or peace.

Key concepts in this chapter

Global governance
Hegemony
Institutions
International organisations
International private law
International public law
Multilateral conferences
Non-govenmental organisations
Public international unions
Regimes
Specialised agencies

Suggested readings

- Joyner, C. C. (ed.) (1997) *The United Nations and International Law* (2nd edition). Cambridge: Cambridge University Press. This provides an excellent introduction to contemporary international law on a policy-issue by policy-issue basis with a focus on the multilateral organisations that are now most often the sites of amendment to treaty law.
- Ofuatey-Kodjoe, W. (1977) *The Principle of Self-Determination in International Law.* New York: Nellen Publishing Co. A good discussion of the constitution of international society, the new legal principles that allowed European international society to be acceptable to larger world, and the consequences of decolonisation for international law.
- Weiss, T. G., Forsythe, D. P. & Coate, R. A. (1997) *The United Nations and Changing World Politics* (2nd edition). Boulder: Westview Press. Probably the best contemporary text on the UN system.
- Murphy, C. N. (1994) *International Organization and Industrial Change: Global Governance since 1850.* Cambridge: Polity Press. A historical and transformation-oriented analysis of global institutions.
- Keohane, R. O. (1984) *After Hegemony: Co-operation and Discord in the World Political Economy.* Princeton: Princeton University Press. This is the paradigmatic neo-liberal study.
- Haas, P. M. (1990) *Saving the Mediterranean: The Politics of International Environmental Co-operation.* New York: Columbia University Press. The path-breaking analysis of the role of an epistemic community in the formation of an important international regime.

7

Non-state actors in International Relations

Louise Vincent

This chapter in outline

- Introduction
- Intergovernmental organisations (IGOs)
- Liberation movements, secessionist groups, terrorists and criminal organisations
- International non-governmental organisations (NGOs) and transnational social movements (TSMs)
- Multinational corporations (MNCs)
- Individuals
- Conclusion

Introduction

International Relations was traditionally thought of as the study of relationships between states. However, it is now increasingly recognised that states are not the only actors that have an impact on international politics. We live in a world in which state boundaries are increasingly porous. People no longer only act politically within the confines of the state or in the name of any particular state. A large number and variety of non-state actors that act across state boundaries have come to occupy an important place on the world stage. But how do these non-state actors change the way we think about international relations? Do they represent rivals to state power? What is their political significance? Do non-state actors make a difference in world affairs?

Since the 1960s and early 1970s, realist theory, which focused on interactions between states (*see* Chapter 3), has come under pressure as the number, size and power of non-state actors have increased significantly. In the 1960s, it was already pointed out that some multinational corporations (MNCs) owned assets whose total value was more than the gross national product (GNP) of certain states. Advances in communications technology opened the way for non-state actors such as environmental groups and human rights advocates to play a greater role in world politics. Innovations in cross-border transport, computer networks and telecommunications were enabling these actors to influence the ideas, values and political persuasions of large numbers of people around the globe. Scholars argued that they were having a significant impact on questions of politics, morality and peace. In short, the surge in transnational activity suggested that the state might not be the most important **variable** for explaining world events.

Non-state actors come in a variety of forms: economic, social, ecological, technical and scientific, religious, ethnic and many more. While their rise in profile does not necessarily mean that we are witnessing the imminent demise of the nation-state, it does call for a new approach to International Relations, an approach which sees the world as multidimensional and characterised by multiple, complex interactions rather than interactions between states alone.

Intergovernmental organisations (IGOs)

An increasingly dense mesh of international relationships, ranging from security and commercial to social interactions, has brought about the need for greater co-ordination between governments. The organisations that facilitate such collaboration are called intergovernmental organisations (IGOs) (*see* Chapter 6). More than 94% have appeared since 1940, making them largely a post-war phenomenon. Although these organisations are made up of states, they act as single actors and sometimes their policies and actions contravene the interests of any single member state. Most deal with economic issues and they tend to have overlapping memberships, particularly in Europe where many countries belong simultaneously to such organisations as the North Atlantic Treaty Organisation (NATO), the European Community (EU), the Nordic Council and others (Holsti, 1995:64).

Perhaps the best known IGO of all is the United Nations (UN). Its predecessor, the League of Nations, was founded as part of the peace settlement after World War I. The League did not prove very successful and there were important gaps in its membership. The United States (US), for example, never became a member. It went out of formal existence in 1946 when its property and personnel were transferred to the UN. The formation of the latter was spurred by World War II. Officially formed in October 1945, the declared purposes of the UN are to maintain international peace and security; to develop friendly relations among states based on respect, equal rights and the self-determination of peoples; to co-operate in solving economic, social, cultural and humanitarian global problems; and to promote respect for fundamental freedoms and human rights

(Said *et al.*, 1995:113). (*See* Chapter 6 for an in-depth discussion of IGOs.)

The UN has come in for criticism for its seeming inability to act decisively to prevent or resolve conflict situations. The armed conflicts in the former Yugoslavia and in Rwanda are cases in point. The organisation faces severe structural constraints, which include the dominance over decision-making enjoyed by the Security Council powers, severe financial limitations and the principle of **sovereignty** that restricts the extent to which the UN can play a role in conflict prevention and resolution. Partly as a result of the growing recognition of these constraints on the UN, greater emphasis is now being placed on the need for regional IGOs such as the Southern African Development Community (SADC) to play a leading role in peacekeeping, as well as development and democratisation initiatives. Other examples of regional IGOs include the Organisation of African Unity (OAU), the League of Arab States and the EU. Because they are smaller and often have a more cohesive membership than a world body such as the UN, regional actors have the potential to be more efficient in achieving the objectives of intergovernmental co-operation.

Liberation movements, secessionist groups, terrorists and criminal organisations

These organisations have in common the fact that they challenge the authority of existing states and may act extra-legally to achieve their aims. They frequently threaten either the continued existence of a state as a whole or aspects of its legal norms and values. Compared with many small states, some of these actors have a great deal of influence in developing and promoting issues on the international agenda.

The Palestinian Liberation Organisation (PLO), for example, has had a significant impact on world politics. In many ways, the PLO acts like a state. For example, it has diplomatic relations with several governments and observer status at the UN (Holsti, 1995:61). Thanks to its popular support, the PLO has been an influential actor in the Middle East peace process, easily equalling the impact of states that are party to the conflict.

Like liberation movements, secessionist groups seek independence and nationhood of their own. They reject identification with the nation-state in which they happen to find themselves. There are many examples throughout the world, including the Basques in Spain, the Kurds in the Middle East, the Quebecois of Canada, a segment of the Afrikaner population in South Africa, the Tamils in Sri Lanka, the Tibetans in China and the Corsicans in France. The significance of these organisations lies in the fact that the most far-reaching conflicts that the world has seen since 1945 have taken the form of ethnic disputes. The call for national self-determination appears as a countervailing trend in a world characterised by increasing integration and homogeneity.

Sometimes separatist movements resort to **terrorist** tactics to achieve their aims. The Basque separatist organisation, ETA, for example, co-ordinated a campaign of bombing, shooting and kidnapping in Spain between 1968 and 1998. Over these three decades, some 750 deaths could be attributed to Basque militants. Nationalist groups of this kind often have links with one another. For example, ETA has a long history of friendship with the Irish Republican Army (IRA) and the leader of its political wing, Gerry Adams.

Far from being outdated by the ending of the Cold War, terrorism offers a low-cost, potentially high-yield weapon for the weak, with relatively little risk to the perpetrators. Thanks to the increased porosity of state borders, international terrorist groups are able to operate transnationally with relative ease. The ready availability of weapons, explosives and technologically sophisticated timing and triggering devices, along with the global communication revolution, have made possible such tactics as co-ordinated attacks in several countries, faxed death threats and comparison of target lists by computer. The bombing of a federal building in Oklahoma City in 1995, which killed 168 people, was carried out with a pipe bomb – assembly instructions for these weapons are freely available on the Internet. Terrorists now have the opportunity to operate in cyber space to destroy or manipulate information for their own purposes (Terrorism Research Centre: 'The Basics of Terrorism', Part 6).

World leaders have highlighted terrorism as a significant challenge facing the global community. While the frequency and magnitude of terrorist activity remains relatively low, terrorism nevertheless has wide influence. Terrorist acts easily capture media attention. This magnifies the desired effect, which is to instil fear and thereby influence public opinion or government policy. As a result, terrorist organisations are able to have an impact on world politics that is far out of proportion to their small numbers of supporters and tiny financial resources.

Like terrorist groupings, International Criminal Organisations (ICOs) operate across borders and often use violence to achieve their aims. The difference is that ICOs are motivated purely by the pursuit of profit rather than political goals. In the same way as the current context of greater global interdependency facilitates the activities of terrorists, the transfer of goods, people and money through the world economy also aids the transportation of drugs, arms and illegal aliens, and the rapid movement of dirty money, contract killers and contraband.

Crime tends to grow rapidly during periods of social and political transition, which are usually accompanied by such features as the relaxing of border controls, the increased movement of goods and people, and the social and economic hardships that are typically a feature of the emergence of free market economies. These circumstances have provided the conditions under which organised crime has grown in recent years in countries such as South Africa and the former Soviet Union. In both cases, crime extends into state structures, including the criminal justice system.

The result is that in Southern Africa, international crime is now a far greater threat to the individual security of citizens than the somewhat distant prospect of invasion by a foreign power. Police intelligence estimates that there are more than 190 crime syndicates operating in South Africa. These include elements of the Russian Mafia, which are involved in diamonds and weapons smuggling; Chinese triads, which have specialised in the trade of endangered species; and Nigerian drug rings.

Similarly, in Russia, estimates suggest that there are as many as 8 000 criminal organisations (Williams, 1997:27). The Russian Mafia is thought to control more than 40% of the country's economy. One of Russia's biggest domestic problems is the infiltration and criminalisation of the banking sector. Criminals have also made inroads into the country's tax base. Not only do they not pay tax, but they have also usurped the state's tax collection role. Russian customs figures show that duties are paid on only 35 out of every 1 000 cars imported. Many customs warehouses are entirely controlled by the Mob.

In countries such as Italy and Colombia, criminal organisations have attacked the state directly, killing judges and police officers. But the political impact of ICOs is usually felt less directly – in the form of corruption that makes it difficult for state institutions to function properly. ICOs also pose significant economic threats. Criminal capital can crowd out legitimate investors in emerging economies. Large amounts of illegal money in an economy render the task of economic management difficult. The consequences of drug trafficking include loss of productivity, and increased health care and law enforcement costs (Williams, 1997:36–37).

ICOs make the task of regulating the global political system more difficult. Codes of conduct, principles of restraint and responsibility, and norms of behaviour are meaningless to criminal organisations. Attempts to prevent arms proliferation, for example, depend on co-operation among suppliers and the ability to isolate rogue states. ICOs operate outside such internationally established norms of conduct and their non-compliance is difficult for even the most powerful states to sanction.

International non-governmental organisations (INGOs) and transnational social movements (TSMs)

International non-governmental organisations (INGOs) are non-profit, service-oriented interest groups that operate across several countries. Examples of some of the world's largest INGOs include the World Federation of Trade Unions with a membership of over 125 million and the World Federation of Democratic Youth with over 100 million members. The number of INGOs first began to increase after World War I, with the creation of such organisations as the International Federation of Trade Unions, the International Federation of University Women and the International Chamber of Commerce. INGOs grew even more rapidly after World War II, but it was the founding of the human rights organisation Amnesty International (AI) and the environmental grouping the World Wildlife Fund (WWF) in 1961 that laid the foundations of the powerful, independent INGO community of today (Spiro, 1995:47).

The explosion of INGO activity over the last three decades reflects the broader trend of **globalisation** that has allowed territorially dispersed individuals to develop common agendas and objectives at the international level. INGOs have also benefited from an international context in which there has been a shift of focus from traditional national security concerns to non-traditional human security issues that are typically not confined within state borders, such as crime, disease, human rights abuses and poverty. On traditional security matters, decision-making was highly centralised under the authority of

states. On such issues as human rights and the environment, by contrast, INGOs have the capacity to act directly and independently and to initiate genuine international co-operation in ways that can often supersede the abilities of states. In their influence over the media and their ability to collect, marshal and disseminate information, INGOs have frequently been able to lay claim to a greater fund of resources than many states (Spiro, 1995:48).

In recognition of their growing political importance, INGOs are now formally accredited by a number of international organisations. A consultative relationship has been established between INGOs and the UN through Article 71 of the UN Charter. Currently, approximately 20 000 INGOs from every part of the world have entered into a relationship with the UN system. INGOs with UN Economic and Social Council (ECOSOC) consultative status may participate as observers in sessions of the Council, submit oral or written statements, and present their views at important intergovernmental forums. Most UN agencies and programmes, including the UN Children's Fund (UNICEF), the UN Educational, Scientific and Cultural Organisation (UNESCO) and the UN High Commission for Refugees (UNHCR), have also established mechanisms for INGO relations.

INGOs very often grew out of or maintain links with another set of very important global actors, namely transnational social movements (TSMs). The main difference between an organisation and a movement is that the former usually has a formal structure and a permanent secretariat or controlling body. In contrast, social movements are loose, informal collections of people who share the same political or social goal, and who take co-ordinated actions to achieve that goal. TSMs are social movements whose members are spread throughout the world, and who maintain contact with each other and sometimes undertake joint actions.

The best examples of TSMs are the anti-slavery movement of the early nineteenth century, the anti-Apartheid movement of the 1960s,

1970s and 1980s, and the world-wide feminist movement. Because of the progress made in global communications in our era, it becomes easier for individuals who feel the same about issues to make and keep contact, and to raise the level of awareness amongst the world's public at large about their concerns. One such example is discussed in the extract in Box 7.1.

The growth in the international profile and political significance of INGOs and TSMs has led to the proposition from some scholars that alongside other processes of globalisation there has emerged a **global civil society** (Wapner, 1995:313). In its original usage, the concept of civil society referred to domestic contexts. However, the idea of civil society may be beginning to make sense on a global level thanks to the interpenetration of markets, the growing homogenisation of values and meaning systems, and the proliferation of collective, transnational activities.

While the contrast between the state and civil society does not necessarily mean that relations between the two are conflictual, they often are. In the African context where states are frequently perceived as weak in the face of the demands of global accumulation and powerful external actors, an independent and vibrant civil society may be viewed as a threat to state legitimacy and power. This has meant that African states have not always been wholeheartedly welcoming in their response to INGOs and these organisations have at times come in for heavy criticism from states that feel threatened by their independent, sometimes critical stance.

When international aid funds go directly to INGOs, for example, states may lose control over the form and direction of development. In countries such as Kenya and Nigeria, environmental INGOs are seen as part of broader anti-government opposition. In these instances outside aid to local groups may be perceived as foreign intervention trying to diminish existing state power and authority. In December 1997, for example, President Nelson Mandela, in his report to the 50th National Conference of the African National

Box 7.1: 'Network guerrillas'

When the leaders of the member states of the Organisation for Economic Co-operation and Development (OECD), the club of rich nations in the world, recently wanted to formulate rules to protect the investment of MNCs in host countries, one TSM put a spoke in their wheel. This is how a reporter, Guy de Jonquières, describes it (*Financial Times*, 98.04.30):

'... fear and bewilderment have seized governments of industrialised countries as they struggle to draft rules for the treatment of foreign investment. To their consternation, their efforts have been ambushed by a horde of vigilantes whose motives and methods are only dimly understood in most national capitals.

This week the horde claimed its first success and some think it could fundamentally alter the way international economic agreements are negotiated.

The target of their attacks was the Multilateral Agreement on Investment (MAI) being negotiated at the OECD, [and the attackers were] a loose coalition of NGOs from across the political spectrum. They included trade unions, environmental and human rights lobbyists and pressure groups opposed to globalisation.

The opponent's [against the MAI] decisive weapon is the Internet. Operating from around the world via web sites, they have condemned the proposed agreement as a secret conspiracy to ensure global domination by multinational companies, and mobilised an international movement of grassroots resistance.'

And they won! The MAI negotiations were suspended in April 1998.

Congress, lashed out at those non-governmental organisations (NGOs) which, he said, had set themselves up as critical watchdogs of government:

'Pretending to represent an independent and popular view .... they lack the issue driven mass base that is the defining feature of any real NGO and are therefore unable to raise funds from the people themselves. This has also created the possibility for some of these NGOs to act as instruments of foreign governments and institutions that fund them to promote the interests of these external forces.'

Potential threats to the authority of the state notwithstanding, in the past ten years or so official development programmes have increasingly made allowance for various forms of collaboration with INGOs. The African Charter for Popular Participation in Development and Transformation (Arusha Charter), adopted jointly in 1990 by African and international associations, African governments and UN organisations, is an example of official recognition for the role that local and international NGOs are expected to play in African recovery. The Charter is a proposal for a form of development involving both the democratisation of African institutions and the active participation of civil society.

On a global level, INGO networking and advocacy efforts have produced results that include the Global Forum and Earth Summit in Rio in June 1992, the Vienna Human Rights Conference in 1993, the Cairo Population Conference in 1994, the World Summit for Social Development in 1995 and the Beijing World Conference on Women in 1995.

INGOs have proved enormously successful at providing humanitarian assistance, particularly with respect to the direct delivery of relief aid, mobilisation and advocacy. The work of Amnesty International led to the adoption by the UN of the Declaration and subsequently the Convention Against Torture, and the work of the International Commission of Jurists contributed to the drafting of the Council of Europe's Convention on torture. In October 1991, the UN estimated that the financial resources of the world's six largest INGOs involved in direct emergency assistance and development amounted to $1,2 billion. Today, humanitarian NGOs, both local and international,

render assistance to some thirteen million people around the world. Their activities include food distribution, immunisation and health care, installing water pumps, distributing seeds and farming tools, and repairing vital installations.

NGOs such as the WWF, Friends of the Earth, Greenpeace, Conservation International and Earth Island Institute have had a significant impact on the creation of global regimes for environmental protection. The budgets of some of the largest of these organisations is greater than the amount spent by most countries on environmental issues and millions of people throughout the world are members of these organisations.

The activities of environmental INGOs are not confined to the North. The WWF, for example, has offices in over twenty countries, several of these in Africa. Dedicated to protecting endangered wildlife and wildlands, the Fund has structured a game management system in Zambia that incorporates local residents in anti-poaching and conservation efforts, and the channelling of revenues from tourism and safaris back into the neighbouring communities that surround reserves. This approach also informs the WWF-initiated Kilum Mountain project in the Cameroon, which is developing nurseries for reforestation, reintroducing indigenous crops, and disseminating information about the long-term effects of environmentally harmful practices.

INGO activity differs from conventional state responses to international political concerns. Rather than directly lobbying state officials, their activity takes place far from the halls of formal political power. INGOs work with ordinary people to try to enhance local capacity for carrying out sustainable development projects. They are often able to reach the most disadvantaged sectors of communities more effectively than governments and their growing professionalism and access to resources is matched by a decline in government funds for social programmes in many parts of the world.

Of course, INGOs also have many weaknesses.

They are unable to use the threat of economic, military or political sanctions. They lack physical resources and do not have the same diplomatic immunity and other privileges of government bodies and representatives. They are very heterogeneous and their different approaches to issues can often hinder efforts to co-ordinate their activities. They are also hamstrung by international law and the principle of sovereignty that often makes it difficult for them to act in contexts where states perceive them as a threat.

Multinational corporations (MNCs)

MNCs are privately owned business enterprises organised in one society with activities in another growing out of direct investment abroad (also called **foreign direct investment**). Until the late 1960s, most MNCs were based in the US or Western Europe. Over the past three decades, the list has grown to include Japan as well as MNCs from some developing countries such as the Korean-based Hyundai Corporation. We can distinguish at least three different types of MNCs. Most important are industrial corporations that make goods in factories. An example is the Ford Motor Company, which has over 300 000 employees in thirty countries. Financial corporations, such as banks, also operate multi-nationally. Japan is the leader here with Japanese banks making up around twenty-three of the fifty largest banks in the world. Service corporations such as the McDonald's fast-food chain are a third type of MNC (Goldstein, 1996:374–375).

There are a large number of multinational corporations in the world. According to a UN Conference on Trade and Development (UNCTAD) report, at the beginning of the 1990s there were at least 37 000 parent companies that controlled over 206 000 foreign affiliates in the world. More than 90% of these parent firms have their headquarters in developed (OECD) countries, but almost a half of all foreign affiliates of multinational corporations are located in developing countries. The world largest 100 MNCs (excluding those in banking and finance) controlled assets of about $3,5 trillion in 1992 (UNCTAD, 1994:3–5). The assets of some of the largest MNCs, such as Unilever, IBM, General Motors, British Petroleum and Mitsubishi, far outstrip the economic capabilities of small states. In 1995, the top 100 MNCs had foreign sales in excess of $2 trillion, foreign employment of close to six million people and foreign assets (assets outside their home countries) of around $1,7 trillion. Only about twenty-five states in the world have a gross domestic product (GDP) that exceeds the turnover of the largest MNC, General Motors (GM). In comparison with General Motor's yearly revenue (income) of over $100 billion, an international organisation such as the UN, with an annual revenue of less than $10 billion, is dwarfed. But what, if any, is the political impact of such immense concentrations of wealth and control over economic resources?

In general terms, MNCs have an interest in both economic and political stability. An MNC makes long-term investments and it therefore wants to be certain that a country's currency and other economic circumstances such as rates of taxation, import duties and so on are reasonably stable. Similarly, it will want to be certain that its investment is not threatened by the prospect of war or revolution. So MNCs prosper in a stable international atmosphere that permits freedom of trade, movement and capital, all governed by market forces with minimal government interference. They therefore act as a strong force for economic liberalisation in the world economy. This makes MNCs very controversial, especially in the developing world where trade unions and governments often perceive them as posing a threat to the economic sovereignty of a state, and as the agents of neo-colonialism. On the other hand, governments of developing countries are appreciating more and more that MNCs are sources of new investment capital, and that their foreign direct investment (FDI) results in new job opportunities and the inflow of new technology.

The decisions that MNCs make about

when and where to invest can have important implications for a developing country's economic structure, tax revenues, level of employment and consumption patterns. While developing countries have experienced a boom in FDI by MNCs in recent years, Africa remains marginalised (*see* Box 7.2).

In theory, when an MNC invests in a country, the relationship is mutually beneficial – the host government gains taxes and economic growth while the MNC gains profits. But conflict can arise, for example about the rate at which the MNC is taxed. If a government does not create an attractive investment environment, the MNC has the option to choose to invest elsewhere. However, once fixed investments have been made, the MNC cannot move to another country without incurring huge expenses. MNCs use a variety of means to influence host governments with regard to these and other issues. They may

---

Box 7.2:   Foreign direct investment by multinational corporations (MNCs)

Foreign direct investment (FDI) outflows, 1996/7

US, EU and Japan	85% of all FDI outflows (mostly going to Europe)
Western Europe	50% of all FDI outflows (mostly going to the US)
US	$85 billion
Asia	$47 billion (an increase of 10% on the previous year)

Foreign investment inflows, 1996/7

Total	$350 billion
Developing countries	$129 billion (34% of total)
Asia	$81 billion (63% of all foreign investment flows to developing countries)
Latin America	$39 billion (30% of all FDI to developing countries and an increase of 52% on the previous year)
Brazil	$10 billion
Mexico	$7,5 billion
Argentina	$4,3 billion
Africa	$5 billion (60% of this to Nigeria and Egypt and an overall decrease from a 10% share of FDI during the 1980s)
China	$42 billion (33% of all FDI to developing countries and 50% of total FDI into Asia)
Singapore	$9 billion (Asia's second largest FDI recipient)
India	$2,6 billion (an increase of 34% on the previous year but still only just over a quarter of investment in Singapore, although its economy is four times as large)
The 48 least developed countries world-wide	less than 2% share of total FDI inflows (32 of these countries are in sub-Saharan Africa)
Central and Eastern Europe	$12 billion in 1996 (compared to $14 billion in 1995)

UNCTAD Press Conference, 3–19 September 1997

---

hire lobbyists, use advertisements to influence public opinion or resort to illegal means such as bribes. A large part of their influence lies in the fact that they are able to avoid certain states and favour others with their investments.

Individuals

We are all, as individuals, actors in international relations. Whenever we make an economic decision that has implications across national borders – such as buying an imported item of clothing, or going to see a film that was made in another country, or visiting another country – we participate in international relations. If we are fortunate enough to live in a democratic country, our individual decisions on who to vote for can also affect the way in which our country's official relations with the outside world (foreign policy – *see* Chapter 5) are conducted.

Thus, all individuals are actors in international relations. However, some individuals are more important actors than others, maybe because they have a high moral standing (President Mandela, or Mother Theresa, for instance), or because of an important religious position that he or she occupies (the Pope, head of the Roman Catholic Church, for instance). Other individuals become important actors because of their personal wealth.

In the same way as some of the world's largest MNCs command budgets that dwarf the GDP of small states, the personal wealth of some of the world's wealthiest individuals can also make them important actors on the world stage. A good example is Hungarian-born American financier and philanthropist, George Soros, who makes money by anticipating economic shifts around the world. In 1992, Soros predicted that the British pound would lose value. He borrowed billions of pounds and converted them to German marks. When the pound collapsed on 16 September 1992, he repaid the pounds he had borrowed at a lower rate than he had originally paid and pocketed the difference. His profit was $1 billion (*Time Magazine*, 150,9). In total, his personal fortune is an estimated $5 billion.

Thanks to a personal philosophy of promoting what he calls 'open societies', Soros's influence is not purely economic but also political. His foundations, which exist in forty countries throughout the world, have the explicit political aim of expanding civil liberties, promoting a free press and political pluralism. To this end, he has donated more than $350 million a year worldwide since 1994. In 1997, he announced his intention to open nine new foundations in Southern Africa. In some cases, his personal aid to countries exceeds that of US government foreign aid (*see* Table 7.1).

Some commentators criticise super-wealthy individuals like Soros for being impulsive, arrogant and politically naïve, for confining their aid to friends and for lacking in accountability or public scrutiny. In Albania, Kyrgyzstan, Serbia and Croatia, Soros's foundations have been accused of shielding spies and breaking currency laws. The Prime Minister of Malaysia, Mahathir Mohamad, has repeatedly accused Soros of mounting politically motivated attacks on his region's currencies. In 1997, Soros shut down his foundation in Belarus after the authoritarian president, Aleksandr Lukashenko, fined a Soros foundation $3 million for alleged tax violations. His employees have been assaulted and threatened with imprisonment or financial sanction for alleged crimes. What is certain is that individuals like Soros are not regarded as politically irrelevant, especially by small, weaker states that feel their influence most acutely.

Conclusion

People across the globe today have more opportunities for contact with one another than ever before. This has made possible a far greater awareness of the global context and the emergence of common political goals that are no longer confined within national borders and that challenge national governments as the sole claimants of political loyalties. environmentalists, peace activists, humans rights watchdogs, women's

Table 7.1: Comparison between US and Soros aid in 1996

	Amount Soros gave in 1996	US aid in 1996
Russia	$24 198 000	$108 140 000
Hungary	$15 769 000	$15 096 000
Ukraine	$15 323 000	$141 100 000
Yugoslavia	$11 180 000	nil
Albania	$10 219 000	$19 900 000
Romania	$10 180 000	$28 680 000
Bulgaria	$9 326 000	$27 865 000
Bosnia	$8 869 000	$245 294 000
Poland	$7 568 000	$44 445 000
Belarus	$6 019 000	$4 600 000

Open Society Institute; US Agency for International Development. Reported in *Time Magazine* (1997), 1 September, 150,9

groupings, consumers and even criminals now operate internationally, following in the footsteps of early non-state actors such as the Catholic Church and the international labour movement.

Rather than International Relations being understood as the study of the relationships between states, we now understand the global political system as one that is inhabited by a wide variety of actors and agents in addition to states. Some have a greater impact on global issues than others whether by placing an issue onto the international diplomatic agenda, publicising an issue or raising citizen consciousness, lobbying national governments and international organisations or seeking an outcome through direct action, sometimes involving the threat or use of force (Holsti, 1995:64).

Does this mean that the state is being eclipsed as the main actor in international politics? States can still legitimately claim to represent the people of a particular territory across a wide range of interests and issues. Non-state actors, in contrast, tend to concern themselves with single issues and their claim to representativeness is far less clear. Their right to exist and operate in a specific territory rests on the consent of the state. On the other hand, access to international media, the Internet, air travel and so on means that states are no longer able to control the political allegiances and interests of their citizens. Non-state actors provide the vehicle for citizens to act transnationally in concert with people of different nationalities in distant countries. As the world economy becomes increasingly integrated, events in one country can have an immediate impact across the globe. For all these reasons International Relations is now about the study of actors other than the state as much as it is about the relationships between states.

Key concepts in this chapter

Foreign direct investment
Global civil society
Intergovernmental organisations
International non-governmental organisations
Multinational corporations
Non-state actors
Sovereignty

Suggested readings

- No. 2 of Vol. 44 of the *Journal of International Affairs* (1991) was a special edition dealing with global environmental politics. *International Affairs* (1995), Vol. 71, No. 3 also had a special edition on 'Ethics, the Environment and the Changing International Order'.

- Much of the literature on social movements focuses on the activities of these movements in the North. An attempt to look at social movements in the South is Wignaraja, P. (1993) *New Social Movements in the South. Empowering the People.* London: Zed Books.

- A comparative look at social movements, including Germany's Green movement, Poland's Solidarity and Peru's Shining Path, is Zirakzadeh, C. (1997) *Social Movements in Politics. A Comparative Study.* London: Longman.

- For a historical appraisal of the UN see Haas, E. (1986) *Why We Still Need the UN. The Collective Management of International Conflict, 1945–1984.* Berkley: Institute of International Studies. For a more recent study, see Simons, G. (1995) *UN Malaise. Power, Problems and Realpolitik.* Basingstoke: Macmillan. See also the UN's Internet site at http://www.un.org/.

- Watch the journal *Transnational Corporations* for articles on the role of non-state actors in the economic realm. See also UNCTAD's annual *World Investment Report*, which can be ordered from the UN.

8

Africa in the global system, 1600 to decolonisation

Egosha E. Osaghae

This chapter in outline
- A brief theoretical overview
- Africa before 1600
- From 1600 to partition
- From colonisation to decolonisation
- Conclusion

Most of the forty-eight independent states of **sub-Saharan Africa** (SSA) came into being in the late nineteenth and twentieth centuries. The states were created by European colonisers (the Portuguese, British, French, Dutch, Belgians, Spaniards, Italians and Germans) in their quest to maximise individual national shares of the evolving global capitalist system. The only exceptions were Ethiopia, Liberia and South Africa. Ethiopia, the oldest independent state in SSA, survived the colonial assault. Liberia, which was founded in 1822 by the American Colonisation Society, a non-governmental agency, to re-settle freed (black) slaves from the United States of America, became independent in 1847 to join Ethiopia as the only two independent modern states in SSA at the time. In the case of South Africa, its amalgamated white republics formed a Union in 1910, and by 1931 were independent of British colonial rule.

The nature of Africa's relations with the outside world, and its **colonisation** and **decolonisation**, raise a number of interesting questions. Why did European (and other external) powers take over control of Africa? What was the purpose of colonialism? If, as some say, it was a civilising mission to uplift the so-called backward Africans, why was it necessary to conquer them, to subject them to forced labour, in short, to deny them the very essence of civilisation? How did European control affect the participation of Africans in world affairs, for example, in World Wars I and II (1914–1918 and 1939–1945 respectively)?

How did Africans go about reclaiming their independence, and what were the local and transnational (for example, pan-Africanism) currents of the nationalist movements? Why were Southern African countries some of the last to be decolonised? Did the granting of independence mean that European powers no longer needed Africa? If not, why did they grant independence? These are some of the questions this chapter will attempt to answer.

A brief theoretical overview

The period under review in this chapter was critical in the development of SSA as an integral part of the international system, as it witnessed the high point of the opening up of the continent to external forces. This led up to colonisation and the integration of Africa into the global system. The period ends with the efforts of Africans to reclaim their independence, the process that is known as decolonisation. One interesting theoretical question raised by the advent of external forces in Africa is, why was Africa subjected to the forces of imperialism and colonialism?

Perhaps the most general explanation would be that Africa is a part of the globe and, although most parts of the continent are said to have been isolated for a long time, they could not continue to be so for ever. Reasons of necessity, curiosity (Africa was referred to as the 'Dark Continent'), scientific development and trade were bound to lead people from other continents to Africa, in the same way that the so-called 'New World', including the Americas and Australasia, were opened up. Such reasons indeed led to the opening up of Africa. Explorers and navigators led the way, then missionaries, merchants and, finally, state agents followed. Trade proved to be the most important of all, boosted as it was by Africa's strategic location (Mazrui, 1977).

At a time when the oceans provided the only routes for world trade, Africa was critical for trade with the Mediterranean, India and the Far East. Thus states located around the strategic Nile (Egypt, Ethiopia and Sudan) and on the Indian Ocean route (the islands of Comoros, Madagascar and Mauritius, as well as the eastern seaboard and South Africa) were points of some of the earliest contacts with the outside world and of the scramble among external powers for influence and control. As the trans-Atlantic trade increased in importance, coastal states also became nodes of contact and scramble. Trade rivalries and other considerations led to the establishment of the first colonial territories along the seas – the Portuguese built fortified trading posts in coastal cities such as El Mina and Luanda, the Dutch took over the Cape in South Africa to strengthen their control of the Indian Ocean trade, and the Arabs established **sultanates** in Zanzibar and the Comoros islands.

By contrast to the coastal areas, the hinterland remained isolated for a long time. Perhaps the only exceptions were the areas, principally the Sahel states, that were involved in the trans-Saharan trade with North Africa and the Mediterranean, which began as early as the tenth century. These areas also became the earliest parts of the hinterland to come under Islamic influence and control. The situation of these hinterland states provides another reason for the opening up of Africa – it had immense resources that were in demand in other parts of the world and, in return, Africa needed goods and services produced in these places.

Some of the resources that attracted the earliest traders to Africa included salt, iron, ivory, gum arabic, gold and slaves, while the goods demanded by Africans at the time included firearms and luxury items like textiles and spirits. Gold in particular was a major factor, as there were myths about hidden gold deposits and other treasures in Africa. Such myths were reinforced by the huge gold deposits in Ashanti in what became the Gold Coast, and the wanton display of gold wealth by Mansa Musa, emperor of the ancient Mali Empire, who, when on pilgrimage to Mecca in 1327, was said to have taken with him over fifteen tons of gold loaded on camels. The discovery of diamond and gold in South Africa somehow reinforced the myths and accelerated the gold rush, as well as the establishment of a colony by European settlers.

The other major reason that brought outsiders to Africa was religion. Christianity was introduced to the ancient Ethiopian highland states as early as the fourth century, while Islam came through Arab intrusion into the Indian Ocean islands and North Africa. Both religions were introduced at the behest of major powers of the time (the Roman and Ottoman empires and Portugal), whose imperialist ambitions were justified on the grounds of religious propagation. This was especially true of Islam, which permitted the declaration of 'holy wars' against supposedly infidel communities, in addition to being theocratic. It was as such that fundamentalist Muslim groups such as the Almoravids conquered the old Ghana Empire in 1010, and so-called pagan ruling classes that resisted conversion were overthrown. Christianity may not have been propagated by such openly violent means, but it is widely known that Christian missions that came to Africa, beginning in the fifteenth century, were forerunners to the colonial enterprise and in many cases were instrumental in the establishment of colonial rule.

The foregoing explanations can be easily fitted into the categories of theories – realist, liberal and transformative – outlined in Chapter 3. Realist theories see colonialism as the product of **realpolitik** on the part of rival European powers, whose overriding interests were economic and strategic. These involved securing the strategic trade routes, protection of sources of raw materials, labour and markets for finished products, and the acquisition of colonial territories to enhance power status (*see* Muir, 1970; Robinson & Callagher, 1981). In this scheme, the interests of the scientifically marginalised Africans who lacked the technology to successfully repel European invasion were secondary, which explains why colonies were partitioned without regard to Africans, their histories, and their ethnic and cultural affiliations, and why colonies were made to serve the interests of the colonisers rather than the colonised. It also explains why the continent became an arena for power play among the European powers, which, for example, led to the use of Africans to propagate the interests of the powers in the two World Wars.

The transformative theories, of which the most frequently cited are those of Hobson (1902) and Lenin (1939), on imperialism overlap with realist theories, but emphasise economic factors centred on the growth of capitalism. Colonialism is attributed to the rise of monopoly capital and surplus and the consequent quest for new investments and markets following the Industrial Revolution in Europe (*see* Box 8.1). For Lenin, it was the ruthless competition for new investments and profit that led to the outward movement of capital or imperialism; hence he saw imperialism as the highest stage of capitalism. Critics of these theories argue that African trade was not crucial to European industry, and that with the exception of South Africa, capitalist development was not really significant on the continent prior to the 'scramble' for Africa. While this may be so, the contributions of Africa to the growth of Western capitalism and industrialisation, beginning from the use of slaves on plantations in the Atlantic islands and the New World, cannot be underestimated.

On the opposite side of realist and materialist theories is liberal theory, which justifies colonialism on the grounds that it was a civilising mission. According to this theory, the Christianised, industrialised and racially superior Europeans had the responsibility – what has been called 'the white man's burden' – of civilising Africans of the 'Dark Continent' and saving them from the state of nature in which they were said to live (*see* Box 8.1).

Having provided a theoretical overview, in the rest of the chapter we will analyse the main issues of Africa's relations with the outside world in the period under review. As a background, we first briefly examine the situation of Africa up until 1600.

Africa before 1600

Several states existed in Africa as long ago as two thousand years and relations with the outside world pre-date those of the period from 1600. Some of the oldest and most advanced of the states of the period were those of the middle Nile Valley and the Ethiopian Highlands – Axum, Amharinya, Abyssinia, the progenitor of modern Ethiopia, Meroe and Sennar – all of which had trade and religious links with places as far away as Asia. Thus, the Ethiopian highlands states,

Box 8.1: Theories of colonialism

Realist theory: imperialism as power

'[T]he attempt to provide security for the state … compels the state to try to control its own environment. In practice this means the extension of its influence over other states. Such control directly challenges the security of these states and so the competition becomes a conflict over rival spheres of influence dominated by the technological capacities of the competing systems of "influence". Imperialism is thus a direct consequence of the security dilemma.'

Reynolds (1981:24)

Liberal theory: colonialism as a civilising mission

'The political and philosophical justification was that the "advanced" white powers would act as tutors or trustees for their Asian or African wards who, in the fullness of time (and this was conceived in terms of hundreds of years), would be capable of behaving in a civilised manner.'

Tinker (1977:8)

Transformative theory: the economic taproot of imperialism

'Overproduction in the sense of an excessive manufacturing plant, and surplus capital which cannot find sound investments within the country, forced Great Britain, Germany, Holland, France to place larger and larger portions of their economic resources outside their areas of present political domain, and then stimulate a policy of political expansion so as to take in the new areas.'

Hobson (1902:56)

beginning with Axum, embraced (Coptic) Christianity as early as the fourth century, while Sennar in the middle Nile was converted to Islam by the eighth century (*see* Curtin *et al.*, 1995).

Other famous states that emerged later included the Sahel states of Ghana, Mali, Songhai, Hausa, Kanem-Bornu and Darfur, as well as the rain forest empires of Benin, Ashanti and Oyo in West Africa. To the eastern, central and southern parts of the continent, including the Great Lakes region, where state formation is of relatively more recent origin, dating in some cases to the nineteenth century, the notable states included Buganda, Bunyoro, Rwanda, Kikwa, Kongo, Lozi, Luba, Lundi and Zimbabwe (or Monomotapa). Some of these states emerged in a milieu of slave raids, ravaging war-lordism and so-called inter-tribal wars, which were instigated by slave-dealing Arab and European traders. Finally, the states in the southern-most end of the continent, especially in present-day South Africa, were still in the process of formation by the time the European settlers arrived in the seventeenth century. In fact, the *mfecane* (the Zulu word for 'breaking or crushing'), which was central to state formation over parts of Southern Africa, did not happen until the early nineteenth century.

Despite Africa's relative technological backwardness, many of these states attained relatively high levels of development. Indeed, the levels of development – for example, as manifest in the stone works and mines of ancient Zimbabwe, whose ruins are to be seen to this day (as in Great Zimbabwe), the sophisticated metal craft work in Benin, which produced the famous bronze works, and the iron smelting technology in many parts of the continent – were sometimes considered too high for 'backward' Africans and were accordingly attributed to external influences. Thus the Phoenicians were credited with the stone works of Zimbabwe, while iron smelting is said to have been developed in western Asia, finding its way to Africa through Egypt (Griffiths, 1995). Some of these claims may very well have been part of the racial theory of European superiority that was used to justify the colonial enterprise.

What cannot be denied, however, is that, contrary to the popular view that Africa was isolated, some parts of the continent had long-established relations with external powers and that these affected their development, positively as well as negatively, prior to 1600. Some scholars believe that the advent of external forces, especially European capitalism, is responsible for the underdevelopment of Africa, which, they argue, was developing along its own paths before it was drawn into relations of unequal exchange in the global capitalist system. One of the most popular of these scholars was the late Walter Rodney, whose famous book is entitled *How Europe Underdeveloped Africa* (1972).

There were basically two strands of these external relations. The first involved Muslim-Arabs who came into Africa through the Indian Ocean trade (which linked Africa to Asia) and the trans-Saharan trade (which linked Africa to the Mediterranean). To secure control of the Indian Ocean trade the Arabs established sultanates in Zanzibar, and the Comoros and Madagascar islands. Large parts of the Horn, eastern coast, the Sahel and other hinterland areas closest to North Africa, which were involved in the trans-Saharan trade, also fell under Islamic influence and conquest.

One aspect of the Islamic push that had devastating effects on state formation was the trade in slaves. In fact, some of the attacks on so-called infidel communities were official slave raids (*ghazwa* or *salatiya*). There were two columns of the slave trade involving Muslim states. One was that by the Arab rulers of the island of Zanzibar, a major slave trade centre, who employed slave labour procured from the Zambesi hinterland to work on the island's clove plantations, and for export to Arabia, the Persian Gulf and Asia. The other was the trans-Saharan slave trade, which saw the exportation of thousands of African slaves to Arabia, India, the Ottoman Empire and North Africa, though the numbers were nowhere near those of the later trans-Atlantic slave trade.

The second strand of external relations, which

proved far more consequential for Africa as it involved the integration of the continent into the world capitalist system on unfavourable and unequal terms of exchange (*see* Box 8.2) and fundamental changes in political and socio-economic formations, was that with the Europeans.

Historical evidence suggests early European influence (for example, the rulers of the Ethiopian highlands states were converted to Christianity as early as the fourth century), but this did not become sustained until the entry of the Portuguese, who established trade, religious and diplomatic links with various parts of Southern, Central (Kongo and Angola) and West Africa (Warri, Benin and Ashanti), as well as Ethiopia in the fifteenth and sixteenth centuries. Explorers and missionaries led the way in this enterprise, but as the needs of the Portuguese changed, colonial relations gradually replaced earlier 'diplomatic' relations. Thus, by 1651, a treaty of protection was signed with the Kingdom of Kongo, and by the end of the seventeenth century, Angola had become the first substantially European colony in Africa.

Portuguese interests in coming to Africa were

Box 8.2: Unequal and unfavourable terms of exchange: the example of cotton in the 1900s

'[T]he cotton grown by African ... peasant farmers was fed into the Lancashire textile mills, via the flourishing port of Liverpool, and the cloth which the mills produced was exported back to Africa by European trading companies. However, while the price which the producer received for his cotton fluctuated widely, and often downwards, the price which he had to pay for imported cloth constantly increased. The unequal and exploitative nature of this exchange ... contributed to the capitalist development of Europe at Africa's expense.'

Tordoff (1997:31)

strategic and only partially to civilise. First, as a Christian (Catholic) state, it was to Christianise and halt the spread of Islam in the Horn, which necessitated strategic alliances with Ethiopia against Egypt and the Ottoman Empire. Secondly, in terms of trade, the aim was to secure the East Indian and trans-Atlantic trade routes and dominate the trade between the north and the Mediterranean. To this end, on the eastern coast they defeated the Arabs, who had dominated the East India trade and built fortresses in Mombasa, Mozambique and port cities on the west coast. The Portuguese were, however, dispossessed of these strategic holdings and the advantages they enjoyed as European pioneers on the trade routes by the entry of the Dutch, English, French and other Europeans into the lucrative East India trade route and the trans-Atlantic slave trade.

As was the case with the Portuguese, Christian missionaries, such as the French Capuchin missionaries in Senegal, and explorers pioneered the entry of the other European powers into Africa. But what increased the European traffic to Africa was, firstly, the rush to control the lucrative East India and trans-Atlantic trade routes and to tap gold and the other mythical precious stones of Africa, and, secondly, the rise of the plantation economy in the 'New World', and the consequent demand for slave labour. The first slaves from Africa were procured by Portugal in 1444 to work the plantations in the Atlantic islands of São Tomé and later Brazil and the island colonies. Thereafter the trade in slaves blossomed to involve virtually all the major Western European powers at the time, including the United States (US).

From 1600 to partition

This period saw the deepening of European penetration into and domination of Africa. This increased the rivalry over trade and territorial advantages among the various powers leading up to what is popularly known as the 'scramble for Africa'. What gave rise to this scramble were the changing demands of capitalist development in Western Europe. This set a pattern of **externalisation** in which changes in Africa were henceforth to be elicited by external rather than internal forces. Before the Industrial Revolution, it was merchant capitalism and plantation economies that needed secured trade routes (the Nile, East India and trans-Atlantic routes), access to gold and other precious metals, and slave labour. With the exception of a few fortresses and colonial holdings along the coast (notably the Cape and Angola), these demands did not require the Europeans to possess colonies or move inland.

After the Industrial Revolution, the demand switched to so-called legitimate goods, mostly raw materials from Africa, and markets for finished products. This not only required penetration beyond the coastal areas into the hinterland, but also, inevitably, colonial conquest and control (*see* Box 8.3).

Of all the events of the period between 1600 and partition, the trans-Atlantic slave trade was arguably the most significant. To be sure, there was domestic slavery and slave trade with the Arabs before the trans-Atlantic slave trade, but this were nowhere near the latter in terms of the volume and scope of the trade, and its overall negative consequences on Africa. The trans-

Atlantic slave trade, which involved all the major Western European countries at the time (Portugal, France, the Netherlands, Britain, Spain, Belgium, Denmark and Prussia) as well as the US, Brazil and Cuba, lasted for nearly four centuries – from the fifteenth to the early nineteenth century – though it was at its peak in the period 1750–1850. Estimates of the number of slaves taken from Africa vary, but it is believed that no less than eleven million Africans were sold into slavery in the trans-Atlantic slave trade, of which about 20% died in slave raids in the hinterland or on the slave ships (Curtin, 1969; Lovejoy, 1983).

The majority of the slaves were 'exported' to the New World – the Americas and the Caribbean islands especially – where they worked the (sugar) plantations. Slaves were also sent to parts of Africa where there were plantations. For example, slaves from Angola and Kongo were taken to the Portuguese islands of São Tomé and Cape Verde and initially to the Gold Coast where they were exchanged for gold, from Kilwa and Zanzibar to the French plantations in Mauritius and Reunion, and from other parts to South Africa, which was already a settler colony. Slaves also worked the Portuguese coffee estates of Cazengo in the Angolan hinterland.

The effects of the slave trade are generally well known. Internally it exacerbated violence, interstate conflicts, social turbulence and insecurity of life, and, because of the large volume of men, women and children taken from Africa, it decimated production and economic development. At the external level, the slave trade was a major factor in the rise of plantation economies and the process of capital accumulation that made the Industrial Revolution possible. It facilitated the development of shipping and new patterns of consumption and thereby enhanced world trade. The trade also laid the basis for the African diaspora, as the ancestors of most of the blacks in the US, Latin America, Asia and other far parts of the world were taken to these places as slaves (Wilson, 1977).

In 1807, Britain officially abolished the slave

Box 8.3: The new phase of imperialism (late nineteenth century)

With time, it became clear that coastal control was no longer sufficient to serve the needs of the new imperial order: 'Governments were required which could smash the power of ruling classes, construct telegraph lines and railways, impose uniformly peaceful conditions and permit coastal traders direct access to free [hinterland] peasant producers'.

Freund (1984:88)

trade, followed by the French, Scandinavian and Dutch colonies and the US, Cuba and Brazil (not until the 1880s), although for a long time after abolition, the trade continued in several parts of Africa. Why did the Europeans abolish such a profitable trade (we are told that the prices of slaves were far higher than those of goods bought for sale in Africa)? It seems that economic necessity, especially the capitalist imperative of free enterprise, more than the humanitarian arguments advanced by the anti-slavery movements was the main reason.

Another reason was that revolts by slaves such as that which overthrew French authority in Hispaniola (now Haiti) in 1791 made slave-holding an increasingly high-risk business. Such underlying reasons were, however, submerged by the humanitarian reasons given by those who saw the abolition as reinforcing the European claim to moral superiority. This ultimately provided a justification for colonisation, beginning with the resettlement of freed slaves in Sierra Leone and the stationing of consuls by the British in the ports of Bathurst, Calabar, Gold Coast, Lagos and Zanzibar, and the French in Senegal to ostensibly enforce the stoppage of slave trade and ensure the smooth flow of legitimate goods.

The other landmark of this period was the colonisation of South Africa. The process began when the Dutch East India Company established a permanent base at Cape Town in 1652 to provide a rendezvous and supply base for merchants and ships on the Indian Ocean trade. A small group of company workers pioneered the influx of settlers who overtime dispossessed the Khoisan and Nguni-speaking (Xhosa, Zulu and Pedi) peoples who inhabited the area. The settlers were a mix of Dutch, French, Germans and Scandinavians who evolved a distinctive (Boer) society served by the Afrikaans language. Under the protection of Dutch rulers, the settler colony developed an agricultural economy that was built around wheat, grains and vineyards. This necessitated the importation of slave labour from Asia, Madagascar and Mozambique. By the eighteenth century, the Cape had become the first settler colony in Africa.

However, between 1795 and 1806, the Cape fell under the British, who were also interested in controlling the strategic trade route and exploiting the mythical deposits of gold and other precious stones that were believed to be hidden in Southern Africa. Under British rule, the Cape prospered as a centre of wine and wool production. But British imperialism, which did not go down well with the Boer settlers in the Cape, triggered off the famous trek into the hinterland areas. The trek brought the Boers into confrontation with the Xhosa and other indigenous groups in the famous frontier wars. With superior weapons and the backing of colonial authorities, the Boers won most of the wars and quickly established the republics of the Orange Free State and Transvaal. Meanwhile, Natal, which was the fourth colony in South Africa, was already under the control of the British. Formal colonial rule began in the Cape with the 1853 constitution, which gave powers of self-government to an elected assembly whose electors included a small minority of black property owners. In Natal, which did not enjoy such smooth racial relations, indentured labourers were imported from India, from 1860, to work the sugar plantations.

The influx of European workers and investments that followed the discovery and subsequent mining of diamonds in Kimberley (1870) and gold in Johannesburg (1886) changed the complexion of imperialism in South Africa. Britain quickly annexed the adjoining areas of Lesotho, Bechuanaland and Zululand to consolidate its control and secure labour reserves. It was also the time to deal with Afrikaner nationalists who resented British rule because, among other reasons, the British encouraged the large-scale immigration of British artisans and capitalist farmers into South Africa. Afrikaners were not ready to lose the privileges they already enjoyed as white settlers. The conflicts between the Afrikaners and the British colonialists resulted in the famous Anglo-Boer War of 1899–1902, which has been described as the greatest imperial war fought by Britain on African soil. It took about

300 000 soldiers from Britain and other parts of the British Empire to subdue the Afrikaners, who resorted to guerrilla warfare. The war finally ended in 1902 with the signing of the Peace of Vereeniging.

This paved the way for the unification of the four white colonies in 1910 following the withdrawal of the British imperialist government. This, and the fact that the country became a republic in 1961, is generally taken to mean independence for South Africa. But this is mistaken because the so-called independence was for the whites only, not blacks, Indians and coloureds, who thereafter were oppressed under a colonial system of racial discrimination, exclusion and exploitation that was accentuated after the Afrikaner Nationalist Party captured state power in 1948. The blacks had to fight for their independence, which only came in 1994. The black labour reserves of Bechuanaland, Basutoland and Swaziland were left out of the Union, and designated as High Commission territories under British control.

The good fortune of South Africa encouraged Cecil Rhodes's British South Africa Company to move further inland with British support to annexe the areas around Lake Malawi and Ndebeleland, which subsequently became Southern Rhodesia, in search of gold and other precious stones. Rhodesia turned out to be unlike South Africa, and this made land alienation and agriculture the basis for settler accumulation and prosperity. Southern Rhodesia became self-governing in 1923.

The final event of the period was the partition of Africa, which came in the aftermath of the scramble for colonies by the European powers. The changes in demands brought by industrial capitalism precipitated the scramble as already indicated, but it was accentuated by a number of factors. First was the economic depression that Europe went through in the 1870s, which increased the desperation to secure protected sources of raw materials and markets. Next was the fierce rivalry for control of the strategic Congo basin and the Nile. The British, French and Portuguese opposed the ambition of King Leopold II of Belgium to control the whole of the Congo basin as a personal empire, while the struggle to control the strategic upper Nile region brought the British, in alliance with Egypt, close to war with the French, in alliance with Ethiopia, at Fashoda in 1898. Third was the entry of Italy and a newly unified Germany, who were late-comers to the scramble, but who managed to secure some colonies. Italy gained a foothold in Somalia, Libya and Eritrea after it was defeated by Ethiopia at the battle of Adowa, although Ethiopia later fell briefly to Italian rule between 1936 and 1941; Germany got what are now Cameroun, Togo, Namibia and German East Africa (mainland Tanzania, Rwanda and Burundi).

It was against this background that the European powers met at Berlin in 1884/85 to reach a peaceful settlement on how to share Africa. Though it had no colonial claims in Africa, the US also participated at the conference, whereas Africa, whose fate was to be determined, was not represented at all. On the basis of effective occupation, as well as amity and trade treaties, which were accepted as valid claims to ownership, the entire continent was arbitrarily partitioned, leading to the creation of 'artificial' states. The claims of Portugal to Mozambique, Angola and Cape Verde were validated. The British got most of East and Southern Africa, and shared Central and West Africa with the French. The Germans and Italians got the territories indicated earlier, while Spain had only the tiny island of Fernando Po and mainland Rio Muni (*see* Table 8.1 for colonial possessions). The period immediately following the Berlin conference up until World War I was devoted to consolidating colonial holdings. This process is popularly known as 'pacification', which is misleading, considering that it involved the conquest of those areas that had not effectively been subjugated and other military 'mopping up' operations.

Table 8.1: Independence dates of sub-Saharan African states

Country	Independent	Independence from
Angola	1975	Angola
Benin (formerly Dahomey)	1960	France
Botswana (formerly Bechuanaland)	1966	Britain
Burkina Faso (formerly Upper Volta)	1960	France
Burundi (formerly Ruanda-Urundi)	1962	Belgium
Cameroun	1960	France
Cape Verde	1975	Portugal
Central African Republic (formerly Oubangui Chari)	1960	France
Chad	1960	France
Comoros	1975	France
Congo (People's Republic of)	1960	France
Congo (Democratic Republic of, formerly Zaïre)	1960	Belgium
Côte d'Ivoire	1960	France
Djibouti (formerly French Territory of the Afars and ISSAs)	1977	France
Equatorial Guinea (formerly Spanish Guinea)	1968	Spain
Eritrea	1991	Ethiopia
Ethiopia Colonised briefly	(1936–1941)	Italy
Gabon	1960	France
Gambia	1965	Britain
Ghana (formerly Gold Coast)	1957	Britain
Guinea	1958	France
Guinea-Bissau (formerly Portuguese Guinea)	1974	Portugal
Kenya	1963	Britain
Lesotho (formerly Basutoland)	1966	Britain
Liberia	1847	American Colonisation Society
Madagascar	1960	France
Malawi (formerly Nyasaland)	1964	Britain
Mali (formerly French Soudan)	1960	France
Mozambique	1975	Portugal
Mauritania	1960	France
Mauritius	1968	Britain
Namibia (formerly South West Africa)	1990	South Africa
Niger	1960	France
Nigeria	1960	Britain
Rwanda (formerly Ruanda-Urundi)	1962	Belgium
São Tomé	1975	Portugal
Senegal	1960	France
Seychelles	1976	Britain
Sierra Leone	1961	Britain
Somalia	1960	Italy and Britain
South Africa		
(independence for white minority)	1961	Britain
(non-racial democracy)	1994	White minority regime
Sudan	1956	Britain
Swaziland	1967	Britain
Tanzania		
(Tanganyika)	1961	Britain
(Zanzibar)	1963	Britain
Togo (formerly French Togoland)	1960	France
Uganda	1962	Britain
Zambia (formerly Northern Rhodesia)	1964	Britain
Zimbabwe (formerly Southern Rhodesia, Rhodesia)		
(unilateral independence for white minority)	1965	Britain
(non-racial democracy)	1980	White minority regime

From colonisation to decolonisation

In this final section, we examine the landmarks of the period from colonisation or the establishment of formal colonial rule to the termination of that rule through the process of decolonisation (*see* also Chapter 9).

Let us begin with the forms of colonial rule that are usually analysed in terms of how the policies of the colonial powers differed. British rule was indirect and decentralised; French (and Portuguese) rule was assimilationist and centralised, as the colonies which were grouped into two federations (**Afrique Occidental Francais** and **Afrique Equatorial Francais**), in the case of the French, were administered as extensions of the mother country; Belgian rule was direct and brutal; and so on. But these differences were more in degree than kind as colonial policies were more similar and pragmatic than is often assumed. Where it suited the needs of the colonial enterprise, there was direct or indirect rule, a settler or non-settler colony, more or less forced labour, taxation, land appropriation, colonial peoples were citizens or subjects, and nationalist forces were tolerated or repressed.

Colonial economies in particular had a common profile. They were dominated by a few European trading firms such as Unilever and Compaigne Francais de l'Afrique Oriental, which engaged in commerce rather than production. Next, the colonies were **monocultural**, that is, dependent on one or a few cash crops (such as cocoa, sisal, oil palm, groundnuts, cotton and rubber) or minerals (such as copper, tin, diamond and gold). This made their economies susceptible to the vagaries of the world market; any time there was a decline in prices or depression in the Western capitalist countries, African economies were thrown into crises, including those deriving from foreign debts.

Thirdly, colonial economies were labour intensive: labour was required to produce surplus in the mines and plantations, to build railway lines and roads, and for portage. Forced labour and forced cultivation were common (in Kenya, Africans were forbidden to grow coffee). In South Africa and other mining centres such as the copper belt of the Belgian Congo and Northern Rhodesia, a system of migrant labour in which black areas constituted labour reserves developed. In addition, all colonies without exception were expected to be financially self-supporting and not constitute any burden on the mother country (this explains the small numbers of colonial officials and the composition of colonial armies by locals, amongst others).

The structures of the colonial state were developed only in so far as they were sufficient to enforce law and order (the army, police, judiciary and prisons) and develop infrastructure (the railways, roads, ports, marketing boards and communication facilities), which facilitated the penetration of capital, extraction of resources and the export/import trade. The colonial state was in effect a 'tribute-taker' rather than an 'organising agency' for capitalism (Freund, 1980:112). The welfare and development of the colonised peoples counted for little. Education, science and technology in particular were underdeveloped and, with the exception of South Africa where industrial growth took early roots, too little European capital and labour were invested to bring about meaningful development. Notwithstanding, the emerging colonial economies attracted commercial merchants from other parts of the world: the Greeks, Lebanese, Jews and Indians.

Given the similarities in colonial forms, perhaps the most important distinction was that between settler and non-settler colonies. Settler colonies were those that had communities of European settlers and in almost all cases developed systems of racial hierarchy and discrimination, which reserved the best privileges and resources, especially land, for whites. South Africa, Northern and Southern Rhodesia, Kenya and, to a lesser extent, French Cameroun and Senegal, and Portuguese Angola and Mozambique were the most notable of the settler colonies. Non-settler colonies, on the other hand, had few Europeans: typically colonial officials, missionaries and merchants (it is said that harsh weather conditions and tropical diseases deterred European settlers from West Africa). In general, the road to independence was more difficult in settler colonies where white settlers were unwilling to relinquish the privileges the racially stratified systems bestowed on them; in almost all cases, the nationalists were forced to resort to armed liberation struggle. In non-settler colonies, on the other hand, it was relatively easier for the nationalists to negotiate independence.

Next, we shall consider the roles of Africans in the two World Wars and the effects of the wars on Africa. For the most part, the colonies were drawn into the wars as appendage actors by their colonial masters who were the main combatants (Portugal, however, maintained a neutral position and so its colonies were not drawn into the wars). Being independent, South Africa and Liberia were exceptions (the other independent state, Ethiopia, was under Italian rule by the time of World War II), but only South Africa played a direct role in both wars, though in alliance with the British. General Jan Smuts, the country's prime minister, was a member of the British war cabinet during World War II, and played a major role in the formation of both the League of Nations (1920–1945) and the UN (1945–), the international organisations formed to keep peace after the wars. The roles of the other Africans entailed, firstly, the drafting and conscription of colonial subjects into enlarged native regiments, notably the British West African Frontier Force (WAFF), the French Tirailleurs, the German Schutztruppen and the Belgian Force Publique. In World War I, Britain used close to one million East Africans in the fight against the Germans in Tanganyika, and in the WAFF in the fight in Cameroun.

Secondly, the colonies were obliged to contribute huge sums to the home countries' war efforts funds, and this led to the imposition of higher taxes and increased production of export commodities. Third, the wars involved fighting

on African soil. World War I extended to North Africa, and the German colonies of German East Africa, Cameroun and South West Africa. In World War II, the Italian colonies of Somalia and Eritrea in the Horn, and North Africa were the battlegrounds in Africa, but this time, African soldiers fought outside Africa in large numbers. About 80 000 of them are said to have been killed during the German invasion of France, while Britain deployed its four African regiments in India and Burma.

As can be well imagined, the World Wars had important consequences for Africa. To begin with, they led to the re-partitioning of colonies. Following the defeat of Germany in World War I, its colonies were re-partitioned among the victorious powers under the mandate scheme of the League of Nations: South West Africa went to South Africa, Cameroun and Togo were split between France and Britain, Ruanda-Urundi was given to Belgium, and German East Africa (renamed Tanganyika) went to Britain. After World War II, these colonies became trustee territories under the UN system. Under this system, colonial authorities of the trustee territories were required to submit annual reports and prepare them for independence within a specified period. Territories of defeated Italy also underwent some changes after World War II: Ethiopian independence was restored; Somaliland was left in Italian hands with the guarantee of independence after ten years; Eritrea was granted autonomy within Ethiopia, which proceeded to establish colonial type rule there; and Libya was quickly granted independence in 1951.

We now turn to national liberation (a form of **nationalism** that accompanied decolonisation), which refers to the various anti-colonial and independence movements that forced the demise of colonisation. The anti-colonial strand of nationalism began with the initial resistance to colonial rule in the period preceding and immediately following the partition. This was followed by the first wave of nationalism by small groups of (mostly coastal) educated élite who demanded greater political accommodation and social mobility within the colonial administration and economy rather than self-government. There were also strikes by labour unions for better wages and working conditions and resistant movements by indigenous churches, which were formed to counter the Europeanness of Christianity. These became politicised as the nationalist movement gathered momentum.

Nationalism as opposition to aspects of colonial regimes later gave way, in the period after World War II, to nationalism as a movement for independence and the termination of colonial rule. One movement whose development coincided with the progress of African nationalism in this sense was **pan-Africanism**, an ideological movement that at once sought the unity of Africans in Africa and the diaspora, as well as the emancipation and progress of Africans from colonial bondage (Ajala, 1974). The idea of pan-Africanism was developed by Africans in the diaspora (notably Henry Sylvester Williams, Marcus Garvey, William DuBois and Edward Blyden). This is reflected by the fact that the first Pan-African congress of 1900, which criticised the racist regimes in South Africa and Rhodesia, was attended by only four African delegates (eleven were from US and ten from the West Indies).

Subsequent congresses, which continued to have a preponderance of Africans in the diaspora, took place in Paris (1919), London and Brussels (1921), London and Lisbon (1923), New York (1927) and Manchester (1945). The Manchester congress was the turning point in the movement. Not only were the majority of participants Africans from the continent, including Kwame Nkrumah who became secretary general, but African liberation was also adopted as the ideology of pan-Africanism. As an ideology of African liberation, pan-Africanism tied African independence to unity and emphasised that the independence of one country was meaningless without the independence of all. The consciousness provoked by this was crucial to the formation of the Organisation of African Unity (OAU) in 1963.

The tempo of nationalism heightened all over Africa after World War II. The events and aftermath of the war itself contributed to this. The war had been fought in the name of upholding the right of people to self-determination, and African nationalists, including those who had fought in the war and had been exposed to new ideas, were no longer ready to accept any suggestion that their own right to self-determination was in any way secondary. In this, they received a boost from the 1941 Atlantic Charter declaration by President Roosevelt of the US and British Prime Minister Winston Churchill, and the charter of the newly formed UN, which reaffirmed the rights of all peoples to self-determination. What was more, the independence of a number of Asian and North African countries – India/Pakistan, Burma, Ceylon (Sri Lanka), Vietnam, Morocco, Libya and Tunisia – showed that the right to self-determination was within reach. The Cold War that ensued in the aftermath of World War II between the US and its Western allies on the one hand, and the Union of Soviet Socialist Republics (the USSR) and its socialist allies on the other further changed the configuration of global politics in favour of the colonies, which were subsequently to be wooed for support by the ideologically opposed power blocs. Other factors that stoked the tempo of nationalism included rapid urbanisation, the increasing reliance of colonial economies on labour, which made strikes by labour unions that had been given legal recognition politically significant, and the proliferation of political parties and organisations demanding one political right or the other, as did the African veterans who had fought in Europe and Asia.

Much of the increased tempo of nationalism involved political agitation and mobilisation by the more assertive nationalists, who had formed independence-seeking political parties, and widespread strikes by labour unions. Only in a few places like Kenya (the Mau Mau) and Cameroun was armed struggle adopted as a means of independence at this stage. Increased nationalist agitation led the colonial authorities to expand African legislative representation, democratise local government, abolish forced labour, liberalise political space to allow formation of political organisations, expand access to education and appoint Africans to top civil service positions. But reforms were no longer sufficient to satisfy African demands. They now wanted independence.

However, no colonial power contemplated immediate independence at this stage. Even the British, who were regarded as liberal, only contemplated self-government within the **Commonwealth**. The French and Portuguese continued to regard their colonies as extensions of the mother country, although the French took the important step of dissolving the two federations under the Loi Cadre of 1956; this made it possible for the countries to become independent individually. The Belgians were very far from reform – in the Congo secular education and municipal elections were only introduced in the late 1950s. As for the settler colonies of Southern Rhodesia and South Africa, the question of independence simply was out. Yet, the drama of decolonisation happened very fast. In 1960, most SSA countries became independent, with Sudan (1956), Ghana (1957) and Guinea, which voted against continued association with France in the 1958 referendum, leading the way (*see* Table 8.1).

Decolonisation, whose defining element was the termination of colonial rule followed in most cases by the withdrawal of the colonisers, was more like a scramble out of Africa. The point was not simply that Africans fought for independence but also that, firstly, the changes in world affairs, including the Cold War – what Harold Macmillan, the British prime minister, called the 'winds of change' in his famous speech to the South African parliament in Cape Town in 1960 – no longer favoured colonial domination, and, secondly, with the rise of multinational corporations (MNCs) and advancements in air travel and communications, global capitalism had grown to a point where it no longer depended on the physical control of colonies.

Neo-colonialism, which involves exploitation by remote control, then took over. This meant that the Europeans could withdraw after preparing the former colonies for neo-colonial domination. For the French, preparing for withdrawal entailed agreements on defence, currency and foreign aid, all reaffirming its 'big brother' role with its former colonies at independence. These arrangements enabled France to place its stooges in power, thereby making nonsense of independence. The British were more subtle, but their attempts to follow the French example by signing defence pacts (such as the Anglo-Nigerian defence pact) were not as successful. In any case, membership in the Commonwealth by virtually all former colonies at independence guaranteed that the British would continue to exert some influence in their affairs. The Belgians failed to prepare their colonies for independence (at independence, the Congo had very few people with secondary school education and only sixteen university graduates), and it was hardly surprising that Congo-Kinshasha was plunged into civil war soon after independence (the same happened to Rwanda and Burundi).

However, the winds of change failed to sway Portugal, which, despite some (cosmetic) reforms such as reducing forced labour and opening up Angola to non-Portuguese investors, hung on tenaciously to its colonial possessions, even increasing the traffic of settlers, mostly unemployed Portuguese, to Africa and land alienation. Portugal's intransigence helped to make Southern Africa not only the last bastion of white rule in Africa, but also the theatre of a complex armed struggle that involved freedom fighters in individual countries and in the sub-region as a whole, as well as the Cold War power blocs, which found the struggles and contradictory forces conducive to their war for allies.

The overthrow of the Salazar regime in Portugal in 1974 accelerated the collapse of its African empire, with Mozambique, Guinea-Bissau and Angola becoming independent in 1975. The independence of these countries was a big boost to the liberation movements in Rhodesia, South West Africa (renamed Namibia in 1968) and South Africa, which now established bases in them (as well as the other frontline states of Lesotho, Tanzania and Zambia). This was the major reason for South Africa's attacks on these countries (despite security pacts such as the Nkomati Accord with Mozambique in 1984) and its active support for opposition movements (UNITA, the National Union for the Total Independence of Angola, in Angola and RENAMO, the *Resistencia Nacional Moçambicana*, in Mozambique).

The scenario was, however, different in Rhodesia. Northern Rhodesia and Nyasaland had pulled out of the Rhodesia/Nyasaland federation and become independent in 1964, and in 1965, a unilateral declaration of independence (UDI) was effected by Ian Smith's white minority government. Sanctions imposed in the aftermath of UDI by Britain were sabotaged by South Africa (and Portuguese authorities until 1974), which strongly backed the Salisbury government. The minority government attempted some 'multiracial' reforms such as giving fifteen of sixty-five legislative seats to Africans under the 1969 constitution, and the creation in 1978 of an internal settlement government with Abel Muzorewa as prime minister, but these could not stop the armed struggle. One of the factors that delayed the success of liberation was the division within the ranks of the movements after the Zimbabwe African National Union (ZANU) broke away from the Zimbabwe African People's Union (ZAPU) in 1963. But independence came soon after ZANU and ZAPU agreed to form an alliance after the Lancaster talks in 1980.

This left Namibia and South Africa itself as the last bastions of white colonial rule in SSA (the other colony, Eritrea, became independent of Ethiopian rule in 1991, after many years of armed liberation struggle following the overthrow of the Mengistu regime). In Namibia, the South West African People's Organisation (SWAPO) had launched a guerrilla war against South Africa in 1966 after sustained appeals to the UN for independence had failed. A 1971 declaration by the International Court of Justice at The

Hague and a number of UN resolutions that South Africa's occupation of Namibia was illegal failed to sway the country's authorities. Rather, they attempted to annexe Namibia as South Africa's fifth province and even introduced a homelands policy to incorporate the country. Shorn of the strategic protection offered by the old white empire, the independence of Namibia became a last-ditch survival bargaining chip for South Africa. The presence of SWAPO guerrillas in Angola provided the setting, as the withdrawal of Cuban forces from Angola was tied to the independence of Namibia. Eventually in 1990, after a series of complicated negotiations involving the US (which pursued a policy it called 'constructive engagement'), the USSR, Cuba and South Africa, both Cuban and South African troops withdrew from Angola, and Namibia was granted independence.

It was soon after this that the 'preparation' for the termination of white supremacist rule in South Africa began. A combination of mounting internal and external opposition to the Apartheid regime and important changes in the global system finally brought the Apartheid regime to the negotiating table in 1990. Alongside the armed struggle by the exiled liberation movements (mainly the African National Congress, ANC, and the Pan Africanist Congress, PAC), there were the defiance and opposition activities of the United Democratic Front (UDF), students and other groups, as well as an escalation of strikes by the (mainly black) labour unions, all of which rendered the country ungovernable and raised the stakes of preserving Apartheid. Although some reforms were introduced in the interest of protecting capital (business), such as the relaxation of influx control laws, the mainstay of the Apartheid regime's survivalist tactics remained, as before, force and repression.

Mounting pressure from the international community, including the UN, Commonwealth, OAU and individual countries, also accelerated the decolonisation process in South Africa. The pressure involved moral persuasion, **isolation** of the country and economic, defence and sporting

sanctions that were imposed by various world bodies and enforced by individual countries. Although the sanctions were violated by several Western countries (notably Britain, the US and Japan) whose nationals continued to invest in South Africa, they proved to be a potent weapon used by the international community to terminate Apartheid.

The other external factor that can be regarded as the last straw that broke the back of the Apartheid regime was the changing character of the international system. The changes that had direct consequences for South Africa were the end of the Cold War following the collapse of the USSR and the socialist bloc, and the global wave of **democratisation**. While the end of the Cold War removed the final shield for Apartheid as the regime exploited its strategic position as the outpost of Western capitalism to the fullest, even to the point of justifying its brutal suppression of the liberation movements in the name of fighting communism, the global democratisation wave simply rendered authoritarianism of a racial-colonial kind untenable. These were the circumstances that led to the negotiations between the National Party government and the ANC, the main liberation movement, beginning from 1990, and ultimately to the end of Africa's decolonisation process in the holding of South Africa's first democratic elections in April 1994.

Conclusion

This chapter has analysed the different phases of Africa's relations with the outside world from 1600 to the end of Apartheid in South Africa in 1994. The period witnessed colonial-type contacts with the Arabs, the slave trade, which was replaced by trade in legitimate goods in the aftermath of the Industrial Revolution in Europe, colonisation, which led to the creation of most of the states to be found in SSA today, and, finally, the decolonisation movement, which culminated in the granting of political independence to the new states. These various processes marked the

integration of African states into the global system on the unfair terms of unequal exchange. These terms, which have been preserved by the neo-colonial structures established in the aftermath of colonisation, make the countries dependent on the global superpowers and render them weak actors in international relations.

Key concepts in this chapter

Colonisation
Decolonisation
Imperialism
National liberation
Neo-colonialism
Self-determination
Settler society
Unequal terms of exchange

Suggested readings

- Hanlon, J. (1986) *Beggar Your Neighbours: Apartheid Power in Southern Africa.* London: James Currey, provides detailed examination of South Africa's destabilising roles in Southern Africa and how the country supported the retention of white regimes in the region.
- Imperialism has been a major factor in the explanation of colonialism and neo-colonialism in Africa. Some of the best analysis of this subject can be found in Nadubere, D. (1982) *Imperialism in East Africa* (vol 1: *Imperialism and Exploitation*; vol 2: *Imperialism and Integration*). London: Zed Books.
- A good overview of the history of Africa from colonisation to decolonisation is found in Gifford P. & Louis, W. R. (eds) (1988) *Decolonisation and African Independence.* New Haven: Yale University Press. For a more detailed historical account a recommended text would be Afigbo, A. E., *et al.* (1993; 1996) *The Making of Modern Africa* (vol 1: *The Nineteenth Century*; vol 2: *The Twentieth*

Century). London: Longman.

- For analyses of different colonial experiences and their aftermath, see Newitt, M. (1981) *Portugal in Africa: The Last Hundred Years.* London: C. Hurst. See also Gifford, P. & Louis, W. R. (1971) *France and Britain in Africa.* New Haven: Yale University Press.
- There are a number of good studies on pan-Africanism. One of these is Geiss, I. (1974) *The Pan-African Movement.* London: Methuen.
- The slave trade has been the focus of a number of studies, though there are still disagreements on the actual volume of the trade and its impact on Africa. Amongst others, see Davidson, B. (1961) *The African Slave Trade.* Boston: Little Brown, and Lovejoy, P. E. (ed.) (1981) *The Ideology of Slavery in Africa.* Cambridge: Cambridge University Press.

9 | Africa in the contemporary world

Roger Southall

This chapter in outline
- One Africa or many?
- Independence, dependence and decline
- The Cold War in Africa
- Africa and the Middle East
- Structural adjustment and political liberalisation
- Beyond the millennium: disaster or development?

Africa is becoming *less* important to the outside world at the very same time as it is becoming *more* subject to external dictates and constraints. This **marginalisation** is both economic and political. On the one hand, whilst Africa is attracting *less* interest from major economic actors (notably multinational corporations, MNCs, and international banks), its economic strategies and choices are becoming *increasingly* determined by Western-dominated bodies such as the **World Bank**. On the other hand, Africa has become *less* important politically and strategically to world powers with the end of the Cold War, but it is becoming *increasingly* subject to political demands imposed by external creditors. Africa, in short, is today subject to **post-neo-colonialism**: domination not by the former colonial powers and foreign capital, but by international financial institutions (IFIs) (Callaghy, 1991:39–41).

There are those, labelled **Afro-pessimists**, who believe that Africa's marginalisation has left it so behind the rest of the world that, in effect, it has no future other than one of continuing backwardness, poverty, corruption, disorder and misrule. In contrast, there are those who believe that the post-Apartheid, post-Cold War era offers the opportunity for an **African Renaissance**, a decisive shift by Africa towards economic growth, stability and democracy. Yet, such **Afro-optimism** is better tempered by a sympathetic realism that stresses that a better future for Africa is obtainable, but only as a result of the adoption of appropriate and alternative goals and strategies. These may leave Africa at the bottom of the global pile for the foreseeable future, but they will serve to replace resignation and despair with hope and determination by Africans themselves that they *can* take control of their own destiny.

One Africa or many?

When Kwame Nkrumah, the visionary pan-Africanist and first president of Ghana, declared that 'Africa must unite!' he was claiming that Africans could challenge global disparities of power only by pooling the resources of their economically weak and politically divided continent. In contrast, if they failed to unite, Africa would become subject to **neo-colonialism** and **balkanisation**.

Nkrumah was referring principally to the way in which Africa had been carved up by the colonial powers, and arguing that these divisions were artificial and could be overcome by an act of political will. In the event, his call went largely unheeded. Some nationalists opposed the breakup of the colonial federations of French West and Equatorial Africa; Leopold Senghor led Senegal into a pre-independence union with French Soudan in the Federation of Mali (but this broke up just two months after independence in 1960); and Julius Nyerere offered to delay the independence of Tanganyika if this would further the cause of East African unity. But these were merely minor interruptions in a process that saw African colonies proceed to their separate political independence. Occasional attempts to unite states subsequently nearly all failed (the union of Tanganyika with Zanzibar to create Tanzania in 1964 being a rare exception). In turn, the dream of the **Casablanca Group** of states, who proposed that the realisation of **pan-Africanism** required a political union or federation of independent African states, dissolved into the compromise of the **Organisation of African Unity** (OAU), which at its formation in 1963 endorsed the rival conception of the **Monrovia Group**, which argued that African countries would not give up their hard-won independence, and that African harmony should be pursued through continental, international co-operation. Africa was already driven by realism rather than by idealism in international affairs. Today, rather than speaking in unison, there is often a cacophony of voices emanating from over fifty individual African states.

Nkrumah's call for unity may have been premature, yet the balkanisation of Africa highlighted the massive extent of divisions. Africa was fragmented, *inter alia*, by its over two thousand languages; by its religious and cultural differences between Arab and sub-Saharan Africa; by its partition by the colonial powers (Britain, France, Belgium, Portugal, Italy and Spain – and by Germany before World War I); and by its vastness, physical terrain and lack of communications infrastructure. African history had forged many connections across the continent before the arrival of the Europeans, yet in an important sense, it was the construction of a global international system, centred upon the European nation-states and their colonial empires in the nineteenth century, which created the modern idea of 'Africa' as an entity. It was precisely in reaction to the colonial intrusion that nationalists from diverse parts of the continent discovered their commonality and 'Africanness' (Mazrui, 1963). Yet, just as colonialism precipitated this awareness, so it promoted divisions that carried over into the post-colonial era. The political map inherited at independence was based largely on the economic and strategic needs of European imperialists, and entrenched huge differences in size (Sudan is 240 times larger than The Gambia) and in their potentials for nation-formation, development and stability (Gordon, 1996:55).

These divisions were to be hugely exploited by Great Power competition during the Cold War. Even when this cause of conflict was over, all sorts of differences remained. Thus, by the 1990s, the World Bank was identifying three groups of countries in sub-Saharan Africa (SSA): those that were mired in civil strife and social unrest; those (mainly in Eastern and Southern Africa) that had adopted the Bank's macroeconomic reforms and were moving ahead with a development agenda; and those where macroeconomic reforms had only just commenced or had not commenced at all (World Bank, 1995:vi–vii).

When we talk about 'Africa's' relations with the contemporary world, we must be aware of such differences and be cautious about making generalisations.

Independence, dependence and decline

Pre-colonial African societies were no strangers to self-rule, but the new states of decolonised Africa were essentially artificial, colonial creations. Many were extremely small; virtually all were relatively if not very poor; and none of them had been adequately 'prepared' for independence (Tanganyika, for instance, became independent with just six graduates). Elaigwu (1993) argues that in these circumstances, the supreme political struggle in the post-colonial era was to achieve greater coherence in nationhood and greater stability in statehood. But politics also became very much a struggle by rival groups (competing tribes, classes and élites) for resources (wealth, jobs, education and state allocations) that were, in general, in extremely short supply. In these circumstances, the political structures of the new states tended to be simultaneously highly contested and very fragile, and in consequence extremely vulnerable to external influence.

The economies inherited by the new states were underdeveloped and disjointed, with production of a few basic commodities (cash crops or minerals) geared for export and with very small domestic markets. This rendered their development prospects dependent upon the world price of their raw material exports. During the latter half of the 1960s – the 'decade of independence' – these prices were rising, providing the basis for some optimism concerning the future. However, caught short by the oil crisis of 1974 (which saw massive hikes in the price of oil imports), the large majority of African countries (save the few oil-exporters – Libya, Nigeria, Gabon, Angola and Congo), were hit by a marked deterioration in their **terms of trade**, plunging them into debt. Meanwhile, for a variety of reasons (including commitment by a large number of African states to nationalisation of significant sectors of their economies), the level of foreign investment remained low: Africa as a whole attracted only 3% of the world total of such investment between 1965 and 1983. Governments were faced with growing populations and development needs (health, education, infrastructure) but with declining revenues. All this had negative consequences for the rate of growth, which for low-income countries in Africa (the vast majority) declined from 3,9% (or 1,3% per capita) during 1965–1973 to 2,7 (–0,1% per capita) during 1973–1980 (Coquery-Vidrovitch, 1993:301–15). African states, whose needs at independence dictated a search for foreign aid, rapidly became locked into a dependence upon their donor patrons.

In the main, the new states remained tied to their former colonial powers. White governors made way for African presidents, colonial civil servants were replaced by African successors and a new breed of 'expatriate' consultants or aid workers, and hurriedly developed colonial legislatures blossomed (for the moment, at least) into parliaments. However, independence failed to give African governments control over their economies. Indeed, the new states became subject to a new form of imperialism. According to Nkrumah (1965:ix), the essence of this new condition of 'neo-colonialism' was that:

'the state which is subject to it is, in theory, independent and has all the outward trappings of international sovereignty. In reality its economic system and thus its political policy is directed from outside'.

Nkrumah went on to comment that in extreme cases, the troops of the imperial power might garrison the territory of the colonial state and control its government, but that more often neo-colonialist control was exercised through economic or monetary means.

The continuing military influence of the ex-colonial powers was highlighted by the role of the armies bequeathed to the new African states. These were often small and were supposed to have inherited European military traditions, which stressed an abhorrence of military rule, yet the early years of independence saw numerous cases of intervention into the political arena by new African armies: fourteen significant cases between January 1963 and the end of February 1966, and by early 1968 there had been nineteen successful military coups (Gutteridge, 1975:1). The reasons for such intervention were diverse, ranging from protests about pay and conditions to full-blown attempts to capture control of the state, and they were also related to such factors as a lack of legitimacy, lack of hierarchy, and the retention of white officers corps and/or lack of experience of African successors. Yet, the key factor was that the fragility of the new states was such that these armies possessed the 'potential and propensity' to overthrow the existing civil order.

Nkrumah viewed his own overthrow by the military in 1966 as fomented by interests that, in reaction to the socialist orientation and anti-Western thrust of his regime, wanted to re-assert neo-colonialist influence in Ghana. In contrast, although British troops intervened at governments' requests to suppress army mutinies that broke out in Tanganyika, Uganda and Kenya in 1964, the British government generally exhibited a marked reluctance to become involved militarily in African affairs and retained little capacity for speedy intervention on the continent. Against this, most former French colonies signed defence pacts with France, which allowed the former colonial power to station troops on their soil, this being deemed an aid to the stability of their regimes, (as in 1964 when the French intervened to quell an uprising against President Mba's regime in Gabon). These arrangements provided for various interventions to preserve pro-French regimes (as in Côte d'Ivoire in 1964 and 1968), or to replace those no longer acceptable to France (such as the coup against Emperor Bokassa in the Central African 'Empire' in 1979) (Chinweizu, 1993:775). Yet by the 1980s even French forces were to be progressively withdrawn in favour of a highly mobile formation that was established in France for rapid reaction to foreign crises. Overall, the fact that Africa was of only marginal significance to their security interests meant that both France and Britain mainly remained on the sidelines. Allegations that the former colonial powers were systematically involved in promoting coups against unsympathetic regimes are therefore overstated (Gutteridge, 1975:17).

Neo-colonialism operated, rather, at the psychological and economic levels. After independence, noted Ruth First (1970:70), 'metropolitan economic interests stayed behind, and so, too, did a deeply enduring subservience to colonial standards and attitudes'. This was reinforced by direct lobbying by white interests with political decision-makers, and by the influential presence of whites within the highest echelons of the post-colonial bureaucracies. This latter phenomenon was most marked in the former French colonies, for France retained a much closer direct involvement with these through the French community than did Britain through the Commonwealth (the loose intergovernmental 'club' that linked the member states of the former Empire). In contrast, former British colonies seemed rather more ready to diversify their international connections by calling upon the growing swarm of Scandinavians, Canadians, Italians, Germans and so on who were available to offer their advice and technical expertise (Hodder-Williams, 1984:203–204).

There was also economic diversification. The most important development initially was the trend towards multilateral relations within the European Economic Community (EEC). Despite opposition from Germany and the Netherlands, France insisted in 1957, at the time of the signing of the Treaty of Rome (which founded the EEC), that the whole of the European Common Market be opened up to the French and Belgian colonies in Africa. The consequent relationship revolved around three features:

1. the gradual opening up of the markets of 'associated' African countries to the exports of all the member EEC states;
2. the opening of EEC markets to the produce of the associated countries, under special preferential arrangements; and

3. the inauguration of an economic and social investment programme in the associated countries financed by the European Development Fund (EDF).

The initial gains were limited. But as time wore on, in successive rounds of negotiations with the EEC (Yaounde I and II in 1963 and 1966, and Lome I, II and III in 1975, 1980 and 1986), African states began to be more demanding of the special multilateral relationship. They wanted help in developing their economies, notably in the industrial sector, and wanted to obtain an export-price stabilisation programme (to offset the adverse effects upon their economies of wild fluctuations in the world prices of raw materials). In the event, the Lome Conventions represented a major turning point, as following the admission of Britain into the EEC in 1973, the number of associated states – in the Caribbean and Pacific as well as in Africa – rose dramatically. In particular, the establishment in 1975 of STABEX, which to some extent stabilised commodity prices, especially of agricultural produce (by establishing a fund that to some extent compensated exporting countries when world prices of their products fell below a certain level), and in 1980 of SYSMIN (intended to accomplish the same objective for minerals) went some way to establishing greater equity in world trade. Nonetheless, whilst conceding preferential tariffs on the primary products exported by the ACP countries, the EEC continued to want free access to ACP markets (Coquery-Vidrovitch, 1993:302–303).

African countries wanted more than a better return upon their traditional exports. As well as taking control of their economies, they wanted to industrialise. For many governments, this entailed, on the one hand, the adoption of interventionist policies, sometimes dressed up as 'African socialism'; on the other, it implied a bid to attract international investment by Western MNCs.

Increased government control over the 'advanced' industrial sector rarely changed

African countries' ties to the international capitalist system. If anything, it worked to augment their dependence upon Western MNCs and financial institutions as most of the new governments adopted an orthodox Western development programme. Although this provided for the substantial 'Africanisation' of management, the strategy required the maximisation of agricultural and mineral exports to earn the foreign exchange needed to finance the import of machinery and equipment that was needed for the expansion of industry. Where governments sought greater control of operations, for instance by purchasing majority shareholdings of the local subsidiaries of MNCs, they remained dependent upon Western technical expertise and technology, especially in large-scale mining enterprise. Overall, therefore, whilst African economic strategies allowed for a diversification of the sources of overseas investment (notably by encouraging an inflow of capital from the United States and Germany), they did little to challenge continuing dependence on the West (Seidman & Makgetla, 1980:44–53).

This is not to say that African leaderships were without choice. Indeed, the differential responses from Sekou Toure of Guinea and from Houphouet-Boigny of Côte d'Ivoire to the offer of independence by France in 1958, and the alternative economic paths adopted by even neighbouring states – rural socialism by Nyerere in Tanzania, capitalism by Kenyatta in Kenya – indicate that African governments enjoyed significant autonomy (Hodder-Williams, 1984:201). Yet, all were constrained by their historical inheritance of dependence. But, as stressed by Leys (1975:27), the degree to which a country could be characterised as neo-colonial was related to the extent to which the new ruling classes were linked to foreign capitalist power. Furthermore, neo-colonialism was only a phase in historical development, and was likely to give way to other forms or stages of imperialism.

The Cold War in Africa

Prior to decolonisation, Africa was of marginal significance to the competing superpowers. For the United States (US), Africa was (and still is) of far less significance than Asia, the Middle East and Latin America. Initially, therefore, the continent became a **NATO** (North Atlantic Treaty Organisation) protectorate (Chinweizu, 1993:773), under which prime responsibility for keeping ex-colonies within the capitalist camp lay with the former colonial powers, and only when 'communist subversion' was deemed a serious threat did the US intervene directly. But growth of Soviet bloc influence in Africa, and the coming to power of several pro-Soviet and even Marxist regimes, meant that by the mid-1970s the US was becoming much more directly involved in defence of Western interests in Africa.

Serious Soviet interest in Africa was only awakened after World War II, when direction of diplomatic and material aid to anti-colonialist movements was seen as a means for weakening international imperialism. Support for these movements was also granted in recognition that, given the lack of a strong working class in Africa, the leading role in the struggle for national liberation lay with the emergent bourgeoisie and national intelligentsia (Thiam & Mulira, 1993:802).

The independence of African states in the 1960s appeared to offer major opportunities for advance by the Union of Soviet Socialist Republics (the USSR) in an era when the superpowers were prone to adopt a bipolar view of the world, which suggested that they should directly engage the enemy in every serious conflict around the globe. In Africa, this saw the US battling Soviet influence in the Congo. But after bipolarity (*see* Chapter 4) brought the world to the verge of a nuclear war over the Cuban missile crisis in 1963, the superpowers began to accept that conflicts in the third world need not require their involvement or even opposition. Indeed, both the US and the USSR backed the federal government of Nigeria during its civil war against secession by Biafra (1967–1969) where the latter received support from the likes of France, Portugal and South Africa. Nonetheless, the USSR's perception of African nationalism as an anti-imperialist force, and the encouragement it received from states such as Ghana, Mali and Guinea, which rapidly adopted a radical rhetoric and struck up close relations with Moscow, fanned expectations that Africa would be drawn into the socialist orbit.

This simplistic view was rapidly overtaken by events, as African states proved neither reliably socialist nor stable. Two of the most radical regimes were replaced by military coups in Ghana in 1966 and Mali in 1968, followed by the fall of the left-leaning Obote in Uganda in 1971. Meanwhile, the difficulty of African terrain was compounded by the preference of many African states for **non-alignment** between the superpowers, along with the realisation that the USSR could not match the West in the provision of material aid. In addition, some states proved fiercely independent: Egypt expelled the Soviet Union following acute differences in 1973 (just eight months after the delivery of massive consignment of Soviet arms), whilst General Numeiry's government in Khartoum crushed the Sudanese Communist Party (for involvement in an attempted coup) in 1971. These developments indicated that the road to socialism in Africa would be long and hard, and forced a reappraisal of Soviet strategy. Indeed, precisely because of the tendency for African regimes to be replaced, intimate relationships with individual leaders or governments came to be viewed as dangerous (Hodder-Williams, 1984:220–225).

The split in communist ranks between the USSR and China added a further complication. China believed that its own semi-colonial experience put it in good stead to aid decolonisation. However, the assertion by Prime Minister Zhou En Lai in the early 1960s that Africa was 'ripe for revolution' offended more African leaderships than it pleased, and severely blunted China's impact, which was also compromised by that country's absorption with its own affairs during the years of the Cultural Revolution. Subsequently, however, its furnishing of support (including workers willing to work with their bare hands) for the costly Tanzania-Zambia railway project (TAZARA), which Western powers had declined to fund, brought it back into the reckoning. The Chinese challenge for socialist leadership in Africa was also heightened by its provision of aid to a number of liberation movements, notably the Zimbabwe African National Union (ZANU) in Zimbabwe and the Pan Africanist Congress (PAC) of South Africa, which were in competition with rival organisations (ZAPU, the Zimbabwe African People's Union, and the ANC, the African National Congress, of South Africa), which were supported by the Soviet Union (Thiam & Mulira, 1993:804–806).

The increasing complexity of international affairs in Africa meant that the Soviet Union came to have more regard for a country's strategic importance than for its socialist credentials. This in turn meant that, to some extent, African countries were able to play the superpowers off against one another; for example, the radical Derg government in Ethiopia lost US aid after it declared for Marxism-Leninism and concluded an arms deal with the USSR in 1977. In turn, the Somali government of Siad Barre – then in conflict with Ethiopia over the Ogaden – terminated its own links with the USSR and subsequently (in 1980) became a military client of the US (Samatar, 1988:132–143).

But it was precisely because the influence of both the USSR and China increased in strategically sensitive zones of the continent from the mid-1970s (when the US was still bruised by defeat in Vietnam) that Africa was drawn more closely into the orbit of superpower military competition.

This conflict was most intense in Southern Africa, where Western enthusiasm for political decolonisation stopped short of concerted efforts to bring democracy to countries under Portuguese colonial and white settler minority rule. Indeed, continuing occupation of Angola and Mozambique by Portugal, a NATO ally, was seen as providing a shield against nationalist assaults upon white power in South Africa, which, despite its embarrassing ideological espousal of racial superiority via Apartheid, was seen as offering protection for extensive Western investment and for strategic control of the Cape sea route. Growing Soviet support, both diplomatic and military, for selected liberation movements was soon to transform South Africa into a bastion against communism, notably after Ethiopia 'fell' to the Soviet Union in 1977 and right wing governments assumed power in Britain (1979) and the US (1980) under Margaret Thatcher and Ronald Reagan respectively.

The scene for confrontation had been set by the Portuguese coup of 1974 and the resultant abandonment by Portugal of its African colonies. In Mozambique, where the OAU had called for power to be shared between the three major liberation movements, the Soviet Union opted to go beyond the conventionally accepted practice of merely arming and training its clients by backing the MPLA to an unprecedented degree. When the Movimento Popular de Libertacao de Angola (MPLA) initially swept aside the challenge of its domestic competitors, Moscow chose to recognise its regime as the legitimate government. Worse, for the West, was that Nigeria and most of the rest of Africa followed suit. In the face of its past failures in post-colonial Africa, and irked by the slowly but surely growing ideological challenge posed in Africa by China, Moscow badly needed a success. Angola provided it with just the right opportunity.

Direct military involvement would have been at the risk of direct confrontation with the US. As an alternative, therefore, as well as pouring arms and other logistical aid into Angola, the Soviet Union persuaded Cuban troops to assist the MPLA in their post-1976 civil war with their rivals. The strategy was a peculiarly appropriate one: the Cubans were inspired by Fidel Castro's revolutionary fervour, their army was competent, the majority of its personnel were black or brown, Spanish was closely related linguistically to Portuguese, and – what was more – Cuba was

heavily indebted to the USSR and thus readily persuaded to earn its keep (Hodder-Williams, 1984:225).

The alteration of power relations in Southern Africa compelled the West to cash in its chips in Rhodesia. South Africa, which had hitherto provided both military and logistical support to the illegal regime, swiftly concluded that its continuing survival was not viable. A settlement was forged with all the competing nationalist forces, which was meant to secure victory for the United African National Congress of Bishop Abel Muzorewa, who was seen as a safe non-Marxist alternative to Robert Mugabe's Chinese-backed ZANU and Joshua Nkomo's Soviet-backed ZAPU. In the event, the extent of Western miscalculation was such that ZANU secured a victory in the 1980 elections, which enabled it to take power on its own. But, although ZANU subsequently used North Korean troops to quell internal dissent, the Chinese advance in Africa was subsequently snuffed out by Soviet gains.

The final act of colonialism lined up the cast as follows: the USSR, indirectly, and Cuba, directly, backed the MPLA in Angola, whereas UNITA (the National Union for the Total Independence of Angola) was supported indirectly by the US and directly by South Africa. South Africa's particular interest was in denying the South West African People's Organisation (SWAPO) (also backed by the Soviet Union) a base in Angola from which they could establish a military and political presence in Namibia. In Mozambique, the Frente de Libertacao de Mocambique (FRELIMO), also professedly Marxist and aided by the USSR, was confronted by a rebel movement, Resistencia Nacional Moçambicana (RENAMO), which was founded by the Smith regime in Rhodesia but which, after 1980, operated out of South Africa, and had extensive military and intelligence support from the South African security forces. Whilst Namibian independence was stalled by US insistence on 'linkage' (the demand that a democratic settlement in Namibia had to be linked to a Cuban departure from Mozambique), the growing efforts of the

ANC to launch an armed struggle in South Africa itself were contained by Pretoria's shift to 'destabilisation'. This was a strategy that, from the early 1980s, imposed heavy military costs (such as a brutal raid upon Maseru in 1982) upon regional countries that were deemed to be providing safe havens or direct logistical support to the ANC. Because of its own alliance with the South African Communist Party (SACP) and support from Moscow, the ANC was easily depicted by both Pretoria and Washington as being communist rather than nationalist (Hanlon, 1986).

A number of factors eventually led to a democratic settlement in Namibia in 1989. These included the increasing financial burden to Pretoria of continued heavy military involvement in that country and across the border in Angola; a shift in the military balance of forces, notably by the Soviet Union's provision of modern fighters, which gave superiority in the skies to Angola over the ageing planes of the South African air force; and Western pressure via the United Nations (UN) upon both Pretoria and SWAPO to broker a compromise constitution.

South Africa's withdrawal from Namibia was rapidly followed by President de Klerk's announcement in February 1990 that he was unbanning the ANC and other movements in preparation for talks about a democratic settlement. The internal pressures upon the government that led to this were numerous: the costs of containing popular revolt, the contradictions between racial restrictions and the modern industrial economy, divisions within the ruling party and so on. But externally, by far the most telling factor was the collapse of communism. By 1989, the Communist Party of the Soviet Union had wholly lost its domestic legitimacy; the Berlin Wall had crashed, the Eastern European satellite states had begun peeling away; and the USSR could no longer aspire to its status and pretensions as a superpower.

At the very same time as the SACP was wrestling with the ideological implications of the terminal crisis of Russian communism, support for the ANC and SACP was drastically cut back. In turn, the collapse of the 'communist threat' deprived Pretoria of backing by the US and its Western allies, who were now keen to rid themselves of the embarrassment of backing Apartheid. Both the liberation movements and the white regime were drastically weakened, and the key political and military leaders on both sides were forced to recognise that outright victory over the other was beyond their capacity.

As South Africans, they were all faced with the choice of chaos or compromise. Over the course of the next four years, they worked towards the latter, which was sealed by South Africa's first democratic election in April 1994 and the subsequent formation of an ANC-led government of national unity (GNU) under the leadership of President Nelson Mandela.

Africa and the Middle East

Anti-colonial movements had emerged in both North and sub-Saharan Africa after 1945, but whereas decolonisation struggles in the former region highlighted Arab and Islamic sentiments, those further south were guided by universal political values such as self-determination. Arab involvement in Black African independence campaigns was minimal, whereas Black African troops were used by the French against the nationalists in Algeria.

The ambivalent relationship between Arab and Black Africa was initially overcome with the founding of the OAU, which rebuffed ideas of Arab-led African unity (peddled by President Nasser of Egypt) in favour of formalised inclusion of the Arab states in African institutions. The framework for an agreement was laid: North African states would back OAU decisions regarding African liberation movements in international forums, whilst Black Africa would support Arab states in their conflict with Israel over Palestine.

In practice, the pursuit of Afro-Arab unity has been extremely uneven. Chazan & Levine (1991) outline three phases. First, from 1957 to 1973, economic and political ties were elaborated slowly, in the face of a push into Africa, which, by the late 1960s, saw Israel having established diplomatic and other linkages with some thirty-three newly independent countries. But this began to unravel with the 1967 war, which led to Israel occupying Egyptian territory. The OAU voted in 1971 for an Israeli withdrawal and by 1973, all but four African states had broken off diplomatic relations with Jerusalem.

The period 1973 to 1978 saw Afro-Arab relations consolidate, as Israel became increasingly isolated. Key Arab states – Iraq, Saudi Arabia, Syria, Qatar and South Yemen – established diplomatic missions in Africa, as the 1973 oil crisis and the skilful use of financial aid – nearly 25% of all development assistance to the continent during the 1970s – yielded a dramatic increase in Arab assistance, investment and trade in Africa. In 1977, a first Afro-Arab Summit was held in Cairo to firm the alliance.

However, from around 1979–1980, the Arab-African connection began not to dissolve but to weaken and diversify. The causes were multiple. Divisions between Arab states in their responses to the Camp David Accord (which saw Egypt break ranks with Arab efforts to isolate Israel by negotiating a peace deal with Jerusalem) were carried into the OAU; the rise of Islamic fundamentalism gave cause for concern for a number of African governments; the recurrence of a series of boundary demarcation and identity conflicts (notably those concerning POLISARIO Front's bid to wrest Western Sahara from Morocco, the Somali-Ethiopian war over the Ogaden, and the civil war between the Arab Muslim north and the African Christian/animist South in Sudan) tested Arab as well as African allegiances; the rise of Muammar Qadhafi and subsequent Libyan adventurism in Chad aroused anxiety in neighbouring states; and African resentments were provoked by the uneven allocation of Arab aid, with over 50% being directed to just two states, Mauritania and Sudan (both members of the Arab League),

whilst the indebtedness of non-oil producing African states spiralled to pay for oil imports (mostly from Arab producers) whose cost had risen from $700 million in 1973 to some $11 billion in 1980. Finally, and not least important, Black African states reacted adversely to growing evidence of covert links between various Arab states and South Africa in the form of arms deals between Pretoria and Somalia, Iraq and Morocco, purchases of gold by Saudi Arabia and the United Arab Emirates, and the supply of oil and oil-products by a number of Middle East oil producers.

These stresses and strains provided the opportunity for something of a recovery by Israel of its position in Africa. Aid, trade and military links were to some extent resumed, although the large majority of African states preferred to keep relationships relatively informal. Against this, few Black African states could reconcile themselves with how, from the mid-1970s, Israel had forged a close military and diplomatic relationship with South Africa. Meanwhile, Black Africa had rallied to the cause of Palestinian self-determination, and by 1988, some thirty-one states had established full diplomatic relations with the Palestinian Liberation Organisation (PLO).

African states had by now indicated that whilst they would adopt a principled stance regarding Palestinian self-determination, their relations with the Arab states themselves would be determined by considerations of pragmatic self-interest.

Structural adjustment and political liberalisation

By the early 1980s, most African states – whatever their forms of government, whatever their ideologies – were heavily indebted (*see* Chapter 2). As a result, they were driven into the arms of international financial institutions (IFIs), notably the International Monetary Fund (IMF) and the World Bank, which offered to provide the necessary credit only if African governments would agree to make sweeping economic reforms.

Major controversy surrounds the reasons for Africa's economic malaise, but there is widespread agreement that the origins of the debt crisis lie, in considerable part, in the limitations of the development model adopted at independence, albeit with variations from country to country. As elaborated above, this saw African states attempting to maximise revenues from the export of primary commodities (crops and minerals) in order to pay for capital imports that were needed to develop physical infrastructure and local industries. Whether driven by local or foreign investment, these industries were typically geared to capturing protected local markets rather than to competing internationally. Ironically, therefore, the greater the success of internally oriented local industry, the greater the need for capital imports, and the worse the balance of trade. Meanwhile, external indebtedness was also being increased by the rising cost of public services and in most states by the '**rent-seeking**' behaviour of an expanding civil service. Easy access to 'petrodollars' (savings invested in commercial banks by oil-producing states and subsequently re-lent to needy borrowers) initially enabled African (and other third world) states to negotiate the immediate effects of the 1973 oil crisis, but by the early 1980s, many African countries were so heavily indebted that they could not repay their loans. Bankruptcy forced them to turn to the IMF and World Bank (Williams 1994).

The 'structural adjustment programmes' (SAPs) imposed upon their African borrowers by the IMF and World Bank (*see* Table 9.1) typically involved a lifting of all market restrictions, such as the relaxation of tariffs and taxes, to encourage inward investment and external trade; a concomitant liberalisation of the labour market, to lower wage costs; and a radical cutback of government expenditure, involving the abolition of price controls and subsidies on basics, such as food and fuel, the raising of charges for services (such as health and education), the reduction of the number of government employees and the

Table 9.1: IMF and World Bank

Country	Period of formal engagement
Benin	1987–
Burkina Faso	1991–
Burundi	1986–
Cameroon	1989–
Central African Republic	1987
Chad	1987–1991
Congo	1987–1990
Côte d'Ivoire	1981–1988
Gabon	1988–
Gambia, The	1986–
Ghana	1985–
Guinea	1986–
Guinea-Bissau	1985–
Kenya	1980–
Madagascar	1987–
Malawi	1981–
Mali	1988–
Mauritania	1987–
Mozambique	1987–
Niger	1986–
Nigeria	1986–
Rwanda	1991–
Senegal	1981–1983
	1986–
Sierra Leone	1986–1987
Tanzania	1987–
Togo	1983–
Uganda	1987–
Zambia	1986–1987
Zimbabwe	1991–

Ponte (1994:556)

IDA structural adjustment lending under SAL, (1980–1985), SFSSA and SPA (1980–1993)	World Bank structural adjustment lending under SAL (1986–1993)	IMF SAF	IMF ESAF
SAP I, 1989; SAP II, 1991	–	1987–1992	1993
SAP I, 1991	–	1991–1992	1993
SAP I, 1986; SAP II, 1988; SAP III, 1992	–	1986–1990	1991–1993
–	SAL 1989	–	–
SAP I, 1987; SAP II, 1998; SAP III, 1990	–	1987–1991	–
–	–	1987–1991	–
–	SAL 1987	–	–
–	SAL I, 1981; SAL II, 1981; SAL III, 1986	–	–
–	SAL 1988	–	–
SAP I, 1986; SAP II, 1989	–	1986–1988	1988–1991
ERP 1985–1986; SAP I, 1987 (supplemented 1988); SAP II, 1989 (supplemented 1991)	–	1987–1988	1988–1992
SAP I, 1986; SAP II, 1988 (supplemented 1992)	–	1987–1990	1991–1993
ERP 1985–1986; SAP I, 1987; SAP II, 1989	–	1987–1990	–
SAL I, 1980; SAL II 1982	–	1988–1991	1989–1992
–	–	1987–1990	1989–1992
SAL I, 1981; SAL II, 1983; SAP III, 1985	–	–	1988–1993
SAP I, 1991	–	1988–1991	1992–1993
SAP I, 1987	–	1987–1988	1989–1993
ERP 1992	–	1987–1990	1990–1993
SAP 1986	–	1986–1988	1988–1991
-	SAP I, 1986*	–	–
SAP I, 1991	–	1991–1993	–
SAP II, 1986; SAP III, 1987 (supplemented 1989) SAP IV, 1990 (supplemented 1991–1992)	SAL I, 1980	1986–1988	1988–1992
–	–	1986–1987	–
–	–	1987–1991	1991–1993
SAL I, 1983; SAP II, 1986; SAP III, 1988 (supplemented 1989, 1990); SAP IV, 1991	–	1988–1989	1989–1993
ERP 1988 (supplemented 1989); ERP II, 1990 (supplemented 1991–1992); SAP I, 1992	–	1987–1989	1989–1993
ERP 1986; ERP 1991 (supplemented 1992)	–	–	–
SAP I, 1991	–	–	1992–1993

Notes: SAF = Structural Adjustment Facility; ESAF = Enhanced Structural Adjustment Facility; ERP = Economic Recovery Programme; SAP = Structural Adjustment Programme; SAL = Structural Adjustment Lending; SPA = Special Programme of Assistance; SFSSA = Special Facility for Sub-Saharan Africa

Notes: * = Nigeria did not formally receive loans from the international finance institutions under the structural adjustment facilities. The SAP launched in 1986 was accompanied by a $425 million loan from the World Bank, called a 'Trade Policy and Export Development Loan', and an IMF stand-by agreement for SDR650 million. (SDR = Special drawing rights, the 'currency' of the IMF).

privatisation of nationalised industries. Central to this strategy was a devaluation of fixed and overvalued currencies, and a shift towards unfettered foreign exchange, the latter which was designed to encourage exports, discourage imports and eliminate unofficial currency markets and smuggling. This focus upon export-led growth and the minimalist state was designed to create an 'enabling environment', one that maximised the opportunity for market forces to operate freely (Callaghy, 1991:51).

There has been little agreement about the results of SAPs save that they have been remarkably uneven. Generally speaking, the IFIs insist that, despite the mistakes they have made, structural adjustment is working. The World Bank concedes that SSA countries not pursuing SAPs performed better during 1980–1984 than those that were, but argues that the situation was reversed thereafter. From 1987 through 1990, data for twenty core reforming countries is said to indicate that gross domestic product (GDP) grew by 4% a year, exports and investment grew even faster and a decline in real per capita consumption was arrested. In contrast, the economies of non-reforming countries deteriorated or stagnated. GDP growth slowed to an average of 2,2% a year, investment increased moderately but gross savings fell, and real per capita consumption continued to decline (Husain & Underwood, 1991:16).

Against this, a host of critics not only dispute the basic argument that reforming countries have outperformed non-reformers, but also argue that what success has been obtained is fragile and has often been achieved at too great a cost. Some reforming countries may have succeeded in attracting foreign capital, yet too often the measures they have taken have increased rather than decreased the level of foreign debt (the major point of the exercise). Furthermore, the emphasis on export promotion and openness to international markets in reforming countries such as Ghana, Uganda, Tanzania and Côte d'Ivoire 'has [had] negative (sometimes disastrous) consequences for food supplies, the viability of local

manufacturing, investment in social overhead capital and infrastructure and the welfare of the poorest and weakest members of society' (Bush & Szeftel, 1994:152).

Broadly speaking, the debate about SAPs was conducted throughout the 1980s between the 'neo-liberals', who favoured reform as envisioned by the IFIs, and the 'structuralists', who argued that the cure has been worse than the disease. Central to their disagreement was that whereas the former viewed the state (especially as it was found in post-colonial Africa) as the key obstacle to growth, the latter located the main barriers to development in the combination of social and economic structures, both internal and external. Not surprisingly, the structuralist position was favoured by many African governments and, not least, the UN's Economic Commission for Africa, which continued to argue the virtues of Africa pursuing a strategy of internal self-reliance rather than engaging with the world economy. However, by the end of the decade, the World Bank had shifted from its previously vehemently anti-statist position to one that recognised that the experience of fast-growing Asian economies indicated that, whilst the production of goods should be left to the market, the state could take a leading role in building human resources, and administrative and physical infrastructural capacity (Callaghy, 1991:57–62).

This policy shift combined with a global development – the revolt against authoritarianism – to produce an emphasis on political conditionality by the IFIs. The demand for the minimal state gave way to the search for 'good governance', for a state that would provide a socio-economic environment that would facilitate structural reform by, *inter alia*, attacking corruption, fostering transparency and accountability to representative bodies, promoting the rule of law, and encouraging public debate and participation.

In the context of the early 1990s, this liberal agenda fairly swiftly became transformed into an explicit call for political pluralism and liberal democracy. This combined with growing internal popular pressures upon some authoritarian governments (these often generated by the social stresses generated by economic reform) to liberalise politically. In Southern Africa, for instance, a return to multipartyism and competitive elections saw incumbent ruling parties replaced in Zambia and Malawi, and a military regime replaced by a democratically elected government in Lesotho. But, as ever, the results of conditionality were uneven and the lessons remain confusing, as much to real-life participants in the African drama as to analysts.

As the continent approaches the new century, the IFIs and African rulers alike remain uncertain whether political conditionality promotes or throws up more obstacles to sustained economic reform (Baylies, 1995).

Beyond the millennium: disaster or development?

This all-too-brief review indicates that the restructuring of African countries' relations with the external world since the 1960s has been a very mixed experience. African dignity and self-assurance has been enhanced by decolonisation and liberation from white minority oppression, but the post-colonial aftermath has thrown up as many dilemmas as it has resolved, whether these relate to wars between states, wars within states, ethnic conflict, or the problems of combining the quest for growth with the construction of civil order in the face of countless counter-pressures. If many of these difficulties were entrenched and extended by the Cold War, the key question posed by the post-Cold War period is whether Africa can avoid further marginalisation.

In all probability, there are no straightforward answers, nor are there answers that apply equally to each and every state or region. Any dichotomy between Afro-pessimists, who predict that African states seem set to become more peripheral (for example, Harbeson & Rothchild, 1991:1), and Afro-optimists, who predict that 'Africa will

prosper' (Mbeki, 1997), is consequently overdrawn. The more likely outcome is that the different states of Africa face a variety of different futures, depending on a wide array of factors ranging from the policies they adopt, the leadership they enjoy, their possession of resources, their proximity to markets, and their skill or good fortune in avoiding being drawn into civil or international conflicts.

Nonetheless, it is apposite to conclude with three observations. The first is that, given current global economic trends and Africa's own improving but still poor performance, it seems likely that increasing dependence and marginalisation are likely to be the lot of many if not most (especially sub-Saharan) countries. Differentiation between the already relatively advantaged and the less advantaged states is likely to increase. A 'third world' Africa will co-exist alongside a nightmarish 'fourth' and 'fifth world' Africa, perhaps even *within* the confines of a single state.

Second, despite the limitations imposed by a post-neocolonial world order, African states will retain a marked degree of political and economic choice. This will not relate, as it did for the first generation of leaders, to the extent to which African countries should strive for self-reliance rather than dependent development, for an indebted, poverty-stricken, technologically backward Africa now has no realistic choice but to engage with the world economy. Instead, African states will be called on to play a central role in deciding the balance between state and market, for although many of them are presently very weak, the IMF and World Bank now recognise that it is necessary for the capacity of states to be increased if neo-liberal strategies are to be effectively implemented. Paradoxically, stronger states will be more able to make real decisions about how they should interact with the external market. In turn, this could enhance the capacity of African states as a bloc or set of blocs to assert their collective interest in world forums, perhaps to challenge ways in which the rules of the global game favour the rich at the expense of the poor.

Third, although the constraints imposed by the global system severely limit the range of options available to African states, they do not justify an intellectual surrender, for there will be alternatives to the strategies touted by the IFIs:

'It is possibly time to worry rather less about who will dominate the world-system next or where the challenges to it will come from: they will not come from Africa. Nor is Africa likely to produce another Korea or even Malaysia, in the early decades of the next century. In the immediate future we need a more basic approach to Africa's crises and solutions, one which sets more modest, and achievable targets' (Bush & Szeftel, 1995:299).

Such an agenda is very distant from the grandiose visions held for Africa by its political leaders at independence, but it is probable that it will be of considerable greater value to the continent and to its citizens over the course of the coming century.

Key concepts in this chapter

Afro-optimism
Afro-pessimism
Cold War
Dependence
Marginalisation
Neo-colonialism
Neo-liberalism
Pan-Africanism
Post-neocolonial world order
Structural adjustment

Suggested readings

For good reviews of the current political and economic challenges faced by Africa in view of global trends, see
* Callaghy, T. (1991) 'Africa and the world economy: caught between a rock and a hard place.' In Harbeson, J. & Rothchild, D. (eds). *Africa in World Politics*, pp. 39–68. Boulder: Westview Press;
* Gordon, A. & Gordon, D. (1996) *Understanding Contemporary Africa*. Boulder: Lynne Rienner Publishers;
* Coquery-Vidrovitch C. (1993) 'Economic changes in Africa in the world context.' In Mazrui, A. *Africa since 1935. General History of Africa*, Vol. VIII, pp. 285–316. California: Heinemann & UNESCO; and
* Harbeson, J. & Rothchild, D. (1991) *Africa in World Politics*. Boulder: Westview Press.

The relations between Africa and the Middle East are discussed very usefully in
* Harbeson, J. & Rothchild, D. (1991) 'Africa in post-Cold War international politics: changing agendas.' In Harbeson, J. & Rothchild, D. (eds). *Africa in World Politics*, pp. 1–15. Boulder: Westview Press.

An excellent case study of neo-colonialism in action is
* Leys, C. (1975) *Underdevelopment in Kenya: The Political Economy of Neo-Colonialism*. London: Heinemann Educational Books.

Current World Bank thinking on Africa can be sampled in

* World Bank. (1995) *A Continent in Transition: Sub-Saharan Africa in the Mid-1990s*. Oxford: Oxford University Press.

10 | Africa's international relations

Maxi Schoeman

This chapter in outline
- Introduction: the features of the African state
- Aspects of African states and their impact on the international relations of these states
  - Poor, quasi states
  - Armed conflict between and inside states
  - African unity: whose unity at what cost?
- Patterns of African international relations
  - Non-state and 'de-stated' international relations
  - International relations at the state level
- Conclusion

Introduction: the features of the African state

A number of characteristics distinguish Africa and African states from the rest of the international system (*see* Chapter 4). These are, *inter alia*, as follows:

- Statehood was imposed on African societies, resulting in artificial borders (*see* Box 10.1) that in many instances separated communities and even created 'new' ethnic groups. Furthermore, African states are underdeveloped and weak, a condition related to the artificiality of these states and therefore, to some extent, to the legacy of colonial rule.

- Africa is the least developed continent on earth, suffering the highest levels of human insecurity, deprivation and poverty. It is the women who suffer most and they are often referred to in the literature as 'the poorest of the poor'. Sub-Saharan Africa (SSA) has the highest percentage of **absolute poverty** in the world with 62% of its population living in this condition, compared with 25% of Asia's population and 35% of Latin America (Todaro, 1997:44).

- In the aftermath of the Cold War, Africa is suffering from a number of intra-state civil wars and from other forms of violent social upheaval and conflict. The nature of this conflict is captured in the term **new conflict paradigm**. Some of these conflicts originated during the Cold War era and have persisted or intensified throughout the 1990s.

- Since the early years of independence, the distinguishable feature of intra-African relations has been the endeavour by African governments to pursue and manage African politics on a continental scale. This objective finds its ultimate expression in the idea of **African unity** or **pan-Africanism** and is institutionally embodied in the Organisation of African Unity (OAU).

Box 10.1: A perspective on the problems of colonial demarcation

'From the viewpoint of what was subsequently to become Africa's "international relations", the colonial interlude, however short, was critical. The previously fuzzy borderlands between indigenous centres of government, together with the large areas which possessed no formalised government structures at all, were replaced ... by precisely demarcated frontiers of the sort that European concepts of statehood deemed necessary. As has often been pointed out, these frontiers were rarely guided by any concern for the identity of indigenous states, societies or ecological units, though some precolonial monarchies were redefined as colonial territories; in some cases, such as what are now the [Democratic Republic of] Congo and Zambia, the process of demarcation reached an astonishing level of cartographical improbability.'

Clapham (1996:31)

The above characteristics form the central theme of this chapter and the extent to which they drive inter-African relations forms the lens through which these relations are studied in this chapter. The purpose is to describe and explain how African states *and* societies interact on the basis of and as a result of the characteristics identified above. In this way, students are made aware of the fact that in Africa, relations across national borders are not conditioned or conducted only in the formal sphere, that is, between governments as the representatives of states. There are many ties at the societal and economic levels that also make for interaction between countries and this interaction in turn influences the foreign, and quite often domestic, policies of governments.

The chapter starts with a discussion of each of the above characteristics. Because Chapter 11 deals in some detail with the first two characteristics, they are given only scant attention while the third and fourth characteristics – those of intra-state conflict and the idea of African unity – are given more detailed consideration. In the next section, the response of African governments to these phenomena and processes is dealt with and attention is also paid to non-state actors that have an impact on relations between states in Africa and African states and the rest of the international system. In this way, we deal with the factors and conditions that shape the external relations of African states and also look at the way in which these relations have been conducted. Students will pick up a basic rule of the study of International Relations in the way that this chapter is written, that is, that it is impossible to discuss international relations without paying attention to the domestic environment, politics and conditions of states. Domestic concerns and issues impact heavily on international relations and need to be considered if the international relations of states are to be understood. The focus in this chapter is mainly on SSA and unless otherwise indicated, facts and figures are derived from *Africa at a Glance* (Africa Institute, 1997).

Aspects of African states and their impact on the international relations of these states

Poor, quasi states

Reference is often made to the artificial way in which the boundaries of states in Africa were determined. The Berlin Conference of 1884 set the scene for what became known as the 'scramble for Africa'. Without regard for existing **systems of rule**, the colonial powers staked their claims to African territories. These claims reflected the goals of status and prestige of the colonial states and their economic needs and interests. The **Westphalian** states of Europe developed over centuries to reflect compromises

between rulers and ruled, and rulers amongst each other. These states came to form **units of production** and **units of meaning,** thereby making social, cultural and economic sense. In contrast, African states were 'created' and statehood was imposed at independence regardless of logic or historical, social, economic and political conditions (*see* Schoeman, 1998).

The resulting quasi states (quasi in comparison with their Northern counterparts and their position in the international political economy) were therefore confronted by two major threats to their viability. The first was the skewed distribution of resources across national borders and the second was the lack of social and political coherence inside these states, an aspect that is dealt with in more detail in Chapter 11 and other chapters in this book.

Armed conflict between and inside states

Conflict between states

In stark contrast with the history of Europe, which is littered with inter-state wars up to the end of World War II, Africa has been characterised by relative peace between its states. This does not mean that conflict, tensions and disagreements between states do not occur. There are still numerous border or territorial disputes between African countries, most notably, in the late 1990s, those between Botswana and Namibia over Sedudu/Kasikili Island in the Chobe River (*see* Box 10.2) and the violent clashes between Eritrea and Ethiopia, which flared up in May 1998. Besides the Ethiopean-Eritrean war, these disagreements seldom spill over into actual war between conflicting parties. The most serious inter-state conflicts between African states have been those between Algeria and Morocco in 1963 and between Somalia and Ethiopia in the era 1964–1967 and 1977–1978, both of which were related to border disputes. In studying this section, students are encouraged to make use of the

Box 10.2: A border dispute in Southern Africa

The dispute between Namibia and Botswana over the territorial ownership of Kasikili Island (known as Sedudu Island in Tswana) illustrates two points about African territoriality and borders. The small island in the Chobe River, submerged during certain times of the year (and therefore uninhabitable on a permanent basis) is used by cattle farmers from both countries for grazing and by peasants for fishing. Both countries claim that their people have been using the grazing for centuries. Both countries claim the island. This dispute illustrates the following: colonial borders are in many cases artificial, actually causing disputes rather than settling them. Secondly, as pressure on natural resources increases, such disputes may become more pronounced. In the case of Kasikili Island, there is no longer enough grazing for the number of animals belonging to both 'sides' with the result that relations between the two neighbours have become strained, with Botswana exhibiting a military presence on the island and hoisting the Botswana flag. To dismiss the dispute as insignificant because it concerns a little-known island that is not even inhabited would be a grave mistake. This kind of conflict might actually increase in Africa with its skewed resource-distribution patterns. The dispute also illustrates the value that African states attach to colonial borders and the OAU's 1964 resolution on the inviolability of African borders. In a formal declaration in 1992 Namibia's Foreign Affairs minister declared: '[T]he government accepts the Anglo-German Treaty of 1890 which established the boundary in question between the two countries ... Consequently, Kisikili Island was accepted by both Britain and Germany as forming an integral part of German South West Africa which is today Namibia'. ['The Kasikili Island situation: Statement made in the National Assembly, Namibia, 26 May 1992 by Theo-Ben Gurirab', reproduced in SAPEM (1992:24–27)].

maps provided in this book for general geographic orientation.

A rather unique form of international/inter-state conflict was that of South Africa's **destabilisation** of its neighbours during the late 1970s and the 1980s. This was a combination of internal conflict with external involvement in neighbouring states in an attempt to safeguard and protect the Apartheid regime in South Africa. The military dimension of destabilisation involved support and even active participation in the civil wars in Zimbabwe (at that stage Rhodesia), Angola and Mozambique, and military incursions into Botswana, Swaziland and Lesotho (*see* Barber & Barratt, 1990:parts V and VI).

What does distinguish Africa from the rest of the international system, though, is the very high incidence of civil wars, unrest and armed conflict occurring *within* states, often with spillover effects for neighbouring countries. Although much emphasis is usually placed on the civil wars on the continent in the post-Cold War era, care should be taken not to create the impression that civil war is a phenomenon peculiar to this era. In fact, various forms of civil war and conflict have characterised Africa ever since independence, and even earlier, if liberation wars fought against colonial powers are taken into account. Yet, civil wars increased dramatically after 1989. For the purposes of this chapter two types of civil war can be distinguished in Africa, namely separatist wars or insurgencies, and wars for control of the state. The term 'war' does not necessarily refer to instances of conventional warfare, but to a whole range of violent conflict activities, such as guerrilla warfare and low-intensity armed conflicts.

Armed conflict inside states

Separatist wars

Separatist wars refer to those wars fought by groups within countries, overwhelmingly regionally based, for independence, that is, for the creation of separate states. There are a number of examples of these wars that also had clear-cut international dimensions and saw international involvement, in many cases shaping the relations between African states, and between these states and the external community, both bilaterally and unilaterally. The first was the Congolese civil war of the early 1960s. The country would later be known as Zaïre and again underwent a change of name in 1997, becoming the Democratic Republic of the Congo (DRC). Limited space does not allow for a comprehensive discussion of the Congolese civil war (for more detail, *see* Bennett, 1995:168–171). To give some idea, though, of the scope and intensity of this conflict, we can mention that the Congo crisis involved a struggle for leadership of the country, with, at one stage during the war, four different leaders and factions claiming to be governing the country. It was also a war of secession with the country's richest province, Katanga, and Kasai province fighting for independence from the Congo.

The international dimension to this inter-state war served to complicate and extend the war. On the one hand, the United Nations (UN) attempted to restore order and stability to the country. It launched the UN Congo Operation (ONUC), which turned out to be its most expensive peacekeeping operation in the pre-1990 era, lasting from 1961 to 1963, and eventually managed to retain the territorial unity of the country, though fighting would continue, intermittently, until 1967. On the other hand, the continued Belgian intervention served to prolong the war.

When foreign intervention (extra-continental) in the internal wars of African states is mentioned, it is often taken to refer to the era of the Cold War. In other words, foreign intervention is seen as a product of the rivalry that existed between the United States (US) and the (then) Union of Soviet Socialist Republics (USSR) (as happened in Angola). The Nigerian civil war of 1967–1970 belies this assumption. The war broke out when Biafra declared its independence from the Nigerian federal state. As is so often the case with inter-governmental organisations, intervention in the internal affairs of the organisation's

strongest, biggest and richest members is hardly possible or ever contemplated. The Organisation of African Unity (OAU) was of little, if any, help in bringing the war to an end. But two great powers, Britain (the former colonial power) and France, got involved in the war. In the case of Britain, involvement was, as far as possible, kept out of the public eye – military assistance in the form of arms supplies to the Nigerian government was limited and the involvement was justified in the name of mutual Commonwealth membership. France also avoided becoming too openly involved in the conflict, channelling its support to the Biafran forces through two proxy states – Côte d'Ivoire and Gabon. French involvement stemmed from De Gaulle's African policy, which aimed to build French influence on the continent and particularly in West Africa. One way of doing this, it was reasoned, would be to break up the strongest Anglophone country in the region (Nigeria). French military support was instrumental in prolonging the civil war by eighteen months.

A last example in the category of separatist internal wars in Africa is that of Ethiopia and the decade-long struggle for Eritrean independence. The struggle for Eritrean independence was led by the Eritrean People's Liberation Front (EPLF) and involved a low-intensity war from the 1950s until independence was eventually gained in 1993. Eritrea does not, however, represent 'the first crack' in the rule of the inviolability of African borders as accepted by the OAU. If anything, it actually reinforces this principle. During the colonial era, Eritrea was administered as a separate Italian colony. After World War II, when the former colonies of the Axis powers were put under UN trusteeship with a view to gaining their independence, the UN General Assembly voted for Eritrea's incorporation into Ethiopia. The Eritrean claim to the right to independence was, in fact, based on the original colonial borders agreed upon by the colonial powers and therefore does not constitute a precedent for other secessionist movements on the continent.

Armed conflict inside states to determine who controls the state

The second category of intra-state conflict in Africa centres on the struggle for control of the state, often involving heavy external intervention and involvement in the conflict. Various further types of this form of civil war or unrest can be distinguished, depending on the identity of the insurgents and the reason for wanting control of the state. We will limit ourselves to two types. The first is that of struggles based on or supported by mass movements or large sections of the population with the aim of gaining control of the government for large-scale democratic transformation. The second type is struggles by small groups, with or without large-scale support from the population, whose aim is control of the state and not necessarily only the government, for personal benefit. The latter is sometimes cloaked in the terminology of the former, yet the new rulers usually quickly revert to their true and original aims once they gain control of the state.

An example of the first type of civil war, aimed at major transformation of the government and regime into a democracy, is that of the liberation struggle of the South West African People's Organisation (SWAPO) in Namibia during the 1960s and 1970s. This low-intensity conflict, largely confined to the northern borders of Namibia in terms of its military dimension, saw large-scale international involvement in the conflict itself, and in its solution, from external states and non-governmental organisations (NGOs).

A second type of intra-state armed conflict, one aimed at personal gain, is much less legitimate in the eyes of the external community, though this does not necessarily mean that external involvement would not be forthcoming in trying to find solutions to the conflict. Furthermore, these wars are often a result of, or aided by, the weakness of the states in which they take place (*see* Chapter 11), thereby complicating foreign intervention even in those cases where it might have been or was forthcoming. The civil war in Somalia in the early 1990s, following decades of steady state and institutional decay, left the international community with the question of how to intervene and with whom to negotiate. In effect, there was no government with which to negotiate and none of the warlords had a clear-cut mandate to negotiate on behalf of the 'state' or had the credentials to imply legitimacy. Clearly, in these cases, civil war is driven by sectional and élitist interests in taking control of the state, often coercing the local population into support or acquiescence and causing indescribable suffering and insecurity to civilians.

African unity: whose unity at what cost?

It was mentioned in the introduction that one of the defining characteristics of inter-African governmental relations is the commitment to manage African affairs on a continental scale and that this aim finds institutional expression in the existence of the OAU. The slogans 'African unity' and 'African solidarity' have become, over the years, rather problematic. The original idea of pan-Africanism and African unity, propagated by the first generation of African leaders, such as Ghana's Nkrumah and Senegal's Leopold Senghor, involved a social movement that would reduce Africa's strong ties with its former colonial masters and the developed world in general, and that would draw the continent together into ever-increasing integration. Yet the very qualities of African states discussed above resulted in the idea of African unity being turned into the unity and solidarity of African governments in the face of internal threats to their survival as rulers and external criticism of their often brutal or authoritarian rule.

The principle of African unity in its distorted version, which supports rulers to the exclusion of the ruled, that is, the *people* of Africa, has made it difficult for international coalitions to form around action against recalcitrant governments or for finding solutions to large-scale internal upheavals in some countries. Add to this economic and other interests, such as regional domination by the 'culprit' state, and the almost impossibility of action becomes clear. African unity may even be an excuse for inaction due to intimidation or fear.

In effect, African unity, so highly prized by African leaders and so often invoked by them at the rhetorical level, whether at economic summits or in the face of state collapse and large-scale abuse of human rights, hides these abuses and deprivations, papers over the structural weaknesses of many African countries and, worse, often serves to protect authoritarian regimes. In the political realm, African unity became the ultimate weapon in defending **juridical sovereignty**, which could be used to prop up failing **political sovereignty**. In the economic sphere, attempts to utilise the concept 'African unity' to promote co-operation with a view to economic development have fared slightly better in the sense that the concept has not been stigmatised. The second part of this chapter deals with various levels of the international relations of African states, covering state and non-state relations, and focusing on bilateral relations with states in the external environment (mostly former colonial powers), regional attempts at co-operation and continental relations as represented by the OAU.

Patterns of African international relations

Paraphrasing Chazan *et al.* (1992:324), the international relations of African states may perhaps best be summarised as the expression and strategies of states with diverse national conditions and a commonality of purpose in the pursuit of economic development and state survival. Various aspects and levels of Africa's international relations can be distinguished, mostly related to the various aspects and characteristics of these states discussed in the first part of this chapter.

The term 'international' relations implies that what is examined here is largely the formal relations between states as conducted at the official, governmental level. Such an approach, though, would lose much of what is important in understanding Africa and we therefore distinguish here between formal relations and non-state or non-governmental relations, starting with the latter. The term 'international' therefore denotes relations *across* borders as well as between groups and governments in different states.

Non-state and 'de-stated' international relations

When we examine the international relations of Africa in the case where these relations do not pertain only to formal relations between the governments of countries, two patterns of cross-border or transnational non-state interaction can be distinguished. The first is that of cross-border alliances and contacts that may be largely ascribed to the artificiality of African borders. These are non-state international relations. Such interaction may not necessarily have any direct or obvious impact on any of the governments involved, that is, on the state at the formal level, but may make **nation-building** difficult, because the primary loyalties of people may not be to the state, but to a specific group that transcends national borders. This does not mean, though, that such relations are not important in their own right. Depending on our perspective, particularly the place accorded to *people* in the way that we study international relations, and on our definition of and expectations of the functions of the state, such relations may be crucial in understanding the socio-economic and political environment in which we find ourselves (*see* Chapter 7, which deals with non-state actors).

If we take as a starting point the assumption that states exist and have developed because they are useful and efficient as a system of rule that mediates relations between people, distributes resources authoritatively and provides security and welfare to its inhabitants, it is clear that much emphasis is placed on what states can do for people. At the same time, African states seldom manage to fulfil these tasks. It is therefore to be expected that other systems of rule or social organisation aimed at fulfilling people's needs, both materially and non-materially, will persist or develop alongside that of the state. The question then becomes whether the state is still a necessary actor. This is one of the most problematic questions to answer, particularly in the context of Africa and in the sense of the relationship between state and population, in other words, in terms of the domestic functions and functioning of the state (*see* Chapters 4 and 11).

Non-state international relations

In certain cases, states as governments, administrations and bureaucracies have collapsed to the point of being largely non-existent. Somalia in the mid-1990s is a case in point. In other cases, the state was taken over and run almost exclusively as a source of revenue and power for the benefit of a personal ruler or a very small élite. In both instances, people had to adapt to the lack of any semblance of government, by setting up their own survival mechanisms and systems of governance. The development of the grass-roots economy in Mozambique, a result of state failure during and in the aftermath of the civil war in that country, is an instance of such a bottom-up attempt at creating order or ensuring survival, or taking advantage of local needs for self-enrichment. This economy developed close ties with, for instance, the South African economy. Many Mozambican traders get their products from South Africa, often by means of smuggling and also through the operations of crime syndicates. Cross-border smuggling of small arms, stolen vehicles and drugs is one of the biggest problems facing both South Africa and Mozambique. Smuggling of other commodities deprives the Mozambican government of much-needed tax revenue in the form of customs and excise duties. This undermining of the state's ability to collect revenue in its turn contributes to the failure of the state to fulfil its functions, thereby further

undermining its legitimacy.

But the operation of informal or black markets across borders is not limited to groups within society as described above. Very often office bearers within governments and governments themselves abuse their positions to participate in and benefit from illegal trading and other business deals with international companies. Such deals are obviously kept secret as far as possible, but from time to time they do come to light. So, for instance, Mobutu, during his presidency of the former Zaïre, signed an agreement with a German company, OTRAG, in 1976, which gave the company a virtual free run of a large area of the country (150 000 square kilometres). The agreement made provision for: 'the right to possess and use the territory without restriction for the purpose of launching missiles into the atmosphere and into space ... and to take all measures which, in the opinion of OTRAG, are related directly, indirectly or otherwise' (Young & Turner, 1985:387–388).

At times, such deals resulted in direct involvement of business people in the politics of the 'host' state. For instance, Clapham relates that the British company LonRho under its previous chairman, Rowland, provided an aircraft in 1971 'at a critical moment to help President Jaafer al-Nemery of Sudan defeat an attempted *coup d'état*' (Clapham, 1996:253). This form of conducting international relations is problematic, particularly because it reinforces the inability of many states, such as Liberia, Nigeria and Sierra Leone, to name but three, to develop political structures with legitimacy that are acceptable to and therefore supported by the population. Corruption and black marketeering become a way of life in which order, stability, predictability and due process of the law play a small, if any, role in building the state or the nation. These forms of relations cannot be classified as 'de-stated' international relations, as are the examples in the following paragraphs. The reason is that although 'states' are involved in these relations, it is a case of individuals within government or the bureaucracy who use their positions and the status conferred upon them as representatives of the state to enrich themselves or to remain in control of the state. For those students who are interested in the impact of corruption on the people of Africa, the novels of Ben Okri and Chinua Achebe, and Es'kia Mpahlele's *Chirundu* will provide a picture of life in such societies.

'De-stated' international relations

The second pattern of international relations that cannot be classified as being inter-state, due to the mix of actors involved in these relations, is also related to what can be termed 'de-stated' international relations. This term refers to instances of international relations between African states and non-state actors where the nature and impact of the relations are of importance to international relations in its broadest sense. The end of the Cold War, and therefore political-strategic interest in Africa, and economic **globalisation** meant the **marginalisation** of Africa and the continent becoming less important in the global economy. The result is less interest in Africa on the side of the once superpowers and other big powers. At the same time, the growth of a strong international civil society has meant that non-state actors in the form of humanitarian relief organisations, other charities, human rights organisations and conservation groups have become increasingly involved in Africa. Their interest in Africa reflects the values and beliefs of these societies and their interaction with African states are very much focused on promoting these values and concerns, often with the consent or even support of their home countries.

An example of such relations between non-state extra-African actors and African states is the increasing interaction between NGOs and African governments, particularly in the case of states suffering internal war. The glaring absence of the UN and of the major powers during and in the aftermath of the Rwanda civil war in 1994, in contrast with the involvement of international NGOs such as *Medecins sans Frontiers*, *Save the Children* and the *International Rescue Fund*, points to the extent to which, in many cases, Western governments are relegating aspects of their policy-making towards African countries to NGOs and their business communities. Clapham (1996:256) refers to this phenomenon as 'the privatisation of North/South relations'.

The trend towards the 'privatisation' of relations is also at least partially induced by the idea of the free market system in its hyper-capitalist form in which all relations are commodified. Governments withdraw (or attempt to withdraw) from the field of social and/or humanitarian aid, as if they were privatising and to some extent subsidising such activities. As a recent book reviewer remarked: 'the emergency aid business grew from a small element in the larger package of development into a giant, global, unregulated industry worth 2 500 million pounds Stirling a year. Most of the money is provided by governments, the European Union and the United Nations' (Rieff, 1997:133). These relief organisations can even, in cases of emergency, call on military protection from the international community in the form of UN peacekeeping assistance, bypassing the African state in which they may be active and in a way showing how little the sovereignty of these states is valued or realisable even within their own borders once they start to lose control.

International aid agencies in the business of providing humanitarian relief and also those involved in nature conservation may therefore become powerful actors on the international scene. They can often command, in terms of their nature and scope of resources, a lot of power and influence over host countries (*see* Box 10.3). This is also particularly true of nature conservation organisations where members sometimes either have little understanding of local African conditions, or show very little respect for *people*, instead concentrating their money, resources and attention on the natural environment (for example, wildlife), with little if any consideration of the effect their policies and actions may have on the people involved. This is clearly illustrated in the displacement of the nomadic Masai people of Tanzania and Kenya from much of the land over which they used to roam for generations in order to make place for game reserves. This expulsion from the land resulted in large-scale deprivation and poverty amongst these people, marked, in particular, by high incidences of child mortality and malnutrition (*The Observer*, 97.04.06). Clapham remarks that 'European conservationists could even support "shoot to kill" policies against wildlife poachers in Africa, with little thought to the controversy aroused by the death penalty for convicted murderers in their own countries' (Clapham, 1996:263). Because so many African countries are dependent on foreign tourists for income, they are sensitive to the way in which these organisations present them to the outside world. A negative report on a country might lose it thousands of dollars in foreign exchange.

This is not to say that the involvement of non-state actors in and with African states is neces-sarily 'bad'. As Rieff rightly notes, humanitarian workers have meant the difference between life and death for tens of thousands of people caught up in civil wars and other disasters in Africa (Reiff, 1997:136). Conservation lobbies have without a doubt contributed to the preservation of many animal and plant species on the contin-ent, often providing the much needed-know-ledge and financial resources that states do not have available (*see* Box 10.3). These non-state actors have the added advantage that they oper-ate in sovereign countries without themselves being sovereign bodies. This means that they can often reach targets or aims that states, because they are bound by the doctrine of sovereignty and the rules of non-intervention (*see* Chapter 4), cannot achieve, thereby providing valuable ser-vices to the international community. The activit-ies, for instance, of human rights organisations have done much to draw international attention to human rights abuses in many African coun-tries and, furthermore, to raise awareness and provide support for human rights activities with-in African societies. These activities are often dif-ficult for foreign governments to address in a direct way with the 'culprit' states and non-state actors therefore provide opportunities for high-lighting such issues and concerns without neces-sarily tarnishing relations between their host countries and the target state or states.

Box 10.3: The power of trans-national NGOs

'During the 1980s the government of Botswana decided to use part of the Okavango Delta's water for urban, industrial and irrigation needs. The people of the Delta were heavily opposed to this proposal, claim-ing that it would damage the ecosystem and also impact negatively on their livelihood, which depends largely on tourism and agri-culture. Greenpeace, an international envir-onmental body, joined in and started a cam-paign against Botswana's diamond industry – part of the Delta's water is used to supply the Orapa diamond mine in the north of the country. The World Conservation Union located in Switzerland intervened and pro-viding their expertise on wetlands, managed to convince the government not to go ahead with their plans for extracting water from the Delta.'

Geographic Magazine, October 1991

International relations at the state level

In this section, we pay attention to the more tra-ditional form of international relations, namely those relations conducted between governments as the formal representatives of states. Despite the increasing participation of non-state actors in international relations, inter-state relations at the formal level remain of importance. This is because states are considered sovereign and independent. States are the highest authority in terms of making enforceable rules for their societies and assuming obligations under inter-national law through the action of treaty-making, or the signing of conventions and resolutions. We will pay attention to various types of international relations. In the first section, the relations between African states and external powers, in particular their former colonial masters, will be discussed. (Because Chapter 13 deals with South–South relations, this chapter does not deal with Africa's relations with other states in the developing world.) This will be followed by a discussion on intra-African relations as reflected by the attempts of African countries to promote their interests through regional/continental co-operation facilitated by the establishment of regional organisations.

Relations with states outside of Africa

Although the idea of pan-Africanism as embraced by Africa's first generation of post-independence leaders included the ideal of independence from the former colonial powers, this proved to be impossible to realise. Colonisation incorporated Africa into a very specific position in the international economic division of labour and this entailed extensive and continuing links with the economies of the former colonial countries (*see* Chapter 11).

Over time, **vertically integrated production and consumer sectors** developed in which the raw materials were an important but first link in a chain of production activities leading from extraction to various stages of refinement to the delivery of the end-product. Copper ore, for instance, would be mined in Zambia, exported to the industrial countries, refined and manufactured in the West to produce and end-product that would then be sold from the West. This meant that although African countries produced the basic commodities, they had very little, if any, access to the skills, technology and other resources needed to add value to these commodities. In order to sell their products, they were, despite the attainment of political independence, still dependent on many of the economic structures established during the colonial era. This necessarily put them in close and continued

contact with the West, and particularly the former colonial powers. Intra-African trade has always been very low, mainly because the economies of African countries are basically the same and very little that is tradable *between* them is produced. Because economic development was of such cardinal importance to these newly independent states, their ties with Western countries were therefore important and few opportunities existed or were created to stimulate intra-continental trade.

But continued interaction between independent Africa and the former metropoles have not been confined to, or cannot be ascribed solely to, economic ties and interdependencies (however asymmetrical). Political ties also characterise the relations between Africa and the North, the latter not only referring to the former colonial powers. These ties have also not always been cordial and tensions between North and South regularly flare up. A case in point was the Nigerian military junta's execution of Ken Sara Wiwo and his comrades in November 1995, which resulted in a serious deterioration of relations between Nigeria and Britain, with countries such as Australia, New Zealand and Canada also strongly criticising Nigeria and calling for sanctions, and even the expulsion of Nigeria from the Commonwealth (Nigeria was suspended). The challenge for African countries has always been to walk the fine line between independence on the one hand, realising the extent of their dependence on the North for economic support and trade, and political support, often to remain in power, on the other hand.

Yet, instances of tensions and conflict between African countries and the former metropoles, most notably France and the United Kingdom (UK), and African criticism of the West did not exclude continuing political ties between these countries and the former colonial powers. African countries have often needed the support, in many instances tangible, of these powers in providing or maintaining their military and political security. It was mentioned above that Britain supported the federal government of

Nigeria during the civil war of 1967–1970 when Biafra wanted to break away from Nigeria. Such support, though manifest at the political level, was often tied up with economic concerns. During the Nigerian civil war, British business interests exerted pressure on their government for support to the Nigerian federal government, though Britain cloaked its stance in terms of support based on respect for the territorial integrity of a fellow member of the Commonwealth.

The relations of some African countries with those of the West, usually the former metropole, can also be explained in terms of the fact that some regimes at times have needed the external support for their continued survival. The most glaring example here is surely the long relationship between the late Mobutu of the former Zaïre and France or, rather, various French governments and presidents. This relationship cannot be described, though, as truly international because although cloaked in official terms of state-to-state relations, the basis was, to a large extent, mutual personal gain on both sides. French interests and Mobutu profited financially, Mobutu managed to remain in power with French military-political support, and France scored politically in expanding and deepening its sphere of influence in central Africa. For both sides, therefore, this was a highly beneficial relationship.

On the other hand, though help was regularly forthcoming when a particular regime was under *threat*, foreign assistance in the case of an actual *coup d'état* hardly ever occurred. Such changes were usually accepted by the external powers, most probably because intervention in such cases would have been too obviously in contravention of national sovereignty. Intervention may also have involved much higher risk than merely assisting in the maintenance of a government. Lastly, such changes seldom threatened the interests (economic in particular) of the former metropoles. At most, the names and faces of the main beneficiaries in government would change, but the business interests of the former colonial power, or other external powers for that matter, were not fundamentally threatened or damaged.

The former colonial powers also maintained other forms of political ties with the new states by, for instance, assisting in maintaining and developing state structures such as bureaucracies. Many African civil servants, military personnel and police officers were, and still are, trained in Britain and other Commonwealth countries. This makes for the forging of various links at various levels between these countries, contributing to the continued existence of strong ties between them. The fact that the former metropoles have the resources to aid their former colonies cannot but make for continued ties and explains the heavy emphasis that extra-continental state actors place on African relations. During the years of the continental (and broader international) struggle against Apartheid and, earlier on, settler control of Rhodesia/Zimbabwe (up to 1980 when Zimbabwe became independent), the support of the West was also encouraged and demanded by African states. These states used their ties with the former colonies, and the influence the Anglophone African countries had in the Commonwealth, to pursue the African ideal of full decolonisation and liberation from racial oppression and discrimination.

Africa's external relations, heavily intertwined with the West despite the ideals of solidarity and independence embodied in the idea of African unity, are thus mainly conditioned by two aspects: economic necessity on the part of Africa and economic interests on the part of the West, and by the political support and access provided by these external powers. Political reasons and economic considerations also determine the extensive relations between the People's Republic of China (PRC) and African states, and the involvement of Japan on the continent. The PRC competed ideologically with the West and with the USSR in Africa (*see* Chapter 9), and more recently with Taiwan. Japan today is the largest donor of aid to Africa (*see* Chapter 1). This largesse is determined, to a large degree, by its desire to gain a Permanent Seat in the UN Security Council.

Relations between African states

In view of the characteristics of African states discussed in the first part of this chapter, it is not surprising that African states have attempted to co-ordinate their interests and concerns through various forms of continental and regional co-operation. Under the umbrella of the OAU (*see* Box 10.4) this ideal of solidarity and unity has been pursued for more than three decades, while economic growth and development formed the centrepiece of many regional co-operation enterprises. In this section, the way in which African states conduct their intra-continental relations at the multilateral level is examined.

Continental relations: the OAU

When we look at the goals and principles of the OAU enshrined in its Charter, it becomes clear that to some extent the organisation has managed to realise some of these goals, albeit in a way that cannot be said to really represent the interests of all the people of the continent. The main objectives of the organisation are:

- to promote the unity and solidarity of African *states*; and
- to protect the sovereignty, territorial integrity and independence of African states.

The other goals of the organisation, such as the eradication of colonialism (and Apartheid), have been realised. But two of the OAU's goals have been neglected, precisely because of the heavy emphasis on the survival of *states* and the protection of sovereignty. These are:

- to co-ordinate co-operation and efforts to achieve a better life for the people of Africa; and
- to promote co-operation within the framework of the UN Charter and the Universal Declaration of Human Rights.

On paper the OAU did, in fact, dedicate a lot of attention to the realisation of these goals, even adopting an African Charter on Human and People's Rights in 1981 and establishing a Conflict Management Mechanism in 1994 in order to address African conflicts. Under the latter a rather innovative idea has also been incorporated, namely that of an African Peace Council of elder 'statesmen'. This 'Elders' Council for Peace' consists of former heads of state and governments who enjoy good standing and legitimacy on the continent and who may therefore be able to bring their good offices to bear on trying to solve disputes and conflicts. This innovation, though, is still to be tested. The Council consists at present of former leaders of the stature of Nigeria's Obasanjo, Senegal's Senghor, Tanzania's Nyerere and Zambia's Kaunda. One can well imagine that South Africa's President Mandela will be included in the Council after his retirement from public office in 1999. The Council, which will operate in an *ad hoc* and rather informal way, may turn out to be of particular value for the purpose that it has been created. This is so because it is based on the African tradition of 'leadership of the elders', a concept based on respect for and obedience to your elders and on traditional dispute resolution methods developed in African societies.

Given the large numbers of intra-state conflicts in Africa, the heavy emphasis of continental co-operation to protect the sovereignty of states, and the troubled history of neglect and abuse of ordinary Africans, African states, as represented by the OAU, face a difficult task. They have to reconcile these seeming contradictions of state sovereignty on the one hand, and the need for intervention in the case of civil war and other bloody intra-state conflicts that cannot be dealt with effectively or justly by governments on the other. This challenge has now been taken up by the OAU in the form of the above-mentioned Conflict Management Mechanism and proposals for an African peacekeeping force. It is difficult, though, to believe, given the history of continental relations, that states, particularly the bigger states, will agree to intervention by armed peacekeeping forces, whether African or composed and mandated by an organisation like the UN. The presence of 'foreign troops' on a country's

Box 10.4: The Organisation of African Unity

'The Organisation of African Unity was formally established on 25 May 1963 and therefore Africa commemorates 25 May as 'Africa Day'. The OAU consists of four major institutions. The first one is the Assembly of Heads of State and Government which meets once a year to discuss matters of mutual concern. The chair of the organisation rotates on an annual basis, usually with the head of the state that hosts the summit as the newly elected chair. So, for instance, President Robert Mugabe of Zimbabwe was the 1997/98 chair of the organisation and was succeeded by President Blaise Compaore of Burkina Faso who hosted the 1998 summit of the Assembly. The second institution is the Council of Ministers that meets at least twice a year and is supposed to take up the issues identified by the Assembly. The third central organ is the General Secretariat headed by the general secretary. The General Secretariat has to implement directives from the Assembly and Council of Ministers. The fourth institution is the Commission of Mediation, Conciliation and Arbitration. The Commission was established to realise the undertaking of member states to settle all their disputes in a peaceful way. It consists of 21 members elected by the Assembly from a list of qualified individuals whose names are submitted by member states and they serve five-year terms. The OAU also established the Co-ordinating Committee for the Liberation of Africa which was based in Tanzania. This became the most important committee of the organisation, tasked with the implementation of a liberation strategy for those territories still under colonial rule. It later became the main channel of African resistance to Apartheid and served to focus international attention and opposition to Apartheid.'

Khapoya (1994:285–286)

territory is a sensitive one because it is such a visible and 'conclusive' proof of its own inability to deal with problems and crises. Rather, it would seem that success would be more forthcoming in concentrating all possible efforts on the prevention and containment of conflicts. This is so because such efforts, sometimes referred to as quiet diplomacy, often involve less visible intervention and may, therefore, be more acceptable and efficient.

At this point, it is necessary to make two remarks regarding the relations between African states. The first is that the fact that the bigger states do not or would not tolerate intervention in their domestic politics is certainly not something unique to Africa, but one of the basic characteristics of inter-state relations. The history of the activities of the UN Security Council and the International Monetary Fund (IMF) provide but two examples of the way in which major powers intervene in domestic matters of smaller countries while not allowing such intervention in their own domestic spheres.

The second point concerns the idea of African unity. There is no lack of examples of serious problems, conflicts, differences and disputes between these countries. The very establishment of the OAU was dependent on a compromise between three very different schools of thought on the idea of African unity and the objectives of the organisation. These were the Brazzaville, Monrovia and Casablanca groups, though the Brazzaville and Monrovia groups had a lot in common (*see* Khapoya, 1994:282–288). Differences at times even threatened the continued existence of the organisation. Summits have often been boycotted by states who were involved in disputes and who felt that they were being unfairly treated or judged by fellow African countries or who had differences of opinion with the host state and/or its allies.

But African unity does not only, or so much, concern intra-continental support and agreement as it depicts a united front to the external environment. In other words, though African states may have conflictual relations, often of a serious nature, the main idea is that criticism of each other should be confined to within the continent and not to be made in forums outside the continent or in a public manner that would in any way be seen as opposing a fellow African state.

Regional relations

The idea of African unity also encompasses regional co-operation. As is discussed in Chapter 11, African states face many difficulties in terms of economic and other dimensions of development. Small markets, lack of infrastructure, expensive transport, narrow-based economies, heavy dependence on exports of primary commodities and few opportunities for intra-continental trade are some of the problems faced by these countries. From the early years of independence, therefore, these states have attempted to promote regional co-operation for development. Such co-operation promises bigger markets, the sharing of burdens and benefits, a stronger voice in multilateral negotiation forums (such as the World Trade Organisation, WTO), as well as the possibility that closer economic ties will promote confidence-building and provide incentives for the prevention of conflict and the peaceful settlement of disputes.

Despite many attempts at regional co-operation and integration, many of these attempts have failed or have had limited success. The main reason for failure or small success is perhaps the tendency of regional organisations to view (and therefore to follow) the integration process adapted by the EU. The fact of the matter is, however, that the European countries differ politically and economically in major ways from African countries. Whereas the fifteen members of the EU have similar political values and forms of government (liberal democracies) that create an environment conducive for the necessary harmonisation of policies, African forms of government differ markedly – even amongst close neighbours.

European economies are widely diversified and produce a very broad range of products and commodities. In this way, intra-regional trade is promoted within a large market in which the buying power of people maintains and encourages the demand for highly industrial and other expensive manufactures and products. The members of the EU also share similar levels of development, thereby ensuring that the benefits of free trade are more or less equally distributed. Within free trade areas, the most developed member state usually benefits most from the agreement. Such 'unequal benefit' may obstruct or even destroy regional co-operation, in the process creating or exacerbating tensions between members.

The above is exactly what happened in the East African Community (EAC). It consisted of three states – Kenya, Uganda and Tanzania – and was a regional free trade area that had been established during the colonial period. Kenya, as the most developed member of the group, also attracted the most foreign investment and therefore the most economic benefit from the arrangement. The political ideologies of the three states were also widely divergent, resulting in conflicting economic policies. During its existence, the EAC was regularly racked by crises and conflict over the distribution of economic gains. Despite various negotiations and measure adopted to address these problems, it disintegrated in 1977. Three years later, Tanzania became one of the founding members of the Southern African Development Co-ordination Conference (SADCC). The border between Tanzania and Kenya was closed for six years and it was only in the mid-1990s that the three countries, now exhibiting less clashing political ideals and economic principles, started once again to explore the possibility of re-establishing the EAC.

Furthermore, the path towards economic integration requires that member states give up some areas of economic decision-making to the supranational body, while the results of free trade are only realised in the longer term. Such loss of economic autonomy is anathema to most African countries, who view it as a threat to their sovereignty. Emulating the European economic growth path is therefore not an appropriate method for African countries to follow, either to promote regional co-operation or to pursue development objectives.

An organisation such as the Southern African Development Community (SADC) (dealt with in detail in Chapter 14), though it had much more modest goals, proved to be more successful than most other attempts during the 1970s and 1980s at regional co-operation in Africa. The reason was that it focused on promoting development in the member countries and in strengthening and building the necessary infrastructure to optimise the economic activities of its members. So, for instance, rather than promoting free trade at a very early stage, it concentrated on co-ordinating development projects in the field of transport and communication, thereby preparing the ground for later closer co-operation in the form of freer trade across borders.

One of the most well-known African regional groupings is ECOWAS – the Economic Community of West African States – whose members consist of Anglophone West African states. Nigeria, being the biggest state in West Africa, took the lead in establishing this organisation in 1975 with a view to achieving a common market between its sixteen member states over a period of fifteen years. The problems of such integration schemes, as just mentioned, prevented the organisation from attaining its goals and over the years, high levels of tension between members were not uncommon. As so often happens, the domestic needs and interests of member countries from time to time threatened to derail the organisation. In 1983, shortly before an election, Nigeria decided that thousands of Ghanaians working in Nigeria had to return to Ghana (also an ECOWAS member) in order to create jobs for Nigerians. This decision resulted in serious acrimony between the two countries. The same happened in 1985 and the border between Nigeria and Ghana was closed for long periods during the 1980s. At the root of the conflict was the fact that the decision to allow the free movement of labour within the

community was a too sophisticated and politically sensitive step to have been taken so early in the existence of ECOWAS. In the end, this misjudgement inhibited the growth of co-operation between member states, pointing to the importance of appropriate policies at the appropriate time not only to promote co-operation for mutual economic benefit, but also to maintain peaceful relations between members.

It is clear, therefore, that despite the practical need for regional co-operation between African states, the road to integration is a difficult one, demanding, above all, the political will of leaders to succeed, as well as the correct choice of co-operation approach and development projects. Ties with extra-regional countries, particularly the former colonial powers, the nature and structure of African economies and above all the fear of loss of sovereignty still inhibit close co-operation (*see* map section for maps of economic groupings in Africa).

Conclusion

Africa's international relations, whether relations with its external environment or with fellow African countries, are largely determined by and best understood in the light of the 'African condition'. International relations are very much concerned with and influenced by domestic circumstances and needs. At the same time, international conditions and trends and the structure of the system – the way in which power is distributed – influence the domestic policies of countries. So, for instance, most African countries have had to accept structural adjustment policies (SAPs) along with their conditionalities as laid down by the IMF. In many cases, though, IMF intervention has been necessitated or facilitated by the way in which African governments failed to develop and implement efficient policies. Therefore, we can also conclude that African international relations are characterised by imperfections in the ways in which Africa governs itself. Both the international community and

African states themselves have to take the responsibility of ensuring a better future for the continent.

Key concepts in this chapter

De-stated international relations
Juridical sovereignty
Non-state international relations
Pan-Africanism
Political sovereignty
Quasi states
Regional co-operation
Separatist wars

Suggested readings

There are literally hundreds of books available that deal with Africa, with the international relations of African states and with the conflicts and crises besetting the continent. Apart from the sources used in this chapter, the following will assist students to gain a better knowledge and understanding of Africa and of the specific (though limited) issues that are dealt with in this chapter. Before listing these, though, I would like to emphasise a point made in the chapter. It is necessary for students, I believe, to increase their knowledge and understanding of Africa not only through reading about the history and contemporary political economy of the continent, but also by means of studying African literature. The work of Chinua Achebe, Ben Okri, Bessie Head, Es'kia Mphahlele, Mariama Bai, Sembene Ousmane, Buchi Emecheta and Wole Soyinka, to name but a very few, are of great value.

Suggested readings of a more direct political and economic nature are:

- Ake, C. (1981) A *Political Economy of Africa*. New York: Longmans.
- Amin, S. (1990) *Maldevelopment*. London: Zed Books.
- Cheru, F. (1989) *The Silent Revolution in Africa*. London: Zed Books.
- Hay, M. & Stichter, S. (eds). (1984) *African Women South of the Sahara*. London: Longman.
- Jackson, R. (1990) *Quasi-states: Sovereignty, International Relations and the Third World*. Cambridge: Cambridge University Press.
- Oliver, R. & Fage, J. (1990) *A Short History of Africa* (6th edition). London: Penguin Books.
- Sandbrook, R. (1993) *The Politics of Africa's Economic Recovery*. Cambridge: Cambridge University Press.
- Shaw, T. & Aluko, O. (eds). (1984) *The Political Economy of African Foreign Policy*. New York: St Martin's Press.
- Young, C. (1994) *The African Colonial State in Comparative Perspective*. New Haven: Yale University Press.
- Zartman, W. (ed.). (1995) *Collapsed States: The Disintegration and Restoration of Legitimate Authority*. Boulder: Lynne Rienner Publishers.

11 | The post-colonial African state and its problems

Eghosa E. Osaghae

This chapter in outline
- The post-colonial state in sub-Saharan Africa
- Why is the post-colonial state weak?
- The problems of the post-colonial African state
  - Internal problems
  - External problems
- The future of the post-colonial state

The ability of states to perform the roles expected of them as central actors in the international system depends on a variety of factors. These include economic capacity, that is, the extent to which a state possesses resources and is able to manage and deploy them in the furtherance of development and other national interests; technological and industrial capacity, including military capacity; and political stability, or the extent to which the government of a state is legitimate and political relations are not subjected to the shocks of civil war, military coups and frequent acts of rebellion or disobedience by the citizenry. In general, states that have economic and technological capacity and are politically stable tend to be more powerful actors in the international system than those that are less endowed with these attributes. This tells us a lot about why the mostly poor, technologically dependent and politically unstable sub-Saharan African (SSA) states are such weak actors, subject to interference from outside Africa and dependent on other actors. To be effective in international relations, to make their claims to sovereignty real, they must have economic, technological and political capacities. But none of this tells us why the states came to be as they are in the first place. The aim of this chapter is to find out why the post-colonial African state is weak and, on that basis, analyse the problems that incapacitate it.

The post-colonial state in sub-Saharan Africa

What do we mean by the term state, and to what extent does the post-colonial state in Africa meet the criteria of statehood (*see* also Chapter 4)? Before attempting to answer these questions, let us first clarify the meaning of the post-colonial African state, which is our specific focus, and the context in which its problems will be discussed. The term post-colonial state refers to the post-independence or contemporary state in Africa. This distinguishes it from the *pre-colonial state*,

which existed before colonisation (*see* Chapter 8) and the *colonial state*, which was the main instrument of colonial subjugation and exploitation.

The reader may be wondering why we refer to a singular post-colonial state rather than plural post-colonial states; after all, there are forty-eight contemporary states in SSA. The reason is that with the exception of Ethiopia, which was colonised only briefly, most of the states were created by colonial rulers, suffered colonial subjugation and exploitation (the defining elements of the colonial experience were similar despite differences in colonial policies) and, largely for these reasons, present basically the same character and face similar problems – problems of legitimacy, national cohesion, political stability and economic development. The post-colonial state discussed here is the typical African state.

It should, however, be emphasised that, although the problems of the post-colonial state are discussed in general terms, there are variations in their scope and intensity. States that have enjoyed relatively long periods of stability and **good governance** (like Botswana, Tanzania and Côte d'Ivoire) have fared better than others, which are either undemocratic (like Mobutu's former Zaïre), have been held captive by military rule (like Nigeria) or have been embroiled in civil war (like Somalia and Sudan). Moreover, oil-rich countries like Nigeria, Gabon and Angola are potentially better off than countries whose export commodities have had a long run of unfavourable prices in the world market. The picture is certainly complex and important differences will be highlighted in this chapter, but these are essentially differences of *degree* rather than *kind*, which underscores the point made earlier that post-colonial African states face basically the same problems.

We can now return to the notion of statehood. A state exists when it meets the following criteria:
- It has a definite territory and boundaries.
- It has a definite population (citizens), on whose individual and collective capabilities, skills and patriotism, as well as the

technologies and resources available to them, the strength of the state greatly depends.

- It has a government that, following Max Weber's (1964) classical definition, has a monopoly of force within the territory.
- It is formally independent, meaning that its government is recognised by other states and international law and conventions as **sovereign**. This makes the state, no matter how quasi, weak or powerful it may be, formally equal to other states (Brownlie, 1979; Jackson, 1990). (*See* also Chapter 4.)

To examine the extent to which the state in Africa meets these criteria, we shall rely on the analysis of Jackson & Rosberg (1982) who have classified the criteria into what they call 'empirical' criteria, which enable us to directly observe and verify the existence of a state (the first three criteria above), and the 'juridical' criteria, which define a state in terms of its legal status under international law and conventions (the fourth criterion). Following this, they argue that many states in Africa exist more in juridical terms than in empirical terms. This is particularly true of states embroiled in prolonged civil war – Liberia (1990–1997), Chad (1970s–1980s), Somalia (1980s–1990s) and Rwanda (1990s) – which went without recognisable governments for long periods, and whose citizens were forced to flee to many other countries as refugees and displaced persons.

But even in those states not at war, empirical statehood is problematic. There is a long catalogue of such problems: some states face serious problems of contested citizenship, as citizens are more loyal to separatist groups than the state (the Oromo and Tigreans in Ethiopia and Casamance in Senegal, for example); boundaries are fluid and contested (Nigeria and Cameroun over the Bakassi peninsula; Ethiopia and Eritrea over disputed territory), although it is remarkable that the artificial boundaries created by former colonial powers have largely been maintained; many governments do not have the monopoly of force and are frequently challenged by armed opposition groups (Uganda, Sierra Leone, Nigeria, Congo-Brazzaville, the Democratic Republic of Congo [the DRC], the Central African Republic, Burundi, Rwanda and so on); and the foreign debts owed to the industrialised countries and the multilateral financial organisations controlled by them – the World Bank and the International Monetary Fund (IMF) – severely limit their ability to function as sovereign states. Under these circumstances, Jackson & Rosberg are right in their conclusion that while many states would fail the strict test of empirical statehood, they do not cease to be states in the juridical sense (*see* also Tordoff, 1997:28).

The foregoing serves as a useful introduction to an analysis of the problems of the African state. It shows that the typical African state is weak (the weakness has also been described in terms of the state being soft, underdeveloped or a quasi-state). The manifestations of weakness are generally well known (*see* Clapham, 1995; Chazan *et al.*, 1992; Tordoff, 1997), and include the following:

- A chronic crisis of legitimacy, which involves the absence of country-wide support for government, serious challenges to its authority by important segments, which sometimes leads to civil war, and disorderly succession to power through military coups, inconclusive or stage-managed elections, rebellion by so-called war lords and their like.
- A low degree of national integration marked by the tendency of citizens to attach greater importance to ethnic, racial, religious and regional affiliations than identification with and a show of loyalty to the state.
- Poor governance and management of the ubiquitous but mostly inefficient public sector accentuated by corruption, personal rulership and the absence of democratic rule and principles of **transparency** and **accountability**.
- A crisis of penetration, involving the inability of the state to effectively establish or extend its authority over large parts of the country (especially parts that are separatist) and sectors of national life (such as effective policing

and security of national boundaries, collection of taxes, customs and excise duties, and enforcement of key legislation, especially on matters of a moral nature). In short, this crisis manifests itself in the fragility of state structures, 'the absence or weakness of effective political institutions in society' (Huntington, 1968).

- Economic weakness and widespread poverty. According to a report on Africa's development in 1995, 'Africa's economic performance continued ... to be the lowest among all developing regions, as real economic growth reached 5.5 per cent in the developing world [Africa's was a low 1.9 per cent]' (ADB, 1995:13).

- Dependence on the industrialised countries for technology and manufactured goods, which are imported at exorbitant prices. The degree of dependence is heightened by the dependent food culture, which involves the consumption of imported food items like wheat, canned food and food supplements, and the strategy of **import substitution industrialisation** (ISI), which entails the importation of technology, spare parts and raw materials to produce goods locally that were previously imported (often at lower prices and better quality).

Why is the post-colonial state weak?

We shall discuss these problems in some detail shortly, but first, we should find out why the African state is so weak, and why these problems persist. There are basically two ways to explain the weakness of the African state. The first, which we shall call the historical and structural explanation, sees it as the product of colonialism, while the second emphasises post-colonial failures. The historical explanation hinges on the fact that most contemporary African states were created by colonial powers in the interests of their colonial (and neo-colonial) enterprise rather than in the interests of the colonised Africans. It is argued that the problems of the post-colonial state derive from the nature of its progenitor, the colonial state (*see* Ake, 1994; Young, 1994). The point here is that the effects of colonialism did not end with the attainment of independence; they continued, albeit in more subtle ways, under neo-colonialism.

To begin with, the colonial state was arbitrarily created without regard to ethnic affinities and historical political boundaries, or for that matter the wishes of Africans, with the result that several peoples/nations were split across new boundaries under different colonial authorities, and formerly hostile communities were lumped together in the new states. Moreover, the institutions of the colonial state (the bureaucracy, police, military, legislature, judiciary and the monetary system) were imported wholesale from the mother country and imposed on Africans, whose societies were at a different level of political and institutional development. Essentially, the colonial state was a *tribute-exacting* military state whose main purpose, far from the welfare of the colonised, was to facilitate the colonial enterprise through maintenance of law and order, forced labour, taxation, exploitation of resources, import/export trade and other objectives of colonialism, including capital accumulation for the colonial powers.

Because of the inherent disjuncture or divergence of interest between state and society, the colonial state suffered from endemic crises of integration, legitimacy and penetration.

- The colonial agenda had no room for the transformation of the state into a nation. The imported state model was bereft of the type of nationhood that had emerged in nineteenth-century Europe. It was also not in the interest of the colonisers that the colonised peoples should be united in a single nation.
- The small size of the colonial bureaucracy made effective penetration difficult.
- The colonial state was deemed illegitimate by the colonised because it did not serve the interests of the colonised, and this was the main reason for its overthrow.

In the economic sphere, the colonial state was characterised by a structure of unequal exchange through the integration of African states into the global capitalist system as dependent and exploited formations. This involved monoculturalism, or the dependence of the national economy on only one or a few export commodities, and monetisation, which entailed the introduction of currencies that were tied to those of the **mother country** as the medium of exchange. It also involved the domination of the economy by one or a few European commercial enterprises, the introduction of import substitution policies, and the accumulation of foreign debt to offset fiscal and balance of payments deficits during periods of economic depression (1930s) and the two World Wars. It has also been suggested that the period of actual colonisation (about 1870 to 1960, less than 100 years) was too short for European capital and modernity to penetrate 'traditional' societies or set the stage for any meaningful capitalist development (Freund, 1984).

With regard to politics, the late introduction of institutions of democratic politics and the exclusion of Africans from the political arena until the eve of independence meant that many countries became independent without having mastered the intricacies of modern democratic politics.

We would expect that, given the abnormality and weakness of the colonial state inherited at independence, the leaders of the post-colonial state would at least do away with the structures that made the state illegitimate and unable to serve the developmental needs of the colonised. One view, represented by Ake (1994), holds that they did not. As he argues, decolonisation only involved the replacement of the colonial rulers by indigenous rulers *without any fundamental change in the character of the colonial state*. The problems of the post-colonial state are accordingly attributed to the structural continuities between the colonial and post-colonial states. Thus, the prevalence of authoritarian and military regimes can be seen as a continuation of the military character and law-and-order orientation of the colonial state. Similarly, the lack of accountability of political leaders is attributed to the continued disjuncture between state and society, and the economic problems of the post-colonial state are blamed on the structural dependence established by the colonial regime.

While also emphasising the structural impediments created by the colonial state, the opposing view to this says that attempts have been made to transform the state after independence, and blames the weakness of the post-colonial state on the failures of these attempts, which in fact worsened the problems in certain respects (*see* Mamdani, 1996). Some of the initial attempts hinged on the ideology of African socialism, which emphasised the communal (and classless) character of indigenous systems of production and distribution (*see* below).

Other notable efforts at transforming the post-colonial state in the first two decades of independence (1960–1980) included nationalisation or governmental acquisition of enterprises previously owned by private (mostly European and South African) companies, which were subsequently run as part of governmental administration as **parastatal corporations**; nation-building schemes, including attempts at rural-urban and élite-mass integration; expansion of the manufacturing sector, mainly through import substitution; and welfarist schemes, which promised rural development, increased access to education, better health care and employment (an example was Obote's Common Man's Charter in Uganda – *see* Minogue & Molloy, 1974).

Other notable efforts at reforming the post-colonial state included:

- democratisation based mostly on the model of the one party system, which was said to express African democracy;
- attempts at redressing relations of unequal exchange in global relations through membership of cartels of commodity-producing countries, which aim to ensure favourable prices in the world market (such as the Cocoa Producers Alliance and Organisation of Oil Exporting Countries); and

- the formation of common markets and economic unions, such as the East African Community (EAC), the Economic Community of West African States (ECOWAS), the Southern African Development Community (SADC) and the proposed African Economic Union.

Necessary as these attempts obviously are, they have not been sufficient to transform the state in any fundamental way. Instead, they have sometimes had the unintended consequence of engendering undemocratic rule, disempowering **civil society**, over-centralising government and causing run-away expansion of the public sector, all of which have complicated the crisis of legitimacy faced by the post-colonial state.

The second explanation focuses on the problems of the post-colonial state as originally African, and some analysts even go to the extent of suggesting that the problems exist because Africans are not capable of governing themselves (so-called **Afro-pessimism**).

The factors emphasised here are those of (over)population as the rate of population growth surpasses that of economic growth, corruption, including the variants of **prebendalism**, **personal rulership**, **neo-patrimonialism**, the over-expansion of the public sector for purposes of extending the patronage system, poor governance and a low level of nation-building as indicated by prevalent ethnic, regional and religious conflicts. A typical example of this explanation is the World Bank's analyses of Africa's economic problems, which highlight the failures of the post-colonial state in terms of poor governance and state intervention in most areas of national life, which has resulted in the multiplication of parastatals and an over-bloated and inefficient public sector. The lack of democracy (especially of accountability), an undeveloped private sector, corruption, and the marginalisation of women and the poor are also highlighted (World Bank, 1989).

A critical look at these factors cannot fail to show us that, while they are plausible, that is,

self-evidently true, they seem to beg the question by positing manifestations of the problems (which themselves need to be explained) as the causes. One reason for this is that the explanations overlook the deeper historical roots of these problems, which, as we saw earlier, originated as a result of colonialism. Perhaps the point they make, which has merit, is that the period since colonial rule ended (nearly forty years ago in most cases) has provided ample time for African countries to solve their problems (after all, the failures of the attempts discussed earlier cannot be blamed on colonialism). But such views underestimate the enduring effects of colonialism and neo-colonialism.

The gist of neo-colonialism is simply that independence was granted only after colonial powers had entrenched structures of dependence through:

- military pacts or defence agreements, which gave former colonial powers responsibility for defending the country and government against external attack and internal insurrection;
- the creation of a **comprador bourgeoisie**, a class of local entrepreneurs and public officials who acted as dependent local agents of foreign capitalists (for instance, Freund [1984:241] has described African state officials 'as agents of Western capital, in power to execute its demands much as colonial officialdom once was');
- dependency-creating foreign aid;
- the affiliations of the currencies of the new states to those of the mother colony, such as the French franc and the British pound; and
- continued domination of the economy by **multinational corporations** (MNCs).

The foregoing designs assured continuity of imperial control without colonial occupation and rule, which is why neo-colonialism is described in Chapter 8 of this book as 'colonialism by remote control'. In a similar vein, the external factors that have greatly contributed to the problems of the post-colonial state are not given sufficient emphasis. These mostly have to do with **relations of unequal exchange** in international relations, the effects of Cold War rivalries, **foreign debt** and the imposition of market reforms by Western powers in the post-cold war era, which are discussed below.

From the insights of the two competing explanations, it can be concluded that the problems of the post-colonial African state can be explained *both* in terms of the structural continuities with the colonial state and failures of the state in the post-independence period. This means that the explanations are complementary rather than strictly contradictory.

The problems of the post-colonial African state

Internal problems

Most of the internal problems suffered by the post-colonial state derive from what the French scholar Jean-Francois Bayart (1993) calls its 'totalising' tendency, that is, the state's attempt to dominate and control virtually all areas of national life – political, social, economic and cultural. This tendency followed the centralist approach to development, nation-building and political stability adopted by most states after independence during the era of the Cold War in which the Soviet models of development often found approval in Africa. The colonial state did not do much in these areas because it was more responsive to the dictates of the colonial enterprise than the interests of the colonised. In a sense, therefore, the attempt was to fill the gaps left by the colonial authorities and redress the anomalies and imbalances inherited from them.

Problems of development

Let us begin with development (*see* also Chapter 15). At independence, very few African countries had a viable private sector and national

bourgeoisie that were able to generate capital and play the roles expected of them in the development process. The few private enterprises that were engaged in small-scale manufacturing, banking, insurance and trading were owned by foreign, mostly European, entrepreneurs and MNCs. This led the post-colonial state into becoming an entrepreneur, by establishing parastatals. In countries like Tanzania and Zambia, major firms belonging to Europeans were nationalised (in Zimbabwe this included the ownership of the leading newspaper), while in others, notably Kenya and Nigeria, indigenisation programmes that sought to create a local bourgeoisie and effect local control of the private sector were launched. Nationalisation and indigenisation did not, however, mean the end of domination of the economies by the foreign MNCs as many MNCs simply Africanised their management cadres to give the wrong impression that they were now controlled by locals.

Several countries, especially those which were formerly settler colonies (Kenya and Zimbabwe), embarked on redistribution schemes, especially with regard to land appropriated by white settlers. Redistribution policies were also introduced to correct the lopsided composition of the civil service and military (in the case of the military, the colonial **warrior tribe policy** led to a preponderance of soldiers from one or a few ethno-linguistic groups). In Nigeria, for example, it was necessary to increase the number of Northerners in the federal civil service to balance the preponderance of Southerners. Also, a quota system of recruitment to the army was introduced in 1958 to offset regional imbalances. Finally, there was an expansion of educational, health, and other social welfare facilities and services, which were rightly believed to underlie the development process.

These undertakings, which were said to be aimed at development, had two direct effects on the state. First, they led to the centralisation of authority and the rapid expansion of the public sector, which in most cases ended up being overbloated, corrupt and inefficient. This was more so because parastatals and public sector employment were expanded to feed the **patronage system**, which sustained incumbent rulers in power by rewarding loyal supporters of the ruling party and military faction, as well as relatives and friends of top government officials – what is known as **patrimonialism**. In pre-1980 Liberia for instance, membership of the ruling True Whig Party and America-Liberian origins were necessary requirements for public service jobs, contracts, scholarships and so on.

The second effect was that the limited resources of the already poor African countries were overstretched. The favourable prices of export commodities in the 1960s and early 1970s enabled the rapid expansion of educational, health and infrastructural facilities. But from the late 1970s, there was a precipitous decline in these prices. This forced many states to rely increasingly on foreign aid and loans. This was the background to the foreign debt crisis and the **structural adjustment programmes** (SAPs) that have crippled most African countries since the late 1970s (these are discussed under external problems below).

Political problems

If the centralisation of development efforts brought such serious problems, the consequences of hegemonic nation-building and political stability were no less serious. Once again, it was the failure of the colonial state that necessitated these tasks. Given the arbitrary manner of their creation and the lumping together of different and sometimes hostile (ethnic, regional and racial) groups, most African states were, at independence, artificial states that, if not carefully held together, could disintegrate. The eruption of civil war in the Congo and Nigeria soon after independence and many others thereafter (Chad, Sudan, Liberia, Ethiopia, Rwanda, Burundi, Sierra Leone and so on), as well as strong challenges to central authority and separatist movements in several others (Senegal and Ethiopia), clearly showed how urgent this task was.

One party rule

Most post-independence African leaders felt that the best way to arrest potential or real disintegration and political instability was to discourage or prevent the expression of differences that threatened national cohesion. They consequently outlawed or suppressed opposition parties, which were accused, with some justification, of promoting ethnic and regional divisive interests. Autonomous non-governmental organisations (NGOs), including private or independent radio, television and newspapers that made up civil society, also suffered the same fate. These steps inevitably led to the emergence of *de jure* and *de facto* one party systems (typically the party that led the independence movement and won overwhelming majorities in general elections). In the 1960s and 1970s, one party rule was very popular in Africa. Even the few countries that remained formally multiparty, like Botswana, Gambia, Mauritius and later Zimbabwe, were one party dominant.

The rise of the one party system was also closely linked to the adoption of centralist ideologies, notably African and Afro-Marxist socialist ideologies that hinged on centrally planned economies and a central role for the state in the economy. African socialism was said to represent an attempt to return to the old or indigenous African system of socio-political organisation that colonialism had destroyed. One of the notable attempts to practise African socialism was President Julius Nyerere's *ujamaa* (familyhood) in Tanzania, which led to the establishment of village co-operatives as primary units of production and distribution. The one party system was projected as the political correlate of African socialism, an expression of African democracy that was said to be characterised by consensus, absence of class conflict, group rather than individual rights, and unalloyed loyalty to the community represented by the king or chief (in this case, the president), all of which were conducive to one party rule. In reality, however, much of the rhetoric and ideology had little support in African history.

A typical one party system was largely undemocratic. Periodic elections were held, and two or more members of the party sometimes contested parliamentary seats, but the electors had no real policy, as opposed to personality, alternatives from which to choose. The rule of law and constitutionality were generally breached, and the rights of citizens, especially those who opposed the party, were habitually denied, press freedom was muzzled, the absence of opposition made for little accountability, etc. One party rule made possible the personalisation of state power, and the emergence of despotic rulers, some of whom became presidents-for-life. Challenge or opposition to incumbent rulers was seen as challenge to the unity of the state.

Military rule

Another form of rule that was widespread and had basically the same effects as one party rule was military rule. In the 1960s, 1970s and 1980s, military rule was a prominent feature of the African political landscape. There was military rule in many countries – Benin, Ghana, Nigeria, Togo, Zaïre, Uganda, Burundi, Mali, Niger, the Congo, the Central African Republic, Liberia, Sierra Leone, Gambia, Guinea and Ethiopia (attempts to overthrow elected governments in Kenya, Zambia and Lesotho were unsuccessful). The reasons for military intervention ranged from institutional factors such as grievances over promotions and salaries of soldiers, and involvement in the suppression of internal uprisings that bred a culture of political efficacy, to the use of the military by groups that lacked viable alternative political platforms from which to compete for state power. Sometimes, also, coups were organised for purely personal reasons stemming from the political ambitions of military officers who became some of the worst dictators in Africa's post-colonial history (like Idi Amin of Uganda, 1971–1979, Mobutu Sese Seko of the former Zaïre, 1965–1997, and Sani Abacha of Nigeria, 1993–1998).

Whatever the reasons for military intervention and rule may be, they point to a major weakness of the post-colonial African state, that is, the susceptibility of civilian government to military control. This is an anomaly because conventional (liberal) wisdom on civil-military relations assumes not only a balance or equilibrium between the civil and military spheres, but also civilian control of the military. But this is not the only problem. Military rule, being inherently unconstitutional, has contributed greatly to the weakening of democratic values such as rule of law, judicial autonomy, accountability, and tolerance of opposition. This weakening has, of course, aided the emergence of arbitrary personal rulership all over the continent.

The state as a poor agent of distributive justice

The ethnic or sectional capture of state power makes it difficult for the state to function as the primary agent of distributive justice. As an agent of **distributive justice**, the state is expected to ensure that public goods, resources and benefits are distributed fairly and equitably. Several African countries pursue policies that aim to ensure at least some distributive justice. A notable example is Nigeria where appointments to cabinet and top political positions, recruitment into the military, admissions to state-owned educational institutions and the distribution of state resources, *inter alia*, are governed by the *federal character principle*, which is enshrined in the constitution to prevent the domination of government by people from one or a few sections of the country by ensuring that the country's diversity is reflected in appointments and the distribution of resources.

In South Africa, a policy of affirmative action, aimed at redressing the gross inequalities in access to jobs and public goods between whites and blacks, has been pursued since the end of Apartheid in 1994. Policies similar to those in Nigeria and South Africa, generally called *ethnic arithmetic formula*, are pursued mostly informally in many other countries. While such policies have obvious political benefits, they also have disadvantages. They tend to reinforce ethnic and racial divisions and encourage nepotism and ascription rather than merit and achievement.

Despite the existence of distributive policies, the post-colonial state finds it difficult to ensure distributive justice. Because it is controlled by people from only one or a few groups in whose favour the distribution of public goods is biased, the state lacks the autonomy or neutrality required to function as an effective agent of distributive justice. It becomes, in effect, an agent of discrimination and sectional domination. Numerous examples abound. Under the Apartheid regime in South Africa, public goods and privileges were the exclusive preserve of the minority whites; in pre-1980 Liberia, the Americo-Liberians dominated the public sphere; in Ethiopia, the Oromos, Tigreans and others allege Amharaic domination of public goods; and in Nigeria, the distribution of resources greatly favour the ruling Northern-Hausa-Fulani-Muslim groups, which have dominated power since independence.

The failure of the state to serve as an agent of distributive justice is one of the major reasons for the chronic problem of **legitimacy** from which it suffers. As it were, the loyalty of members of the groups who are excluded, marginalised or discriminated against cannot be guaranteed; some are then forced to oppose or challenge the state. A recent example that captured world-wide attention was the case of the Ogoni minority group in Nigeria who, *inter alia*, demanded an equitable share of crude oil derived from their area and internal political autonomy.

The 'second independence movement': responses of citizens to the 'failed' state

How did the citizens of the post-colonial state respond to the state's performance, which, viewed against the background of the high expectations of independence, was disappointing? As we have said, those excluded and marginalised confronted the state in a variety of ways. While some fought guerrilla wars and organised military coups to overthrow incumbent leaders, others demanded separation from their present states to form their own states. On the other hand, many ordinary citizens simply **exited** from the state to rely more on the voluntary self-help associations (civics, home town associations, community development associations, savings clubs, co-operatives, farmers' unions and women's organisations), which they formed to provide the social goods the state was unable to provide.

From the 1980s on, however, there was more vigorous and popular resistance against the state, in what has been described as the second independence movement (Anyang' Nyong'o, 1987). This coincided with the wave of democratisation, involving the sacking of authoritarian regimes, that swept all over the world, especially in the socialist countries of the former Eastern bloc, Latin America, Asia and, of course, Africa (*see* Diamond *et al.*, 1988). What catalysed and sustained the resistance was the economic crisis (discussed below) that crippled African states to the point where most of them could no longer discharge even basic functions such as maintenance of infrastructure, payment of workers' salaries, and protection of lives and property.

They were forced to turn to the World Bank, IMF and the international donor community, who made economic or market reforms packaged in structural adjustment programmes (SAPs) a major condition for the much-needed loans. The key policies of SAPs were the privatisation or sale of state-owned corporations, parastatals and commercial enterprises to private entrepreneurs; the down-sizing and rationalisation of the public sector; the removal of foreign exchange controls; currency devaluation; the removal of subsidies on essential goods and services, including food, education and health; export promotion; the attraction of foreign investment; and trade liberalisation.

The implementation of SAPs brought greater misery to the citizens: down-sizing, rationalisation and privatisation saw massive retrenchments of workers and hence increased unemployment; and unprecedented increases in the costs of essential commodities, including food items, social goods and services due to privatisation, withdrawal of subsidies and the devaluation of currencies. These demonstrably increased the gap between citizens and the state, and provoked frequent strikes, riots and demonstrations by workers, retrenched workers, students, professionals, and women. Although a large part of the escalating social and political unrest was devoted to demanding higher wages and opposing unemployment, insecurity of lives and property, and rising costs of living, they were also channelled into demands for political reforms. Through various civil society associations such as labour unions, student unions, lawyers' associations and other professional bodies, and women's organisations, scores of ordinary people, especially in the urban areas, rose to demand the termination of authoritarian rule, respect for fundamental human rights, responsiveness and accountability of rulers to citizens, and reform of the public sector to ensure greater moral probity and equitable access to state power and resources.

The process of democratisation received ample support from the United States (US) and other Western powers, largely because the global wave saw the triumph of (Western) liberal democracy over other competing forms of democracy (socialist democracy and African democracy). Thus NGOs, especially pro-democracy, human rights and opposition groups, received direct material support and indirect support (through condemnation of human rights abuses) from these powers. But by far the greatest external support was the so-called political conditionality – the stipulation that democratisation, good human rights records, liberalisation and market reforms had to be effected before African states could be granted the desperately needed loans and aid. The World Bank, IMF and other multilateral financial organisations also stipulated the same conditionalities, while the United Nations (UN), Commonwealth and other international organisations supported the

process through sanctions and threat of sanctions, isolation, investigations of human rights abuses and the monitoring of multiparty elections. International NGOs such as *Amnesty International* and *Human Rights Watch* also played key roles in these areas.

These pressures yielded some dividends in a number of countries. For example, President Daniel Arap Moi of Kenya was forced by the threat of withdrawal of aid by Britain and others to accept multiparty politics, while military leaders like J. J. Rawlings of Ghana and Blaise Campaore of Burkina Faso had to transform themselves into 'democratically-elected' leaders to satisfy the conditionalities for aid. There have also been remarkable changes in countries where political opposition, human rights and press freedom were previously denied. However, many of the changes were cosmetic or superficial, which is to say that despite the trappings of democracy, especially multiparty politics and the writing of new constitutions, the old authoritarian ways inherent in personal rulership and abuse of human rights remained strong (Bratton & Van de Walle, 1997).

The implementation of SAPs further alienated the state from the citizens and so also had a disabling effect on democratisation. Not only were the citizens not consulted before SAPs were introduced, but their implementation forced the state to become (more) authoritarian in order to implement the hardship-inflicting policies and contain the protests, riots and demands. For this reason, the logic of SAPs contradicted the logic of democratisation, and the fact that both were being simultaneously implemented has been identified as one of the reasons for the failure of democratisation in Africa in the 1980s and 1990s.

External problems

External problems refer to those problems emanating from outside the boundaries and control of the post-colonial African state. These problems are fundamental to understanding the problems of the contemporary state in Africa, not only because they are closely linked to the internal problems but also because even if the internal problems could be overcome, the external problems seriously incapacitate the state. The external problems mainly derive from the peripheral location of the state in the global capitalist system and the unequal exchange that characterises its relations with the dominant centres of that system (the industrialised or developed countries who belong to the twenty-nine member Organisation of Economic Co-operation and Development, the OECD, and the **G-8**). We have already seen how colonialism and neo-colonialism fostered the integration of African states into the global system as sources of raw materials and markets for finished products.

Since independence, most states in SSA have remained monocultural, that is, dependent on the export of one or a few cash crops (cotton, cocoa, groundnut, rubber, sugar, tea and coffee), animal products (cattle, beef, hides and skins, and fish) or minerals (copper, oil, diamonds, gold, uranium, bauxite and iron ore) for their foreign exchange earnings. With the exception of South Africa, they are not industrialised and are technologically dependent on the industrialised powers. African countries continue to attract the least amount of direct foreign investment (DFI) of all developing areas, making Africa as a whole the poorest and most marginalised of all the world's continents. For example, of the US$153,2 billion and US$159 billion net financial resources flow from the OECD countries to developing countries in 1992 and 1993 respectively, not only was Africa's share the least, but it was the only one that decreased, from US$24,1 billion to US$19 billion, in the same period (ADB, 1995:4).

These characteristics have serious implications for the role of African states in the global system. In particular, the dependence on one or a few export commodities makes the economies susceptible to the vagaries (some say manipulations) of international markets, as unexpected falls in the prices of these commodities tend to affect the countries directly and often adversely. At such points of diminishing resources and revenues, they are forced to resort to loans from the World Bank, IMF and other international creditors to offset **balance of payments** deficits and other financial problems. The total external debts of SSA countries have been on the increase since 1970. The enormity of the debt burden can only be appreciated when it is realised that a large proportion of the revenue accruing from exports (an average of 28,8% in 1993 and 35,4% in 1994), which should have been spent on developing or maintaining infrastructure, social services and so on, goes into servicing foreign debts (that is, paying the interests on the loans).

The burden of foreign debts is of such magnitude that several countries are simply not in a position to service the debts, much less repay them. Many of them have accordingly asked for their debts to be written off or for repayments to be rescheduled on more convenient terms. This leaves them at the mercy of creditors who have exploited the situation to exercise various kinds of direct and indirect control over their governments and economies in a new form of domination that has been described as the recolonisation of Africa. Chief amongst these have been the stipulation of democratisation, liberalisation and market reforms as conditionalities for getting new loans or debt relief through rescheduling of repayments.

As we have already discussed democratisation, the focus here will be on liberalisation or market reforms. At the core of the reforms embodied in SAPs is the removal of state control or regulation over economic, social and political activities such as foreign exchange, tariffs, trade restrictions, parastatals and civil society, and their subjection to the forces of free trade, demand and supply. The overriding objective is to down-size the over-bloated, inefficient and corrupt public sector and reduce the overbearing role of the state, which the World Bank blames for the woes of post-colonial African countries, and to expand the role of the private sector, including most foreign private investors, in the development process. The fact that SAPs are imposed by the World Bank/IMF and implemented under their direct supervision has put a question mark on the sovereignty of African states and their ability to perform as autonomous actors. At the same time, though, commentators agree that economic reform is desperately needed in SSA.

The future of the post-colonial state

This chapter has shown that most states have been crippled by an economic crisis primarily caused by political instability and malgovernance, which is complicated by diminishing resources and the debt overhang. The so-called market reforms imposed as a conditionality for new aid, loans and debt relief have not brought much relief, especially not for governments reeling under heavy budget and balance of payments deficits, and dependent on the World Bank and IMF to fund budgets and pay workers' salaries. They have not brought relief to the citizens either, but have brought in their wake poverty, massive unemployment, emigration of citizens to other countries, the inability of the state to perform its core functions and decaying infrastructure, all of which have elicited social unrest and political tensions. They have also failed to attract the expected foreign investment, as African states continue to receive the least DFI of all developing areas. The overall miserable state of the economy is well summarised in the observation that the economies of most African countries were worse off in the 1990s than they had been in the 1960s and 1970s, the first two decades of independence.

On the political side, the situation is not much better. Decades after independence, most countries are still plagued by political instability and lack of national cohesion. One party rule and military coups and rule have become far less frequent than they were in the 1960s, 1970s and 1980s (by 1998, Nigeria was the only country on the continent under effective military rule and virtually all other countries were at least

formally multiparty states). The democratic struggle has also yielded some dividends as we saw, not the least of which are greater concern with issues of constitutionality, human rights, accountability and autonomy of civil society, but the hallmarks of the crisis of legitimacy – political turbulence and threats to the continued survival of the state – remain prevalent.

Several countries are embroiled in civil war of differing scale (Burundi, Rwanda, the Central African Republic, the Congo, Somalia, Sierra Leone and Uganda), while others have been on the brink of disintegration. In those that recently ended civil wars, a relapse into violence has occured (Angola, Liberia and the DRC), and a few are plagued by separatist movements (Ethiopia, Senegal, Mali, Niger and Mauritania). Almost all other states suffer from one form of serious political turbulence or another. These range from hotly disputed electoral processes and outcomes to incessant anti-government riots, strikes, and demonstrations.

Given this gloomy picture, what can we expect in future? Will African states be recolonised as some Afro-pessimists predict or, in fact, recommend? Ali Mazrui, the distinguished African political scientist, for example, recommends a system of benign colonialism under which powerful African countries (Nigeria, Egypt and South Africa) would serve as colonial-type centres of growth in their respective sub-regions. Will states like Nigeria, Zaïre, Sudan, Somalia and Sierra Leone, which are threatened by serious internal conflicts, disintegrate? If so, what would the map of Africa look like in the twenty-first century? It is highly unlikely that African states will be recolonised. This is not only because the era of colonialism is over, or because Africa remains marginalised in terms of global capitalist investment, but because the phenomenal advances in telecommunication (electronic mail and the Internet), which have further integrated the world into a global village, make re-colonisation too costly.

As for the other questions, two points are all that need to be made. First, African states have shown a remarkable capacity for survival. So far, no state has split into two or more states on account of civil war. Even those such as Chad, Sierra Leone, Liberia, Sudan and Somalia, which had two or more rival governments in the course of civil war, did not fall apart. The survival of these countries owes much to the self-preservationist inclinations of the leaders of warring factions and most ordinary citizens as it does to the efforts of third-party mediators and peacekeeping forces to ensure the survival of the states and their international juridical identities. The second point is that the boundaries inherited from the colonial era, arbitrary as they are, have been substantially maintained, thanks to the efforts of the Organisation for African Unity (OAU) to prevent and minimise boundary problems on the continent. It seems unlikely that African leaders will support the disintegration of any state, as this is likely to threaten their own fragile systems. For these reasons, the map of Africa is not likely to change in the twenty-first century despite the chronic weaknesses and failures of the post-colonial state. But for African states to make real their claims to sovereignty, to be less susceptible to foreign influence and manipulation, and to become strong actors in international relations, they need to have the economic, technological and political capacities that would make them strong rather than the weak states they presently are.

Key concepts in this chapter are

Colonial state
Distributed justice
Good government
Import substitution
Neo-colonialism
Patronage
Post-colonial state
Structural adjustment
Weak state

Suggested readings

- The literature on the nature and problems of the post-colonial African state, including the political economy of the problems and relations between state and society, is vast. See, *inter alia, Presence Africaine,* Paris (1983) Special issue on 'The problematic of state in Africa', Nos 32/34; Rothchild, D. & Chazan, N. (eds) (1988) *The Precarious Balance: State and Society in Africa.* Boulder: Westview Press; Sandbrook, R. (1985) *The Politics of Africa's Economic Stagnation.* Cambridge: Cambridge University Press; Ergas, Z. (ed.) (1987) *African State in Transition.* London: Macmillan; Davidson, B. (1992) *The Black Man's Burden: Africa and the Curse of the Nation-State.* New York: Times Books.

- For analyses of political and economic reforms since the 1980s, see Wiseman, J. A. (1996) *The New Struggle for Democracy in Africa.* Aldershot: Avebury.

- For analyses of the world system and the development and consolidation of Africa's peripheral location within it, see various writings by the foremost world system theorist, Immanuel Wallerstein. In particular, see *The Modern World System* (3 volumes – 1974, 1980, 1989). New York: Academy Press. Also see Mazrui, A. A. (1978) *Africa's International Relations: The Diplomacy of Dependency and Change.* London: Heinemann.

12 | Making foreign policy in South Africa

Garth le Pere & Anthoni van Nieuwkerk

This chapter in outline
- Introduction
- The African National Congress (ANC) in exile
- South Africa's foreign policy and its settings
  - The Domestic environment
  - The regional environment
  - The international environment
- Foreign policy actors
  - The Department of Foreign Affairs (DFA)
  - The president and deputy-president
  - Parliament
  - The Department of Trade and Industry (DTI)
  - The Department of Defence (DoD)
  - The intelligence community
  - Other departments
  - Civil society
- Analysing a foreign policy decision
  - The decision to normalise relations with the People's Republic of China (PRC)
  - Applying the Allison models
- Concluding remarks

Introduction

This chapter concerns itself with processes that underpin and inform the making of foreign policy in South Africa. It attempts to describe and analyse the typical dilemmas that confront decision-makers and policy-makers as they grapple with difficult and at times seemingly intractable problems in foreign policy. As is evident from Chapter 5, foreign policy is made within analytically distinct domestic, international and psychological environments. Such environments tend to be infinitely elastic. As Frankel explains, '[t]heoretically, the environment of foreign policy decisions is limitless, it embraces the whole universe. Any domestic matter may impinge on foreign policy and require adjustment; any problem in any part of the world may call for urgent attention – even outer space and the moon are now included' (Frankel, 1968:3). However, in practice the environment is 'circumscribed', to use Frankel's term, by a range of factors and these include how a country defines its national goals, geographical location, military capability, level of economic development and type of government, how it perceives itself *vis-à-vis* the international system, and the types of resources it disposes of to influence other states in order to advance its own putative interests.

With this in mind, this chapter will explore the trajectory and evolution of foreign policy in South Africa, concentrating essentially on the period that marks South Africa's transition to a democracy since April 1994. An illustrative case-study is included, which demonstrates the problematic nature of foreign policy-making with regard to establishing diplomatic relations with the People's Republic of China (PRC).

It should be borne in mind that during the period of Nationalist Party (NP) rule from 1948 to 1994, South Africa was treated as a **pariah state** by the international community. The general opprobrium incurred because of **Apartheid** policies had a profound impact on the way South Africa was treated internationally and the manner in which it responded to external censure and sanctions. Successive Apartheid governments adopted defensive, reactionary and combative strategies in order to offset the impact of relative international isolation and punitive measures. Foreign policy-making was highly centralised, idiosyncratic yet rational if understood in Vale and Mphaisha's terms as a 'response to a series of strategic problems that confront decision-makers at any given moment' (*see* Chapter 5). Further, foreign policy was the exclusive preserve of the executive head of government (the prime minister or president) and 'his' foreign minister. In this scheme of things, according to a practitioner during the Apartheid years, '[p]olicy formulation was therefore limited to a handful of individuals who constituted a special kind of élite. For all practical purposes, Parliament played no role in foreign policy and the role of Cabinet tended to be limited to acquiescence or approval' (Sole, 1994:104; *see* also Geldenhuys, 1984:71–105). Under President P.W. Botha, institutional mechanisms such as the State Security Council (SSC) were also established to meet the challenges of the 'total onslaught'. This 'militarisation' of policy meant that the full might of South Africa's military machine was deployed in the region to contain an ostensible communist threat and to weed out African National Congress (ANC) guerrilla bases. Foreign policy was thus a response to perceived and real threats to South Africa's increasing marginalisation in world affairs. There were widespread calls, for example, from the United Nations (UN), the **Commonwealth** and the **Non-Aligned Movement** (NAM) for political and economic sanctions against South Africa while the ANC's foreign policy in exile was directed at isolating the country by carrying the UN declaration to the world that 'Apartheid was a crime against humanity'.

The African National Congress (ANC) in exile

While in exile, the ANC established a network of offices in a range of international capitals such as

Moscow, Oslo, London, New York, New Delhi, Havana and Egypt, and by 1990, it had twenty-eight strategically located diplomatic offices abroad. According to Thomas, the ANC's foreign policy in exile rested on three pillars:

1. to isolate South Africa by publicising the injustices of Apartheid and to call for the imposition of sanctions;
2. to forge political and ideological alliances with sympathetic countries and other liberation movements in support of the armed struggle; and, more controversially,
3. to project itself (with the PAC) as the 'sole legitimate representative of the South African people' (Thomas, 1996).

The task of ANC country representatives was to conduct an aggressive diplomatic campaign directed at influencing the host country's attitude towards the South African government of the day. This campaign certainly gained momentum after the dramatic student uprising in 1976 and the ANC and PAC gained new-found respectability and growing stature, especially among Western countries. It successfully mobilised international public opinion and operational support, primarily because, as Lodge explains, 'underneath the shelter afforded by sympathetic government, the organization developed resources well beyond the capacity of internally based South African political movements' (Lodge, 1987:26–27).

Once the ANC assumed power after April 1994, it had to come to terms with what amounted to a double transition. First, there was the imperative to refocus philosophically and re-adjust politically from being 'first among equals' in the liberation movement to becoming the governing political party. The ANC-led **government of national unity** (GNU) had to register a decisive normative and moral break with the past and assume challenging new responsibilities relating to nation-building, democratic governance and institutional restructuring. Second, there was the imperative to understand the tectonic shifts in world order, following the collapse

of the bipolar world and the end of the **Cold War**. This meant crafting a foreign policy that, while sensitive to the needs of internal transformation, would, nevertheless, reflect a recognition of the altered international relations terrain, as well as adopt a 'pragmatic internationalism' towards engaging with a globalising environment.

South Africa's foreign policy and its setting

As early as 1993, Nelson Mandela articulated several principles that would underpin South Africa's future foreign policy (Mandela, 1993:87). These principles were further elaborated in March 1994, when the ANC published a comprehensive foreign policy document entitled 'Foreign Policy Perspectives in a Democratic South Africa'. This document advances seven principles that ought to guide the conduct of South Africa's new foreign policy:

1. a belief in and preoccupation with human rights that extends beyond the political, embracing economic, social and environmental dimensions;
2. a belief that just and lasting solutions to the problems of humankind can only come through the promotion of democracy worldwide;
3. a belief that justice and international law should guide relations between nations;
4. a belief that international peace is the goal to which all nations should strive;
5. a belief that South Africa's foreign policy should reflect the interests of Africa;
6. a belief that South Africa's economic development depends on growing regional and international economic co-operation; and
7. a belief that South Africa's foreign relations must mirror a deep commitment to the consolidation of its democracy.

For the ANC, the struggle for an Apartheid-free South Africa was in many ways a struggle for fundamental **human rights**. It is no coincidence, therefore, that the promotion of human rights has been canonised as a cornerstone in its foreign policy. Furthermore, the emphasis on the promotion of democracy and adherence to **international law** embodies the values and norms enshrined in South Africa's new constitution. It is worth noting that South Africa's neighbours suffered immeasurable harm in aiding and supporting the struggle for liberation. A range of African countries also provided the ANC and PAC with material support and formal diplomatic recognition while in exile. Much of the continent thus enjoys a special relationship with the ANC and vice versa, and Africa's elevation to a foreign policy priority is thus not surprising. There are elements of a neat, logical symmetry between the ethical and normative constructs of its domestic policies and the idealist foundations of its foreign policy. The domestic public policy emphasis on democracy, justice and human rights is refracted in the foreign policy principles listed above. The Reconstruction and Development Programme (RDP) White Paper (1994), for example, also refers to the importance of rebuilding the South African economy in partnership with its regional neighbours and the necessity for integrating trade and foreign policy as part of a broader strategic approach to strengthen South-South co-operation (*see* Chapter 13).

The leitmotif governing foreign policy has been labelled 'universality', which is essentially the opening of foreign and local doors in the same reconciliatory spirit that has characterised South Africa's own domestic transformation. The noble intentions and the affirmation of certain values in its foreign policy notwithstanding, the realisation and implementation of such intentions and values have proven, in practice, to be an ongoing dilemma and a vexing problem. In the view of one analyst, South Africa's 'foreign relations could be said to be lacking the necessary broad orientation and strategic purpose' (Mills, 1997:19). The classical challenge confronting South Africa is that of developing appropriate operational and psychological milieux for foreign policy. This includes what

Hermann calls 'regime orientation', which can be described as 'the shared political system belief of authoritative decision makers about their country's relationship to its external environment and the roles of government appropriate for pursuing the belief' (Hermann, cited in Walker, 1987:277). In South Africa's case, the visionary and enlightened principles in its foreign policy form a more or less coherent belief system or world-view. However, there seems to be less consensus among the key decision-making élite about the substance and goals of policy and what has proved to be much more problematic is the processes by which policy is made. Besides ideological, organisational and systemic considerations, this is substantially conditioned by the domestic and external environments. While domestic factors are a critical ingredient in how foreign policy is made, the focus of foreign policy is the external environment. In the words of Frankel, '[t]he ghosts of the theories of sovereignty linger with us and the physical delimitation of frontiers persists but in fact states have completely forfeited the hard shell of impenetrability ... Their domestic affairs have become a matter of foreign concern which states cannot ward off by insisting on national sovereignty' (Frankel, 1968:66). A country's foreign policy has to be communicated, explained and executed in its external environment. Foreign policy goals depend on external actions, reactions and interactions for their realisation, efficacy and impact (*see*, for example, Box 12.1 below). It is worthwhile then to examine briefly the different environments in which South African foreign policy is made.

The domestic environment

The basic objectives of a country's foreign policy are determined within a domestic context. Seen through the domestic prism of ensuring national security, welfare and economic growth, the means of achieving these reside increasingly in the external environment. There are several national attributes that are important for a

Box 12.1: Thinking about foreign policy, by Vusi Mavimbela*

'It helps to reflect on foreign policy issues that are driven not by self-importance or emotional subjectivity but by well-thought-out guidelines and policy positions that are to the benefit of more fundamental ideals.

The first guideline relates to the concept of global governance as an aspect of globalisation. As the nation-state gravitates towards greater integration into the world, two dialectically opposite forces impact on it: one is centrifugal, the other centripetal.

The nation-state is increasingly surrendering part of its sovereign power to regional, continental and global institutions, such as the Southern African Development Community (SADC) and the Organisation of African Unity (OAU). At the same time, it is developing increasing power in its citizenry as they mobilise organs of civil society to demand for expanded democracy.

Greater devolution of power helps to compensate for power lost to larger foreign institutions. In that context, drastic initiatives such as the decision to commit military troops in foreign lands should be the function primarily of institutions rather than the subjective preserve of individual nation-states. If we encourage individual initiatives, we are likely to undermine the cohesiveness of the very institutions we have set up to serve as our governors in global affairs.

Similarly, organs of popular expression become indispensable if the nation-state hopes to sustain such drastic and expensive initiatives as conducting wars in foreign lands.

The second guideline relates to the fact that a nation-state's foreign policy is like the Greek god Janus – it has two faces looking in opposite directions. Foreign policy both expresses and reflects domestic policy. The form of the nation-state's interaction in the global village, as well as the content of that interaction, also tells the world about the extent of the frontiers of freedom that the state allows its own citizenry.

The third point to consider is that genuine democracies do not go to war against each other. Every time a war breaks out between nation-states, it is certain that at least one is not a genuine democracy.

The operational concept in this instance is 'democracy'. So, the moment a nation-state commits troops in foreign wars is the moment it enters murky political waters.

The fourth point is that what governs international relations is neither friendship nor an idealistic sense of camaraderie, but interests. The correct definition of these interests helps to guide proper engagement with the world around us.

South Africa has made the African Renaissance the cornerstone of its interactions with the world, especially within our continent. Our national interest is underpinned by this continental and global vision. Any talk of the renewal of our country, region and continent can be predicated only on a stable and peaceful Africa, committed to the principles of democracy and respect for human rights; a region and continent guided by clear and deliberate socio-economic development programmes.

Those who define their interests narrowly are likely to miss the picture of the bigger things that should underpin the national interest.'

The Sunday Times – 98.09.13
*Special adviser in Deputy-President Thabo Mbeki's office

---

country's foreign policy and these include its history, geostrategic location, economic prowess, military power and resource endowments (Kegley & Wittkopf, 1993:60–70). These taken together permit and constrain a country's ability to act and interact with its external environment.

South Africa's domestic environment has been drastically altered after the formal demise of Apartheid following the elections in April 1994. The domestic imperatives of transforming society and consolidating democratic gains have to do battle with ethical and welfare concerns of addressing the historical legacies of Apartheid, especially as these affect the state's ability to meet very basic needs. Although now abandoned, the government's RDP formed the policy template for addressing the injustices of the past while contemplating the need to maintain the South African economy on a path of sustained growth. The Growth, Employment and Redistribution (GEAR) strategy was inaugurated as the government's response to the country's macroeconomic challenges. This translated into a robust external offensive in search of increasing direct investment, new markets for export, and development aid for infrastructural and human resources development.

After a near half century of relative isolation, South Africa's passage from an authoritarian system of government to a democracy has brought it into close and intimate contact with much of the world. Its enunciated foreign policy goals (enshrined in the concept of 'universality') are to form alliances with countries and regional blocs as well as partnerships with international organisations and transnational corporations for the purpose of reconstructing the social and economic fabric of its society.

The regional environment

South Africa's regional relations have also benefited from its transition. In a rather ironic twist, it has now become one of the main guarantors of regional security and, by its example, has strongly promoted regional norms of democracy and human rights. South Africa's destructive campaign of destabilisation and inter-state hostilities during the Apartheid era have been replaced by a co-operative philosophy and a professed intention 'to become part of a movement to create a new form of economic interaction in the region based on principles of mutual benefit and interdependence' (ANC, 1994). The RDP White Paper (1994) further enjoins the new government to 'negotiate with neighbouring countries to forge an equitable and mutually beneficial programme for increasing co-operation, co-ordination and

integration'. As a measure of its commitment to regional development, South Africa joined the Southern African Development Community (SADC) in 1994 (*see* Chapter 15).

While policy-makers continue to be preoccupied with the demands of domestic restructuring, their stated commitment to regionalism and regional integration in Southern Africa is fraught with differing and contradictory interpretations. A more welfarist approach stresses an affirmative action type of intervention by South Africa, which will assist underdeveloped countries. At the other extreme are those who advocate an 'open' regionalism based on competition and comparative advantage. South Africa – whether the regional hegemon or partner – is thus forced to steer a middle path between these regional and global pressures for promoting the region's development (*see* Awhireng-Obeng & McGowan, 1998). Whatever the case, South Africa's overwhelming economic superiority and military and political dominance will be a focal point for the region's growth, and its own development, in turn, will prove decisive for the entire region.

The international environment

South Africa's own transition more or less coincides with major shifts and changes in the global order. The most egregious of these are the disintegration of the Soviet empire and the unprecedented impact of **globalisation** on the world economy. As commonly understood, economic globalisation implies a rapid increase in economic interaction across borders, and results in the inability of national governments to keep exclusive control over macro-economic policy making. Unfettered and unruly market forces have become important agents and forces of change, although one should not underestimate the resilience of states to resist the negative impact of these market forces (Hirst and Thompson, 1996).

A developing country such as South Africa is, and one whose economy is very 'open' (dependent on trade and foreign investment), is particularly vulnerable to the pernicious effects of unbridled market forces. In responding to global market pressures, it has to continue to attract foreign investment, establish globally competitive credentials and commit the country to economic liberalisation by subscribing to the trade rules of the **World Trade Organisation** (WTO). Although consistent trade liberalisation also has obvious benefits for South Africa (such as giving its exports greater and freer access to other markets, and lowering the price of imported goods), the unbridled behaviour of financial market forces impose a difficult set of economic and political circumstances and choices on South Africa. In order to secure its democratic gains and to further make advances in welfare provision and poverty alleviation, South Africa's foreign policy tools, and those who hone them, will need to come to terms with these imponderable factors in the international environment.

This has dire consequences for South Africa's economic prospects. In the face of having to respond to global market pressures, it has to continue to attract foreign investment, establish globally competitive credentials and commit the country to economic liberalisation.

Foreign policy actors

Traditionally, the most important persons involved in a country's foreign affairs are its head of government and the foreign minister. Whether the head of government be president, or prime minister, that person 'is formally the key figure in all foreign policy decisions. According to international law and practice, the head of government, as the political leader of the people, officially speaks for the state in international relations and exercises ultimate authority in the area of foreign policy' (Said *et al.*, 1995:39). The foreign minister, in turn, is a specialist with a good technical grasp of the complexities of day-to-day decisions and an appreciation of the larger internal and external environments in which the head of government has to operate. In addition, the foreign minister is the administrative head of the

foreign ministry and plays a decision-making and advisory role (Said *et al.*, 1995:40).

However, foreign policy principles and priorities have been formulated and planned by multiple actors in post-Apartheid South Africa. While the primary locus of expertise in and implementation of foreign policy is the Department of Foreign Affairs (DFA), it often finds itself in competition if not at odds with a range of other actors who also shape policy. These include the president, the deputy-president, cabinet, parliament, parliamentary committees dealing with foreign affairs and trade, other state departments, such as the Department of Trade and Industry (DTI), the Department of Defence (DoD) and civil society components such as non-governmental organisations (NGOs) (Muller, 1997:70; *see* also Figure 12.1). This is understandable in view of the widening scope of international relations and the blurring of the traditional demarcation lines between domestic and foreign affairs – what Keohane & Nye (1997) have called 'complex interdependence'. Foreign policy agendas now include issues as diverse as investment, migration, energy, inflation, food security, human rights, and the environment. Government leaders thus 'find it increasingly difficult to set priorities, avoid contradictory targets, and maintain a sense of national interest and direction. Since the alternatives are more numerous and less clear-cut, the task of choosing becomes more complex' (Karvonen & Sundelius, 1987:7). In an era that stresses the importance of global financial markets, international trade linkages and information technology, the management of the foreign policy agenda becomes a task for multiple bureaucratic players.

If we refer back to the exposition offered in Chapter 5 of the models of foreign policy-making, contemporary international relations requires an explanatory compass that incorporates and syntheses elements of all of Allison's three models: the rational actor, the organisational process and bureaucratic politics.

The multiplicity of actors involved in policy formulation within South Africa encourages

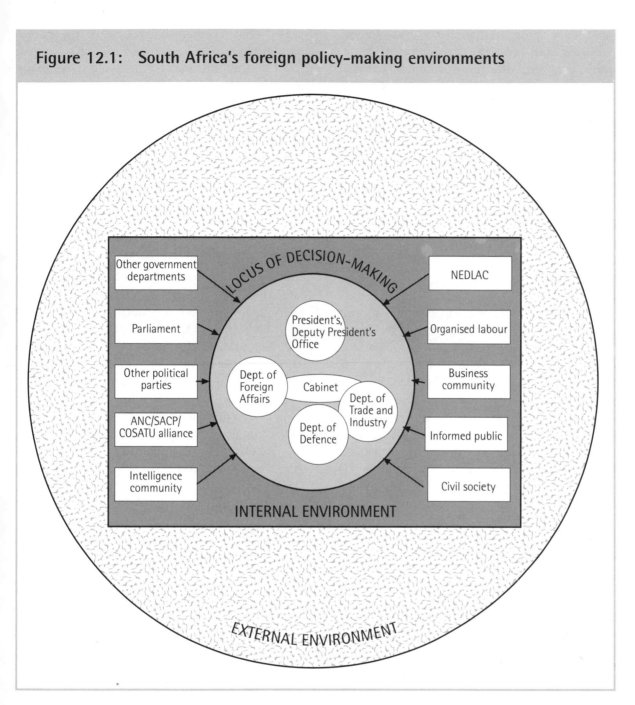

Figure 12.1: South Africa's foreign policy-making environments

LOCUS OF DECISION-MAKING

Other government departments

Parliament

Other political parties

ANC/SACP/COSATU alliance

Intelligence community

NEDLAC

Organised labour

Business community

Informed public

Civil society

President's, Deputy President's Office

Dept. of Foreign Affairs

Cabinet

Dept. of Trade and Industry

Dept. of Defence

INTERNAL ENVIRONMENT

EXTERNAL ENVIRONMENT

accusations of incoherence, inconstancy and opaqueness (Muller, 1997:69). Let us examine some of the actors in terms of their place in the policy-making processes.

The Department of Foreign Affairs (DFA)

The DFA is headed by a minister and a deputy minister. Of all state departments, its role as the new custodian of foreign policy has been mired in controversy and contestation. To begin with, it inherited a highly fragmented and ideologically polarised staff, and the integration of the old bureaucracy with the new government's corps of officials has not been a smooth process. One view holds that South Africa's foreign policy circles are divided between an 'internationalist' and 'neo-mercantilist' camp. Officials representing the previous Apartheid government belong to the latter group, and 'consistent with the logic of neo-realism, emphasised the importance of trade and self interest over all else'. The 'internationalists' were mainly those who returned from exile or 'were in favour of a demonstrably greater degree of solidarity with the collective problems of the developing world' (Van der Westhuizen, 1998:444).

An essential component in a country's foreign policy machinery is its diplomatic service (*see* Chapter 4). It is through this medium of communication that countries conduct their relations. Maintaining missions abroad is an expensive business, as is evident from Table 12.1. South Africa's missions vary in size and structure. Its largest embassy is in the United States (US) with fifty-five staff members (including consulates-general), followed by the United Kingdom (UK) with forty staff members and Germany with twenty-five. Indeed, the expenditure priorities on foreign missions in developed counties has not matched South Africa's rhetoric about promoting South-South co-operation as a foreign

policy goal. Former chairperson of the parliamentary portfolio committee on foreign affairs, Raymond Suttner, was therefore led to complain in 1995 that 'of R645 million budgeted for foreign missions only approximately R105 million was allocated to missions in Africa' (Suttner, 1996:140).

The president and deputy-president

President Harry Truman, US president from 1945 to 1952, once remarked that 'the President makes foreign policy' (cited in Frankel, 1968:21). In South Africa's case, given President Mandela's towering personality, international prestige and stature, this would not be an inaccurate postulate. His command and seeming domination of every major foreign policy decision and issue has been so complete that he almost overshadows the role of the DFA, cabinet and parliament. However, cabinet and, to a lesser extent, parliament maintain checks and balances on presidential authority. Procedurally, the president has to consult and get the approval of cabinet on every major foreign policy decision. This notwithstanding, in the view of Mills, 'it has meant South Africa's image (and its foreign policy) tends largely to be equated with the President's profile. As a result, policy has often followed his public statements, rather than the other way around' (Mills, 1997:24).

President Mandela fits the image of the 'hero-in-history'. It is no hyperbole to equate his role in South Africa with that of other great leaders in history who have dramatically shaped and determined the outcomes of human affairs. These would include figures such as Winston Churchill, Franklin D. Roosevelt, Mikhail Gorbachev and Fidel Castro.

The deputy-president, and likely future president, is also a very skilled diplomat and international statesperson. While in exile, Thabo Mbeki was the ANC's chief diplomat and his outlook is distinctly internationalist. Like President Mandela, he has had a hand in fashioning the contours of South Africa's foreign relations. He has, for example, been the prime architect of

Table 12.1: Department of Foreign Affairs (DFA) expenditure, 1996/7 (R'000)	
Administration	94 361
Foreign relations	835 904
Foreign representation	202 467
Total	1 132 732
DFA, Office of the Auditor General, March 1997	

reconfiguring South Africa's relations with the US and Africa. With regard to the former, Mr Mbeki is co-chairman with US Vice-President Albert Gore of the Bi-National Commission, which meets twice a year to enhance and consolidate the countries' bilateral relations. In Africa, he has articulated a visionary policy framework around the concept of an 'African Renaissance', which advocates a renewal of the continent by seeking African solutions to African problems (*see* Box 12.2 and Chapter 10). In addition, the

Co-ordination and Implementation Unit (CIU) in the Office of the Deputy-President facilitates policy co-ordination across government. One of four professional units in the CIU is specifically concerned with international relations.

Parliament

Parliament in South Africa is made up of the National Assembly and the National Council of Provinces. The main function of the National

---

Box 12.2: Africa is a rebel with a cause. Excerpts from a speech by Thabo Mbeki

'An ill wind has blown me across the face of Africa. I have seen the poverty of Orlando East and the wealth of Morningside in Johannesburg. In Lusaka, I have seen the poor of Kanyama township and the prosperous residents of Kabulonga. I have seen the slums of Sirulere in Lagos and the opulence of Victoria Island. I have seen the faces of the poor in Mbare in Harare and the quiet wealth of Borrowdale.

And I have heard the stories of how those who had access to power, or access to those who had access to power, of how they have robbed and pillaged and broken all laws and all ethical norms to acquire wealth.

Their measure of success is the amount of wealth they can accumulate and the ostentation they can achieve, which will convince all that they are a success, because, in a visible way, they are people of means. Thus they seek access to power or access to those who have access to power so that they can corrupt the political order for personal gain at all costs. In this equation, the poverty of the masses becomes a necessary condition for the enrichment of the few and the corruption of political power, the only possible condition for its exercise. It is out of this pungent mixture of greed, dehumanising poverty, obscene wealth and endemic public and private corrupt practice, that many of Africa's *coups d'état*, civil wars

and situations of instability are born and entrenched.

The African Renaissance demands that we purge ourselves of the parasites and maintain a permanent vigilance against the danger of the entrenchment in African society of this rapacious stratum. The call for Africa's renewal is a call to rebellion. We must rebel against the tyrants and the dictators, those who seek to corrupt our societies and steal the wealth that belongs to the people. We must rebel against the ordinary criminals who murder, rape and rob, and conduct war against poverty, ignorance and the backwardness of the children of Africa.

Surely there must be politicians and business people, youth and women activists, trade unionists, religious leaders, artists and professionals from the Cape to Cairo, from Madagascar to Cape Verde who are sufficiently enraged by Africa's condition in the world to want to join the mass crusade for Africa's renewal.

It is to these that we say, without equivocation, that to be a true African is to be a rebel in the cause of the African Renaissance, whose success in the new century and millennium is one of the great historic challenges of our time.'

Office of the Deputy-President, 12 August 1998 (speech delivered at Midrand and televised by SABC)

Assembly as set out in the constitution is to represent the people by 'providing a national forum for public consideration of issues, by passing legislation and by scrutinizing and overseeing executive action'. The National Council of Provinces, in turn, represents the interests of the nine provinces at national level and it does so 'by participating in the national legislative process and by providing a national forum for public consideration of issues affecting the provinces' (South African Constitution, 1996:Article 42). Parliament thus has a distinct constitutional duty in the process of government and 'is the pre-eminent institution through which the public expresses its views concerning foreign policy' (Suttner, 1996:136). The role of parliament in foreign policy is important for ratifying treaties and evaluating draft policy documents, and for appropriating funds and approving departmental budgets. Furthermore, the parliamentary portfolio committee on foreign affairs is a specialist, activist multiparty body of representatives that ensures that the oversight and review function is properly executed and that democratic procedures and principles are observed.

The Department of Trade and Industry (DTI)

Investment and foreign trade, especially with regard to gaining preferential access to developed countries' markets, have become important instruments in South Africa's economic development, its export diversification and industrialisation strategy. As a consequence, since 1994, the DTI, now headed by Mr Alec Erwin, has emerged as the chief steward of South Africa's bilateral and multilateral trade diplomacy and it boasts a formidable team of negotiators. It is generally responsible for encouraging foreign direct investment (FDI), expanding transnational commerce, negotiating trade deals with countries and regional blocs, and representing the country in multilateral bodies such as the WTO and the **UN Conference on Trade and Development** (UNCTAD). It has, for example,

developed South Africa's negotiating mandate for a free trade agreement with the fifteen-member European Union (EU), which is its largest and most important trading partner. Closer to home, the DTI has been instrumental in the crafting and promotion of a free trade protocol in SADC. Its objective is to introduce a progressive reduction of tariff and non-tariff barriers to trade within the region to the extent that all intraregional trade is substantially free by 2006 (*see* also Chapter 14).

The Department of Defence (DoD)

The role of the military establishment has changed quite fundamentally since 1994. During the Apartheid years when concerns about national security and 'total onslaught' were synonymous with defence, the military and its senior officials enjoyed unparalleled influence in shaping policy. After 1994, the official discourse has embraced a widened, people-centred definition of security, which incorporates political, economic, social and environmental dimensions (DoD, 1996). The military and DoD have simply become one of several, albeit important, actors in the decision-making process. As security matters and arms sales have become a more critical feature of South Africa's foreign relations, so has the profile of the DoD become prominent. In regional security matters, the South African National Defence Force (SANDF) has played a key role in the operational planning of the SADC Organ for Politics, Defence and Security, and although far from settled and contentious, an increasing role for the SANDF is contemplated in continental peacekeeping, peace-building and conflict prevention (*see* Solomon & van Aardt, 1998).

With regard to arms sales, a cabinet committee was established to guide the terms of selling and exporting of conventional arms. It is called the National Conventional Arms Control Committee (NCACC) and is chaired by Professor Kader Asmal, the Minister of Water Affairs and Forestry. Importantly, other cabinet members of the NCACC include the Ministers of Defence;

Trade and Industry; Arts, Culture, Science and Technology; Constitutional Affairs; Public Enterprises; Intelligence Services; Foreign Affairs; and Safety and Security.

The DoD also represents South Africa where bilateral defence matters are concerned. Thus, for example, the Defence Minister represents South Africa on a sub-committee dealing with defence and security at the US-SA Bi-National Commission.

The intelligence community

Intelligence services acquire information that might be deemed important for a country's decision-making processes. The archetype of cloak and dagger activities of the Soviet Union's KGB (Committee of State Security) and US's CIA (Central Intelligence Agency), involving espionage and sabotage, belonged more to the Cold War era. In the present information age, more sophisticated means can be brought to bear on the intelligence-gathering function. However, where there are separate military and civilian intelligence agencies, a struggle usually ensues between centripetal and centrifugal forces

(Frankel, 1968:51). Military intelligence tends to be highly centralised, concentrated as it is around its respective branches, and it is a potential centre of power. Civilian intelligence might have several arms and hence its decentralised and often unco-ordinated nature. The two often vie for influence in policy.

In South Africa, there are various agencies charged with the intelligence function. The civilian bodies are the National Intelligence Agency (NIA) and the South African Secret Service (SASS). Their military counterpart is called the Military Intelligence Agency (MIA) and to obviate the struggle referred to above, all their work is centrally co-ordinated by the National Intelligence Co-ordinating Committee (NICOC). These agencies jointly and separately provide information on internal and external security and related matters to all important decision-makers in government. They are consequently in a position to substantially influence how a particular foreign policy problem is understood, conceptualised and resolved. This is particularly the case with regard to the new security challenges confronting South Africa. The role of intelligence thus cannot be exaggerated in combating

Table 12.2:   South Africa's top ten trading partners, 1997 (R'000)

Exports to	Amount (R'000)	%	Imports from	Amount (R'000)	%
United Kingdom	13 449	22,3	Germany	20 436	22,7
United States	9 746	16,1	United States	15 879	17,6
Japan	9 304	15,4	United Kingdom	14 972	16,6
Germany	5 653	9,4	Japan	13 025	14,5
Zimbabwe	5 439	9,0	Italy	5 594	6,2
Switzerland	3 867	6,4	Iran	5 296	5,9
Belgium	3 621	6,0	France	4 236	4,7
Netherlands	3 327	5,5	Taiwan	4 103	4,6
Taiwan	3 169	5,2	Netherlands	3 308	3,7
South Korea	2 818	4,7	Sweden	3 110	3,5
Total	60 393	100,0		89 959	100,0

'A Study of South Africa's Major Trade and Investment Partners',
SA Foundation, Occasional Paper, No. 1, April 1998, p. 7.

the scourge of international crime syndicates, drug cartels, illicit arms trade, money laundering schemes and illegal migration (Landsberg & Masiza, 1996:28–33).

Other departments

It should be clear by now that there are a wide array of departments that, in one way or another, are involved in foreign affairs. In South Africa's case, examples would include the following departments:

- Arts, Culture, Science and Technology – negotiates the transfer and exchange of scientific and technological knowledge from other countries.
- Environmental Affairs and Tourism – responsible for the implementation and monitoring of international environmental agreements.
- Finance – represents South Africa in international financial institutions such as the **World Bank** and **International Monetary Fund** (IMF).
- Justice – represents South Africa at international forums such as the International Court of Justice and implements international legal treaties.
- Sport and Recreation – facilitates South Africa's re-integration into international sporting bodies such as the Olympics, World Rugby Union and International Football Federation.
- Home Affairs – develops and implements a policy for immigration to South Africa based on international conventions.

Civil society

While states remain the dominant actors in international politics, new participants now include non-state actors such as business, transnational interest groups and NGOs such as trade unions and churches (*see* Chapter 7). South Africa is no exception in its number of non-state actors that exert an influence on foreign policy or at least attempt to do so. The business community, constantly in search of new opportunities, especially

in Africa, has made ample use of the offices of the DTI and DFA in facilitating contact or promoting trade missions.

When in June 1996 the DFA released its equivalent of a foreign policy White Paper, the 'South African Foreign Policy Discussion Document', it invited a cross-section of academic and other NGO interests to a forum where they tried to prioritise the goals set out in the document. To some extent, the views of civil society on issues of South Africa's foreign relations are known. During the Apartheid years, regular but limited (whites only) opinion surveys were conducted that attempted to capture the 'public mood'. More recently, surveys among all South Africans have been launched, and one can now speak of 'South African public opinion on foreign policy'.

Analysing a foreign policy decision

This section presents a case-study analysis of the foreign policy process. In this case, we have chosen to investigate one of the new South African government's first and most difficult foreign policy challenges – that of 'normalising' its relations with the People's Republic of China (PRC). This analysis of the policy process draws on insights gained from Chapter 5, namely Allison's three models of decision-making.

The section concludes with a brief assessment of the applicability and efficacy of the theoretical model.

The decision to normalise relations with the PRC

In 1994, the newly elected government in South Africa faced the challenge of implementing a number of anticipated policy departures from that of the previous Apartheid government.

Foreign policy was one such area of departure, and it soon became evident that the new administration had indeed designed a fundamental shift in policy orientation – precipitated by the ANC's thinking on the matter and publicly announced by its leadership (its elements are described earlier in the chapter). To recapture briefly, in 1993 the ANC announced its Asian foreign policy orientation. It proclaimed that:

'Although some of our peoples and the liberation movement have had important links with Asian countries and peoples, South Africa under the existing regime has had only limited contact with this important region of the world. A democratic government will vigorously seek to extend South Africa's economic relations with Asian countries' (ANC, 1993:16–17).

This opened the way for a reconsideration of South Africa's diplomatic relations with Taiwan (the Republic of China) with whom the Apartheid government had had strong relations. Because of these relations, Communist China (the People's Republic of China) refused to have diplomatic relations with South Africa.

The ANC also stated that '[i]n issues of recognition, we will be guided by international law and practice at the United Nations' – a clear reference to the fact that South Africa at that time had not established diplomatic relations with the PRC.

However, as Raymond Suttner – an ANC member of parliament – observed in 1995, foreign policy is not made on a clean slate. In his view, the new government had inherited relationships, but there was also the issue of the absence of relationships with various states. Consequently, in his view, 'it has to decide whether or how to continue relationships. It also has to decide whether or not to establish new relationships and on what basis' (Suttner, 1995:4). Furthermore, the core of the problem with regard to China was the Apartheid legacy:

'There is an inherited relationship with Taiwan, resulting from a shared isolation during the Apartheid years. Taiwan was one of the few entities with whom South Africa could form diplomatic relations and interact relatively closely. On the other hand, there are only unofficial relations with the PRC. This is surely an untenable and unsustainable situation' (Suttner, 1995:4).

However, not all South Africans were convinced that the situation was unsustainable. Despite the fact that the new government was clear in its intention to normalise its relationship with the PRC, many voices offered alternative views and recommendations. Between 1994 and 1997, three schools of thought emerged: those advocating diplomatic recognition of the PRC, which automatically implied the downgrading of diplomatic relations with Taiwan; those urging the continued diplomatic recognition of Taiwan, which meant unofficial relations with the PRC; and, finally, those who urged the so-called option of dual recognition of Taiwan and the PRC.

On Thursday, 28 November 1996, leading newspapers in South Africa announced the new government's most dramatic foreign policy decision to date in colourful headlines: 'Shock as SA dumps Taiwan for China' (*The Star*) and 'SA breaks ties with RoC – full links with red China' (*The Citizen*). Indeed, in a surprise announcement the previous day, President Mandela had stated that South Africa would award diplomatic recognition to the PRC and therefore downgrade relations with Taiwan. Not to be outdone, Chinese commentators followed suit: 'A wise strategic decision – written in celebration of establishment of China-South Africa relations' (Qiang & Zhonggui, 1997).

Why was this decision so dramatic and shocking? Paradoxically, Mandela's announcement was both expected, and surprising – expected because increasingly for the government the question was not the shifting of diplomatic relations, but the timing of it; surprising because the announcement came without any warning, prompt or alert. President Mandela communicated the decision to Beijing and Taipei only one day earlier, and South African observers and even departmental representatives were all caught off guard.

On what basis then, did South Africa's foreign

policy-makers reach this dramatic decision? Why was the decision delayed for so long? Expectations were that the new government, upon taking office in 1994, would not delay in normalising its relationship with a global power. Who were involved in the process, and what were the pressures that came to bear on it?

Applying the Allison models

'In any policy situation there will be elements of choice (rational actor), routine (governmental process) and contest (bureaucratic politics), but they will not be the same for all the participants, or at all times, or in all policy fields' (Colebatch, 1998:81, as cited in Chapter 5).

As argued in Chapter 5, by using Allison's models, foreign policy decision-making processes can be 'mapped' or framed in three ways to explain what happens when groups in a government meet, deliberate and recommend options. These are known as the rational actor model, the organisational process model and the bureaucratic politics model.

The rational actor model

The activity of foreign policy-making, in this model, occurs between identified players who have set goals and who make clearly defined and informed choices about how to achieve them. In Allison's model, the challenge for the decision-maker is to make a choice between competing alternative options. A range of assumptions underlie this approach: the existence of a centrally controlled, informed and value-maximising government; behaviour that follows calculated choices from informed and rational leaders; and a government that will act on the basis of either opportunities or threats originating from the international environment.

If this model is applied to the situation at hand, what does it explain, and what can we learn? If we assume that the South African state

acted as a unitary actor, that its leaders were well informed and that they made a rational choice between competing alternatives, then we can argue that the South African foreign policy-makers were faced with a fairly straightforward situation. They had to consider three scenarios and choose one way forward. These scenarios were:

1. maintain the status quo, which meant maintaining full diplomatic relations with Taiwan and limited relations with the PRC;
2. reverse the status quo, which meant delinking diplomatically from Taiwan and establishing diplomatic relations with the PRC; or
3. develop a new option, which meant attempting to establish diplomatic relations with both Taiwan and the PRC.

As part of the decision-making process, the South African government would have had to consider the implications of these three competing alternatives, before coming to a final decision.

Choosing the first or third option (status quo and dual recognition) would have meant an apparent continuation of the strong trade and investment links between South Africa and Taiwan. This possibility was strengthened by the Taiwanese who, in anticipation of the decision, sent numerous messages to South Africa promising an increasing flow of investment and development aid (Mills, 1995:92–94). However, it would also have meant foregoing the economic opportunity of allowing South Africa to fully benefit from the growing Chinese market, and, furthermore, would have prevented South Africa from counting the PRC as an ally in its international relations. By all accounts, these two considerations weighed heavily on the minds of the decision-makers. As for the dual recognition option, despite arguments by some analysts (Breytenbach, 1994; Daniel, 1995; Sono, 1995; Geldenhuys, 1995), as well as the Taiwanese, favouring South Africa exercising this option, it was evident to most observers that this would simply not have been allowed by Beijing.

This left the South African government with

the option of reversing the status quo. The implications of delinking from Taiwan in order to establish diplomatic relations with the PRC meant a serious consideration of the damage Taiwan might cause to South Africa by withdrawing or suspending investment and co-operation agreements. Indeed, the Taiwanese took great pains to convince South Africa of the negative fall-out associated with this option. The PRC in turn made a great effort to convince South Africa of the benefits it stood to gain if it went the recognition route.

Both the DFA and DTI developed cost-benefit assessments of the option favouring PRC recognition at the cost of Taiwan, and in both cases came to the conclusion that, despite some negative fall-out from Taiwan, South Africa stood to gain immeasurably from normalised relations with the PRC (*see* Medhurst, 1995; Kuper, 1995). The main benefits were seen to be economic (increased two-way trade and investment flows to South Africa), as well as political (not having diplomatic relations with a permanent Security Council member was seen as untenable). These views were presented to the South African cabinet, which on two occasions considered their options. However, the final decision was left in the hands of the president, who eventually made the announcement in September 1996.

What does the model not explain? The assumptions on which this model rests are, in the view of most analysts, unrealistic because they simplify the decision-making world (*see* Chapter 5 for an overview). The main criticism would be the unrealistic assumption that governments are centrally controlled, rational and informed. In the case at hand, evidence suggests quite the opposite. The South African government was not the only actor in the process; many influences and pressures were brought to bear on the process – from academics, political parties, the business community, and external actors such as the Taiwanese and PRC governments. The rational actor model cannot adequately explain these dynamics. A further criticism would be that we cannot automatically assume that decision-makers act 'rationally' or with full or complete information at hand. Both Taiwan and the PRC used carrots and sticks in an attempt to persuade the decision-makers of a particular point of view. In our case, decision-makers were frequently exposed to emotional appeals for 'friends to stay together', as well as subtle techniques of manipulation and influence (in the case of Taiwan, so-called 'chequebook diplomacy'). The PRC used more direct methods, such as warning South Africa that unless they recognised the PRC, the PRC would prevent them from using Hong Kong (after the UK handed it over to the PRC in 1997) as a transit point for their national airline or as a base for their export and import operations.

The organisational process model

This model rests on the understanding that the pursuit of policy is determined by the routine behavioural habits of the organisation involved in the decision. In contrast with the rational actor perspective, governments are not the proverbial 'black box' or unitary actor in the making of policy; instead, governments consist of a number of loosely allied organisations, each with a life and experience of their own. As the authors of Chapter 5 argue, to view policy-making in this way encourages parochialism because each organisational unit's goals and objectives emerge as a set of constraints that define acceptable performance. Furthermore, experience suggests that standard operating procedures are slow to change with the net result that organisational behaviour within the government is formalised, sluggish or inappropriate in crisis situations.

How applicable is this model to the recognition of the PRC? On the one hand, we have to appreciate the insight that governments are not unitary actors, and the recognition that various 'loosely allied organisations' make up a government. Unfortunately, there seems to be an uneasy fit, given the nature of the decision-making organisations involved. Essentially the foreign policy behaviour of the new government in

South Africa in the first years of existence cannot entirely be characterised as 'routine', and, as a matter of fact, it took it many months – and in the case of the foreign ministry, even a few years – to settle down and develop routine behavioural habits. This was due to the nature of the transition from Apartheid rule to democratic decision-making, which involved complex structural and procedural transformations (Evans, 1995).

The model makes sense only to the extent that it suggests that we should investigate the role that different governmental departments might have played in determining the ultimate decision. It is true that at least two departments (the DFA and DTI), as well as the Office of the President (and perhaps others) played a role in the process. However, we have to look elsewhere for a richer and more nuanced explanation of the process.

The bureaucratic politics model

As with the previous model, this approach begins by assuming that government is not a unitary actor in the making of foreign policy. The central focus is on conflict and co-operation between departments charged with the decision-making and administration of foreign policy, and suggests that the outcome of this dynamic is more important than the issue. Indeed, as argued before, 'specialised bodies (in government) have different interests and powers, and the policy process is about power relationships and bargaining between them' (Chapter 5). Furthermore, the individuals within these bodies are not a monolithic group either. They are 'players' in a competitive game of politics. As such, the players compete for resources, attention and the right to frame the policy question. The result is conflict, although it can, and often is, about the building of coalitions between competitors. The outcome of these political struggles affects policy output. The central players in this process are political leaders and senior public servants, each of whom enjoys considerable organisational discretion in foreign policy-making. Their respective and

often very distinctive roles are guaranteed by the principle of bureaucratic decentralisation.

As has become evident by now, the search is for a rich and inclusive approach to better explain the foreign policy decision at hand. The third model indeed brings us closer to a better understanding of the complexity of the process. We learn, for example, that we can identify distinctive roles played by a variety of political leaders and senior public servants. In the South African case, determining a foreign policy position regarding the PRC became subject to a competition for resources, attention and the right to frame the policy question. In the event, the policy process became characterised by power relationships and bargaining between various specialised bodies in government.

Some examples might illustrate this insight. At the level of departments, competition ensued between the DFA and DTI for the 'right to frame the policy question', where the former – by way of its powerful director-general – reserved the right to inform and advise cabinet and the president on the position to take. As is now known, this position was basically in favour of maintaining the status quo. The DTI, on the other hand, had developed a well-researched position that favoured the reversal of the status quo as soon as possible. The challenge was then to influence the senior decision-makers (cabinet and the president) ahead of the other, and this created tension and resulted in a delay in decision-making. Moreover, intra-departmental competition and bargaining ensued. The section in foreign affairs responsible for Asia developed a policy recommendation similar to that of trade and industry, but because of the director-general's preference for the status quo option, was not able to get its message directly delivered to the senior decision-makers.

At the ministerial level, it appeared that cabinet had not developed a unified position, with some ministers – notably the defence minister – favouring one option (maintaining the status quo) and others favouring rapid normalisation of the relationship with the PRC. One factor, which heavily influenced this unhealthy state of affairs, was the role played by the Taiwanese. They went to great lengths to impress upon senior politicians the advantages of not breaking off relations with Taiwan, going so far as to treat many cabinet members and over 200 parliamentarians to lavish, all-paid for, visits to Taiwan. This became known as Taiwan's 'chequebook diplomacy', and we should recognise its impact in the sense that it succeeded in delaying the policy decision for many months, if not years.

Contributing to this competition over policy was the role played by interests outside the state. These can broadly be described as the media, academics and business. Once again, the position taken by these players was not a unified one. The media and foreign policy analysts tended to send conflicting messages to government, advising either the maintenance of the status quo or a rapid normalisation of relations with the PRC. Business tended to promote the position that would best favour their medium- and long-term interests, namely diplomatic recognition of the PRC (of all players they were probably most aware of the economic importance of, and opportunities provided by, the Chinese market, which would soon include Hong Kong under Chinese governance).

Lastly, a factor not readily recognised by any of Allison's models relates to the role of political parties and individuals. In the South African case, this would refer to the role and influence of the ruling party, the ANC and its senior leader, President Mandela. Similar to departments involved in the policy process, a fair amount of inter- and intra-party competition developed in order to influence the decision. The ANC, the South African Communist Party (SACP) and COSATU – the three partners of the ruling alliance – all developed positions on the situation and although they shared the same end goal, at various times came up with varying strategies. The SACP and COSATU, for example, found it difficult to understand why the government appeared to delay the inevitable, namely to normalise relations with the PRC (a delegation of the

SACP visited Beijing in early 1996). Under pressure from party members, as well as its alliance partners, Foreign Minister Nzo visited the PRC in 1996 to 'investigate' the relationship, and was informed by the Chinese leadership in no uncertain terms that neither dual recognition nor maintaining the status quo was acceptable to the PRC. In addition, the parliamentary portfolio committee on foreign affairs – chaired by the ANC – travelled to both Beijing and Taipei to gather first-hand information on the question. Again, the committee received the same message from the PRC. Finally, shortly after the announcement on 27 November 1996, the ANC sent a delegation to Beijing, led by its deputy general secretary, Ms Cheryl Carolus.

The personality of the president played a crucial role in the policy process. Evidence suggests that he was reluctant to downgrade the country's diplomatic relationship with Taiwan. Firstly, he tended to take the foreign ministry's director-general's policy advice at face value, and did not cross-check it with other bureaucratic sources. In fact, in an effort to overcome this problem, officials who advocated the 'recognise PRC now' strategy eventually resorted to subtle techniques of bypassing the foreign ministry's director-general in order to get direct access to the president. Secondly, he was very conscious of his cabinet colleagues' prevarication on the issue – remember that at that time the cabinet was also composed of representatives of other parties, who took a strong stance in favour of maintaining the status quo. It seems that the president was not prepared to force a decision, preferring instead to persist with a consensus decision-making approach. Thirdly, one has to consider the question of the impact of financial support by the Taiwanese for the ANC's 1994 electoral campaign. Although disputed, it appears that up to $10 million was donated to the ANC, and in some analysts' views this contributed significantly to President Mandela's high regard for Taiwan as 'a friend of South Africa'. This relationship appears to explain his statements in October 1994 that 'South Africa doesn't break relations with countries unless a country does something wrong which causes us to break relations. We are prepared to enter into diplomatic relations with China but we are not going to break our relations with Taiwan' (*Financial Mail* (SA), 12 August 1994).

In the end, the eventual decision was announced by President Mandela himself, from his home in Johannesburg rather than from his office in Pretoria, and with very little advance warning to either the Chinese diplomatic representatives or his own cabinet and foreign ministry. This suggests that he reluctantly came to the conclusion that the reversal of the status quo was the only feasible option open to the South African government and that his government would be better off with a clear, recognisable foreign policy position on China.

Assessment of the Allison models

What can we learn from this case-study? First, the Allison models do not provide all the answers to the questions around the foreign policy-making process, and neither should we think that they were designed to do so. Rather, they provide us with a useful analytical tool to probe and investigate the nature and intricacies of the policy process. They should perhaps also be read as approaches on a continuum, ranging from state to bureaucratic interests. Allison provides us with a crucial insight – that of the reality of power relationships and bargaining between different interests involved in the policy process. This reinforces one of the points made in Chapter 5, namely, that 'foreign policy is invariably made by the interaction of many individuals operating in various organisational settings who bargain, negotiate and compromise with each other, often many times over'.

Applying Allison's models to this particular case reveals an important shortcoming. The three approaches do not really recognise the important role of actors outside the state – both domestic and international. In our case, we had to factor in the role and influence of civil society interests as

well as that of the PRC and Taiwan. After all, for the latter, much more was at stake and when the South African decision became known, it was seen as a bitter blow to Taiwan's quest for international recognition as an independent entity. In fact, some commentators are of the opinion that this decision might have activated the last chapter in the fractious PRC-Taiwanese relationship; reunification of the two now appears to be only a matter of time (Singh, 1997:58).

Concluding remarks: assessing government's performance

In this chapter we have briefly covered some of the many ways in which the scholar of International Relations can analyse the making and implementation of foreign policy in South Africa. We have focused on the various contexts (domestic, regional, global) related to South Africa's foreign policy, and have highlighted the various actors involved in the making and execution of policy. These actors can be found on various levels of analysis: the individual level (the Minister of Foreign Affairs, for instance); the bureaucratic level (individual state departments, for instance); and the national level (where the South African state is treated as a single, rational actor). We have also illustrated the usefulness of using explicit theoretical models to analyse a specific foreign policy decision.

Echoing Chapter 5 (and what was said in Chapters 1 and 3 about normative theory), this chapter also emphasises the importance of raising ethical questions in the academic study of foreign policy. Although realists are probably correct to emphasise that foreign policy decisions are influenced by many factors apart from moral considerations, we believe that liberals do have a point when they argue for giving moral considerations the weight they deserve. There is a special responsibility on South Africa in this regard. The very possibility of a post-Apartheid South Africa was secured through, amongst others, the foreign policies of states that objected to

Apartheid on moral grounds. As such, the making of the new South Africa was a moral act, and any post-Apartheid government will have to honour that by giving issues related to human rights and democratisation an important position in foreign policy making. At the same time, though, moral considerations in foreign policy will only come into their own once fundamental changes have been made to the economic and political structures of the international system. As a developing country, South Africa also has a special responsibility to help effect fundamental change in order to eliminate undeserved privilege and marginalisation in the world.

Key concepts in this chapter

Bureaucratic politics
Foreign policy
Foreign policy actors
Morality in foreign policy
Organisational process
Policy-making
Post-Apartheid
Rational actor

Suggested readings

- Barber, J. &. Barratt, J. (1990) *South Africa's Foreign Policy: The Search for Status and Security, 1945–1988*. Johannesburg: Southern Book Publishers. A comprehensive examination of the impact of domestic policies and international pressures on the conduct of South Africa's foreign relations until 1988.
- Geldenhuys, D. J. (1984) *The Diplomacy of Isolation: South Africa's Foreign Policy-making*. Johannesburg: Macmillan. A useful treatment of the making and conduct of South Africa's foreign policy from 1945 to 1984.
- Mandela, N. (1993) 'South Africa's future foreign policy,' *Foreign Affairs* 72(5). This article articulates the principles, norms and values that inform the new South Africa's foreign policy.
- Landsberg, C., Le Pere, G. & Van Nieuwkerk, A. (eds) (1995) *Mission Imperfect: Redirecting South Africa's Foreign Policy*, pp. 70–77. Johannesburg: Foundation for Global Dialogue and Centre for Policy Studies. Reflections on South Africa's foreign policy, one year after the democratic elections, by a range of experts.
- *South African Yearbook of International Affairs* . Published annually by the South African Institute for International Affairs. Has useful data and coverage of South Africa's bilateral relations, global events and foreign policy issues.
- Thomas, S. (1996) *The Diplomacy of Liberation*. London: IB Tauris, is a critical study of the exiled ANC's foreign relations and diplomacy from 1960 to 1990.

13 | Southern Africa in South-South relations

Chris Alden

This chapter in outline
- The rise of the South
- The challenge of diversity in the South
- The institutions of the South respond
- The integration of Southern Africa into the Global South
  - North Africa and the Middle East
  - Latin America
  - East and Southeast Asia
  - South Asia and the Indian Ocean Rim
- The future of the South
- Conclusion

One of the areas of concern for students of International Relations is the question of equity and justice in the global system. Many scholars contend that the international economic and political situation in the world favours the interests of a minority of people, namely the privileged classes in the industrialised states. In turn, the interests of the majority of the world's population are undermined or marginalised by the prevalent global political and economic arrangements (*see* Chapter 2). This contention, known as the 'North-South debate', has had a major impact on international relations ranging from the negotiations on international trade to the reform of the United Nations (UN) Security Council.

One important aspect of the North-South debate is the question of whether it is not possible for states in the South to stand together or at least to co-operate internally in order to offset some of the negative consequences of North-South disparities and inequalities. In this chapter we review steps that have been taken along these lines, and try to determine what prospects do exist for South-South co-operation.

For Southern Africa, the emergence of the idea of South-South co-operation offers both a bulwark against the superior political and economic resources wielded by the industrialised states and a realistic alternative to North-South trading patterns that have dominated international exchange since the colonial era. Furthermore, all of the states of the Southern African region have committed themselves to seeking ways to improve co-operation between Southern Africa, the rest of Africa, Latin America, Southeast Asia and other parts of the developing world. For these reasons, it is crucial that Southern Africans understand the emergence of the South and its role in influencing the international system, as well as Southern Africa's part in this dynamic process.

The rise of the South

Although the term 'the South' (also sometimes referred to as 'the Global South') sounds like a geographical term, it actually has more of a political, economic and ideological meaning today. 'The South' is a term used to describe those regions of the globe that have in common a political, social and economic history rooted in the inequalities of a colonial past. As the levels of economic development have evolved amongst the countries of the South over the last few decades, the concept has come to signify more than geographic proximity or the notion of a shared history. 'The South' is increasingly understood to be an ideological expression for the range of concerns facing developing regions, which themselves are growing in economic and political diversity and experience.

Complementing the concept of the South is the idea of the North. Originally, the North referred to those industrialised states of Western Europe and North America that historically had embarked upon colonial and imperial missions to secure their economic and political well-being. As in the case of the South, changing economic and political circumstances have altered this narrow geographic and historical understanding of the North to take into account the rapid industrialisation in Asia and Latin America, as well as the emergence of pockets of modernity in otherwise developing countries such as South Africa and Brazil. Today the 'Global North' represents the perspectives and interests of the industrialised regions that include the **Group of 7** (G-7) and the institutions of the Bretton Woods system.

The impetus for the development of the concept of 'South' came from the transformative Marxist critique of the international global economy (*see* Chapters 2 and 3). Rooted in the work of the UN's Economic Commission for Latin America (ECLA) under the chairmanship of Raul Prebisch, the critique suggested that the world economy was essentially divided into a centre and periphery, with the centre composed of industrialised states of the northern hemisphere

The terminology used to classify the poorer regions of the world tells a complex story. The use of the phrase 'third world' is drawn from the ideological divide between the capitalist oriented countries led by the United States (the first world) and the socialist-oriented countries led by the Soviet Union (the second world). The recently decolonised countries were designated as the third world. The term 'the South' gained popularity as a way of further distinguishing the interests of the states in Africa, Asia and Latin America from those of the industrialised North. The development of an enriched concept, the 'Global South', which transcends the geographic and ideological parameters of the past, has come into being in recent years as a way of capturing the growing economic and social differentiation between and within countries of the South and North.

In addition to these different terms, there are three main systems of classification of poor countries promoted by the United Nations (UN), the Organisation for Economic Co-operation and Development (OECD) and the World Bank based primarily on measuring relative income levels between countries. The UN designates the forty-four poorest countries as 'least developed', the eighty-eight non-oil exporting countries as 'developing' and the thirteen petroleum-rich countries of OPEC (the Organisation of Petroleum Exporting Countries) as oil-exporting, developing countries. The OECD divides the third world into sixty-one 'low-income countries' (LICs), seventy-three 'middle-income countries' (MICs), eleven 'newly industrialising countries' (NICs) and the thirteen members of OPEC. Finally, the World Bank divides 125 countries with populations in excess of one million according to their per capita income levels – as low income, middle income, upper middle income and high income.

(the 'North') and the periphery comprising undeveloped former colonial territories in the southern hemisphere (the 'South'). Prebisch and his followers held that the nature of the existing trade relationship between the centre and the periphery inhibited the development of the countries of the South beyond that of a narrow political and economic élite. However, distinct from traditional Marxist theorists, they believed that this situation was not deterministic or immutable, but that through unified pressure brought about by the South, the terms and structure of its trading relationship with the North could be altered to ameliorate conditions in the South.

With the growth in membership in the UN during the 1960s, developing states were increasingly confident that they could use the world body to place their concerns on the international agenda. The establishment of the **UN Conference on Trade and Development** (UNCTAD), created in 1964 after intense lobbying by UN representatives of the South (known as the **Group of 77**), marked the commencement of a formalised and ongoing dialogue between North and South on the nature of the relationship between them, and what to do about the enduring inequalities between the two regions. The discussions are held at a series of conferences every four years and range from the technical issues regarding trade to broader questions involving the re-ordering of the fundamental relations between the North and the South. The three principal demands put forth through the UNCTAD process in its early days were:

- a call for change in the international structures of the world economy;
- an improvement in the conditions influencing the ability of the South to export manufacturing products; and
- an improvement in the international terms governing commodity trade of the South (*see* also Chapter 2 for a discussion of these demands and others, which later formed the

core of the demand for a **New International Economic Order**, NIEO).

Paralleling the development of this form of transformative critique of the global economy was the establishment of an alternative international political structure to the dominant bipolar Cold War system. Following a conference in Bandung, Indonesia, in 1955, many newly independent states in Africa and Asia, together with ideologically neutral states outside of the formal alliances promoted by the United States (US) and Soviet Union (USSR), launched the Movement of Non-Aligned Countries, better known as the **Non-Aligned Movement** (NAM), in Belgrade, Yugoslavia, in 1961. The movement was animated by a set of basic principles centring on the promotion of sovereign independence in the political sphere and collective self-reliance in the economic sphere. The idealism that motivated NAM is captured in this excerpt from the then Indonesian President Sukarno's address to the delegates:

> 'What can we do? We can do much! We can inject the voice of reason into world affairs. We can mobilise all the spiritual, all the moral, all the political strength of Asia and Africa on the side of peace. Yes, we! We, the peoples of Asia and Africa, 1,400,000,000 strong, far more than half the human population of the world, we can mobilise what I have called the "Moral Violence of Nations" in favour of peace' (Harris, 1986:11).

Contrary to expectation and despite intense pressure from both without and within the organisation, NAM managed to maintain its independence from the politics of the Cold War, as well as periodic conflicts between members to go on to be a leading forum for the articulation of the political concerns of the South. Included amongst its founding aims was a call for 'economic development (and) economic co-operation amongst the participating countries' and an agreement to provide 'technical assistance to one another ... in the form of experts, trainees, pilot projects and equipment for demonstration purposes; exchange of know-how and establishment of national and where possible regional training and research institutes' (Sobhan, 1987:3). These ideas, often referred to as economic co-operation amongst developing countries (ECDC) and technical co-operation amongst developing countries (TCDC), were to form the basis for South-South co-operation.

The success of the oil embargo by OPEC in 1973 (*see* Chapter 2) gave further impetus to more radically minded states to press for an accelerated

Box 13.2: The Non–Aligned movement (NAM)

NAM is a grouping of states representing the interests of the developing world. Conceived by the leading independent states at a conference in Bandung, Indonesia, in 1955 and officially launched in Belgrade, Yugoslavia, in 1961, NAM derived its initial impetus from a desire to avoid being drawn into the polarising alliances of the Cold War. With the ending of Soviet and American conflict in the late 1980s, NAM shifted its emphasis to primarily promoting the development concerns of the South on the international stage. It is guided by five principles: respect for territorial integrity; mutual non-aggression; mutual non-interference in internal affairs; equality and mutual benefit; and peaceful co-existence. NAM consists of 114 members, meets every three years under the leadership of a new chair and makes its decisions on the basis of full consensus. It has a permanent bureau in New York to lobby for its interests as well as to facilitate co-operation with the Group of 77, and has recently established a research institution, the South Centre, in Geneva and a training centre, the NAM Centre for South–South Technical Co-operation, in Jakarta. South Africa chairs the body in the period 1999–2001.

review of North-South relations through the call for a NIEO in 1975. This was coupled with a more aggressive stance on questions such as the promotion of armed struggle in Southern Africa. In many respects this was the highpoint of optimism for a negotiated and radical restructuring of the world economy, with expectations that the South's new-found power would serve as a lever to open Northern markets and financial coffers as never before. However, by 1979 the fallout from the second oil shock and the concurrent collapse of non-oil commodity prices, and the rising debt problem in many developing countries, had shaken the economies of the South and underscored their continued dependence upon trade and finance from the industrial North. Coupled with this were the difficulties in maintaining unity amongst members of producer cartels such as OPEC, which, despite the rhetoric of solidarity, demonstrated the limits of joint action in propping up commodity prices. All of these factors contributed to bringing to an end the most active phase of militancy in the South. While the UNCTAD process resulted in modest successes in the realm of institution-building and the insertion of elements of concern to the South within the Northern-dominated agenda, the South had failed to achieve a re-ordering of the relationship through the NIEO.

At the same time that pessimism was gripping much of the developing world, a new phenomenon began to make its impact felt upon the North-South debate. The remarkable achievements of the export-oriented approaches adopted by some states in East Asia and Latin America, using the newly established **Generalised System of Preferences** (which granted privileged access to Northern markets for selected manufactured goods from the South, a key demand of UNCTAD), underscored the growing power of the so-called **newly industrialising economies** (NIEs). Utilising a combination of low labour costs, an undervalued currency and selective state-supported incentives to embark on an aggressive export-oriented strategy, these countries were able to commence a

rapid trajectory of growth that defied the predictions of structuralist economists. (Harris, 1986) One of the most successful of the NIEs, Singapore, went from a per capita income of $1000 in 1965 to over $15,000 in 1995 (Lingle, 1996:61). Asia's form of corporate capitalism, which brought together semi-authoritarian regimes in a close relationship with local businesses and the banking sector, suggested to many observers that there was an 'East Asian Model' for development that could be transposed on struggling economies in other parts of the third world. This notion was taken up by the World Bank and became a standard reference point for many of the **structural adjustment programmes** (SAPs) that were imposed upon selected states around the globe (World Bank, 1993).

Buoyed by their initial achievements, the NIEs were soon unnerved by the onset of a world-wide economic recession in the first half of the 1980s, which was characterised by a drop in international trade and a fall in commodity prices. The annual growth of imports from NIEs by the industrialised countries, which had averaged 4,5%, 7,7% and 10,1% for Latin America, Africa and Asia respectively between 1970 and 1981, dropped dramatically to –8,4%, –6,1% and –0,3% between 1982 and 1985. (The South Centre, 1993:15) Furthermore, NIE inroads into the markets of the North based on lower factors costs (lower labour costs in the area of textile production, for example) were threatened by growing protectionism in the industrialised countries, which sought to limit the trade in cheaper manufactured goods from the South. Rather than focusing exclusively on the seemingly limited opportunities offered by trading with the North, voices in the South began to promote more strongly the notion of enhancing co-operation between the growing economies of the South.

The Caracas Plan of Action, adopted by the Group of 77 countries in 1981, provided the most comprehensive elaboration of the strategies and advantages to be achieved through enhanced co-operation between developing countries. Eight sectors were identified as crucial to furthering the aims of collective self-reliance: trade, finance, industrialisation, science and technology, food and agriculture, energy, raw materials and technical co-operation. South-South co-operation focused upon four rationales:

1. the relative comparative advantage of conducting South-South trade versus North-South trade;
2. the notion that greater dynamic gains for the economies of the South were possible through promoting South-South trade;
3. the importance of diversification of markets, which offered the South relief from fluctuations based upon exclusive reliance upon the North; and
4. that South-South co-operation would serve the ideological objective of strengthening the principal of collective self-reliance.

This ideal of South-South co-operation sought to build upon the institution-building initiatives of the previous decade in which most developing countries joined a regional or sub-regional organisation. At the time, the hope was that economies of scale achieved through regional co-operation would encourage regional industrialisation through the application of **import substitution policies**. While most of the regional organisations never realised these ambitions, in some cases tentative co-operation was to lay the foundation for the new proposals adopted by the South. In the meetings that followed the gathering at Caracas, the establishment of the Association of State Trading Organisations (ASTRO) of developing countries, coupled with increased access to trade-relevant data through UNCTAD, served to promote the interests of South-South trade. In the area of financial co-operation, progress was made in implementing multilateral clearing arrangements that cut down on the transaction costs of doing business between developing countries. However, the ambitions to create a South Bank, which would entail substantial financial commitments from member states, were not realised. Significantly, the thrust of South-South co-operation remained

Box 13.3: South–South co-operation and African development

South-South co-operation is the promotion of economic action amongst developing countries at the bilateral, regional and global levels to achieve the aims of collective self-reliance. The economic and technical co-operation envisaged in South-South co-operation includes an expansion of trade, as well as co-operation in the industrial and financial sectors, science and technology, food and agriculture and a range of other related areas. The rationale informing such co-operation is that collective economic interactions between countries of the South will promote mutually beneficial development by taking advantage of enlarged markets, economies of scale and complementarities while at the same time reducing dependency upon the industrialised countries of the North.

According to an OECD report, South-South co-operation is more feasible in the late twentieth century than in the past because of the accumulation of technical knowledge across a range of institutions in the South. However, 'the process of technological accumulation is proceeding at a far slower rate in Africa. Yet the need to stimulate firms in Africa to solve restructuring problems, and to innovate in the course of rehabilitation, is critical to the sustainability of development on that continent' (Mytelka, 1994:14). The question facing leaders in Africa, in an era that has seen development assistance from the industrialised countries to Africa falling annually, is to what extent can South-South co-operation serve as a panacea for the development ills facing the continent?

solidly within the state sector, ignoring the emergence of dynamic enterprises in the private sector of countries such as Singapore and Malaysia.

On the eve of the ending of the Cold War, which had given rise to the NAM, the assessment of South-South relations and, more specifically, co-operation was decidedly mixed. While there had been some concrete achievements in the areas of trade, finance and industrialisation, the gap between stated objectives and actual implementation or realisation was large indeed. Reviewing the history of South-South relations in 1987, a former Chairman of the Group of 77 declared that:

> 'The truth of the matter is South-South is no more than a pious slogan where the bureaucracies (of developing countries) at home are concerned. The bureaucrats may be willing to say nice things about it in the speeches they write for their leaders and friendly things in their own speeches and attend meetings and seminars (usually with some enthusiasm if these are in New York or Geneva, less so if they are held somewhere in the South) but when it comes to concrete action or budgetary allocations for a South-South programme, the response is invariably negative' (Sobhan, 1987:26).

The ending of the Cold War, which saw both the assertion of American dominance and the tentative emergence of multipolar centres of power (*see* Chapter 4 for a discussion of multipolarity), brought about a re-assessment of the principal contours of the international system. The old political and economic structures shaped by ideological conflict, from which the leaders of the developing world had sought to distance themselves at Bandung, gradually gave way to a complex web of political and economic relationships that reshaped or founded new institutions to reflect the changes to the international system. The resurgence of ethno-nationalism in Yugoslavia in the early 1990s, which brought about the breakup of one of the founding members of NAM, and the concurrent creation of exclusive **trading blocs** in the North in the form of the **European Union** (EU) and the **North American Free Trade Agreement** (NAFTA), served to reinforce the dangers facing the interests of developing countries. Thus, for the leaders of the South the challenges posed by the new international environment were every bit as

difficult and divisive as those that had confronted them over the previous thirty years.

The challenge of diversity in the South

Much of what bound the countries of the South together, creating a sense of unity of purpose that translated into international action in such settings as the UN, was tied up in a common sense of shared political history and economic experience. However, the gradual transformation of the international economy during the 1970s and 1980s brought with it a growing divergence in the character of the economies of the South, and consequently gave rise to a new set of equally divergence concerns. The first significant crack in the monolith of unity amongst developing countries was the emergence of the oil rich states, whose fabulous wealth provoked envy in both North and South. With the exception of the radical states of North Africa and Iran (and these regimes employed their wealth principally in the service of causes that suited their national goals) there appeared to be only limited desire on the part of the leadership of the OPEC states to use their income to ameliorate conditions in the developing world. A second fissure in the South came with the rise of the NIEs, especially those in East and Southeast Asia, whose strong adherence to market capitalism flew in the face of the socialist rhetoric that marked much of the discourse pervasive in the North-South debate. As Malaysia and Indonesia expanded at a phenomenal rate, bringing them closer to the economic standing of the poorer industrialised countries of the North, they began to assume some of the interests of middle-level economies with a range of trade and investment concerns that, at times, were at odds with the needs of their poorer neighbours. The recognition of these concerns caused the leaders of these states, along with other sub-regional powers in 1989, to create a new forum, the Group of 15, which sought to articulate the specific interests of the leading economies in the South. With combined trade worth US$800 billion in 1997, the Group of 15 was capable of promoting initiatives such the Business Investment Forum, a centre providing data and technical support for South-based companies interested in doing business in other parts of the world (*The Star Business Report*, 11 May 1998).

At the same time, that rapid growth was transforming the economies of Asia (and, to a lesser extent, Latin America), the crisis in Africa highlighted the emergence of a new class of impoverished countries. Saddled with enormous debt, spiralling fuel costs, low prices for primary commodities and bloated, inefficient state sectors, these economies experienced a relative decline in per capita income during the 1980s. The spectacle of famine, exacerbated by civil war or external intervention, struck countries such as Bangladesh, Ethiopia and Mozambique and helped to create the impression that some sectors of the South were, in the words of American Secretary of State Henry Kissinger, 'basket cases'. Dependent upon external debt relief and emergency humanitarian assistance, this so-called 'fourth world' of impoverished states were in marked contrast to their brethren NIEs, and this divergence of interests began to place stress upon the sense of unity of purpose that lay at the heart of the concept of the South.

The institutions of the South respond

At the ninth and tenth NAM summits held in Belgrade, Yugoslavia and Jakarta, Indonesia, in 1989 and 1992 respectively, the question of the relevance of non-alignment in the absence of the Cold War was hotly debated. Unwilling to turn away from the institutions and issues that had served the interests of the developing world for decades, the leaders of the South re-committed themselves to supporting the NAM process by adapting it to the new global circumstances. Specifically, NAM was charged with providing a

political platform to articulate the concerns of the developing world within the changing dynamics of North-South and South-South interactions. To reinforce this position, in 1989 the South Commission, later institutionalised as the South Centre, was established as a research institution to investigate technical areas such as intellectual property rights and trade from a 'South' perspective. Recognising the importance of multilateral institutions in the new international environment, NAM called for a reform of the UN Security Council so as to include permanent representatives from the developing countries. At the same time, spurred on by the creation of the **World Trade Organisation** (WTO) in 1995, UNCTAD belatedly acknowledged that its role as the premier forum for negotiating the terms of the North-South relationship had been effectively eclipsed by events. The organisation responded by moving away from its confrontational approach to the question of economic co-operation between the North and the South, and it altered its reporting methodology to reflect the dominant neo-liberal perspective on international economic affairs. Taken together, these efforts were aimed at reconceptualising the key institutions of the South, and setting the South on a new course that, in conjunction with the new-found wealth of the NIEs, expanded the range and depth of activities pursued in the name of the developing world.

In the area of trade relations, the rapid growth in parts of Asia and Latin America allowed for the pursuit of South-South co-operation as never before. Harnessing the new information technologies to the aggressive spirit of export-oriented economies, the Group of 15 led the way in forging bilateral and multilateral agreements in the areas of mutual trade and technology transfers. The emergence of parastatal or South-based multinational corporations (MNCs) has encouraged, for the first time, the development of substantial foreign direct investment (FDI) from one developing country to another. Business associations representing the interests of South-based multinationals have sprung up in the capitals of developing countries and these companies are even listing on stock exchanges outside their home territories. This reinvigoration of the notion of South-South co-operation, coming against the background of NIE fears of being denied access to markets in the North, has become a cornerstone of the South's response to the new international environment.

Complementing the elevation of South-South co-operation has been the introduction of a novel ideological dimension to the North-South debate. Primarily driven by the Asian NIEs, the new approach challenges the belief that the universal values enshrined in institutions such as the UN are, in fact, applicable to all societies. Indeed, the suggestion in leadership circles of some Asian NIEs is that human and labour rights, as well as 'Western-style' democracy, are merely representative of the interests of the dominant powers (Lingle, 1996:37–60). It followed from this approach that the North's overemphasis on rights and concurrent negligence of responsibilities is dangerous to the interests of Asian states and, amongst the more paranoid governments, is declared to be a propaganda weapon wielded primarily to thwart their economic challenge to the older industrialised states. Another defining feature of the ideology of the South is its continued adherence to the notion of the sanctity of territorial sovereignty. Beset by weak or artificial institutions and territorial boundaries, as well as a history of internecine ethnic conflict, leaders in countries of the South have argued, since the founding of NAM, that the fragility of the post-colonial state warranted an especially generous approach to the maintenance of internal order over that of traditional democratic concerns. The result has been, with some glaring exceptions in the Horn of Africa and South Asia, the general adherence to the principle of non-interference in the internal affairs of another state (Asante, 1996:48–49).

Finally, with the seemingly reduced UN role in peace maintenance since the disaster in Somalia in 1993, the South is increasingly making common cause in the area of regional security. Security co-operation for states of the South is understood to incorporate both traditional security concerns, such as concerted diplomatic (and even military) action against outside forces, as well as a strong emphasis on the need for nation-building and preventive diplomacy. The case of the **Association of South East Asian Nations** (ASEAN), a regional organisation constituted by the ten states in Southeast Asia, typifies this approach. Established during a period of great instability in the region, its initial development aims were overshadowed by the immediacy of security concerns involving politico-territorial ambitions of states in the 1950s and 1960s, such as Sukarno's Indonesia and Mao's China. The result was that ASEAN held as a cardinal principle the sanctity of non-intervention of member states (and outside states) in the internal affairs of others. ASEAN has used quiet diplomacy to register its concern over breaches in security, co-ordinated regional military operations as a deterrent to aggression, as well as attempted to negotiate settlements through the employment of conflict resolution techniques. More recently, the organisation has been actively involved in the mediation of regional disputes such as the Vietnamese withdrawal from Cambodia and competing territorial claims in the South China Sea.

The integration of Southern Africa into the Global South

Southern Africa, the last significant zone of conflict in the anti-colonial struggle and the Cold War, was, in many respects, ill-prepared for the changes that shook the international system during the 1980s and early 1990s. Nevertheless, with a history of regional involvement in South initiatives centred primarily on the question of decolonisation and Apartheid, as well as support for UNCTAD's ambitious plans to renegotiate the terms of trade in commodities, Southern Africa did contribute to the development of the South's agenda. That said, beyond multilateral forums such as the UN, NAM and UNCTAD, there was very little interaction between the states of Southern Africa and the rest of the South in the area of bilateral trade or investment. The perception of persistent conflict, natural disaster and poor governance all conspired to restrict interest by South-based business concerns. However, these attitudes have changed dramatically in the 1990s, spurred on by the international spotlight on the commercial and political possibilities of a democratic South Africa.

North Africa and the Middle East

Relations with the states of North Africa and the Middle East have been complex owing to the history of volatility in the regions. In the case of the Middle East, the Apartheid government had developed close ties with Israel and, until the Shah's overthrow in 1979, Iran, which manifested itself in close military co-operation (including the sharing of nuclear technology with Israel) and sanctions-busting in the area of petroleum. Concurrently, the exiled liberation movements received diplomatic, financial and military support and training at various times from Nassar's Egypt, Ben Bella's Algeria and Qaddafi's Libya. With the advent of democracy in South Africa, official relations with the Middle East have broadened considerably to incorporate the new government's regional networks. Specifically, Pretoria has developed ties with the Palestinian authority, Syria, Iran, Algeria and Iraq. In the case of North Africa, the African National Congress's (ANC's) traditional support for the Polisario in the former Spanish colony of the Western Sahara (annexed by Morocco in 1975) continues to divide what is an otherwise stable relationship between the two states (Lambrechts, 1996:140–157). Equally, the South Africa government's hosting of opposition figures from Palestine and Algeria have signalled an unwillingness to adhere uncritically to the wishes of unrepresentative governments.

In the economic sphere, trade relations between North Africa and the Middle East and Southern Africa are developing rapidly, primarily in the areas of arms sales, petroleum products and agricultural products. The South African arms manufacturer, DENEL, has embarked upon an aggressive strategy of marketing its products to Syria, Algeria and Saudi Arabia and has managed to sign deals worth millions of dollars. At the same time, Iran has taken a high-profile position in promoting the petroleum industry in South Africa and Mozambique, while South African agricultural products have found new markets in the Middle East.

Latin America

Relations with Latin America and the Apartheid government were relatively close as many of states in the region were subject to authoritarian rule throughout the 1970s and 1980s. The transition to democracy in Argentina, Brazil and Chile in the latter half of the decade marked a cooling of diplomatic relations that was not to change until the advent of democratic government in South Africa. As far as the region goes, ties of communist solidarity resulted in tens of thousands of Cuban troops assisting Angolan government troops in their war against South Africa and the rebel movement UNITA (the Union for the Total Independence of Angola) from 1975 to 1988. While the signing of the New York Accords in 1988 ended substantive Cuban involvement in the region, since coming to power the ANC has made a special show of underscoring its relationship with Cuba in opposition to American efforts to isolate the island. Brazil retains its historical interest in Angola based upon enduring cultural links derived from the colonial slave trade, and it has discovered in the emergent South Africa, a society that mirrors many of its own concerns. In terms of regional multilateral relations, South Africa and Namibia joined the states of South America in endorsing the Zone of Peace and Co-operation in the South Atlantic in 1997, and the newly established Valdivia Group co-ordinates environmental and scientific policy between Argentina, Australia, Brazil, Chile, New

Zealand, South Africa and Uruguay.

In the economic sphere, the states of the Southern Cone (Argentina, Brazil, Chile and Uruguay) have repeatedly declared their interest in strengthening South-South co-operation in the economic and technical areas (Leysens and Fourie, 1997:160–161). South Africa's trade with Brazil and Argentina increased by 65% and 35%, respectively, between 1995 and 1996. South African mining interests have been active in Brazil and Chile and analysts see potential for further development. The governments of the region have also entered into discussions about securing regional fishing rights in the South Atlantic. Interestingly, trade links between the South and Southern Africa, and particularly the MERCOSUR countries, were being promoted in the late 1990s by Malaysia, who saw market and investment opportunities in the region.

East and Southeast Asia

Since the end of Apartheid, relations between Southern Africa and East Asia have grown enormously bringing together two regions that have, in the main, had little prior contact. In the political sphere, the Southern African states of Tanzania, Zimbabwe, Mozambique and Namibia have had the most extensive ties with East Asia in the form of political and military co-operation with China and North Korea during the Cold War. This included financial support and military training for liberation movements such as Namibia's South West African People's Organisation (SWAPO) and Mozambique's FRELIMO (the Front for the Liberation of Mozambique), and the secondment of North Korea's notorious 5th Brigade to Matabeleland, Zimbabwe, in the early 1980s to assist in wiping out opposition to President Robert Mugabe's rule. Turning to South Africa, the diplomatic relationship with Malaysia, Indonesia, China and Taiwan has proved to be the most important to the new ANC-led government. The success of Malaysia's affirmative action policies, coupled with its cultural affinities with South Africa's

'Cape Malay' population, gave impetus to a relationship that has been already solidified through substantial Malaysian investment (see below). In the case of Indonesia (which also shared a common Dutch colonial history with the Cape), the ANC's support for the cause of the annexed territory of East Timor has been a source of friction between Pretoria and Jakarta. During President Mandela's visit to Indonesia in 1997, he took the unprecedented step of demanding a meeting with jailed Timorese opposition leader, Xanana Gusmao, and urged the government to embark upon a negotiated settlement to the dispute. Finally, the diplomacy of recognition impeded the rapid development of relations with China and Taiwan for the first few years of the government of national unity (GNU). Inheriting the National Party's (NP's) official position of support for Taiwan, the new government stalled on according China exclusive diplomatic recognition while it debated the merits of retaining ties with both governments. Beijing's insistence that diplomatic recognition be accorded to itself alone, backed by its position on the UN Security Council and a concern that South Africa would lose lucrative trade opportunities with the world's fastest-growing economy, spelled an end to this situation (notably, Taiwan retains official ties with other states in the region, including Lesotho and Swaziland).

In the economic sphere, as part of its contribution to breaking Tanzanian and Zambian dependency upon the transport network of the then Rhodesia and South Africa, China provided financial and technical support for the construction of the TAZARA railway in the 1970s. More recently, Korean MNCs such as Hyundai and Samsung have been active in promoting trade links with Southern Africa – they built an automobile assembly plant in Botswana in the early 1990s and have embarked on joint ventures with locally based electronics manufacturers. Malaysian investment has been particularly prominent in the region, and Malaysian companies have invested US$3,4 billion in petroleum production, telecommunications and property, making Malaysia the second-largest source of new investment in South Africa between 1994 and 1998. Malaysian interests have expanded into Zimbabwe as well, and they have secured a contract to rehabilitate a hydro-electrical project in Hwange. While Taiwanese companies are present in both South Africa and the rest of Southern Africa, it is the rapid growth of trade with China, both through state-owned trading companies and private concerns that has caught the attention of observers. Equally, South African businesses are investing in China in the areas of food and beverage processing and production, financial services, mining and related areas.

South Asia and the Indian Ocean Rim

In the case of South Asia, links between the states of Southern Africa have been long-standing in economic, political and cultural terms. Beyond the history of intra-regional trade and nineteenth-century immigrant labour from the sub-continent to Southern Africa, Mahatma Gandhi's twenty-three year sojourn in South Africa, during which time he developed his strategy of non-violent political action, left an indelible mark upon relations between the two countries. Independent India took a highly publicised stance in the early days of the UN on the Apartheid question and, in the years that followed, maintained close ties with the anti-Apartheid movement in exile through the old Gandhian network. Ironically, the new South African government's position against nuclear proliferation is more in keeping with the spirit of that pacifist ethos than is India's, and with the recent resurgence in military activity in the region, it seems inevitable that Delhi and Pretoria will come into conflict. South Africa's surprisingly muted response to the testing of nuclear devices by India and Pakistan during 1998 stands in marked contrast to its prominent stance against proliferation during the discussions leading to the signing of the Non-Proliferation Treaty in 1995 (*see* below). Coupled with this issue is the question of the disputed territory of Kashmir,

which has divided India and Pakistan for nearly fifty years and remains an impediment to closer ties between the two regions. This could also be said of the Tamil insurgency in Sri Lanka, which reportedly draws support from the Tamil-speaking population in South Africa.

In the economic sphere, while trade has dominated the relationship between the two regions for generations, during the Apartheid era India and Pakistan were strict adherents to the sanctions movement. Merchant trade across the Indian Ocean brought not only prosperity to Southern Africa, but also encouraged immigration from the Indian sub-continent to Africa. More recently, the establishment of an India-Africa interest group in 1996, bringing together representatives of government and industry from both regions, is a further indication of the growing importance of relations. In fact, bilateral trade between South Africa and India was valued at US$600 million in 1997 and the India-South African Joint Commission has set a target of US$1 billion by the year 2000 (Gujral, 1998:126–127). In keeping with this, India has looked to South Africa to play a role in promoting formal regional ventures such as the Indian Ocean Rim initiative. Despite the optimistic forecasts for trade relations, sceptics have suggested that India's strong manufacturing base could damage Southern Africa's nascent industries. (Obeng, 1997:105)

In many respects, the Indian Ocean Rim initiative is the fullest expression of South-South cooperation to have emerged in the aftermath of the Cold War and has provided South Africa and Southern Africa with an opportunity to play a formative role in its development. In early 1995, the concept of an Indian Ocean Rim initiative was formally launched by President Mandela on an official visit to India. From this point the debate has gathered momentum and developed around a number of issues, including trade, investment opportunities and even security cooperation. South Africa, India, Australia and Mauritius, as representative of the four strategic 'points' of the Indian Ocean with either significant economies and/or access to their respective continental interiors, were the driving forces behind this initiative. This initiative was formalised in 1997 with the adoption of the **Indian Ocean Rim Association for Regional Co-operation** (IOR-ARC) by fourteen states bordering the shores of the Indian Ocean. Although Mandela's initial comments regarding tourism, science and technology and culture were more encompassing, South African involvement in the evolution of the IOR-ARC has ensured that it does not become a trading bloc but retains a looser structure (Nkhulu, 1995:13–18).

The future of the South

In spite of decades of effort devoted to de-linking the economies of the South from those in the industrialised world, the future of the South is still intimately linked with the North. But the growing volume of trade between countries of the South is an indication that South-South co-operation is a reality and is providing the hoped for alternative to reliance upon Northern markets. Indeed, the fact that the economic crisis in Southeast Asia, that began in July 1997, has had an impact on stock exchanges world-wide is a sure sign that mutual dependency is more complete today than it was thirty years ago when the institutions of the South were first established.

That being said, there are a number of challenges to deepening co-operation amongst the states of the developing world. One of them, already alluded to in this chapter, is the growing diversity and, consequently, a divergence of interests among the economies of the South. Another concern is the emergence of North-South trading blocs, such as the **Asia-Pacific Economic Co-operation** (APEC), which brings together the most developed and the less developed nations in the Asia-Pacific region in a single forum. The implications of APEC and NAFTA is that states in the South will no longer identify exclusively with other developing countries, but will find common cause to act in concert with

regional partners. Recognition of the potential damage to solidarity of purpose in the South has led Malaysia to propose the establishment of an East Asian Economic Caucus within the APEC structure in an effort to ensure that the developing countries still operate as a coherent force.

At the same time, the political aspirations of the South are changing in response to the new international environment. The eventual permanent inclusion of states from the developing world on the UN Security Council, the result of intense lobbying by the NAM states, will for the first time give the South its own voice at the highest level in the organisation. How this will be exercised remains to be seen, but there are already indications that divisions amongst members of the South will be as apparent as acts of solidarity. For example, the difficulties raised by the disintegration of Yugoslavia and the plight of Muslim-dominated Bosnia caused widespread dissent within NAM, between those favouring solidarity with fellow Muslims and those concerned about the implications of intervention. The principle of non-intervention in internal affairs (which was overridden in the case of the liberation struggles in the former Rhodesia and South Africa, when countries of the South argued that the nature of the regimes in power necessitated a violation of the principle of non-interference) will continue to be a source of division within the developing world. The post-Apartheid government in South Africa, as a regional leader and beneficiary of this approach, seems poised to make the case for selective intervention – at least in the diplomatic sphere – in internal matters. As already demonstrated in South Africa's actions in Indonesia and Nigeria, this is sure to cause conflict between the democracies and the authoritarian regimes of the South.

With respect to the security dimensions of South-South relations, the continued unwillingness of the UN to support peacekeeping operations in the developing world (something that, given financial constraints, will not change with the advent of a reformed Security Council) places the burden of security increasingly upon the regional groupings of the South. The question of institutional and financial capacity remains an impediment to effective action on the part of regional organisations, though efforts such as the African Crisis Response Initiative (initiated by the USA) demonstrate a willingness on the part of the industrialised nations to make provisions for the funding and training of regional organisations. Coupled with these logistical concerns is the recognition that political will may be lacking on the part of regional organisations to deal with arms proliferation in the South. The recent militarisation of many NIEs in Asia is particularly troubling. In this regard, South Africa's active participation in the armaments industry is a contributing factor in the destabilisation of regional conflicts, as diverse as Rwanda and Algeria.

Conclusion

The prospects for improved South-South relations offers substantial opportunities for Southern Africa to promote its own concerns in conjunction with those of other developing countries. Firstly, through institutions such as UNCTAD and NAM, Southern African can find a voice for its particular interests in the all-important international debates on security, trade and development. At the same time, Southern Africans can act to influence these institutions to incorporate their concerns in the areas of human rights and conflict prevention. Secondly, South-South co-operation promises to provide technical and financial assistance through trade and development co-operation between Southern Africa and other parts of the South. The growing political and economic power of the South will go a long way towards ensuring that the idealistic slogans of the past can find fulfilment in the realities of the present.

Key concepts in this chapter

New International Economic Order
Non-Aligned Movement
North-South conflict
South-South co-operation
The North
The South

Suggested readings

For general discussions of South-South co-operation see:

- Asante, S. K. B. (1996) 'Contemporary Africa: India and South-South co-operation', *South African Journal of International Affairs*, 4(1).
- Mytelka, L (ed.). (1994) *South-South Co-operation in a Global Perspective*. Paris: Development Centre OECD.
- Sobhan, F. (1987) *Opportunities for South-South Co-operation* (ISIS Issue Paper). Kuala Lumpur: Institute of Strategic and International Studies.
- Sridharan, K. (1998) 'G-15 and South-South co-operation: promise and performance', *Third World Quarterly*, 19(3).

The South Commission (now the South Centre) is the general think-tank of the South. Its thinking can be sampled in:

- The South Commission. (1990) *The Challenge of the South: Report of the South Commission*. Oxford: Oxford University Press.
- The South Centre. (1993) *Facing the Challenge: Responses to the Report of the South Commission*. London: Zed Books.

The World Bank's analysis of the Newly Industrialised Economies can be found in:

- World Bank. (1993) *The East Asian Miracle*. Washington DC: World Bank.

14 | The regional sub-system of Southern Africa

Patrick J. McGowan

This chapter in outline

- Historical development
- The structure of Southern Africa today
- The Southern African regional sub-system
  - Economic interactions
  - Organisational interactions
  - Political interactions
- Conclusion

What is 'Southern Africa'? If we use a political definition, we can say that 'African' countries are the fifty-three independent states that are members of the Organisation of African Unity (OAU), which has its headquarters in Addis Ababa, Ethiopia. Forty-seven of these states are on the African continent and six are islands in the Atlantic and Indian Oceans. Using a geographical definition, we could say that Southern Africa comprises the twenty-two African countries whose national capitals are situated south of the equator. Stretching from Kenya on the east to Gabon in the west, and encompassing all the states south of that line (*see* Map 8), this vast region is larger than Canada – eleven million square kilometres versus ten million square kilometres – and in 1995 had more people than the United States (US) – 264 million versus 260 million. But to geographers and political scientists, this region is known as sub-Equatorial Africa (SEA), which emphasises its geographical character.

Because this is a textbook on International Relations, this chapter will use an international organisation, the Southern African Development Community (SADC), to define Southern Africa. This region comprises the fourteen members of SADC, all of whom are in SEA (*see* Box 14.1). As Map 9 shows, twelve members are on the southern part of the African continent, with the Democratic Republic of the Congo (DRC) being the most northern and South Africa being the most southern. Two members are tiny islands in the Indian Ocean – Mauritius and the Seychelles.

Thus defined, Southern Africa is a vast region of 9,3 million square kilometres, representing 39% of sub-Saharan Africa's (SSA's) area (*see* Table 14.1). With an estimated population of 187,4 million in 1995, Southern Africa contains 25,8% of Africa's people. But, because South Africa is in the region, SADC's **gross domestic product** (GDP) in 1995 was US$178,7 **billion**, representing 43,9% of Africa's GDP, and fully 60,2 % of the GDP of SSA. From this, we can see that Southern Africa is Africa's economic powerhouse. Moreover, as this chapter will show,

Southern Africa is historically, infrastructurally, economically and politically Africa's most coherent and integrated region. Indeed, it represents a **regional sub-system**, centred on South Africa, that is of considerable importance within the international system of states (*see* Chapters 4 and 10) and the global economy (*see* Chapter 2).

Historical development

Over thousands of years Bantu-speaking African peoples with the knowledge of iron making and mixed agriculture (livestock and crops) spread south and east from what are now Cameroon and Nigeria, finally reaching the Eastern Cape Province of South Africa around the year 1000 AD. Once settled, they often established sophisticated political systems, such as the Kongo Kingdom in what is today known as Angola (*see* Box 14.2) and the Zulu Empire in what is now South Africa's KwaZulu-Natal Province (*see* Box 14.5), as well as the prosperous Shona mining and trading states of fifteenth-century Zimbabwe, one of which built the famous Great Zimbabwe (*see* Box 14.8). Along the East African coast, Arabs and Persians (today's Iranians) established city-states, such as on the island of Zanzibar (*see* Box 14.6), that actively participated in an Indian Ocean trade network that reached as far as China.

Beginning in the late fifteenth and early sixteenth centuries, Portuguese explorers and merchants began making contact, via the sea, with people in parts of Southern Africa – particularly in Angola and Mozambique. They were followed by the **Dutch East India Company** (VOC), which founded Cape Town in 1652. Then came the British who created the Cape Colony, which was finally taken from the Dutch in 1805, and the Natal Colony, which was annexed in 1844. At this time, many **Afrikaners** trekked inland from the Cape and eventually established two white-minority Republics in what is now northern South Africa. Finally, in the eighteenth and nineteenth centuries, the French took control of many Indian Ocean islands, including modern-day

Box 14.1: The states of the Southern African Development Community (SADC)

Official name of country	Capital	Date of Independence	Head of state (Oct. 1998)	Form of government	Official languages
Angola, Republic of	Luanda	11 November 1975	President Jose E. dos Santos	Unitary republic	Portuguese
Botswana, Republic of	Gaborone	30 September 1966	President Festus Mogae	Unitary republic	English, Tswana
Congo, Democratic Republic of	Kinshasa	30 June 1960	President Laurent-Desire Kabila	Unitary republic	French
Lesotho, Kingdom of	Maseru	4 October 1966	King Letsie III	Unitary kingdom	English, South Sotho
Malawi, Republic of	Lilongwe	6 July 1964	President Bakili Muluzi	Unitary republic	English, Chewa
Mauritius, Republic of	Port Louis	12 March 1968	President Cassam Uteem	Unitary republic	English, French
Mozambique, Republic of	Maputo	25 June 1975	President Joaquim Chissano	Unitary republic	Portuguese
Namibia, Republic of	Windhoek	21 March 1990	President Sam Nujoma	Unitary republic	English
Seychelles, Republic of	Victoria	26 June 1976	President Albert Rene	Unitary republic	English, French-Kreole
South Africa, Republic of	Pretoria, Cape Town*	31 May 1910	President Nelson Mandela	Federal republic	English**
Swaziland, Kingdom of	Mbabane	6 September 1968	King Mswati III	Unitary kingdom	English, Siswati
Tanzania, United Republic of	Dar es Salaam	9 December 1961	President Benjamin Mkapa	Unitary republic	Swahili, English
Zambia, Republic of	Lusaka	24 October 1964	President Frederick Chiluba	Unitary republic	English
Zimbabwe, Republic of	Harare	18 April 1980	President Robert Mugabe	Unitary republic	English

Esterhuysen (1998)

Notes: * Pretoria is the national administrative capital and Cape Town the seat of Parliament; the Constitutional Court sits in Johannesburg; the national Appeal Court in Bloemfontein. ** South Africa has eleven official languages: English, Afrikaans, Ndebele, North Sotho, South Sotho, Siswati, Tsonga, Tswana, Venda, Xhosa and Zulu.

Mauritius and the Seychelles – both of which were eventually incorporated into the British Empire.

In the last quarter of the nineteenth century, the European 'scramble' for Africa, which represented the high water mark of European **imperialism**, led to the complete colonisation of all of Southern Africa (*see* Chapter 8 and Boxes 14.2 to 14.8). Modern-day Angola and Mozambique remained Portuguese colonies, but with vastly expanded territories. The German Empire seized German South-West Africa

Box 14.2: The political history of Angola

Portugal colonised parts of present-day Angola, including the famous Kingdom of the Kongo, as early as 1483, but colonial rule over the entire territory was not completed until the late 1800s. For much of its history, colonial Angola was a major source of slaves for the infamous Atlantic slave trade (most went to Brazil, which is why Angola is called 'the mother of Brazil'). Besides slavery, Portuguese colonial rule also involved forced labour, the exploitation of the territory's agricultural and mineral riches, and the settlement of up to 500 000 Portuguese.

An anti-colonial war of national liberation began in 1961, which involved three mutually hostile liberation movements. A military *coup d'état* in Portugal in April 1974 led to Angola's independence on 11 November 1975, with the MPLA (Movement for the Popular Liberation of Angola) forming the national government in Luanda. The country immediately slid into a civil war during which more than 500 000 Angolans lost their lives. The MPLA was supported by as many as 50 000 Cuban troops (1988 figures) and advisors from the Soviet Union (USSR); Jonas Savimbi's UNITA (Union for the Total Independence of Angola) was supported by South African troops and money and equipment from the US and China; and the FNLA (National Front for the Liberation of Angola) was covertly supported by Zaïre and the US. Also involved in the war were SWAPO (the South West African Peoples' Organisation), which was fighting to liberate Namibia (then known as South West Africa) from South African control, and the ANC's (African National Congress) Umkhonto we Sizwe (Spear of the Nation) troops, who were

fighting Apartheid in South Africa. Thus, the war was a classic Cold War proxy war.

With the coming to power of Mikhail Gorbachev in the USSR in 1985, the Cold War began to end and complex negotiations led to a cease-fire agreement in Angola with planned multiparty elections; the withdrawal of Cuban and South African troops; and the independence of Namibia on 21 March 1990. No longer supported by the US and South Africa, UNITA broke the cease-fire after it lost the September 1992 multiparty elections to the MPLA. It financed its forces via diamond smuggling from northern Angola through Zaïre. By 1998, after the ending of Mobuto's dictatorship in Zaïre in May 1997 and despite the involvement of the United Nations (UN), the major world powers and the new South Africa, the fighting had still not stopped and elements of UNITA continued with the war against the MPLA government.

Between 1975 and 1991, Angola was 'ruled' by the MPLA as a legal single-party system. Its first President, Dr Agostinho Neto, died in 1979. He was succeeded by President Jose Eduardo do Santos, who was first elected by the MPLA, but in 1992 was popularly elected by the people.

This potentially rich country, because of its petroleum, diamonds and other minerals and excellent agricultural land, has been at war almost continually since 1961. It will take decades to overcome the legacy this war has left; for example, there are still millions of land mines in Angola that kill or maim people daily.

Esterhuysen (1998); Ramsay (1997)

Box 14.3: The political history of the Democratic Republic of Congo (DRC)

Most West European countries participated in the imperialist scramble for Africa in the last quarter of the nineteenth century. The small and neutral Kingdom of Belgium did so, but with a difference. It was Belgian King Leopold who was the chief colonialist. He created his own company and carved out in Central Africa what became known as the Congo Independent State in 1879 – his own personal possession. Leopold's agents exploited the country and its people without mercy (*see* Joseph Conrad's novel, *The Heart of Darkness*). This caused an international outcry and led to the transfer of control to the elected government of Belgium in 1906 and the territory became the Belgium Congo.

Belgium's rule of the Congo lasted until 30 June 1960. Colonialism Belgium style involved the systematic development of the Congo's agricultural and mineral resources with little investment in the people – education and most health care were left in the hands of missionaries, and the colonial government played little role in developing **human capital.**

With little preparation and only a handful of Congolese university graduates (just sixteen), independence in June 1960 came very quickly. The new Democratic Republic of the Congo (DRC), with its capital in Kinshasa, slid rapidly into anarchy. The army mutinied almost immediately and the first Prime Minister, Patrice Lumumba, was assassinated. The mineral-rich Katanga Province (now Shaba Province) led by Moise Tshombe, as well as South Kasai Province, tried to secede from the Congo and were only prevented from doing so by a massive UN military intervention. Between 1960 and 1965, prime ministers came and went and there were significant Cold War covert operations by the Americans, Belgians, French, Russians and Chinese. Among the causes of this instability were the Congo's size (equal to one-quarter of the US) and its ethnic diversity (over 200 different ethnic groups speaking nearly 700 languages).

In 1965, with the support of the American Central Intelligence Agency (CIA), General Joseph Desire Mobutu (more recently known as Mobutu Sese Seko, the 'all powerful one') seized power and ruled as military dictator until 1971, after which single-party elections kept him in power as 'elected' president until May 1997. Mobutu's thirty-two-year rule of the renamed Zaïre was marked by strong support from Western powers, repression of political opposition and the gradual destruction of the economy and its infrastructure due to poor policies (for example, the nationalisation of mines and industries), and massive corruption and incompetence (for example, by 1990 the **real wages** of urban workers had fallen to 2% of what they had been in 1960).

Indeed, Mobutu's regime was a classic **kleptocracy** (a government of thieves) in which he was the chief patron-thief and ruled the country through a complex system of corrupt **patron-client relationships**. For example, in the early 1990s the foreign debt of Zaïre was equal to the Mobutu family's wealth – some US$5 billion! The constitution, parliament and courts were shams, mainly serving public relations purposes.

In early 1997, a long-time political opponent of Mobutu, Laurent-Desire Kabila, launched a rebellion in Eastern Zaïre. Kabila was supported by Rwanda and Uganda. His rebellion was successful because, with the end of the Cold War, Mobutu was no longer a valued ally of the Western powers; indeed he was a historical embarrassment. Also important was the dislike of his regime by ordinary Congolese and the incompetence of his army. In May 1997, Kabila's forces entered the capital, Kinshasa, and Mobutu fled the country and died of cancer soon after in exile.

Kabila renamed the country the Democratic Republic of the Congo, or the DRC. Unfortunately, he has governed the DRC just as poorly as Mobutu. In September 1998, a new civil war broke out in the country with the rebels being supported by Rwanda and Uganda and with Kabila receiving military support from the governments of Angola, Namibia and Zimbabwe. This threatened to become a major regional security crisis.

The DRC's political history is unfortunate because the country is unbelievably well endowed with minerals, excellent agricultural land and vast hydroelectric potential (13% of the world's total). At present, it is a potentially rich country with very poor people. With good governance and foreign investment (which will not happen without good governance), the Congo's potential is great.

Esterhuysen (1998); Ramsay (1997)

(Namibia) and German East Africa (Burundi, Rwanda and mainland Tanzania), which it lost to the Union of South Africa and Great Britain in World War I (1914–1918). Belgian King Leopold created the Congo Free State that came under Belgium's colonial control in 1906 (*see* Box 14.3). The remainder of Southern Africa became part of the British Empire – Botswana, Lesotho, Malawi, Mauritius, Seychelles, South Africa, Swaziland, Zanzibar, Zambia and Zimbabwe. The white-minority Union of South Africa achieved limited independence in 1910 and became a republic in 1961. In 1924 white-minority Southern Rhodesia (Zimbabwe) was granted self-governance, with the United Kingdom (UK) only responsible for defence and foreign policy.

European colonialism and white-minority rule in South Africa and Southern Rhodesia introduced into Southern Africa modern technology, capital, management techniques and populations of European origin who seized African land and exploited African labour. Almost everywhere in the region African peoples resisted these processes, often in violent wars and through rebellions, but they were always eventually defeated and subjugated because of the whites' superior military technology and tactics. Also introduced by the colonialists and white settlers was a paradoxical mix of racism and Christianity. In addition, the Europeans established the current boundaries of the fourteen Southern African states, which have not changed in 100 years (except for Tanzania, which lost Burundi and Rwanda to Belgium in 1919 and merged with Zanzibar and Pemba islands in 1964).

Nevertheless, the European presence and abundant African labour brought the entire region into the global political economy and began its modern economic development. How the African peoples (now including millions of persons of European and Asian origins) achieved their independence from colonialism or liberation from white-minority rule is described in Boxes 14.2 to 14.8 (for the smaller SADC countries, the process was largely similar).

The processes just described led to Southern Africa's **incorporation** into the global political economy as a **peripheral** region. South Africa was a significant exception because of its vast mineral wealth and industry, which developed rapidly, beginning in the 1920s. Thus, South Africa emerged as a **semi-peripheral** power of considerable importance to the rest of the world and the regional **hegemon** within Southern Africa.

It was the discovery and mining of minerals throughout the region that drove this process and ultimately created today's Southern Africa. Diamonds were discovered at Kimberly in 1871 and on the Witwatersrand, vast deposits of gold were found in 1886. A classic 'gold rush' followed. Capital to develop mines initially came from abroad, particularly from Great Britain and the US; hence the major mining corporation in South Africa is called the *Anglo-American Corporation*. The growth of the mining industry created a railroad building boom, rapid urbanisation, as in Johannesburg, improved farming to feed the miners and cities, the first stages of industrialisation to supply the mines, great wealth for the Rand Lords (mine owners) and the **proletarianisation** of both African and white mine workers.

British desire to control the gold fields was the main cause of the famous Anglo-Boer War of 1899–1902 between the British Empire and the two Boer Republics of the Orange Free State and the Transvaal. The Afrikaners were defeated and in a grand political compromise, the quasi-independent Union of South Africa under exclusive white-male rule was founded in 1910 (white women only got the vote in 1930).

Eventually, significant mineral deposits were found in most Southern African states: Angola (petroleum and diamonds), Botswana (diamonds), the Congo (cobalt, copper and diamonds), Namibia (diamonds), South Africa (besides gold and diamonds, platinum group metals, coal and chrome), Tanzania (diamonds), Zambia (copper and cobalt) and Zimbabwe (chrome, coal and gold). Countries without

Box 14.4: The political history of Mozambique

During the 1500s, after the Portuguese sailor, Vasco da Gama had sailed into the Indian Ocean (in 1498), his country established a system of forts/trading posts along the East African coast, from Mombasa, Kenya, in the north to Lourenço Marques (LM, present-day Maputo) in the south. Thus began Portugal's colonial rule in what is now Mozambique. The Portuguese did not penetrate into the interior, except for the Zambesi River valley, until the late 1800s.

Colonial rule in Mozambique was similar to that in Angola, with forced labour, exploitation of African labour and land, and the promotion of white, Portuguese settlement as features. Because of its location on the Indian Ocean, Mozambique's participation in the Atlantic slave trade was less than Angola's, but slaves were sent to the Middle East, the Dutch Cape and Brazil. After the discovery of gold on the Witwatersrand in 1886, colonial Mozambique became a major supplier of migrant labour to the South African mines, with the colonial authorities in Mozambique being paid in gold by the mines for each worker provided. With the expansion of railroads and roads in Southern Africa, the Mozambican ports of LM, Beira and Nacala became important outlets for trade between South Africa, Southern and Northern Rhodesia (Zimbabwe and Zambia) and Nyasaland (Malawi) and the rest of the world.

In 1962, FRELIMO (the Front for the Liberation of Mozambique), led by American-educated Dr Eduardo Mondlane, was formed. In 1964 it launched a war of national liberation from Tanzania and soon gained control of most of northern Mozambique, where it established its own government, schools, clinics, and so on. At a cost of at least 30 000 lives the fighting continued until 1974, when a *coup d'état* in Portugal brought to power a military regime committed to independence for Portugal's African colonies. Mozambique gained independence as a unitary republic on 25 June 1975, and at the time had an illiteracy rate of 93%.

FRELIMO created a single-party state with a Marxist-Leninist (that is, communist) policy line. Because Dr Mondlane had been assassinated by Portuguese agents in 1969, the first president was his successor as leader of FRELIMO, Samora Machel. Machel died in a suspicious aeroplane crash in South Africa in October 1986 (his widow, Mrs Gracia Machel, is today a senior UN official and the wife of President Nelson Mandela of South Africa). Joaquim Chissano was elected president by FRELIMO in the same month, and in a multi-party election in 1994, his term as president was extended.

The newly independent FRELIMO government made some fateful decisions in 1975/76 that have affected the country to this day. First, it decided to support the war of liberation in white-settler Rhodesia and the ANC's struggle against Apartheid in South Africa. It closed the Beira Corridor to Rhodesian trade (particularly hurtful for Rhodesia was the closing of the oil pipeline from Beira to Rhodesia). It also encouraged Robert Mugabe's ZANU (the Zimbabwe African National Union) forces to attack Rhodesia from bases in Mozambique. In retaliation, the white-minority government of Ian Smith in Rhodesia organised, financed and equipped RENAMO (the Mozambican National Resistance), which initiated a civil war in Mozambique. When Rhodesia became the independent, majority-ruled Zimbabwe in 1980, with Mugabe as prime minister, support for RENAMO was passed to Apartheid South Africa because of FRELIMO's support for the ANC, which had important facilities in Maputo. The civil war continued until 1992, when a cease-fire was brokered by Italy and the Catholic Church. The infrastructure in Mozambique that survived the successful war of independence was destroyed in this civil war. It also cost at least 1 000 000 lives and made 7 000 000 Mozambicans refugees. No Southern African nation paid a higher price for opposing white-minority rule in Southern Africa.

The second fateful decision was the adoption, in 1975, of rather rigid Marxist-Leninist political-economic policies, which was supported by the then Soviet Union (USSR) and some theoretical merits and faults are of communism in industrial societies with large working classes in need of a better deal, it has proven totally inappropriate in peasant societies such as Mozambique, where both the workers and capitalists are tiny minorities (90% of the population are rural peasants). The civil war and policies such as the collectivisation of agriculture alienated many peasants from the FRELIMO government. Hence, in the reasonably free and fair multiparty elections held in October 1994, RENAMO got 38% of valid votes to FRELIMO's 44%.

President Chissano's government has learned from past mistakes. In 1990, a new, multiparty constitution was adopted and the Marxist-Leninist policies were scrapped. As of 1998, Mozambique is at peace for the first time since the early 1960s. It has a multiparty political system and an open, market-oriented economy. While it still has a large, inefficient and often corrupt bureaucracy (a British company now runs the Mozambican Customs Service because of the corruption and incompetence of the previous civil service Customs Department) and is one of the poorest countries in the world, with one of the world's largest foreign debts per capita. Foreign investment, particularly from South Africa, is flowing in and the prospects for the country are better than they have been since independence in 1975. An example is the Maputo Corridor project, which will upgrade the infrastructure of the port of Maputo and the road and rail links of Maputo to the industrial heartland of Gauteng Province in South Africa. Today, Mozambique's greatest problems are meeting the needs of its 18 million people and avoiding becoming a total economic colony of South Africa. This is a vast improvement when compared with the country's problems in the past.

Esterhuysen (1998); Ramsay (1997)

mineral wealth, such as Lesotho, Malawi and Mozambique, provided workers for the mines via the migrant labour system. One such migrant worker was Malawi's first president, Dr Kamuzu Banda, who literally walked to South Africa as a young man to work in the Rand's gold mines. Throughout the region, Africans were subordinated to the interests of white capital in the mines, farms and growing industries.

Southern African minerals were exported to the developed countries of the North, particularly Europe and North America (and Japan beginning in the 1950s). In exchange, Southern Africa imported manufactured capital and consumer goods. This long-distance **division of labour** completed the region's incorporation into the global political economy.

Thus, well before World War II Southern Africa had become a regional subsystem economically based on mining, but with significant modern agriculture for export, such as wine and tobacco, and to feed the mines and growing cities. There was also important industry in South Africa and Southern Rhodesia producing intermediate and **finished manufactured goods**. An infrastructure of roads and railroads reached from Cape Town and Durban in South Africa to as far north as the Congo's copper belt with offshoots to the Portuguese ports of Lobito in Angola and Beira and Lourenço Marques (Maputo) in Mozambique (Tanzania was linked to this network in the 1970s; *see* Map 10). Generally, the colonial authorities (Portugal and Great Britain) and independent South Africa cooperated in economic projects and infrastructural development, but there were no common economic or political institutions except for the Southern African Customs Union (SACU) (to be discussed later in this chapter).

The structure of Southern Africa today

Table 14.1 presents basic indicators for the fourteen Southern Africa states. With the exception of Lesotho, Mauritius, the Seychelles and Swaziland, these are large countries, often many

Box 14.5: The political history of South Africa

South Africa has one of the most complex and tragic histories of any country in the world. Stone Age cultures, the Khoi and San, inhabited most of what is now South Africa, Botswana and Namibia for thousands of years. Around 300 AD black African peoples with their more advanced technologies (for example, iron and mixed agriculture) began to enter what is now South Africa from the north, and they gradually pushed the Khoisan aside. They reached the Ciskei around 1000 AD. Then, in 1652, the Dutch East India Company established Cape Town and white settlement began. Two simultaneous processes ensued: the further spread of Bantu-speaking Africans throughout most of eastern and northern South Africa, including the formation of the Zulu Empire by Shaka Zulu in the early nineteenth century; and the gradual spread of whites from Cape Town into the interior of the country, as well as direct British settlement in the Eastern Cape and Natal. A series of wars were fought in the Eastern Cape, in Natal and in the interior between the whites (both Afrikaners and British) and various Bantu-speaking peoples, particularly the Xhosas and Zulus. While Africans won some famous battles, because the whites had access to superior European military technology, they always won the wars.

By the 1880s, what is now South Africa comprised four political units, all under white-minority rule: the Cape of Good Hope Colony and Natal Colony, which were parts of the British Empire, and two internationally recognised, independent Boer (white-minority, Afrikaans-speaking) Republics – the Orange Free State and the South African Republic (later the Transvaal Republic). With the discovery of diamonds at Kimberly in 1871, quickly annexed by the British to the Cape, and the discovery of gold on the Rand in 1886, the modern history of South Africa began. Two wars were fought between the British and their colonial allies against the Boer Republics, the last being the famous 'Anglo-Boer War' of 1899–1902, which led to the defeat of the Afrikaners and the creation of the Union of South Africa in 1910 as a self-governing, white-minority ruled dominion within the British Empire. Full independence was granted by an Act of the British Parliament (the Act of Westminster) in 1931.

Between 1652 and 1931, the 'non-white' populations of South Africa (Africans, people of mixed origin, known as coloureds, and Asians from India) experienced slavery until the 1830s, and then race-based segregation (Indians began to arrive in the 1860s and were never enslaved). Except for a few coloured voters in the Cape, they were all politically disenfranchised. Africans, particularly outside the Cape, were segregated into 'Native Reserves' and only entered the white economy and cities when their labour was needed – on white-owned farms, in the mines and as domestic workers.

In 1912, the South African Native National Congress was founded to speak for African interests. It soon became the African National Congress (ANC), the oldest liberation movement/political party in SSA. South Africa participated in World War I (1914–1918) and conquered German South-West Africa (Namibia), which it ruled until 1990. The country, under the leadership of Field Marshal and Prime Minister Jan Smuts, fought on the Allied side in World War II (1939–1945) in Africa and Europe against the Italian Fascists and German Nazis. Members of the South African military also fought on the UN side (mainly South Koreans and Americans) in the Korean War (1950–1953) against communist North Korea and China.

In the period 1910–1990 politics in South Africa was dominated, firstly, by the struggle between Boer and Britons (English-speaking South Africans) for control of the government. In the 1948 elections, Afrikaner nationalism finally triumphed and the National Party (NP) ruled the country until 1994. The NP began immediately to implement its core policy of Apartheid (separateness), which sought to make South Africa 'white man's' country with the African population becoming 'citizens' of ten ethnically-based homelands (for example, Venda, Ciskei and the Transkei). At least 3,5 million blacks were forcibly removed from their long-held homes and dumped in these homelands.

Led by the ANC and then also by the Pan-Africanist Congress (PAC), African nationalism became the second major political force in this period. African nationalists fought the implementation of Apartheid and in 1960 began an armed struggle to end this system and to achieve freedom and equality for all South Africans. Many blacks and some whites died in this struggle and thousands of others, such as President Nelson Mandela, spent years in prison because of their political beliefs and their actions in support of these beliefs (for example, when Mr Mandela was sentenced to life in prison for 'treason', he was the leader of the ANC's armed wing, Umkhonto we Sizwe [Spear of the Nation]).

The 1980s were a very troubled decade with internal rebellion against Apartheid, countered by states of emergency and repression (often involving illegal murders and torture); armed struggle by the liberation movements (the ANC and PAC); and international military, economic, financial, cultural and sporting sanctions against the NP government and its policies. The economy suffered a severe collapse in 1985, from which it only began to recover in the second half of 1993.

On 2 February 1990, new State President F. W. de Klerk announced to a startled world that his government was unbanning all opponents and that Mr Mandela and other political prisoners would be released forthwith (Mr Mandela was freed on 11 February). Complex negotiations then began amidst a climate of political violence that resulted, ultimately, in the Interim Constitution in November 1993 and, finally, an adult franchise, democratic election in April 1994, which was decisively won by the ANC. Mr Mandela become the first black president in the history of South Africa in May 1994.

Today, South Africa has one of the most democratic constitutions in the world (adopted in 1996) and is rapidly developing a democratic political culture based on human rights. The country is the military and economic powerhouse of the African continent (which is why President Bill Clinton of the US spent four days in South Africa on an official state visit in March 1998). How a democratic South Africa will use its political and economic power and moral authority in Africa is one of the big questions in African international relations. At the same time, it must deal with the legacy of Apartheid, which has left South Africa one of the most unequal societies in the world, with widespread poverty and unemployment amidst the riches of the few.

Esterhuysen (1998); Ramsay (1997)

times larger than typical European states. The DRC, Angola and South Africa are particularly large (the Congo equals one-quarter of the US), which has hampered the development of both Angola and the Congo. With the exception of the Congo Basin and much of coastal Mozambique, the region is a high plateau with occasional mountain ranges. This means that all the region's major rivers, such as the Congo and Zambesi, have rapids or waterfalls near the coast, which makes them unsuitable for use as transportation networks (compare this to the Mississippi River system in the US or the Rhine River in Europe).

The Congo, South Africa and Tanzania have relatively large populations, but are all much smaller than major European countries such as France, Germany and Great Britain. There are four important features of the region's **demography**:

1. first, these populations have been growing rapidly since the 1950s (with the exception of Mauritius and the Seychelles) at rates of about 3,0% a year in the period 1990–1995;

2. second, the (mainly) sexually transmitted HIV and AIDS are widespread in the region, particularly in the Congo, Zambia and Zimbabwe. (This may sharply reduce future population growth and will have massive impacts on the region's economy);

3. third, the region contains six **mini-states** with populations of two million or less, which are never likely to develop diversified economies nor count for much in international politics;

4. finally, a large population alone does not translate into strength and influence in international relations. Rather, it is the population's level of development in terms of health, knowledge, skills and income that counts in the world today (this is measured by the UN Development Programme's **human development index**, or HDI).

Table 14.1: Basic indicators for Southern African countries

Country	Area in km², 1995	Estimated population in thousands, 1995	Total GDP in US$ millions, 1995	Real GDP per capita in PPP$, 1994	HDI value, 1994	HDI rank*, 1994
Angola	1 246 700	11 500	3 722	1 600	0,335	157
Botswana	581 730	1 550	4 318	5 367	0,673	97
DRC****	2 344 858	43 500	8 025	429	0,381	142
Lesotho	30 355	2 000	1 029	1 109	0,457	137
Malawi	118 484	10 000	1 465	694	0,320	161
Mauritius	2 040	1 130	3 919	13 172	0,831	61
Mozambique	801 590	18 000	1 469	986	0,281	166
Namibia	824 268	1 600	3033	4 027	0,570	118
Seychelles	455	80	487**	7 891	0,845	52
South Africa	1 219 090	37 859***	136 035	4 291	0,716	90
Swaziland	17 364	950	998	2 821	0,582	114
Tanzania	945 087	29 000	3 602	656	0,357	149
Zambia	752 618	19 000	4 073	962	0,369	143
Zimbabwe	390 759	11 200	6 522	2 196	0,513	129
SADC total	9 275 398	187 369	178 697	3 301‡	0,516‡	n/a
South Africa as % of SADC	13,1	20,2	76,1	n/a	n/a	n/a

Esterhuysen (1998); United Nations Development Programme (1997) **Notes:** * rank out of 175 countries; ** preliminary 1996 census results; *** GNP 1995; n/a = not applicable; **** Democratic Republic of Congo; ‡ Average

HDI ranges from high human development (1,000 to 0,800), to medium development (0,799 to 0,500) to low human development (0,499 to 0,000). In 1997, Canada scored highest on HDI with a score of 0,907; Sierra Leone in West Africa was ranked last out of 175 states with a score of 0,176; and the middle-ranking country (87 on the list) was the Dominican Republic in the Caribbean with a score of 0,718. Collectively, the fourteen SADC members manifest poor human development. Only the tiny island Republics of Mauritius and the Seychelles are in the high development category and one-half of Southern Africa from Lesotho to Mozambique are in the low group, with Angola, Malawi and Mozambique being among the least developed countries in the world. These conclusions are reinforced by these countries' very low **real GDP per capita in purchasing power parity (PPP)**

US$. Despite its wealth and advanced economy, South Africa ranks only ninetieth in the world because, under Apartheid (1948–1994), the country did not invest in all its people. Hence, in 1992, had the white minority population been a separate country, it would have ranked twenty-fourth in the world, along with Spain (0,878), whereas the vast African majority in the country would have been number 132 on the list, just ahead of Congo, Brazzaville (0,462) (UNDP, 1994:98).

As discussed in more detail in Chapter 15, Southern Africa shows a pattern of systematic human underdevelopment, poverty and **socio-economic inequality** caused by colonial exploitation, extensive warfare beginning in the 1960s, the impact of Apartheid and racism on South Africa, and regional and economic mismanagement by many independent governments (*see* Boxes 14.2 to 14.8). However,

Table 14.2: Southern Africa's transportation and communications infrastructure

Country	Railway track in kilometres, 1990	Paved roads in kilometres, 1990	Number of major ports, 1998	Air freight in millions of tonnes, 1991–1993	Telephones (estimated) in thousands, 1990–1993	Number of host computers, July 1998
Angola	2 900	8 600	3	113	40,3	2
Botswana	1 600	1 600	LL*	8	48,0	581
DRC**	4 000	2 800	0	42	40,0	0
Lesotho	2	570	LL	1	19,0	17
Malawi	780	2 400	LL	15	50,0	0
Mauritius	0	1 700	1	334	75,0	370
Mozambique	3 150	5 300	3	47	66,0	83
Namibia	2 380	4 100	1	84	92,0	668
Seychelles	0	n/k	1	70	n/k	7
South Africa	21 425	58 000	7	1 285	5 200,0	213 818
Swaziland	370	510	LL	4	25,0	398
Tanzania	3 570	3 600	1	16	140,0	143
Zambia	2 190	6 500	LL	47	92,0	241
Zimbabwe	2 745	15 800	LL	154	300,0	844
SADC total	45 112	111 480	16 2	220	6 187,3	217 172
South Africa as % of SADC	47,5	52,0	n/a	57,9	84,0	98,4

Esterhuysen (1998); Network Wizards   Notes: *LL = landlocked country with no sea ports; n/k = not known; n/a = not applicable; ** Democratic Republic of Congo

Botswana, Mauritius and Namibia have managed their economies well and have promoted the development of their citizens. This lack of human development sharply reduces the region's capacity to compete in the world and makes it more difficult to implement its plans for regional economic integration and peace and stability, as called for in SADC's founding treaty.

The column in Table 14.1 reporting the economic size of each SADC country, as measured by total GDP in millions of US$ in 1995, is significant. It shows that South Africa is the economic giant of the region, with its economy being more than three times bigger than the rest of the region combined and seventeen times bigger than the region's second-largest economy – the Congo. This provides South Africa with a **structural power** (*see* Chapter 2) that results in great infrastructural, military and political advantages in comparison to any other Southern African state and, indeed, to the region as a whole.

This is reinforced by Table 14.2, which summarises the region's infrastructure of transportation and communication. Given its vast size, the Southern African region has an underdeveloped road and railroad transportation system (*see* Map 10). For example, the huge country of Canada, with only 27,8 million inhabitants in 1992, had 93 545 kilometres of railroads and 250 000 kilometres of paved roads in comparison to SADC's 45 112 kilometres and 111 480 kilometres respectively. But, as we have seen, Canada ranked first in human development in 1997, whereas most of SADC is underdeveloped. Only South Africa looks reasonably developed in road and rail transport as it accounts for only 13% of the region's area, yet it has around 50% of its railroads and paved roads.

Box 14.6: The political history of Tanzania

The United Republic of Tanzania comprises two parts, each with a distinct history before 1964 – mainland Tanganyika, and Zanzibar and Pemba islands in the Indian Ocean. Zanzibar and Pemba were settled by Arabs from Oman and elsewhere after 1000 AD; the islands also received many Persians (Iranians), whose descendants are known as Shirazis. The islands were ruled by an Arab Sultan (monarch) and became a slave-trading centre, exporting African slaves captured in the interior of Eastern and Southern Africa to the Middle East and India. As a consequence of the trade, the majority of the population on the islands was then African in origin. In an effort to end this trade, which was exposed to world opinion by the missionary and explorer David Livingstone, Great Britain imposed a Protectorate on Zanzibar in 1890, which lasted until independence on 9 December 1963. Almost immediately after independence, in early 1964, the majority African population rose in a revolution, seized political power and killed many ordinary Arabs and Shirazis. Chaos ensued and in order to prevent Cold War interference, President Julius Nyerere of Tanganyika quickly negotiated a merger, thus creating, on 24 April 1964, the United Republic of Tanzania.

Mainland Tanganyika was populated by Bantu-speaking Africans well before the time of Christ. German explorers initiated European contact with these peoples, signing treaties of protection with African chiefs and leaders, who probably did not fully understand the implications of these treaties, as defined by **international law.** So, in 1885, the German Empire proclaimed a Protectorate over the entire territory (including present-day Rwanda and Burundi) and called it German East Africa. Once the African people understood that they had lost their independence, they launched the so-called Maji-Maji ('water-water' in Kiswahili) rebellion, in 1905/6, which was viciously suppressed by the Germans.

During World War I (1914–1918), there was much fighting in the territory between the German colonial army (which was never defeated) and British colonial forces from Kenya and the Rhodesias. When Germany lost the war, the territory was given to Great Britain in 1919 as a League of Nations Mandate, which it was supposed to rule in the interest of the local population. In fact, Tanganyika Territory was ruled little differently from other British colonies in Africa, with the exception that white settlement was not actively encouraged. At the end of World War II (1939–1945), Tanganyika became a British United Nations Trust Territory, and the implication was clear that the British should prepare the country for eventual independence.

In the 1950s, African nationalists, led by school-teacher Julius Nyerere, began to demand independence. This was achieved on 9 December 1961. Nyerere became prime minister and then president in 1962. In 1967, with the Arusha Declaration, President Nyerere introduced Ujamaa (literally, familihood), or African Socialism Tanzanian-style, and Kiswahili was made the official national language. A single-party system was introduced in 1965, but with regular elections between opposing candidates from the ruling Chama Cha Mapinduzi (CCM) party.

Ujamaa, with its (sometimes forced) collectivisation of agriculture in a villagisation programme, and the establishment of many state-owned industries failed miserably, and Tanzania became one of the poorest and most aid-dependent economies in Africa. But the political reforms were a brilliant success, and except for a failed military coup in 1964 before the reforms were begun, Tanzania has been one of the most politically stable and peaceful countries in post-colonial Africa. It also has a reasonably good human rights record and only mild levels of corruption.

President Nyerere retired in 1985 with the status of an honest African elder statesman (or 'Mzee' in Kiswahili). He was succeeded by President Ali Hassan Mwinyi (1985–1995). Constitutional reforms restored a fully democratic, multiparty system in 1992. In controversial multiparty elections held in October-December 1995, present President Benjamin Mkapa was elected with 62% of the vote. Parliament now includes the majority CCM party and two major and two minor opposition parties.

Under Mwinyi, and particularly under Mkapa, economic policy has changed completely and

Tanzania is now a market-oriented economy; most state firms have been privatised, such as the State Brewing Company that is now profitably one-half owned by South African Breweries. In recent years, positive economic growth has returned and currently there is a boom in mineral exploration and mining in Tanzania. If properly managed, the country could be a great destination for eco-tourism – the Serengeti Plains and various watersports, such as scuba diving off Zanzibar and Pemba islands, are already major tourist attractions.

Esterhuysen (1998); Ramsay (1997)

Similar conclusions apply for sea and air transportation. In the period 1991–1993, South Africa accounted for 58% of the region's air freight, which means that it has a greater number and more efficient airports than the rest of the region, and air freight usually involves high value to weight goods. If information were available for 1998, South Africa's proportion would probably be much higher because of the great growth in the number of international airlines servicing South Africa since the end of Apartheid.

South Africa has seven of the region's sixteen ports, and its ports are much larger and more efficient (for example, able to handle cargo containers) than those found in the rest of the

Table 14.3: Armed forces, military expenditure and arms trade in Southern African states

Country	Total active forces, 1995	Total military expenditure in US$ million, 1995	Expenditure as % of budget, 1995	Arms exports in US$ million, 1995	Arms imports in US$ million, 1995
Angola	127 000	300	31,0	0	1600
Botswana	6 100	225	5,2	0	30
DRC***	67 100	125	0,8	0	10
Lesotho	2 000	33	13,0	0	0
Malawi	10 400	21	0,7	0	0
Mauritius	7 260	11	0,4	0	0
Mozambique	49 800	58	7,3	0	160
Namibia	8 000	65	2,0	n/k	n/k
Seychelles	1 100	n/k	4,0	n/k	n/k
South Africa	196 500*	3 720	2,8	60	0
Swaziland	25 400	22	n/k	0	0
Tanzania	58 500	89	3,9	0	70
Zambia	24 400	62	1,4	0	0
Zimbabwe	70 000	233	6,0	0	0
SADC total	653 560	4 964	6,0**	60	1 870
South Africa as % of total	30,1	74,9	n/a	100,0	0,0

Esterhuysen (1998); Ramsay (1997); Allen (1998)
Notes: * includes 61 500 full-time forces and 135 000 ready reserves; ** average percent; n/k = not known; n/a = not applicable; *** Democratic Republic of Congo

region. Also notable is that SADC contains six landlocked countries, a far higher proportion than is found in the European Union (EU) or the Association of Southeast Asian Nations (ASEAN). Recent research (Sachs, 1997) has shown that being landlocked is a distinct handicap for development and it makes these countries highly dependent upon South Africa's extensive and efficient port and transportation systems for their trade with the rest of the world.

We live in a global, informational economy (McGowan, 1997). Therefore, a nation's communications infrastructure is an important indicator of its global competitiveness and links to the rest of the world. In this respect, within SADC, South Africa is in total command. Its 5,2 million telephones, essential for fax transmissions as well as long-distance conversations, represent 84% of the region's total. In terms of **host computers**, its lead is even greater, as it has over 98% of the region's total hosts. Host computers are essential for electronic mail (e-mail) and for using the **Internet** for research and economic activity. In this respect, South Africa resembles a small, developed European country – in July 1998 it had more hosts than Austria, the Russian Federation, Poland and the Czech Republic, and on a per capita basis it ranked twenty-fifth in the world, just behind Italy and Spain.

Our look at transportation and communications infrastructures in Southern Africa reinforces the picture of South Africa being in a different international league from its SADC partners. In other words, inherited structural imbalances in Southern Africa make South Africa the regional hegemon. How South Africa will use its power in the region is one of the big questions in the region's international relations (*see* Ahwireng-Obeng & McGowan, 1998; McGowan & Ahwireng-Obeng, 1998).

Great economic strength and an extensive infrastructure should translate into considerable relative military power for South Africa, and this is confirmed in Table 14.3. As discussed in Chapter 4, military power has always been an essential aspect of state power in international relations because of **international anarchy** and the **doctrine of self-help** in which all states claim the **sovereign right** to use military force to defend themselves and to promote their **national interests**.

In 1995, Angola was involved in a civil war between the MPLA government and UNITA rebels (*see* Box 14.2) and therefore had the second largest military in the region. However, as it did not have its own arms industry, it was a large importer of military goods. To a lesser extent the same applies to Mozambique, whose civil war ended only in 1992. With the exception of South Africa, most Southern African states have small armed forces and small defence budgets. These military forces are for defensive purposes and they possess little capacity to launch a sustained war on a neighbour. Moreover, they are all importers of military equipment. Besides the armed forces of Angola and Mozambique, only Zimbabwe's armed forces have much real military experience, having served in Mozambique during that country's civil war and in several UN peacekeeping exercises elsewhere in Africa.

On the other hand, Table 14.3 reveals yet again that South Africa is much stronger than its SADC neighbours. Including its ready reserves, it has the largest military in the region. Moreover, while small and with outdated equipment by world standards, the South Africa Navy and Air Force are the most powerful in the region. Even though it spent less than 3% of its budget on the military in 1995, because of its economic size South Africa accounted for 75% of the region's military spending. Moreover, the SANDF (South African National Defence Force) has extensive experience in warfare, having fought Cubans and MPLA forces in Angola until 1989, having fought SWAPO forces in Angola and Namibia until the same year, and having fought ANC and PAC units within South Africa itself and in much of the Southern African region. Experienced elements from the ANC and PAC forces have been integrated into the SANDF and its new Commander, Siphiwe Nyanda, is a former Umkhonto we Sizwe general.

Box 14.7: The political history of Zambia

Although Northern Rhodesia became a British Protectorate and part of the British Empire in 1924, the territory was created by South African imperialism. In 1889, the Cape Colony politician and mining magnate Cecil John Rhodes organised and financed the British South Africa Company (BSACO). Rhodes's dream was to create a continuous British territory 'from Cape to Cairo' and to use force if necessary to do this. In 1890, BSACO forces were sent north of the Limpopo River by Rhodes and conquered what are now Zambia and Zimbabwe, which were originally known as Northern and Southern Rhodesia. As a private company, the BSACO ruled Northern Rhodesia until 1924, when it became a British Protectorate that was ruled by the Colonial Office in London.

While significant deposits of gold and diamonds were never found, Northern Rhodesia was exceptionally well endowed with vast deposits of copper and cobalt, which were developed by British and South African mining houses (for example, the Anglo-American Corporation), from the 1920s. A major mining industry developed on the 'Copper Belt' and included a large and eventually unionised working class of African miners. To this day copper and cobalt remain Zambia's principal exports.

In 1953, the British government formed the Central African Federation, grouping together what are now Malawi, Zambia and Zimbabwe under a federal government in Salisbury (now Harare) in Southern Rhodesia. Only white adults had the vote so the tiny white minority in the Federation controlled it and its policies (essentially Southern Rhodesian whites). This led to the growth of African nationalism, which sought independent, majority-rule in all three territories.

In Northern Rhodesia, nationalist Kenneth Kaunda formed the United National Independence Party (UNIP) to struggle for independence. There were many strikes, protest marches and imprisonments after the formation of UNIP and the Federation. By the early 1960s, the British realised that the Federation could not be made to work and ended it in 1963. They then moved quickly to hold multiparty elections in Northern Rhodesia in January 1964. These were decisively won by Kaunda and his UNIP. Independence was granted to Zambia on 24 October 1964. UNIP won the second multiparty election in 1968, but in 1972, Zambia amended its constitution and the country became a single-party system with UNIP as the only legal party. After 1976, the government ruled with state-of-emergency powers.

Kaunda and the UNIP were guided by the philosophy of 'humanism' – a mild form of African socialism. In 1969, all Zambian industry, including the mines, was 51% nationalised. This turned out to be an economic disaster of major proportions. As urbanisation, unemployment and poverty grew, opposition to the UNIP grew and was suppressed. Due to its massive economic problems, a **structural adjustment programme** (SAP) was imposed on Zambia by the World Bank and International Monetary Fund (IMF). This added to popular discontent with the ruling party.

Under pressure from domestic opponents and foreign aid donors, the government reluctantly amended the constitution in December 1990 to restore a multiparty system. In an August 1991 election, Kaunda and his UNIP were defeated by a huge majority by Frederick Chiluba and his Movement for Multiparty Democracy (MMD). Mr Chiluba was re-elected President in November 1996 in elections that the UNIP and ex-president Kaunda boycotted.

During 1998, the Zambian economy was being rapidly privatised, with Anglo-American again involved in mining. Mr Kaunda and his opposition UNIP party are regularly harassed by the government and the MMD. Chiluba's government has shown high-level corruption, including drug trafficking, frequent ministerial resignations and an inability to address the country's economic problems, such as 200% inflation. Today Zambia is a poor, copper-dependent, unstable democracy. However, the country has great agricultural and eco-tourism potential which, with proper investment and training, could balance its dependence on minerals.

Esterhuysen (1998); Ramsay (1997)

Box 14.8: The political history of Zimbabwe

Present-day Zimbabwe has an important pre-colonial past. By the 1400s, a series of (Chi)Shona-speaking states had emerged that prospered through their trade in gold, ivory and other goods with Indian Ocean merchants who had contacts as far away as China. These states built stone settlements known as 'zimbabwes', the most important being Great Zimbabwe near modern-day Masvingo. In the 1600s, these states declined, possibly because of disruption by the Portuguese of the Indian Ocean trade or because of declining food production relative to population growth. Today Shona speakers represent about 80% of the population.

The second-largest ethnolinguistic community (16%) are Ndebele speakers (Ndebele is a dialect of Zulu) who created a militarily strong Ndebele kingdom around Bulawayo in the 1840s. The Ndebele and their leaders refused to be forcibly incorporated into Shaka Zulu's empire and moved to what is now northern South Africa. There they fought Afrikaner voortrekkers who had horses and guns. Unable to defeat the Afrikaners, but knowing Shaka's military tactics, they moved north under their king, Umzilagazi, and conquered much of modern Zimbabwe.

Zimbabwe's early colonial history was similar to Zambia's, but with three key differences. White settlement under BSACO rule was significant, even though most whites arrived in Southern Rhodesia after World War II (1939–1945). They never numbered more than 5% of the total population, but they did seize 50% of the best land for the farming of tobacco and other crops. Second, in 1921 the settlers were offered the option of joining the Union of South Africa as a fifth province or self-government as a British Crown Colony. By a narrow margin they chose self-government, so in 1924, BSACO rule was ended and Southern Rhodesia became a white-minority, self-governing colony, and Britain was responsible only for foreign affairs and defence. Thus, the third difference is that Zimbabwe was never under the direct rule of a European colonial power, which makes the country unique in African colonial history.

Even though it never officially embraced Apartheid, Southern Rhodesia developed into a highly segregated society with whites in control of farming, mining and business. Blacks worked for whites or engaged in subsistence agriculture in the 'Native Reserves'. This combination of black labour and white skills, capital and technology created Africa's second most developed economy after South Africa's. But, as the first prime minister of the Central African Federation said, the relationship between blacks and whites was like the relationship between a horse and its rider!

Southern Rhodesian whites were the principal beneficiaries of the Central African Federation (1953–1963) and they fought hard to keep it. They failed in this and, in 1962, voted into power the Rhodesian Front Party (RF). The RF was led by Ian Smith, whose aim was to maintain white-minority rule at any cost. When negotiations with the British government broke down, Smith's RF made its Unilateral Declaration of Independence (UDI) in 1965. This led to the suppression of the two major liberation movements: Joshua Nkomo's Zimbabwe African People's Union (ZAPU) and Robert Mugabe's Zimbabwe African National Union (ZANU).

No other country officially recognised Rhodesia's 'independence', but South Africa and the Portuguese colonial authorities in Mozambique rendered Smith's regime significant economic and military aid. The second consequence of UDI was mandatory economic sanctions imposed by the UN in 1967. Unfortunately, these never worked. In addition, there was never a chance that Britain would use force against 'fellow whites' who were in rebellion against their common Queen.

Because of this, both ZANU and ZAPU launched a war of national liberation in 1966. The war was long and bitter, costing thousands of (mainly African) lives. After the fall of Portuguese colonialism, Mugabe's ZANU fighters attacked from independent Mozambique while Nkomo's forces operated from Zambia. In 1976, ZANU and ZAPU formed the Patriotic Front (PF). Cosmetic political reforms in 1978–1979 only intensified the fighting. At Lancaster House (London) in 1979, negotiations among Smith, Mugabe, Nkomo and their parties produced an agreement to end the war and hold all-race elections in 1980. The elections were won by ZANU, with ZAPU becoming the minority party in parliament (the voting was strongly on ethnolinguistic lines).

Zimbabwe became independent on 18 April 1980, with Robert Mugabe as prime minister and then president. Regular elections have continued, but often with many irregularities. In 1990, ZANU and ZAPU merged to form ZANU-PF and Nkomo became the second vice-president. The 1995 parliamentary and 1996 presidential elections were boycotted by the opposition and today Zimbabwe has become an increasingly corrupt, *de facto* one party state.

Considering the bitterness of the war between 1966 and 1979, Mr Mugabe has had considerable success in racial reconciliation, although many white settlers chose to relocate to South Africa and elsewhere. As whites owned 50% of the best farmland, land redistribution (reform) to blacks has been a key issue. To date this has not produced a large, new class of prosperous black commercial farmers. While Zimbabwe has mines and some industry, it is essentially an agricultural country exporting tobacco and other crops to the world. These crops are still produced, mainly by a few thousand white farmers. Economic mismanagement and corruption have forced Zimbabwe to accept a SAP, which means that its monetary and fiscal policies are largely dictated by the World Bank and the IMF in Washington, DC.

Esterhuysen (1998); Ramsay (1997)

South Africa also has the only significant arms industry on the African continent. Much of the SANDF's excellent equipment, such as its world-class artillery and attack helicopters, is made in South Africa by various divisions of Armscor, and the country is the world's tenth-largest arms exporter. While detailed statistics are never published, South Africa's Minister of Defence has often said that military equipment is South Africa's single-largest manufactured export and that foreign sales in 1997 amounted to around US$260 million. It is deeply ironic that this arms industry grew as a consequence of the international arms embargo against Apartheid in the 1970s and 1980s!

The overall picture is that South Africa is militarily dominant in Southern Africa; indeed, it is the major military power in SSA. So far, the new South Africa has been reluctant to use this power in such activities as peacekeeping in Africa, in part because the integration of personnel from the old SADF (South African Defence Force), the armies of four former 'homelands' and the ANC and PAC cadres is not complete and because the SANDF is heavily involved in support of the South African Police Service for domestic law and order purposes. Nevertheless, Western powers such as the US are keen for South Africa to take a lead in 'policing' SSA, and South Africa may find it hard to resist such pressures, particularly given that such a role would enhance its status in Africa and its bid for a permanent seat on a restructured UN Security Council.

Our examination of the structural features of Southern Africa has resulted in an analysis that demonstrates South Africa's power in comparison to its regional neighbours; a power that is growing because of the economic and political problems of the larger SADC states: Angola, the DRC, Mozambique, Tanzania, Zambia and, especially, Zimbabwe, the only other state in the region with a somewhat diversified economy and a disciplined military. The other SADC states that are well governed with growing economies – Botswana, Mauritius and Namibia – are mini-states in terms of their very small populations, none of which is larger than metropolitan Cape Town. They can never threaten South Africa; indeed as the next section will show, in the cases of Botswana and Namibia, they are highly dependent on South Africa.

The Southern African regional sub-system

The existence of a regional sub-system within the global political economy must be demon-

Table 14.4: External trade of SADC countries

Country	Imports in US$ million, 1995	Exports in US$ million, 1995	Value of main exports as % of total exports, 1994–1996	Value of imports from main source as % of total 1994–1996	Value of exports to main buyer as % of total, 1994–1996
Angola	1 748	3 508	Petroleum (95%), diamonds	France (23%), Portugal	US (65%), Germany
Botswana*	1 907	2 130	Diamonds (70%), copper-nickel	South Africa (78%), EU	EU (74%), South Africa
DRC**	581	1 028	Diamonds (35%), copper, cobalt	Belgium (15%), South Africa	Belgium (37%), US, Italy
Lesotho*	821	143	Manufactured goods (85%), wool, mohair	South Africa (82%)	South Africa (53%), US
Malawi	491	325	Tobacco (70%), tea, sugar	South Africa (36%), Zimbabwe	South Africa (15%), Germany
Mauritius	1 959	1 537	Textiles/clothing (57%), sugar	South Africa (12%), France	UK (34%), France, US
Mozambique	784	169	Shellfish (52%), cotton, nuts	South Africa (44%), Zimbabwe	Spain (16%), South Africa
Namibia*	1 196	1 353	Diamonds/minerals (58%), fish	South Africa (85%), EU	UK (37%), South Africa
Seychelles	204	25	Fish (90%)	UK (20%), Singapore	UK (43%), Germany
South Africa*	30 555	27 860	Minerals (37%), gold (21%)	EU (44%), US, Japan	EU (27%), SACU (23%)
Swaziland*	825	800	Sugar (17%), woodpulp	South Africa (97%)	South Africa (58%), EU
Tanzania	1 619	639	Coffee (18%), cotton	UK (10%), Kenya, Japan	Germany (10%), Japan, India
Zambia	1 258	781	Copper (60%), cobalt	South Africa (28%), UK	Japan (18%), Thailand
Zimbabwe	2 241	1 885	Tobacco (21%), gold, minerals	South Africa (38%), UK	South Africa (13%), UK
SADC total	46 189	42 183	n/a	n/a	n/a
South Africa as % of SADC	66,2	66,0	n/a	n/a	n/a

Esterhuysen (1998)
Notes: * SACU member; ** Democratic Republic of Congo; n/a = not applicable

Country	Economic activity	South African firm or group
Angola	Banking	Investec Bank
	Electric power	Eskom
	Mineral exploration	Trans Hex International
		Anglo-American Corporation
	National parks	South African Parks Board
	Textiles	Zhauna
Botswana	Banking	Standard Bank of South Africa
	Brewing	South African Breweries
	Hotels/resorts	Conservation Corporation Africa
		Protea Hotels
		Sun International
	Mining (diamonds)	De Beers
		Anglo-American Corporation
	Telecommunications	NZ Telecoms Ltd.
Congo	Banking	Standard Bank of South Africa
	Diamond sales	De Beers
	Farming	Individual families
	Hydroelectricity	Eskom
	Mining (copper)	JCI Limited
	Mining (copper/cobalt)	Iscor
	Mineral exploration	Trans Hex International
	Railways	Spoornet
	Water treatment/sewage	Aquazur Ltd.
Lesotho	Banking	Standard Bank of South Africa
	Brewing	South African Breweries
	Electric power	Eskom
	Hotels/resorts	Sun International
	Mineral exploration	JCI Limited
Malawi	Hotels/resorts	Protea Hotels
	Mining	Gencor Limited
	Mining (monazite)	Rareco
Mauritius	Hotels/resorts	Protea Hotels
	Reinsurance brokering	Forbes Group
Mozambique	Aluminium smelting	Gencor/Alusaf
	Banking	Standard Bank of South Africa
	Brewing	South African Breweries
	Cashew nut factory	Anglo-American Corporation
	Cellular telephones	Alcatel Alsthom
	Coking cole	JCI Ltd.
	Electrical power	Eskom
	Farming	Sacada
	Iron briquettes	JCI Ltd.
	Mining	Gencor Limited

(Mozambique continued)	Mineral exploration	Gencor Limited, Anglo-American Corporation
	Natural gas	IDC
	Railways and ports	Spoornet
	Retailing	Pepkor
	Shipping	Unicorn
	Supermarkets	Shoprite/Checkers, Pick 'n Pay
Namibia	Banking	Standard Bank of South Africa
	Hotels/resorts	Sun International
	Liquid oxygen/nitrogen	Afrox
	Oil exploration	Sasol
	Mineral exploration	Anglo-American Corporation
		Anglovaal Ltd.
		Trans Hex International
	Mining (zinc)	Iscor
	Supermarkets	Pick 'n Pay
Swaziland	Banking	Standard Bank of South Africa
	Brewing	South African Breweries
	Electricity	Eskom
	Hotels/resorts	Protea Hotels
		Sun International
	Mineral exploration	JCI Limited
Tanzania	Airlines	South African Airways
	Banking	Standard Bank of South Africa
	Brewing	South African Breweries
	Hotels/resorts	Conservation Corporation Africa
		Protea Hotels
	Mineral exploration	Anglo-American Corporation
		Iscor
		JCI Limited
		Randgold
Zambia	Banking	Standard Bank of South Africa
	Brewing	South African Breweries
	Electricity	Eskom
	Hotels	Southern Sun
	Manufacturing/retailing	Pepkor
	Milling	Anglo-American Corporation
	Mineral exploration	Anglo-American Corporation
		Anglovaal
		Gencor Limited
		JCI Limited
		Phelps Dodge SA
	Mining (copper)	Anglo-American Corporation
		Avim
Zimbabwe	Banking	Standard Bank of South Africa
	Bank services	Sagacious Systems
	Cellular	Payphones Maxtel
	Electricity	Eskom
	Hotels/resorts	Protea Hotels

(Zimbabwe continued)	Hotels/resorts	Conservation Corporation Africa
	Industrial alcohol	Sentrachem Ltd.
	Manufacturing	Pepkor
	Mining	Amalia
		JCI Limited
	Mineral exploration	Anglo–American Corporation
		Trans Hex International
	Retail clothing	Pepko
	Supermarkets	Pick 'n Pay
	Textiles	Frame Group
	Water treatment/sewage	Aquazur Ltd.

Ahwireng-Obeng & McGowan (1998:22–24)

strated by historical, economic, international organisational and political analysis. The previous discussion of the historical development of Southern Africa and Boxes 14.2 to 14.8 demonstrate the interconnected history of the region. The analysis of the structure of the region in Tables 14.1 to 14.3 showed the basic features of Southern Africa and the economic, infrastructural and military strength of South Africa in comparison to the rest of the region.

In International Relations theory, being a system implies both regular **interactions** and **interconnectedness**. When interactions reach a critical level, they create interconnectedness among the system's members. Interactions may be on a relatively equal basis, as they are in the EU among its most important members (Britain, France, Germany and Italy), in which case we can say they are balanced or symmetrical. On the other hand, interactions may be relatively unequal, or asymmetrical, as in NAFTA (the North America Free Trade Agreement), which groups the very powerful US with the much less powerful Canada and Mexico.

Interconnectedness refers to the fact that members of an international system are **interdependent**, which means that they are affected by each other's actions. They therefore share what is called **mutual vulnerability**. When vulnerability is largely one-sided, as between Mexico and the US in NAFTA, we can speak of asymmetrical

interdependence, or **dependence**. Very importantly however, even though Mexico is dependent upon the US, the two countries share mutual vulnerability, which gives Mexico some bargaining strength *vis-à-vis* the US. In a similar fashion, while the countries of Southern Africa may be asymmetrically interdependent or dependent upon South Africa and the industrialised countries of the North, this does not mean that they are powerless to influence their 'exploiters' if they grasp the notion of mutual vulnerability.

Economic interactions

In a strong regional sub-system, a high proportion of trade in goods and services will be among the members and there will be much **foreign direct investment** (FDI) in each other's economies. Thus, in NAFTA, Canada is the US's number one trade partner in the world, and Mexico ranks third after Japan. For both Mexico and Canada, the US is their largest export market. Similarly, in the EU over 50% of Denmark's trade is with the other fourteen EU members. Levels of FDI within NAFTA and the EU are correspondingly high.

This is not presently true of SADC, but the situation is rapidly changing. In 1994 SADC's total trade (exports plus imports) amounted to some US$75 billion, but somewhat more than 80% was with non-SADC members outside Africa. As Table 14.4 shows, with the sole exception of Mauritius (which has undergone **economic structural transformation**), all SADC members still depend on *the very same* commodity exports to the industrialised countries of the North that were initiated during colonial times. SADC's economies are **competitive**; for example, both South Africa and Zimbabwe compete to sell chrome ore and chrome products to the rest of the world, as do the Congo and Zambia with copper. It makes no sense to sell each other chrome or copper.

But there is a growing economic **complementarity** between post-Apartheid, industrial South Africa and the rest of the region. South Africa increasingly sells manufactured products and services to SADC countries and imports from them raw materials, food products such as fish and shrimp, hydroelectricity and some labour. This trade is exploding. South Africa's exports to non-SACU, SADC countries grew by 53,2% in 1994 and by 31,5% in 1995. The problem is that this trade is very unequal. In 1995 (when the DRC and the Seychelles were not yet members of SADC), South Africa exported R26,2 billion worth of goods to the eleven other SADC members and imported only R4,7 billion from them – a ratio of 5,6 to 1 (Ahwireng-Obeng & McGowan, 1998:5). **Invisible trade** in banking, consulting, education, tourism and other services may account for another 20% or more, and it is even more in South Africa's favour. These trends have increased since 1995 and have caused numerous complaints and tensions from the SADC members who depend so heavily on South Africa (*see* McGowan & Ahwireng-Obeng, 1998, for details).

The pattern of trade and investment within the Southern African region is between South Africa on the one hand and the rest of SADC on the other hand. There is little trade and investment among the other members of SADC. As Table 14.4 shows, there is variation among SADC members in the degree to which they depend on trade with South Africa. Particularly dependent on South Africa are the four other members of SACU: Botswana, Lesotho, Namibia and Swaziland. South Africa is also a very important trading partner for Malawi, Mozambique, Zambia and, particularly, Zimbabwe, with South Africa being its largest trading 'partner'.

These patterns are reinforced by the fact that Johannesburg is a **global city** that is increasingly being used by the major multinational corporations (MNCs) and service companies as a base for their operations in the entire Southern African region. Gauteng Province's well-developed transportation and communications infrastructure (*see* Table 14.2) and the presence of other businesses there create **economies of scale** and **positive externalities** that are very attractive for corporations connected to the major multinationals located in the centres of the global political economy, such as London, New York and Tokyo.

FDI within the SADC region shows a similar pattern. South Africa increasingly makes investments in other SADC countries, but there is next to no SADC investment in other SADC countries or in South Africa. Table 14.5 reports new South African investments in other SADC countries for the period 1992–1997, and the total is worth billions of rands. For example, South African investments in Zambia in 1997 reached US$180 million, making it the largest foreign investor in the Zambian economy. It is clear that the South Africa economic presence in the rest of the region is very strong and growing rapidly.

This examination of economic interactions has shown that Southern Africa is a coherent regional sub-system within the global political economy, but one with a very different structure from all other such sub-systems. It is a sub-system with one economic pole, South Africa, around which the other thirteen states in the region interact with greater or lesser degrees of dependence. The political and business leaders of these states thus have a 'love-hate' attitude toward South Africa. They resent their dependence on South Africa's economy, but have no practical alternative to trade and investment with South Africa as long as they wish to develop their countries and businesses. This pattern of asymmetrical interdependence is reinforced by an examination of interactions within regional international organisations.

Organisational interactions

Within Southern Africa, there are three international organisations that promote patterns of economic and political interactions among their members and thereby create a high degree of regional interconnectedness. The first is the Common Monetary Area (CMA), whose members are Lesotho, Namibia, South Africa and Swaziland. The second is the Southern African Customs Union (SACU), which includes members of the CMA plus Botswana. The third, and largest, is the Southern African Development Community (SADC), which groups together the five members of SACU and nine other states to the north and in the Indian Ocean (see Map 9).

The CMA was created in 1974 after the independence of Lesotho and Swaziland and while Apartheid South Africa still controlled South West Africa (Namibia). The CMA places the national currencies of Lesotho, Namibia and Swaziland at a par with the rand, and both the rand and their own currencies circulate in their respective economies. Within the CMA, common currency exchange controls apply. There is also free movement of funds among member countries as well as access to South African capital markets (Leistner, 1995:271).

For the three smaller members of the CMA, it makes their currencies fully convertible into foreign currencies such as the US dollar or the British pound, which is an advantage in doing international trade and investment. The CMA also promotes trade with the much larger South African economy as members can use rands or their own currencies to settle accounts. The ability to raise funds in the large South African capital market is another decided advantage. The disadvantage is that their **monetary policies** – such as interest rates and the rate of growth of

their **money supply** – are basically determined by the South African Reserve Bank in Pretoria. Thus, a key element of the members' national sovereignty has been surrendered in order to tie their currencies to the rand.

SACU is the oldest and most effective instance of economic integration on the African continent. Founded in 1910 at the height of the colonial rule, the SACU Treaty was renegotiated in 1969 after Botswana, Lesotho and Swaziland had achieved independence. Its present membership also includes Namibia and South Africa. Zambia has expressed an interest in joining SACU. The present treaty creates a **customs union** among the five members, that is, a **common external tariff** toward all non-member countries and the duty-free movement of goods and services (but not persons) among the five members. Customs and excise duties collected on imports into SACU are pooled and by means of a complex formula are distributed among members, with the smaller states receiving disproportionately larger shares. SACU does not have a secretariat. Common tariff levels are set at the recommendation of South Africa's Board on Tariffs and Trade. Most duties are collected by the South African Department of Customs and Excise and the Trade and Industry Department in Pretoria acts as SACU 'co-ordinator' (Esterhuysen, 1996:61–62, 76).

Both the CMA and SACU are very important to their members, but for different reasons. For South Africa the BLNS (Botswana, Lesotho, Namibia, Swaziland) states represent captive markets; indeed, taken as a group, they are South Africa's single-largest export market (in 1995 the BLNS bought R16,5 billion worth of South African goods, whereas the UK bought only R8,6 billion). South Africa also runs a massive trade surplus with the BLNS states – R13,3 billion in 1995 (Ahwireng-Obeng &McGowan, 1998:3, 5). Also, SACU reinforces South Africa's structural power as was demonstrated by its ability to intervene successfully in the repeated bouts of political instability in Lesotho.

For the BLNS states SACU's common revenue

pool (CRP) provides an important share of total government revenue – in 1995 about 16% of Botswana's, 50% of Lesotho's, 30% of Namibia's and 50% of Swazi revenues. Also, the BLNS get more from the CRP than they contribute to it: in 1994/95 they contributed 16% to the CRP and received 31% of revenues. Finally, selected industries are located in the BLNS states because of their duty-free access to the South African market, for example, the Hyundai auto assembly plant in Botswana; Swazi sugar, sugar-based products and consumer-oriented assembly plants; the Namibian fishing industry; and many of Lesotho's thirty-one textile companies.

SADC originated in 1980 as the Southern African Development Co-ordination Conference (SADCC), the same year that Zimbabwe became independent. African nationalism had triumphed in Southern Africa and all countries in the region were now under majority rule, except for South Africa and South West Africa (Namibia), which was occupied by South Africa. As part of the '**frontline states**' strategy to confront Apartheid and assist in the liberation of the two remaining white-minority regimes in the region, SADCC sought to reduce its members' economic, transportation and political dependence on South Africa and to co-ordinate foreign aid and investment in the region.

SADCC failed in these goals and as the 1990s began the region was more dependent on South Africa than it had been in 1980. In 1988, an agreement was reached to end foreign military intervention in Angola and to grant independence to Namibia, which was achieved in March 1990 (*see* Box 14.2). Then, in February 1990, State President F. W. de Klerk unbanned the South African liberation movements and released from prison most political prisoners, such as Mr Nelson Mandela (*see* Box 14.5). Clearly, confronting Apartheid in Namibia and South Africa was no longer at the top of the region's political agenda. After Namibia joined SADCC, its leaders negotiated a new treaty and SADC came into being at an international conference in Windhoek, Namibia, on 17 August 1992. SADC's secretariat is located in Gaborone, Botswana.

There were ten founding members of SADC, and they have since been joined by South Africa (1994), Mauritius (1995), the Democratic Republic of the Congo and the Seychelles (1997) (*see* Table 14.1). SADC's formal and legally binding treaty contains much more ambitious objectives than did the SADCC agreement:

'a) achieve development and economic growth, alleviate poverty, enhance the standard and quality of life of the peoples of Southern Africa and support the socially disadvantaged through regional integration;

b) evolve common political values, systems and institutions;

c) promote and defend peace and security;

d) promote self-sustaining development on the basis of collective self-reliance, and the interdependence of Member States;

e) achieve complementarity between national and regional strategies and programmes;

f) promote and maximise productive employment and utilisation of resources of the Region;

g) achieve sustainable utilisation of natural resources and effective protection of the environment;

h) strengthen and consolidate the long standing historical, social and cultural affinities and links among the peoples of the Region' (SADC, 1995:6).

The treaty has common economic, environmental, political and peace and security goals for its members. This represents a big step forward in consolidating Southern Africa as an interconnected regional sub-system in international relations.

Of particular importance are SADC's goals of promoting regional economic integration, environmental sustainability and peace and security. Regarding integration, on 24 August 1996 the SADC heads-of-state signed a Trade Protocol, which aims 'to establish a **Free Trade Area** in the

SADC Region' (SADC, 1996:3). The protocol will come into effect once it is ratified by two-thirds of SADC's members. By the beginning of 1998, only three members had ratified the protocol – Botswana, Mauritius and Tanzania. The Free Trade Area (FTA) is intended to be similar to NAFTA and will be in full operation eight years after ratification. In the meantime, tariff and non-tariff barriers to trade are being gradually reduced. The Trade Protocol can be criticised on a number of grounds, such as its failure to address **supply-side measures** as in the link between trade and investment (Mayer & Thomas, 1997:346). Nevertheless, it sets an ambitious and important target that would make Southern Africa a unique region on the African continent.

Because of the size and importance of their economies, the protocol will not come to much until it is ratified by Zimbabwe and, in particular, South Africa. South Africa has not moved quickly to ratify the treaty, although there are strong theoretical reasons to believe that a FTA in Southern Africa will mainly benefit South Africa (*see* McGowan & Ahwireng-Obeng, 1998) because of its economic size and relatively advanced level of industrialisation and economic sophistication.

Besides minerals, Southern Africa's greatest comparative advantage in the global political economy is eco-tourism, which is vitally tied to environmental issues. Attracting tourists to the region from overseas requires preservation of the region's ecology of animals, plants, landscapes and peoples, as well as the provision of enhanced infrastructure and the maintenance of law and order, peace and security. On average around the world, every thirty tourists create one new job, so the employment and economic growth potential of the 'leisure industry' in the region is vast.

The work of SADC is divided up among its members with each having responsibility for co-ordinating SADC activities in a given sector of economic **functional co-operation**:
- Angola: Energy
- Botswana: Agricultural research; Livestock production; Animal disease control
- Lesotho: Environment and land management; Water
- Malawi: Inland fisheries, forestry and wildlife
- Mauritius: Tourism
- Mozambique: Culture and information; Transport and communications
- Namibia: Marine fisheries and resources
- South Africa: Finance and investment
- Swaziland: Human resource development
- Tanzania: Industry and trade
- Zambia: Mining; Employment and labour
- Zimbabwe: Food, agriculture and natural resource food security
(Chipeta *et al.*, 1997:38–39).

This illustrates why SADC has not yet matched its goals with concrete achievements. Mauritius, in the Indian Ocean, far away from the region's main tourist destinations – Cape Town, the Kruger Park, the Okavango Delta, the Serengeti Plains, Victoria Falls – has prime responsibility for promoting the region's tourist potential. Moreover, the sectorial responsibilities of Botswana (animal disease control), Lesotho (environment and water), Malawi (wildlife) and Mozambique (transportation and communications) all affect tourism. This creates great problems of co-ordination. Finally, most SADC members have very weak institutional capacities to co-ordinate co-operative efforts within such a large region. Hence, expert consultants have recently called for a major reorganisation of SADC's structure (Chipeta *et al.*, 1997), but little has been done so far to implement their recommendations.

Many SADC states also belong to competing organisations that divert attention from SADC's goal of greater economic co-operation. Ten SADC members belong to the Common Market for Eastern and Southern Africa (COMESA), which was originally founded in 1981. The coastal states of South Africa, Mozambique and Tanzania also belong to the newly created Indian Ocean Rim Association for Regional Co-operation (IOR-ARC). Both COMESA and IOR-ARC seek greater economic integration among their members. This presents problems of co-ordination and prioritisation for many SADC states, which may result in important issues not getting the attention they deserve.

Political interactions

Our discussion of the historical evolution of Southern Africa and the seven boxes (Boxes 14.2 to 14.8) describing the political histories of the major states of the region demonstrate that its peoples and **polities** have had extensive political interactions for more than 100 years. It was Cape Colony imperialism (through Rhodes) that created Zambia and Zimbabwe. There was much co-operation among African nationalists in the region who were struggling to achieve independence from Britain and Portugal (a number were educated at Fort Hare University in South Africa). Having achieved independence, states in the region formed the frontline states organisation to give assistance to liberation movements: Tanzania to FRELIMO; Zambia to ZAPU; Mozambique to ZANU and the ANC; Angola to the ANC and SWAPO; and almost all majority-ruled states to the ANC and the PAC after 1976. On the other hand, there was often close co-operation among white-minority Rhodesia, South Africa and colonial Portugal.

Thus, beginning in 1961 with the revolt in Angola until the present (*see* Box 14.2), wars were fought throughout the region. The basic cause was the intransigence of white-minority Rhodesia, Apartheid South Africa and the Portuguese colonialists to negotiate a peaceful transfer to majority-rule, as had been the case in Botswana, Lesotho, Malawi, Mauritius, Seychelles, Swaziland, Tanzania and Zambia. The wars were of two types:

1. **wars of national liberation**, in which the nationalists often received assistance from **communist bloc** countries such as East Germany and the Soviet Union, as in Angola, Mozambique, Namibia, South Africa and Zimbabwe, and in which Portugal and South

Africa received assistance from the US; and
2. sometimes related **civil wars** between different factions within and from outside given states: Angola from 1975 to 1997, the DRC on several occasions, including late 1998, and Mozambique between 1976 and 1992; all three involved neighbouring African states and Cold War participants from the East and West (*see* Boxes 14.2 to 14.4).

Particularly devastating for the region was the forward defence of Apartheid by the P. W. Botha regime in the 1980s in which South Africa launched repeated 'cross-border' attacks as far north as Lusaka in Zambia against ANC facilities and local civilians, and in which South Africa supported RENAMO in Mozambique and UNITA in Angola.

Except for Angola and the DRC, all these wars have ended and Southern Africa is more peaceful than at any time since 1961. In addition to the instability and conflict in the DRC and Angola, the major security problems confronting the region today are illegal immigration, particularly into South Africa, and organised crime syndicates involved with arms smuggling, drug trafficking and automobile theft and smuggling. These problems are not classical military security issues and fall into a grey area between criminal anarchy and organised violence (*see* Kaplan, 1994).

From a classical military security perspective, the major problems facing the SADC states today are to preserve and consolidate the peace that presently exists, to ensure that the peace accord in Angola is implemented, and to end military interventions in the Congo. SADC's Organ for Politics, Defence and Security has that responsibility. Created in July 1994 in Windhoek, Namibia, the Organ has been chaired by President Robert Mugabe of Zimbabwe since its inception. Unfortunately, as of 1998, the Organ exists 'merely on paper as an ill-defined and rather unwanted appendage to the Southern African Development Community' (Malan, 1998:17).

The basic problem is a dispute between South

Africa and Zimbabwe over the relationship between the Organ and the SADC Summit of Heads of State and Government. President Mandela currently (1998) chairs the Summit and has taken the position that the Organ should not be independent, but subordinate to the Summit. President Mugabe rejects this view and wants to keep the Organ separate and flexible in the tradition of the now defunct frontline states. This dispute led to an acrimonious SADC Summit in August 1997 in Blantyre, Malawi, that failed to resolve the matter (Malan, 1998:15–16; McGowan & Ahwireng-Obeng, 1998). Thus, SADC does not have a well-organised and functioning peace and security organ, which is dangerous for the region given its history of instability and warfare.

There are also tensions within both SACU and SADC arising from South Africa's hegemonic role in the region. In August 1994, the new South Africa called for renegotiations of the 1969 SACU Treaty because of its origins in the Apartheid era. By August 1998, the negotiations were still deadlocked, primarily because South Africa, on the one hand, and the BLNS states on the other could not reach agreement on such matters as CRP shares, protection against unfair South African trading practices, and whether or not SACU should have a permanent Secretariat like the SADC. Given that the BLNS states represent South Africa's largest export market and that there are such huge power differences between South Africa and the BLNS states, South Africa's tough negotiation stance reflects its desire to protect what its leaders perceive to be its legitimate interests.

South Africa's export and investment drive into the rest of Southern Africa has created serious tensions in the region because of its one-sided nature. In the words of President Mugabe of Zimbabwe: 'South Africa cherishes the notion that because it is the most developed country in the region it can use other SADC countries as receptacles for its goods while protecting its own industries' (McGowan & Ahwireng-Obeng, 1998). This sentiment is widespread among political and business leaders in the Southern African region. South African must act as a more equal partner if it wishes to avoid serious, economic-based political disputes.

As of 1998, political interactions in the Southern African region are much improved because the region is now free of the scourges of European colonialism and Apartheid. This is not to say that the region is free from political tensions and potential conflicts, as the border dispute between Botswana and Namibia along the Chobe River illustrates. Hence, an effective SADC-related regional Organ for Peace and Security needs to be created as a priority.

Conclusion

There can be no doubt that a regional political-economic sub-system exists in Southern Africa, and this makes the region unique in comparison to the rest of the continent where similar sub-systems do not exist. This regional sub-system is similar to MERCOSUR in South America and ASEAN in Southeast Asia. Properly organised and led, SADC has the potential to promote the economic and human development of the region and its peoples and to enhance regional peace and security. Unfortunately, SADC is not even coming close to its potential in these areas.

What is really happening is that, with the end of Apartheid, old patterns are re-emerging in which South Africa dominates the region infrastructurally, economically, militarily and politically. The Apartheid period, 1948–1994, resulted, to a great degree, in isolating South Africa from the region and the world. This has ended, and South Africa's hegemony grows almost daily. While there appears to be no practical alternative to this, it has already created tensions in the region. South African hegemony and the possible marginalisation of the region in the global system (*see* Chapter 9) are the two major issues confronting Southern Africa today. Neither problem has simple, easy-to-agree-to, solutions.

Key concepts in this chapter

Customs union
Free trade area
Hegemony
Interconnectedness
Mutual vulnerability (interdependence)
Periphery
Regional sub-system
Semi-periphery

Suggested readings

- Esterhuysen, P. (1998) *Africa at a Glance: 1997/8*. Pretoria: Africa Institute of South Africa. A useful compilation of relevant international relations data on all countries of Africa. Includes many easily readable graphs and charts.

- Ahwireng-Obeng, F., & McGowan, P. J. (1998) 'Partner or hegemon? South Africa in Africa', *Journal of Contemporary African Studies*, (Part 1) 16(1):5–38; (Part 2) 16(2):165–196. This recent two-part article describes and explains South Africa's increasingly hegemonic role in South Africa since the fall of Apartheid in 1994. It contains much relevant data and statistics and demonstrates the existence of a distinct Southern African sub-system, centred on South Africa, within the global political economy.

- Ramsay, F. J. (ed.) (1997) *Global Studies: Africa*. Guilford, CN: Dushkin/McGraw-Hill. An overview of the African continent, its problems and prospects. Includes profiles of every SSA country and a collection of timely articles on specific African topics. An excellent reference book for undergraduate International Relations students.

- Bowman, L. (1968) 'The subordinate state system of Southern Africa', *International Studies Quarterly*, 12:231–261; and Grundy, K. (1973) *Confrontation and Accommodation in Southern Africa: The Limits of Interdependence*. Berkeley: University of California Press. These two studies provide today's readers with a historical perspective on the Southern African regional sub-system.

- Swatuk, L. A. & Black, D. R. (eds) (1997) *Bridging the Rift: The New South Africa in Africa*. Boulder: Westview Press. A recent volume that examines the Southern African region from a variety of perspectives that are relevant to the International Relations student, with special emphasis on South Africa's role in the region.

15 | Dimensions of sustainable development in Southern Africa

Fred Ahwireng-Obeng

This chapter in outline
- Introduction
- The meaning of development
- The development problem in Southern Africa
  - The development problem in general
  - South Africa's share of the development problem
- Sustainable development in Southern Africa: challenges and possibilities
  - Challenges
  - Possibilities

Introduction

The challenges to sub-Saharan Africa's (SSA's) economic development are not likely to diminish as long as external and internal forces continue to cause marginalisation of the continent. External forces are a result of the new world order and the insistence of donors on human rights and political democracy; internal forces are caused mainly by the economic crises in many countries. To the extent that marginalisation and the lack of **sustainable development** reinforce one another, we can think of four levels of the phenomena – continental, regional, national and sub-national.

At the continental level, sub-Saharan Africa (SSA) is failing to respond to large-scale structural adjustment programmes (SAPs). It is in need of a significant 're-awakening' to counter the steady decline of global interest and concern about its well-being. Most regions of Africa are facing marginalisation, and attempts to counter the trend by promoting regional integration have invariably failed. At the national level, many small countries, including those in Southern Africa, are particularly disposed to marginalisation. The emergence of a democratic South Africa poses the problem of another kind of marginalisation for some countries in the region – a reduction of their economic sovereignty and political standing. Finally, within individual countries, poor rural communities, especially women and the youth, are prone to increasing marginalisation, as governments are obliged to reduce **budget deficits** and tighten **monetary policy**.

Given these developments and the difficulties and opportunities they cause, this chapter explores four issues: the concept of and debate about development; how development is measured; the development problems of the region; challenges and possible alternative solutions.

The meaning of development

Our task in this section is to provide essential elements of the term **development** as it means different things to different people. This will then become a working definition that will enable us to appreciate the problems and challenges facing the Southern African region and determine alternative solutions.

Prior to the 1970s, development was understood, largely, as an economic phenomenon in which rapid increases in **gross national product (GNP)** would translate into economic opportunities such as jobs, or create the conditions for the equitable distribution of the economic and social benefits of economic growth. Thus, economic development was taken to mean economic growth, measured by an increase in the GNP. The growth process itself comes about as a result of either or both of two changes. One is an expansion of or additions to the use of current economic resources, such as land (by finding new sources of raw materials or using materials that were not in use before), labour (by increasing the size of the labour force either through population growth or by changing working patterns), or capital (by increasing the stock of **physical or human capital** or both).

The other change that can cause economic growth to occur is an increase in **productivity**, that is, operating more efficiently with the resources that producers use. Productivity increases may also occur by increasing the degree of specialisation or through technological advancement. Growth, as explained above, should be clearly differentiated from **business cycles**, which means the recurring ups and downs in the economy that take place over time.

When a nation's population growth rate is taken into account, another economic index of development emerges. This is the growth rate of **income (output) per capita** or **per capita GNP**. A positive per capita growth rate means that the nation is expanding its output at a rate faster than the growth rate of its population. Normally, the levels and rates of growth of 'real' per capita GNP (monetary growth of GNP per capita minus the rate of **inflation** or increase in general level of prices) are used as measures of the overall well-being of a population. In other words, they are a measure of how much of real goods and services are available to the average citizen for **consumption** and **investment** (Todaro, 1994:14).

As an economy continues to grow, alterations in its occupational structure, that is, changes in the structure of production and employment, occur, so that agriculture's share of both declines while that of manufacturing and service industries increases. There are two reasons for this. First, the share of income spent on food rises as income rises, so that resources shift away from agriculture to the other sectors. Second, productivity grows faster in manufacturing and service industries than in agriculture, thus increasing the shares of the latter in the national output at the expense of agriculture. Either way, this phenomenon accompanies economic growth and is called **structural transformation**. Therefore, the size of agriculture's contribution to national output is taken as an index of the level of development. Characteristically, for economies with agricultural resources, a relatively large agricultural sector is an indication of a low level of development.

These economic measures of development have usually been supplemented by non-economic **social indicators** such as, *inter alia,* gains in literacy, schooling, health conditions, services and housing. The **human development index** (HDI) (referred to in Chapter 14) is an attempt to compress economic and non-economic measures of development into a composite index.

During the 1950s and 1960s, many countries experienced rapid economic growth without the expected improvements in the well-being of their populations. **Absolute poverty** was widespread and there was an increasing unequal distribution of income, usually accompanied by rising unemployment and worsening social indicators. This experience led to a redefinition of development as a *'multi-dimensional process involving major changes in social structures, popular attitudes and national institutions,* as well as the acceleration of economic growth (and employment), the reduction of inequality and the eradication of poverty' (World Bank, 1991:4 – *see* Box 15.1).

There are three basic values that relate to fundamental human needs, which provide a practical guide to a deeper understanding of development, as sought universally by individuals and societies. These are sustenance, self-esteem and freedom. *Sustenance* refers to life-sustaining basic human needs, including food, shelter, health and protection, the critical shortage of which leads to a condition of **absolute underdevelopment**. By *self-esteem* is meant a sense of worth and self-respect, of not being used as a tool by others for their own needs. This component of development is variously termed as respect, dignity, honour, identity and recognition in different societies, cultures and population groups. What is essential is that it is dispensed on grounds other than material achievement. *Freedom,* or human freedom to be precise, is taken to mean an emancipation from alienating material conditions of life and from social slavery, caused by nature, ignorance, other people, misery, institutions and dogmatic beliefs. Freedom in this sense involves an expanded range of choices for societies and their members. The concept also embraces such aspects of political freedom as personal security, the rule of law, freedom of expression, political participation and equality of opportunity (Todaro, 1994:17–18).

Thus, development is both a normative concept and a reality of life. It is a process that all societies experience as the way of obtaining a 'better life'. Whatever this better life means is subjective to an extent. But the process itself must be driven by three central objectives: increase the availability and widen the distribution of basic life-sustaining goods; raise the standard of living to include not only higher incomes but also more jobs, better education, and greater attention to cultural and humanistic values; and expand the scope of economic and social choices. Most important is the concept of sustainable development, that is, patterns of development that permit future generations to live at least as well as current generations. An overview of the concept is given in Box 15.1.

Box 15.1: Concepts and measurements of poverty and human development

Absolute and relative poverty

Absolute poverty refers to poverty measured against a standard of minimum requirement, while relative poverty refers to poverty measured against the well-being of others in the same community. With respect to income, a person is absolutely poor if her income is less than the defined income poverty line, while she is relatively poor if she belongs to a bottom income group (such as the poorest 10%) of a population.

Functions and capability

The functions of a person refer to the valuable things the person can do or be (such as being well nourished, living a long life and taking part in the life of a community). The capability of a person stands for the different combinations of functions the person can achieve; it reflects the freedom to achieve functions.

Ultra–poverty

Ultra-poverty is said to occur when a household cannot meet 80% of the FAO-WHO minimum calorie requirements, even when using 80% of its income to buy food.

Incidence of poverty

The incidence of poverty, expressed as a headcount ratio, is simply an estimate of the percentage of people living below the poverty line. It does not indicate anything about the depth or severity of poverty and thus does not reflect the conditions of those already in poverty.

Depth of poverty

The depth of poverty can be measured as the average distance below the poverty line, expressed as a proportion of that line. This average is calculated over the entire population, poor and non-poor. Because this measure shows the average distance of the poor from the poverty line, it is able to show a worsening or improvement of their conditions.

Severity of poverty

The severity of poverty can be measured as a weighted average of the squared distance below the poverty line, expressed as a proportion of that line. The weights are given by each individual gap. Again, the average is formed over the entire population. Since the weights increase with poverty, this measure is sensitive to inequality among the poor.

Transient and chronic poverty

Transient poverty refers to short-term, temporary or seasonal poverty, and chronic poverty to long-term or structural poverty.

Vulnerability

Vulnerability has two faces: external exposure to shocks, stress and risk; and internal defencelessness, that is, a lack of means to cope without suffering damaging loss.

Poverty lines and ways of measuring poverty

1. **Poverty lines for international comparison.** A poverty line set at $1 (1985 PPP$) a day per person is used by the World Bank for international comparison. This poverty line is based on consumption. A poverty line of $2 (PPP$) a day is suggested for Latin America and the Caribbean. For Eastern Europe and the CIS countries, a poverty line of $4 (1990 PPP$) has been used. For comparison among industrial countries, a poverty line corresponding to the US poverty line of $14,40 (1985 PPP$) a day per person has been used.

2. **National poverty lines.** Developing countries that have set national poverty lines have generally used the food poverty method. These lines indicate the insufficiency of economic resources to meet basic minimum needs in food. There are three approaches to measuring food poverty:

   • **Cost-of-basic-needs method.** This approach sets the poverty line at the cost of a basic diet for the main age, gender and activity groups, plus a few essential non-food items. A survey then establishes the proportion of people living in a household with consumption (or sometimes income) below this line. The basic diet may consist of the least expensive foods needed to meet basic nutritional requirements, which is the typical adult diet in the lowest consumption quintile or the investigator's notion of a minimal but decent diet. The choice of both the food and the non-food components included is necessarily arbitrary.

- **Food energy method.** This method focuses on the consumption expenditure at which a person's typical food energy intake is just sufficient to meet a predetermined food energy requirement. Dietary energy intake, as the dependent variable, is regressed against household consumption per adult equivalent. The poverty line is then set at the level of total consumption per person at which the statistical expectation of dietary energy intake exactly meets average dietary energy requirements. The problem with this method is the caviar caveat: groups that choose a costly bundle of foods are rewarded with a higher poverty line than that for eaters that are more frugal.
- **Food share method**. This method derives the cost of a consumption plan to acquire just sufficient nutrients. If the cost of basic nutrients is a third of total consumption, the poverty line is fixed at three times that cost.

All three approaches are sensitive to the price level used to determine the cost of the bundle, and all three concentrate mainly on calories or dietary energy, because protein deficiency due to inadequate economic resources is perceived to be rare in most societies.

In industrial countries, national poverty lines are also used to measure relative poverty. The European Commission has suggested a poverty line for these countries of half the median adjusted disposable personal income.

The concept of human development

The process of widening people's choices and the level of well-being they achieve are at the core of the notion of human development. Such choices are neither finite nor static. But regardless of the level of development, the three essential choices for people are to lead a long and healthy life, to acquire knowledge and to have access to the resources needed for a decent standard of living. Human development does not end there, however. Other choices, highly valued by many people, range from political, economic and social freedom to opportunities for being creative and productive and enjoying self-respect and guaranteed human rights.

Income clearly is only one option that people would like to have; though, it is an important one. But it is not the sum total of their lives. Income is also a means, with human development the end.

Human development index (HDI)

The HDI measures the average achievements in a country in three basic dimensions of human development – longevity, knowledge and a decent standard of living. It is a composite index that contains three variables: life expectancy, educational attainment (adult literacy and combined primary, secondary and tertiary enrolment) and real GDP per capita (in PPP$).

Human poverty index (HPI)

The HPI measures deprivation in basic human development in the same dimensions as the HDI. The variables used are the percentage of people expected to die before the age of forty, the percentage of adults who are illiterate, and overall economic provisioning in terms of the percentage of people without access to health services and safe water and the percentage of under-weight children under the age of five years.

Gender–related development index (GDI)

The GDI measures achievements in the same dimensions and variables as the HDI does, but takes account of inequality in achievement between women and men. The greater the gender disparity in basic human development, the lower a country's GDI compared with its HDI. The GDI is simply the HDI discounted, or adjusted downwards, for gender inequality.

Gender empowerment measure

The gender empowerment measure indicates whether women are able to actively participate in economic and political life. It focuses on participation, and measures gender inequality in the key areas of economic and political participation and decision-making. It thus differs from the GDI, which is an indicator of gender inequality in basic capabilities.

United Nations Development Programme (1997: 13–14)

The development problem in Southern Africa

The development problem in general

Like the rest of Africa, most of Southern Africa is facing a serious economic crisis, which has resulted in a lack of development. As a result, people have become hopeless and increasingly disinterested in making efforts to work towards development. This vicious circle has reinforced underdevelopment in the subregion.

The economic crisis is partly the outcome of colonialism, as well as civil wars, such as those that broke out in Angola and Mozambique, and the destabilisation of neighbouring states by the former Apartheid regime. It is also attributed to the failure of some MNCs to demonstrate corporate social responsibility in the region. The overwhelming evidence, however, is that it is predominantly the result of poor development policies and their careless implementation in the majority of countries in the region (Hope & Kayira, 1996:881–894).

In most of post-independent Southern Africa, the state intervened directly in the development process. For most African leaders, the period immediately after independence in the 1960s was an opportunity to exercise greater authority and power over their populaces and territories. Development policy was formulated by the state and the role of markets was undermined. Policy was implemented by leaders' political and personal agents, who used the state's financial and other resources to reward themselves. This was the beginning of the deterioration of the quality of African leadership, which was the main catalyst for the deepening crisis that provoked the structural adjustment programme (SAP) policy reforms in the region.

In almost all the fourteen Southern African

Table 15.1:   Southern African countries – some poverty indicators

Country	% population in poverty (1984–1995)	Life expectancy at birth in years (1995)	Gini Coefficients (1991–1995)
Angola	–	47	–
Botswana	43	68	–
Democratic Republic of Congo	–	–	–
Lesotho	55,6	61	0,56
Malawi	82	43	–
Mauritius	11	71	–
Mozambique	–	47	–
Namibia	–	59	–
Seychelles	–	72	–
South Africa	45,7	64	0,58
Swaziland	50,2	58	–
Tanzania	57,6	51	0,38
Zambia	64,3	46	0,46
Zimbabwe	25,5	57	0,56

Esterhuysen (1998); United Nations Development Programme (1997); United Nations, *Africa Recovery* (several issues) countries that have been forced to implement SAPs, generally the impact has been disastrous. They have resulted in mass unemployment, declining **real incomes**, rising inflation, increased imports with recurrent **trade deficits**, net **capital outflow**, mounting **external debts**, neglect of basic needs, cruel hardships and growing inequality. Poorer countries are particularly hard hit and often threatened with social and political discord and economic collapse.

The hardest hit fall into the following categories:

- victims of droughts or ecological degradation whose incomes are depleted;
- the poor – usually rural, female-headed households pushed by land deficit on to more marginal lands;
- peripheral or isolated households;
- small producers;
- victims of war – loss of access to health, education and water;
- members of the urban informal sector facing more competition from retrenched public servants;
- urban wage earners whose real wages have fallen due to sharp price increases (Green, 1991:36–37).

The impact of adjustment is particularly severe on women as it causes an imbalance in the household economy. The process affects households through:

- a decline in income through decreases in money wages and levels of employment for employees and through declines in profit margins (due to a disproportionate increase in production costs) and product demand for the self-employed;
- increasing food prices;
- a fall in levels and changes in the composition of public expenditure that lead to increases in the cost of using public utilities; and
- changes in working conditions, through changes in number of working hours, intensity of work, job security, fringe benefits and legal status.

Finally, with regard to environmental issues, Southern Africa has persistently suffered drought, advancing desertification, deforestation, soil erosion, pollution and the increasing threat of the dumping of toxic waste from the North. This has worsened the lack of sustainability in the development of the region.

The negative human impact of the crisis is indicated by the poor HDI – *see* Table 14.1 in Chapter 14 – but more directly by the high rate of poverty, low life expectancy at birth, and high **Gini Coefficient** (*see* Table 15.1).

The available data on the rate of poverty shows that it is only in Botswana, Mauritius and Zimbabwe that the proportion of the population below the absolute poverty line is less than 50%. Thus, poverty is a major challenge facing the Southern African region, and it is worsened by high rates of population growth.

According to Table 14.1, the fourteen states in the Southern African Development Community (SADC) have an estimated population of about 187 million people, and South Africa, Tanzania and the Democratic Republic of Congo (DRC) have the largest populations. Botswana, Mauritius, Namibia and Swaziland have populations of under 2 million. Persistently high **fertility**, mainly due to early child bearing, and a rapid decline in **mortality** since the 1960s due to relatively improved health have resulted in a fast-growing population (above 2% per annum) despite new challenges posed by HIV/AIDS. Consequently, countries of the region have a young age structure, the average being sixteen years. The **dependency ratio**, or the number of dependants supported by one worker, is, therefore, very high.

Another important factor is population distribution. Immigration into the region is not a major contributor to the rapid population growth rate. However, armed conflicts, drought and the quest for formal sector employment have increased rural-urban migration to about 10% per annum (70–80% of the population lives in rural areas). Also, the manufacturing sectors of these economies have steadily lost their ability to absorb labour. As a result, rapid urbanisation is accompanied by increasing rates of urban unemployment and increased pressure on national resources for the provision of social services, health, housing and so on. Apart from Botswana, where there is an oversupply of housing, poor housing has created an environmentally hazardous situation as a result of overcrowding and the spread of squatter settlements. This situation contributes to material poverty and is often quoted as a source of social conflict.

Contributing further to poverty is the poor performance of Southern African economies. While only Botswana, Mauritius, Mozambique, Namibia and Seychelles recorded positive growth rates in the GNP per capita in the period 1986–1996; the rest of the region recorded negative growth rates. Declining growth rates (and hence increased poverty) are associated with income inequality, which can be measured by the Gini Coefficient. The available estimates of the Gini Coefficient for Lesotho, Tanzania, Zambia and Zimbabwe for the period 1991–1995 are high, ranging from 0,46% for Zambia to 0,56% for Zimbabwe. The 0,58% for South Africa is a particularly high indicator of inequality (*see* Table 15.1: A Gini coefficient count of 1,0 is an indicator of complete inequality; a count of 0,0 is an indicator of complete equality in a population).

The failure of Southern African economies to grow at a pace that would provide for increased employment in the formal sector and reduced national poverty rates has led to a significant expansion of the informal economy. The sector has become a major absorber of female labour in the region and provides the opportunity for demonstrating entrepreneurial ability. It absorbs 80% of urban workers in Zambia and accounts for 51% in Tanzania. In South Africa, the sector provides between 20 and 30% of employment among the economically active population. As we would expect, all governments in the region have, in varying ways, given prominence to the role of the informal sector in their respective economies.

In addition to providing employment and contributing to the national product, the informal sector is a significant source of credit in the rural sector of Southern Africa, where the absence or ineffectiveness of institutional lending and the limited access to formal credit are deeply felt. Outside the rural sector, the informal sector offers a wide range of financial services to small-scale savers and entrepreneurs. The most common of informal sector finance is the rotating savings and credit associations – ROSCAS.

South Africa's share of the development problem

South Africa, as a leading economy in the region, has its fair share of the development problem. South Africa's importance in world trade was much less by the beginning of the 1990s than at the end of the 1970s. Between 1965 and 1985 it shed most of its share of world trade to the **newly industrialising economies** (NIEs) because of rapid increases in the costs of Apartheid structures and security and changes in the global economy. The National Party (NP) state was forced to 'liberalise' by diplomatic, demographic and strategic pressures, and to 'privatise' in response to pressures from external creditors and economic trends, in particular declining trade, profit and investment (Shaw, 1997:253–267). These developments ultimately 'trickled down' to worsen the already poor HDI performances.

The forced reforms steadily undermined the 'state capitalist' system, created by the NP after 1948, well in advance of the current stage of crisis, which may be dated from 1985, when intense and widespread rebellions induced a combination of further reforms and repression.

South Africa's non-African exports have historically been primary products, with agricultural commodities, raw and semi-processed minerals, gold and diamonds being the most important. However, technological and policy changes in the world economy have led to more gold mines and an increase in the production of gold coins elsewhere in the world. At the same time, the production cost of gold mining in South Africa has kept rising. Prospects for the prices of other South African mineral exports – chrome, nickel, zinc, copper and uranium prices – are dim as the country continues to lose market shares in most of these minerals.

Responses to the political and economic crisis by the state, the people and the private sector have been variable. The Apartheid state's response was to restructure state capitalism into a form of 'corporatism', that is, a coalition of private capital, Afrikaner nationalist state capital and international capital. The new black majority government has, since 1994, pursued a policy of infusing black capital, through various forms of black economic empowerment deals, into this South African corporatist structure. This trend is compatible with the **neo-liberal** policies of the **Growth, Employment and Redistribution** (GEAR) strategy and the affirmative stance of the **Reconstruction and Development Programme** (RDP).

Popular response to the shrinking state and formal sectors due to the adjustment has been the expansion of the informal sector, as is the case in other Southern African countries. In South Africa, such informal structures as shebeens and illegal and criminal activities have accompanied continued under-employment and unemployment.

On the other hand, the 'economic' response of the formal private sector to the two-edged pressures of economic crisis and sanctions during the Apartheid era was to diversify sectors, locales and partners. As multinational corporations (MNCs) withdrew from South Africa in response to the sanctions campaign, large South African companies such as Anglo-American and Rembrandt diversified out of mining by buying their **shares**. This trend is in line with the current government's policy of deconcentration, competition and beneficiation or value addition, and reflects some of the government's responses to globalisation. Franchising, licensing, outsourcing to concentrate on core business and decentralisation of management are other dimensions of the

trend. In addition, the steady penetration of South African exports – visible and invisible – as well as capital, into Africa may represent the extension of the diversification that began in the 1980s.

This combination of high-cost Apartheid, structural responses of the state, the private sector and the populace to both internal and external forces and the new economic order of the 1990s have conspired to undermine the fabric of the South African economy. All this has marginalised the majority of the disadvantaged black population. Indeed, the economy, despite popular belief, is structurally weak and vulnerable with respect to sectors, partners, debt, foreign capital, technology and demand. Since South Africa is the dominant economy in the Southern African region, the historical contradiction of conflict and co-operation in the region can be directly traced to the history of the South African political economy.

Sustainable development in Southern Africa: challenges and possibilities

Challenges

South Africa has joined at least two major Southern African regional organisations since 1994 and appears to be working hard at developing a programme of promoting sectoral co-operation and restructuring trade relations with its neighbours. A number of protocols have been signed, including an understanding to establish a Southern African Power Pool and an agreement on shared watercourses. Discussions with Mozambique to develop road, rail, port and tourism facilities in the Maputo Corridor are progressing. The adoption of a trade and development protocol in 1996, which calls for the adoption of a **free trade area** within eight years, marks the beginning of the process of trade integration in the region. These are positive developments, but expectations of what South Africa can bring to a new partnership must be matched against South Africa's poor economic performance and rather low HDI in relation to other countries in the region. In this sense, Southern Africa faces many challenges (Davies, 1998:40–50).

The region will have to design a comprehensive framework for regional co-operation and integration that takes full account of the development problems we have discussed in this chapter. It has to define its shared efforts, how these efforts fit in with and complement those at the African continental level, and how the Southern African region should position itself as a regional sub-system in a global context. In particular, the region will have to work out a

Box 15.2: Forms of regional economic integration

Four forms of integration can be distinguished:
1. free trade areas that eliminate trade barriers between their members;
2. customs unions, in which member states enjoy duty-free access to each other's markets and adopt a common external tariff;
3. common markets, which extend the customs union by freeing the movement of capital and labour between members; and
4. economic unions, which aim to co-ordinate members' economic policies.

The Organisation of African Unity's (OAU's) Lagos Plan of Action (1980) envisaged dividing Africa into four common markets, which would merge in the year 2000. Under the plan each subregion was to pass through the three stages of free trade area, customs union and, finally, economic union. Obviously, not much of this plan has materialised.

shared vision of what integration is intended to achieve, how to manage conflicts and prevent disintegration, co-ordinate the economic, political, social and cultural dimensions of development, and how to inter-relate macroeconomic policy, finance, trade and investments, production activities and the goods, services and factor markets. These are conceptual, strategic and practical issues that must be placed at the top of the regional agenda if equitable, mutually beneficial, growth-oriented and sustainable development is to be realised in the Southern African region.

In pursuing these tasks the region will have to recognise that it is characterised by many of the factors that have contributed to the failure of regional co-operation efforts in Africa: a lack of diversity in tradable goods; a low level of intragroup trade and high level of extra-group trade; insufficient means of payment; and political immaturity.

Possibilities

The history of Southern Africa over the last hundred years has created a region in which transport, monetary and financial matters, migrant labour, regional trade and other activities are very uneven. As a result, national problems and policies often spill over into neighbouring countries. For instance, when SAPs were applied in an unco-ordinated manner in countries within the region – resulting in reduced production, deindustrialisation, unemployment, and political and social disorder – South Africa took the initial brunt of the impact through the influx of millions of illegal migrants. This is a major problem for the new South African government as it poses the risk of political and social instability. For all governments in the region, these issues challenge the prospects of a regional approach to sustainable development.

On the other hand, the similarity of macroeconomic policy in all the countries due to SAPs may make co-operation easier to achieve. There are other common features that could make co-operation easier: all countries in the region except Swaziland, now have a multiparty political system; relative peace is now restored in both Mozambique and KwaZulu-Natal in South Africa; the four members of the Southern African Customs Union (SACU) are strongly integrated in the South African economy; and South Africa, which has economic and resource dominance in the region, has become more strongly integrated with the rest of the region through water, energy, transport and communication.

The crucial issue then is whether these apparent advantages can be transformed into reality. In other words, what possible mechanisms can be employed, including **regional integration**, to achieve sustainable development in Southern Africa? In examining this issue, it is fair to argue that any practical method will depend on two related factors: current trends in the world economy and political will among the states of the region (Van Aardt, 1997:252–265).

An important aspect of the first factor is globalisation of capitalism, finance, manufacturing and services. The general acceptance and dominance of capitalism in the world political economy cannot be disputed. The Southern African region, which is made up of predominantly developing countries, undoubtedly conforms to this trend. South Africa's GEAR strategy amply reflects this. Thus, the dictates of the global market will significantly influence the form and implementation of regional development in Southern Africa.

The globalisation of manufacturing is particularly likely to impact on Southern Africa in two ways. First, technological developments have increased the substitution of raw materials with synthetic inputs thereby reducing the demand for and the prices of primary commodities, which are the principal exports of countries in the region. On the other hand, the cost of manufactured goods, the major imports in the region, has increased. This has had the effect of not only marginalising the region, but also limiting its ability to earn foreign exchange for developmental activities.

The second global trend – **regionalisation** – has become accepted as a means of maximising regional economic opportunities, increasing political influence in the global system and realising socio-economic objectives. Various factors, however, mitigate these expected benefits of regionalisation. First, the Southern African market lacks effective **purchasing power** because of widespread poverty. Second, although South Africa is an economic giant in the region, the enormous demands on its government to provide jobs and to meet the huge socio-economic backlogs might discourage closer integration efforts. Most important, there is no guarantee from the failed experience of SSA that regionalisation is the surest route to economic progress.

Indeed, there are various views and approaches to development, but since current global trends limit these options to the **neo-classical model** as prescribed in the SAPs, and since SAPs have failed to translate into the objectives of development, there is little prospect that these prescriptions will stimulate sustainable development in Southern Africa.

Finally, despite bilateral agreements and the recently signed free trade agreement, Southern African states are yet to demonstrate a political will or the commitment to create, implement and maintain a regional development mission.

We have mentioned earlier that short-term domestic pressures may prove too strong for the new South African government to ignore. Hence, what is clear is that for South Africa, the national interest will probably be given priority over regional issues, that is, a 'South Africa first' approach to economic growth and development will be adopted.

There are genuine fears among policy-makers and producers in the region about the 'benefits of regional co-operation'. South African labour is concerned about the loss of jobs in those areas where other SADC countries hold a **comparative advantage** – Kenya in wood, furniture and paper products and Zimbabwe in textiles, leather and footwear. These fears, coupled with the rise of nationalism among black South Africans following their new-found freedom, are serious but less tangible obstacles to regionalisation.

Environmental issues may, however, hold good prospects as focal points for co-operation. Increasingly, the mutual desire to exploit natural resources, particularly water, for direct domestic and commercial use as well as a source of hydro-electric power has brought Southern African states together. It is estimated that South Africa will run out of water between 2020 and 2030 unless steps are taken to address the problem. Similarly, most other states in the region have historically suffered water shortages in varying degrees. Worse still, environmental problems have been exacerbated by unsustainable resource use, such as overgrazing around boreholes, small-scale gold panning, uncontrolled exploitation of mangrove forests and over-exploitation of fish stocks, as well as siltation and pollution of the region's dams, lakes, rivers and wetlands. Thus, both the need for 'water security' and improved use of natural resources are likely to strengthen the urge for co-operation (Shaw, 1997).

The desire for hydroelectric power for industrial development is very strong and is, therefore, another source of engagement of people and institutions in the region. Invariably, civil society, business and government in the various states will have to search for common ground on which to co-operate for the sake of sustainable development practices.

Key concepts in this chapter

Common market
Economic integration
Free trade area
Human development
Marginalisation
Poverty
Regionalisation
Sustainable development

Suggested readings

- Adedeji, A. (ed.) (1993) *Africa within the World: Beyond Dispossession and Dependence*. London: Zed Books (in association with African Centre for Development and Strategic Studies, ACDESS). This book gives an account of the Africanist view of Africa's increasing marginalisation and explores strategies to reverse it.
- Onimode, B. (1992) *A Future for Africa*. London: Earthscan Publications Ltd. (in association with the Institute for African Alternatives, IFAA). The President for IFAA, Professor Bade Onimode, makes a strong case for relaunching Africa's development in the 1990s.

The following three publications focus on the new South Africa's role in Africa in the 1990s:

- Adedeji, A. (1996) *South Africa in Africa: With or Apart?* London: Zed Books.
- Swatuk, L. R. & Black, D. R. (eds.) (1997) *Bridging the Rift: The New South Africa in Africa*. Boulder: Westview Press.
- Handley, A. & Mills, G. (eds.) (1988) *South Africa and Southern Africa: Regional Integration and Emerging Markets*. Johannesburg: South African Institute of International Affairs.

A very good account of Africa's failure at regional co-operation is given in;

- Aly, A. A. H. M. (1994) *Economic Cooperation in Africa: In Search of Direction*. Boulder: Lynne Rienner.

An up-to-date account of the thesis that South Africa is behaving towards Southern Africa as a selfish benign hegemon is given in a two-part publication:

- Ahwireng-Obeng, F. & Mcgowan, P. (1998) 'Partner or Hegemon? South Africa in Africa', *Journal of Contemporary African Studies*, (Part 1) 16(1):5–38; (Part 2) 16(2):165–196.

Using the Internet to gather information on International Relations

Patrick J. McGowan

What is the Internet and why is it important to you?

The **Internet** (the Net) is a global network, or **matrix**, of computers linking millions of persons and organisations around the world. It is an electronic medium for transferring words, images and sound between people, similar to printing them on paper or sending tapes, CDs and videos, but much faster and cheaper. It is much like postal and telephone systems in that if you have a postal address, you can send and receive mail to and from anywhere in the world, and, if you have access to a telephone, you can receive and make telephone calls from and to any other telephone in the world (as long as you can afford to pay for the calls you make).

Similarly, you can 'surf' the Net *if* you own or have access to a **client computer** – usually a personal computer (PC) of your own or one provided by your university; *if* that PC is linked to a telephone line via a **modem** or by other means; *if* the PC runs the appropriate software (**e-mail** and Internet **browser** programmes); and *if* the PC is linked via the telephone line to a **service provider** (as a student, your university's computing centre is your service provider).

Once this is in place, you can make contact with any similarly linked computer in the world, no matter where it is, and you can then access its Internet files. If your connection to the Internet is through a commercial service provider via your own PC, you will have to pay for the time you are **online** (the price of a local telephone call plus your service provider's fees). In South Africa, some universities charge a fee for student use of the Internet.

As this textbook argues, we now live in a global information society which has a profound impact on society, the economy, government and international relations. Indeed, the development of the Internet may be as revolutionary and transformative as was the invention of the printing press more than 500 years ago in Europe.

Given that there are more telephones in New York City alone than in all Sub-Saharan Africa, there is a real danger that Africa will be further marginalised if Africans do not get onto the Internet. However, on a positive note, the proper use of **information technology** (IT), such as the Internet, can permit African countries and their citizens to leapfrog development obstacles. Unfortunately, in many African countries, state telecommunications monopolies, with vested interests in obsolete technologies and high-cost structures, are obstacles to more rapid IT development, including access to the Internet.

As Table 14.2 shows, South Africa has a well-developed IT infrastructure, similar to smaller developed countries of Europe such as Denmark or Austria. Indeed, in January 1998 the country ranked twenty-fifth in the world in terms of **host computers** per capita, just behind Italy and Spain. This indicates that South Africa is well positioned for Internet-based economic and research activity. The only 'developing' countries ranking higher than South Africa were Singapore (tenth) and Hong Kong (seventeenth) (*The Economist*, 1998). With an estimated 213 818 host computers in July 1998, South Africa ranked as the twentieth most connected to the Internet country in the world (Network Wizards, 1998).

The rest of the countries in sub-Equatorial Africa (SEA) have underdeveloped infrastructures, but there are big differences between countries, such as between Namibia and Angola. In July 1998 only the Democratic Republic of the Congo (DRC) and Malawi did not have links to the **World Wide Web** (also referred to as the Web or WWW), but they were connected to the Internet via e-mail. Most countries in the Southern African Development Community (SADC) and their state telecommunications services need to do more to connect their citizens to the Internet. Even in South Africa, there are great inequalities in access to the Internet between urban and rural populations and between communities, and these must be addressed (*see* World Bank, 1997).

Because of poverty, **balance-of-payments** crises and other economic and political problems, the growth of many African university library holdings has been limited. The good news is that the Internet can give you access to much of the world's research resources at little cost, whatever the problems may be in your local university library.

People, organisations, businesses and governments everywhere have recognised the importance of the Internet for their lives, their work and even for their recreation. Because of this, the so-called 'information superhighway' is growing explosively. As recently as July 1993 there were merely an estimated 1,78 million host computers linked to the Internet. Four-and-a-half years later, in January 1998, the number had grown to 29,67 million. Similarly, estimated *domains* (or unique Web addresses) grew from 26 000 in July 1993 to 10 380 858 by January 1998 (Network Wizards, 1998). Wouldn't we all like to have a savings account that grew so fast!

The bottom line for you as a university student, and future university graduate, is this: *if you cannot use the Internet productively, you will not be able to get a good job after graduation, much less rapidly advance in your chosen career*. For this reason, the authors of this textbook regard this Appendix as essential to your entire university education, not only for your first course in International Relations.

What you can do with the Internet

This depends on what kind of access you have to the Internet and what you want to do with the Net. Using the Internet is like going to a shopping mall filled with hundreds of libraries and bookstores. The time you spend using the Net will depend on what information you want, how quickly you can find it and how much you like surfing the Internet.

The minimum connection to the Internet is the ability to send and receive e-mail (electronic mail). All countries in Southern and Eastern African now have this capacity. E-mail service makes it possible for you to communicate with other individuals and organisations anywhere in the world, and to do this rapidly and cheaply. Even if you only have e-mail access to the Internet, you can access WWW files via e-mail (for more information, *see* African Policy

Information Centre, 1997).

A more advanced capacity on the Internet is the World Wide Web, which electronically links Web documents containing text, pictures, images and sound. Each Web file begins with a '**home page**' that is linked to other files. By January 1998, there were at least 10,4 million home pages on the Web.

Businesses use their home pages to market their products and services globally; universities have home pages to describe their teaching and research departments and to recruit students; governments have home pages that contain official publications and documents. Indeed, organisations of every possible type have home pages.

For university students like you, the most important use of the Web is for research. Just think of the Web as being a gigantic electronic library that is global in its holdings. Whatever undergraduate course you take, there will be vast resources on the Web to extend your knowledge beyond your textbooks, lectures and local university library. This appendix has a list of home pages that are useful for research in International Relations.

How to use the Internet

If your personal or university PC is connected to the Internet as described above, then using the Net is really quite simple.

You will first need to establish an e-mail account and address. Your university computer centre or commercial service provider will help you to do this. Actually using e-mail is straightforward. Programmes for e-mail, such as Pegasus, require you to enter the address of the person or organisation to whom you are sending a message (essential), the subject of the message (optional but preferable), and the addresses of those to whom you wish to send copies (also optional), for example, a **listserve** or **mailing list** of others interested in the subject.

When you log onto your PC, use your **mouse** to click on the icon of your e-mail programme.

Then, click on the 'send mail' icon. Enter the required information, and then type in your message, and click 'send'. Through a host of direct and indirect computer networks, your message is on its way! This is much like writing a letter to someone on a piece of paper, except that it is so much faster (your e-mail will arrive at its destination, *anywhere* in the world, within a few minutes to a few hours), and it is cheaper!

E-mail addresses usually take the following format: *anyname@anycomputer.locationofcomputer.antypeofserviceprovider.country*. Thus, my addressis: *mcgowanp@zeus.mgmt.wits.ac.za*. The name is my last name plus the initial of my first name; the computer providing this service is a Wits computer called 'zeus'; its location is 'mgmt.wits', which represents the Faculty of Management at Wits; the service provider is a university – 'ac'; and the country is South Africa – 'za'.

Receiving e-mail is just as easy. Once you are online your e-mail programme will have an icon for opening mail – often an opened envelope. Simply click on this icon and your e-mail program will download messages that have come to your e-mail address or 'mailbox'. Then, highlight a message, and click 'open' and you can read it and use your programme's 'reply' icon to send an answer.

You will quickly find that e-mail is your preferred means of communicating with individuals and organisations all around the world. It is cheap, it operates 24 hours a day – so if you are in Harare, you don't have to worry about what time it is in Tokyo or New York – and you can always print hard copies of the messages you send and receive by clicking on the 'print' icon.

A second useful feature of e-mail is that you can join mailing lists or electronic distribution lists that are Internet versions of conventional subscription or membership postal mailing lists. Mailing lists cover a huge range of topics, many of which deal with various aspects of International Relations and African affairs. Each list is run by a 'moderator' who uses a computer program called a listserv to maintain and control membership of the list and what is communicated among the list's members. When you send an e-mail message to a mailing list, everyone on the list receives it and when one or more list members responds to you, everyone on the list receives their response(s) as well.

A good example of such a mailing list run by a listserv programme is the one set up by the South African newspaper, *The Mail & Guardian*, which provides a forum for discussing general South African affairs. You can join by sending an e-mail message. Simply fill in the address [majordomo@wmail.misanet.org], type in the single word 'subscribe' for your message, and then send the e-mail. Within a day or so, you will begin to receive list messages. To leave the list, send a similar message to the majordomo programme with the single word 'unsubscribe' in the message. But, be careful with this Internet option. If you join too many active lists, you will be spending all your time deleting e-mail messages in your mailbox that you really do not want to read!

The second and even more powerful component of the Net is the World Wide Web. To access the Web your PC must operate a Web browser programme such as Netscape Navigator or Windows Explorer. We will give an example using Netscape. After logging on to your computer, click on the Netscape icon and the Netscape home page (or some other page, if your Netscape programme is set up that way) will quickly appear on your screen. At the top of the screen is a 'tool bar' with various options; click on the 'open' button. A window will appear. Type in the **URL** (or Web address) of the site you wish to visit and hit 'enter' on your keyboard. Depending upon the time of day, the amount of traffic on the Web, the amount of graphics on the home page and your modem's speed (plus various other factors), the home page of that URL will appear on your monitor's screen sooner or later.

For example, if you entered the URL for the African National Congress (ANC) [http://www.polity.org.za/], the Web home page of the ANC will soon appear. This home page contains many more than links to the ANC. This Web page is simply a text file written in a language called **HTML**, or Hyper Text Markup Language. Each of the underlined words, as well as the icons at the top (for example, What's New), represent **hypertext links** to other Internet computer files. So, if you wish to learn about COSATU (the Congress of South African Trade Unions) or Internet resources related to South Africa, you just click on these highlighted words and your computer and the Internet will quickly take you there – you are now surfing the Net!

Surfing the Internet is like browsing in a bookstore or library, hence the term *browser* for the computer programme that does this for you electronically. All URLs like the ANC's begin with '**http://**'. The major exception is any file organised via consecutive menus, called a '**gopher** file' (a system for storing and accessing computer files on the Internet, mainly text documents, developed before the WWW). A gopher address always begins with 'gopher://'.

The standard format for URLs is *http://anycomputer.locationofcomputer.typeofserviceprovider.country/directory/filename*. In this Appendix, a list is given of the URLs that are useful for the study of International Relations. An extemely useful one is Political Resources on the Internet [http://www.agora.stm.it/politic]. In the URL for this for this Web page, the 'www' represents a computer linked to the Web; the computer is located at 'agora'; the service provider is 'stm'; the country, 'it', is Italy; the directory, or general computer file, is 'politic'. All of the files linked to this home page would come after 'politic/', but are not given here. Note that if you are sitting in Pretoria or Lusaka, you are now linked to a computer and its Web files in Italy! Amazing, isn't it!

Once you have found a useful Web file you may save it on your hard disk (drive 'C'), or on a diskette (drive 'A'), or you may print it by clicking on your browser's 'print' icon. If you are going to be visiting the Political Resources site on the Internet a lot, and we think you will, then click on the **Bookmarks** at the top of the screen and then on 'add bookmark,' and the URL will be saved by Netscape and you can visit it again by simply opening your bookmarks file. This can be done for any useful home page.

What do you do if you want to visit a particular home page and you do not know its URL? You must use a Web **search engine** such as Altavista [http://www.altavista.digital.com/]. A search engine permits you to search the Web in any language. All you need do is type in the name of the organisation you wish to visit, such as 'African National Congress', and then click on the 'search' icon and within a few seconds or minutes, Altavista will provide you with a list of all home pages on the Web that have those three words in their page. This also works for concepts such as 'Peace and Conflict Studies'.

If you have understood the above (and please use the Glossary to help you understand the words and terms in bold), you are now ready to enter the information superhighway. Even if you have never worked with an Internet-linked PC before, your instructor has, as have at least some of your fellow students in your introductory International Relations course. They, and the staff of your university's computing centre, will be glad to help you get started. Don't be shy! Surfing the Internet will enrich your undergraduate university experience; indeed, it may change your life. And, it is fun!

Useful Web sites for International Relations reading and research

The following are a selection of WWW sites that International Relations students will find useful. The sites are listed by geographical regions, with particular emphasis on Africa, and by topics. Please note that the WWW is always undergoing change, so the URLs may no longer be correct, and the content and links we describe here may have changed by the time you begin to use this list. If the URL does not work, use one of the Net search engine programmes supported by your browser by entering key words, like 'World Bank', and you will easily find the new URL. Recall that all URLs begin with 'http://'. We have omitted this in the list, so remember to add it. Finally, remember that URLs are case sensitive, so they must be typed into your 'open' window *exactly* as given here.

General International Relations sites

- *Academic Council on the UN System* [www.brown.edu/Departments/ACUNS/]. The major Web site for information about international institutions of both a global and regional character.
- *Foreign Affairs Guide to International Relations On the Internet* [www.foreignaffairs.org/links.html]. An invaluable starting point for almost any International Relations research topic. Also very good for current events links.
- *International Relations Gateway* [www.aber.ac.uk/~inpwww/resour.html]. A general purpose International Relations gateway maintained by the Department of International Relations, University of Wales, Aberystwyth.
- *International Network Information Center* [inic.utexas.edu/]. This gateway at the University of Texas (US) has many links to international sites, which are organised on a regional basis.
- *Multilaterals Project Web Site* [www.tufts.edu/fletcher/multilaterals.html]. A site containing many major international treaties and the charters of international organisations.
- *Omnivore* [www.way.net/omnivore/index.html]. Truly global in scope, Omnivore is an easy-to-use point of entry for the many sources of news on the Web.
- *Parliamentary and Presidential Elections around the World* [www.geocities.com/~derksen/election. htm]. If an election is held somewhere, the

voting results and much more will be found here.

- *Political Resources on the Internet* [http://195.62.33.1/politic/]. This Italian home page provides listings of political sites, sorted by country, with links to parties, organisations, governments, media and more from all around the world. An alternative URL [www.agora.stm.it/politic/] is available.
- *Political Science Resources* [www.psr.keele.ac.uk/]. Dynamic gateway to sources available via European addresses listed by country name.
- *Political Studies Association International Government Sites* [www.Igu.ac.uk/psa/intgovt.htm/]. A directory of all the home pages of governments around the world.
- *Research Guide to International Law on the Internet* [www.spfo.unibo.it/spolfo/ILMAIN.htm]. Maintained by the Faculty of Political Science, University of Bologna, Italy, this is a useful gateway to international law.
- *The United Nations Organisation* [www.unsystem.org/]. The UN Web site contains information on its activities, resolutions, debates and links to all members of the UN system. An alternative URL [www.unicc.org/] is also available.

Maps relevant to International Relations

- *John R. Borchert Map Library* [www-map.lib.umn.edu/news.html]. Located at the University of Minnesota (US), this site has as very useful collection of 'maps in the news'.
- *Magellan Geographix Interactive Atlas* [www.maps.com/DOCS/atlas.html]. An electronic atlas with maps of all countries of the world, and their major cities. Linked to a 'maps in the news' page with a searchable archive of previous maps in the news.

Global issues

- *The Committee for a Sustainable Future* [csf.colorado.edu/]. The CSF page provides information to pages dealing with ecology, economics, peace and conflict studies.
- *Democracy Net* [www.ned.org/]. Created by the National Endowment for Democracy (US), this site covers democracy and democratisation world-wide.
- *Stockholm International Peace Research Institute* [www.sipri.se/]. Excellent Swedish source for information on disarmament, arms control and the arms trade.
- *The World Health Organisation* [www.who.ch/]. Located in Geneva, Switzerland, the WHO is the major public health organisation in the world, fighting diseases such as Aids malaria, and ebola.
- *United Nations Environmental Programme* [www.unchs.unon.org/]. The major international organisation working on global environmental problems.
- *US Arms Control and Disarmament Agency* [www.acda.gov/]. Information on arms control and disarmament negotiations and issues on a global scale.
- *US Institute of Peace* [www.usip.org/]. Located in Washington DC, the site contains information by and about the USIP. There are links to Web sources relating to international conflict resolution, negotiation theory and peace studies.

International Political Economy

- *BBC OneWorld Online* [www.oneworld.org/]. This site provides links to most of the important NGOs working in the field of sustainable development and North–South relations.
- *International Monetary Fund* [www.imf.org/]. The major international organisation responsible for world monetary

affairs. Responsible for structural adjustment programmes (SAPs) in Africa and elsewhere.

- *Praxis: Resources for Social and Economic Development*
  [www.ssw.upenn.edu/~restes/praxis.html]. Created by a Professor of Social Work at The University of Pennsylvania (US), this site contains links to most Web sites dealing with development and international economic issues.

- *United Nations Conference on Trade and Development*
  [www.unicc.org/unctad/en/enhome.htm]. UNCTAD is the major UN organisation dealing with North-South issues, particularly global economic and development issues.

- *United Nations Development Programme*
  [www.undp.org/]. A major source of information and analysis on global efforts to promote development in the South and former communist states.

- *The US Agency for International Development*
  [www.info.usaid.gov/]. USAID focuses on development issues world-wide and has a great deal of material dealing with Africa.

- *The World Bank*
  [www.worldbank.org/]. The International Bank for Reconstruction and Development (the World Bank) has the world's best data and information on the social and economic conditions in *all* countries of the world.

- *World Trade Organisation*
  [www.wto.org/]. The WTO is the central organisation in the world's trade regime and the site includes information on a host of international trade issues, including intellectual property rights.

Important media for Southern African International Relations students

- *Africa News Online*
  [www.africanews.org/]. This is the gateway site with the most up-to-date current news,

which covers the entire continent and includes feeds from the Pan Africa New Agency (PANA) in Dakar and the All African Press Service (AAPS) in Nairobi.

- *Africa Online*
  [www.africaonline.com/]. The site contains links to all African newspapers and magazines that are on the Web. Excellent for current events and news.

- *The BBC Online*
  [www.bbc.co.uk/]. The British Broadcasting Corporation is the most respected radio and television source of international news reporting in the world.

- *Business Day Online*
  [www.bday.co.za/]. South Africa's leading business and financial daily newspaper, with a good, searchable archive.

- *CNN Online*
  [www.cnn.com/]. A US 24-hour video news channel. News, updated every few hours, includes text, pictures and film. Good external links.

- *The Economist*
  [www.economist.com/index.html]. This is the leading British weekly magazine reporting and analysing world economic and political events and trends.

- *The Financial Mail*
  [www.fm.co.za/]. South Africa's leading weekly financial and business magazine.

- *Financial Times*
  [www.ft.com/]. This London daily newspaper is the best source of global economic and financial news.

- *The Independent Online*
  [www.inc.co.za/]. Daily news on South Africa, Africa and the rest of the world from independent newspapers such as the *Johannesburg Star* and the *Cape Argus*.

- *The Mail & Guardian*
  [www.mg.co.za/mg/]. This outstanding South African weekly newspaper has one of the best sites on the Web. Focus is on South Africa and then the rest of Africa.

- *Le Monde Diplomatique*
  [www.ina.fr/CP/MondeDiplo/]. If you read French, this is the world's best newspaper reporting on international relations issues.
- *Nando News Network*
  [www2.nando.net/nt/world/]. Links to almost all virtual newspapers and news services in the world, including the Pan African News Service.
- *The New York Times*
  [www.nytimes.com/]. This excellent American newspaper provides very good coverage of international affairs and US foreign policies.
- *The Times of London*
  [www.the-times.co.uk/]. One of the world's great newspapers. Very good for British and European news and events.
- *The Washington Post*
  [www.WashingtonPost.com/]. An excellent American newspaper with very good coverage of international affairs and US government politics and policies.

Online reference works

- *Encyclopedia Britannia*
  [www.eb.com/]. The world's greatest reference encyclopaedia.
- *Social Science Information Gateway*
  [sosig.esrc.bris.ac.uk/]. An online catalogue of quality-controlled Internet resources relevant to social science education and research.

Virtual reference libraries

Many South African University libraries are now online. Use SunSITE Southern Africa (listed below) to get to them by clicking on 'universities'.
- *Columbia University African Studies Internet Resources*
  [www.columbia.edu/cu/libraries/inadv/area/Africa/]. A very good, online library that makes available the resources of this major 'Ivy League' university.

- *Harvard University Library*
  [www.harvard.edu/home/library/]. This is the largest university research library in the world.
- *Northwestern University's M. J. Herskovits Library of African Studies*
  [www.library.nwu.edu:80/africana]. This is the largest university collection of research materials on Africa in North America It includes 245 000 books and 2 800 scholarly journals.
- *Unisa Library*
  [www.unisa.ac.za/netcat/index.html]. The Library at the University of South Africa is the largest in Southern Africa, and much of its materials are online.
- *US Library of Congress*
  [www.cweb.loc.gov]. The world's largest research and reference library has vast materials on Africa and International Relations.
- *World Wide Web Virtual Library: International Affairs Network*
  [www.pitt.edu/~ian/ianres.html]. Located at the University of Pittsburg (US), this electronic library focuses on links dealing with international relations.
- *Yale University Library Southern African Collection*
  [www.library.yale.edu/african.html]. The largest collection of books, journals and government documents dealing with *all* the countries of Southern Africa.

Internet regional information services

- *Altavista*
  [www.altavista.digital.com/]. A very popular and useful search engine. Developed by Digital Corporation (USA), one of the world's leading manufacturers of computers and computer software.
- *HotBot*
  [www.hotbot.com/index.html]. Voted by *PC Computing* magazine in late 1997 as the best search engine on the WWW.

- *Yahoo*
[www.yahoo.com/]. One of the best search services on the Web. Open www.yahoo.com/Regional/Regions/Africa/ and you will be able to do keyword and hypertext searches of African events, countries, topics. Substitute Asia for Africa and you can do the same for Asia, and so on.

Africa

- *Africa South of the Sahara*
[www.sul.stanford.edu/depts/ssrg/africa/guide.html]. Located at Stanford University (US), this site is an excellent gateway for electronic information on sub-Saharan Africa that is very well organised.
- *African National Congress Home Page*
[www.polity.org.za/]. This site contains a large array of information on the ANC and its history as well as links to useful Internet resources dealing with South and Southern Africa.
- *A–Z of African Studies on the Internet*
[www.library.uwa.edu.au/subibs/sch/sc.ml.afr.html]. A useful alphabetical index of electronic African materials created by Peter Limb.
- *Index on Africa*
[www.africaindex.africainfo.no/]. Produced and maintained by an alliance of Norwegian NGOs, this site provides a comprehensive guide to Africa on the Internet.
- *Pana News Agency*
[www.africanews.org/PANA/]. The Pan African News Agency has current news from thirty-six correspondents in Africa, and working relationships with forty-eight national news agencies in Africa.
- *Southern African Development Community*
[www2.sadc-usa.net/sadc/home.html]. The home page of SADC with information on the organisation and links to its fourteen member countries.
- *SunSITE Southern Africa*
[sunsite.wits.ac.za/home.html]. This is an excellent gateway for Web resources dealing with South and Southern Africa.
- *UN Economic Commission for Africa*
[www.un.org/Depts/eca/]. Located in Addis Ababa, Ethiopia, the UNECA is a general clearing house for information and research on African development issues.
- *University of Pennsylvania Africa Studies Center*
[www.sas.upenn.edu/African.Studies/AS.html]. This site brings together most Internet resources dealing with Africa, organised by each African country and by topics.

Asia

- *ASEAN*
[www.asean.or.id/]. The Association of South East Asian Nations (ASEAN) groups the tiger economies of Southeast Asia. The site is a comprehensive gateway for this subregion.
- *Asian Studies*
[coombs.anu.edu.au/WWWVLAsianStudies.html]. The Australian National University's comprehensive Web site for research on all Asian nations.
- *India Index*
[www.ubcnet.or.jp:80/jin/ind_gen.html]. General information about India, including news, politics and the economy.
- *Inside China Today*
[www.insidechina.com/]. Recent information on China and related sites for China, Hong Kong, Macao and Taiwan.
- *Japan Policy Research Institute*
[www.nmjc.org/jpri/]. Focuses mainly on Japan-US relations.
- *South-East Asia Information*
[sunsite.nus.sg/asiasvc.html]. Comprehensive site for information on *all* the countries of Southeast Asia.

Europe

- *EUROPA*
[europa.eu.int/]. Information on the European Union's goals and policies, history,

institutions, publications and statistics.

- *Politics-Russia, USSR & Eastern Europe* [bib10.sub.su.se:80/sam/spruss.htm]. Text-only information about Russia, the USSR and Eastern Europe.
- *Organisation for Economic Cooperation and Development* [www.oecd.org/]. The OECD groups the twenty-nine most advanced industrial democracies. Very good comparative statistics and other information, including their foreign aid programmes.
- *Russia & Eastern Europe Network Information Center* [reenic.utexas.edu/reenic.html]. Comprehensive gateway to Web resources on the former Soviet Empire in Eastern Europe, Russia and Central Asia.

Latin America (including Mexico, Central America and The Caribbean)

- *Latin American Studies* [lanic.utexas.edu/las.html]. Comprehensive gateway of Web resources for Latin America, broadly defined.
- *Mexico's Index* [www.trace-sc.com /mex-gov.htm]. Mexican news, government Web map and links for culture, history and politics.

North Africa and the Middle East

- *ArabNet Site Directory* [www.arab.net/]. Web links to twenty-two Arab-speaking countries with a standardised category system.
- *The Middle East Network Information Center* [menic.utexas.edu/menic/]. Comprehensive, well-organised gateway for Web resources on this region of the world, including North Africa.
- *Middle East Security* [www.me-dialogue.demon.co.uk/]. For information on Middle Eastern military and security issues.

North America

- *American Studies Web* [www.georgetown.edu/crossroads/asw/]. If you are researching any aspect of US history, foreign policies and role in international relations, this is a good place to start.
- *Statistics Canada* [www.statcan.ca/start.html]. Site includes information on land, people, economy and government as well as links to other Canadian government sources.
- *The US Central Intelligence Agency* [www.odci.gov/cia]. Includes information about the CIA and very useful annual publications such as the *CIA World Factbook*, *Factbook on Intelligence* and *Handbook of International Economic Statistics*, and CIA maps.
- *The US Congress Home Page* [www.thomas.gov/]. The House of Representatives and Senate play important roles in US foreign policy. Current legislation and other documents are here.
- *The US Department of State* [www.state.gov/index.html]. Organised by categories dealing with world regions and major states and by topics such as human rights. Also contains information about the State Department, its activities and US foreign policy positions.
- *The White House and Executive Branch* [www.whitehouse.gov/]. Gives access to the US President, statements and press briefings and to the departments of the Executive Branch of the US government.

Suggested readings

- Africa Policy Information Centre (1997) *Africa on the Internet: Starting Points for Policy Information.* [http://www.igc.apc.org/apic/bp/inetall. html]. A comprehensive guide to the Internet with special reference to African affairs.

- Deibert, R. J. (1998) 'Virtual resources: International Relations research resources on the Web', *International Organization,* 52:211–221. A good discussion of the WWW and International Relations resources found on it.
- *The Financial Mail Navigator.* [http://www.atd.co.za/fm/fmnavigate.html]. A useful, brief guide to the Internet produced by the South African business magazine, *The Financial Mail.*
- *International Organization.* [www-mit press.mit.edu/IO]. The home page of a major journal in international political economy.
- *The Internet Journal of African Studies.* [www.brad.ac.uk/research/ijas]. The first electronic scholarly journal dealing with African affairs.
- *The Journal of World-System Research.* [http://csf.colorado.edu/wsystems/jwar.html]. An electronic journal dealing with a major approach to International Relations and International Political Economy.
- O'Leary, T. & O'Leary. L. I. (1996) *Internet.* New York: McGraw-Hill. A comprehensive description of the entire Internet, including electronic mail and the WWW.
- Polman, K. (1998) 'Evaluation of Africa-related Internet resources', *African Affairs,* 97:401–408. A useful review of Internet resources for African studies.
- World Bank (1997) *Internet Connectivity: Africa.* [http://www.worldbank.org/aftdr/connect/connect.htm]. Links to a wide variety of documents relating to the Internet and Africa.

B Careers in international relations

Kato Lambrechts

Introduction

One of the wonderful things about globalisation (*see* Chapters 1 and 2) is that it has opened up so many new employment opportunities for students who have successfully completed a university or technikon degree or diploma with International Relations as a major subject. As more and more aspects of life become exposed to international actors and influences, employers are increasingly recognising the need for qualified people who have an understanding of, and can critically evaluate, global events. The study of International Relations is unique in that it provides students with the opportunity to acquire these types of intellectual skills.

A qualification in International Relations can lead to careers in the following areas:
- the diplomatic service;
- the international offices of Departments of Labour, Trade and Industry and Defence
- the international section of parliament;
- the National Intelligence Agency (NIA);
- the international telecommunications industry;
- international journalism;
- the tourism industry;
- management consultancies;
- research institutions, such as the Foundation for Global Dialogue, the Centre for Policy Studies and the South African Institute of International Affairs;
- regional or national organisations that promote foreign trade and investment, like WESGRO;
- the headquarters or branch offices of international governmental organisations, such as the United Nations (UN), the World Trade Organisation (WTO), the Southern African Development Community (SADC) and the Commonwealth;
- international non-governmental organisations (INGOs), such as Amnesty International (AI) and the World Economic Forum;
- international relief agencies, such as Save the Children and OXFAM;
- multinational corporations (MNCs);
- the export and import business sector; and
- international offices of universities and technikons.

Southern African students of International Relations need to pay careful attention to the combination of subjects they choose at an undergraduate level, since this will determine their future career options. For example, a student who majors in International Relations and Economics will have different initial career opportunities from a student who majors in International Relations and Law.

Besides English, Southern African students will find it extremely useful to be proficient in one or more of the following languages: Arabic, French, Japanese, Mandarin Chinese, German, Portuguese or Spanish.

On the postgraduate level (Honours and Masters), the universities of Southern Africa provide wonderful opportunities for students to further their general study of International Relations, or to specialise in fields such as international development, international management, diplomacy, regional integration, international organisations, international economics, international environmental affairs and international co-operation in science and technology.

This Appendix outlines opportunities that are available to students of International Relations in the public, private and non-governmental non-profit sectors. For each sector, career opportunities, relevant institutions and the educational qualifications and experience you will need are outlined. Examples of successful career paths that International Relations graduates interviewed by the author have followed as well as possible career paths in the UN system are also provided.

Careers in the public sector

Career opportunities for Southern African students of International Relations in the public sector are varied. These often depend on the student's area or areas of specialisation and expertise within the broad field of International Relations. The first and traditional career opportunity is that of a *diplomat*. The main functions of a diplomat are to represent his/her home country and to communicate information between governments. Other duties include the protection of national citizens and their property abroad, gathering information in the host state for policy-makers in their own government and providing advice to those who formulate policies in their own government. Occasionally, diplomats have to make important policy decisions themselves. Finally, diplomats have to represent their governments in the host state.

The international co-operation or foreign affairs departments of governments in Southern Africa employ diplomats. The minimum qualification that is required for acceptance to a government's diplomatic training programme is an undergraduate degree in International Relations or Political Science, or a related discipline. However, candidates who *only* have an undergraduate qualification are usually required to have previous work or political experience before they are admitted to the programme. Candidates with a postgraduate qualification in International Relations are not required to have previous work experience. Trainees have to pass the examination set by the diplomatic training programme before they can start building their careers as diplomats.

A second career opportunity in the public sector is as an *international lawyer*. Many governments employ specialists in international public law to deal with legal aspects of bilateral and multilateral relations between states. Specialists in public international law provide legal advice and litigate on issues as diverse as human rights, environment, trade, fishing and crimes committed across borders. Governments also employ specialists in private international law as consultants to provide legal advice on financial, trade and investment issues.

Government departments such as foreign affairs and trade and industry hire specialists of international public and private law. The UN and its agencies, the WTO and regional economic and political organisations, such as SADC, also hire specialists of both public and

Box B.1: Natalie's career

Thirty-year-old Natalie graduated with a Master's degree in International Studies in 1992 from the Graduate Institute of International Studies at the University of Geneva, with the assistance of a scholarship from the UN. She specialised in International Economics, Politics and History. During her stay in Geneva, she worked as an intern and a volunteer at several non-governmental and governmental organisations, such as AI, the Programme to Combat Racism, the Geneva office of the Organisation of African Unity (OAU) and Defence for Children International. Since her student days, therefore, she has been exposed to the international human rights movement and has learned organisational, administrative, research, writing and advocacy skills through her various internships.

She returned to South Africa after completing her degree and worked as a special projects officer in a non-governmental organisation (NGO) that provides credit to women in rural areas for micro and small business development. One of her principal projects during this time was to initiate preparations among NGOs for the fourth UN World Conference on Women in Beijing, which took place in 1995. She subsequently opened a co-ordinating office for the Beijing Conference in collaboration with other NGOs and served as project co-ordinator in this office. Her job involved fundraising, project co-ordination and promotional and advocacy work on a national scale.

After the Beijing Conference she joined the Department of Foreign Affairs (DFA) and completed a four-month training course. Natalie was subsequently posted to the embassy in Paris, where she was still serving at the time of writing, as counsellor for multilateral affairs. In this capacity, she supervises multilateral economic issues, human rights, international exhibitions and other issues pertaining to international organisations and multilateral affairs in France. She deals daily with the French and other governments as well as local associations and academic institutions in France.

Box B.2: United Nations (UN) recruitment information

Recruitment of young professionals

Junior professionals and professionals are recruited through National Competitive Recruitment Examinations. These are organised as a matter of priority in countries inadequately represented among the UN staff or the UN Secretariat. The UN administers these examinations in a number of occupational groups, including economics, legal affairs, political affairs, public information and social development. To qualify for junior professional positions, the candidate must possess a first-level university degree and be thirty-two years or younger. For professional positions, a candidate must possess an advanced university degree, have four years of professional experience and be thirty-nine years old or younger. Fluency in either English or French is required for both positions. All those who meet these criteria and believe in the purposes and ideals of the UN are encouraged to apply to:

United Nations, Division for Staff Development and Performance
Policy and Specialist Services
Office of Human Resource Management, Room S-2590
New York, NY 10017, USA

Recruitment for middle and higher level posts

It is the general policy of the UN to announce all vacancies other than those at the entry level. In filling these vacancies, it makes special efforts to recruit from as wide a geographic area as possible, in order to achieve as closely as possible equitable representation among member states. To be considered for these posts, candidates must possess an advanced university degree, as well as relevant professional experience. Normally, a minimum of six years' professional experience is required. Information on currently vacant positions is available at the UN Headquarters in New York, UN information centres throughout the world, and other offices of the UN family such as the UN Development Programme (UNDP). Information may also be obtained from the foreign ministry of the respective member states and certain educational or professional institutions such as universities. In order to identify the best and the brightest, the UN uses competitive recruitment methods such as assessment centres. The Secretariat maintains a computerised roster of qualified candidates for these posts. Interested candidates should contact:

United Nations Staffing Support Section
Division for Planning, Recruitment and
Operational Services
Office of Human Resource Management,
Room S-2555
New York, NY 10017, USA

United Nations (UN) Headquarters Internship Programme

The UN Headquarters Internship Programme is offered to students enrolled in postgraduate degrees to promote their understanding of major problems confronting the world and give them insight into how the UN attempts to find solutions to these problems. The programme is conducted in three two-month periods in a year – from mid-January to mid-March, from mid-May to mid-July, and from mid-September to mid-November. As the UN has no provision in its budget for paying interns, all costs connected with internships must be borne by interns themselves or by their sponsoring institutions or governments. Interested candidates should contact:

United Nations Internship Programme
Division for Staff Development,
Performance, Policy and Specialist Services
Office of Human Resource Management,
Room S-2580
New York, NY 10017, USA

United Nations (UN) Volunteer Programme

UN volunteers need a professional qualification and an interest in humanitarian relief, democratic support, electoral monitoring, conflict resolution, peace-building and community work. Interested candidates should have at least five years' experience and should contact:

United Nations Volunteer Programme
Division for Staff Development,
Performance, Policy and Specialist Services
Office of Human Resource Management
New York, NY 10017, USA

private international law. A postgraduate degree in International Legal Studies is a minimum qualification for this career. A postgraduate degree in International Studies/Relations will advance the opportunities of anyone who wants to pursue a career in international law. Legal experts in multilateral institutions are usually required to have at least five years' legal experience and be fluent in English and/or French. It is also useful to note that MNCs, particularly those who focus on international finance, trade and investment law, also hire specialists in international private law.

A third career option in the public sector is to become an *international development worker*. This typically involves fieldwork as a programme officer for a development organisation in a developing country, or as a desk officer or researcher for a development organisation in a developed country.

Institutions that offer career opportunities in development work include the UNDP, the International Labour Organisation (ILO), the UN Conference on Trade and Development (UNCTAD), the World Bank, the Development Bank of Southern Africa (DBSA) and the African Development Bank (ADB). A postgraduate degree in International Studies/Relations, focusing on international political economy and international development, is a minimum qualification. Often, these organisations require a taught Masters degree or postgraduate diploma in Development Management and Administration, Public Finance or a specific area such as health, education, gender studies or rural development.

A fourth career opportunity in the public sector is in the field of *public management of international trade* (there are, of course, also many career opportunities in the private sector related to trade, for example in the import and export business). Governments employ foreign trade representatives to represent their trade interests in other countries or at multilateral economic institutions, to gather trade information and to make policy decisions on trade matters. Foreign trade experts are also required to work on trade,

Box B.3: World Bank recruitment information

Young Professionals Programme

This programme is a starting point for careers in the World Bank group. The programme has been designed for highly qualified and motivated young people skilled in areas relevant to the Bank's operations, such as economics, finance, education, public health, social sciences, the environment and natural resource management. The programme provides the opportunity for professional development through on-the-job experience and exposure to the World Bank group's operations and policies. Each year, the World Bank accepts about thirty candidates into the programme. Young professionals start with two rotational assignments, lasting up to one year each in different departments, which provide a broad overview of the World Bank group's work. The type of assignment is based on the person's qualifications and personal preferences, as well as institutional staffing needs. All young professionals are on probation for the duration of their rotational assignments and they can apply for a permanent position upon successful completion of these assignments.

Summer Employment Programme

This programme is open to students who are nationals of the World Bank's member countries. The goal of the programme is to offer successful candidates an opportunity to improve their skills as well as the experience of working in an international environment. To be eligible for the programme, candidates must possess an undergraduate degree and be enrolled in a full-time Master's or Doctorate degree course. This programme seeks candidates in the following fields: economics, finance, development (in the areas of public health, education, the environment, nutrition and population), social sciences, agriculture, the environment, private sector development as well as other related fields. Fluency in English is required. Prior relevant working experience, computing skills as well as knowledge of languages such as French, Spanish, Arabic, Portuguese, Russian and Chinese are advantageous.

Interested candidates for both programmes should contact:

The World Bank, Staffing Centre
1818H Street, NW
Wahington DC, 20433, US

---

investment and industrial-related policy issues in their home government. Furthermore, regional groupings such as SADC, and its member states appoint programme officers and researchers to work on political and economic issues concerning regional integration, both in national governments and at the SADC headquarters in Gaborone, Botswana.

Institutions that offer career opportunities in the public management of international trade are government departments dealing with trade issues and the SADC Secretariat. A postgraduate qualification in International Studies, specialising in International Political Economy and International Trade, is required for a career as a foreign trade representative. The trade and industry departments of governments will appoint International Relations graduates with-

out experience at a junior level (for example, as a trade advisor) and they can build their career through continued education, that is, through special economics training courses. For a senior level post, previous experience in the private or non-governmental non-profit sector is required, as well as a postgraduate degree in Economics.

A fifth career opportunity for students of International Relations in Southern Africa is in *international peacekeeping*. In order to fulfil its peacekeeping role, the UN is involved in a number of operations in different regional of the world, known as UN Peacekeeping Operations. These operations rely partly on military forces provided directly by the member states of the UN, known as the 'blue helmets', but they also rely on civilian staff to monitor the observance of human rights, to manage human resources, to

Box B.4: Marobo's career

Twenty-five-year-old Morabo completed an Honours degree in International Relations in 1995. He specialised in International Political Economy, Crisis Management and International Development. The next year he was offered a post in his department as a tutor, moderating small group discussions and assessing student essays. He also occasionally lectured second-year students. During this time, he worked for ten hours a week as an intern at a foreign policy NGO. He did research and wrote reports on national foreign policy-making, organised and attended workshops on foreign policy in conjunction with the government, and attended a human rights conference in Mozambique under the auspices of the NGO as part of his research

work. He also wrote a paper on foreign policy in the working paper series published by his department. In 1998, he decided to embark on a new career path in an international organisation. He was offered a job as an administrative officer in the education department of the UN Educational, Scientific and Cultural Organisation (UNESCO). In his new job, Morabo will assist in establishing a UNESCO Secretariat in South Africa. To do this, he will divide his time between administration, budgeting and research. Although his work currently involves mostly administration, Morabo was hired because of his experience in project co-ordination as an intern and his advanced understanding of the international system.

manage material resources and for other aspects of the peacekeeping operation. Generally, positions are offered in the following fields: political affairs, legal affairs, human rights, election monitoring, humanitarian assistance and public information.

To serve on a UN peacekeeping mission, applicants need an advanced university degree in a relevant discipline (for example, International Relations) and fluency in either English or French. Fluency in languages such as Arabic, Portuguese and Spanish are an added advantage. Generally, candidates for peacekeeping missions need at least four years of relevant professional experience, especially in developing countries, to qualify for a position.

Finally, students of International Relations can pursue a career in *academia*. Academics lecture and do research at universities or technikon departments. To become a tutor in a university or technikon department, students need an Honours degree in International Relations. A junior lecturer should have a Master's degree and a senior lecturer a Doctorate in International Relations. A senior lecturer should also have a significant publishing record (that is, books and articles in accredited journals). At a junior level,

tutoring experience is required and at a senior level, significant lecturing experience is required. Both public and private universities, as well as technikons and business schools, employ lecturers in International Relations.

Careers in the private sector

Career opportunities for Southern African students of International Relations in the private sector are expanding for the reasons elaborated in the introduction. This section will discuss three broad career options in the private sector. Firstly, Southern African students of International Relations can pursue a career in *international business*. This includes setting up your own international business, or working for an established international business.

National or multinational corporations often seek specialists to research and identify market opportunities throughout the world, as they wish to expand the markets for their services or manufactured goods. The duties of such specialists may vary, but generally a solid knowledge of a particular geographical area and basic economics is required.

Box B.5: Brenda's career

Twenty-eight-year-old Brenda completed an Honours degree in International Relations in 1993, specialising in African Politics, International Political Economy and International Organisations. She started working at a foreign trade promotion organisation as a researcher on African markets in 1994. She had to research barriers to trade in African markets; source and consult with clients who wanted to enter foreign markets for the first time or expand the scope of their products within a given market; and compile statistical analyses of various African countries. She was hired because of her postgraduate qualification in African Politics and International Political Economy. The company sent her on courses to train her in market research and numerical skills. These skills, coupled with her research experience and broad political knowledge of Africa, qualified her for her current job as a manager of the foreign trade promotion division of a corporate merchant bank that is expanding its interests in Africa. In her new job, she has to provide trade and technical information to clients, run trade and finance seminars for clients, produce and market trade publications, and host foreign delegations for economic briefings. She also has to liaise regularly with foreign parastatals and trade organisations.

Institutions offering career opportunities in international business include foreign trade organisations, chambers of commerce, merchant banks and MNCs. A postgraduate degree in International Relations, focusing on the international political economy and a geographical area, is a minimum entry requirement. At a managerial level, employers require previous experience in and knowledge of foreign markets, as well as basic economic training.

Secondly, students of International Relations can pursue a career in *international communication*. Job opportunities in this field range from that of a journalist to an information officer in international organisations or the foreign relations departments of governments. A journalist specialising in international affairs writes feature articles, as well as reports on international events and issues for newsmagazines and daily and weekly newspapers. An information officer in a foreign affairs department or international organisation writes press releases and public information documents relating to foreign policy and international issues.

News magazines such as the *Southern African Political and Economic Monthly*, *African Topic*, *Leadership Magazine*, *Time*, *Newsweek* and *The Economist* all offer career opportunities in journalism, as do daily and weekly newspapers and press agencies in Southern Africa. The UN offers various positions for public information officers and the foreign affairs and trade departments of governments also employ press liaison officers. A minimum requirement for interns at a newspaper or news magazine is an undergraduate degree in a relevant discipline (such as, International Relations). At a more senior or editorial level, reporting and writing experience, as well as a degree or diploma in journalism, are necessary. For a career in public information, a degree or diploma in Communication Studies

Box B.6: A career in public information at the United Nations (UN)

Positions in the field of public information involve a wide range of activities in the areas of production of UN press releases and information materials, both in print and on-line. The assignments may include providing all official coverage of UN meetings, conferences and programmes for delegations, the media and NGOs at UN Headquarters and around the world, as well as the production of thematically-integrated publications, radio, television, video and photographic products. Other major activities are the handling of promotion campaigns for media coverage of international conferences, observances and special events, conducting public tours and responding to public enquiries.

would be an advantage.

A third career option in the private sector for Southern African students of International Relations is that of *finance and investment research* and *business management*. There are a wide range of jobs in in this field, from doing research on goods and money markets in different regions of the world, to managing investment portfolios for investment companies and administering businesses in various regions of the world.

MNCs and investment and consulting firms, such as Frankel Pollak and Andersen Consulting, offer career opportunities in finance and investment research and business management. To pursue a career in this field, a student should take Economics and International Relations as majors in an undergraduate degree. An

International Relations Honours degree, focusing on a specific geographical and political region as well as the international political economy, coupled with a Masters degree in Business Administration would allow a student to enter a company at a middle-management level. At a junior level, companies often employ promising students without any prior experience or training in business management and instead provide on-the-job training.

Non-governmental non-profit sector

This section will explore three possible career paths in the non-governmental, non-profit (or voluntary) sector. This sector comprises mostly national and international NGOs engaged in research, advocacy, conflict resolution and development work.

A first career option is that of a *programme or project officer*. Such a person co-ordinates workshops, conferences and research and development projects related to all areas of international affairs. Entrants at a junior level do not need any previous experience, but for a more senior position, applicants need previous project co-ordination experience. An Honours degree in International Relations (or a related discipline) with a specialisation in an appropriate sub-field is a prerequisite. A researcher does qualitative and quantitative research on specific themes such as conflict resolution, foreign policy and international trade organisations. To pursue a career in research, students need at least a Masters degree in International Relations, specialising in a specific sub-field. For example, to work as a researcher at AI or Human Rights Watch, students need to focus on a geographical area, as well as international human rights issues. A development worker identifies, prepares, evaluates and manages development projects in developing countries. This includes training. A postgraduate degree in International

Box B.7: David's career

Twenty-seven-year-old David completed his undergraduate degree in 1993, majoring in Private Law and Political Studies and continued with an Honours degree in International Relations, focusing on the international political economy and East Asia. He then did one year of language study in Asia and today he speaks fluent Mandarin Chinese. During his postgraduate study, he also took correspondence courses in Economics up to a third-year level. While in Asia, he was first offered a job as a research editor at an investment firm as a result of his language skills and understanding of the global political and economic system. He is now working at a securities firm as a research analyst and conducts research on goods and money markets in Japan, Korea and Southeast Asia. He was offered this job because of his background in economics, his language and analytical skills, and his understanding of the global system. The company that employs him at present also sent him on an investment analysis course to further enhance his understanding of international finance. He was recently promoted to assistant fund manager of a portfolio investment fund for East Asia.

Studies/Relations, either combined with a post-graduate degree in Development Management, or a focus on international development as a functional stream, is a prerequisite for this career. Previous experience in development organisations as an intern, project officer, researcher or fieldworker is a requirement for the manager of a programme or project. Students should thus seek internships or even do voluntary work in development organisations.

Organisations that offer the above career opportunities in Southern Africa and elsewhere include research institutes affiliated to universities and independent national or international NGOs. These include organisations such as Women and Law and Development in Africa (in Botswana), OXFAM (in most SADC countries), the Southern African Research and Documentation Centre (in Mozambique), the Foundation for Global Dialogue (in South Africa) and the Southern African Regional Institute for Policy Studies (in Zimbabwe).

Conclusion

There is hardly any sector of private and public life that is not being internationalised today. This means that opportunities for people with a qualification in IR are constantly expanding. Studying IR also helps one to understand other cultures – a skill much in demand in today's workplace.

Suggested readings

- Holsti, K. J. (1977) *International Politics: A Framework for Analysis* (3rd edition). New Jersey: Prentice-Hall. Holsti explains the changing role of diplomats in a chapter entitled 'The Instruments of Policy: Diplomatic Bargaining'.
- Barnard, D. (1997) *The Southern African Development Directory*. Johannesburg: Human Sciences Research Council. This directory lists

Box B.8:   Palesa's career

Twenty-seven-year-old Palesa completed an Honours degree in International Studies in 1993, specialising in International Political Economy, the Political Economy of Southern Africa, Research Methodology and International Law. She then worked as an intern at a foreign policy research institution for ten months. After that, she was offered an internship at a US Foundation, doing research on technological developments and environmental protection. Her specialisation in the international political economy and previous experience as an intern made her the favoured candidate for the internship. Back in South Africa, she worked simultaneously as an intern to co-ordinate a project on Southern Africa at a research institution and as a co-ordinator of the international desk at an umbrella organisation for NGOs in South Africa. She recently started working at an NGO as a research and education officer on international labour issues. Her research focuses in particular on the impact of crises in the international economy on working women and she also designs and runs training programmes for women workers in the labour movement. She was offered the job because of her political understanding of international labour issues, her previous research and project co-ordination experience as well as her academic background in International Political Economy.

all NGOs in Southern Africa.
- http://www.unsystem.org/. This Web site gives an overview of the activities of the UN, and has information on job opportunities in the UN.
- http://www.worldbank.org/. This Web site gives an overview of the activities of the World Bank, and has information on job opportunities in the World Bank group.
- http://www.pitt.edu/~ian/resource/schools.htm. This Web site gives information on postgraduate degrees offered by universities world-wide in the field of International Relations.

Bibliography

Abbravanel, M. & Hughes, B. (1973) 'The relationship between public opinion and governmental foreign policy'. In *Sage International Yearbook of Foreign Policy Studies*, edited by McGowan, P. pp. 107–134. Beverly Hills: SAGE.

Adar, K. G. (1987) 'A note on the role of African states in Committee I of UNCLOS III', *Ocean Development and International Law* 18(6):665–681.

Adar, K. G. (1994) *Kenyan Foreign Policy Towards Somalia, 1963–1983*. Lanham: University Press of America.

ADB (1995) *African Development Report 1995*. Abidjan: Africa Development Bank.

Adedeji, A. (ed.). (1996) *South Africa and Africa: Within or Apart?* London: Zed Books (in association with African Centre for Development and Strategic Studies, Ijebu-Ode, Nigeria).

Africa Institute (1997) *Africa at a Glance: Facts and Figures 1995/6*. Pretoria: Africa Institute of South Africa.

African National Congress, (1993) *Foreign policy in a New Democratic South Africa*. Johannesburg: African National Congress.

African Policy Information Centre (1997) *Africa on the Internet: Starting Points for Policy Information*. [http://www.igc.apic/bp/inetall.html]

Ahwireng-Obeng, F. (1997) 'A sceptical view of South Africa within the IOR-ARC', *South African Journal of International Affairs*, 5(1):97–109.

Ahwireng-Obeng, F. & McGowan, P. J. (1998) 'Partner or Hegemon? South Africa in Africa: Part one', *Journal of Contemporary African Studies*, 16(1):5-38.

Ahwireng-Obeng, F. & McGowan, P. J. (1998) 'Partner or Hegemon? South Africa in Africa: Part two', *Journal of Contemporary African Studies* 16(2):165–196.

Ajala, A. (1974) *Pan-Africanism*. London: Deutsch.

Ake, C. (1994) *Democratisation of Disempowerment in Africa*. Lagos: Malthouse.

Alden, C. (1998) 'Solving South Africa's Chinese puzzle: democratic foreign policy making and the "two China" question', *Discussion Papers in International*

Relations, 2(1):1–18.

Allen, J. L. (1998) *Student Atlas of World Politics.* Guilford: Dushkin/McGraw-Hill.

Allison, G. T. (1969) 'Conceptual models and the Cuban missile crisis', *American Political Science Review* 63(3):689–718.

Allison, G. T. (1971) *Essence of Decision: Explaining the Cuban Missile Crisis.* Boston: Little, Brown.

Aly, A. A. H. M. (1997) 'Post-Apartheid South Africa: implications for regional co-operation', *Africa Insight* 22(1):24–30.

Aly, A. A. H. M. (1994) *Economic Co-operation in Africa: In Search of Direction.* Boulder: Lynne Rienner Publishers.

Annan, K. (1998) 'The causes of conflict and the promotion of durable peace and sustainable development in Africa.' Report of the Secretary General on the work of the Organisation A/52/871, United Nations, New York, 13 April.

Annan, K. (1998) 'The quiet revolution', *Global Governance,* 4(2):123–138.

Anyang' Nyong'o, P. (1987) *Popular Struggles for Democracy in Africa.* London: Zed Books.

Asante, S. K. B. (1996) 'Contemporary Africa: India and South–South co-operation', *South African Journal of International Affairs,* 4(1):27–55.

Balaam, M. D. and Veseth, M. (1996) *Introduction to International Political Economy.* Englewood Cliffs: Prentice-Hall.

Baldwin, D. A. (ed.) (1993) *Neorealism and Neoliberalism: The Contemporary Debate.* New York: Columbia University Press.

Barber, J. and Barratt, J. (1990) *South Africa's Foreign Policy: The Search for Status and Security, 1945–1988.* Johannesburg: Southern Book Publishers.

Bayart, J. (1993) *The State in Africa: The Politics of the Belly.* London: Longman.

Baylies C. (1995) '"Political Conditionality" and Democratisation', *Review of African Political Economy,* 22(65):321–338.

Bello, W. & Rosenfeld, S. (1990) *Dragons in Distress: Asia's Miracle Economies in Crisis.* San Francisco: Institute for Food and Development Policy.

Bennett, A. LeRoy (1995) *International Organizations: Principles and Issues* (6th edition). Englewood Cliffs: Prentice-Hall.

Beresford, D. (1998) 'SA crime is getting organised', *Mail and Guardian,* 13–19 February.

Berridge, G. R. (1997) *International Politics: States, Power and Conflict since 1945.* New York: Harvester Wheatsheaf.

Bloomfield, L. P. (1974) *The Foreign Policy Process: Making Theory Relevant.* Beverly Hills: SAGE.

Booth, K & Smith, S. (eds.) (1995) *International Relations Theory Today.* Cambridge: Polity Press.

Boutros-Ghali, B. (1992) *An Agenda for Peace.* New York: United Nations.

Bowle, J. (1962) *A New Outline of World History.* London: George Allen and Unwin.

Bratton, M. & van de Walle, N. (1997) *Democratic Experiments in Africa: Regime Transitions in Comparative Perspective.* Cambridge: Cambridge University Press.

Bratton, M. (1989) 'Beyond the state: civil society and associational life in Africa', *World Politics,* 41:407–30.

Braudel, F. (1982) *The Wheels of Commerce* (Vol. II of *Civilisation and Capitalism, 1400 to 1800*). London: HarperCollins.

Bresler, F. (1992) *Interpol.* London: Penguin.

Breytenbach, W. J. (1994) 'The Chinese dilemma: dual recognition is the ultimate solution', *The South African Journal of International Affairs,* 2(1):50–61.

Brown, S. (1992) *International Relations in a Changing Global System: Toward a Theory of the World Polity.* Boulder: Westview.

Brownlie, I. (1979) *Principles of Public International Law* (3rd edition). Oxford: Clarendon Press.

Bull, H. (1977) *The Anarchical Society: A Study of Order in World Politics*. New York: Columbia University Press.

Bulmer, S. & Scott, A. (eds) (1994) *Economic and Political Integration in Europe: Internal Dynamics and Global Context*. Oxford: Blackwell.

Bush, R. & Szeftel, M. (1995) 'Taking leave of the twentieth century', *Review of African Political Economy*, 65:291–300.

Buzan, B. (1996) 'The timeless wisdom of realism?' In *International Theory: Positivism and Beyond*, edited by Smith, S. Booth, K. & Zalewski, M. pp. 47–65. Cambridge: Cambridge University Press.

Buzan, B., Jones, C. & Little, R. (1993) *The Logic of Anarchy: Neorealism to Structural Realism*. New York: Columbia University Press.

Caldwell, L. K. (1992) *Between Two Worlds, the Environmental Movement and Policy Choices*. Cambridge: Cambridge University Press.

Callaghy, T. (1984) *The State-Society Struggle*. New York: Columbia University Press.

Callaghy, T. (1991) 'Africa and the world economy: caught between a rock and a hard place'. In *Africa in World Politics*, edited by Harbeson, J. & Rothchild, D. pp. 39–68. Boulder: Westview.

Camillieri, J. A. & Falk, J. (1992) *The End of Sovereignty: The Politics of Shrinking and Fragmenting World*. London: Edward Edgar.

Carlsnaes, W. & Muller, M. (eds) (1997) *Change and South African External Relations*. Johannesburg: International Thompson Publishing.

Carlsnaes, W. (1986) *Ideology & Foreign Policy. Problems of Comparative Conceptualization*. Oxford: Basil Blackwell.

Carr, E. H. (1961) *What is History?* Harmondsworth: Penguin Books.

Carr, E. H. (1966) *The Twenty Years' Crisis, 1919–1939*. London: Macmillan

Carruthers, S. (1997) 'International History, 1900–1945.' In *The Globalization of World Politics: An Introduction to International Relations*, edited by Baylis, J. & Smith, S. pp. 49–69. Oxford: Oxford University Press.

Central Intelligence Agency (1997) *CIA Factbook 1997*. [http://www.odic.gov/cia/publications/nsolos/wfb-all.htm].

Chazan, N. & LeVine, V. (1991) 'Africa and the Middle East.' In *Africa in World Politics*, edited by Harbeson, J. & Rothchild, D. pp. 202–227. Boulder: Westview.

Chazan, N., Mortimer, R., Ravenhill, J. & Rothchild, D. (1992) *Politics and Society in Contemporary Africa*. London: Macmillan.

Chinweizu. (1993) 'Africa and the capitalist countries.' In *Africa Since 1935. General History of Africa, Vol. VIII*, edited by Mazrui, A. pp. 769–797. London: Heinemann.

Chipeta, C., Lue, B. V. & Atkinson, K. (1997) *Review and Rationalisation of the SADC Programme of Action, Volume 2: Main Report*. Gaberone: SADC Secretariat, April.

Chopra, J. (ed.) (1998) *Peace Maintenance Operations*. Boulder: Lynne Rienner.

Clapham, C. (1995) *Third World Politics: An Introduction*. London: Croom Helm.

Clapham, C. (1996) *Africa and the International System: The Politics of State Survival*. Cambridge: Cambridge University Press.

Colebatch, H. K. (1998) *Policy*. Minneapolis: Minnesota University Press.

Connor, W. (1987) ' Ethnonationalism'. In *Understanding Political Development*, edited by Weiner, M. and Huntington, S. pp. 196–220. Boston: Little Brown.

Coquery-Vidrovitch C. (1993) 'Economic Changes in Africa in the world context.' In *Africa since 1935. General History of Africa, Vol. VIII*, edited by Mazrui, A. pp. 285–316. London: Heinemann.

Cottam, R. W. 1977) *Foreign Policy Motivation: A General Theory and a Case-study*. Pittsburgh: University of Pittsburgh.

Couloumbis, T. A. and Wolfe, J. H (1978) *Introduction to International Relations: Power and Justice* (1st edition) Englewood Cliffs: Prentice-Hall.

Couloumbis, T. A. and Wolfe, J. H. (1986) *Introduction to International Relations: Power and Justice* (3rd edition) Englewood Cliffs: Prentice-Hall.

Cox, R. W. (1987) *Production, Power, and World Order: Social Forces in the Making of History*. New York: Columbia University Press.

Cox, R. W. (1992) *Globalization, Multilateralism, and Democracy*. Providence: Academic Council on the UN System.

Cox, R. W. *et al.* (1995) *International Political Economy: Understanding Global Order*. London: Zed Books.

Crabb, C. V. (1968) *Nations in a Multipolar World*. New York: Harper and Row

Craig, A., Griesel, H. & Witz, L. (1994) *Conceptual Dictionary*. Kenwyn: Juta.

Curtin, P. D. (1969) *The Atlantic Slave Trade: A Census*. Madison: University of Wisconsin Press.

Curtin, P. D., Feierman, S. Thompson, L. & Vansina, J. (1995) *African History: From Earliest Times to Independence* (2nd edition). London: Longman.

Dahl, R. (1957) 'The Concept of Power', *Behavioural Science* 2:201–215.

Daniel, J. (1995) 'One China or two? South Africa's foreign policy dilemma'. Unpublished paper.

Danziger, J. N. (1991) *Understanding the Political World: An Introduction to Political Science*. New York: Longman.

Darcy de Oliveira, M & Tandon, R. (1996) 'The emergence of global civil society', *Issues of Democracy*, 1(8):18–21.

Davidson, B (1974) *Africa in History: Themes and Outlines*. New York: Collier Books.

Davidson, B. (1978) *Africa in Modern History*. London: Penguin.

Davidson, B. (1992) *The Black Man's Burden: Africa and the Curse of the Nation-State*. Oxford: James Currey.

Davies, M. (1995) 'South Africa's relations with the PRC and the ROC, 1949–1995: the question of diplomatic recognition'. Unpublished M.A. thesis, University of the Witwatersrand.

Davies, R. (1996) 'South Africa's economic relations with Africa: current patterns and future perspectives'. In *South Africa in Africa: Within or Apart*, edited by Adedeji, A. pp. 167–192. London: Zed Books.

Davies, R. (1997) 'Promoting regional integration in Southern Africa: an analysis of prospects and problems from a South African perspective'. In *Bridging the Rift*: *The New South Africa in Africa*, edited by Swatuk, L. A. & Black, D. R. pp. 109–126. Boulder: Westview.

Davies, R. (1998) 'South Africa and Southern Africa'. In *South Africa and Southern Africa: Regional Integration and Emerging Markets*, edited by Handley, A. & Mills, G. pp. 40–50. Johannesburg: South African Institute for International Affairs.

De Rivera, J. (1968) *The Psychological Dimension of Foreign Policy*. Columbus: CE Merrill.

Department of Defence (1996) 'Defence in a Democracy': White Paper on National Defence for the Republic of South Africa. Pretoria: Department of Defence.

Deutsch, K. W. and Singer, J. D. (1964) 'Multipolar Power System and International Stability', *World Politics* XVI (April):390–406.

Diamond, L., Linz, J. J. & Lipset, S. M. (eds) (1988) *Democracy in Developing Countries, Volume 2: Africa*. Boulder: Lynne Rienner.

Dougherty, J. E. & Pfaltzgraff, R. L. (1981) *Contending Theories of International Relations*:

A Comprehensive Survey. New York: Harper & Row.

Dunn, W. N. (1994) *Public Policy Analysis: An Introduction* (2nd edition). Englewood Cliffs: Prentice-Hall.

Eagleburger, L. S (1989) 'The 21st century: American foreign policy challenges.' In *America's Global Interests: A New Agenda,* edited by Hamilton, E. K. pp. 242–260. New York: Norton.

Eigen, L. D. & Siegel, J. P. (eds) (1993) *The Macmilllan Dictionary of Political Quotations.* New York: Macmillan.

Elaigwu J. (1993) 'Nation-building and changing political structures.' In *Africa since 1935. General History of Africa, Vol. VIII,* edited by Mazrui, A. pp. 435–467. London: Heinemann.

Elrod, R. B. (1989) 'The Concert of Europe: A Fresh Look at an International System.' In *International Conflict and Conflict Management* (second edition), edited by Matthews, R. Rubinoff, A. & Gross Stein, J. pp. 448–457. Ontario: Prentice-Hall.

Esterhuysen, P. (comp.) (1996) *Africa at a Glance, 1996/7.* Pretoria: Africa Institute of South Africa.

Esterhuysen, P. (comp.) (1998) *Africa at a Glance, 1997/8.* Pretoria: Africa Institute of South Africa.

Evans, G. & Newnham, J. (1992) *The Dictionary of World Politics; A Reference Guide to Concepts, Ideas and Institutions.* New York: Harvester Wheatsheaf.

Evans, L. H. (1995) 'The challenges of restructuring'. In *Mission Imperfect: Redirecting South Africa's Foreign Policy,* edited by Landsberg, C, Le Pere, G. & Van Nieuwkerk, A. pp. 70–77. Johannesburg: Foundation for Global Dialogue; Centre for Policy Studies.

Fairbank, J, Reischauer, E. & Craig, E. (1989) *East Asia: Tradition and Transformation.* Boston: Houghton Mifflin.

Feldstein, M. (1996) 'Security experts warn of loose nukes', CNN Interactive News, 12 March.

First, R. (1970) *The Barrell of a Gun: Political Power in Africa and the Coup d'Etat.* Middlesex: Penguin.

Fomerand, J. (1996) 'UN conferences: media events or genuine diplomacy?' *Global Governance,* 2(3):361–75.

Foundation for Global Dialogue. (1996), *The Ninth Conference of the United Nations Conference on Trade and Development: South Africa Preparing for the Agenda* (FGD Occasional Paper No. 5). Johannesburg: FGD.

Frankel, J. (1968) *The Making of Foreign Policy.* London: Oxford University Press.

Frankel, P. (1984) *Pretoria's Praetorians: Civil Military Relations in South Africa.* Cambridge: Cambridge University Press.

Freund, B. (1984) *The Making of Contemporary Africa: The Development of African Society since 1800.* London: Macmillan.

Geldenhuys, D. J. (1984) *The Diplomacy of Isolation: South Africa's Foreign Policy Making.* Johannesburg: Macmillan.

Geldenhuys, D. J. (1987) 'South Africa's international isolation', *International Affairs Bulletin,* 11(1):29–37.

Geldenhuys, D. J. (1995) *South Africa and the China question: The Case for Dual Recognition* (East Asia Project Working Paper No. 6). Johannesburg: University of the Witwatersrand.

Ghils, P. (1992) 'International civil society: international non-governmental organisations in the international system', *International Social Science Journal,* 44:417–431.

Gill, S. and Law, D. (1988) *The Global Political Economy: Perspectives, Problems and Policies.* New York: Harvester Wheatsheaf.

Gilpin, R. (1987) *The Political Economy of International Relations.* Princeton: Princeton University Press.

Gjural, I. K. (1988) *A Foreign Policy for India.* New Delhi: Ministry of External Affairs.

Goldstein, J. (1996) *International Relations.* New York: Harper Collins College Publishers.

Gordon, A. & Gordon, D. (1996) *Understanding Contemporary Africa.* Boulder: Lynne Rienner.

Gordon, D. (1996) 'African politics.' In *Understanding Contemporary Africa,* edited by Gordon, A. & Gordon, D. pp. 53–90. Boulder: Lynne Rienner.

Gray, H.P. (1995) 'The modern structure of international economic policies', *Transnational Corporations,* 4(3):49–66.

Green, R. H. (1991) 'The broken pot: the social fabric, economic disaster and adjustment in Africa.' In *The IMF the World Bank and the African Debt: Volume 2 – The Social and Political Impact,* edited by Onimode, B. pp. 31–55. London: Zed Books and the Institute for African Alternatives.

Griffiths I. (1984) *An Atlas of African Affairs.* London: Routledge.

Griffiths, I. L. (1995) *The African Inheritance.* London; New York: Routledge.

Groom, A. J. R. & Light, M. (eds) (1994) *Contemporary International Relations: A Guide to Theory.* London: Pinter.

Gulick, E. V. (1955) *Europe's Classical Balance of Power* . Ithaca: Cornell University Press.

Gutteridge, W. (1969) *The Military in African Politics.* London: Methuen.

Gutteridge, W. (1975) *Military Regimes in Africa.* London: Methuen.

Haas, E. (1953) ' The balance of power: prescriptive concept, or propaganda?' *World Politics* 5(July):442–477.

Hanlon, J. (1986) *Beggar your Neighbours: Apartheid Power in Southern Africa.* London: Catholic Institute for International Relations; James Currey; Indiana University Press.

Harbeson, J. & Rothchild, D. (1991) 'Africa in post-Cold War international politics: chang-ing agendas.' In *Africa in World Politics,* edited by Harbeson, J. & Rothchild, D. pp. 1–15. Boulder: Westview.

Harbeson, J. & Rothchild, D. (1991) *Africa in World Politics.* Boulder: Westview.

Hargreaves, J. D. (1988) *Decolonisation in Africa.* London: Longman.

Harris, P. (1986) *The End of the Third World.* London: Penguin.

Harvey, C., & Lewis, S. R. Jr. (1990) *Policy Choice and Development Performance in Botswana.* New York: St Martin's Press.

Havenga, M. (1995) 'The dilemma of the two Chinas: an economic perspective.' In *South Africa and the two Chinas dilemma,* edited by The SAIIA Research Group, pp. 32–46. Johannesburg: South African Institute of International Affairs; Foundation for Global Dialogue.

Hayek, F. von (1960) *The Constitution of Liberty.* London: Routledge & Kegan Paul.

Hettne, B. (ed.). (1995) *International Political Economy: Understanding Global Disorder.* London: Zed Books.

Hirst, P. & Thompson, G (1996) *Globalisation in Question.* Cambridge: Polity Press.

Hobsbawm, E. J. (1975). *The Age of Capital: 1848–1875.* London: Weidenfeld and Nicolson.

Hobson, J. A. (1902) *Imperialism: A Study.* London: Allen & Unwin.

Hodder-Williams, R. (1984) *An Introduction to the Politics of Tropical Africa.* London: George Allen & Unwin.

Hoffman, S. (1981) *Duties Beyond Borders: On the Limits and Possibilities of Ethical International Politics.* Syracuse: Syracuse University Press.

Hoffmann, S. (1972) ' Weighing the Balance of Power', *Foreign Affairs* 59(July):618–643.

Holden, M. (1996) *Economic Integration and Trade Liberalization in Southern Africa: Is there a Role for South Africa?* (World Bank Discussion

Paper No. 342). Washington DC: World Bank.

Holsti, K. J. (1991) *Peace and War: Armed Conflicts and International Order 1648–1989.* Cambridge: Cambridge University Press.

Holsti, K. J. (1992) 'Power, Capability, and Influence in International Politics.' In *The Global Agenda: Issues and Perspectives* edited by Kegley, C. and Wittkopf, E. pp. 9–21. New York: McGraw-Hill.

Holsti, K. J. (1995) *International Politics: A Framework for analysis.* Englewood Cliffs: Prentice-Hall.

Holsti, K. J. (1995) *International Politics: A Framework for Analysis* (7th edition). Englewood Cliffs: Prentice-Hall.

Holsti, O. R (1962) 'The belief system and national images', *Journal of Conflict Resolution,* 6:244–252.

Hoogvelt, A. (1997). *Globalisation and the postcolonial World: the new political economy of development.* Basingstoke: MacMillan.

Hope, R. & Kayira, G. (1996) 'The economic crisis in Southern Africa: some perspectives of its origins and nature', *Development Southern Africa,* 13(3):881–894.

Hsü, I. C. Y. (1995) *The Rise of Modern China (5th edition).* Oxford: Oxford University Press.

Huntington, S. P. (1968) *Political Order in Changing Societies.* New Haven: Yale University Press.

Huntington, S. P. (1991*) The Third wave: Democratization in the Late Twentieth Century.* Norman: University of Oklahoma Press.

Hurrell, A. (1995) 'Crisis of Ecological Viability? Global Environmental Change and the Nation-State'. In *Contemporary Crisis of the Nation State?* edited by Dunn, J. pp. 146–165. Oxford: Blackwell.

Husain, I. & Underwood, J. (eds) (1991) *African External Finance in the 1990s.* Washington, DC: World Bank.

Inukai, I. (1993) 'Why aid and why not? Japan and sub-Saharan Africa.' In *Japan's Foreign Aid – Power and Policy in a New Era,* edited by Koppel, B. M. & Orr, R. M. Boulder: Westview.

Isaak, R. A. (1995) *Managing World Economic Change : International Political Economy* (2nd edition). Englewood Cliffs: Prentice-Hall.

Jackson, R. H. (1983) *The Non-Aligned, the UN and the Superpowers.* New York: Praeger.

Jackson, R. H. & Rosberg, C. G. (1982) 'Why Africa's weak states persist: the empirical and the juridical in statehood', *World Politics,* 35(1):1–24.

Jackson, R. H. (1990) *Quasi-States: Sovereignty, International Relations and the Third World.* Cambridge: Cambridge University Press.

Jervis, R. (1968) 'Hypotheses on misperception', *World Politics,* 20(3):454–479.

Johnson, A. G. (ed.) (1995) *The Blackwell Dictionary of Sociology.* Oxford: Blackwell.

Johnson, P. (1991) *The Birth of the Modern: World Society 1815–1830.* London: Weidenfeld and Nicolson.

Kaplan, M. A. (1962) *System and Process in International Politics.* New York: Wiley.

Karvonen, L. & Sundelius, B. (1987) *Internationalization and Foreign Policy Management.* London: Gower Publishing.

Kautilya (1992) 'The strategy by which rulers should protect their interests.' In *Basic Texts in International Relations,* edited by Luard, E. pp. 126–129. London: Macmillan.

Kegley, C. W. (1995) *Controversies in International Relations Theory: Realism and the Neoliberal Challenge.* New York: St Martin's Press.

Kegley, C. W. & Wittkopf, E. R. (1997) *World Politics: Trend and Transformation* (6th edition). New York: St Martin's Press.

Kennedy, P. (1987) *Rise and Fall of the Great Powers.* New York: Random House.

Keohane, R. O. & Nye, J. (1977) *Power and Interdependence*. Boston: Little Brown

Keohane, R. O. & Murphy, C. N. (1992) 'International institutions'. In *Encyclopedia of Government and Politics*, edited by Hawkesworth, M. & Kogan, M. Vol. 2, pp. 871–886. London: Routledge.

Keohane, R. O. (1984) *After Hegemony: Co-operation and Discord in the World Political Economy*. Princeton: Princeton University Press.

Khapoya, V. (1994) *The African Experience: An Introduction*. Englewood Cliffs: Prentice-Hall.

Kukreja, S. (1996) 'The Development Dilemma: NIC's and LDC's.' In *Introduction to International Political Economy*, edited by Balaam, M. D. and Veseth, M. pp. 311–338. Englewood Cliffs: Prentice-Hall.

Kuper, K. (1995) *The Two Chinas Debate in South Africa: A Political Economy Analysis of the Issues and Some Policy Proposals*. Pretoria: Department of Trade and Industry.

Lambrechts, K. (1996) 'South Africa and the Maghreb: Past, Present and Future'. In *Paris, Pretoria and the African Continent: The International Relations of States and Societies in Transition*, edited by Alden, C. & Daloz, J. P. London: Macmillan.

Landsberg, C. & Masiza, Z. (1996) *The Anarchic Miracle: Global (Dis)order and Syndicated Crime in South Africa*. Johannesburg: Centre for Policy Studies.

Lee, L. T. (1995) 'A history of the PRC's policy towards Taiwan'. In *South Africa and the Two Chinas Dilemma*, edited by The SAIIA Research Group, pp. 19–31. Johannesburg: South African Institute of International Affairs; Foundation for Global Dialogue.

Leistner, E. (1997) 'Regional co-operation in Sub-Saharan Africa', *Africa Insight* 77:112–123.

Leistner, Erich (1995) 'Considering the methods and effects of regional integration.' In *South Africa in the Global Political Economy*, edited

by Mills, G. Begg, A. & Van Nieuwkerk, A. pp. 265–279. Johannesburg: South African Institute of International Affairs.

Lenin, V. I. (1939) *Imperialism: The Highest Stage of Capitalism*. New York: International Publishing Co.

Levinson, L. L. (1963) *The Left Handed Dictionary*. New York: Collier.

Leys, C. (1975) *Underdevelopment in Kenya: The Political Economy of Neo-colonialism*. London: Heinemann.

Leysens, A. & Fourie, P. (1997) 'Relations with Latin America'. In *Change and South African External Relations*, edited by Carlsnaes, W. & Muller, M. pp. 149–173. Johannesburg: Thompson.

Lindblom, C. E. & Braybrook, D. (1963) *A Strategy of Decision*. New York: Free Press.

Lindblom, C. E. & Braybrook, D. (1968) *The Policy-making Process*. Englewood Cliffs: Prentice-Hall.

Lingle, C. (1996) *Singapore's Authoritarian Capitalism: Asian Values, Free Market Illusions and Political Dependency*. Barcelona: Edition Scirocco.

Lodge, T. (1987) 'State of exile: The ANC of South Africa 1976–1986', *Third World Quarterly* 9(1):1–27.

Lovejoy, P. E. (1983) *Transformations in Slavery: A History of Slavery in Africa*. Cambridge: Cambridge University Press.

Luard, E. (ed.) (1992) *Basic Texts in International Relations*. London: Macmillan.

Lumsdaine, D. H. (1993) *Moral Vision in International Politics: The Foreign Aid Regime, 1949–1989*. Princeton: Princeton University Press.

Macridis, R. C. (ed.) (1976) *Foreign Policy in World Politics* (5th edition). Englewood Cliffs: Prentice-Hall.

Mamdani, M. (1996) *Citizen and Subject: Contemporary Africa and the Legacy of Late Colonialism*. Princeton: Princeton University

Press.

Mandela, N. (1993) 'South Africa's Future Foreign Policy', *Foreign Affairs* 72 (5):86–97.

Mandela, N. (1997) Address to 50th National Conference of the African National Congress at Mafikeng, 16 December.

Marx, K. (1935) 'Theses on Feuerbach'. In *A Handbook of Marxism*, compiled by Burns, E. pp. 228–231. London: Victor Gollancz.

Mawlawi, F. 'New conflicts, new challenges: the evolving role of non-governmental actors', *Journal of International Affairs*, 46(2):391–413.

Mayer, M. J. & Thomas, R. H. (1997) 'Trade integration in Southern African Development Community: prospects and problems', *Development Southern Africa*, 14(3):327–353.

Mazrui, A. A. (1963) 'On the concept of "We are all Africans"', *American Political Science Review*, LVII(1):88–97.

Mazrui, A. A. (1977) *Africa's International Relations: The Diplomacy of Dependency and Change*. London: Heinemann.

Mazrui, A. A. (ed.) (1993) *Africa Since 1935. General History of Africa, Vol. VIII*. London: Heinemann.

Mbeki, T. (1996) Statement of Deputy President Thabo Mbeki on the occasion of the adoption by the Constitutional Assembly of 'The Republic of South Africa Constitution Bill 1996', 8 May.

Mbeki, T. (1997) Speech to the South African National Assembly, 10 June.

McGowan, P. J. (1997) 'The global informational economy and South Africa.' In *Change and South African External Relations*, edited by Carlsnaes, W. and Muller, M. pp. 279–311 Halfway House: International Thomson Publishing.

Meacham, C. J. (1997) *How the Tiger Lost its Stripes: An Exploration into the Endangerment of a Species*. New York: Harcourt Brace.

Medhurst, R. (1995) 'The effect of Taiwan's pressure on South African foreign policy.'

Pretoria: Foreign Service Institute.

Meier, G. & Seers, D. (eds). (1985) *Pioneers in Development*. Oxford: Oxford University Press.

Mill, J. S. (1983) *On Liberty*. Harmondsworth: Penguin.

Miller, H. (1996) 'A critique of anarchy.' In. *International Politics*, edited by Art, R. C. & Jervis, R. pp. 70–75. New York: Harper Collins.

Mills, G. (1995) 'The Case for Exclusive Recognition.' In *South Africa and the two Chinas dilemma*, edited by The SAIIA Research Group, pp. 81–99. Johannesburg: South African Institute of International Affairs and Foundation for Global Dialogue.

Mills, G. (1997) 'Leaning all over the place? The not-so-new South Africa's foreign policy.' In *Fairy Godmother, Hegemon or Partner: In Search of a South African Foreign Policy* edited by Solomon, H. pp. 19–34. ISS Monograph Series 13. Midrand: Institute for Security Studies.

Minogue, M. & Molloy, J. (eds) (1974) *African Aims and Attitudes: Selected Documents*. London: Cambridge University Press.

Mittelman, J. (ed.). (1996) *Globalization*. Boulder: Lynne Rienner.

Mohr, P. *et al.* (1995) *Economics for South African Students*. Pretoria: JL van Schaik.

Morgenthau, H. J. (1962) 'A political theory of foreign aid', *American Political Science Review*, 56:301–309.

Morgenthau, H. J. (1978) *Politics Among Nations: The Struggle for Power and Peace* (5th edition) New York: Alfred A. Knopf.

Mortimer, R. (1996) 'ECOMOG, Liberia and regional security in West Africa.' In *Africa in the New International Order: Rethinking State Sovereignty and Regional Security*, edited by Keller, E. & Rothchild, D. pp. 149–164. Boulder: Lynne Rienner.

Moynihan, D. P. (1993) 'Congress and the UN',

presentation to the annual meeting of the Academic Council on the United Nations System held at the International Monetary Fund, Washington, DC, 23 June.

Mphaisha, C. J. J. (1997) *Conference Diplomacy and Ocean Resource Development. Zambian Papers 19*. Lusaka: University of Zambia.

Muir, R. (1970) *The Expansion of Europe: The Culmination of Modern History*. New York: Kennikat Press.

Muller, M. (1997) 'The Institutional Dimension: The Department of Foreign Affairs and Overseas Missions.' In *Change and South African External Relations*, edited by Carlsnaes, W. and Muller, M. pp. 51–72. Johannesburg: International Thomson Publishing.

Murphy, C. N. (1987) 'Learning the national interest in Africa', *TransAfrica Forum*, 4(1):49–63.

Mytelka, L (ed.). (1994) *South-South Co-operation in a Global Perspective*. Paris: Development Centre OECD.

Nagel, E. (1971) *The Structure of Science*. London: Routledge & Kegan Paul.

Neack, L., Hey, J. A. & Haney, P. J. (eds) (1995) *Foreign Policy Analysis: Continuity and Change in its Second Generation*. Englewood Cliffs: Prentice-Hall.

Nel, P. R. (1998) 'A society of communities? A report card of diversity and the state system 350 years after Westphalia'. Unpublished paper delivered at the International Pluralism Colloquium, Living Difference: Towards a Society of communities', 24–27 August 1998, University of the Witwatersrand, Johannesburg.

Network Wizards (1998) *Internet Survey July 1998*. [http://www.nw.com/zone/]

Network Wizards [http://www.nw.com/zone/WWW/dist-bynum.html]

Nkrumah, K. (1965) *Neo-colonialism: The Last Stage of Imperialism*. London: Panaf Books.

Nkuhlu, M. (1996) 'South Africa and the concept of the Indian Ocean Rim: a strategic, political and economic analysis.' In *South Africa and the Indian Ocean Rim: Obstacles and Opportunities* (FGD Occasional Paper No. 4). Johannesburg: FGD.

Nossal, K. (1998) *The Patterns of World Politics*. Scarborough: Prentice-Hall.

Nye, J. (1993) *Understanding International Conflicts: An Introduction to Theory and History*. New York: Harper Collins.

Nye, J. (1993) *Understanding International Conflicts: An Introduction to Theory and History*. New York: Harper Collins.

O'Keefe, P. (1988) 'Toxic terrorism', *Review of African Political Economy*, 42:84–90.

Obeng, F (*see* Ahwireng-Obeng)

Oden, B. (1996) *Southern African Futures: Critical Factors for Regional Development in Southern Africa* (Discussion Paper No. 7). Uppsala: Nordic Afrika Institute.

Onimode, B. (1996) 'The state of the African political economy'. In *South Africa in Africa: With or Apart?* edited by Adedeji, A. pp. 101–117, London: Zed Books.

Onimode, B. (ed.) (1991) *The IMF, The World Bank and the African Debt: The Social and Political Impact*. London: Zed Books.

Orkin, M. (ed.) (1989) *Sanctions Against Apartheid*. Cape Town: David Philip.

Papp, D. S. (1994) *Contemporary International Relations* (fourth edition). New York: Macmillan.

Ponte, S. (1994) 'The World Bank and "Adjustment in Africa"', *Review of African Political Economy*, 22(66)December:539–558.

Qiang, Z. & Zhonggui, Z. (1997) 'A wise strategic decision', *Contemporary International Relations*, 7(12):15–20.

Raffer, K. & Singer, H. (1996) *The Foreign Aid Business: Economic Assistance and Development*

Co-operation. Cheltenham; Edward Elgar.

Ramsay, F. J. (ed.) (1997) *Global Studies: Africa*. Guilford: Dushkin/McGraw-Hill.

Ray, J. L. (1992) *Global Politics* (5th edition). Boston: Houghton Mifflin.

Reynolds, C. (1981) *Modes of Imperialism*. New York: St Martin's Press.

Rieff, D. (1997) 'Charity on the rampage: The business of foreign aid', *Foreign Affairs*, January/February:132–138.

Robinson, R. & Gallagher, with Deny A. (1981) *Africa and the Victorians: The Official Mind of Imperialism*. London: Macmillan.

Rodney, W. (1972) *How Europe Underdeveloped Africa*. London: Bogle-L'Ouverture.

Roosevelt, F. D. (1958) 'A new bill of rights.' In *Liberalism: Its Meaning and History*, edited by J. Salwyn Schapiro, pp. 184–185. New York: D. van Nostrand.

Rosecrance, R. N. (1966) : 'Bipolarity, Multipolarity, and the Future', *Journal of Conflict Resolution* 10(September):314–327.

Rosenau, J. (1961) *Public Opinion and Foreign Policy*. New York: Random House.

Rothstein, R. L. (1979) *Global Bargaining: UNCTAD and the Quest for a New International Economic Order*. Princeton: Princeton University Press.

Russett, B. and Starr, H. (1981) *World Politics: The Menu for Choice*. San Francisco: W. H. Freeman.

Sabine, G. H. (1961) *A History of Political Theory* (3rd edition) New York: Holt, Rinehart & Winston.

Sachs, J. (1997) 'The Limits of Convergence: Nature, Nurture and Growth', *The Economist*, June 14.

SADC (1995) *Declaration Treaty and Protocol of Southern African Development Community*. Gabarone: SADC Secretariat.

SADC (1996) *SADC Protocol on Trade*. Maseru: SADC Secretariat, August.

Said, A. A. & Lerche Jnr., C. O. & Lerche III, C. O. (1995) *Concepts of International Politics in Global Perspective* (4th edition). Englewood Cliffs: Prentice-Hall.

Sakamoto, Y. (ed.) (1994) *Global Transformation: Challanges to the State System* . Tokyo: United Nations University.

Samatar A. I. (1988) *Socialist Somalia: Rhetoric and Reality*. London: Zed Books.

Schoeman, M. (1998) 'Celebrating Westphalia's 350th birthday: reflections on the state of the state in Southern Africa', *The South African Journal of International Affairs*, 5(2):1–20.

Seidman, A. & Makgetla N. (1980) *Outposts of Monopoly Capitalism: Southern African in the Changing Global Economy*. London: Zed Press.

Shaw, T. (1994) 'The South in the "New World (dis)order": towards a political economy of third world foreign policy in the 1990s', *Third World Quarterly*, 15(1):17–30.

Shaw, T. (1997) 'Post-apartheid South(ern) Africa in the new international divisions of labour and power: how marginal?' In *Bridging the Rift: The New South Africa in Africa*, edited by Swatuk, L. A. & Black, D. R. pp. 23–40. Boulder: Westview.

Singer, M. R. (1972) *Weak States in a World of Powers: The Dynamics of International Relationships*. New York: Free Press.

Singh, S. (1997) 'Sino-South African relations: Coming Full Circle'. *African Security Review* 6 (2), pp. 52–59.

Smith, M. J. (1986) *Realist Thought from Weber to Kissinger*. Baton Rouge: Louisiana State University Press.

Sobhan, F. (1987) *Opportunities for South-South Co-operation* (ISIS Issue Paper). Kuala Lumpur: Institute of Strategic and International Studies.

Sobhan, R. (1992) 'Changing patterns of interdependence: the need for symmetry in North–South adjustment processes', *The Round Table*, 324.

Söderbaum, F. (1996) *The New Regionalism and the Quest for Development Co-operation and Integration in Southern Africa.* Lund: University of Lund (Department of Economics).

Sole, D. (1994) 'South Africa's foreign policy assumptions and objectives from Hertzog to De Klerk', *South African Journal of International Affairs*, 2(1):104–113.

Solomon, H & Cilliers, J. (1996) 'People, poverty and peace: human security in Southern Africa', *IDP Monograph Series*, 4, May.

Solomon, H. and Van Aardt (eds.) (1998) *Caring Security in Africa.* ISS Monograph Series, 20. Midrand: Institute for Security Studies.

Sono, T. (1995) 'The case for dual recognition.' In *South Africa and the two Chinas dilemma*, edited by The SAIIA Research Group, pp. 72–80. Johannesburg: South African Institute of International Affairs and Foundation for Global Dialogue.

Southall, R. (1995) 'A critical reflection on the GNU's foreign policy initiatives and responses.' In *Mission Imperfect: Redirecting South Africa's Foreign Policy*, edited by Landsberg, C. Le Pere, G. and Van Nieuwkerk, A. pp. 39–44. Johannesburg: Foundation for Global Dialogue and Centre for Policy Studies.

Spanier, J (1975) *Games Nations Play* . New York: Praeger.

Spiro, P. (1995) 'New global communities: non-governmental organisations in international decision-making institutions', *The Washington Quarterly*, Winter:45–56.

Sprout, H. & Sprout, M. (1962) *Foundations of International Politics.* Princeton: D. van Nostrand.

Spruyt, H. (1994). *The Sovereign State and its Competitors.* Princeton: Princeton University Press.

Sridharan, K. (1998) 'G-15 and South-South co-operation: promise and performance', *Third World Quarterly*, 19(3):357–374.

Stewart, F. (1987) 'Money and South-South co-operation', *Third World Quarterly*, 9(4):1184–1205.

Strange, S. (1988) *States and Markets: an Introduction to International Political Economy.* London: Pinter Publishers.

Strange, S. (1991) 'An eclectic approach.' In *The New International Political Economy*, edited by Murphy, C. & Tooze, R. pp. 32–50. Boulder: Lynne Rienner.

Strange, S. (1996) *The Retreat of the State.* Cambridge: Cambridge University Press.

Strange, S. (1998) *Mad Money: A Sequel to 'Casino Capitalism'.* Manchester: Manchester University Press.

Stubbs. R. & Underhill, G. (eds). (1994) *Political Economy of the Changing Global Order.* London: Macmillan.

Suttner, R. (1995) 'Dilemmas of South African Foreign Policy: The Question of China'. In *South Africa and the Two Chinas Dilemma*, edited by The SAIIA Research Group, pp. 4–9. Johannesburg: South African Institute of International Affairs and Foundation for Global Dialogue.

Suttner, R. (1996) 'Brief review of South African foreign policy since April 1994.' Unpublished paper.

Suttner, R. (1996) 'Parliament and foreign policy process.' In *South African Yearbook of International Affairs*, edited by Mills, G. pp. 136–143. Johannesburg: South African Institute of International Affairs.

Tandon, Y. (1997) 'Globalization and the South: the logic of exploitation', *International Politics and Society*, 4:29–48.

The South Centre. (1993) *Facing the Challenge: Responses to the Report of the South Commission.* London: Zed Books.

The South Commission. (1990) *The Challenge of the South, Report of the South Commission.* Oxford: Oxford University Press.

The Terrorism Research Centre

[http://www.terrorism.com].

Thiam, I. D. & Mulira,J. (1993) 'Africa and the socialist countries'. In *Africa since 1935. General History of Africa, Vol. VIII*, edited by Mazrui, A. pp. 798–828. London: Heinemann.

Thomas, C. & Wilkin, P. (eds). (1997) *Globalization and the South*. London: Macmillan.

Thomas, S. (1997) *The Diplomacy of Liberation: The Foreign Relations of the African National Congress Since 1960*. London: IB Taurus.

Thompson, V. B. (1987) *The Making of the African Diaspora in the Americas 1441–1900*. London: Longman.

Thomson, D. (1950) *England in the Nineteenth Century: 1815–1914*. Harmondsworth: Penguin Books.

Thucydides (1985) *History of the Peloponnesian War*. Harmondsworth: Penguin.

Thurow, L.C. (1992) *Head to Head: Coming Economic Battles Among Japan, Europe, and America*. New York: William Morrow.

Tinker, H. (1977) *Race, Conflict and the International Order: From Empire to United Nations*. London: Macmillan.

Todaro, M. (1994) *Economic Development* (5th edition). New York: Longman.

Todaro, M. (1997) *Economic Development* (6th edition). New York: Longman.

Tordoff, W. (1997) *Government and Politics in Africa* (3rd edition). Bloomington; Indianapolis: Indiana University Press.

UNCTAD (1997) *Trade and Development Report*. New York: United Nations.

UNCTAD. (1994) *World Investment Report: Transnational Corporations, Employment and the Workplace*. New York: United Nations.

UNCTAD. (1997) Press Release, UNCTAD/1848, 17 September.

United Nations Development Programme (1994) *Human Development Report, 1994*. New York:

Oxford University Press.

United Nations Development Programme (1997) *Human Development Report, 1997*. New York: Oxford University Press.

Vale, P. (1997) 'Understanding the upstairs and the downstairs: prospects for a post-apartheid foreign policy'. In *Niche Diplomacy: Middle Powers and Global Change*, edited by Cooper, A. pp. 197–214. London: Macmillan.

Van Aardt, M. (1996) 'A foreign policy to die for: South Africa's response to the Nigerian crisis', *Africa Insight*, 26(2):107–119.

Van Aardt, M. (1997) 'Factors influencing development prospects in South Africa.' In *Change and South African External Relations*, edited by Carlsnaes, W. & Muller, M. pp. 253–267. Johannesburg: International Thompson Publishing.

Van der Westhuizen, J. (1998) 'South Africa's emergence as a middle power', *Third World Quarterly* (19)3:435–455.

Van Nieuwkerk, A. (1996) 'Unpacking the foreign policy black box', *Global Dialogue*, 1(2):1–2.

Van Nieuwkerk, A. (1998) 'South Africa's foreign policy mood: moral internationalism or commercial realism', *Global Dialogue*, 3(1):7–8.

Vaquez, J. (ed.) (1990) *Classics of International Relations*. Englewood Cliffs: Prentice Hall.

Viotti, P.R. & Kauppi, M.V. (eds) (1993) *International Relations Theory: Realism, Pluralism, Globalism*. New York: Macmillan.

Vogt, M. A. (1992) *Liberian Crisis and ECOMOG: A Bold Attempt at Regional Peace-Keeping*. Lagos: Gabumo.

Walker, S. (1987) 'Role theory and the origins of foreign policy.' In *New Directions in the Study of Foreign Policy*, edited by Hermann, C. *et al.* pp. 269–284. Boston: Allen & Unwin.

Wallerstein, (1979) *The Capitalist World-Economy*. Cambridge: Cambridge University Press

Wallerstein, I. (1974) *The Modern World System:*

Capitalist Agriculture and the Origins of the European World Economy in the 16th Century. New York: Academic Press.

Wallerstein, I. (1979) *The Capitalist World Economy.* Cambridge: Cambridge University Press.

Wallerstein, I. (1996) 'The inter-state structure of the modern world system.' In *International Theory: Positivism and Beyond*, edited by S. Smith, S. Booth, K. and Zalewski, M. pp. 87–107. Cambridge: Cambridge University Press.

Walt, S. M. (1998) 'International relations: one world, many theories', *Foreign Policy* 110(Spring):29–48.

Walter, A. (1993) *World Power and World Money.* New York: Harvester Wheatsheaf.

Walters, R. S. & Blake, D. H. (1992) *The Politics of Global Economic Relations* (4th edition). Englewood Cliffs: Prentice-Hall.

Walters, R. S. and Blake, D. H. (eds.) (1992) *The Politics of Global Economic Relations* (fourth edition). Englewood Cliffs: Prentice-Hall.

Waltz, K. N. (1967) 'International Structure, National Force, and the Balance of World Power', *Journal of International Affairs*, 21:215–231.

Waltz, K. N. (1979) *Theory of International Politics.* London: Addison-Wesley.

Waltz, K. N.(1990) 'Realist thought and Neorealist theory. In *Evolution of Theory in International Relations* edited by Rothsted, R. pp. 21–38. Columbia: University of South Carolina Press.

Wapner, P. (1995) 'Politics beyond the state. environmental activism and world civic politics', *World Politics*, 47:311–340.

Wayman, F. W. & Diehl, P. F (1994) 'Realism reconsidered: the realpolitik framework and its basic propositions'. In *Reconstructing Realpolitik*, edited by Wayman, F. W. & Diehl, P. F. pp. 3–28. Ann Arbor: University of Michigan Press.

Weber, M. (1964) *The Theory of Social and Economic Organisation* (edited by Parsons, T.). New York: Free Press.

Weiner, M. & Huntington, S. P. (eds) (1987) *Understanding Political Development: An Analytic Study.* Boston: Little, Brown.

Weiss, T. G. (ed.) (1998) *Beyond UN Subcontracting: Task-Sharing with Regional Security Arrangements and Service-Providing NGOs.* New York: St Martin's Press.

Wemping, H. (1996) 'An analysis on the relationship between the new South Africa and Africa.' Paper presented at the Conference on the Prospect of Political and Economic Development in South Africa. Beijing: Institute of West Asian and African Studies, June 1996.

Wilkinson, P. (1996) 'Blood is spilling all over the world', *Mail and Guardian*, 2–8 August.

Williams, M. (1994) *International Economic Organisations and the Third World.* Hertfordshire: Harvester Wheatsheaf.

Williams, P. (1997) 'Transnational organised crime and international security: a global assessment.' In *Society Under Siege. Crime, Violence and Illegal Weapons. Towards Collaborative Peace Series* (Vol. 1), edited by Gamba, J. pp. 11–41. Halfway House: Institute for Security Studies.

Wilson, H. S. (1977) *The Imperial Experience in Africa since 1870.* Minneapolis: University of Minnesota Press.

Wong, Y. (1994) 'Impotence and intransigence: state behaviour in the throes of deepening global crisis', *Politics and the Life Sciences*, 13(1):3–14.

World Bank (1991) *World Development Report.* New York: Oxford University Press.

World Bank. (1989) *Sub-Saharan Africa: From Crisis to Sustainable Growth.* Washington, DC: The World Bank.

World Bank. (1993) *The East Asian Miracle.* Washington DC: World Bank.

World Bank. (1995) *A Continent in Transition: Sub-Saharan Africa in the Mid-1990s*. Oxford: Oxford University Press.

World Bank. (1998) *African Development Indicators 1997*. Washington DC: World Bank.

Young, C. & Turner, T. (1985) *The Rise and Decline of the Zairian State*. Madison: University of Wisconsin Press.

Young, C. (1994) *The African Colonial State in Comparative Perspective*. New Haven: Yale University Press.

Zartman, I. W. (1995) 'Introduction: posing the problem of state collapse.' In *Collapsed States : The Disintegration and Restoration of Legitimate Authority* edited by Zartman, I. W. pp. 1–11. Boulder: Lynne Rienner.

Zartman, I. W. (ed.) (1997) *Governance as Conflict Management: Politics and Violence in West Africa*. Washington DC: Brookings Institution.

Acronyms

AAPS	All-African Press Service
ACDSS	African Centre for Development and Strategic Studies
ACP	African, Caribbean, and Pacific Countries
ADB	African Development Bank
AI	Amnesty International
ANC	African National Congress (South Africa)
APEC	Asia-Pacific Economic Co-operation
ASEAN	Association of Southeast Asian Nations
ASTRO	Association of State Trading Organisations
BLNS	Botswana, Lesotho, Namibia, Swaziland
BOP	Balance of payments
BSACO	British South Africa Company
BSFF	Buffer Stock Finance Facility
CAP	Common Agricultural Policy
CCFF	Compensating and Contingency Financing Facility
CCM	Chama Cha Mapinduzi Party (Tanzania)
CIA	Central Intelligence Agency (US)
CIS	Commonwealth of Independent States
CITES	Convention on International Trade in Endangered Species of Wild Fauna and Flora
CIU	Co-ordination and Implementation Unit
CMA	Common Monetary Area
CMEA	Council for Mutual Economic Assistance

COMECON	*see* CMEA
COMESA	Common Market for Eastern and Southern Africa
COSATU	Congress of South African Trade Unions
CPSU	Communist Party of the Soviet Union
CRP	Common revenue pool
DBSA	Development Bank of Southern Africa
DDG	Deputy Director General
DFA	Department of Foreign Affairs (South Africa)
DG	Director General
DoD	Department of Defence (South Africa)
DRC	Democratic Republic of Congo
DTI	Department of Trade and Industry (South Africa)
EAC	East African Community
ECA	Economic Commission for Africa (UN)
ECDC	Economic co-operation amongst developing countries
ECLA	Economic Commission for Latin America
ECOMOG	A peace force established by ECOWAS
ECOSOC	Economic and Social Council (UN)
ECOWAS	Economic Community of West African States
ECSC	European Coal and Steel Community
EDF	European Development Fund
EEC	European Economic Community
EPLF	Eritrean People's Liberation Front
ESAF	Enhanced Structural Adjustment Facility
ETA	Basque Fatherland and Liberty Group
EU	European Union
FAO	Food and Agricultural Organisation
FDI	Foreign direct investment
FGD	Foundation for Global Dialogues
FNLA	Frente Nacionale de Libertacao de Angola (National Front for the Liberation of Angola)
FRELIMO	Frente de Libertacao de Mozambique (Front for the Liberation of Mozambique)
FTA	free trade area
G-7	Group of 7 (seven major industrial states)
G-8	G-7 plus Russian Federation
G-77	Group of 77 (developing countries)
GATT	General Agreement on Tariffs and Trade
GDI	gender-related development index
GDP	gross domestic product
GEAR	Growth, Employment and Redistribution Strategy (South Africa)
GNP	gross national product
GNU	government of national unity (South Africa)
GPE	Global Political Economy
GPS	Generalised System of Preferences
HDI	human development index
HPI	human poverty index
HTML	Hyper Text Markup Language
IBM	International Business Machines
IBRD	International Bank for Reconstruction and Development (World Bank)
ICO	International Criminal Organisation
IDA	International Development Association
IFC	International Finance Corporation

IFI	international financial institution	MIA	Military Intelligence Agency (South Africa)
IGO	intergovernmental organisation		
ILO	International Labour Organisation	MIC	middle-income country
IMF	International Monetary Fund	MIGA	Multilateral Investment Guarantee Agency
INGO	international non-governmental organisation		
		MMD	Movement for Multiparty Democracy (Zambia)
INTELSAT	International Telecommunications Satellite Organisation	MNC	multinational corporation
IO	international organisation	MPLA	Movimento Popular de Libertacao de Angola (Movement for the Popular Liberation of Angola)
IOR-ARC	Indian Ocean Rim Association for Regional Co-operation		
		NAFTA	North American Free Trade Agreement
IPC	integrated programme for commodities		
		NAM	Non-Aligned Movement (official title is Movement of Non-Aligned Countries)
IPE	International Political Economy		
IR	International Relations		
IRA	Irish Republican Army	NATO	North Atlantic Treaty Organisation
ISI	import substitution industrialisation	NCACC	National Conventional Arms Control Committee (South Africa)
ISIS	Institute of Strategic and International Studies		
		NEDLAC	National Economic Development and Labour Council (South Africa)
ISO	International Sugar Organisation		
IT	information technology	NGO	non-governmental organisation
ITO	International Trade Organisation	NIA	National Intelligence Agency (South Africa)
JIT	just in time (production)		
KGB	Committee for State Security (Russian initials of Soviet Union's main body for national security)	NIC	newly industrialising country (see NIE)
		NICOC	National Intelligence Co-ordinating Committee (South Africa)
KMT	Kuomintang (ruling party in Taiwan)		
		NIE	newly industrialising economy
LIC	low-income country	NIEO	New International Economic Order
MAI	Multilateral Agreement on Investment	NP	National Party (South Africa)
		OAU	Organisation of African Unity
MERCOSUR	Common Market of the South (economic integration project in South America in which Argentina, Brazil, Paraguay, Uruguay, and Chile – as associate member – are engaged)	ODA	official development assistance
		OECD	Organisation for Economic Co-operation and Development
		ONUC	United Nations Congo Operation
		OPEC	Organisation of Petroleum Exporting Countries
MFN	Most Favoured Nation principle (in GATT and WTO)		
		OXFAM	International group of independent,

	non-governmental humanitarian-relief organisations founded in Oxford, UK
PAC	Pan Africanist Congress (South Africa)
PANA	Pan African News Agency
PC	personal computer
PLO	Palestine Liberation Organisation
POLISARIO	*Frente Popular para la Liberación de Saguía el-Hamra y del Río de Oro* (Popular Front for the Liberation of the Western Sahara and Rio de Oro)
PPP	purchasing power parity
PRC	People's Republic of China
RDP	Reconstruction and Development Programme (South Africa)
RENAMO	*Resistencia Nacionale Mocambicana* (National Resistance Movement of Mozambique)
ROSCAS	rotating savings and credit associations
SACP	South African Communist Party
SACU	Southern African Customs Union
SADC	Southern African Development Community
SADCC	Southern African Development Co-ordination Conference
SADF	South African Defence Force (old)
SAF	Structural Adjustment Facility
SAFTO	South African Foreign Trade Organisation
SAIIA	South African Institute of International Affairs
SALT	Strategic Arms Limitation Talks
SANDF	South African National Defence Force
SAP	structural adjustment programme
SASS	South African Secret Service
SEA	sub-Equatorial Africa
SSA	sub-Saharan Africa
SSC	State Security Council (South Africa)
STABEX	Stabilisation of Export earnings (an EU stabilisation system offering the ACP states funds to finance their agricultural sectors when they encounter difficulties because of falls in export earnings)
START	Strategic Arms Reduction Talks
SWAPO	South West Africa People's Organisation
SYSMIN	An EU financial facility assisting qualifying ACP state's mining sectors in situations where economic viability is under pressure
TAZARA	Tanzanian-Zambia Railway
TBVC	Transkei, Bophuthatswana, Venda, Ciskei
TCDC	technical co-operation amongst developing countries
TNC	transnational corporation
TRIM	Trade Related Investment Measures (GATT and WTO)
TRIP	Trade Related Intellectual Property Rights (GATT and WTO)
TSM	transnational social movements
UDF	United Democratic Front (South Africa)
UDI	unilateral declaration of independence (Zimbabwe)
UK	United Kingdom
UN	United Nations
UNCHR	United Nations High Commission for Refugees
UNCTAD	United Nations Conference on Trade and Development
UNDP	United Nations Development Programme

UNESCO	United Nations Educational, Scientific and Cultural Organisation	USA	United States of America
UNICEF	United Nations Children's Fund	USSR	Union of Soviet Socialist Republics
UNIDO	United Nations Industrial Development Organisation	WAFF	West African Frontier Force
UNIPO	United National Independence Party (Zambia)	WESGRO	Western Cape Investment and Trade Promotion Agency
UNITA	Uniao para a Independencia Total de Angola (Union for the Total Independence of Angola)	WHO	World Health Organisation
		WTO	World Trade Organisation
UNO	*see* UN	WWF	World Wildlife Fund
US	*see* USA	WWW	World Wide Web
		ZANU	Zimbabwe African National Union
		ZAPU	Zimbabwe African People's Union

Glossary

absolute poverty: a situation in which a population is able to meet only its bare subsistence essentials (food, clothing, shelter) to maintain minimum levels of survival. In many instances of the developing world there are people who cannot even maintain such survival levels.

absolute underdevelopment: extreme level of **underdevelopment;** that is; a situation in which the well-being and choices of a population are drastically curtailed.

accountability: the democratic principle that government should be answerable to those affected by its decisions.

actor: any entity or person engaged in international activities.

African Renaissance: a term associated with Thabo Mbeki, who has argued that the post-Apartheid, post-Cold War era opens the possibility for a decisive shift by Africa towards economic growth, stability and democracy. The word *renaissance* means 're-birth', and is used mainly to refer to the revival of art and letters in Europe in the fourteenth to sixteenth centuries, influenced by classical (Greek and Roman) models.

African unity: a doctrine developed during the 1950s by a number of Africans who later became the first generation of post-independence leaders on the continent. It refers to the unity of the whole continent in terms of relations with the external world, and in efforts to address colonialism, apartheid, development and other issues of mutual concern. Although initially providing for *all* Africans, over time it became a doctrine used by African governments to support one another's survival and to ward off criticism (*see* also **pan-Africanism**).

Afrikaners: a collective noun for the Afrikaans-speaking descendants of European settlers in South Africa.

Afrique Equatorial Francaise: one of the two French colonial federations. Formed in 1908 and with headquarters in Dakar, it comprised eight colonies: Dahomey, Guinea, Ivory Coast, Senegal, Mauritania, Soudan (now Mali), Niger, and Upper Volta (now Burkina Faso).

Afrique Occidental Francaise: the other French colonial federation that was founded in 1902. It has four colonies: Gabon, middle Congo, Oubangui-Shari, now Central African Republic, and Chad. Its headquarters was in Brazzaville.

Afro-optimism: the belief that despite Africa's many problems, recent developments — notably the end of the Cold War and the shift towards democracy in key African countries — provide a genuine opportunity for the continent to achieve sustained economic growth and **good governance**.

Afro-pessimism: the belief that Africa's economic and political record in terms of economic growth, poverty, disorder and misrule is such that the continent's future is bleak.

agreement: a) any mutual understanding between actors; b) consent issued by a host state once an ambassador of the sending state has submitted his or her letters of credence. It indicates that the host state has accepted the mission headed by the ambassador.

alliance: a formal agreement between two or more states to co-ordinate their responses to specified military situations.

analysis: the mental process of identifying and examining the parts of a whole.

anarchical: adjective derived from **anarchy**.

anarchy: in general the word refers to the absence of governmental authority. In International Relations it refers to the absence of a central governing authority in the international state system. This amounts to a drastic decentralisation of power in international affairs.

Apartheid: the official policy of racial discrimination and social and political segregation followed in South Africa between 1948 and 1994.

arbitration: a process for resolving disputes in which a third party makes a binding decision through an ad-hoc forum. In arbitration the disputants agree on the issues to be resolved, on who the judge or arbitrator will be, and that the resolution proposed by the arbitrator will be honoured by the disputants.

Asia-Pacific Economic Co-operation (APEC): a regional grouping concerned with promoting trade and co-operation between states in the Asia-Pacific region.

Association of South East Asian Nations (ASEAN): a regional grouping concerned with promoting development and co-operation in cultural and security matters between members. Founded in 1967, it consists of Thailand, Vietnam, Singapore, Malaysia, Indonesia, Brunei, Laos, the Philippines and Myanmar (Burma).

assumption: a belief accepted as true for the sake of an argument.

authoritarian state: a state characterised by a system of government in which the power of the leaders or leader is unconstrained by legal principles or by popular vote.

balance of payments: the official record of a country's transactions with the rest of the world. It consists of two accounts, the *current account* and the *capital account*. All the sales of goods and services to the rest of the world (exports), and all the purchases of goods and services from the rest of the world (imports) are recorded in the *current account*. All the purely financial flows in and out of a country, for instance the purchase and sales of assets such as bonds and shares, are recorded in the *capital account*. When a country imports more than it exports, it has to finance that deficit on the current account with an inflow of capital into the capital account. If that does not happen sufficiently, and if the country does not have sufficient reserves to cover the shortfall, we say that that country experiences a **balance-of-payments deficit**.

balance-of-payments deficit: *see* **balance of payments**.

balance of power this term can be used in at least four different ways. Firstly, it can refer to any distribution of power, as in the sentence 'there is a precarious balance of power in East Asia'. Secondly, it can be used to refer to situations in which power is distributed equally between two or more powers. Thus, one can say that 'there was a balance of power between the USA and the USSR during the Cold War'. Thirdly it can refer to a deliberate policy choice on the part of a third state to act as a balancer between two or more other states in order to maintain the peace. Thus, Britain followed a balance-of-power policy during much of the nineteenth and early twentieth centuries in its dealings with

European powers. Finally, the word can also be used in phrases such as 'the balance-of-power system' to describe historical multipolar systems, in which a number of powers – perhaps five or six – maintained shifting alliances amongst themselves in order to prevent any one power from dominating the rest (the so-called 'Concert of Europe' after 1815 is an example).

balance of uncertainty: refers to uncertainty associated with a multipolar system in which three or more powers compete and in the process escalate the possibility of conflict.

balkanisation: the division of an area into small and mutually-antagonistic states. The term was first used to describe Imperial Russia's divide and rule policy towards Balkan states in the late nineteenth century.

billion: a thousand million.

bipolar: an international system which contains two dominant centres of power around which other states cluster. Usually contrasted with a **unipolar** system where there is one, all-powerful **hegemon** (Rome in antiquity, for instance), or with a **multipolar** system.

bookmarks: an option in your browser programme that allows you to save the location of a Web page (its **URL**) for future use.

Bretton Woods system: the economic rules, institutions and decision-making procedures established by the July 1944 Agreement signed by 44 states at Bretton Woods in the USA. It created the **International Monetary Fund** (IMF) and the International Bank for Reconstruction and Development (IBRD or **World Bank**), and later, in 1947, the **General Agreement on Tariffs and Trade** (GATT). The IMF and The World Bank were to be responsible for the regulation of international financial affairs, with the US dollar as the dominant currency, while GATT oversaw the **liberalisation** of trade.

browser: a software programme that displays files from the Web on your computer. Popular browsers include Netscape Navigator, Mosaic, Microsoft Explorer, and Lynx (for text-only display).

budget deficit: the amount by which budget expenditure exceeds budget revenue.

bureaucratic politics model: a view of policy-making that emphasises the role of bargaining and compromises among the contending government departments that exert influence on the foreign policy choices of leaders.

business cycles: the pattern of upswing (expansion) and downswing (contraction) that can be discerned in economic activity over a number of years. One complete cycle has a trough, an upswing (or boom), a peak, and a downswing.

capital flight: a rapid increase in the outflow of capital from a country. This places tremendous stress on the country's currency, because investors want to sell the local currency for foreign currencies in order to take their money out of the country.

capital flows: the volumes of private foreign investment, public grants, loans, and other funds that flow into (capital inflow) and out (capital outflow) of a country over a given period.

capital outflow: *see* **capital flows**.

capitalism: an economic system that is based on the private ownership of the means of production, and the utilisation of wage labour. In capitalism, markets are used to determine the relative prices of factors of production and of goods and services.

cartel: an alliance of firms or states who join together to restrict the supply of a particular product or service in order to increase its cost.

Casablanca Group: a grouping of African leaders, led by Kwame Nkrumah of Ghana, who, prior to the foundation of the OAU, argued that the success of **pan-Africanism** required a political union of all independent African countries.

chain-ganged: a term used to describe a form of alliance between states in which state A binds itself, without any preconditions, to another state (B). When B gets involved in a war with a third state (C), the chains of the alliance between A and B pull A into the war as well, even if A did not want to go to war. Germany was chainedganged with Austria-Hungary before the First World War, and when Austria-Hungary's confrontation with Russia began, Germany was sucked into it as well.

civil society: the non-governmental segment of the public realm, comprising a variety of voluntary non-governmental organisations that function to check the power of the state.

civil wars: armed conflict between political factions within the same country.

client computer: the individual computer you are working on, when connected to a 'host' or 'server' computer.

Cold War: an era of ideological, economic, political, and diplomatic confrontation between the USA and its allies on the one side, and the USSR and its allies on the other. It lasted from 1947 until the breaking down of the Berlin Wall (which symbolised the division between a communist Eastern and a capitalist Western Europe) in 1989.

Cold War proxy war: an armed conflict in the developing world, promoted or supported by the USSR or the USA as a means of challenging or checking the power of the other during the **Cold War**.

collective security: a security system within which aggression by one state results in a joint response by all the other states.

colonisation: the process, usually of conquest, by which an imperial power imposes direct or indirect political, economic and cultural control over a foreign country or people. The word originates from the Latin word *colonus*, which means 'a farmer'. Colonisation in the nineteenth and twentieth centuries was often associated with the settlement of the colony by numbers of settler-farmers from the imperial **mother country**.

Comintern: also known as the Third Communist International. A Communist organisation founded in 1919 by Vladimir Lenin. The aim of the Comintern was to co-ordinate and promote the move towards socialism in various parts of the world. The Comintern was abolished in 1943, as a reconciliatory move by the Union of Soviet Socialist Republics to its war-time allies.

Common Agricultural Policy (CAP): The European Union's plan of action to support their farmers through financial and others incentives.

common external tariff: found in **customs unions**, where the member states establish one, shared **tariff** that is applied to non-members.

Commonwealth (of Nations): a voluntary international association of 52 states that have historical links with the British Empire. Britain is also a member of this organisation, and the British monarch is nominally Head of the Commonwealth. All of the former British colonies in SSA, except Sudan, are members (as is Mozambique, although it was a Portuguese colony).

communist bloc: a **Cold-War** term used to refer to the USSR and its allies.

comparative advantage: a principle used to explain the existence and the benefits of international trade. This principle claims that any two states will benefit if each specialises in those services and goods that it can produce more cheaply than the other state, and buys those goods and services that the other state can produce more cheaply.

competitive: an adjective derived from the noun 'competition', which denotes activities involving a striving for superiority in a quality.

complementary (economies): economies that produce different products, permitting a **division of labour** and mutually beneficial trade according to the principle of **comparative advantage**, e.g., country A makes and sells computers to country B and, in return, buys wine from country B.

comprador bourgeoisie: local business persons who collaborate with more developed countries and their businesses to exploit a weaker, developing country economically. Comprador élites are often involved in export/ import businesses.

consumption: The buying and using of goods and services. Consumption is one of the three main economic activities in modern societies (the others are production and exchange).

containment: a United States foreign policy during the Cold War, initiated by President Harry Truman, and aimed at limiting the expansion of the Soviet sphere of influence.

core: the central, privileged position in the global

system and its **division of labour**.

coup d'état: A French word meaning, literally, 'a strike of the state' – the very rapid and illegal overthrow of a government, violently or non-violently, and its replacement by a new set of rulers. In Africa, *coups* have often been executed by the military.

critical thinkers: a specific group of authors in International Relations who challenge what they perceive to be the orthodox beliefs and assumptions of the discipline. Some of them are influenced by transformative Marxism and by feminist theories. Others find inspiration in post-modernist thinking in the human sciences, that is, approaches that emphasise the constructed and, therefore, relative nature of all knowledge.

customary international law: law based on the established practices of sovereign states in their relations with each other.

customs and excise duties: taxes on goods imported into a country or **customs union**. Among the poorer countries of Africa, these duties are an important source of government revenue.

customs union: an international association of states who agree to abolish tariffs among themselves, set a common tariff on goods coming from outside the union, and divide the income from the tariffs that are levied.

data: discrete pieces of information that one can use to analyse and explain trends or events. For instance, counting the votes of states in the UN General Assembly (*yes*, *no*, or *abstentions* produces data that is useful for analysising political alliances in the General Assembly.

de facto: Latin — indicates that something exists in fact, whether by right or not.

de jure: Latin, meaning 'rightfully' (by right of law).

decolonisation: the process of ending colonial rule, which involves (sometimes violent) nationalist struggles and a period of preparation for independence for colonial peoples. In SSA it began with the independence of Ghana in 1957 and ended with the independence of Namibia in 1990.

democratisation: literally the transfer of power to the people (*demos* is the Greek word for 'people'. The process of transforming **authoritarian** and totalitarian systems of government into a system in which the fundamental rights of the individual, rule of law and democratic values, such as accountability and constitutionality, are upheld.

demography: (the study of) the statistical record of births, deaths, diseases, ageing patterns, etc. as illustrating conditions of life in a community.

dependence: a relationship of unequal reliance in the interactions between two or more actors. The inequality exists in the fact that the one, weaker actor is exposed to much higher levels of vulnerability in the relationship than the other, stronger actor.

dependency ratio: a ratio is a quantitative relation between comparable magnitudes determined by the number of times one contains the other. A dependency ratio is used to indicate how many times actor A is more dependent on actor B than the reverse. If a dependency ratio of 1:5 applies, actor A is five times as dependent on B than B is on A.

dependency theorists: a group of theorists who are sympathetic towards the developing world, who argued that the poverty and degradation experienced by many developing countries is caused by the high levels of vulnerability they experience in their relationship with the industrial countries.

destabilisation: the name given to the regional policy implemented by the South African government during the late 1970s and the 1980s. The purpose of this policy was to undermine the economies of southern African states who were perceived to be 'pro-Communist', and who sympathised and assisted the liberation movements. Destabilisation also had a military dimension in that resistance movements, such as UNITA in Angola and RENAMO in Mozambique, were given support by the South African government, and the South African Defence Force attacked so-called terrorist bases in neighbouring countries (Swaziland, Lesotho and Botswana, amongst others) from time to time. On the other hand, countries who were willing to withdraw support for the ANC and PAC were given economic rewards by the Apartheid government.

détente: the deliberate relaxation of tension/hostilities between conflicting parties. Associated primarily with a policy of co-operation and restraint established by the Nixon Administration in 1969 *vis-à-vis* the Soviet Union. President Nixon's main strategy was to promote an environment based on co-operation between the two superpowers. The Soviet Union also adopted this strategy towards the US.

development: the ability of a community to advance in terms of the well-being and range of choices experienced by its people.

developmental state: a state that adopts policies to increase the international competitiveness of its economy, while improving the standard of living of its population (e.g. Japan since WW II).

dialectical: adjective of 'dialectic', a noun that refers to an evolutionary process (or a form of reasoning) characterised by opposition and contradiction. According to dialectic theory, every historical or social tendency (or thesis) calls forth a contradictory counter-tendency (or antithesis). This contradiction is then resolved in a synthesis which, in turn, forms a new thesis, on a higher plane, which will eventually again evoke a new antithesis, and so the process continues. Transformative Marxism makes use of this idea to explain how change from one economic system to another takes place.

diplomacy: sometimes wrongly used as a synonym for **foreign policy**, this word refers to the official practices through which actors (mostly states) communicate and negotiate with one another.

distributive justice: principled way of distributing rewards and responsibilities in a community. The principle used is one of rewarding people on the basis of the contributions they make to common efforts, and of their need for fair and equal treatment.

division of labour: occurs when a production process is broken up into different steps or parts, each of which is performed by an individual worker or group of workers. In the modern world economy, such division of labour occurs not only within specific production plants, but also between production plants, often scattered across national boundaries, and also between different countries.

doctrine of self-help: a set of beliefs which emphasises that **anarchy** compels each state to rely on its own resources in an attempt to secure its survival. This often leads to selfish behaviour on the part of states, according to the doctrine.

Dutch East India Company: formed in the early 1600s this merchant-trading joint stock company created a commercial and territorial empire in the Indian Ocean and Southern Africa in the seventeenth and eighteenth centuries. In 1652 it founded Cape Town in what is now South Africa. The Company was highly profitable for its investors.

East Timor: former Portuguese-controlled territory, invaded and annexed by Indonesia in December 1995.

ecology: used in two senses: either in the sense of 'the study of the biological and physical environment on Earth'; or in the sense of 'the environment itself'.

economic integration: a process that is followed by two or more states to promote the co-ordination and sometimes eventual unification of their economies. Early steps in economic integration usually involve policies that are aimed at enhancing the free flow of money, goods and labour across borders.

economic structural transformation: this happens when a country significantly changes what it produces and sells to the world. Historically, Mauritius sold sugar to the rest of the world. Today its major exports are manufactured: textiles, clothing and consumer electronics.

economies of scale: reductions in the average cost of a product in the long run, due to an expanded level of output.

e-mail: electronic mail; exchange of messages between computers. A popular e-mail programme is Pegasus, but there are many similar programmes.

emerging markets: a group of developing countries and transitional countries (countries in Eastern Europe making the transition from communism) that were identified by The World Bank in the 1990s as being particularly ripe for foreign investment. Once a term of endorsement, it has become rather notorious after the Asian financial crisis of 1997 and 1998, which led to **capital flight** from many of the once-favoured emerging markets.

epistemic communities: groups of scientists and policy-makers who share an understanding of a particular policy issue and jointly influence international policy making.

equilibrium: a situation that obtains when the parts of a system balance one another in such a way that no fundamental change can take place in the system.

ethnonational groups: one of the non-state transnational actors in international relations. They consist of people from the same ethnic or national group who have organised themselves across the national borders that divide them. Examples include the Kurds and the Palestinians.

European Union (EU): an economic and political union of fifteen states in (Western) Europe.

exit: (from the state): the withdrawal of segments of the citizenry from the state into parallel self-governing structures (such as community development associations) usually in response to the state's tyranny and poor performance.

external debt: sometimes termed foreign debt, this represents what a country owes foreign lenders – other governments, investors in other countries, international organisations, and foreign banks – from which it has borrowed in the past.

external sovereignty: *see* **sovereignty**.

externalities: the social costs of economic activities (such as exploitation of the environment) which are not included in market costs. A concrete example would be the affects on you of my economic activities. If these are positive, you benefit; for instance, when my bee-keeping results in the pollination of your fruit trees. When negative, you lose, as when my paper pulp factory pollutes your fishing water downstream.

extraterritoriality: the legal principle which allows a country to maintain jurisdiction (final say) over its embassies on the territory of other states.

fertility (rate): the number of children born alive, annually, per 1000 women in the child-bearing age bracket (normally 15–49 years).

feudal: *see* **feudal era**.

feudal era: a political-economic system found in medieval Europe and Japan based on ownership of farmland by an aristocracy (lords, princes, kings), and the farming of the land by serfs, who had to give much of their produce to the aristocracy in exchange for use of the land and for protection from invaders. An essentially rural economy with only a small role for markets.

financial markets: national and international markets for securing credit through buying and selling financial instruments, such as private and government bonds, currencies, securities, and debt.

finished (manufactured) goods: products bought by a consumer, such as a television, or a machine tool bought by a manufacturer. The first is a personal consumption good, whereas the later is a capital good used in the manufacture of other goods.

floating exchange rate system: one of the systems used to determine the relative value of currencies. Governments can fix the value of their currency relative to other currencies, or they can let it 'float', that is, allow supply and demand market forces to determine its value.

foreign aid: a collective name for all forms of assistance from one country (the donor) to another (the recipient) country. It may be private, from an NGO, or official, from states or international organisations such as the UN. We normally distinguish, as far as official aid is concerned, between foreign military aid and official development assistance (ODA). The latter is aimed at promoting development, and is administered by official (government) institutions in the donor and the recipient countries. It consists of grants, cheap loans, and technical assistance. There are two types of ODA: bilateral ODA (involving one donor and one recipient state) and multilateral ODA (where more than one donor state or more than one recipient state co-ordinate their policies).

foreign debt: *see* **external debt**.

foreign direct investment (FDI): investment by nationals of one state in the economy of another state, aimed at gaining control over a certain instrument of production or service, such as a factory or a bank.

foreign policy: all of the actions that a government takes in its dealings with the world outside its borders.

free markets: the production, buying and selling of goods and services without interference of government or anyone else under conditions of competition among many producers and consumers. In free markets, prices are determined by the demand for goods and services and their supply.

free trade: the condition in which there are no tariffs or other barriers to the exchange of goods and services between countries. Conventional economic theory argues that free trade will maximise global welfare. But, it is an ideal that has never fully operated in the world of self-interested states.

free trade area: a form of economic integration between two or more states in which there exists free internal trade among member countries, but each member is free to levy a different external tariff against non-member nations.

Frontline States (FLS): a grouping of states in Southern Africa, started in the early 1970s by Tanzania and Zambia. The FLS lobbied for the liberation of Namibia, South Africa and Zimbabwe from exclusive white-minority rule. As other states in the region gained their independence, they joined the FLS.

fungibility: a term used to discuss power capabilities of states. One capability is fungible when it is transferable across issue areas and can be used instead of another capability. An important insight linked to this concept is that capabilities are not always equally effective. For instance,

whether military power is effective or not depends on the issue area. When A wants to invade B, A's military superiority will determine the outcome. When states A and B compete for investment from a multinational corporation, though, A's relative military might is not of much use. In this case, military power has a low fungibility.

G-77: a coalition of the world's poorer nations, formed in 1964 at the UNCTAD summit in Geneva, with the aim of collectively pressing for a major restructuring of the unequal world economy. Originally there were 77 members, but this coalition has grown to 124 members in 1997. It continues to be a major forum for regular consultation amongst developing countries within the United Nations system, and to pressurise the wealthier nations of the world into making economic concessions in their dealings with the developing world.

G-8: (formerly **G-7**) group of leading industrialised countries – USA, Britain, Germany, France, Italy, Japan and Canada. Russia was admitted as the eighth member (for political discussions) in 1998. By means of regular summits, these states manage the world economy to their best interest.

General Agreement on Tariffs and Trade (GATT): an intergovernmental organisation formed in 1947 as part of the **Bretton Woods system**. It promoted free trade and the **most-favoured-nation principle**. It was replaced in 1995 by the World Trade Organisation.

generalised system of preferences (GSP): trade rules which grant privileged access to markets in the North for selected manufactured goods from the South.

genocide: the practise of exterminating a whole population, or a sizeable part of the population, belonging to a specific ethnic, national, racial, or religious group. Examples include the mass extermination of Jews during WW II, the mass killings of Bosnian Muslims during the civil war in Bosnia during the early 1990s, and the mutual slaughter of Hutus and Tutsis in Burundi and Rwanda during the 1990s. In 1948, the UN

General Assembly accepted a resolution that outlaws genocide.

Gini coefficient: an aggregate numerical measure of income inequality in a country, ranging from 0 (perfect equality) to 1 (perfect inequality). The higher the value of the co-efficient, the higher the inequality of income distribution; the lower it is, the more equitable the distribution of income.

Glasnost: a Russian word referring to the policy of political and economic 'openness' initiated by former president of the Soviet Union, Mikhail Gorbachev.

global city: a city that plays a global role, for instance as a major financial centre (London), or as a source of global cultural inspiration (Paris, for instance).

global civil society: transnationally linked non-governmental public sphere (*see* **civil society**).

global conference system: a name for the periodic **multilateral** conferences on global issues that has been institutionalised over the last quarter-century. Some scholars and policy makers see the system as the equivalent of a 'legislative branch' of an emergent global government.

global governance: a relatively informal system of regulation at a global level that combines global treaties, conferences, and the regulatory actions of great powers and powerful private agencies.

globalisation: the rapid deepening, widening and speeding up of interaction between individuals, organisations, and states across national and natural boundaries. The current phase of globalisation is associated with the universalising of a set of norms and rules that govern many aspects of life which were previously determined nationally. Its effects are deemed to be the emergence of a global (Americanised) culture, the firm entrenchment of liberal economic and political principles globally, and the 'retreat of the state' from some public-policy issue areas.

gold exchange standard: a monetary system whereby currency values are fixed in terms of a stable gold value, in order to prevent the volatile fluctuation of **rates of exchange**. It came into being after WW II and replaced the gold standard system. In the gold standard system, currencies were also defined in terms of gold but, in addition, money supplies were linked to gold, and **balance of payment deficits** were settled in gold. These latter two aspects fell away with the introduction of the gold exchange standard.

good governance: a composite of efficient, transparent and accountable government.

gopher: a menu-based system for accessing files on the Internet; now often reached through the Web.

Government of National Unity: The first government of democratic South Africa which represented all parties, and which won enough popular votes to qualify for representation in the cabinet.

gross domestic product: *see* **gross national product**.

gross national product (GNP): an economic indicator of the total value of the goods and services produced by the nationals (citizens and permanent residents) of a particular country in any one year. GNP should be distinguished from **gross domestic product (GDP)** which expresses the total value of all goods and services produced within the boundaries of a country in one year. GDP, therefore, also contains the value of the goods and services produced by non-nationals on the territory of the country in question. GDP is a good measure to use when investigating the level of economic activity in a country, and economic growth is usually indicated in terms of the percentage growth or decline of the GDP from one year to another. GNP, on the other hand, gives a better indication of the standard of living of the citizens of a particular country. It is widely used in cross-country comparisons, where the GNP of a country is divided by the total population of that country, which gives a value of GNP per capita (literally, 'per head' of the population).

Group of 77: *see* **G-77**.

Growth, Employment and Redistribution Strategy (GEAR): the economic policy of the **GNU** in South Africa, introduced in June 1996. It attempted to attract **FDI** to South Africa, by making the economy more investor friendly, and by emphasising export-led growth.

Hansa (Hanseatic) league: a trade and security alliance of major trading cities and towns in Northern Europe. It existed in one form or another from the fourteenth to the nineteenth century.

hegemon: the dominant **core** power in the world at any time. Hegemons try to provide order for the international system, as they are best positioned to benefit from it. There have been three hegemons since the sixteenth century: Holland, Great Britain and the United States.

hegemonic power: a state that holds hegemony within international society. Synonym of **hegemon**.

hegemony: unchallenged leadership exercised by, for instance, one state over other states, or by an economic class over other classes. It comes from the Greek word *hegeomai* which means 'to lead'.

home page: for a given URL, the first page of text and images that your browser loads onto your computer monitor. It will contain 'hypertext links' to sub-pages and to related home pages.

host computer: a computer which provides or 'serves' files to 'client' computers linked to it, such as your PC.

HTML: hypertext mark-up language; a set of standard codes used to prepare pages for display on the Web.

HTTP: hypertext transfer protocol; the set of rules that regulate the transfer of files over the Web.

human capital: productive investments embodied in human persons. They include skills, abilities, ideals and health resulting from expenditures on education, on-the-job training programmes and medical care.

human development index (HDI): a measure devised by the UNDP that uses life expectancy, literacy, educational attainment, and income to assess a country's human development performance.

human rights: the civil, economic and social rights that people can claim because they are human beings.

hypertext link: highlighted names, addresses or icons on a Web page. When you click on the link with your 'mouse', your browser connects you to that site on the Web.

identity: an indicator of belonging to a group. Both individuals and groups have a propensity to develop a sense of who they are, often by constructing a sense of who they are not.

ideology: a dogmatic set of ideas that pretends to explain the world, and that usually propagates one or other ideal form of society.

imperialism: the deliberate projection of a state's power beyond the area of its original jurisdiction with the object of creating and controlling a larger coherent political and administrative unit. Modern imperialism coincided with the expansion abroad, from the 1500s, of European states, the United States and Japan, to gain control of vast territories in Asia, Africa, Latin America and the Middle East which were turned into colonies. Marxists explain this as resulting from capitalism's need for raw materials and new markets. Realists see it as an expression of the power rivalries of the major powers.

import substitution industrialisation (ISI): a strategy of industrialisation in which previously imported goods are manufactured locally, and local industry is protected from foreign competition. It entails importation of technology and, in some cases, labour and raw materials.

import substitution policies: *see* **import substitution industrialisation**.

income per capita: what is earned, on average, by a population (*see* also **gross national product**).

incorporation: inclusion, sometimes of foreign territory to make it part of the 'home' territory of a state.

Indian Ocean Rim Association for Regional Co-operation (IOR-ARC): a regional grouping concerned with promoting trade and co-operation between member states bordering on the Indian Ocean.

Industrial Revolution: the economic transformation in Western Europe during the nineteenth century, from predominantly agrarian economies to economies centred on machine production in factories. The Industrial

Revolution is usually said to have begun in England in the late 1700s.

inflation: a rise in the general level of prices in any one state, usually linked to a rise in production costs.

information technology (IT): the machines, ideas and knowledge that make electric and electronic communication possible between individuals and organisations. IT began with the telegraph in the middle of the nineteenth century. The most recent IT innovation is the World Wide Web. 'Spy satellites' that some governments rocket into space, are very advanced and expensive forms of IT.

integration: the unification of two or more separate states, their economies, and their societies into a single social, economic, and political system.

intelligence: the result of (or the activity of) collecting and evaluating information about other countries, or about domestic challenges to the security of the state.

interactions: a collective noun for all the various contacts between international actors.

interconnectedness: a situation which results from high levels of regular **interactions** between actors.

interdependence: a situation of mutual dependence, defined as mutual sensitivity and mutual vulnerability, that can develop between **interconnected** actors. Not all interdependence is symmetrical, however. Symmetrical interdependence obtains when every actor is affected in the same way and to the same extent by occurrences affecting another actor with which it is interconnected. Liberals argue that the many ties that bind nations in today's world make them interdependent, and more sensitive to each other's fears and desires. Realists argue that interdependence does not necessarily lead to a decline in conflict, but may actually increase the potential for conflict: each point of interconnectedness is a potential site of conflict, they argue.

intergovernmental organisation (IGO): an international organisation that is created by an agreement or treaty between states.

intermediate manufactured goods: manufactured products used to make **finished goods**, such as the steel, aluminium and plastics used to make many parts of automobiles.

internal sovereignty: *see* **sovereignty**.

international anarchy: *see* **anarchy**.

international commercial law: *see* **international law**.

international institutions: persistent and connected sets of rules (formal and informal) that prescribe behavioural roles, constrain activities, and shape expectations of states and other international actors in their relations with each other.

international law a set of binding principles, rules, and procedures for arbitration that governs the transnational interaction of actors. We distinguish between international private law (that is, law pertaining largely to routinised transnational interaction between or among non-state actors), and international public law, also called public international law (law applicable largely to state-state relations). International commercial law is a part of public law and deals with international commercial interactions, such as trade between states.

International Monetary Fund (IMF): one of the so-called **Bretton Woods** institutions that were formed in 1944 at Bretton Woods in the USA to manage the post-war world economy. The IMF is a specialised agency of the United Nations, which seeks to maintain stability in the monetary system in the world and, in particular, in the value of currencies. It helps countries that have serious **balance of payments** problems by giving them low-interest loans. In return, the IMF demands that these countries apply strict measures to curb the financial problems that led to the balance of payments deficit in the first place (so-called **structural adjustment programmes**). Membership of the IMF is restricted to those states who are also members of the World Bank. Like the World Bank, the IMF has a system of weighted voting, which gives power to affect outcomes to those states that make the biggest financial contributions.

international non-governmental organisation: international bodies that have a permanent address and a secretariat, and whose members are private citizens from more than one country.

international organisations institutions with an international membership, and which have a permanent headquarters or secretariat. We distinguish between **intergovernmental organisations (IGOs)**, that were created by agreement between states (such as the UN or SADC), and **non-governmental international organisations (INGOs)**, that were created by agreement between private individuals and groups (such as Amnesty International and the Red Cross). IGOs can be further subdivided according to whether they have universal membership or not, and according to the range of issue areas with which they deal.

international public law: *see* **international law**.

international religious movements: religious movements with members in more than one country, who maintain a form of contact with one another. While an **international organisation** always has a permanent secretariat or headquarters, a movement usually has not achieved that level of institutionalisation.

international society: sovereign states that recognise each other's sovereignty and share a set of expectations of each other's behaviour, are said to constitute a society with at least some shared norms and values. Due to the universalisation of the modern state, some authors claim that such a society is in existence today, and that it softens the harsher qualities of international **anarchy**.

Internet: broader definition: all the computers in the world that can communicate with each other by e-mail; same as the Matrix. Restricted definition: all the computers in the world that can communicate with each other using a standard set of rules called **TCP/IP**.

investment: expanding productive activity by purchasing capital goods such as machinery and equipment, or increasing financial resources by buying and selling financial instruments.

invisible trade: the export or import of services such as banking, insurance, shipping, consulting and tourism.

isolation: a severance of international ties with or by a particular state or government. A state can follow a policy of isolation when it tries to minimalise its links to the outside world (Albania in the 1980s, for example). A group of states can isolate a particular state if they want to punish it for one reason or another. Apartheid South Africa was an isolated state.

juridical sovereignty: formal authority vested in a state to exercise authority over a specific territory, and to enter into agreements with other like units in the international system. It is a legal status given to states by other states in the international system.

kleptocracy: rule by thieves or by leaders who are only interested in enriching themselves.

League of Nations: a global intergovernmental organisation that was formed after WW I in order to prevent war amongst nations, and to promote respect for public international law. The League failed in its aims, however, and was replaced by the United Nations in 1945.

legal doctrine: the opinions of prominent legal scholars that serve as one source of international law.

legitimacy: the quality of having your rule accepted as legal and just.

less(er) developed countries (LDCs): the majority of countries in Asia, Africa and Latin Americe which, when compared with the industrialised or most developed countries (MDCs), have low economic growth rates, low per capita incomes, low living standards, high population growth rates and, generally, are economically and technologically dependent on the MDCs.

levels of analysis: a methodological term which indicates that we can choose between different levels when we analyse or explain events in international relations. We can either focus on leaders and their attributes (individual level), states or societies and their characteristics (state or national level), or we can focus on attributes of the system as a whole (system level).

liberalisation: a process whereby a greater degree of freedom is introduced into an issue area. Political liberalisation implies lifting of restrictions on individual and collective freedom of opinion and assembly, and other forms of political expression. In the economic sphere, it refers to a process whereby state-applied rules and regulations are lifted, and market forces are given wider scope.

listserve: one of a number of automatic software programmes for maintaining a mailing list; others include major-domo and listproc.

mailing list: a set of e-mail addresses, all of which receive the same message.

macroeconomic policy: plan or course of action which focuses on the economy as a whole, specifically aimed at managing employment and production levels, determining levels of income and expenditure, limiting inflation, and ensuring economic growth.

marginalisation: the propulsion of weak states to the edge or margin of the global political economy in terms of weight, opportunity and influence.

Marshall Plan: a package of grants and loans extended by the United States to Western Europe, to facilitate its reconstruction after World War II.

matrix: all the computers in the world that can communicate with one another by e-mail.

mercantilism: a state policy that stresses the idea of the accumulation of national wealth (measured in terms of gold and silver) in order to increase state power.

MERCOSUR (or MERCOSUL): a regional grouping concerned with promoting trade between member states in South America. It consists of Argentina, Brazil, Paraguay and Uruguay. Chile is an associate member.

mini-states: states with very small populations (Swaziland), or small land areas (Mauritius), or both. Their very small size implies that their economies can never be very complex and that they are seldom influential in international relations. Hong Kong and Singapore are distinct exceptions to this generalisation.

misperception: a wrong evaluation of a state of affairs. Thus, we say that someone was subjected to a misperception when s/he miscalculated the strength or weakness of an opponent or his/

her own strength, or when s/he misjudged the intentions of another actor (*see* also **perception**).

modem: a device for transferring electronic signals between computers and telephone lines.

monetary policy: official measures used by central banks to influence the availability and price of money (as the means of exchange) in a national economy.

monetary relations: relations pertaining to means of exchange.

monetary system: the set of global rules and institutions dealing with means of exchange. It determines how one currency can be exchanged for another, and how **rates of exchange** are determined.

money supply: the amount of money circulating in an economy, comprising notes and coins, and all deposits with monetary institutions.

monocultural: being of or consisting of one culture only.

Monrovia Group: a group of African leaders, led by Alhaji Abubakar Tafawa Belewa, Prime Minister of Nigeria, who, prior to the foundation of the **OAU**, rejected the idea of a political union of African states in favour of a looser, intergovernmental organisation. This group's view prevailed at the time of the foundation of the **OAU**.

mortality (rate): yearly number of deaths per 1000 of the population.

most favoured nation (principle): a principle of free trade that demands that any favourable treatment (such as preferential tariffs) extended by one state to another must be granted to all other states as well.

mother country: the home country of a colonial power.

mouse: the palm-sized control mechanism for a personal computer.

multilateral: adjective pertaining to activities in which more than two states co-ordinate their policies.

multilateral conferences: diplomatic meetings, frequently on a specific topic, which more than two states attend and which often produce treaties that are signed and ratified by many parties. As a way of establishing law, multilateral conferences stand somewhere between traditional state-to-state diplomacy and the legislative activity of domestic parliaments, city councils, etc. Multilateral conferences share characteristics of traditional diplomatic interactions and of national legislatures.

multinational corporations (MNCs): private companies that have their headquarters in one country, but also have concerns, acquired through foreign direct investment, in one or more other countries (*see* also **transnational companies**).

multipolar: an international system that contains more than two dominant centres of power.

mutual dependence: *see* **interdependence**.

mutual vulnerability: *see* **interdependence**.

nation: a people who regard themselves as comprising a distinct cultural, geographic and political **identity**.

national interest: a) the goals and objectives of a state's foreign policy; b) a set of enduring concerns that the state wants to protect.

nationalism: an **ideology** that makes the nation the focus of highest political loyalty and the centre of political identity.

nation building: the process of fostering the growth of unity and a shared identity in a country that is characterised by divisions and cleavages within society. Engendering respect for, and the acceptance of, national symbols, such as a flag, a national anthem, national sports teams, etc. are strategies of nation building. Often, however, nation-building is used as a ruse for building the power of the state.

nation-state: one form of the 'territorial state' (others are city-states and empires) in which the people comprising the nation are the ultimate source of the state's legitimacy. With the growth of **nationalism** as an **ideology** in the nineteenth century, the norm grew that, ideally, every nation should have its own state. Today, the term is often used simply as a synonym for 'state'.

national liberation (struggle): the political, economic, and cultural struggle by subjucated people to be free from foreign rule, and to set up an independent **nation-state**.

NATO (North Atlantic Treaty Organisation): a collective defence alliance formed in 1949 by the victorious Western powers, and headed by the USA, to contain and counteract perceived USSR-led communist expansionism.

negotiation: involves an engagement in discussion by two or more parties to reach an agreement over a disputed issue. Negotiating in 'good faith' is based on the assumption that the parties concerned are interested in resolving the issue.

neo-classical model: an economic model proposed by economists who, beginning in the 1970s, built on the tradition of classical economists and believed that market forces, if left to themselves, would solve the problems of unemployment and recessions.

neo-colonialism: control of a former colony which is politically independent by an outside power or powers, especially through domination of its economy.

neo-liberal: adjective derived from neo-liberal economic thinking, which proposes that economic growth can best be achieved under conditions of minimal state involvement in the economy (*see* also **neo-classical model**).

neo-patrimonialism: a political ideology / system in which rulership is personalised (despite the official existence of a written constitution), and in which the leader is often seen as 'the father of the nation'. It is sustained by selective distribution of favours and material benefits.

new conflict paradigm (NCP): term given to describe the new type of conflicts that the UN and other international organisations have to deal with in the post-Cold War era. These conflicts are intra-state and take the form of civil wars or large-scale civil upheaval, often with negative spill-over effects, such as large numbers of refugees, into neighbouring countries.

new international economic order (NIEO): a term that came to the fore during the 1970s when a group of developing countries, known as the Group of 77, started to use international organisations, such as the General Assembly of the UN and UNCTAD (United Nations Conference on

Trade and Development), to aggregate and propagate their suggestions and recommendations for change in the international economy. Their ideal was to create a more equal international economic system that would also benefit developing countries and assist them in their development. The developed countries, particularly the USA, were less enthusiastic, and although many undertook to provide development assistance to developing countries, the main objectives of the NIEO have not been realised.

newly industrializing countries (NICs): a small group of countries at a relatively advanced stage of economic development and closely linked to the international trade, finance and investment system. These include Argentina, Brazil, Greece, Hong Kong, Mexico, Portugal, Singapore, South Korea, Spain and Taiwan.

newly industrialised economies (NIEs): the economies of **newly industrialised states (NICs)**.

Non-Aligned Movement: a popular name for the Movement of Non-Aligned Countries, which is an intergovernmental movement comprising 114 developing countries that meet regularly (with a Summit of Heads of State and Government every three years) to discuss global issues of common concern relating to development, trade and security. It was founded in Belgrade, Yugoslavia, in 1961, and in 1998 had 114 full members, plus some thirty observer members. It is committed to principles of disarmament, the peaceful settlement of disputes, South-South co-operation, North-South dialogue and reform of the UN Security Council. It has no permanent secretariat (why it is called a movement), and has a rotating presidency that changes every three years. At the Twelfth Summit of NAM, South Africa was elected president of NAM for the period 1998 to 2001.

non-alignment: a foreign policy pursued by many developing countries during and after the Cold War. In terms of this policy, developing states refused to 'take sides' for/ against military alliances of the major powers, wanted to solve international disputes by peaceful means, and promoted principles of equality and mutual recognition of sovereignty between states.

non-governmental organisation (NGO): any organisation not set-up or controlled by the state.

non-tariff barrier: a form of economic protectionism involving obstacles to free trade of goods and services across borders that do not involve an import tax or duty. A quota on the number of units of a product that can be imported in a year is such a barrier. Today states use non-tariff barriers much more than tariffs to restrict the inflow of imports in order to protect domestic industries.

North American Free Trade Agreement (NAFTA): a regional trade grouping consisting of Canada, the United States and Mexico.

North Atlantic Treaty Organisation: *see* **NATO**.

online: when your client computer is turned on and linked to the Internet, you are online.

Organisation for Economic Co-operation and Development (OECD): The twenty-nine most industrialised countries of the world belong to this organisation, which has its headquarters in Paris, France. It promotes economic co-ordination and co-operation between these states.

Organisation of African Unity: a Pan-African organisation, formed in 1963, which has its headquarters in Addis Ababa, Ethiopia. All independent African states, except Morocco, are members.

Organisation of Petroleum Exporting Countries (OPEC): a producer's **cartel** established to co-ordinate actions in order to fix and maintain petroleum prices.

organisational process (model): a view of decision-making that argues that decisions are determined by routine procedures and practices in organisations.

pan-Africanism: refers to one or all of the following: a) a movement began by Africans in the diaspora (especially in the USA and the Caribbean) which aimed at greater affinity with Africans on the continent and, if possible, a return to Africa; b) an ideology of unity amongst

African states, irrespective of colonial boundaries and differences; and c) an ideology of African liberation, particularly with reference to the white-settler regimes of Eastern and Southern Africa.

parastatal corporations: commercial enterprises owned partly or completely by the state.

pariah state: a state that is internationally **isolated** because its internal policies and external conduct are deemed to violate international law and practice. Apartheid South Africa was a pariah state.

patrimonialism: a manner of running households and families in which the father rules, and grants privileges to, and demand absolute fidelity from, his spouse(s) and children (*see* **neo-patrimonialism**).

patronage system: a system of governing in which ties of personal obligation between a superior (the patron) and a subordinate (the client) are used to obtain loyalty and obedience. Widespread in history and in contemporary Africa, it is usually associated with high levels of corruption.

patron-client relationship: *see* **patronage system**.

Peace of Westphalia: the Treaties of Münster and Osnabruck that ended the Thirty Years' War in Europe in 1648. These treaties codified some aspects of our modern notion of state sovereignty, and 1648 is often seen as the starting-date of the modern inter-state system.

peacekeeping: traditionally, the positioning of armed international observers to help belligerents maintain an agreed upon cease-fire. Since the end of the Cold War this term has been used more loosely to refer to any multilateral action using armed force to help establish or maintain peace, especially in situations of protracted domestic conflict.

Peloponnesian War: extended armed conflict between the two 'alliances' of ancient Greece, one led by Athens (a democratic, commercial and sea-oriented state), and the other by Sparta (an oligarchic, land-oriented, inward looking state). The first Peloponnesian War started in 461 BC, and ended in a peace treaty in 445 BC. The

second Peloponnesian War broke out in 431 BC, when Sparta decided that the growing power of Athens was upsetting the **balance of power** amongst the Greek city states, and it went to war against Athens and its allies. In 404 BC, Athens was finally defeated, having suffered an anti-democratic revolt by oligarchs in 411 BC.

per capita GNP: *see* **gross domestic product**.

perception: the result of a cognitive process by which an individual selects, organises, and evaluates stimuli from his/ her external environment. In International Relations we are particularly interested in how the leaders of states perceive the motives and goals of other states (*see* also **misperception**).

perestroika: a Russian word, meaning 'restructuring' or 'reformation'. Associated specifically with the policies introduced by President Mikhail Gorbachev to reform the government and the economy.

periphery: a subordinate position in the global system and its international division of labour in which a peripheral area is often colonised and made to produce agricultural and mineral commodities. Contrast to **core** and **semi-periphery**. Today, most of SADC is a peripheral zone in the global system.

personal rule: the personalisation of state power by the head of state or government, whose preferences rather than any codified system of laws shapes the exercise of authority.

policy: course or general plan of action adopted by a government or NGO.

political sovereignty: *see* **sovereignty**.

polities: plural of 'polity' which means 'a form or process of civil government', or 'politically organised society'. Sometimes used as a synonym for 'political system'.

portfolio investment: investment by nationals from one country in the financial and equity (**share**) markets of another country. In contrast with **foreign direct investment**, portfolio investment is aimed not at gaining control over means of production, but at making speculative profits from price fluctuations on these markets.

positive externalities: *see* **externalities**.

post-neocolonialism: continued domination of former colonies, not by their former colonisers, but by international financial institutions, notably the International Monetary Fund and World Bank.

power: the ability to affect outcomes and/ or to get others to do what they otherwise would not have done. This ability in international affairs may be determined by resources such as military might, economic strength, or size (so-called 'hard' power). It can also be determined by moral standing or cultural dominance (so-called 'soft' power). We can also distinguish between 'relational' power, the ability of A to change the behaviour of B as a result of the resources that A can bring to bear on B, and 'structural' power, which is the ability to make the rules in an issue area, according to which all other actors must behave.

prebendalism: the abuse of public office or privileges to serve personal and private ends, principally to enrich the individual. Originates from the Latin word that means a (public) grant or pension.

productive: a quality of being that enables one to deliver services or make goods efficiently.

proletarianisation: the process of turning a group of people into wage labourers (proletariat).

propaganda: organised propagation of a doctrine or beliefs. It is used to change the views of a target group, in order to get the target group to act in a desired fashion.

protectionism; the outcome flowing from policies that are aimed at restricting imports in order to encourage the growth of domestic production of goods.

proxy war: armed conflict in which the belligerent parties fight indirectly through allies or surrogate parties.

public good: any good enjoyed by all, but for which everyone does not take responsibility. A public road is a public good, for instance: we all use it, but no one but the local authority takes responsibility for it. 'Who will look after the production of public goods' is a classic problem in any situation of collective action in international relations. For instance, all of us in Southern Africa will benefit if the wars in Angola and the DRC are stopped. But which of these countries' neighbours will take the responsibility (and pay the price of the costs involved) for securing peace? Some realists believe that it is the function of a **hegemon** to secure public goods.

public policy-making: the process whereby authoritative plans or courses of actions are devised on public issues.

purchasing power parity (PPP) US$**: a way to measure the relative cost of living by determining how much citizens of various countries around the world can actually buy in US$ terms in their home countries. Often called 'international dollars', this complex procedure takes into account the fact that many consumption goods, such as haircuts or heating/ cooling a home, are not traded internationally and may be more or less expensive in different countries. Estimating per capita incomes in PPP$ terms gives a more accurate picture of the real income and local living standard terms than an estimate based upon the prevailing exchange rate between the US$ and the local currency would provide. In general, using PPP$ does not change wealth estimates among the developed countries of the North, but it does increase the estimated individual **incomes of people in the developing countries of the South because certain goods and services are sometimes cheaper there than in the North.

rapprochement: a diplomatic term to describe the initiation of friendlier relations between two or more former rivals.

rate of exchange (or **exchange rate**): an indication of the value of one currency measured against another currency. In December 1998, the exchange rate of the US dollar against the SA rand was just over 5,80 rands to one dollar.

ratification: affirmation of a treaty by the legislative body of a state which has negotiated and signed the treaty. Ratification serves to make the treaty 'the law of the land' in the countries that ratify.

rational actor model: a view of foreign policy decision-making that presents states as single calculating units who are trying to optimise their goals/ interests.

RDP: an economic development policy introduced by the **GNU** in 1994 as the Reconstruction and Development Programme.

real GDP per capita in purchasing power parity US$: the **gross domestic product** of an economy, as measured in PPP determined US$, discounted for the effects of inflation and divided by the total population. A widely used measure of the relative wealth of countries, whatever their population size.

real income: the earnings of an individual/ household measured in terms of the real (inflation discounted) price of goods and services it can purchase.

real wages: a person's salary discounted for its reduced purchasing power brought about by inflation.

realpolitik: a German word, referring to policies that seek to maximise a state's power in the **anarchical** international system.

Reconstruction and Development Programme: *see* **RDP**.

regime: this term is used in at least three senses. The first and popular usage is as a pejorative synonym for government. Thus, opponents of Apartheid used to refer to the government of Apartheid South Africa as 'the Pretoria regime'. A second usage, more restricted to political science, describes the way in which power is distributed in a political system. Thus, we say that 1994 saw a transition from an 'authoritarian regime' to a 'democratic regime' in South Africa. Transitions from authoritarianism (or totalitarianism) to democracy are called 'regime changes'. A third use is found in the literature on international relations. Here, a 'regime' is a set of basic understandings, rules and expectations shared by the actors involved, and covering a specific area of policy.

regional integration: the process of closer economic co-operation and/ or unification between neighbouring states.

regional organisations: intergovernmental organisations whose members are limited to a specific part of the world.

regional protectionism: the co-ordination of policies between a group of states who (usually) belong to a regional organisation, and who want to protect their regional market from foreign products with which they cannot or do not want to compete.

regional sub-system: a group of states and their economies where interactions among the members are significant, resulting in **interconnectedness**. Sub-systems usually have common economic and political institutions and are formed among geographically neighbouring states (SADC or the EU, for example).

regionalisation (= creating regional trading blocs): creating an economic coalition among countries within a geographic region, usually characterised by liberalised internal trade and uniform restrictions on external trade, designed to enhance regional economic integration and growth.

relational power: *see* **power**.

relations of unequal exchange: (trade) relations in which the values of goods exchanged are not commensurate. In many cases of North-South exchanges, the prices of primary products exported from the South have declined, while that manufactured goods imported from the North have risen.

roles: the functions that a state performs in the international system. Some states are 'defenders of human rights', while others are 'regional leaders', for example.

ROSCAS: rotating savings and credit organisations consist of between six and forty members who pool their money in a fund. The fund is held by a group leader who is informally selected from among the members, and who is responsible for periodically collecting a fixed share from each member. The money collected is then given, in rotation, as a lump-sum payment to each member of the group, thus allowing them to finance expenditures much sooner than if they had had to rely on savings efforts of their own.

sanctions: cover a broad spectrum of constraints on

economic, military, sporting, cultural, and other relations, imposed by members of the international community or sections of it on a country, to pressurise it to act in certain ways.

search engine: various computer programmes that search for and retrieve Web pages and documents via keywords or 'hypertext links'; popular engines include Altavista, HotBot, Infoseek and Yahoo.

semi-periphery: an intermediate position in the global system and its division of labour, in which the semi-periphery has simultaneously core and peripheral characteristics. Brazil, Turkey, South Africa and Indonesia are classical semi-peripheral countries today.

service provider: a company or organisation which makes its host computer(s) available to clients for Internet access, for example, all the universities in Southern Africa, or the Internet Solution in South Africa.

service sector: fast growing part of the economy in which not products, but intangible services are produced and traded. The waiter in a restaurant serves you food (products), but s/he gets paid for the service that s/he provides. Similarly, the motor mechanic gets paid for the service s/he provides in fixing your car. The insurance and banking industries are also examples of service industries.

share: one of a number of equal portions in the nominal capital of a company entitling the owner of the share to a proportion of distributed profits.

social indicators: measures of the welfare levels in a society.

socio-economic inequality: refers to the skewed distribution of income, land or other assets among a nation's population. When a small part of the population has most of the wealth, and the majority has little, this is said to be a situation of relative inequality. South Africa and Brazil are among the most unequal countries in the world, and the Netherlands and Taiwan are among the most equal.

Southern African Development Community: a regional grouping of fourteen countries in Southern Africa and the Indian Ocean, established for the purpose of promoting regional **integration** and development.

sovereign: supreme and exclusive legal authority with exclusive right to make policy on a territory, which is so recognised under international law.

sovereignty: the right to exclusivity in making and applying rules for a distinct territory (**internal sovereignty**), and the right to participate equally in the international community, with all the duties and privileges this entails (**external sovereignty**).

specialised agencies: relatively independent organisations affiliated to the UN system that carry out most of the UN's work, other than the work of conflict avoidance and peacekeeping which is conducted by the Security Council.

state: this word has three specialised meanings: a) a synonym for 'country'; b) a reference to the set of central and local institutions in a society that make and apply policy for that society; c) refers to a legal entity that possesses a permanent population, a well-defined territory, and a government capable of managing public affairs (including having foreign relations with other states).

structural adjustment programme: a package of economic reforms recommended by the **World Bank** and **International Monetary Fund** to bring about liberalisation in countries who applied for assistance from these institutions. The key policies include currency devaluation, removal of subsidies on goods and services, privatisation and trade liberalisation.

structural power: *see* **power**.

structural transformation: *see* **economic structural transformation**.

structure: people use the word in many ways: a) it may refer to the rules and institutions of a particular organisation or organised behaviour. Thus, we may speak of how a manager changed the structure of a corporation in order to make it more profitable; b) it is used in economic analysis to indicate the prevalent production and distribution patterns in a specific economy. For instance, people say that the structure of the South African economy must change to make it less dependent on gold exports. Similarly, **structural adjustment programmes** aim at changing the prevalent practices in certain economies (see **economic structural tranformation**); c) realists use the term structure when they speak of the way in which the units of the international system (states) are arranged in terms of their relative power and functions; d) transformative Marxists and dependency theorists use the term to mean the fundamental features of the global economy, namely, who owns the means of production and the pattern of how every country fits into the global division of labour. In its most general sense, therefore, the word 'structure' can refer to any persistent pattern of ordering.

sub-Saharan Africa (SSA): is used to refer to Africa excluding the North African countries of Algeria, Egypt, Libya, Morocco, Sahrawi Democratic Republic (Western Sahara), and Tunisia.

sultanate: an Islamic state headed by the sultan who plays a double role as both political and spiritual leader.

supply-side (economics): policies or measures aimed at increasing the aggregate supply of goods and services in the economy. Supply-side economists are usually in favour of cutting government spending, bringing down tax rates, and reducing the number of rules and regulations to which producers have to adhere. The combination of these things, they believe, will allow producers to be more productive, and ensure cheaper goods and benefits.

sustainable development: an approach to development which emphasises that today's development cannot deplete the Earth's natural resources and destroy the environment upon which future generations will be dependent.

system: any set of interconnected parts or units in which the behaviour of one part will affect other parts. We distinguish between mechanical systems (such as the internal combustion engine of a car), biological systems (such as the human body), and social systems (such as a university).

When we speak about the 'world system', we refer to the **interconnected** totality formed by all the actors in the world, plus their relationships with one another.

system of rule: the interconnected set of mechanisms through which a society or community organises and orders itself so as to regulate the distribution of resources, rights and obligations.

tariffs: a tax or import duty which is imposed on imported goods and services. Governments use tariffs to raise revenue, discourage imports, and to protect local industries from foreign competition.

taxonomy: a systematic classification of a class of things or issues.

TCP/IP: Transmission Control Protocol/ Internet Protocol; the set of rules by which computers on the Internet communicate.

terms of trade: the ratio between indices of export prices and of import prices. The better the ratio is in favour of export prices, the better the economic well-being of that particular country.

terrorism: indiscriminate use of violence to achieve political goals.

terrorist: a person who uses **terrorism** to achieve his/her goals.

trade deficit: the shortfall that arises when a country imports more than it exports in a specific period of time. Trade deficits have to be financed from the capital account of the **balance of payments** or from the country's foreign reserves. The opposite of a trade deficit is a trade surplus.

trade related intellectual property rights (TRIPs): intellectual property rights (IPRs) are ownership rights vested in inventors (patents), artists and authors (copyright), and in the original developers of trade marks. The term TRIPs was popularised during the Uruguay Round of trade negotiations, as it was one of the trade issues that was placed high on the agenda by the United States, who wanted stricter enforcement of IPRs to protect its inventors and artists from illegal copying of their products.

trade related investment measures (TRIMs): a GATT-WTO agreement that deals with the doing away of rules which certain states implemented to ensure that foreign companies investing in their country were restricted in what they could import. The purpose of the agreement was to remove a specific obstacle to trade, but it has taken away some of the relational power that states had over foreign corporations operating on their territory.

trading blocs: groupings of countries that promote trade amongst themselves by lifting trade restrictions, and follow joint policies on trade with countries outside of the bloc.

transnational corporation (TNC): increasingly used instead of the term **multinational corporation**. A TNC is a business enterprise that is organised in one country but which maintains activities in others. These activities flow from direct investment abroad (**FDI**), such as erecting and operating a factory in a country other than the one in which the business has its headquarters. The definition of a TNC, therefore, excludes businesses that only own shares in companies in other countries.

transnational social movements (TSMs): (also TSMOs) are voluntary groupings of individuals and organisations (often NGOs) from different states working to achieve a common goal, as in the international anti-Apartheid movement.

transparency: the conduct of governmental and political affairs in an open and above-board fashion so that the media and public know what is going on.

treaty law: international law established by formal **agreements** between states.

tripartism: a manner of making **macroeconomic policy** that is characterised by close co-operation between government, the private sector and labour.

typology: a study or list of different types of the same phenomenon. Thus, one could, for instance, draw up a typology of different types of war, by distinguishing between them according to how many countries were involved, or how many casualties there were, etc.

UN Conference on Trade and Development (UNCTAD): a UN body whose primary mission is to promote trade and development for developing countries through more favourable terms of trade and increased foreign aid.

UN trust territories: colonies confiscated by the victorious powers from Germany after the World War I and from Italy after the World War II. Subsequently administered by other states on behalf of the League of Nations before 1948, and of the United Nations Organisation after 1948, with a view to eventual independence.

underdevelopment: an economic situation in which there are persistent low levels of living standards, low income per capita, low rates of economic growth, poor health services, high death rates, high birth rates, high unemployment and dependence on foreign economies.

unipolar system: a system in which power is concentrated in a single major hegemon. The period immediately after the end of World War II was dominated by the United States, both at the economic and military levels, and has been described as unipolar.

unit of meaning: the state as a 'unit of meaning' refers to the fact that it becomes important to people not only as a **unit of production**, i.e. satisfying their needs (economically, socially, in terms of security, etc.), but also as a place to which they owe allegiance and attach loyalty.

unit of production: *see* **unit of meaning**.

URL: uniform (or universal) resource locator; the address of a file on the Internet.

Uruguay Round: a multilateral round of trade negotiations (1986–1994) under the auspices of GATT, aimed at further reducing trade barriers on a variety of goods.

USSR: the Union of Soviet Socialist Republics that came into being between 1917–1924, after the communist revolution in Russia and the incorporation of some neighbouring countries and territories. The USSR was also known as the Soviet Union, and it consisted of fifteen semi-federal republics, all communist controlled, under the strict rule of Moscow. It was dissolved between 1989 and 1992, with the Russian Federation acting as the successor state to the USSR.

variable: anything that can be measured and can change.

vertically integrated production and consumer sectors: a term associated with mineral extraction and the manufacturing of products with a high raw material content. A firm that produces finished goods which require large amounts of a specific mineral, for instance copper, will create affiliates to produce copper so as to ensure control of a resource of which it is also a consumer (and not only a producer). Through such vertical integration, extraction, production and consumption, the firm ensures its supply of the mineral in a seller's market.

war: large-scale armed conflict between or within states.

warrior-tribe policy: a colonial policy of recruiting people from the 'warrior tribes' (who were believed to be the best fighters) into colonial armies.

wars of national liberation: *see* **national liberation**.

welfare state: a form of state which uses government intervention in the economy to ensure maximum employment and generous social benefits for the work force.

Westphalian: a term used to describe the modern state system. *See* **Peace of Westphalia**.

World Bank: one of the so-called **Bretton Woods** institutions formed in 1944 (see **International Monetary Fund**). The World Bank actually consists of three institutions, namely the International Bank for Reconstruction and Development (IBRD), the International Development Association (IDA), and the International Finance Corporation. The IBRD (the institution which most people have in mind when they speak of the 'World Bank') was originally started in order to build up the economies of the states which had been devastated by WW II. Today, its main aim is to provide loans and technical assistance for development projects, mainly in the developing world. Membership is restricted to those states that are also members of the IMF. Like the IMF, the Bank has a system of weighted voting which gives power to affect outcomes to those states that make the largest financial contributions.

World Trade Organisation: an international body, established in 1995, to regulate and set rules for trade in goods and services among countries and regional blocs. It is the successor to the **General Agreement on Tariffs and Trade (GATT)**.

World Wide Web (WWW or Web): documents, including voice and video, on computers around the world that are linked to one another using a set of standard procedures called http, or the hypertext transfer protocol.

xenophobia: hatred and fear of foreigners.

zero-sum game: any competitive or co-operative undertaking in which a gain for one side results in an equal loss for the other side.

Index

Entries are listed in word-by-word alphabetical order. Those in bold can be found in the Glossary, on page 311. The list of Acronyms is on page 306.